German Political Philosophy

From the Reformation to the present, German political philosophy has done much to shape the contours of theoretical debate on politics, law, and the conditions of political legitimacy; many of the most decisive and influential theoretical impulses in European political history have originated in Germany. Until now, there has been no thorough history of German political philosophy available in English. This book offers a synoptic account of the main debates in its evolution.

Commencing with the formal reception of Roman law and the constitutional reforms in the Holy Roman Empire in the late fifteenth century, *German Political Philosophy* includes chapters on:

- the political ideas of Luther, Zwingli and Melanchthon in the Reformation;
- the natural-law theories of the early German Enlightenment;
- Kant, Hegel and the age of German idealism;
- romanticism and historicism;
- the Young Hegelians and Karl Marx;
- legal positivism and organic theory;
- Nietzsche, Weber and early sociology;
- neo-Kantianism in the late nineteenth century;
- constitutional theory in the Weimar Republic;
- the critical theories of the Frankfurt School;
- post-1945 sociological functionalism;
- Jürgen Habermas and Niklas Luhmann.

At the heart of this book is the claim that, despite – or perhaps because of – the great upheavals and ruptures in the history of state-formation in Germany, there are certain recurrent themes and concerns that persist through these discontinuities to give a distinctive character to German political reflection. This valuable book will be of great interest to political philosophers, intellectual historians, lawyers and historical sociologists.

Chris Thornhill is Professor in Politics at the University of Glasgow. His recent books include *Political Theory in Modern Germany*; *Karl Jaspers: Politics and Metaphysics* (also published by Routledge); and, as co-author, *Niklas Luhmann's Theory of Politics and Law.*

Routledge Studies in Social and Political Thought

1 Hayek and After
Hayekian liberalism as a research programme
Jeremy Shearmur

2 Conflicts in Social Science
Edited by Anton van Harskamp

3 Political Thought of André Gorz
Adrian Little

4 Corruption, Capitalism and Democracy
John Girling

5 Freedom and Culture in Western Society
Hans Blokland

6 Freedom in Economics
New perspectives in normative analysis
Edited by Jean-Francois Laslier, Marc Fleurbaey, Nicolas Gravel and Alain Trannoy

7 Against Politics
On government, anarchy and order
Anthony de Jasay

8 Max Weber and Michel Foucault
Parallel life works
Arpad Szakolczai

9 The Political Economy of Civil Society and Human Rights
G. B. Madison

10 On Durkheim's *Elementary Forms of Religious Life*
Edited by W. S. F. Pickering, W. Watts Miller and N. J. Allen

11 Classical Individualism
The supreme importance of each human being
Tibor R. Machan

12 The Age of Reasons
Quixotism, sentimentalism and political economy in eighteenth-century Britain
Wendy Motooka

13 Individualism in Modern Thought
From Adam Smith to Hayek
Lorenzo Infantino

14 Property and Power in Social Theory
A study in intellectual rivalry
Dick Pels

15 Wittgenstein and the Idea of a Critical Social Theory
A Critique of Giddens, Habermas and Bhaskar
Nigel Pleasants

16 Marxism and Human Nature
Sean Sayers

17 Goffman and Social Organization
Studies in a sociological legacy
Edited by Greg Smith

18 Situating Hayek
Phenomenology and the neo-liberal project
Mark J. Smith

19 The Reading of Theoretical Texts
Peter Ekegren

20 The Nature of Capital
Marx after Foucault
Richard Marsden

21 The Age of Chance
Gambling in Western culture
Gerda Reith

22 Reflexive Historical Sociology
Arpad Szakolczai

23 Durkheim and Representations
Edited by W. S. F. Pickering

24 The Social and Political Thought of Noam Chomsky
Alison Edgley

25 Hayek's Liberalism and Its Origins
His idea of spontaneous order and the Scottish Enlightenment
Christina Petsoulas

26 Metaphor and the Dynamics of Knowledge
Sabine Maasen and Peter Weingart

27 Living with Markets
Jeremy Shearmur

28 Durkheim's Suicide
A century of research and debate
Edited by W.S.F. Pickering and Geoffrey Walford

29 Post-Marxism
An intellectual history
Stuart Sim

30 The Intellectual as Stranger
Studies in spokespersonship
Dick Pels

31 Hermeneutic Dialogue and Social Science
A critique of Gadamer and Habermas
Austin Harrington

32 Methodological Individualism
Background, history and meaning
Lars Udehn

33 John Stuart Mill and Freedom of Expression
The genesis of a theory
K. C. O'Rourke

34 The Politics of Atrocity and Reconciliation
From terror to trauma
Michael Humphrey

35 Marx and Wittgenstein
Knowledge, morality, politics
Edited by Gavin Kitching and Nigel Pleasants

36 The Genesis of Modernity
Arpad Szakolczai

37 Ignorance and Liberty
Lorenzo Infantino

38 Deleuze, Marx and Politics
Nicholas Thoburn

39 The Structure of Social Theory
Anthony King

40 Adorno, Habermas and the Search for aRational Society
Deborah Cook

41 Tocqueville's Moral and Political Thought
New liberalism
M. R. R. Ossewaarde

42 Adam Smith's Political Philosophy
The invisible hand and spontaneous order
Craig Smith

43 Social and Political Ideas of Mahatma Gandhi
Bidyut Chakrabarty

44 Counter-Enlightenments
From the eighteenth century to the present
Graeme Garrard

45 The Social and Political Thought of George Orwell
A reassessment
Stephen Ingle

46 Habermas
Rescuing the public sphere
Pauline Johnson

47 The Politics and Philosophy of Michael Oakeshott
Stuart Isaacs

48 Pareto and Political Theory
Joseph Femia

49 German Political Philosophy
The metaphysics of law
Chris Thornhill

German Political Philosophy

The metaphysics of law

Chris Thornhill

Routledge
Taylor & Francis Group
LONDON AND NEW YORK

First published 2007
by Routledge
2 Park Square, Milton Park, Abingdon, Oxon, OX14 4RN

Simultaneously published in the USA and Canada
by Routledge
270 Madison Avenue, New York, NY 10016

Routledge is an imprint of the Taylor & Francis Group, an informa business

Typeset in Times New Roman by Taylor & Francis Books
Printed and bound in Great Britain by Biddles Ltd, King's Lynn

British Library Cataloguing in Publication Data
A catalogue record for this book is available from the British Library

Library of Congress Cataloging in Publication Data
A catalog record for this book has been applied for

ISBN10: 0-415-31238-8 (hbk)
ISBN10: 0-203-96640-6 (ebk)

ISBN13: 978-0-415-31238-7 (hbk)
ISBN13: 978-0-203-96640-2 (ebk)

For Hermione, Grace and John

Contents

Acknowledgements

There are various debts of gratitude that I must acknowledge in committing this book to print. I am grateful to the staff of the British Library for their courtesy and unfailing assistance in providing the books and documents that I have required over recent years. I am grateful to King's College London for granting me study leave in 2003 to conduct research for the book. I would also like to thank the AHRB for providing very generous research funding to support some of the research on this book. I am grateful to Routledge publishers and their editors for working with me in such cordial manner on this and other publications and for showing that even in the accelerated reality of contemporary academic production in the UK it is still possible for authors actually to enjoy working with publishers.

During my work on this book, I have had the good fortune to find myself in the company of a number of excellent scholars and intellectuals in different fields of academic inquiry, and many of these people have greatly influenced my thought. Over the past decade, for example, I have been lucky enough to name Darrow Schecter amongst my best friends, and I think it is fair to say that all aspects of my work have been influenced by him in one way or another. Over recent years I have also been engaged in intermittent debate with Drew Milne, and the traces of his thinking are always in my mind. My friend Michael John has put me right or offered new light on so many historical points that I cannot begin to enumerate them. My various experiences of academic collaboration with Michael King and Alan Norrie have also been both pleasurable and enduringly stimulating. William Outhwaite has also been magnificently supportive towards me, and it is not possible for me to thank him sufficiently for all the assistance that he has given to me. Further recognition of my intellectual gratitude is due to Samantha Ashenden, Matthew Bell, Andrew Chitty, Jean Clam, Robert Fine, Gert-Joachim Glaeßner, Stephen Jacobson, Simon Jarvis, Stiljan Jotov, Paul Key, Margarete Kohlenbach, Cecile Laborde, Douglas Moggach, Alan Olson, Jan Palmowski, Ralf Rogowski, Jeff Seitzer and Seishu Yasu. All of these people have influenced my thinking on various questions, either through years of collaboration and collegiality, or simply through short theoretical or historical exchanges.

A note on texts and translations

Whilst I was writing this book, I was often forced to make a number of difficult decisions about the scholarly editions that I have chosen to use. This book refers to texts originally published in German, Latin, French and English, and the publication of these works spans well over five centuries. Many of these texts have appeared in more than one original edition, which often have varying claims for authority and preference, and many have also appeared in a number of English translations. In some respects, the method by which I have selected original texts and editions for reference may appear slightly unusual. As far as possible I have tried to consult established scholarly editions, normally using, for instance, Latin editions of works published first in Latin and subsequently in German. At times, however, I have deviated from this policy. This is particularly the case in my discussions of works written and published during the Reformation era, where I have sometimes referred to the original pamphlet publications and sometimes even to first German translations of works whose original language of publication was Latin. I have followed this course because, where possible, I have tried to trace the evolution of specifically German debates on political problems, and in using the most widely circulated versions of influential texts I have tried to capture something of the revolutionary spontaneity and the rapid changes of mind that marked the pamphlet wars and the theological controversies of the 1520s and 1530s. This approach has naturally involved a balancing of considerations of scholarly accuracy against considerations of historical authenticity and discursive evolution. In most instances, especially in the Reformation era where translations enjoyed immediate and widespread theoretical resonance, the latter consideration has prevailed.

In addition to this perhaps rather controversial method, I have also decided not to refer to any recognized English translations in this book. The reason for this is that the available translations of the different original works are of extremely variable quality, and in many cases it is difficult to judge which translation should be used; moreover, many of the original texts have never been fully translated. Consequently, the task of selecting consistently or comparably high-quality translations of the works covered here is almost impossibly complicated, and reference to works in translation could never approach a reasonable standard of uniformity. Therefore, all translations from German, Latin and French are my own, and I naturally accept responsibility for whatever deficiencies they might have.

Introduction

The primary purpose of this book is to set out a synoptic account of the history of German political philosophy and political theory from the Reformation to the present. At the heart of this work is the claim that, despite, or perhaps because of, the great upheavals and ruptures in the history of state formation in Germany, there are certain recurrent themes and concerns that persist through these discontinuities and give a distinct character to German political reflection. Indeed, the book argues that the very fact that German political thought has evolved in a historical framework in which the institution of stable and centralized political systems has been very fitful, and in which the process of state foundation has commenced and recommenced in very different ways at different times, means that certain questions surface repeatedly across different historical periods. For this reason, the second purpose of this book is to identify the principal problems of German political thought, to examine their genesis and the forms of their recurrence, and to interpret the founding objectives of theorists working in this philosophical tradition.

In addressing these issues, this book adopts an encompassing definition of what constitutes political theory or political philosophy, and texts from distinct intellectual disciplines – from politics, philosophy, sociology, public law, private law, ecclesiastical law, theology and historiography – are at times included in this definition. Works are considered here if they contribute to debates of principle on the necessary political and constitutional form of Germany and if they provide a theoretical account of the necessary conditions of political order in Germany. It is fundamental to the intentions of this work that a broad thematic focus is deployed, and that it emphasizes the politically shaping force of arguments posed in a number of different vocabularies. Indeed, central to this work is a concept of theoretical secularization, which argues that the problems and the concepts of political theory are often distilled from, or express responses to, points of theological or legal-theological debate, that legal and political principles evolve through a reshaping or a transformation of paradigms first pertaining to religion or religious conceptions of law, and that theological or legal-theological ideas retain impact in political debate even when the specifically religious content of these problems has begun to diminish in relevance.

What is German political philosophy?

Before attempting to examine the underlying motivations and evolutionary history of German political philosophy, it is necessary to give an account of its major characteristics. This is attempted below.

It has recently been argued that it is a commonplace to claim that German political philosophy is primarily concerned with the state.[1] This may well be true. However, this is one of those commonplaces with which it remains difficult to disagree, and the claim that there exists a strong element of statism in German political thought has not become any less true simply because it has often been voiced. First, therefore, it is arguable that most German political philosophers and theorists, whether from liberal, conservative or even socialist traditions, have tended to interpret the state as the supreme organ of social coordination, and they have often imputed to the state a structural dignity over and against the rest of society. German political theory generally sees the state as universally accountable for determining and representing the principles by which society is ordered, and as embodying principles of unity and cohesion (whether national, cultural or consensual), which cannot be deduced from a foundation of particular social interests. For this reason, more progressive elements of German political thought often have a pronounced reformist component, which places responsibility for social change and transformation in the state itself, not in associations or factions external to the state. Above all, German political thought usually defines the state as the precondition of human freedom, not as its limit or adversary. In fact, it often sees the question about the necessary nature of the state as inseparable from the question about the necessary nature of human freedom.

Second, it can be argued that German political thought often approaches questions about political order as *exceptional* or *paradoxical* questions. This means, first, that it often focuses on clarifying the relation between state and law, it often views the aspect of freedom or voluntarism in power and the aspect of reason or normative necessity in law as antinomies, and it is commonly called to account for the formation of power outside any firm normative setting. At the centre of German political philosophy, consequently, is an endeavour to resolve the exceptionality of power, and to articulate positive conditions to reconcile the antinomies of law and state. Second, this means that, as it sees the formation of power as originally outside normative preconditions, German political thought recurrently shows a sceptical attitude towards claims for absolute legal validity in the exercise of power, and it is marked by a series of distinct attempts to unmask as simplified, or as paradoxical, the constructs by means of which power explains itself as legally justified or rational. Consequently, throughout its history German political theory has attempted, in constantly new configurations, to reinterpret and reconsolidate descriptions of the sources of valid law, and to place and re-place both law and state on new foundations.

For this reason, the category of *legitimacy* has a fully centralized role in German political theory. Legitimacy is usually conceived as the characteristic of a state that unifies the antinomies of reason and law and freedom and power, but this category is widely burdened with anxiety. In general, German political thought is deeply preoccupied with constructing sustainable analyses of the relation between law and power, with overcoming paradox and exceptionalism in power, and with the construction of a state founded, not in paradoxical claims to authority, but in fully authenticated law. The pervasive German concern with the institution of the *Rechtsstaat* can be traced to this fact.

Third, in its approach to questions of legitimacy, German political philosophy often differs from the general normative or social-contractarian tendencies prevalent in other lines of political philosophy, especially in Britain and the USA, it is often sceptical towards purely normative analysis of legitimacy, and it often addresses the problem of legitimacy in *historical,* or, latterly, in *sociological* terms. This means, for instance, that the models of legitimacy propagated in German political thought are often of an interpretive nature. Rather than determining the unique and ideal conditions of morality or utility under which a political system may or may not be accorded legitimacy, they tend to describe the historical and sociological processes leading either to the production of legitimacy, or to its forfeiture, and to interpret the quality of legitimacy in its distinct societal and historical environment. For this reason, the tradition of abstract or ahistorical normative theory does not have a fully central status in Germany, and German political theory cannot easily be separated from interpretive methodologies originating in historiography. Kant and the representatives of the neo-Kantian tradition are clearly the major exceptions to this argument. However, in many ways, as discussed below, Kantian thinking has a distinct status in German political thought, and most major post-Enlightenment perspectives have evolved through a primary disagreement with Kantian ideas.

Fourth, it is also arguable that German political philosophy is marked by periods of deep hostility to formal *ius-naturalism,* and that much German political philosophy rejects universalizing natural-legal models of political legitimacy. In this respect, this book argues that there are two quite distinct lines of natural-law theory, and that these serve very different purposes in the history of political theory and political formation. First, it argues that there exists a tradition of scholastic natural-law theory, which predated the evolution of the modern European states, and against which the theorists of European state-building originally reacted. Second, it argues that there also exists a tradition of post-scholastic or eclectic natural-law theory, which directly served the consolidation of legal order in the early European states, and which provided a frame of reference within which these states could explain themselves as natural and legitimate. This second tradition usually placed itself in direct opposition to scholastic ideas of law, which were specifically bound to the Thomist orthodoxy of the Roman Catholic church. Against this background, then, this book argues that the first evolution of German political thought in the sixteenth century was shaped by a rejection of the universalist implications of scholastic natural law. Subsequently, however, through the later sixteenth century and the early Enlightenment of the seventeenth century there developed a powerful tradition of practical natural-law philosophy in Germany, which provided commentary and justification for the emergence of particular forms of state and law. Natural-law thinking, consequently, is surely not marginal to the tradition of German political thought. However, at the very origin of German political philosophy stands an antagonistic approach to natural law, and this remained resonant through subsequent theoretical epochs. The periods of most intense state-building in Germany – the era after the Reformation, the era after the French Revolution, and the period of unification under Bismarck – had their great theoretical expressions in the endeavour to dislocate political order from universal-juridical ideals and to provide an account of political order as internally or organically cohesive. Indeed, the concrete conditions of German political history have been often such that the major political thinkers have, during periods of transition and instability, found themselves in immediate opposition to philosophical traditions, notably to late-medieval Roman Catholicism and to the ideals of post-revolutionary France, which were rooted in paradigms of natural law.

Fifth, related to these points is the fact that German political thought is usually marked, at different junctures and across very different points in the political spectrum, by an attitude of great scepticism towards *capitalism,* by a reluctance to embrace trade and economic independence as forces of human improvement, and by a critique of legal-political outlooks that *materialize* law around particularist economic interests. German political thought tends consequently to reject the claim that private interests, and above all *private law,* can on their own provide a foundation for political order. As a result of this, it is very difficult to find views on political legitimacy conforming to standard positions in the canon of liberal thought: that is, views that see the legitimacy of a state as depending on a maximum of private autonomy, on negative freedom of the person against the state, on guarantees of individual economic liberty, and on the restriction of executive power. Even avowedly liberal positions in the history of German political philosophy are inclined towards a very affirmative view of the state: they commonly see the state as the public embodiment and the structural prerequisite of private freedom, and they refuse to give private interests, especially private economic interests, any primacy over public order. The conception of the state as an oppressive or coercive order, whose authority must be checked by strictly guaranteed protection for private interests, is thus not common in German philosophy, and the classic early-liberal idea of the social contract as a means of demarcating a sphere of private autonomy outside the state has limited influence. Obviously, as will be discussed, there are very important exceptions to this, but classical-liberal examples of privatism and possessive contractarianism play a relatively marginal role in German political thought.

Sixth, in consequence, it is also arguable that German political philosophy tends to view the relation between politics and law in *substantial* terms. It views legitimate law not as a medium of technical administration, nor as an institution for defending private interests in society, nor as a formal set of ius-natural norms or prescriptions. Instead, it claims that law possesses legitimacy only in so far as it shapes or reflects a political order that gives publicly evolved expression to primary or integral human attributes, emphases and freedoms, so that law which merely secures particular motivations or interests is not seen as legitimate. On these grounds, German philosophy is often shaped by Aristotelian assumptions about the politicality of human nature, which assert that politics is the realm of human freedom, and that the original political characteristics of human beings must be imputed as the foundation for law. As an extension of this point, then, German political philosophy is in most cases consolidated around a *political anthropology.* It sees questions of political form and necessity as related to fundamental questions of human self-realization, it construes the ideal state as an expansion of human personality, and its inquiry into the character of the legitimate state often leads into an inquiry into the nature of the ideally realized and liberated person. The legitimate state, therefore, is often conceived as one which manifests ideal human characteristics *in the form of law,* and a legal state framed by legitimately positivized laws is an immediate extension of the legitimate human being. This anthropological dimension to German political thought also reinforces its scepticism regarding atomistic or privatist conceptions of order.

Seventh, as a result of this, it is also often the case in German philosophy that conceptions of political order are related to the essential questions of *philosophical humanism.* These conceptions are often expressed with a political-pedagogic inflection, and they assert that the legitimate state must be an expressly human state, allowing and positively enabling a full realization of ideal human freedom and ideal human attributes. Therefore, whilst it tends to avoid purely prescriptive accounts of legitimacy, German political thought might be seen to develop its normative implications by offering theoretical accounts of ideal human nature, and by insisting that a state must elaborate this ideal as the necessary substructure of its own authentic legitimacy.

Eighth, most specifically, it can also be shown that German political philosophy has a particular relation, both historically and conceptually, to *metaphysics* or especially to *metaphysics in the law.* German political philosophy tends to react against legal-political views that stabilize the necessary preconditions of government as external to the political order itself, it commonly opposes analysis that sees legitimacy in politics as a condition of static compliance with norms or purposes that are not produced by the political order itself, and it denies that the politics of the human world is incorporated into an overarching unity of reason or is underpinned by perennial essences or laws. It is perhaps not uniquely characteristic of German political thought that it opposes metaphysical deductions of law and legitimacy. The reaction against metaphysics is clearly a formative element of all political humanism, in all European countries. However, the critique of political and legal metaphysics is particularly strong in German political reflection, and it forms an enduring dialectical source of debate and controversy between theories and orthodoxies. At the origin of German political thought, in fact, is the assertion that metaphysical deductions of legitimacy are *paradoxical,* that they derive the origin of order from false or conveniently manufactured constructs of rational causality or necessity, and that rational or metaphysical laws suppress the constitutive aspect of freedom in legitimacy. In consequence, German political thought repeatedly identifies paradoxical elements in metaphysical claims about the law, and it repeatedly attempts to locate the origin of law away from metaphysical postulates, to place the source of legitimacy on fully free foundations, and to illuminate the rationality of the laws as a non-paradoxical or non-metaphysical rationality. It is for this reason that German political philosophy tends to reject both natural-law ideals and private-law ideas of the state's personality; at different junctures private-law and natural-law ideals are repudiated for imposing a falsely metaphysical system of norms on the political realm of human freedom. It is for this reason, also, that it ties its inquiries into the conditions of legitimate order to inquiries into the nature of the human being, human freedom, and human self-formation. Throughout the evolution of German political philosophy, there is a recurrent tendency to see the beginning of politics where metaphysics ends, and to see politics as deeply enmeshed with the constitutive conditions of human existence, which are only fully elaborated where humanity and politics are distinct from metaphysics. Throughout the history of German political philosophy, consequently, questions about law's necessary positive form are inextricably bound to questions about the form of humanity and about the character of humanity as distinct from metaphysics. It is in fact a distinctive feature of German political philosophy that it often elides the question of law's positivization into the question of human nature and human distinction.

Ninth, consequently, this relation between politics, humanism and metaphysics means that the analysis of the relation between *legitimacy* and *legality* in German philosophy is also closely connected with metaphysical debates, and that, even in contemporary debate, political philosophy is concerned with the task of placing the state on a foundation of non-metaphysical laws, and so of underwriting its legitimacy as a human polity. The central task of German political philosophy might in fact be seen as the attempt to account for a legitimate polity as a sphere of free human self-legislation, in which laws give rational sanction to freedoms and obligations which, distinct from all formal or abstractly universalized principles, human beings freely identify as their own.

Tenth, it can also be argued that German political philosophy customarily concentrates on the founding question of all political thought, namely the question: 'What is politics?' In fact, summarizing all nine points given above, it can be concluded that German political reflection relies, first, on the definition of politics as a sphere of human practice, which is distinct both from private or material interests, and from narrowly purposive motives. Second, then, it also views politics as a distinct location of positive human freedom and accountability, whose laws cannot be explained as reflecting prior norms or metaphysically imputed obligations and values. Politics, thus, is the original and defining fact of the distinctively and authentically human world, and political agents are responsible for ensuring that their political freedoms are not undermined or imperiled by metaphysically imposed norms or constraints. On these grounds, questions of humanism and metaphysics and questions about law and political legitimacy converge in German political thought, and authentic humanity and legitimate politics are both construed as conditions that evolve at the end of metaphysics, through the primary human faculties of self-legislation and self-creation.

The formation of modern German politics I: the problem of capitalism

In more recent history, it is not difficult to discern a number of socio-political factors that might explain why German political philosophy has these broad characteristics. The statist and anti-privatist elements of German political thought can be explained, in part, through consideration of certain aspects of modern German political and economic history. First, it might be argued that the basic evolution of modern German states was driven by a reaction against the politics of private law. The model of statehood that emerged in the German territories during the early modern period was an estate-based system of governance and delegation, in which the coercive public power of the state executive and the private interests of the estates were dualistically balanced against each other, and in which princes purchased the compliance necessary for government by granting private-legal concessions and entitlements to members of the estates. This estate-based order remained influential into the nineteenth century, and by this time it was widely perceived as a retrograde and debilitating intrusion of late-medieval patterns of government by privilege, which obstructed the path to a fully modern and fully public form of statehood.[2] For this reason, both liberal and nationalist theorists of the nineteenth century usually saw concessionary modes of governance rooted in private law, or in the dualistic separation of private and public law, as insufficiently or incompletely realized examples of statehood, which failed to generate a genuinely cohesive or genuinely *political* ethic of identity and legitimacy. The hostility to purely privatist politics is therefore central to the more recent processes of state-building in the German territories.

In addition, though, there are a number of specific points in the political and economic history of Germany that might explain why most political theorists, even those of liberal orientation, express great caution in recognizing the private-legal freedoms of the modern economy as a source of socio-political liberty, human progress, or legal validity. Capitalism developed very late and very quickly in Germany, and the existence of an economically independent and self-reliant capitalist class has not always been a precondition for German political reflection in the same way that it has, for instance, for modern British, American or even French political thought. Indeed, whereas in other countries capitalism played a constitutive role in forming the state, the states of modern Germany were often formed in spite of capitalism, they often experienced capitalism as a threat to their own structure, and, almost from their inception, they were surrounded by more highly evolved capitalist states. Owing to their economic backwardness, the small German states of the pre-1789 era commonly assumed quite distinctive mercantilist features, using protectionist policies, high tariffs and high levels of state intervention in industrial enterprise in order to consolidate their domestic political and economic systems against the much more advanced economies of the Atlantic seaboard. This often prevented the emergence of a fully autonomous civil society in the German states, it ensured that, well into the nineteenth century, much economic activity was conducted under partial state control, and it meant that many quasi-corporate associations, such as guilds and corporations, exercised political and economic influence in many parts of Germany for longer than in other western European countries. Through the first epochs of political liberalism, therefore, most especially the aftermath of the French Revolution and the era around 1848, capitalist interests were relatively weak, and they were ultimately appeased by processes of limited political reform, which left the pre-capitalist structure of the state largely intact. Ultimately, in fact, high capitalism developed with extreme rapidity towards the end of the nineteenth century, in the decades following the unification of Germany under Bismarck in 1870–71. However, this led, in turn, to a rapid and alarming polarization of social classes and political interests in Imperial Germany, and it placed great strain on the relatively archaic and unrepresentative political system of this era. In fact, the evolution of the state of Imperial Germany, not as a national democracy, but as an authoritarian executive, which balanced anti-liberal constitutional policies with a cautious liberalization of the sphere of private law and civil law, reflected the fact that this was a state which was deeply challenged by increasing economic pluralization and which struggled fully to integrate the interests of the social classes generated by capitalism. Similarly, the constitutional structure of the Weimar Republic established in 1919, providing for corporatist or even mixed-economic processes of collective bargaining and codetermination, reflected the fragile political-economic climate after the First World War, and it sought desperately (and unsuccessfully) to find a formula for integrating diverse and often highly antagonistic social and economic classes into a unitary political process. Indeed, because of the failures of liberal political integration in Imperial Germany, the democratic system of 1919 was forced to try to incorporate the middle class and working class in the democratic political apparatus at the same time, a task which proved too difficult in a political culture with a relatively weak tradition of democracy. Subsequently, the types of authoritarian capitalism that evolved after the Wall Street Crash of 1929, and which culminated in the assumption of power by the National Socialist Party (NSDAP) in 1933, also underlined the susceptibility of the German political apparatus to transformation as a consequence of international economic forces and crises. The only fully committed liberal-capitalist state in Germany, the Federal Republic of Germany, was, in part at least, constitutionally imposed by the Allied Powers after 1945.

All in all, therefore, the formation of statehood in German political history is inextricably intertwined with complex and at times catastrophic experiences of capitalism. As a result of this, German political theorists have, in different contexts, been obliged to address acute questions about how the socially disaggregating forces of economic autonomy stimulated by capitalism might be brought together under one political apparatus, which, until 1918–19, was founded in pre-capitalist social structures. Similarly, they have been forced to address questions about how the political system might stabilize itself in face of social divisions arising from rapid and precarious processes of capitalization. Notably, in consequence, German political theory has often responded to capitalism by adopting an attitude of gradual political-economic reformism. Through this attitude, it has sought to assimilate and implement the legal principles of capitalism whilst attempting to preserve the role of the state as a neutral and constant source of order above civil society, and so to counteract the polarizing elements of the unregulated economy. Similarly, German political theory and German politics have been marked by very strong traditions of welfarism and economic collectivism, designed to integrate the autonomously evolving economy into a system of cross-class collaboration and socially palliative distribution. In consequence, at a very early stage in the evolution of capitalism Germany developed a tradition of welfare-statism, and a high degree of welfare provision has remained characteristic of German politics in all its transformations since the latter decades of the nineteenth century. Even the model of social capitalism or Rhineland capitalism pioneered after 1945 can be viewed as a late position in a political tradition, which is reluctant to recognize the capitalist economy as a motor of progressive transformation, which ascribes a high degree of economic steering authority to the political system, and which views principles of economic democracy or codetermination as fundamental to political and economic stability.

It is also important to observe that the major processes of legal foundation and codification which have introduced capitalist law in Germany tended, at least until after 1866, to originate outside Germany and this, too, has provoked hostility to pure capitalism and pure capitalist laws. The debates surrounding the reception of Roman law as the earliest foundation for clarifying rights of ownership and exchange will be addressed extensively below. It is sufficient to note here that the reception of Roman law has always been fiercely contested in Germany, especially in eras of intense legal and political upheaval, and it has often been viewed as corrupting the (allegedly) more cooperative and organic laws indigenous to Germany. In the sixteenth century, for example, Roman law contributed in important ways to the volatile political and economic climate leading to the Reformation. In the seventeenth century, hostility to the Holy Roman Empire expressed itself in scepticism about the value and applicability of Roman law. Through the latter part of the nineteenth century, then, legal and political theory was broadly split between Romanist and Germanist jurists. In this controversy, the Germanists looked to Germanic legal concepts as devices through which alternatives to pure capitalist ideas of freedom, personality and entitlement could be proposed, and they saw the principles of purposive and possessive autonomy sanctioned under Roman law as offering only very insubstantial preconditions for acceptable economic and political order. However, the hostility to pure capitalist law was most obvious in the debates concerning the assimilation of Napoleonic law after the completion of the Code Napoléon in 1804. The Code Napoléon established the juridical foundation for a modern capitalist exchange economy, setting principles for freedom of contract, freedom of labour, and free circulation of goods, and most German states either experienced a direct imposition of the Code or they incorporated select elements of it into their own legal systems. Nonetheless, as discussed below, this process of assimilation was often fraught with debates about the compatibility of French and German legal ideals, and it was shaped by the sense that German legal culture contains its own ingrained ideas of ownership and obligation, which cannot be distilled from pure capitalism. In short, capitalist law has often been tainted by its association with political ideas both external and apparently hostile to the German political tradition, and discussions about German law have commonly demanded that legal culture should be based in cohesive shared identities and cooperative models of personality under law, not in an aggregate of autonomous or singularly purposive individuals.

The formation of modern German politics II: Roman law, feudalism, and the problem of secularization

To understand the more fundamental concerns of German political philosophy, however, it is necessary to consider the political processes that marked the era of Reformation in Germany. The Reformation was the period in which German political culture and German political thought began to assume distinctive features, and it is possible to discern in this era certain political-theoretical and historical developments that shaped the entire subsequent history of political thought in Germany. Most particularly, this period saw the consolidation of the characteristic political humanism, the anti-metaphysical attitudes and the exceptionalism that distinguished later political thought in Germany. To interpret the implications of the German Reformation, however, it is also necessary to give a brief account of the ways in which this period marked, first, a response to the legal and political problems of the late Middle Ages and, second, a very distinctive and unusual transitional stage in the passage from feudalism to the modern political order.

On the first point, it is important to note that the age of the German Reformation (1517–55) occurred against the background of intense upheaval, not only in religion, but also in the law. The Reformation was a response, at a most obvious level, to legal debates within the church concerning the nature of papal power. Through the fifteenth century the papacy had resolutely attempted to reconsolidate itself as a papal monarchy after the disastrous schism of 1378–1417 and the Hussite rebellion in Bohemia. During this century, the papacy had reacted against and suppressed the more constitutional or delegatory principles of government that had been promoted by the conciliar movement during the schism, and it had sought once again to assert papal power as the source of all authority in the church.[3] In their later demands for a limitation of the power of the pope and the abandonment of papal monarchy, the leading figures of the Reformation saw themselves as recommencing an earlier tradition of ecclesiastical constitutionalism, and as reviving some of the ambitions of the conciliarist movement. In this respect, the Reformation drew on a vital tradition of legal-constitutional protest within the late-medieval church, and it brought to an end the attempt of the papacy to reinstate the monarchical foundations of the church.

To a still greater degree, however, the Reformation was also a response to legal and constitutional occurrences outside the church, and it refracted the secular legal struggles and controversies that had dominated late medieval political life in the German territories. Prior to the Reformation, the fifteenth century had witnessed a period of protracted legal and constitutional reform in the Holy Roman Empire, in which different political groups vied for control of the law. The result of this was that legal power and the instruments of its application were progressively displaced from the traditional and personal locations of feudal law, and were now increasingly organized in positive and relatively consistent and centralized form. The latter part of the fifteenth century, in other words, saw an incremental process of political formalization in the Holy Roman Empire, and by 1500 the empire had – arguably, at least – obtained the basic, although still very rudimentary, characteristics of an early modern state. By this time, the empire possessed the foundations of a governmental executive (*Reichsregiment,* established in 1500), it had a centralized judicial system with a fixed court (*Reichskammergericht,* established in 1495), it had a universally implemented penal order (the *Landfriedensgesetz* of 1495), which undermined the feudal law and imposed generally consistent conditions of legal order throughout the territories, and it was in the process of developing a set of regional authorities (*Reichskreise*) to facilitate administration in the German territories of the empire. In conjunction with these innovations, the empire was also beginning to deploy representative methods of political decision-making. By 1500, the informal moving courts of the medieval empire were gradually giving way to more formal imperial diets,[4] which arrived at decisions on a majoritarian basis, with established quota of territorial representatives.[5] In addition, the empire was also instituting an early taxation system, intended both to replace the ancient feudal techniques for levying armies and resources and to finance an independent judiciary for the new court. Some of these institutions, notably the governmental executive (*Reichsregiment*), were suspended shortly after their establishment. However, this executive was founded again in the early 1520s, and it formed an important locus of controversy during the early Reformation.

Importantly, these processes of political centralization and early state-building were very closely bound up with the introduction of Roman law in the German territories of the empire. The reception of Roman law, initially stimulated by Gratian's codification of the canon law in the middle of the twelfth century, had exerted pervasive influence throughout the whole history of late medieval Germany. However, the reception of Roman law was accelerated and formalized at the imperial Diet of Worms in 1495, where it was decided that Roman law should be taken as the basis for legal ruling in cases where the findings of common law were equivocal or unclear.[6] It was at the same diet, in fact, that the Imperial Court was established; this court primarily applied Roman law, and it served to intensify the dissemination of principles of Roman law through the empire.[7] The year 1495 did not mark the end of the reception of Roman law or the elimination of Germanic law in the German territories. On the contrary, the assimilation of Roman law continued through the following century, and the writings of glosses and commentaries on Roman law – *Pandektenwissenschaft* – remained the chief activity of German jurists until well into the nineteenth century. However, the Diet of Worms in 1495 gave formal sanction to Roman law as the foundation of imperial law, and the political institutions evolving in the empire around 1500 were strongly coloured by the distinctive features of Roman law. Roman law led to the formation of an independent professional class of lawyers and a bureaucratic judiciary; it transformed the application of legal rulings into an activity quite distinct from the local and less predictable medieval techniques for exercising power; and it made the imperial state, as a set of organs distinct from other areas of society, the primary seat of accountability for passing and enforcing laws. Through this process, law was detached from its customary forms and it was applied, from above, as a formal or positive medium for codifying and enacting more generalized prerogatives.

Whilst marking the consequences of the controversies about the law in the fifteenth century, the establishment of the court applying Roman law also formed a culminating moment in a longer history of rivalry over Roman law, and over the form of the law per se, in the German regions of the Holy Roman Empire. This history reached back to much earlier questions of legal organization and to much earlier controversies over the use of Roman law as a mechanism for the formal organization of political power. These controversies had their most potent expression in the earliest conflicts over the form of the modern state: namely, in the conflicts between the empire and the church in the investiture contests of the late eleventh century and the early twelfth century – during the period, first, of Cluniac and, then, of Gregorian reform. The Gregorian period, most especially, marked the beginning of an era in which the church slowly organized itself in accordance with generalized and regular legal principles, derived from Roman law, and, as an order of monastic autonomy, self-regulation and discipline, placed itself on relatively firm and independent legal foundations.[8] During this era, authority in the church was tied, to an unprecedented degree, to papal power, which in turn was supported by an extensive legatine network for ensuring papal control over priests and bishops. In this form, the church defined its role as a legally ordered representative and enforcer of divine or natural law in the world, and, most importantly, as a hierarchically structured temporal institution, equipped to assert legally enshrined rights against – and, where necessary, *over* – worldly states. Through the Gregorian reforms, moreover, the church began to develop institutional features now considered characteristic of secular states: it evolved new resources for raising fiscal revenue,[9] and, crucially, it acquired legal-administrative powers for codifying law, for issuing and promulgating new laws, and for enforcing positive law through specialized judicial procedures.[10] The Gregorian reforms thus marked a period in which an institutional apparatus used principles of Roman law to found itself as a positive or autonomous, hierarchical and self-determining legal order. In this respect, this period had seminal importance for later historical and political developments, and it initiated a secular process in which Roman law came to act as a primary medium of state formation, institutional self-regulation and legal positivization.

The reorganization of the church through this period of medieval reforms necessarily engaged it in conflict with secular powers. The Gregorian era saw the final collapse of the ancient Carolingian unity of church and state in the Holy Roman Empire, and of the tradition of princely or regional control of the church that had prevailed in the German territories of the empire under the Ottonian and the early Salian rulers.[11] In the German territories, the Gregorian era caused protracted antagonism between church and empire over the extent of lay involvement in church appointments, over the degree to which territorial rulers could influence the church or even claim ownership of it, and over the relative authority of pope, papal legates, emperor and princes. Ultimately, these contests were resolved, at least in part, by the Concordat of Worms, in 1122. This agreement established clear legal distinctions between ecclesiastical and temporal power, it limited imperial influence on the investiture of ecclesiastical potentates, and it ensured that legal jurisdiction in purely ecclesiastical matters was placed outside temporal control and made solely dependent on the institutional will of the church. In this respect, the concordat cemented the concentration of church power already initiated by the Gregorian reforms, as it allowed the church to construct itself as an independent *monarchia,* freely exercising power through law. At the same time, however, the temporal apparatus of the empire also obtained certain benefits from the concordat. The concordat integrated the temporal elements of the church into the feudal system of the empire, it placed the worldly possessions of the church under imperial law so that the empire obtained the right to confer ecclesiastical property, in the form of *regalia,* and it played a significant role in extending the feudal power of the empire over all areas of worldly legislation.[12] For this reason, the concordat might be viewed as the moment in which the secular powers of medieval central Europe began to emulate the process of legal rationalization pioneered by the church, and where they used elements of church law in order positively to separate their own law from contamination by the religious or metaphysical burdens placed on law by the church. After this time, secular authority began gradually to borrow the administrative features of the papal monarchy, to separate the exercise of power from the complex interwovenness of political authority and personal or customary agreement which had marked the pre-Gregorian era,[13] and consequently, like the church, to focus power on single points of authority within an institutional order. In the German regions, in fact, the concordat directly reinforced the power of imperial authority: it defined the empire as the primary bearer of secular political authority; it formalized the extent and the limits of imperial power; and it determined the legal tools by means of which its power could be applied. After the investiture contests, therefore, rulers of the empire increasingly employed concepts of Roman law to define their own legal foundations, and to strengthen their autonomy and their positive jurisdictional authority.[14] Crucially, the *lex regia* of Roman law, containing the principle that law derives from imperial statute, and enunciating the famous principles that the will of the prince has the force of law and that the prince is not bound by the law, helped to liberate imperial power both from the subtle personal and legal nexi of early feudalism and from the limits imposed upon it by the church. Roman law thus provided a crucial set of references in which medieval emperors could underwrite their independence and sovereignty,[15] and it set out categorical legal terms for consolidating and enforcing obligations that had possessed merely personal force under feudal law.[16]

The consolidation of Roman law as imperial law around 1500 therefore constituted the outcome of a long process of *political secularization* and *legal-institutional positivization,* which began as a transformative appropriation of the positive legal forms produced in the church. Indeed, the end of the imperial reforms prior to the Reformation marked the end of an ancient contest over the secular form of the law and over the power of supreme jurisdiction in the law, through which the empire had both freed itself from the sacral corpus of law's validity in the church and arrogated to itself the legal structure initially evolved by the church.[17] By the end of the reforms, the Holy Roman Empire, though still explaining its authority as founded in Carolingian ideas about the unity of church and state, had constructed itself as an institutional apparatus using law as a relatively positive medium of organization, and central to this apparatus was the use of Roman law as a set of authoritative institutes which could be used to authorize and validate positive laws. The constitutional form of the Holy Roman Empire in 1500, consequently, can be seen as the final stage in an epochal process of legal positivization, in which the law was disarticulated from its ecclesiastical or metaphysical foundations, and was now increasingly deployed as a device for transmitting and supporting the power of a relatively cohesive and independent order of state. The immediate background of the German Reformation was thus marked by the end of a lengthy course of secularization, in which, as in other countries, Roman law was brought under the control of a worldly order of jurisdiction, and religious influence on the law became relatively indifferent in the validation of law.

To understand fully the legal configurations impacting on the Reformation, however, it is important to note that the constitutional reforms of the fifteenth century did not only reflect relatively widespread processes of state-building and legal positivization, but they also articulated certain distinctive characteristics in the German passage from the feudal to the post-feudal political order. Most noteworthy in this respect is that fact that the constitutional reforms before the Reformation were not the outcome of consensual or unified political objectives, but were driven to a large extent by a fermenting rivalry between increasingly powerful political classes in the empire, especially the imperial and territorial princes, and the imperial dynasty, the Habsburgs, and their supporters. The reforms, therefore, were shaped by two quite distinct motivations, and the form of state that they instituted was based in a fractious balance between these sets of interests. During the reforms, the imperial princes used the law to consolidate their political position within and against the authority of the empire, and to impose constitutional constraints on the power of the Habsburgs. They thus sought to reform the empire by imposing a concentrated legal order onto it, designed to regularize imperial power, to secure princely influence on crucial areas of administrative competence and to give greater legal protection to princely prerogatives. At the same time, however, members of the imperial party, especially Maximilian I, used the law during the reforms to organize their own authority, to rationalize the instruments of government and to raise concessions from recalcitrant princes. Because of the divergent prerogatives that the reforms manifested, it can be seen that, before the Reformation, the law was a site of intense antagonism, and it was determined by sharply opposed ideas of statehood, jurisdictional influence and legal supremacy. By the end of the reformist era, however, it is notable that the princely faction was becoming increasingly dominant, and that the legal form of the imperial state would necessarily evolve as a constitutionally balanced state, and would bear the hallmark of princely authority.[18] Indeed, it is notable that the earliest attempts to establish conditions of universal legal order in the empire during the thirteenth and fourteenth centuries had been initiated by the bloc around the Emperor as a means of consolidating imperial power.[19] However, these attempts had not been successful, and the law and the court of 1495, instigated mainly by the princes, now acted both as a device for centralizing and generalizing political power and as a mechanism for limiting central authority and for ensuring that power should be subject to independent legal constraint and constitutional restriction.[20]

Perhaps the most important underlying motivation for the imperial reforms and the centralization of jurisdiction in the late fifteenth century was the general decline of the feudal institutions of vassalage and *regalia* in the empire. By the eve of the Reformation, the personal bonds of obligation and obedience uniting the feudal order of the empire had been severely weakened, and the empire could no longer rely on its feudal powers to obtain political or military support to maintain its inner and outer stability, and it was forced to use other means to recruit and maintain armies. At the heart of this process of defeudalization was the fact that power transmitted through *regalia* and cemented in vassalage was rapidly yielding to new modes of politically and economically independent power, founded primarily in the ownership of land. As a consequence of this, early forms of territorial and princely dominion (*Landesherrschaft*) were quickly supplanting the personal bonds of feudal law, and the feudal overlordship of the Emperor was increasingly counterbalanced by new forms and sources of political authority.[21] Indeed, it can be argued in general terms that the feudal governance which had supported the empire in the German territories was characterized by the fact that it had an endemically *centrifugal* nature, and that it was structurally centred on a model of proprietary concession and land tenure, which finally led to its collapse. Although in the strict definition of the word feudalism is usually seen as a centripetal method of administration, in which those bearing power bind their subjects to them by granting land or offices as *regalia,* the territories of medieval Germany instituted a rather distinct type of feudalism. After the first evolution of feudalism in the early medieval period, the Holy Roman Emperor maintained support for his position by granting concessions of territorial authority and jurisdiction to quasi-sovereign regional princes, whose main motives for accepting imperial authority over them primarily was that this bolstered their own power in the empire, and strengthened their jurisdictional authority in their own territories.[22] This process ultimately led to the creation of powerful and self-interested factions within the overarching constitution of the empire,[23] and the regalia granted under feudal law in the empire gradually enabled powerful princes to extract themselves from direct or mandatory obedience to the Emperor.[24] As a result of the Emperor's concessions, therefore, in the late medieval era the ownership of territory increasingly became the foundation for claiming power in the empire, and the pre-feudal apparatus of the empire was progressively hollowed out by the dynamics of this distinctive type of feudalism. The reforms preceding the Reformation in fact directly reflected this process, as they created a constitution that was centred in a strategic balance between the relatively dispersed or centrifugal interests of the princes and the concentrated or centripetal interests of the imperial executive, and which consolidated the imperial state around a conflictual equilibrium between two divergent sets of legal prerogatives.

If the longer process of political formation leading to the Reformation had seen a course of legal secularization, in which empire and church vied for control of the law, it is important to note that this process did not stabilize the means of legal application in one relatively controlled system of jurisdiction. On the contrary, the secular form of the law emerging in the German territories before the Reformation was an intensely exceptional form, marked by a new controversy over its application: whereas the earliest controversies over law's secular form had been controversies between church and state, law was now the site of entrenched conflict between empire and princely estates. This conflict, in fact, was immediately internalized and reflected by Roman law, and in the first stages of its application Roman law offered distinct advantages to both factions in the conflict for control of the law. On one hand, Roman law had clear utility for the imperial faction because of the *lex regia,* which could be manipulated to sanction abstract or proto-absolutist concepts of supremacy.[25] Roman law could thus be constructed as a formal substructure for imperial authority, and it could restrict independent landed power by denying to the territories the right to take law into their own hands in the manner characteristic of feudal law. It is notable, for example, that the major imperial reformist manifesto of the early fifteenth century, the *Reformatio Sigismundi,* expressly demanded that the *lex regia* (*keiserliche rechte*) of Roman law should be systematically implemented by the Emperor in order to create a new framework of legal stability.[26] The anonymous author of this document lamented ecclesiastical influence on monarchical rule,[27] recommended the establishment of imperial courts with a uniform legal code (*ein keyserlich rechtsbuch*),[28] and viewed the imperial promulgation of written law as the most reliable means of reconstituting the divine order of law (*götliche ordnung*) which had been eroded through the rivalry between different legal conceptions.[29] On the other hand, though, Roman law was also a potent political instrument for the factions of landed power benefiting directly from the erosion of feudal ties. Roman law, applied through the central court, could be used to assist the rationalization of power at a local level, to serve the reinforcement of regional states and territories, to secure mechanisms of political representation and judicial control within the constitutional structure of the empire,[30] and so to restrict imperial arbitrariness in the exercise of power.[31] Equally importantly, in its insistence on undivided ownership as the foundation of property relations, Roman law also created more secure foundations for land law, favouring individual ownership against feudal bonds and commonly held property. These ideas obviously promised great advantage to those hoping to give regular legal form to the emerging notion of territorial sovereignty, and they directly supported the centrifugal interests of the princely estates.[32]

Several arguments of particular importance emerge from this historical narrative. First, before the Reformation the German territories of the Holy Roman Empire already possessed a set of institutions close in form and competence to an early modern state. This state naturally had little similarity with modern ideas of the nation state, but it was already very distinct from the personalized or local governance of the high feudal era, and, crucially, it arranged itself as a source of jurisdiction, in which laws were applied in relative independence of religious influence. This early state, however, had certain distinctive characteristics and problems. In keeping with the peculiar character of late feudalism in the Holy Roman Empire, most notably, the constitution of this state was shaped by highly antagonistic conceptions of why it existed and by whom it was to be controlled. The political order created through the period of imperial reform in fact marked a fragile and necessarily fleeting accord between two irreconcilable sets of legal interests, which demanded the establishment of a centralized political order for very different motives. As will be seen, during the Reformation, the fragile constitutional accord between the empire and the princes soon collapsed, and many princes supported the Reformation precisely because they saw it as an opportunity to assert still more emphatically their jurisdictional autonomy within the empire.

Second, then, this historical reconstruction also suggests that the course of state-building and legal positivization in Germany followed a highly unusual pattern. In most other European states the formation of secular law in the late medieval era marked the culmination of the first stage of legal positivization initiated in the investiture controversies, it was carried forward by one relatively cohesive bloc, and it resulted, in the Reformation, in the formation of a uniform state applying law as a uniform legal corpus. In Germany at this time, however, both state and law remained burdened with a high degree of centrifugality and polarization, so that law refracted very disparate ideas of legal necessity and purpose. Whereas in the early medieval era the empire had consolidated its power through the use of

Roman law against the church, in the late medieval era this process of positivization was undermined by the fragmentation of the empire into particularized groups of landed interests, who sought to monopolize the law for their own land-based purposes, and to cement their authority through the use of Roman law against the empire itself. By the eve of the Reformation, therefore, the legal apparatus that had evolved in the German regions was not able to sustain a unitary conception of law's objectives and principles. The era immediately preceding the Reformation might, consequently, be seen to express a *crisis of legal positivization,* arising from the characteristic centrifugality of late feudalism in Germany, in which the law, and especially Roman law, was dominated by an unresolved conflict over jurisdictional power. Indeed, at the risk of dramatic exaggeration, it might be argued that in the German territories the jurisdictional contests of the twelfth century, intent on separating positive law from sacral law, began to revive themselves, in new form, during the era of the Reformation. Whereas in other states the early contests generally created a political order in which monarchical power and jurisdiction could be gradually consolidated over one territory, in Germany they formed a system in which jurisdiction, finally in 1495, was concentrated in the empire. However, this jurisdiction was immediately contested by increasingly powerful landed princes, who sought to detach law from all association with supra-positive sources, here the Holy Roman Empire, and so to control the form of the law in their own lands. The law, in consequence, did not assume a conclusively stable form throughout the Middle Ages, but it remained attached to the exceptionalism and the religiously intonated rivalry of earlier eras. During the Reformation, then, the contest over the law which had originally been fought between state and church was translated into a contest between territories and empire, through which territorial princes sought to exclude external or religiously justified elements of law from their own jurisdictional powers, and in which the earlier political hostility to the ecclesiastical law of the church was converted into a hostility to all law, especially imperial law, notionally supported by Roman Catholicism. The gradual course of positivization in legal production and application, which runs through the history of all European states from the high medieval period to the formation of modern states, was, in short, a deeply discontinuous process in the German territories. This process deviated paradigmatically from the course of legal formation in other countries, especially Protestant countries. In other such countries the Reformation marked a culminating occurrence in the history of legal positivization, in which national legislators and judiciaries finally attained a condition approaching full legal independence from the church, and detached themselves definitively from the religious and metaphysical conceptions of law and legitimacy under the late papal monarchy. In such countries, the Reformation occurred within an institutional setting in which the law was already, to a very large extent, established on independent and positive foundations, and in which institutions creating and applying law could provide a relatively stable normative framework to legitimize the Reformation, and to soften the legal disruption that it provoked.[33] In Germany, however, the Reformation only marked a very early stage, or in fact a recommencement, in the process of legal positivization and state foundation. The effects of the Reformation were most manifest in the *destruction* of existing legal institutions, in the intensification of jurisdictional rivalry between empire and estates, and in the vehement reaction against religious presuppositions underlying imperial legislation. It was not until the latter part of the seventeenth century or even the early part of the eighteenth century that the German territorial states obtained independence from the quasi-sacral or at least religiously burdened legitimacy of the Holy Roman Empire; it was only at this stage that they began to explain their own legal powers and jurisdictional competence in fully functional or secular terms.

Indeed, if the period prior to the Reformation saw the emergence of an apparatus of governance and jurisdiction that was constitutionally centred in a legal relation between imperial executive and territorial princes, the period of the Reformation caused the fragmentation of this apparatus. A first effect of the Reformation was that it enabled territorial states whose regents supported the Evangelical movement to assume for themselves the jurisdictional (and fiscal) competences originally assumed by the church, and so to strengthen their authority over their territory in all aspects of the law.[34] This began most manifestly in 1531, when the Evangelical princes defied the imperial constitution and pledged military support to the Evangelical cause.[35] The later outcome of the Reformation, then, was that the territorial estates gradually prevailed in their constitutional conflict with the empire, which led to the organization of power in smaller, though still centralized principalities. This was first enshrined in the Religious Peace of Augsburg in 1555, which brought to a temporary conclusion the conflict between the Evangelical faction, the Roman Catholic Church, and the Holy Roman Empire, and which – albeit grudgingly – gave partial legal recognition to the jurisdictional independence of individual princes. The settlement of 1555 led to the devolution of important swathes of jurisdictional competence from the church to the regional states, and it marked a major step for the German territories in their attempts to assert independent sovereignty. The year 1555 was the point when the empire, represented by Emperor Karl V, finally accepted that it was not able to monopolize legal application and jurisdiction in the style of a central monarchical executive.[36] It was also the point when the territorial princes began, at first in very fitful manner, to establish a high degree of authority over all courts of law, and to utilize the means of legal application to reinforce their own territorial control. Nonetheless, the aftermath of the Reformation remained dominated by further conflicts over the law and the form of jurisdiction. Most German states did not fully and conclusively consolidate their own courts and their own judicial and prerogative independence until well into the seventeenth century. Indeed, it was only after the great constitutional conflict of the Thirty Years

War (1618–48) that most princes were able to obtain a condition approaching jurisdictional sovereignty in their territories. Even the manner in which the territories ultimately accomplished legal control testifies to the conflict and uncertainty attached to jurisdictional rights after the Reformation. Territories obtained rights of jurisdictional self-regulation through a special privilege (the *privilegium de non appellando illimitatum*) granted by the Emperor.[37] This privilege partly exempted those territories that obtained it from overruling by imperial law, and it allowed them to operate their own courts and to act as the highest sources of jurisdiction for their subjects. This privilege, however, still had its origins in the ancient system of feudal contracts, it still reflected the notional legal superiority of the empire over the territories, and it meant that the territories remained accountable to imperial courts in some areas of legal application. At a most practical level, therefore, legal debate after the Reformation was characterized by an exacerbated uncertainty about the institutional organization and source of the law, and this dragged against the positivization of law as a medium of generalized governance. Indeed, the fact that conflict over the law was normally articulated along confessional fault-lines, with imperial courts favouring Catholic and territorial courts favouring Evangelical interests, meant that even everyday questions about law and appeal remained burdened with religious ideas, and they were difficult to resolve in purely positive legal analysis.[38] The crisis of legal positivization that marked the pre-history of the Reformation did therefore not disappear, but in fact remained one of the most important aspects of the legacy of the Reformation. At the very origin of modern German statehood, in any case, it is possible to identify a fragmentation of the means of legal application, and the formation of political power as a reaction against inherited legal structures. The primary cause of this can be found in the fact that legal positivization did not occur as a linear process, but was obstructed by the constitutional peculiarities of the Holy Roman Empire.

Theology and the law in the Reformation

These problems in the course of legal formation in Germany around the Reformation were also reflected in the religious teachings of the Lutheran Reformation. Indeed, if the practical result of the Reformation was that it disrupted the unitary institutional foundation of the law and articulated a critical moment in the casting of law's positive form, it is also the case that at a theoretical level it disrupted the unitary preconditions of legal validity and authority. The Reformation contained a broad range of distinct legal-political perspectives, and it incorporated a number of quite distinct responses to contemporary legal problems. As will be discussed below, the legal conceptions in the Reformation included a reaction against the concentration of legal power through the imperial reforms, attacks on Roman law, attacks on the constitution of the empire, demands for a return to common law and common courts, plans for the installation of theocratic government by Old Testament law, initiatives to develop independent territorial constitutions, and new ideals of natural law. However, the earliest wave of Lutheran teaching had its focus in a pronounced attitude of universal *anti-legalism,* which both reflected and intensified the juridical exceptionalism in the wider environment of the Reformation.

As in other countries, the most obvious legal aspect of the German Reformation was its vehement hostility to the canon law. In the case of the Lutheran Reformation, however, this hostility assumed a symbolically exceptional character. Martin Luther's burning of the canon law in 1520 gave supreme symbolic form to his desire to order religious life around faith alone, to limit the interference of church courts in everyday life and, in fact, thoroughly to curtail the role of ceremony, regulation and law in all spiritual life.[39] Moreover, all the most important political positions in Luther's theoretical trajectory – for example his anti-legalist commentary on St Paul's *Epistle to the Romans* in 1515–16, his early attack on papal supremacy, his contempt for ceremonies and indulgences, his invectives against theocracy, his notion of the church as an invisible community, his later opposition to Caesaropapism and episcopacy, and his caution in sanctioning the emergence of a state church – were all shaped by a critical attitude to the law, both religious and worldly. Many of these debates suggest that he was fully aware of how the secular concentration of the law was shaping late medieval Europe, and that he clearly comprehended the extent to which his epoch was marked by an intensification of the status and character of the law. However, these debates also show that he was not willing to see religious faith as supporting the evolution of particular secular political forms, and that he saw true faith only at the end of the realm of legal validity. At the very heart of Luther's work, in fact, was the view that the law makes people lose sight of faith, that it lulls them into an illusion of self-reliance and outward justification, and that, in consequence, it causes the damnation of human souls. Luther thus saw the Reformation as a denial of law's absolute authority, and as a denial that the divine will inheres in human law. In this respect, his teachings internalized socially embedded controversies about the existing positive form of the law, and they acknowledged the status of law as a primary object of contestation. Above all, Luther's teachings had the crucial similarity with the wider controversies about the law that they rejected the unitary form of inherited law, and they attempted to separate a realm of human freedom, in faith, from determination by existing legal principles.

In addition to his general anti-legalism, in fact, Luther's theology contained a more determinate legal element, which also intersected with wider legal controversies. Luther's theology, namely, revolved around a deep hostility to legalistic metaphysics, and especially to the *metaphysics of legal justification* promoted by the natural theology of Thomas Aquinas, which had been the main ideological support of the late medieval church, and the reassertion of which was desired by Luther's adversaries in the Roman Catholic camp. Building on the spirit of the Gregorian movement, Aquinas proposed an intellectualist interpretation of divinity, which argued that God's will is an intellectual will, and that this will necessarily wills the existence of a rational order throughout the universe, in which human beings participate if they correctly exercise their powers of reason.[40] For this reason, Aquinas also argued that God had ordained a natural order of law throughout creation, and that this order conducts a simultaneously immanent and metaphysical government in the world.[41] On this account, God's will is formed as an innately rational will, and the qualities of right and goodness which God ordains in law are good and right, not because they are willed by God, but because they are rationally necessary and deducible from the eternal law of God's own rational nature. No act, consequently, is good or right simply because it is commanded by a will. All laws are evaluated independently of the will that ordains them, and rational laws of nature can always be normatively invoked against the will. God himself, therefore, has no freedom that is fully independent of reason; he 'is bound' by his own reason to will certain things and certain laws, and he cannot exercise freedom in willing laws that are not rational.[42] God's will is thus, on the Thomist analysis, an element in a rationally normative structure, and God is always at the same time both will and reason, both absolute freedom and absolute law.[43]

God's rational nature, Aquinas concluded, provides universal natural-moral principles against which worldly human acts might be called to account, and it institutes a realm of supra-positive laws against which all positive or voluntaristic laws are measurable. To be sure, Aquinas insisted that there is a clear distinction between positive law and eternal law or divine law, and he did not claim that human laws can perfectly reflect the divine will or the divine mind. Eternal laws or divine laws, he asserted, are intended to lead man to the goal of 'eternal happiness', whereas natural human law leads only to the goal of civil peace.[44] However, he claimed emphatically that true human law is not absolutely removed from the divine order of the world, and that both eternal or divine law and human law are correlated elements of the divinely founded order. Human law always reflects the idea that the world is governed by 'divine reason',[45] and eternal laws and divine laws have an immediate role in ruling the human community.[46] Central to Thomism is thus the claim that true law is derived from metaphysical law, and that metaphysical law is God's freely exercised reason in the universe. God's reason, moreover, is embodied in the laws of the church, which form the source for all other laws.

Luther's theology passionately opposed these principles. He rejected the Thomist beliefs that human reason can participate in the eternal law,[47] and that human law can be 'derived from natural law and divine law'.[48] Most particularly, he denounced the implication in Thomism that God's will is bound by normative intellectual substances, that God's will creates law in the world because God's own free will is determined by rational laws. God, Luther claimed, is *freedom,* not *reason*: God acts entirely in freedom from all rational norms, and it is utterly hubristic to assume, in the manner of metaphysical natural-law theory, that God and humans share the same reason, so that humans interpret the same laws as God and deduce from God's reason the necessary conditions of secular law. Divine grace, Luther argued, is the sole possible mode of communion between man and God, and community united in God is a community united, not by reason or legal compliance, but by faith alone. In these respects, he derided the elements of natural law, natural theology and natural metaphysics in Thomism as the great heresy at the centre of the Roman Catholic world order. Indeed, his theology contained the crucial anti-Thomist claims that God's freedom has no necessary legal element, that there is no analogy between human reason and divine reason, and that laws or norms pursued by a human will can never assume any degree of conformity with God.

By describing the human being as an agent in a metaphysical structure, Aquinas' ius-naturalism was devoted, in its political implications, to showing that all social and political order exists in a natural-metaphysical normative horizon, and that this horizon imposes clear legal constraints on the exercise of political authority. Luther, however, derided the Thomist assertion that God's freedom is freedom under law, and that the principles of this freedom under law might be deduced by human reason and instituted in the form of worldly law, as a self-serving paradox – a paradox that does violence to God's freedom and that corruptly projects rationalized constructs of divine freedom onto worldly political order. In allowing God's freedom to prevail over God's reason, therefore, Luther indicated that the realm of worldly power is not enshrined in a positive divine will, it is not bound by positive divine laws, and it cannot invoke an absolute legal foundation for its own justification. Luther's anthropology, in consequence, rejected as paradoxical the fusion of divine freedom and rational law in Thomism, and it saw the freedom of the human being as an event brought by grace alone, or by the passive reception of grace, in obtaining which the law, and all acts in conformity with the law, have no constitutive role.

At its most essential level, therefore, Luther's theology saw the human being in its authentic freedom as *outside the law,* and he claimed that human activities under the law can never have the same importance as those above the law, and they can never lead to meaningful human freedom: to freedom leading to salvation. Freedom, he concluded, is an inner condition, and it is determined solely by the *new law* of faith. At the very heart of the Lutheran Reformation, in fact, was the conviction that the most authentic model of the human community, the church, is an invisible community of freedom: it is a 'spiritual body', whose authentic life is always undermined by law.[49] In describing the church in these terms, he imagined the true church as a commune, a *Gemeinde,* in the image of the pneumatically inspirited communities of earliest Christianity, before unity in faith had given way to the legal, constitutional and ceremonial administration of the church under Roman Catholicism. The true *Gemeinde,* he explained, requires little hierarchical or legal distinction between the lay members and the priesthood, it needs little ceremonial order, its laws are simple internal laws of appointment and self-organization, and it has little external representative structure, formalized in a papal or episcopal order. The *Gemeinde* needs no representation, Luther claimed, because all its members share equally and in like manner in the divine spirit, and all are equally and in like manner integrated under the new law of faith. He consequently viewed communities defined by legal order, legal regulation, or legal representation as marked by a deficiency of faith: indeed, such communities stand in the way of faith, and they threaten the eternal well-being of the soul. The very principle that a church might act as an organ of divine representation or mediation through law is, on Luther's view, a corrupt characteristic of Roman Catholic ecclesiastical ideas; it is a characteristic of a church not internally centred on God, but figuring the external or intellectual presence of God's law through a personalized and degraded legal apparatus.[50] Representation through legal hierarchy, in other words, appeared to Luther as a metaphysical principle, in which a distant or external God is transformed and made obscurely *present* in human law and human order. His own idea of the invisible church, in contrast, reflected a vision of a community founded in the substantially *integrated* pneumatic unity of its members. He conceived the invisible church as a community *without metaphysics,* whose bond with God is formed through faith, not through law. This community is the neo-Augustinian community of the New Testament. It sees the manifest *letter* of the Old Testament as giving rise to Pelagian or falsely juridical accounts of religious life, and it identifies the invisible *spirit* of the New Testament as the foundation for an authentic community.

In this respect, in consequence, Luther's work both represented and intensified the wider crisis of legal positivization that shaped the origins of modern German statehood and modern German political reflection. As discussed, the historical setting in which the Reformation occurred was deeply marked by a crisis in the law, in which the linear course of secularization running from the high Middle Ages was interrupted by new controversies over law's secular form, leading to a fateful disruption in the positive formation of law and to the inception of a second stage of legal positivization. Central to this second period of legal organization was a renewed hostility to unitary or universal conceptions of the law, and a renewed attempt, echoing the earliest conflicts between church and state, to expunge all claims to metaphysical validity from the law. The legal undercurrents in Luther's theology assimilated and reproduced elements of this controversial setting: Luther too reacted vehemently against all assumptions of universality in law, he too acknowledged the inherent exceptionality and contestability of law, and he too insisted that claims to absolute validity in law commonly derive from paradoxical or strategic accounts of law's origin.

Underlying both the practical and the theoretical course of the Reformation, therefore, was a revolt against the unitary form of the law and a denigration of the claims to binding or metaphysical validity articulated in this form. Underlying the practical and the theoretical course of the Reformation, moreover, was the sense that freedom from metaphysical law was a freedom to be under own laws, and that at the end of metaphysically authenticated law was the law of freedom. At the same time, however, Luther's relation to the process of legal formation around him was deeply equivocating and dialectical. Whilst promoting a non-metaphysical account of law, his theology had little to say about the necessary principles underlying positive law. On the contrary, in fact, he suggested that secular law, beyond its usefulness in keeping the peace and protecting good people from violence, has no necessary normative origin in divine reason, and true freedom, both the freedom of God and the freedom of humanity, is always freedom to be other than law. Whilst he attacked the pre-humanist unity of natural law that had underpinned Thomism, therefore, Lutheran teaching did little to institute a *human* – or specifically *humanist* – law or to place new law on newly human foundations.[51]

As a consequence of this, a first result of the Reformation, both practically and theoretically, was that freedom was detached from inherited law, that laws had to be explained in relatively contingent manner, without reference to ideas of natural law in Roman Catholicism. States and theories of state emerging from the Reformation were thus called upon to account for their freedom, and to explain, in positive terms, their inner legal structures. In this process, however, Lutheran theology did little to contribute directly to the theoretical consolidation or justification of the freedoms that it made possible.[52] The *Gemeinde* was the formative worldly ideal in Lutheranism, at least in its earliest expressions, but this did not provide for a clear political doctrine. In his conception of the *Gemeinde,* Luther saw the freedom obtained in religion through the liberation of God's freedom from metaphysical law as producing an elevated experience of human freedom. He saw the *Gemeinde* as a community that replaces the legal-theocratic or hierocratic aspects of the Roman church, and that pledges itself, at least in matters of the church, to an inspirited vision of common self-legislation.[53] The vision of the equally and cohesively inspirited community formed the counterweight to the reality of false laws and paradoxical laws which he encountered around him, and the commune integrated under faith appeared as the Lutheran alternative to the Thomist community, represented under law. Nonetheless, although other early Reformers, in early humanist manner, identified the *Gemeinde* as a new source of natural law, replacing the unity of law prescribed and represented by ecclesiastical hierarchy with a unity of law prescribed and enacted by the parish communities, Luther was unwilling to see the *Gemeinde* as endowed with political powers. In this crucial respect, therefore, Luther withdrew before the articulation of a distinct legal-political outlook, and Lutheranism did in fact not concretely produce sustained examples of religious orders based in communal self-administration or a universal priesthood.[54]

As a consequence of this, then, it was a specific characteristic of state formation after the Lutheran Reformation that German territorial states struggled to find distinctive vocabularies for explaining the conditions of their justification and their freedom. The most common immediate institutional consequence of the Reformation was in fact that the territorial states tended to organize their governmental structure in extremely paradoxical manner, often appropriating aspects of the canon law which they had first sought to suppress, gradually modelling their legal systems on the Roman Catholic decretals which they had striven to supplant, and thus, largely, emulating the constitutional forms the Roman Catholic Church.[55] Indeed, the earliest Evangelical commentaries on territorial ecclesiastical law even concluded that Gratian's work was founded in natural law, and should be accepted as an element of Evangelical church orders.[56] This process of borrowing culminated in the institution in the German states of a quasi-episcopal ecclesiastical order, through which states articulated their own legitimacy through direct, yet altered, reference to the legal principles of the empire and the Roman Catholic Church. In the wake of 1555, the jurisdictional powers of the Roman Catholic episcopate were gradually conferred on secular princes to form a state church;[57] these princes, aided by their court theologians, defined their position as the highest representative of a territorial episcopate (*Summepiskopat*), and they assumed a devolved responsibility for affairs of the church.[58] Under this system, princely executives often allowed their legal forms to be retheocratized, and they justified and explained their own freedom by imagining their law as a reflection of God's own will or God's own laws. Philipp Melanchthon, most importantly, set the tone for later reflections when, in the 1540s, he described the prince as the 'shepherd of the law' with responsibility for the 'teaching of religion' and for maintaining orthodoxy in the church.[59] Underlying this consequence of the Reformation, therefore, was a process in which particular states internalized the unity of reason and freedom, which they had first dismembered in the scholastic God, and in which they allowed a paradoxical reference to God's legal authorship to assist them in accounting for and in defending their own laws, which they made as positive laws, distinct from laws covered by original ideas of natural law. After the early Reformation had first denounced God's legal authorship as a metaphysical paradox, which the church, to the detriment of God, had constructed for itself, the later Reformation reacquired this paradox, and it permitted worldly states to use it against the church. The establishment of a state church contributed in numerous ways to the evolution of the early absolutist ecclesiastical regimes in the German territories, in which the *Gemeinde,* above all, played a deeply diminished role. The first era of state-building after the Reformation, therefore, was marked by an inflation of quasi-theocratic reference, not by accountable freedom from false law.

It was, in sum, a distinctive feature of the Lutheran Reformation that it evolved in an exceptional legal climate, and that it created an exceptional freedom in which new states and new laws could emerge. At the same time, however, it only offered a precarious basis for these states and these laws, and it reinforced the wider crisis of legal positivization characteristic of this era. States and theorists of state emerging from the Reformation, although recognizing their freedoms and laws as reliant on the attack on metaphysics expressed by Lutheranism, were therefore unable to call on constitutive political principles in the immediate theologists of Lutheranism, and they were forced to explain the source of law, power and freedom without direct assistance from Luther's own works.[60] If the centre of the Reformation was marked by a dislocation of freedom from reason and by the introduction of legal freedom into the form of the early territorial states, the Reformation did not account for the manifest human form of this freedom or for specifically human laws giving expression to this freedom. The main theoretical legacy of the Reformation, therefore, was that theorists were required to continue the metaphysical rebellion of Lutheranism and, in both personal and political life, to preserve and reinforce the freedoms (the *new laws*) obtained, as God's freedom and human freedom, through the Reformation. Indeed, the freedoms from metaphysics, obtained as the positive form of God's own freedom, were immediately identified as German freedoms, as the freedoms in which German states freely developed and explained their political structure. Yet these states, and their theorists, were also called upon to convert these freedoms into an account of freedom in which freedom could be stabilized under demonstrable laws of freedom, not only under new laws of faith. After the Reformation, therefore, German political theorists received the complex task of imagining God's freedom, and German freedom, as a human freedom, of finding positive legal form for this freedom, and even of reconnecting this freedom with accountably human justifications. At this point, the problem of legal positivization became abidingly inseparable from the problem of humanism, and after the Reformation the need to consolidate the law in consistently positive forms coincided with the need to explain the human authorship of law and to consolidate the conditions on which the human being, after metaphysics, could act as a legislative agent. The freedom obtained in the Reformation was, in any case, initially an exceptional freedom, and subsequent debate returned recurrently to the task of finding a reliable positive and human form for this freedom.

1 The Reformation and the loss of law

Against natural law

The philosophical background of Luther's theology was shaped by a series of debates about the law, so that his religious ideas necessarily evolved, in part, within a set of legal references and discussions. The prevailing philosophical controversy in German universities in the latter part of the fifteenth century was the debate between the realists and the nominalists, in which realists, or the Thomists, represented the so-called *via antiqua,* and the nominalists, or Ockhamists, represented the *via moderna.* The increasingly influential nominalist view in these controversies was founded in the belief that God is essentially *will,* and that God's redeeming freedom in human history is an act of divine will, and is not tied to rational normative preconditions. The nominalists opposed the intellectualist claims of Thomism, they negated the Thomist presupposition that there exists an eternal metaphysical law in nature, or that the universe is an 'organic whole' in which all things are connected ultimately to the divine mind,[1] and they rejected the central Thomist assumption that the church and the state form an insoluble legal unity.[2] The *via moderna,* therefore, contained an attack on the ideas of divinity as an intellectual essence promoted by medieval scholasticism and an attack on the legal and institutional doctrines rising from medieval ius-naturalism, which presupposed that the laws of the world exist in continuity with God's will and God's reason, and that human action and human politics can be evaluated by their proximity to this will and this reason. Underlying the philosophical environment from which Luther emerged there was thus an increasing willingness to construe God's freedom in volitional terms, and to question whether God might be construed as a juridical presence in the world, accessible to human reason and manifest in clear prescriptions for individual moral and collective political order.

The influence of Ockhamist nominalism on Luther was perhaps rather vague and indirect.[3] However, in certain respects Luther's early writings contain an intensification of ideas associated with late medieval nominalism and the *via moderna.* Fundamental to Luther's first writings is the claim that there exists an opposition between faith and law, and that conformity with law cannot bring salvation. Indeed, at the heart of these works is a rejection of the defining view of medieval Thomism: namely, that God's will is evident in the positive legal order of the world, and that human beings can use their rational powers to understand the foundations of this originary metaphysical order and shape their own wills in accordance with it. Instead, Luther saw God as removed and remote, as absolutely free, and so as evident only in faith, not demonstrable or manifest in any metaphysical scheme or any stable system of law. In this, he extended the voluntaristic conceptions of the *via moderna,* and he argued that God exercises his will with absolute freedom in the world, and inhabitants of the world, where they do not have faith, can only despair over their inability to appreciate and obey God's will and God's law. No element of worldly ordinance can, in consequence, be placed on a continuum with God's will, and there is no necessary or intellectual unity either between God's will and human reason, or between God's will and the laws used to govern human societies. No law, Luther indicated simply, can begin to form an adequate reflection of God; no action or works in conformity with law can lead to justification before God; and human reason cannot obtain laws that unite it, in metaphysical knowledge, with God's will.

Luther initially elaborated this opposition between faith and law in his very early interpretation of what was ultimately to become the one of the central texts of Reformation theology: St Paul's *Epistle to the Romans.*[4] Commenting on this Epistle, he explained that obedience to the law cannot lead to human salvation. In fact, obedience to the law leads to pride and 'self-glorification', and it obstructs true faith by promising salvation as the entitled reward for outward human activity.[5] Justification can only occur as a passive experience of grace, which God 'enacts by acting upon us', without any concern for our 'works and deserts'.[6] The path to salvation is through faith alone, not through works demonstrating compliance with law.

In this argument, Luther addressed one of the fundamental problems in the history of Christian doctrine: that is, the problematic relation between the Old Testament and the New Testament, and the relation of Mosaic law to faith in Jesus Christ. In his treatment of this, he followed Augustine's anti-Pelagian approach, and he insisted on the primacy of the New Testament and faith over the Old Testament and law, and he stated that only a direct reading of the New Testament, and the faith that this might inspire, can make salvation possible. This argument referred primarily to the salvation of souls: it claimed that no external displays of devotion or righteousness can lead to justification before God, and that the religious orders that confuse law and faith or place law before faith threaten the souls of their adherents. In addition, however, this argument also contained implications for wider legal and political concerns: it implied that true law is not expressed as natural or material ordinance, but that the true law is the *new law,* the invisible law of a community united in Christian faith alone, and only this law can bring salvation. Unlike purely antinomian or Gnostic theologians, Luther did not entirely reject the Old Testament, or the elements of Christian natural law founded in the Decalogue. He claimed that the moral codes in the Old Testament might be accepted as long as they serve interests of public order and help to protect Christians from the evil deeds of the ungodly. Indeed, his teaching also intermittently expressed a minimal conception of natural law, and he was prepared to accept as natural those laws preserving outer conditions of stability and reflecting a general human interest in peace and security. He, therefore, saw the Old Testament as expressing a natural law of practical utility, which is 'written in the hearts of all men', and contains certain universally acceptable precepts.[7] Nonetheless, he viewed 'natural law' as, by definition, a limited law, and he saw the validity of such law as restricted to the human person in its natural condition, without relevance to the person as a bearer of faith. Moreover, he argued that natural law is the law of the Jews: he described the Decalogue as 'the common law [*Sachsenspiegel*] of the Jews'.[8] Such law is contaminated by worldly pride and false piety, and it is the law of those who 'boast about the law which they have received and brag that they are its adherents and followers.'[9] Above all, natural law is the law of those who cannot ascend to the *new law* of faith and whose legal compliance is limited to outward things, and obedience to this law does not elevate the person to the level of a true Christian.[10] Natural law, in short, cannot express an embracing continuity between divine and human law. It is essential to natural law that it applies to all people, Christians, Jews and heathens, and it cannot be viewed as a medium of grace, which is offered only to Christians.[11] Natural law applies to that realm of natural life where there is no faith.

Luther's early attack on natural law was specifically designed as an attack on Roman Catholicism and on the scholastic orthodoxy of Aquinas, and it immediately touched at the nervous centre of Roman Catholic orthodoxy.[12] Aquinas also argued that compliance with the law of the Old Testament cannot confer grace without faith. However, Thomism assumed a partial continuity between the law of the Old Testament and the faith of the New Testament; it argued that the natural law of the Old Testament anticipates and foreshadows the salvation eventually to be brought by Christ, and that even ceremonial laws bring humanity close to God. Moreover, Aquinas also saw the pope as a privileged interpreter of the eternal law, and he viewed the church as the primary custodian of the law.[13] For Aquinas, in short, God's grace possesses a juridical nature; he saw obedience to laws, sanctioned by the church, as a primary means of obtaining grace, and he saw the church as responsible for guiding people towards legal obedience and towards salvation. Luther, in contrast, argued that faith is corrupted by the law, that belief in natural law exaggerates the extent of human knowledge and allows people to assume salvation without true faith. The belief in natural law, therefore, persuades people that they can be saved without faith, and it dilutes the urgency with which each person seeks salvation through faith. A 'Christian person', Luther explained, 'has enough in faith, so that he does not need works to be pious', and whoever has faith is 'delivered from all commandments and laws.'[14] The institutions of the Roman Catholic Church, he concluded, are founded on the false precondition that the administration of law facilitates salvation, and that God's will can be made legally apparent as a certain path to salvation, and, in offering indulgences and dispensations for sins, they assert their own legal order to the detriment of Christian souls. In his polemics on this matter, he demanded a complete segregation of faith and law, arguing that the church should have power only in the resolution of spiritual questions,[15] and that matters of secular law should be left to 'worldly judges'.[16] 'There is', he concluded, 'no power in the church', except the power of spiritual improvement,[17] and the claim that representatives of the church might possess any legal authority is a Pelagian heresy, which endangers the souls of the members of the church.[18]

The *Gemeinde* and the two kingdoms

Central to the practical implications of Luther's theology is the belief that the church only exists as a pneumatic community, or as a pure community of believers, not as a hierarchical, legally ordered or metaphysically *representative* institution. He saw the church as an invisible community, whose offices are restricted to teaching and biblical interpretation, whose members are united by faith alone, not by law, as *a universal priesthood.* All Christians, he explained, are 'the brothers of Christ' and all are 'consecrated as priests'.[19] In this respect, Luther took the charismatic communes of the early church as the model for a reorganization of ecclesiastical life, and he argued that the principle of universal priesthood meant that the parish or commune (*Gemeinde*) should be seen as the centre of all religious life and should replace the hierarchical order of the Roman Catholic Church. The episcopate and the ordained priests of the Roman church do not truly constitute a *Gemeinde,* he argued.[20] The bishops and the priests of the papacy, he explained, have corrupted the New Testament through the representative legal order that they have imposed upon the church. It is only where it divests itself of law that a church becomes a true *Gemeinde,* founded in faith and truth. In an authentic church, Luther concluded, members of the *Gemeinde* give laws in accordance with the scriptures alone, without reliance on natural laws or any laws external to the common unitary experiences of faith.[21]

In its original articulation, the concept of the *Gemeinde* was not focused solely on the church, and it envisaged an ideal of the self-organizing community, which implicitly expanded beyond religious life and administration. In fact, Luther's early anti-legal strictures reflected a wider attitude, which attacked the concentration of power in both ecclesiastical and secular jurisdiction. The conflation of law and faith in the church, he claimed, had created a realm of 'priestly tyrants', who distortedly interpreted Christianity as a doctrine of 'worldly authority'.[22] In secular life, then, the law served to bolster the standing of the outwardly 'powerful and the wise', whose claims to social dignity were based on illusions of virtue, obtained through law.[23]

In his earliest works, Luther questioned the right of 'worldly princes and rulers' to take common goods from their subjects; he opposed the emerging hierarchical government under Roman law; and he suggested that 'the law and morals of the land', not the newly received Roman law, should act as the basis for legal ruling. God had ordained, he concluded, that 'every land has its own manner and talents, and should be governed by its own simple laws'.[24] The early doctrine of the *Gemeinde* integrated in faith alone was thus first conceived as a radically egalitarian doctrine, which condemned the authority of law in both religious and worldly contexts, which denounced false piety and socially instituted displays of esteem and worth, and which sought to bind all people under shared laws. In this respect, therefore, Luther used his broad anti-legalism as a vehicle for criticizing secular law, and for demanding that all law should draw from a common source. In the *Gemeinde,* he stated, people are bound by internally held laws: 'each is the judge of the other, and in turn also subject to the other', and faith places all people on equal legal footing.[25] Moreover, the members of the *Gemeinde* are, in so far as they are guided by the scriptures, entitled to assume authority for themselves and to organize their communities as they see fit.[26]

Despite this, however, Luther's account of the *Gemeinde* remained highly equivocating in the political role that it imputed to the community united in faith. His idea of the *Gemeinde* was primarily concentrated on questions of religious organization, teaching and appointment, not on the formation of secular or worldly power. Indeed, despite the critical aspects of his earliest reflections on worldly law, in his later theoretical career he was unwilling to accept that the religious community could produce laws for worldly organization. The *Gemeinde,* he argued, has power and freedom only in religious matters, and it only obtains this power and freedom because of its objective inspiration by the New Testament. In all other matters, the *Gemeinde* is obedient to worldly laws. 'Christ speaks' in the *Gemeinde,* Luther stated. But in the world 'the authorities command what they want, and the subjects accept it.'[27] At the heart of his mature idea of the *Gemeinde* is the claim that the realm of the inspirited community, integrated under new laws, cannot determine the realm of natural or objective authority: indeed, it is constitutive of new law that it does not have objective or material force.

In this light, the conception of the law in the early Reformation appears as a complex and dialectical form. At one level, Luther identified the religiously inspired community, divested of the legal, hierarchical and metaphysically representative order of the Roman Catholic Church, as the locus of human freedom and integrity – as the congregation of the universal priesthood. He saw this as a community of equals, bound only by very rudimentary forms of external law and internally united by the invisibly experienced regime of faith. At the same time, however, he saw this community, to a large extent, as the community of faith alone, largely defined by the fact that it is not political. Central to the idea of the *Gemeinde,* therefore, is the belief that worldly power and spiritual power form two quite distinct areas of human existence, or two separate kingdoms, that each of these kingdoms should acknowledge that it is limited by the other, and that neither of these realms can provide laws to organize the other. Worldly power, Luther concluded, should always be free to 'use its office without hindrance', and all attempts to impose 'spiritual law' on worldly authority or to distill maxims for government from religious teaching belong to the quasi-Pelagian legal ideas that characterize the Roman church.[28] To assume that the *Gemeinde* can provide laws for worldly governance presupposes that there is a natural legal unity binding God and the world and that those who have faith also necessarily have knowledge of law. For Luther, however, those who have faith are above the law, and their freedom is determined precisely by the fact that it is not captured in law.

On this basis, then, in the 1520s Luther argued that the freedom from tyrannical law offered by the *Gemeinde* is an inner freedom, or a freedom under the shared inner law of faith. Although his reflections on the *Gemeinde* at times extended into more critical pronouncements on worldly law, he did not consistently see freedom in the *Gemeinde* as a freedom to make laws, and the *Gemeinde* did not provide an expressly positive or natural basis for worldly laws. Indeed, it is specific to Luther's thinking that faith cannot legislate and that new laws cannot be applied to outer nature. Natural law, such as it exists, is defined precisely by the fact that it does not originate in faith or divine reason and that it only applies to the functional necessities of the worldly kingdom. Worldly power, therefore, has a necessary independence from faith and it obtains natural sanction as an order that maintains stability and authority in the world. Luther in fact concluded that 'worldly law and the sword' constitute an 'order in the world' that is specifically ordained by natural law,[29] and he claimed that 'authority, regiment and power' must remain 'as long the world continue to stand'.[30] The order and the authority of the world, however, are distinguished by the fact that they are only supported by very limited laws of nature and have no origin in faith or in the new laws of faith. As two distinct kingdoms, the state must take responsibility for maintaining 'external peace', and the church must help 'make people pious' and oversee spiritual well-being.[31] However, there is no natural link between these kingdoms, and natural law can only apply to the worldly kingdom.

In separating the two kingdoms, Luther's primary ambition was to liberate the church – the *Gemeinde* – from all legal control, to consolidate the church as a place of faith alone and to ensure that members of the church were not deflected from faith by law. This meant, first, that the church had to be protected from worldly rulers. The 'worldly regiment', he explained,

> has laws which stretch no further than over body and goods and the external things on earth. For God cannot and will not let anyone else but himself alone rule over the soul. Therefore, wherever worldly power is brazen enough to give laws to souls, it pulls God into its regiment and seduces and ruins the souls.[32]

Second, however, this argument was also intended to counteract the expansion of ecclesiastical influence beyond questions of faith, and so to protect the church from leaders, such as those in the Roman Catholic Church, who contaminate the church with political ambitions. Representatives of the Roman Catholic Church, Luther claimed, 'have become worldly princes, and rule with laws which are only applied to the body and to goods. [{.. .}] They are supposed to rule souls, internally, through God's word, but they rule externally.'[33] Such conflation of the two regiments, he argued, necessarily obstructs human salvation. Worldly power that assumes spiritual power fails to understand that 'Christians must be governed in faith', and that no worldly authority can rule in this way.[34]

A further motive for Luther's separation of the two kingdoms was simply that he considered worldly power immeasurably less important than religion. Worldly power, he explained, does not have power over souls, and therefore it 'can do no damage'. Worldly power is 'a small thing before God': it is far too small for people to become 'disobedient or disunited' because of it.[35] Religious power, in contrast, causes great damage when it exceeds its limits, where it conflates faith and law, or where it loses sight of its obligation to the human soul. For this reason, in fact, Luther indicated that those who are truly Christian need not concern themselves with matters relating to worldly authority, and they need not devote time properly devoted to the care of their souls to questions of worldly law. The 'worldly regiment', he concluded, is only necessary for those who do not have faith; it is only the unbelievers who 'belong beneath the law'. Those who have faith are obedient to the law if the law is good, because they too are good. And they are also obedient to the law if the law is bad, because they recognize that the law cannot either bring or deny them their salvation.[36] Law, therefore, is not finally necessary for those who are, out of free choice and faith, Christians. For Christians, the only virtue of law is that it might offer them protection from the evil actions of those who are not Christians. Otherwise, law is not of essential importance, and matters falling beneath the law's jurisdiction are relatively incidental.

In addition, however, Luther's idea of the two kingdoms also reflected a great anxiety about *theocracy*. Luther saw all theocratic outlooks as lapsing into the Jewish religious knowledge of the Old Testament and as falsely assuming that precepts for external obedience can bring salvation. Above all, in indicating that God's rule can be instituted on earth, theocracy, for Luther, arrogantly integrates God's freedom into worldly law and it removes the obligation of faith from the individual soul and so distracts the soul from the cause of its salvation. This anxiety was originally expressed as a condemnation of the assertion of worldly authority by the Roman Catholic Church, which Luther saw as a particularly crude manifestation of theocratic monarchy. At the same time, though, through the evolution of his thought he also became intent on differentiating his own stance from the more febrile millenarian movements that attached themselves to the Reformation, and some of his harshest polemics were reserved for those who interpreted Reformation theology as a doctrine of religious self-governance or divinely legitimized insurrection. It is for this reason, primarily, that Luther suppressed the early natural-legal elements in his idea of the *Gemeinde,* that he refused to allow this concept to found a political doctrine, and that he concluded that the new laws of faith are invalidated where they are transformed into laws of government or worldly politics. Indeed, against the more radical millenarianism of the early Reformation, he argued that those united in faith must not use faith for political ends and that they must not refer to faith when opposing political regimes which they perceive as illegitimate. Faith cannot provide principles that authorize objective political order, and, conversely, it cannot provide principles that validate resistance to it. No 'rebellion is justified',[37] he simply concluded, and later he added: 'We cannot resist authority with violence, but only by confessing the truth.'[38]

Natural law, in sum, only exists for Luther as an extremely limited natural law, which justifies worldly order as order, and which entitles worldly order to use coercive force to uphold conditions of stability. No higher or transcendent element of natural law can be summoned to oppose this order: higher or transcendent law is the *new law* of faith in the New Testament, which cannot be politically applied or even made positively manifest. Therefore, whilst Luther dissolved the metaphysical order of scholastic natural law by identifying the *Gemeinde,* not the representative church and its legal apparatus, as the essential expression of human life, he refused to replace the legal metaphysics of Roman Catholicism with any alternative type of theocracy. Indeed, he placed himself firmly against all attempts to reinstate theocratic natural law, or to repair the fractured unity of law under Roman Catholicism. His theology thus left law as a matter of relative indifference, which cannot institute true freedom and in fact impedes the true freedom of faith and the soul.

The idea of the *Gemeinde,* consequently, describes the dialectical core of Luther's legal theology, and it also describes the dialectical core of the legal debates initiated by the Reformation. At one level, Luther actively promoted a positivization of the law; he saw both God and humanity as authentically free of invariably metaphysical law, he claimed that law is a matter of human freedom, whose authority is not authenticated by absolute essences or absolutely external principles of reason. Law, therefore, is a law of freedom: it is a *new law.* At the same time, however, he also expressly diminished the positive authority of the law; he announced that true law, the new law, is only in faith, that objective law has only limited application and, indeed, that the particular freedom offered by the Reformation is undermined by law. This evolved as the main problem in the legal theologies of the Reformation, and controversies on the law during and after the Reformation concentrated on the endeavour to resolve the antinomies arising from Luther's legal attitude and to explain how freedom from metaphysics might also be constructed as a positive human freedom. For this reason, moreover, most of the contemporary debates in which Luther participated were also tied to debates about the law, as the theologians around him recognized the problems in his legal thought, and tentatively configured his teachings to include more reliable legal principles.

Radical theocracy and antinomianism

Luther's views on the two kingdoms marked a move away from the more critical legal implications of his very earliest works. Indeed, it has often been pointed out that the political aspects of Luther's theology underwent a striking transformation in the first half of the 1520s. During these years, Luther consciously dissociated himself from the more radical theologians of the early Reformation, and he hardened his thought into a set of more considered attitudes regarding law and political authority. This was caused, first, by the fact that the Evangelical movement became increasingly volatile whilst he was imprisoned in the Wartburg in 1521–22; this period witnessed feverish outbreaks of iconoclasm and violent reforms of church order in Wittenberg. Then, more pressingly, it was caused by the emergence of the radical Reformation, one strain of which was reflected in the revolutionary ius-naturalism of Thomas Müntzer, and which culminated in the Peasants War of 1524–25.

On the first issue, during the iconoclastic interlude in Wittenberg Luther was deeply concerned that his denial of representative authority to the church could be seen as a mandate for violent acts against ecclesiastical property, and he was alarmed at the idea that his teachings should seen to vindicate lawlessness and insurrection. For this reason, after his release from captivity he turned with particular vehemence on his lapsed disciple, Andreas Bodenstein von Carlstadt, who had played a leading role in the events of 1521–22. During this time, Carlstadt set out a distinctive interpretation of Luther's teachings, which intensified Luther's assault on the canon law, declared the scriptures as the sole basis of legitimate political authority,[39] and insisted that true faith entitled its adherents to act against the law where the law was demonstrably unjust.[40] Carlstadt, who was trained as a lawyer, differed from Luther in that he accentuated the possibility of a metaphysical convergence of the divine law and the human law.[41] He, therefore, rejected the doctrine of the two kingdoms, and he proposed a radical-theocratic theology which directly contradicted Luther's relative legal indifferentism. 'God rules us', Carlstadt claimed, and 'God's kingdom' demands that 'law and regiment' should be established for all things.[42] More emphatically still, he argued that the 'spirit of the law is the will of God', and that God's will must be made manifest in worldly law.[43]

In addition to this, Carlstadt's theology contained an intensely spiritualistic account of ecclesiastical power in which he insisted that the church is founded only in spiritual unity, not in any monopoly of ceremony, and that the laws of the church originate in spirit alone. To a greater extent even than Luther, he saw the church as an invisibly integrated community, and he derided all material or institutional tokens of ecclesiastical authority. For this reason, Carlstadt's invectives focused on Roman Catholic teachings concerning the Eucharist, and he denied that the church could act as a custodian of Christ's real presence in the administration of the Eucharist. The bread and wine of the Eucharist, he claimed, do not contain the flesh and blood of Christ: they are nothing more than 'signs of God's promises',[44] or signs of God's 'word',[45] and it is only possible to partake 'spiritually' in these signs.[46] Elsewhere, he modified this interpretation of the Eucharist and argued that drinking the wine is an act of symbolic 'memory', so that those who drink 'recollect the Lord'.[47] Nonetheless, central to these reflections was the belief that inherited views of the Eucharist serve to consolidate institutional power in the Roman Catholic church and to stabilize the church as a legal administrator of grace. In fact, however, the Eucharist is a symbolic event, which is not tied to any one location, but which integrates all believers equally, independently and invisibly. For similar reasons, he also denounced the use of imagery in churches; images, he explains, 'have no origin in God', and, as they detract from the internally unifying process of spiritual recollection, they should be forcibly removed or thrown down.[48]

It is of the greatest importance for Luther's intellectual trajectory that he deplored Carlstadt's activities in Wittenberg and that he chose to refine his own political views in critical reference to Carlstadt's work.[49] In his debates with Carlstadt, he protested, first, against 'storming the images and breaking the churches'.[50] With still greater consternation, he noted that some of his early followers seemed to interpret his teaching as a rejection of all scriptural orthodoxy and as a purely spiritualist doctrine.[51] This, he warned, might lead to a dereliction of all 'divine order', and might appear to provide justification for insurrection. Indeed, Luther was especially threatened by Carlstadt's view of the Eucharist as a justification for an entirely spiritual or personal interpretation of the Bible, and he was deeply exercised by the sense that the spiritualist denial of Christ's real presence in the Eucharist might lead to the final abolition of the church as an institutional form.[52] In his discussion of the Eucharist, therefore, Luther opposed the fully spiritualistic or symbolist doctrines set out by his fellow Reformers, especially Carlstadt and Huldrych Zwingli, and he set out a doctrine of *consubstantiation* in the Eucharist, which contained a modified version of the Roman Catholic idea that Christ is really present in the bread and wine. Luther's doctrine stated that Christ is omnipresent and universal, thus inspiring a universal church. Yet he saw Christ's presence as especially concentrated in the Eucharist, and so as manifest in the institutional order of an established church, commanding orthodoxy in teaching and worship. This treatment of the Eucharist was shaped by a reluctance fully to accept the reality of the universal and invisible church, and it remained attached to the traditional notion of the church as the custodian of mystery and grace and as the primary receptacle of divine presence.

In these respects, Luther's criticism of Carlstadt turned against the aspects of antinomian thought in Carlstadt's work, and he sought to qualify the idea that a religious community with no institutional order could assume accountability for doctrine and teaching. More fundamentally, however, Luther's opposition to Carlstadt was also affected by the suspicion that Carlstadt's theocratic vision exaggerated the significance of worldly law, that it was excessively influenced by the Old Testament, and that it falsely assumed that faith and law could be united in worldly order. Measures to be taken against the Catholic church, he explained, should be executed by 'worldly authority and the nobility', and the community united in faith should not assume any power of law.[53] During this critical period in the development of the Reformation, therefore, Luther showed himself, in his legal ideas, to be an increasingly conservative thinker, who was clearly unnerved by the prospect that the religious communities liberated from the old ecclesiastical order might assume far-reaching authority for themselves. In his opposition to the antinomian and the legal-theocratic aspects of Carlstadt's work, in fact, Luther's idea of freedom as freedom above law moved perceptibly towards a defence of worldly authority, and an assumption that inner freedom is best preserved under a strong outer state.

Luther's debates with Carlstadt also show certain similarities with his debates with Zwingli. Zwingli shared certain basic principles of political theology with Luther. Like Luther, he endorsed a doctrine of two kingdoms, which separated 'divine justice' from 'human justice' and assigned inferior status to human justice. Like Luther, he described human justice as 'poor' and 'weak' in contrast to divine justice.[54] He too argued that human salvation is only brought by the new law, represented in Christ in the New Testament, and it cannot be measured in legal terms or obtained through legal acts.[55] These arguments led Zwingli to conclude that religious power is based solely in 'the divine scripture', and those who officiate such power do not possess 'authority' in the worldly sense.[56] The church, he explained, is nothing more than the 'community of all pious Christians', and all legal-constitutional ideas of church authority corrupt its invisibly inspiriting character: the 'statutes' of ecclesiastical authority, most especially, are the cause of 'all disturbance' in the church.[57] Nonetheless, echoing Luther's doctrine of the two kingdoms, he also insisted that the sphere of human justice commands obedience as mandated by 'God's ordinance', although the 'poor justice' of this sphere can do little more than create rudimentary conditions of peace and order.[58]

Despite these shared preconditions, however, Zwingli was far closer to theocratic ideas than Luther. The divine word, he argued, must 'rule over all people', and it should, by implication, always limit and determine human justice. All laws, in short, should be 'formed in accordance with the divine will',[59] and the best mode of government is one which 'rules with God'.[60]

Zwingli's doctrine of the two kingdoms also differed perceptibly from Luther's thought in that he insisted on a more integral and metaphysically constitutive relation between the regiments, and he ascribed an important role to divine law as the originating foundation of human law. He stated, for example, that Christ 'forbade all wealth',[61] that Christians should not 'govern like princes',[62] and that worldly 'government and authority', where it is not exercised by 'tyrants', should hold to the word of Christ's teaching.[63] If the 'laws of princes' are against the divine will, he concluded, it is essential to be 'more obedient to God than to men', and resistance to worldly law is fully justified.[64] On these grounds, Zwingli also proposed a doctrine of natural law which is far stronger than the simple utilitarian ideas implied by Luther; he argued that all 'laws connecting us to fellow men' should be 'founded in the law of nature',[65] and that, crucially, the experience of faith provides insights into the laws of nature. Unlike Luther, therefore, he argued that natural law is not peculiar to Jewish or heathen cultures, it is not founded in the merely natural or positive element of human existence, and it in fact coexists with and gives expression to faith. Natural law originates in divine law, and human conduct according with natural law also accords with divine law. Natural law, therefore, can only be 'known through God', and knowledge of 'the law of nature comes solely from the holy spirit'.[66] Zwingli consequently asserted that worldly power should be exercised by 'believing and God-fearing' leaders, and authority should be placed in the hands of judges, who interpret all things 'after the word and ordinance of God'. Under such political conditions, laws can 'become like the divine will', and they possess something of the character of divine law and divine will, for the justice imparted by judges and magistrates is a shadow of true justice.[67]

On these foundations, Zwingli argued that the Bible provides a legal basis for the entire community, so that in a Christian community no one should ever be 'without law', or without legal protection. Law should only be administered by secular courts, not by church authorities, for the proper limits of the church would be exceeded if it assumed duties under civil law: it is the responsibility of the church to help ensure that 'fair courts of law' are established, not actually to preside over these courts.[68] However, Zwingli clearly indicated that the church should play a fully integrated role in the political community, and it should provide a foundation of legal principle on which the wider political community can evolve. He was thus far more emphatic than Luther in his claim that religion should form the substructure of all law, and he moved close to advocating a model of communal or local theocracy, which argued that the Gospel should be applied by secular powers and judges, and which saw the inspirited 'commune' (*Gemeinde*) as the bearer of responsibility for both political and religious decisions.[69]

Zwingli's doctrine of the Eucharist was also directly opposed to that set out by Luther. Whilst Luther's notion of consubstantiation still endorsed aspects of the ceremonial structure of the Roman church, and still espoused a doctrine – albeit diluted – of the real presence, Zwingli, like Carlstadt, argued that the bread and wine of the Eucharist have a merely symbolic content, and simply enact a 'recollection' of Christ's death.[70] He saw the Eucharist as a symbol of Christian communion with Christ's spiritual nature, and he saw participation in this communion as extending beyond the custody of appointed representatives of the church. For this reason, he claimed that the assumption of Christ's 'corporeal' presence in the Eucharist devalues Christ's divine nature and falsely restricts Christ's spirit to one particular place. Like Carlstadt, in fact, he expressly associated the Catholic doctrine of transubstantiation with the corrupting political ambitions of the papacy; he saw the assumption of real presence in the Eucharist as creating a ceremonial order around the church that was designed to sustain the church as a worldly power, asserting a false monopoly over spiritual goods.[71] Indeed, it is generally notable that theologians who supported a spiritualist interpretation of the Eucharist – including Johannes Oecolampadius,[72] and, to a far greater degree, Caspar Schwenckfeld – usually opted for more communal theocratic ideas of law and politics, and they opposed the relative indifferentism of Luther's political theology.[73]

Luther's reluctance to embrace the politically constitutive aspects of the Evangelical movement can also be discerned in the transformation of his attitude towards princely authority through the 1520s. In his earliest writings, as discussed, Luther spoke out against the legal concentration of princely power through the period of imperial reform, and he especially criticized Roman law as an instrument of princely coercion and advocated a simplification of legal procedure. In this regard, he had certain similarities with the leaders of the peasants' uprisings of 1524–25, whose grievances also concentrated on the new legal processes in the post-feudal German territories, and on the erosion of traditions of oral or common law-finding.[74] The peasants protested fervently against the increasing use of Roman law, and they articulated their protests either as a demand for a return to the old common law, or for the establishment of a regime based in divine law.[75] As in the earlier outbursts of iconoclasm, however, in the Peasants War of 1524–25 Luther encountered what he perceived as a distortedly militant or theocratic interpretation of his teachings, culminating in a denial of obedience to princely authority, and after this time his attitude to princely authority changed markedly.

In his writings on princely power, Luther's great antipode (at least in recent historical representations of this era) was Thomas Müntzer, who had originally been influenced by Luther, but who soon transformed Evangelical doctrine into a theocratic programme of political resistance. Müntzer rejected Luther's doctrine of the two kingdoms and his separation of faith and law; he claimed that it is impossible 'to serve two lords, both of whom strive against each other', and he denied that worldly power could be judged by any law other than the pure law of the scriptures.[76] Christ, Müntzer concluded, urges that the 'will of God and his work should be carried out on earth through observation of the law'. Indeed, compliance with divine law on earth is the most necessary sign of faith, and it is only possible to 'distinguish belief from unbelief' by observing outward compliance with the law.[77] This teaching on divine law was intended firstly to provide a justification for resistance against all who exercise power in ungodly manner.[78] However, it also provided the foundation for a communal theocracy that assumed that all people should participate in law-finding and implementing the divine will. The spirit of Christianity, Müntzer argued, can only be fulfilled if the 'whole commune has the power of the sword', and if 'the good old custom of the people' is used as the basis for legal finding and for interpreting 'God's law'.[79] Müntzer thus moved towards a radical-theocratic variant on natural-law ideas, which saw a direct relation between faith and law, and which viewed the peasant commune as the natural manifestation of God's will in law.

Luther's response to Müntzer's ideas was vehemently to condemn the insurrections of the peasants and to support the princes in the violent suppression of the peasant armies.[80] To support this, he denounced all people seeking to 'enact God's scriptures on earth', and he denied that the Bible could be employed to justify any act of political resistance. If the 'worldly regiment' is overthrown, he explained, this leads not to a political order founded in 'God's word' but rather to 'eternal destruction'.[81] It is only heathens, not Christians, he argued, who 'struggle against authority', for only heathens attach such importance to worldly rule. Christians, in contrast, fight only through the cross and through suffering. Their 'victory' lies not 'in governing or in power', but in 'vanquishment and powerlessness'.[82]

Through all these political controversies of the first years of the Reformation, it is evident that Luther's theology was most deeply troubled by the question of theocracy and by the relation between theocracy and natural law. At a most obvious level, like other Reformers he reacted against the quasi-theocratic claims of Roman Catholicism, which, like other Reformers, he reviled as a Pelagian monarchy, unable to maintain the care of souls. However, whilst other Reformers saw this reaction as an opportunity for instituting a different theocracy or a new natural law, Luther's teaching remained fixed on the separation of faith and law and on the disjuncture between absolute reason and worldly power. He consequently refused to replace the metaphysics of scholasticism with a new metaphysics of law, based in the *Gemeinde,* and he insistently stated that law merely pertains to matters of practical regulation under a worldly regime, guided only by limited ideas of utility. In each of the defining controversies of the earliest years of the Reformation, Luther's position turned on the same point. This was, namely, the belief that faith is not politically constitutive, that the new law of faith is a spiritual law, not a secular law, and that natural law is only a limited law, not a metaphysical law founded in faith. Müntzer specifically identified this point in his tirades against Luther; he denounced Luther's purely scriptural, and anti-theocratic idea of faith, and he proposed instead a theology of 'testimony', in which scriptures give witness for worldly action and political upheaval.[83]

Antinomianism and the third use of the law

A more exposed flank in Luther's theology emerged in his debates with the antinomian theologians of the early Reformation, most especially with Johann Agricola. Whilst other Reformers saw the Reformation as providing an opportunity for genuine theocratic governance, Agricola saw the Reformation as leading to an entirely spiritual community, in which all law, but most especially the laws derived from the Old Testament, are abrogated and rendered invalid. Unlike other early Reformers, therefore, Agricola intensified the opposition between faith and law in Luther's own thought, and he denied categorically that any preaching of law can be based in the Christian faith or that any regiment can be supported by God's will.[84] The religion of law in the Old Testament, he argued, is a tyrannical religion, which induces a devastating alienation between humanity and God. Such law cannot 'make people just'; it is 'an office of death', which reduces people to despair and misery over their own inability to fulfil it. It is the law itself, not those who cannot fulfil it, in consequence, which must be 'damned and condemned.'[85] The faith revealed in the New Testament thus stands in full contradiction of the laws of the Old Testament: faith can have no relation to law, it marks the *end of the law,* and the faith disclosed in the New Testament cannot be manifested in any law, either in the law of the church or in the laws of the state.[86] Roman Catholicism, with its ceremonies and masses, is an eminently corrupt religion of law, whereas the Evangelical faith, based in the New Testament, is a religion of 'grace and truth', founded not in a God which issues commandments to humanity, but in a God offering reconciliation through faith and love.[87]

Antinomianism was an element of Evangelical doctrine that shadowed the entire early history of Lutheranism; this was no coincidence, for antinomian elements were surely ingrained in Luther's early works and Luther never unambiguously distinguished his own theology of law from antinomian attitudes. However, in his controversies with Agricola, he set out a nuanced theory of law, through which he placed himself delicately between antinomian views and views susceptible to theocratic interpretation. In these controversies, he maintained his earlier view that law is 'not necessary for justification'; indeed, he described the law as 'truly useless' in helping people obtain salvation. Not enough could be said, therefore, 'against the impotence of the law' and against 'the most pestilential faith in the law' which sees law as a means of ensuring justification.[88] However, he also argued, reinforcing a point in his earlier writings, that law remains necessary because it shows to people that they cannot be virtuous by their own means, and it at least makes people conscious of the need for faith and for grace.[89]

It is impossible 'to know sin without law', Luther concluded, and knowledge of sin is the first precondition of grace.[90] As a consequence, although law is not operative in securing justification, it is essential for creating despair and humility in the human soul, and so for allowing the soul to recognize that it cannot be justified without faith. It is only 'the pernicious' who espouse the fully antinomian claim that 'law should be removed from the church', or that legal obedience is irrelevant for faith.[91] Law cannot replace faith; to argue that law reflects faith, for Luther, is to argue theocratically and to threaten the soul. Nonetheless, law has the power that it stimulates a desperate openness for faith. Faith, therefore, cannot exist where there is no law to be fulfilled, and where there has been no despair over human inability to fulfil the law.[92]

Debates on the role of law in obtaining salvation persisted long after Luther's death, and they only approached a conclusion with the publication of the *Concordia* of 1580, which sought to unify the different strands of Evangelical faith by resolving major points of doctrinal doubt and dispute. Until that time, however, antinomianism remained a constant undercurrent in the Evangelical movement, and Luther's responses to Agricola did little to quell controversy on these questions.[93] In fact, Agricola remained at the centre of confessional disputes in the Evangelical camp, and his work and political ideas continued to act as a powerful irritant to more orthodox Lutherans.[94] It was partly as a consequence of their provocation by Agricola that many of the most influential theologians of the generation after Luther, particularly Matthias Flacius Illyricus and Nicolaus Gallus, dedicated themselves to clarifying Luther's teaching regarding the law.[95] As a result, whilst opposing all compromise with Roman Catholicism and with the Evangelical theologians supporting partial accommodation with the papacy and the empire, Flacius elaborated a distinctively Lutheran doctrine of the third use of the law (*tertius usus legis*). Central to this doctrine was the belief that the law has a pedagogic function in bringing people to salvation, and that those who receive grace are not punished and tormented by the law to the same extent as those who do not receive it.[96] This doctrine, clearly influenced by Melanchthon's earlier ideas, ultimately became a central tenet in the consolidation of Lutheran doctrine in the *Concordia*.[97] Through this doctrine, the later Evangelical theologians agreed on the principle that, although law can surely not bring salvation, those who are saved – or born anew – through faith will naturally behave in accordance with law, and so, by fulfilling the law, they will demonstrate in their own lives that they are saved or reborn.[98] This allowed the later Evangelical theologians to reconnect law and faith, and to show how faith and law are correlated in right action.[99] This, in turn, provided a foundation for a clarification of Evangelical legal ethics, and for a more systematic rebuttal of legal conceptions in the Roman Catholic Church.

Luther's debate with antinomianism, however, was motivated by the disconcerted suspicion that the early Evangelical movement had unwittingly stimulated two distinct radical interpretations of his own doctrine, one of which construed the *Gemeinde* as a source of a new natural law, and one of which denied all law, and so entitled the community of faith to place itself above all legal statute. Indeed, if theocratism and antinomianism appeared to Luther as closely correlated (and equally misguided) responses to his own initial anti-legalism, these responses also marked the weaknesses and the limits of Lutheran accounts of law, and they formed plausible solutions to the problems to which Luther's expulsion of natural law gave rise. It was not until the idea of the *tertius usus legis* was elaborated that the Lutherans finally stabilized a new conception of natural law. In this idea, they argued that law does not fulfil the task of faith and that works under law do not bring salvation, or effect compliance between human acts and divine law. However, they also obtained means to demonstrate that compliance with law is still a necessary signifier of justification, and it indicates a factual unity between human actions and divine will.

Resistance, law and the Holy Roman Empire

As discussed, in the first period of political upheaval after his first rise to prominence in 1517, Luther distanced himself from possible radical and theocratic readings of his work. Central to this was the concept of the two kingdoms, through which he sought to sever the thread of natural law that traditionally attached questions of political order to matters of religious faith. However, a second stage in Luther's reflections on law commenced after 1526, by which time a sizeable group of princes and towns had decided to support the Reformation and had begun to form a proto-constitutional league, united in defiance both of papal power and of Karl V, the Holy Roman Emperor. At this point, Luther also began to ally himself more closely with the early Evangelical princes, and he even altered his teachings to suit the interests of the emerging anti-imperial faction.

Luther's attitude to the constitution of the Holy Roman Empire is not always easy to assess. After Luther's theological disputations with representatives of the papacy and the empire in 1518 and 1521, Karl V made clear his conviction that the Evangelical attack on the juridical ecclesiasticism of Roman Catholicism also entailed an attack on the constitution of the empire. In justifying the excommunication of Luther and the proscription of Lutheran teaching in 1521, he underlined that as Holy Roman Emperor he was obligated to protect the 'sacred ceremonies, laws, ordinances and holy customs' of the Roman Catholic Church,[100] and to maintain the laws of the one universal church through all dominions of the empire.[101] Even after this event, however, Luther was reluctant to question the legitimacy of the empire, at least in the estate-based constitutional form that it had obtained in the late Middle Ages. His attitude towards the consolidation of territorial power against the empire and the increasingly volatile challenges presented by the princely estates to the empire also remained highly circumspect.[102]

As late as 1523, for instance, he derided princes who felt entitled to 'command their subjects as they wish' and to govern like emperors in the German lands.[103] It is, therefore, important to remember that, in their attack on the church, it was not a strategic intention of the early reformers to undermine the constitution of the empire. It might, of course, be argued that their hostility to all conflation of ecclesiastical and worldly law necessarily involved a confrontation with the empire, as the empire derived its symbolic legitimacy through its (albeit factually highly precarious) connection with the Roman Catholic Church. At various points, moreover, the reformers clearly identified the fusion of church and empire effected by Emperor Constantine as one main cause of the impurity of the church, opening the church to heathen political influences.[104] Nonetheless, even at moments of most intense conflict with the empire, the early reformers remained committed to a universal church and they continued to support an imperial constitution.[105]

Despite this, however, Luther's view of the empire was discernibly modified by a number of events in the later 1520s. Following Luther's excommunication, the empire, challenged on other fronts by pressing military threats, began to adopt a more pragmatic approach to the growing religious dissent, and it even showed tolerance towards the freedoms claimed by Evangelical princes. In 1526, most notably, the Diet of Speyer ruled that each prince was entitled to exercise freedom of worship in accordance with his own judgement and conscience. The Evangelical princes viewed this as an important sanction for their own regional authority, and many began at this point to reorganize their churches and to integrate the Evangelical church into the jurisdictional order of their territories. In 1529, however, this strategy of relative tolerance was reversed, and the empire began to pursue a far more repressive policy towards the reformers and their adherents. The Diet of Speyer in 1529 consequently marked a crucial caesura in the relation between the reformers and the empire, and this was directly reflected in the theologies of law promulgated by the reformers. In 1529, the tolerant ruling of 1526 was rescinded, the prohibition of Lutheran teaching was reaffirmed, and 'Imperial fullness of power' was reasserted as the sole authority in legal decisions concerning ecclesiastical politics in the empire.[106] The Evangelical party responded to this by submitting the so-called 'Protestation of Speyer', requesting reconsideration of these decisions, and by intensifying their plans to form a league of Evangelical, or now properly *Protestant,* resistance to protect both the Evangelical cause and the material and territorial advantages which the princes had obtained because of it. These conflicts came to a head at the Diet of Augsburg in 1530, where the Evangelical theologians presented to the imperial executive the *Confessio Augustana,* the articles of faith forming the doctrinal basis of Lutheranism, only to see this refuted shortly afterwards. The aftermath of this diet saw the formation of the League of Schmalkalden, and the beginning of a period of sporadically acute confessional conflict, which had short interludes in 1532, 1548, 1552 and 1555, but which was not fully resolved until 1648. Against this background, Luther's increasing reliance on the protection of territorial princes necessarily meant that he became involved in discussions on validity of the imperial constitution, and that he was called upon to devise theological justification for political opposition to the Emperor and the empire. This, in turn, created the problem that, in order to satisfy the needs of his princely supporters, he was required to revise some of his earlier views on the separation of the two kingdoms and on the sacred duty of outward obedience.

Luther's reluctance to contribute to debates concerning political resistance is apparent in the caution that he exercised in writing on this subject.[107] He stressed repeatedly that his inclination was 'vehemently against rebellion', and that his teachings had always demonstrated his belief that 'one should suffer even the evil deeds of tyrants and not defend oneself'.[108] Moreover, where he did offer a defence of disobedience or resistance, he tried to articulate this in legal terms, so as not to compromise his broader religious ideas. On the concrete question of how far opposition to the empire might be legitimate, he observed simply that such matters should be referred 'to the lawyers', and could not be decided by principles of religious debate.[109] His qualified support for resistance was thus not – or not principally – driven by religious dictates, but, as far as possible, by analysis of legal and constitutional principles. Despite this, however, in his reflections on political obedience after the deterioration of relations between princes and empire, Luther proposed three express and distinct justifications of princely opposition to the empire. First, he argued that, whereas rebellion is never acceptable, there might under some circumstances be cases of legitimate protest or of 'acting against the law', which do not constitute rebellion and possess legal justification. 'A rebel', he explained, is not a person who opposes specific laws on specific grounds, but a person who 'will not suffer' any kind of 'authority and law'.[110] Whoever 'defends himself against the murderous and bloodthirsty papists should not be accused of rebellion', he thus concluded, but should be seen as acting in self-defence, and so as legally in the right.[111] Second, he argued that the decision of the Emperor to suppress free religious worship was itself in contravention of the imperial constitution. Such suppression was 'contrary to imperial and natural law' and to the 'oaths and duties' by which the Emperor is obligated.[112] Refusal to comply with imperial law on this point was consequently fully justified under worldly law, even under the terms of the constitution itself. Third, however, he also asserted that those who adhere to the Evangelical faith have sworn in their baptism 'to abide by Christ's Gospel', and this baptismal obligation must prevail over duties comprising only worldly obligations.[113] On this last point, therefore, Luther clearly invoked a religious justification for opposition to the Emperor. However, even here his argument was worded in a highly circumspect manner, and he indicated that religion authorizes resistance only because of the legal burden that it places on the human being in its worldly actions, and he was careful not to propose a full doctrine of natural law to settle this question.

Despite his caution, however, Luther's willingness to set out a doctrine of religiously founded resistance provided a dynamic legal and constitutional touchstone for the subsequent course of the Reformation. The first constitutions of the Evangelical alliances in the early 1530s, for example, were supported by the conviction, sanctioned by Luther, that resistance to the Emperor was legitimate because such resistance was a defence of the true faith. Similarly, this evolution of Lutheranism into a doctrine of possible resistance also provided legal principles that expedited the spread of the lay Reformation. By 1530, for example, Lazarus Spengler, a leader of the lay Reformation in Nuremberg, was able to declare quite simply that those who 'disobey the edicts of authority which are in accord with divine truth' should be subject to legal punishment, but that those who oppose 'the laws and edicts of authority which are contrary and repugnant to the divine will' should be viewed as laudable and morally upstanding. Tellingly, Spengler also formulated these ideas on the basis of a doctrine of natural law and divine-natural law, which defined the Emperor himself as constitutionally 'subject to divine law'.[114]

In the early 1520s, in sum, Luther had refused to see the uprisings of the peasants against the princes as justified under divine law. In the later 1520s, however, he grudgingly accepted that the uprisings of the princes against the empire were valid under law, even under divine law. By 1530, consequently, the Reformation was beginning to revise its earliest legal stances, and even to enunciate cautious ideas of natural law to provide justification for new conceptions of legal validity, obligation and princely authority. In this, however, it is of the greatest importance that Luther's theoretical reorientation in this matter was grudgingly obtained, and his vacillations show that he opposed the deployment of his doctrine as a basis for legal formation. Moreover, it is also of the greatest significance that the Reformation articulated ideas of natural law, not as aspects of a consistent account of law's status and function, but as exceptional rights, providing a sporadic and precarious foundation for legal order. The first formative or constitutional premise for legal positivization in the early Reformation, therefore, was an exceptional principle, and the *right to reform* (the *ius reformandi*) was first enunciated as a right determined outside the normalcy of law, or as a right deriving from uttermost duress.

Philippism and the godly prince

In Evangelical controversies on the role of law, both in worldly and spiritual order, it was ultimately not Luther, but Melanchthon, who formulated the most systematic and cogent doctrines and who consequently did most to transform Evangelical teaching into a framework for secular legal analysis. Like Luther, Melanchthon first elaborated his ideas in a commentary on

Romans, and he too saw the sense of this epistle as residing in the intimation that 'God's justice' is revealed not through legal conformity in works, but only 'in faith'.[115] Law, therefore, is not able to bring salvation and should be obeyed only through 'force of reason'.[116] Even the 'works of the just, however good they are, do not help bring justice', and law 'can only make people pious in appearance, not in their hearts.'[117] Like Luther, therefore, Melanchthon saw law as obstructing faith, and he saw religious institutions based in law as jeopardizing the souls of Christians.

Melanchthon used this analysis of law to develop an anthropological account of human existence. He argued that human life exists on three levels: human life can exist in *sin,* it can exist beneath the *law,* or it can exist in *grace.* Each of these levels reflects a distinct point in human evolution: *Heathens* exist at the level of sin or nature, *Jews* exist at the level of the law, and *Christians* exist in the realm of faith or grace.[118] The true Christian, therefore, exists only in faith, not under law, and law distracts from faith.[119] For this reason, Melanchthon's attack on the use of law in the church was hardly less emphatic than that of Luther.[120] He rejected all claims that the church might act as a secular legislator,[121] and, like Luther, he saw the legal rituals of dispensation and absolution under the canons as signs of the contamination of the church by the spirit of Pelagianism.[122] The corruption of Roman Catholicism, he argued, was primarily caused by the fact that it defines the church as a 'supreme monarchy', or as the 'highest most powerful majesty in the entire world.'[123] Against this, Melanchthon aspired to a 'common Christian church', which, unlike any 'external polity', is not bound to 'this or that country, kingdom or estate', and he saw the 'mass of people' as the 'true church'.[124] Melanchthon also echoed aspects of Luther's doctrine of the two kingdoms, and he too tended to relativize the significance of the realm of worldly power. The 'preachers of the word', he explained, have direct authority and 'express commandment' from God, whereas the 'realm of the sword and of worldly power' exists without 'express commandment', and it clearly has a subsidiary status.[125] Nonetheless, like Luther again, he insisted on the importance of 'external discipline and morality', and he argued that 'worldly authority' is ordained by God in order to 'keep the peace' and maintain tranquillity in the world. All people, consequently, are 'subject to the sword' by God,[126] and it is categorically forbidden 'to set oneself violently against authority'.[127]

The greatest distinctions between Luther and Melanchthon, however, are evident in their ideas about law, both religious and worldly. As early as the early 1520s, Melanchthon, whilst accepting Lutheran ideas of spiritual justification, became preoccupied with the paradoxes in Evangelical legal ideas, and he set himself the task of resolving these. He ultimately identified a special role for the law in ensuring salvation; indeed, the main principles of this account were later adopted by Luther in his own controversies with the antinomians. Law, Melanchthon explained, has the function that it engenders humility in the soul, that it demonstrates to people that without God they can never fulfil the law and can never be saved, and that it consequently creates a receptiveness for God in an attitude of self-loathing and acute despondency. 'Justification', he explained 'does not occur through the law, but where there is no law there is no transgression, and where there is no transgression there is no fear of the law.' This fear of the law then stimulates 'hatred for the law' and despair over the law; in so doing, it engenders a spiritual craving for freedom from the law, and freedom from the law can only be obtained through faith.[128] In a soteriological inversion of Roman Catholic doctrine, therefore, Melanchthon argued that the law does not 'remove sin'. In fact, the law acts to 'multiply' sin, and so also to multiply the cause of despair.[129] As it multiplies despair, however, law also enlarges the need for faith, for faith follows on the heels of despair. Knowledge of the law, in consequence, is 'vastly important' because it is only through the 'power of the law', which 'terrifies and frightens the conscience', that people can 'experience the Gospel' or feel faith in their hearts.[130] The law, in short, 'shows us the sickness', and the Gospel shows us 'the medicine'.[131]

Even in his early writings, therefore, Melanchthon attributed two distinct positive uses to the law. First, the law exists to maintain outward conditions of peace, discipline and order in the world. Second, it makes people conscious of their sins, so that they despair of themselves, they seek to escape the shackles of the law, and they become open for faith. In this, Melanchthon already gave greater weight to law than Luther was willing to do, and he clearly felt little of Luther's hostility towards legal reasoning in theology. In addition to this, however, the later Melanchthon also proposed an early account of the third use of the law (*tertius usus legis*), which stated that those who have faith fulfil the law because they feel no temptation to do otherwise, and they require law at most to remind them of the duties of faith. By the time the *Concordia* was drafted, this doctrine was taken for granted as a central, although perennially controversial, aspect of Evangelical teaching.[132] It was, however, Melanchthon, not Luther, who formulated this point most comprehensively. He argued that those who have true faith are above the law, and, because they are above the law, they also necessarily behave in accordance with law. Through their faith, in fact, the law is 'written' in their 'mortal hearts' and their inner faith is outwardly reflected in fulfilment of law.[133] Although surely not constitutive of redemption, therefore, Melanchthon saw the law as an important index of faith. We do not 'cancel out the law through faith', he concluded. On the contrary, 'we establish the law' and the law is always both a precondition and a sign of salvation in faith.[134]

As a corollary of these points, Melanchthon, especially after 1522, was also much more engaged than Luther in debate regarding the conditions of legal rule in the secular sphere, and he began to propose a fusion of Evangelical teaching and Aristotelian ius-naturalism. Unlike Luther he did not denounce 'jurists and legal experts' as corrupters of true faith.[135] Rather, he argued that lawyers have a specifically religious function in helping create good laws, and all 'learned people' who serve the cause of worldly law clearly assist in the enforcement of God's will, and in the creation of a world which is transparent to God's will.[136] In fact, after the mid-1520s, Melanchthon set out an unqualified argument for political ius-naturalism, and his account of the first use of the law (the *usus politicus* or *civilis*) far exceeded Luther's understanding of law's functions.[137] He defined law as the 'voice of God',[138] he argued that the 'law of God' is 'inscribed in the minds of men, so that they obtain a rule from God which governs worldly laws',[139] and he explicitly defended a 'law of nature', which 'God has buried in each mind'.[140] Unlike the more fervently theocratic reformers, Melanchthon did not claim that natural law legitimizes common or communal rights in the political community, and his view of natural law was not tied to any early republican ideals. Instead, he saw natural law as a set of norms serving to stabilize human society, to impose regular constraints across society and to promote civil education in moral decency and convention. He viewed Roman law, most especially, as the legal order that is most appropriate for fulfilling such functions. The 'law of the Romans' is superior 'to the laws of all other peoples',[141] and, as a means of guaranteeing universal order, it draws its source directly 'from nature'.[142]

Melanchthon's notion that Christians are naturally law-abiding ultimately became the foundation for perhaps the most far-reaching claim of the Philippist Reformation: the claim, that is, that true Christians inevitably act in unity with the law, that Christian princes pass and abide by good laws, and that states governed by Christian princes have a specific legitimacy under divine-natural law and specifically contribute to the institution of divine law in the world. It is the 'calling of kings', Melanchthon stated, to 'set laws', to 'create peace, and to reinforce the civil regiment with laws and arms'.[143] This calling of kings, moreover, is not restricted to the outward protection of the peace, but also contains spiritual obligations. God makes the king 'a protector of the law',[144] and the 'policies and moral ordinances' that a king enforces demonstrate 'God's marvellous wisdom', and they make all subjects of the king compliant with God's law. The laws passed by a virtuous king therefore allow God to 'be correctly recognized in human society and community', and they enable the pursuit of 'eternal goods' in the worldly polity.[145] If Luther's work intended to dissolve the relationship between ius-naturalism and religion and to justify government on relatively minimal preconditions, consequently, Melanchthon's later writings reunited religion and natural law to form a specifically Evangelical strain of political ius-naturalism. Indeed, whilst Luther's work strongly opposed the normative universality of natural law, Melanchthon set out a compromise between universal-normative and more positive or voluntaristic accounts of the law. He argued on hand that the prince is accountable for passing laws, and that the decision of the prince gives authority to law. Yet, on the other hand, he asserted that the will of the Christian prince is also bound to God, and, as it is bound by God's laws, it contains within it a universal legal order: the decisions of the prince thus stand in for God's decisions, and the prince himself is bound by the norms which these decisions incorporate.

In this respect, Melanchthon's thought assumed seminal importance in the evolution of post-Reformation Evangelical political thought, as it offered a clear practical justification for princely power without papal support, and it created a normative horizon in which princely power could be viewed as legitimately enacting or even replacing metaphysically construed legal ideas. If Luther's work had led to an exceptional view of positive law, therefore, Melanchthon endeavoured to resolve the political problems caused by Lutheranism and to allow the legal antinomies and the exceptionality of Lutheranism to be reconciled in the concept of the *confessional state:* that is, the worldly state governed by a godly and divinely authorized regent. Indeed, in its Philippist expression, the Reformation ultimately transformed natural law from a metaphysical doctrine, which originally weighed against the emergence of positive law and independent statehood, into a set of principles that facilitated the positivization of law and the formation of independent and positively self-justifying states. After Melanchthon, the Evangelical movement abandoned its earlier unreserved critique of theocracy; it allowed the prince to assume the legislative duties formerly allocated by the Roman Catholic Church and sanctioned under the semi-theocratic natural law of this church; and it allowed the princely will, at once bound by and distinct from God's will, to engender law and to define this law as absolutely valid. Indeed, if Luther's first justification of Evangelical law had resulted from an exceptional gesture, recognizing princely law as originating outside normalcy, Melanchthon's natural law converted early Evangelical exceptionalism into an endlessly fraught paradox of legal order, in which the princely will, acting outside inherited natural law, proclaimed itself, like the scholastic God, as both the author and the addressee of natural law, uniting reason and freedom in a set of positive legislative acts. In these early steps towards an Evangelical theocracy, therefore, Melanchthon allowed the discredited paradox of God's legal authorship momentarily to reappear in the state, not as a full theocracy, but as a state that owed its genesis to the abolition of theocracy, but whose laws were still sanctioned by the personally embodied will of God.

The idea of the prince as God's legal representative on earth became increasingly prominent through the early decades of the Reformation. Although Melanchthon first formulated this idea, it was Martin Bucer, the leading reformer in Strasburg and the major influence on the dissemination of Evangelical ideas in England, who gave fullest expression to the belief that the power of the prince should extend beyond the outward preservation of the peace, and so includes powers of divine representation. Bucer claimed that princely rule is 'ordained by God',[146] and that princes contribute to the establishment of 'true religion and to the establishment of God's realm'.[147] To a greater extent even than Melanchthon, therefore, he argued that there is a necessary divine order in the worldly state, and this order is most effectively instituted when pious princes hold office.[148] The natural order of the state is concentrated in the will of the prince, and, as a source of absolute law, the prince possesses control over a specific territory, with full power to regulate preaching, religious instruction and organization of the church.[149]

These early Evangelical doctrines of natural law also stimulated the evolution of legal thought in other areas of legal inquiry. Johannes Oldendorp, for instance, pioneered an early line of Evangelical ius-naturalism, which paved the way both for a revival of private-law teaching in Germany and for a doctrine of public law underpinned by concepts of Evangelical natural law. Oldendorp argued that there exists an 'immutable' natural law, which is observable in all societies, and which forms a uniform basis for the principles of civil law.[150] The spirit of this natural law, he claimed, is most effectively expressed in Roman law, especially in the principle of equity in Roman law: in fact, he viewed 'natural law and equity' as 'one and the same thing',[151] and he argued that the principle of equity constitutes a normative framework in which all laws, both written and unwritten, can be applied and modified.[152] For this reason, Oldendorp also identified ways in which natural law might assist the jurisdictional interests of individual states, and he argued that natural law can act as a powerful foundation for the introduction of new laws and for positive acts of legislation. He stressed that new laws are always necessary, depending on the customs and needs of the republic. Where circumstances change, then, magistrates are entitled to use considerations of 'utility' to decide which new laws should be introduced, and new laws obtain justification through their convergence with principles of natural law.[153] Natural law, he concluded, has its great public value in the fact that it enables reliable and just laws to be introduced with relative facility, and it ensures that new laws are likely to enjoy a high degree of common consent. Indeed, Oldendorp even expanded this argument to demand that legal application throughout Germany should be consistently organized and that uniform and regulated courts should be instituted by imperial command.[154] As in the works of the more legally minded reformers, therefore, natural law acted here as an idea of the law which introduced an element of flexibility into law, and which provided for the consolidation of secular power around accountable judicial explanations of its own authority.

On these grounds, then, it can be concluded that, despite the original anti-legal position of the reformers, the Reformation eventually cleared the terrain for the emergence of positive accounts of legal order, both in state law and in civil law. However, it is also necessary to emphasize, first, that the reformist teachings on law that offered a constructive analysis of natural-legal validity directly contradicted the earliest ideas of Reformation teaching. Second, moreover, it is also important to see that the Evangelical accounts of natural law that reintroduced aspects of theocratic thought into political discourse used elements of theocracy to provide intensely paradoxical accounts of political legitimacy. At the heart of Melanchthon's confessional state, most strikingly, is the abiding paradox that this state invoked metaphysical or universal laws to justify a process through which law was factually detached from metaphysical or universal preconditions, and in which law was gradually reconstructed as a positively constituted and interpretable set of facts and norms. Evangelical natural law was thus founded in the paradox that it allowed the state to *appear* metaphysically valid, yet it practically organized its functions on positive principles. Even in their most abiding normative consequences, therefore, the legal teachings of the Reformation retained an aspect of exceptionalism, and they inflated their quasi-theocratic ius-naturalism, in part, as recognition of their own origin in the end of theocracy and in the end of natural law.

The ecclesiastical constitution

The legal problems and paradoxes of the Reformation are also evident in the debates during the Reformation period concerning the constitutional order of the Evangelical church. As discussed, the constitutional form of the church began to assume concrete contours after the settlement of 1555. This settlement recognized the legal status of the Evangelical church under the Imperial Constitution, it transferred jurisdiction in spiritual matters to the princely estates in territories whose princes had abandoned the Roman church, and it created a legal basis for the eventual evolution of the famous principle of '*cuius regio eius religio*' – that is, that the prince can decide what his people ought to believe, and then impose religious uniformity in his territory. The year 1555, therefore, saw the beginnings of the territorial constitutional system (*Staatskirchenrecht*), in which the prince of an Evangelical state ultimately obtained, under *ius reformandi,* supreme responsibility for all ecclesiastical matters in that state.[155]

Before 1555, however, and especially before the promulgation of the *Confessio Augustana* in 1530, princely control of church was not established, and there was no accepted model of ecclesiastical jurisdiction. In his earlier works, Luther took a latitudinarian approach to questions of church order, arguing that legal and ceremonial questions should not be permitted to burden the Christian conscience or spirit.[156] However, owing to the often eccentric proliferation of religious teaching in the first years of the Reformation, the leading reformers soon decided that they needed consistent instruments of legal control over the church and over the doctrines preached in the church, and they began to design constitutional mechanisms or orders of visitation to oversee orthodoxy in teaching and in services in the church. However, these issues had a number of highly sensitive religious and constitutional implications for the reformers. They raised the question of how the Evangelical Church should relate to worldly power, of how law might be applied in this church, and of how precisely the Evangelical Church was institutionally distinct from the Roman Catholic Church.

In addition, then, the suggestion that princes might govern churches also touched on the constitutional nerve of the relation between princes and empire, and of the extent to which princes could legitimately act against the empire in ecclesiastical politics.

Melanchthon played a leading role in the debates on the institution of a church constitution, and the very earliest models of supervision for the church, for instance the *Order of Visitation* introduced in 1527–28, were largely the product of Melanchthon's ideas. In these documents he expressed the conviction that, although the laws regulating the church could not help bring justification before God, a 'human order of the church' was essential, and the authorities ordained by God in the world should help preserve this order.[157] He therefore concluded that the *external* order of the church necessarily falls under the legal responsibility of the prince, although the *internal* practices of religion are not subject to princely jurisdiction. Article 28 of Melanchthon's *Confessio Augustana* then clearly stated that the inner corpus of the church should be devoted only to teaching and preaching and is thus governed by God's word alone, but that 'worldly authorities' are 'authorized by God' to oversee maintenance of civil peace and 'outward order'.[158] A first ecclesiastical constitution was subsequently proposed in 1538: this was the work of a number of theologians, primarily of Justus Jonas, but also of Melanchthon.[159] This constitution, although never fully enforced, foresaw the establishment of territorial consistories to supervise all ecclesiastical matters and to assume the legislative competences previously accorded, in the Roman Catholic Church, to courts applying the canon law. These consistories drew their jurisdictive power directly from 'the immediate command of the territorial prince',[160] and they initiated a process of legal organization in which the prince ultimately assumed formal rights of *cura ecclesiastica* or final jurisdiction in the church. Indeed, in addition to this, Melanchthon also presided over a short-lived experiment with Evangelical episcopacy in the early 1540s. In his correspondence of this time, he stated that the optimal church order is one which incorporates a consistory and a bishop, both subject to the authority of a 'regional prince', who acts as 'Patronus' of the church.[161] He ultimately urged the appointment of Nicolaus von Amsdorff as Evangelical bishop of Naumburg, and he pressed the claim that episcopal order and princely control were mutually supportive.[162]

Under the influence of Melanchthon's concept of princely natural law, therefore, the Evangelical Church was rapidly integrated into the early territorial states. Luther himself, although not without equivocation, was also complicit in this transfer of power over the church from the papacy to the territorial princes. His willingness to countenance princely custody of the church was already evident in his claims in the 1520s that princes possessed rights of political resistance and independence in religious questions: these arguments implicitly meant that princes could present themselves as *defenders of faith*. Later, he followed Melanchthon in acceding to the recreation of an episcopate in the Evangelical regions, and he endorsed Amsdorff's appointment in Naumburg. He justified this by saying that he had never had the ambition to 'tear down the monasteries'; his Reformation had intended, instead, to 'set an example for how the monasteries should be reformed and governed'.[163] He, therefore, approved the appointment of Evangelical bishops, provided that these had nothing to do with 'worldly goods or power', but were responsible solely for matters pertaining to spiritual order.[164] Despite this, however, Luther's enthusiasm for territorial organization of the church was never more than circumspect, and he saw this as an exceptional solution, pending a resolution more in keeping with Evangelical principles. In the early debates on the territorial constitution, for example, he commented acerbically on the increasing tendency towards territorial regulation of the church in the 1520s and 1530s. Whilst before the Reformation the pope had confused the office of the preacher with the worldly regiment, he argued, the Reformation had now imposed a consistorial constitution that confused the office of worldly power with the office of preaching. Under this constitution, he claimed, 'evil lawyers' tried to 'tell preachers what they are to preach.' He consequently attacked all those 'worldly lords want to run the spiritual regiment', and who wish to be 'transformed into popes and bishops'.[165] Indeed, even in agreeing to the reintroduction of episcopacy, Luther argued that 'worldly powers' could only act as 'bishops of necessity' (*Not Bischove*),[166] exceptionally required to protect the Evangelical Church from its Roman Catholic adversaries. He thus never fully abandoned his earlier scepticism towards the legal organization of the church, and his main intention remained to simplify the church as a place of faith. As in other respects considered above, therefore, in discussions concerning the legal administration of the Evangelical church, a set of legal forms emerged which often contradicted the initial visions of the first Reformers, which assimilated elements of legal order which they had initially reviled, and which expressly justified themselves as exceptional points of law. The evolution of Evangelical church law and church constitutions especially demonstrates how the Reformation struggled to absorb the legal crises that it stimulated and how it maintained itself only by rapidly generating responses to the collapse of legal order in both church and state.

In conclusion, therefore, it can be argued that the Lutheran Reformation responded to a deeply complex legal situation, and it bequeathed a no-less-complex legal legacy. At the very centre of Lutheranism was a rupture between reason and freedom: that is, between God's law and God's freedom, but also between metaphysical ideas of natural law and the human will. Indeed, both practically and theoretically the Reformation undermined the unitary foundation of the law: practically, it allowed newly powerful interests to take possession of the law, to bring division into the inherited legal order and to eliminate the last traces of religious justification from the law; theoretically, it defined all law as other than eternal law, and it restricted the principles valorizing law to a narrow set of functional or utilitarian considerations, which could be positively invoked by many sites of authority. The defining legal implication of the Reformation, consequently, was that law is free, that law is exercised in positive form by positive wills, and that debate about the law must be conducted in positive terms. Indeed, as a corollary of this, the Reformation also contained the necessary implication that statehood in Germany must be a free statehood, and this statehood must explain its legitimacy as other than all metaphysically structured ideas of natural law. In instituting this metaphysical rupture in the law, however, Luther did not provide for a model of legal foundation, and he only allowed for law's value and for freedom under law in highly exceptionalist or contradictory terms. Generally, in fact, he denied that positive acts of human will can create fully valid laws. Valid law, he claimed, is neither human law nor natural law nor divine law: it is the *new law,* and this law exists only in the church and the *Gemeinde,* integrated under faith. Evangelical legal theorists after Luther, therefore, were confronted with a dual problem of positivization. They encountered law as divested of its metaphysical unity with reason and so as requiring positive validation. Yet this positive or this human law, as they encountered it, could not articulate itself as fully valid, because it remained shadowed by the inferiority of law to faith and by its devaluation in the first pronouncements of the Reformation. In the first stage of their theoretical formation, therefore, laws evolving from the Reformation existed on precarious ground, they were forced constantly to negotiate with their own paradoxicality, and most laws explained their positive authority either as exceptionally justified principles, through a parasitic borrowing of legal constructs from models of law which they opposed, or through paradoxical acts of self-validation. It was only in the longer wake of the Reformation that theorists began to reconstruct an integral relation between reason and will and law and power on Evangelical foundations, and to explain how human law could be valid, and how the freedom of statehood could be imagined, after metaphysics, without paradox.

2 The early Enlightenment

The laws of which nature?

The dynamics of state-building and theoretical formation in early modern Germany differed significantly from those in other countries. In other European states, the early modern period was generally marked by a consolidation of statehood: that is, by the increasingly uniform exercise of territorial dominance by one distinct executive structure. In Germany, however, the evolution of statehood followed an altogether more cautious and defensive trajectory. At this time, even the most powerful German states could not construct themselves as independent or assume full responsibility for the basic functions of statehood outside the empire, and the consolidation of their administrative authority concentrated to a large extent on the gradual obtaining and jealous guarding of jurisdictional privileges granted by the empire.[1] Consequently, whilst post-Reformation England saw the rapid reinforcement of an integrated monarchical executive, with control over all courts, church and taxes, the German states only very tentatively assumed analogous institutional features. As a consequence of this, the constitutional debates arising from the early period of state formation in Germany were quite distinctive. In England, for example, constitutional debates arising from the century of Reformation could, to a large extent, assume that the existence of a sovereign and politically independent state was a basic fact of political life. These debates tended to focus on questions of administrative balance within a sovereign state, on the distribution of competence between different levels of judicial authority and, ultimately, prior to the Civil War, on the relation between parliament and monarchy. The constitutional conflicts and settlements of early modern England thus aimed at securing a legally organized accommodation between distinct elements of an already existing and integrated body politic.[2] Central to these conflicts was the assumption that the law and the courts of law had a formative role in the administration of power and that law, anchored in the courts of the common law, could act as a powerful medium for shaping the overarching political order and for limiting arbitrary exercise of power. At the heart of English political thought at this time, therefore, was the belief that law could be contested within the state, and that the structure of the state could be contested and formed by law. In Germany, by contrast, constitutional debates of the same period concentrated mainly on clarifying the relations between the early territorial states and the empire, and the main objective of the participants in these debates was usually to define the empire as a constitutionally obligated polity and to advocate that certain competences, especially rights of jurisdictional control, should be fully detached from the empire and ceded to the territorial states. Underlying these debates was the knowledge that most particular states did not yet have their own fully independent laws or their own fully independent powers of jurisdiction, and that the law was not yet a positive medium of state-building. The territorial states consequently sought to use the law, not, primarily, to organize their own inner structure, but to impose negative constraints or restrictions on the exercise of power by the empire.

Early legal and constitutional discourse in the post-Reformation German states, therefore, was not principally oriented towards the organization of sovereign states, but towards the restriction of the influence of external sources of legal power on emerging territorial states which only possessed limited sovereignty. For this reason, the formation of the territorial states tended to produce *externalized* constitutional orders, which were less concerned with the constitutional balance within the state than with the outer relation between the particular states and the empire. Whilst in other, more integrated polities, the primary contest of early modern constitutionalism was the restriction of state power and the intensification of the law and legally enshrined liberties against the state, in Germany, in many cases at least, the primary contest related to the cementing of state power, and to the exclusion from law of elements which might disrupt the authority of the state. The result of this was that early modern constitutional debate in Germany tended towards more concentrated conceptions of territorial power, which placed limited legal restrictions on the application of power within the territorial state. Naturally, this argument should under no circumstances be taken to mean that early German constitutional theorists uniformly supported princely absolutism and had no interest in the evolution of a balanced constitution in their own territories. Indeed, the contrary is evidently the case; many early constitutionalists sought to define territorial sovereignty as dependent on a balanced relation between the quasi-sovereign competences of the regional princes and regents, and the customary rights, liberties and privileges of the local estates or territorial assemblies (*Landstände*).[3] Nonetheless, constitutional debate in the early German Enlightenment was inevitably concerned, above all, with the relation between territory and empire, and with the protection of rights of territorial jurisdiction against other laws, especially imperial law.[4] Indeed, the question of how power might be balanced or distributed inside the particular territorial states was difficult to pose as long as the relation between territory and empire remained unclarified, and as long as the legal organization of the territories was determined by systems of jurisdiction divided between territories and empire.

In this respect, the early emergence of constitutional debate in the German territories formed a complex continuum with the theological/political conceptions developed during the first period of Reformation. The longer aftermath of the Reformation extended the legal debates of the early Reformation by attempting to consolidate the power of the princes, first obtained by exceptional means, in an enduring constitutional order, and to explain the sources of this order in sustainable normative terms. In this, moreover, the anti-legal revolt in Lutheran theology continued to exercise pervasive influence in constitutional thought. Whereas the early reformers had opposed the external legal domination of the church, the Evangelical constitutionalists in the generations after the Reformation set themselves against the external legal domination of the state by the empire, and they continued in the endeavour to liberate political power from an overarching and universalized legal order and to place German polities under their own laws. In these respects, although now concentrated on questions of worldly order, early constitutionalism in Germany reflected certain primary features of Lutheranism, and it often re-enacted the original anti-metaphysical impulse and the hostility to natural law that had first shaped the Reformation. The theoretical models of statehood that were elaborated at this time were often forced to reformulate, albeit in more secular methodology, the rejection of universal theocracy in the Reformation, and they intensified the earlier attempts to split the implied unity of power and universal law in Roman Catholic ideas of statehood.

Calvinism and natural law

There are important exceptions to the suggestion that early German constitutional thought was united in hostility to ius-natural universalism or that it promoted a concentration of territorial power. Most notably, Johannes Althaus, or Althusius, strongly influenced by the politics of Calvinism in North West Germany, set out a proto-constitutional or early republican account of legitimate political order. Central to this account was the claim that the laws of the legitimate polity must accord with absolute principles of natural right: 'universal law', he argued, is 'the form and substantial essence of sovereignty (*majestatis*)',[5] and all members of the polity, including the prince, are bound by such universal law.[6] Althusius expanded this theory to argue that a state obtains legitimacy under natural law, not as this law is instituted by the will of a regent, but as it is founded by the 'symbiotic universal association' of towns, provinces and regions, which a state incorporates. The state is an emphatically public body, and its laws are not deducible from the personal attributes of princes: the state is the 'property of the people', and the conditions of its sovereignty are derived from 'consensus between the members' of the different associations in which it has its origin.[7] Importantly, Althusius also stated that the agreements between members of the state-founding associations place limits on the power of the highest magistrate and the administrators of the state, and these agreements can be invoked to justify opposition to the state wherever it threatens to descend into tyranny.[8] Indeed, he argued that an organically constructed state requires specific administrative security against tyranny, and it must appoint representatives, called 'ephors' or 'defenders of the republic',[9] who are responsible both for appointing the highest magistrate and for ensuring that the highest magistrate does not contravene the laws or agreements instituting the republic.[10] The ephors, he explained, have the function that, using 'word and deed', they obstruct 'the tyranny of the highest magistrate'.[11] In their capacity as representatives of the people, in fact, the ephors have 'greater power and authority' than the highest magistrate himself.[12]

Fundamental to Althusius' doctrine is a radical-constitutional notion of natural right, which insists that the state, as a public body, is constitutionally independent of its ministers. The state is formed as law and, as such, it exists as an inviolable order, which has a dignity above all particular persons charged with its representation. The majesty or sovereignty of the state is defined by pacts and natural laws, and these 'laws of majesty' must be protected from all abuse – even from abuse by their highest custodians.[13] This natural-legal independence of the state, he explained, originates first in the associational consensus between the organs, which support and produce the state. However, it also originates in a 'religious pact', through which the magistrate promises to God to introduce and preserve the one true religion in the state and to ban all atheists and heretics from the state.[14] Political sovereignty, therefore, expressly requires that the state should integrate the church, and that the magistrate should have authority over the church and preside over the 'ecclesiastical courts', the 'presbyteries', and the 'church consistories'.[15] The integration of the church by the state, however, is not justified as an element of public law or princely authority. Instead, the state's control of the church means that the state is subject to a second constitutive contract: in addition to the contract that it forms with its associated constituents, it is also bound by contract to God, and both contracts impose a natural-legal obligation upon the state. For Althusius, consequently, a contractually founded state is not thinkable without a strict ecclesiastical regime, and the ecclesiastical regime ties the order of state to precise legal duties and responsibilities. The ephors, then, are entitled to denounce as a tyrant any magistrate whose duties in respect of the ecclesiastical regime are not fulfilled.[16] In both civil and ecclesiastical politics, Althusius saw the state as structured around a set of strict laws, which are independent of the state in its personal structure, and he saw sovereignty as constituted and defined by laws, not by persons.

In the same era, David Pareus adapted political elements of Calvinism to the politics of South West Germany, specifically the Palatinate. Pareus put forward a doctrine of radical natural law; he insisted that rights of individual conscience exist independently of political order and have a certain priority over all political legislation, and he asserted that citizens are entitled to use all available means to overthrow tyrannical government.[17] Like Althusius, Pareus also endorsed an integrated ecclesiastical regime, and he argued that territorial rulers hold authority over the church as a public body.[18] However, he also insisted that the church must retain a constitutional distinction from the state, and that church elders are entitled to resist the state in cases of religious and political abuse.[19]

These prominent examples of political Calvinism, however, cannot perhaps be taken as fully representative of early constitutional thought in Germany. Pareus's work, for example, was more pervasively influential in England than in the German states, and it was only at a later point in the evolution of German constitutionalism that the importance of Althusius was fully realized. More mainstream lines of political theory in the early German Enlightenment were motivated by a less unyieldingly universal attitude on questions of legal power and judicial control. Indeed, works outside the Calvinist canon tended to oppose abstract ius-naturalism, to limit the purchase of universal ideas on the self-explanation of political power, and they were attached more to the reinforcement of territorial competence than to its formal restriction.

The empire: a constitutional state?

If the Religious Peace of 1555 set out an interim constitutional settlement, ascribing expanded powers to the territorial princes, provisionally sanctioning territorial independence in religious jurisdiction and promoting independence in other spheres of jurisdiction, it also formed the crux of subsequent constitutional antagonisms. Indeed, the settlement of 1555 was clearly an improvised response to the legal conditions created by the Reformation, and it did not begin to pacify the climate of legal exceptionalism at this time. On the contrary, it merely stabilized a fractious balance of force between princely estates and empire, and it left the authentic foundations of legal order and the boundaries of imperial and territorial jurisdiction unresolved. The accord instituted in 1555 became finally unsustainable after 1607-08, when the Lutheran town of Donauwörth was annexed and forcibly re-Catholicized by the empire and placed under the Catholic jurisdiction of Bavaria. This event led to renewed controversy about the constitutional authorities of the empire and to a polarization of religious groups and the renewed formation of confessional alliances. In many respects, in fact, the Thirty Years War, whose advent was accelerated by the annexation of Donauwörth, marked the final explosion of the constitutional antagonisms which had been hastily appeased in 1555.

The period after 1607, and especially after 1618, gave rise to the discipline of imperial constitutional or public law (*Reichsstaatsrecht*) in the German states, and the evolution of this discipline was strongly shaped by the constitutional and confessional controversies of the era. Indeed, even in its early years, the science of public law was marked by an entrenched division between the lawyers and theorists who saw the empire as a monarchical constitutional form, over which the emperor had personal dominion, and those who saw the empire as a publicly constituted and obligated *state:* that is, as a body politic possessing a binding legal order, and a constitution that balanced power between Emperor and territorial princes. Between 1607 and 1618, for instance, Reinhard König argued in seminal manner that a distinction should be made between the majesty (sovereignty) of the empire and the majesty (sovereignty) of the Emperor. He claimed that the majesty of the empire was a *real* majesty whereas that of the Emperor was a *personal* majesty, and that the personal majesty of the Emperor was derived from and secondary to the real majesty of the empire as a state. It was, König concluded, only as a representative of the real majesty of the empire that the Emperor was entitled personally to make laws, so that the Emperor, as a person, was always subject to the constitutional laws of the empire.[20] Analogously, Matthias Stephani also insisted that the Emperor was bound by oath to the 'laws of the empire'.[21] Christophorus Besoldus argued in similar voice that the empire was defined by a mixed constitution, with power shared between Emperor and estates.[22] Subsequently, Dominicus Arumaeus refined these principles to argue that the majesty inherent in imperial power was derived, not from the person of the Emperor, but *ex capitulatione:* from the compacts agreed between the Emperor and the electors. These contracts, once agreed, formed fundamental constitutional laws that determined how power in the empire was to be exercised.[23] Slightly later, Johannes Limnaeus furthered this constitutional model by claiming that the majesty or the sovereignty of empire resided originally in the empire's constitutional form, and this constitution was the sole bearer of imperial authority. The Emperor, as a person, was thus a protector of this constitution, but this constitution existed independently of the Emperor's personal power, and his personal power was bound by the 'fundamental laws' that the constitution contained.[24] The residue of this argument, in sum, was that the empire was a state with real majesty, which could not be reduced to a dynastic or personal majesty, and the exercise of legal coercion in this state was subject to control by the constitutional form of the state. Naturally, Limnaeus did not wholly diminish the role of the Emperor: he saw the Emperor as the supreme organ in the administration of the empire. However, he construed the state represented by the Emperor as a *status mixtus,* whose power derived from a constitution incorporating princely estates, not from the person of the Emperor.[25] Other major constitutional theorists of this age also set out analogous claims. Benedict Carpzov, for instance, also subscribed to the theory that the empire was a mixed state possessed of a double majesty – combining the personal majesty of the Emperor and the real majesty of the empire. The real majesty of the empire, he stressed, was 'born with the empire', it was based in 'the fundamental laws of the empire', and the personal majesty of the Emperor originated in and was necessarily restricted by this higher majesty.[26] Not all early state theorists in the German territories held this constitutional view of imperial sovereignty. Wilhelm Witzendorff, for example, argued for a monarchical definition of the empire's constitution, albeit with a mixed administrative order.[27] Theodor Reinkingk also supported a monarchical conception of the empire, closer to ideas derived from Jean Bodin. He argued that the Emperor was not bound by the laws of a state, but was entitled independently to promulgate laws.[28] Nonetheless, theories which accentuated the divided personality of the empire, and which ascribed importance to the role of the electors and princes as participant subjects of constitutional law captured the prevailing spirit of constitutional debate in early seventeenth-century Germany.

These arguments for a mixed constitution prepared the ground for the main lines of constitutional theory after 1648, which insisted more confidently on territorial independence and integrity. This took exemplary form in the influential and widely read works of Veit Ludwig von Seckendorff. Seckendorff saw the settlements in the Peace of Westphalia in 1648 as providing for a patriarchal expansion of princely power, and allowing the prince to acquire full legislative sovereignty: the 'power to establish good laws and orders in his land'.[29] Seckendorff fell some way short of supporting fully independent sovereignty in the territories. He argued that the prince was still 'obliged to show obedience' to the 'orders and laws of the empire' and to ensure that his own laws did not contravene the laws 'prescribed to all Germany by Imperial Majesty and all the Estates'.[30] Indeed, he saw the Emperor's majesty as deriving from the fact that he 'has no superior in this world'.[31] However, he also insisted the Emperor was bound to certain constitutional 'conditions', and that the authority of the empire could only be used within a system of territorial balance.[32] At the same time, Caspar Ziegler also asserted that it would be 'absurd' to deny that that the 'supreme power' of the empire resided in any other source but a constitution. He opposed earlier theories of the dual personality of the Emperor, and argued that the majesty of the Emperor resulted from the 'majesty of the entire empire',[33] which had its constitutional origin in the constituent organs of the empire: that is, the princes, each of which rightly exercised the fullness of power in 'his own province'.[34]

The great legal historian of early modern Germany, Hermann Conring, also endorsed a strong theory of the constitution, using an eclectic fusion of historical interpretation and legal deduction to demonstrate the necessary constitutional form of the empire. The Emperor, Conring concluded, was obligated by pacts formed with the princes,[35] and these pacts had constitutionally binding power: even direct resistance to the Emperor was legitimate if the Emperor threatened to contravene the stipulations of this constitution.[36] Of the major constitutional theorists of this period, Conring came perhaps closest to a full discrediting of the empire and to a full advocacy of unlimited territorial sovereignty. He insisted that the imperial state was primarily founded in the imperial princes, not in the Emperor: the state of the empire, he argued, is the 'imperial estates' (*Reichsstände*).[37]

Sovereign jurisdiction and the unity of the law

In their institutional implications, these constitutional doctrines sought to establish both a constitutional order, in which different sources of power countervailed and restricted each other, and an organic order, in which the empire was construed as an integrated order of state, and in which particular institutions had clearly defined competence. More fundamentally, however, these doctrines also marked an endeavour to find alternatives to the externality of law in the Holy Roman Empire and to consolidate the sites of territorial power as cohesive centres of legislation and jurisdiction. The underlying impulse in these debates, consequently, was not a demand for a balanced law, but a demand for law consistently applied in German states, placed on foundations of secure statehood.

After 1648, for instance, Seckendorff emphasized the fact that 'highest judicial power' is an inalienable attribute of princely power, although he also accepted that princes were not permitted to pass laws contravening imperial statute.[38] This view was seconded by Samuel Pufendorf, who saw centralized 'judicial power' as a defining feature of a regular state constitution.[39] Conring also asserted that control of the courts is the supreme hallmark of sovereignty and that a state accountable to foreign courts is not a 'free republic'.[40] Indeed, he argued that regulating 'the business of courts' is the main concern of free states.[41] On this point, Conring reflected critically on universally applied legal models, and he called into question the judicial order of the empire. He described the Roman law promoted and disseminated by the empire and the papacy as lacking natural claim to universal validity and as incompatible with the historically formed legal culture of the German people.[42] In this respect, Conring's work marked the beginning of a long tradition of legal thought, which asserts that Roman law does not have unquestionable authority in Germany, and in fact it served to undermine the indigenous legal and political culture of German states.[43]

It was only at the very end of the seventeenth century and in the first decades of the eighteenth century, however, that political commentators began emphatically to insist on the final consolidation of territorial power, and so also on the full control of the courts of law by the princes.[44] In the early 1690s, Samuel Strykius argued that the prince enjoyed full jurisdiction 'within the limits of his territory'.[45] Johann Peter Ludewig extended the earlier historicist method used by Conring to claim that German territories first existed independently of the empire and were justified in the claims to full sovereignty in law.[46] Burcard Gotthelf Struve claimed similarly that within his territory the prince was entitled to exercise 'the very highest jurisdiction'.[47] Nicolaus Gundling also called on historical examples to argue that territories had an original independence from the empire and could exercise their legal powers as the highest law of majesty.[48] Whilst remaining insistent on the high dignity and authority of the empire, Gundling also defended rights of territorial jurisdiction,[49] and he explained that whoever wishes to exercise majesty must seek to gain control, not only over the process of legislation, but also over the interpretation of laws in the courts.[50] He concluded, therefore, that: 'A king who is not a judge is not a king, and an emperor who is not a judge is not an emperor'.[51] At the same time, Johann Franz Buddeus also stated categorically that sovereignty revolves around supreme jurisdictional power, and that whoever exercises this power must ensure that order and uniformity are maintained in the courts.[52]

Sovereign jurisdiction and the church

These attempts to consolidate territorial jurisdiction against the empire necessarily viewed the Roman Catholic Church, the ancient embodiment of legal externality and universalism, as their great adversary. Above all, they reacted against ecclesiastical constitutions that endowed bishops with independent representative authority under papal rule, and that implicitly claimed that the Roman Catholic Church contained legal principles that transcended territorial jurisdiction. The earliest constitutional lawyers in Germany, consequently, promoted the foundation of ecclesiastical constitutions that subordinated the church to the body politic and restricted the representative independence and the universal claims of religious institutions. In the early seventeenth century, 'episcopal' ideas of constitutional order in the church assumed dominant status in debates in ecclesiastical law in Germany.[53] These doctrines of church order replaced the diffuse proto-constitutional ideas of the sixteenth century with a more stringent account of the state as a legal organ authorized to integrate and protect the church, and they asserted, after 1555, that supervision of the church in a territory was an indispensable element of regional power, and that powers formerly exercised by Roman Catholic bishops were now devolved to worldly regents.

These early episcopal arguments are usually associated with the brothers Joachim Stephani and Matthias Stephani. Joachim Stephani was responsible for the original formulation of the principle *cuius regio eius religio,* which taught that in all external matters spiritual jurisdiction should be fully transferred from the Catholic episcopate to the Evangelical princes.[54] Matthias Stephani elaborated this view to argue that 'secular princes' have a 'dual person': they are both secular and ecclesiastical princes, at once princes and bishops, and they have full external control over the church. In the German territories, he claimed, this transfer of episcopal power was formally recognized in the 'fiduciary contract' of 1555, through which authority over the church had been permanently devolved from imperial authority.[55] In consequence, the princes were authorized to exercise 'dual jurisdiction' over worldly and ecclesiastical matters, with worldly matters to be judged in civil courts and ecclesiastical matters in consistories.[56] At a later date, Carpzov's deeply influential treatise on ecclesiastical law also asserted that 'episcopal rights' – that is, the right to administer and to represent the church – fell under the regalia of territorial supremacy.[57] The prince was consequently entitled to act both as the prince of a given territory and as the bishop of the church in this territory, so wielding a fullness of political and ecclesiastical power. Even Reinkingk, a supporter of imperial monarchy, asserted that the prince should have care of the external direction of the church, and he should oversee doctrinal disputes to ensure that 'no pernicious errors' or 'schisms' erupt from the church to threaten civil order.[58]

The model of princely supremacy over the church in these early episcopal constitutions was, in certain respects, an extension of the neo-theocratic turn that had characterized the later period of Reformation in Germany. These constitutions presupposed that the prince, as defender of peace and faith at the same time, was of the same confession as his subjects, that his power was derived from a unity of co-believers, and that the state was necessarily a confessional state. These integrationist ideas on the relation between church and state did not always find unanimous support. Indeed, certain influential theological views throughout the seventeenth century showed a growing resentment to the external control of the church by the princely states, and they tried to reclaim the anti-theocratic elements of the earliest wave of Lutheran thought. For example, theologians who influenced the early Pietist movement, such as Johann Valentin Andreä vehemently opposed Caesaropapist doctrines, and they demanded the reintroduction of an early-Christian constitution in the church.[59] Later, more clearly pietist thinkers such as Philipp Jacob Spener protested vehemently against the quasi-Roman Catholic 'Babel' of Caesaropapistic governance.[60] Spener denounced the episcopal constitution, in which 'bishops become worldly princes',[61] and he advocated instead the establishment of 'ordinary presbyteries' for the administration of the church.[62] Nonetheless, the early exponents of Lutheran orthodoxy did much to contribute to the consolidation of princely rule in the church, and they too commonly argued that the survival of the Lutheran religion depended on the confessionalization of the state. In the wake of 1555, for instance, Johann Arndt accepted the close relation between church and state, and he denied that church representatives were entitled to oppose the state's encroachment on the church.[63] Arndt emphasized the burden of obedience to authority placed on all Christians, and he saw those exercising princely power as bound to represent 'God's honour', and to 'draw the sword' to protect God's own justice.[64] After 1600, the other great father of Lutheran orthodoxy, Johann Gerhard, warned against the assumption that the constitution of the church is an aspect of princely regalia, and he denied that a princely magistrate might possess 'absolute empire' in the church. He thus clearly restricted the religious power of the church to external control – to *ius circa sacra,* not *ius in sacra.*[65] However, he also endorsed the episcopal constitutional model, arguing that episcopal rights belong to the princes under 'territorial law'.[66] Ultimately, then, even many pietists became sympathetic to the idea of the state church, and they viewed the pious prince as the most important guarantor of religious community and spiritual rebirth. August Hermann Francke is perhaps the most important example of this attitude. Francke argued that the political and ecclesiastical estates had common and concerted responsibility for maintaining order and virtue through society.[67] He therefore identified the pursuit of religious works as a token a civic virtue and distinction,[68] and he sought to fuse church and state as dynamic agents of moral-political engagement.[69] In later forms of pietism, therefore, the legal-political integrity of the first territorial states drew substance from the assumption of the princes that they were defenders of faith, and the Evangelical faith was asserted as a foundation for independent statehood.

In the decades after 1648, the insistence on state control of the church and the integrity of state law against the church became still more emphatic, although articulated on altered preconditions. The Peace of Westphalia gave more fundamental recognition to princely authority in religious matters; it sanctioned the power of the state over the church as an element of secular public law, not as a temporarily devolved liberty; it gave express sanction to the equality of the different confessions, including Calvinism; and it endeavoured to secure conditions of legal tolerance through the empire. The settlements of 1648 consequently deliberately prompted a move away from primarily confessional justifications of worldly power, and they sought to define statehood in more strictly territorial terms. The ecclesiastical/constitutional models that evolved after 1648 are, therefore, usually viewed as conforming to a 'territorial' model: that is, as defining the church as an institution like all other institutions under the public law of the territorial states, and as integrating the church through constitutionally underwritten authority, not through claims founded in confessional identity. This territorial outlook was exemplified in the works of Conring. Conring claimed that the primary concern of the prince must be that the 'state remains tranquil and happy'.[70] For this reason, the prince is required to supervise the church and to appoint bishops, or superintendents, and to ensure that disputes in the church do not threaten to disrupt civil order.[71] The 'best constituted republic', consequently, is one in which the church is placed under 'civil authority' and subject to civil law.[72] The greatest threat to a republic occurs where its cohesive legal order is unsettled by religious bodies, especially those, such as the Roman Catholic Church, using independent legal means to fragment the power of the state.[73] At the same time, Seckendorff also argued that the prince has supreme power in religious matters. This power, he argued, includes the right to make laws regulating the church, and the right to appoint ministers and supervise religious reaching.[74] Although not envisaging a total integration of the church into the state, he accepted that the prince should have final rights of direction in the church, and should, most importantly, preside over and limit the influence of ecclesiastical courts.[75] The prince is therefore the '*episcopus in externis*', with responsibility for the outward administration of the church,[76] especially where matters in the church concern the 'good order', which all 'Christian authority' is required to uphold.[77] Seckendorff differed slightly from his contemporary constitutionalists in that he showed strong sympathy for the original Lutheran conception of self-government by the parish or *Gemeinde,* and he lamented the emergence of excessively hierarchical ecclesiastical orders in the early territorial states.[78] His work stands out as an early model for a collegial constitution in the church, in which decisions on matters of faith are made within a college or councils of religious delegates. Only through this constitution, he argues, might the 'Roman hierarchy' based in 'artificially conceived representation' be supplanted.[79] Nonetheless, Seckendorff also accepted that the final right to reform the church (*ius reformandi*) must reside, according to 'worldly law', in the hands of territorial rulers.[80]

Beyond the seventeenth century, the insistence that the church should be brought under full political control became increasingly emphatic amongst leading constitutional thinkers. Gundling reiterated these earlier claims, asserting that territorial power is founded in the legitimate assumption by territorial rulers of powers fraudulently granted to bishops under Roman Catholic law.[81] The king or prince, he insisted, possessed full *ius reformandi* under territorial law and had unrestricted right to make laws relating to the church.[82] It was in Gundling's theory, in fact, that the attempt in Evangelical ecclesiastical law to limit legal externality came to its clearest conclusion. He argued that the church is ultimately nothing more than an organ under public law, and it is bound by public law in the same manner as all other public organizations. Therefore, wherever matters in the church become relevant for public law or where they threaten the cohesiveness of this law, they are subject to the jurisdiction of the prince.[83] However, where matters of faith only concern the church, the application of public law is not necessary. The prince, consequently, is not enjoined to debate on points of dogma, and, most importantly, he is not entitled to force his subjects to hold to one particular confession; Gundling thus broke with earlier confessionalist models and he defined religious tolerance as a particularly effective way of guaranteeing public security. The exclusion of external law from the state, which had always shaped Evangelical views on state law and ecclesiastical constitutions, thus, finally culminated, around 1700, in the view that religion should be legally neutralized and should enjoy no particular distinction amongst the legal facts of territorial law.

Similar arguments were at the heart of some of the major political-philosophical interventions in the early German Enlightenment – namely, the political doctrines of Samuel Pufendorf and Christian Thomasius, which also sought to curtail the role of religion in the outer life of the polity. Thomasius claimed that the external church should be fully integrated into the state, and he defined the right to control the outer activities of the church as 'one of the inalienable rights of the sovereign power of the state'.[84] Unlike earlier episcopal theorists, however, he did not believe that the church occupied an elevated or constitutive role in the organization of the territorial state; he denied that the legitimacy of princely power requires religious uniformity; and he rejected the idea that the prince might be endowed with elements of episcopal dignity. He concluded that it is misguided to assume, in early Evangelical manner, that the prince might 'represent two persons',[85] the ecclesiastical and the secular, or that he might exercise one set of laws as one person and one set of laws as a different person. The prince has no immediate or privileged mandate to govern the church; indeed, in matters of faith he is naturally obliged to 'follow the rules of Christianity' in the same way as all his subjects.[86] In the church, the prince is merely 'one who listens', and he has no power in questions of doctrine.[87] In fact, he argued that it is impossible for an Evangelical prince to apply worldly power in the government of the church, for the true church is always 'invisible' and it is not subject to legal rule.[88] Thomasius was, therefore, deeply opposed to all types of Caesaropapism and theocracy, which he described as 'tyranny'.[89] For this reason, he also questioned the essential constitutional principle of political Protestantism (derived from the concept of *cuius regio eius religio*): namely, that it is the 'duty of majesty' to 'guide his subjects to true religion'.[90] The prince, for Thomasius, has no authority to impose doctrine as a matter of civil order, or to force doctrinal conformity on his population.[91] Opposing confessionalist ideals of order, therefore, he opted for an altogether more functional approach to religion in politics.[92] As long as the prince preserves the peace, he indicated, it is not eminently important whether the prince is Christian or heathen: the primary natural law of governance, which insists alone that peace must be kept in the realm, cannot distinguish between inner questions of the soul.[93]

Despite this separation of church and state, however, Thomasius also asserted that the obligation of the prince 'to use appropriate coercive measures to maintain external tranquillity and peace amongst his subjects' must override all other rights possessed by churches or other collegial bodies.[94] The prince is consequently authorized to assume full control of the external direction of the church, to appoint ministers, to pass judgements in ecclesiastical courts,[95] to exercise *ius praesidendi* in the consistories,[96] and, crucially, to intervene in the church in cases where religious debates threaten the more general stability of society.[97] For Thomasius, in short, the church is always subject to the fundamentally secular principles of public law, and it is bound by the imperative that peace must be kept in the realm. Indeed, whereas earlier episcopal theories derived the legitimacy of princely power from a neo-theocratic substructure, Thomasius saw stable power as depending precisely on its ability to detheocratize its foundations, to neutralize religious controversy, to exclude from its functions all laws that undermine its integrity and, so, to stabilize a sphere of state power that is not excessively encumbered with religious ideas. The prince, in short, can exercise all the legal rights that come to him as a worldly prince, and these rights are deducible from the need to maintain external peace. The explanation of these rights in metaphysical categories, however, is always likely to detract from the appropriate application of law.

Pufendorf's writings on religion and theology also articulated similar views. On the one hand, Pufendorf showed preference for Lutheranism over other confessions, and he argued that the Lutheran church gives ideal institutional support to the state. However, this argument was not shaped by theocratic considerations, but simply by the functional belief that Lutheranism breeds political obedience, whereas Calvinism, especially, fosters more turbulent, and even democratic, political sentiments.[98] More generally, however, he argued that religion is a matter of inward devotion, and it should not be ascribed undue importance. Debates on the constitutional form of the church are unnecessary because the 'church is not a state', and its contents cannot be represented in any institutional order.[99] The 'doctors of the church', he argued, are 'servants of Christ', not 'public officials of the king', and religious discourse does not provide legitimacy for the state. As a consequence of this, however, the prince must be accountable – at least 'in part' – for the external order of the church, as the doctors of the church have no external political force with which they might defend or organize the church, or with which they might ensure that religious division does not create civil strife.[100] In his exercise of this external care of the church, however, the prince is not obliged to impose religious uniformity on his people, and the prince is allowed, 'with a good conscience', to show tolerance towards religious dissidents.[101]

Two distinct theoretical phases are, therefore, discernible in German constitutional reflection on the relation between church and state throughout and after the period of religious conflict. The earliest post-Reformation constitutionalists, especially those concentrating on ecclesiastical law, sought to minimize the power of external ecclesiastical law by binding church and state together, and by defining confessional identity as a founding principle of the state. These theories were intended to harden the state against external law, and they used theocratic ideas to counteract other, more entrenched modes of juridical theocracy, and to concentrate state power as a distinct element of worldly order in the empire. Subsequently, this outlook gave way to a more obviously positive/secular stance, which sought to detheologize the law or to neutralize religion as a formative element in the law, whilst still defining the external church as an integrated component of public law, under a quasi-absolutist executive. Recent theoretical historians have rightly emphasized the caesura between these theoretical epochs in the course of German state-building, and they have often seen the transition from the 'confessional' to the 'absolutist' state as a secular precondition of modern states, in which the enjoyment of private and religious freedom in the state is presupposed as a natural right.[102] For all the divergence and, indeed, antagonism, between these theoretical epochs, however, both periods were shaped by common objectives, and they might in fact be viewed as related stages in a longer process of legal positivization. Both periods had their centre in the denial of the belief that the church could be ascribed authority that might be translated into politically relevant laws, and they saw the elimination of the legislative autonomy of the church as fundamental to political stability. Above all, both saw the stability of the state as hinging on a reduction of the *legal externality* of the church, and on an expulsion of all metaphysically universalized law from the state. '*Ecclesia est in Respublica*', both claimed, for different reasons: '*non Respublica in Ecclesia*'.[103] Both thus reacted fundamentally, at both a theoretical and practical level, against the universal legal postulates enshrined in the hierarchical structure and juridical independence of the Roman Catholic Church. In endorsing, first, the united kingdom of co-believers, theocratically led by a Christian prince/bishop, or, second, the religiously neutralized territory led by a tolerant and enlightened prince, these stages of constitutional theory were bound together by their intention to institute a legally cohesive state, whose authority and legitimacy were not fractured by universal-metaphysical or formally ius-natural conceptions of political order and legal application. Indeed, the paradox of theocracy in the first stage might actually be seen as a necessary reaction to the acute legal exceptionalism in the first decades after the Reformation, and so as the effective precondition for the second wave of theoretical formation and legal stabilization. Both these stages in legal-theological foundation had at their heart an attempt to demarcate the space of statehood as a realm of positive legal independence in which the state is not obstructed by metaphysical postulates in its political tasks and in which the state itself obtains full power to authorize its own law.

Natural law: the state's own law

If the objective of these constitutional debates was, in large part, to reduce legal externality and to consolidate the positive form of the law, this had implications for the wider evolution of political theory in Germany, and these constitutional arguments converged with the more general development of ideas of natural law. As discussed above, specifically Evangelical approaches to natural law began to evolve in the earliest period of Reformation, and they used natural law, and sometimes Roman law, to cement positive accounts of state authority, against more widely universalized ius-natural theories. In modified manner, this tendency to articulate natural-law paradigms as alternatives to the traditional sources of natural law also became prevalent in early constitutional law, and by the first decades of the seventeenth century it was common for German lawyers and theologians to use principles of natural law to explain the relation between imperial and territorial power, and to determine the constitutional constraints bearing on the personal/dynastic authority of the Emperor. At a very early stage, for example, Balthasar

Meisner argued that laws of the Holy Roman Empire should be accepted by all as 'sacred' and 'inviolable', and that even those representing the empire could be called to account by binding legal standards.[104] Slightly later, König argued that the Emperor was 'bound by divine and natural laws', which were expressed in the constitutional covenants of the empire.[105] Limnaeus argued that the 'fundamental laws' limiting imperial power had the quality of divine laws, or laws of nature, and the legitimate exercise of imperial power could not contravene such laws.[106] Matthias Stephani also insisted that the Emperor was subject to the law 'of nature and of reason'; the Emperor justified his majesty only by 'living by the laws', and by showing compliance with natural law, which was enshrined in the constitutional pacts restricting imperial authority.[107] The Emperor, he claimed, was bound by two sets of fundamental laws – those derived from nature, and those derived from pacts: both sets of laws, however, tended to coalesce in the fundamental laws of the constitution. Later in the seventeenth century, Caspar Ziegler also extended this argument, claiming that imperial majesty was derived from God and that, for this reason, those who wielded imperial majesty were always constrained by the 'directive force of the law', and were not empowered to use power for personal gain or advantage.[108] To 'be bound by laws and to live in accordance with laws', he asserted, was to comply with the very 'nature of majesty' and so to act in accordance with the dignity of empire.[109] The divine laws of state, Ziegler concluded, were in fact manifest in the 'fundamental laws' formed by custom and convention.[110] For this reason, the natural laws forming the majesty of the empire were identical with the laws, pacts and agreements formed between the empire and the princes.

Early conceptions of natural law in German constitutional thought were part of a set of strategies that were intended to elaborate a doctrine of public law and to define the empire as a state – as a publicly accountable constitutional body, comprising publicly accountable organs. The emerging insight in these constitutional theories was that ideas of natural right provided a theoretical instrument with the aid of which the real majesty of the empire could be separated from the personal majesty of the emperor, and that a set of constitutional constraints could be imposed around the emperor. In its first objective, therefore, early German ius-naturalism was committed to the constitutional restriction of power in the empire, and to the balancing of power between distinct centres of jurisdiction. Within a short period of time, however, the aim of effecting a constitutional balance was replaced by the more far-reaching intention of dislocating princely power from the empire, of providing justification for the full concentration of legal power in territorial states and territorial courts and of elaborating cohesive jurisdictional orders independently of any constitutional balance. As the territories loosened their political and judicial apparatus from the empire, then, the constitutional structure of the empire was undermined, and this paved the way, in some instances, for a particularly stringent brand of regional absolutism. In this constitutional process, consequently, natural law was not primarily effective in constructing a realm of supra-positive law or a set of constitutional principles that could be employed to place procedural or normative limits on the state. On the contrary, the main function of natural-law arguments, in early modern Germany, was to establish and defend certain fundamental laws, which conferred independence, not limits, on the evolving sites of territorial statehood, within the dualistic imperial constitution. In the German states, therefore, natural-law theory was commonly devoted to the positive concentration of power and law: in fact, it tended, de facto, to free power, not to bind it, to reduce, not reinforce, the legal constraints on the state, and to facilitate, not curtail, the positively self-legitimizing power of the territories.

This analysis does not wish to suggest that early German natural-law theorists had no commitment to imposing limits on the power of princely states. In the immediate aftermath of the Reformation, to be sure, the improvised nature of political order tended to foster homogenous constitutional orders. Subsequently, however, the general endorsement of princely authority within or against the empire was increasingly flanked by a tentative insistence that subjects or regional estates (*Landstände*) within the territories should be seen as bearers of certain rights and customary freedoms.[111] Indeed, even the early defenders of territorial power stated that such power could not be exercised without any limits. Matthias Stephani, for example, asserted that the prince was 'above the law and outside the law', but he also stipulated that the true Protestant prince was obligated under natural law and forfeited his majesty wherever he violated Christian morality.[112] Later, Seckendorff was prepared to describe the prince as 'God's viceroy on earth', yet he also insisted that the prince was bound to respect certain privileges and procedures in the administration of the courts, in raising taxes, and in guaranteeing religious freedom.[113] As princely authority is granted by God, he reasoned, those who exercise it are bound to act within firm moral constraints.[114] Even Conring, who was surely not without Machiavellian sympathies, argued that princely power is restricted by considerations of utility and practical morality: by the religious piety, the good faith, the modesty and the justice inherent in the character of the true Christian prince.[115]

By the late seventeenth century, then, ius-natural ideas became elements of the conceptual apparatus supporting a doctrine of universal public law, which, even in particular territories, took natural right as a practical guarantee of the rule of law under restricted monarchy. Heinrich Cocceji interpreted public law as a body of politically enforceable norms deducible both from nature and from pacts between citizens,[116] and he defined the rule of law as the 'highest good of the state'.[117] Samuel Cocceji, subsequently, gave a more positivist inflection to his father's teachings on natural law. He argued that law is a positive and autonomous science, and he insisted on the need for a formally independent judiciary, separate from the executive body of the state, which could ensure that the functions of law were systematically defined and implemented.[118] At the same time, Justus Henning Boehmer extended this legal-constitutional analysis to argue that power has no 'absolute foundation' under natural law, and always presupposes specific legal or moral justification.[119] Those charged with the exercise of power are obliged by natural law to maintain conditions of 'peace and tranquillity',[120] and the specific form of this obligation is dictated by 'pacts' constituting the 'fundamental laws' of the polity.[121] Boehmer even defined conformity to natural law, and so to agreed law, as the sole condition under which the exercise of power can be viewed as a 'legitimate faculty'.[122]

It is, therefore, evident that early German natural-law theory cannot be seen as offering a uniform blueprint for unrestricted state power. On the contrary, many influential participants in constitutional debate were committed, especially after 1648, to the institution of a legally ordered territorial state, containing certain guarantees for customary and even – at a later stage – social rights. Nonetheless, the most salient objective of the constitutional theory of this time was to define the state as a politically cohesive and self-authorizing order, and such theory, even where it accepted necessary limits on state power, necessarily viewed jurisdictional pluralism and diversity in the creation and application of law as potentially problematic. The diverse accounts of natural law set out by Stephani, Seckendorff and Conring, for example, defined the limits on princely authority, to a large extent, as constraints deduced by the prince himself or, paradoxically, enacted by the prince in the fulfilment of his own majesty, not as restrictions imposed by any external source. The limiting of power was thus, in many respects, a process of moral *self-limiting* by a Christian patriarch, who was accountable both for making laws and for ensuring that these laws were not in contravention of natural law. Even theorists such as Boehmer, who was deeply committed to the legal circumscription of government, argued that the majesty of state could only be concentrated in *one* place, and that the binding of the prince by natural law did not imply any division of sovereignty.[123] Other theorists of state more inclined to accept a patriarchical or quasi-absolutist state set the binding force of natural law at a lower level still, and they argued, in Hobbesian manner, that the obligation of the prince under natural law is fulfilled wherever he succeeds in keeping the peace.[124] The underlying tendency in most of these early theories of natural law, in consequence, was that they posited natural law as an internal element of the state's own operations, and they determined the source of natural law as the state itself. At the heart of these doctrines was the fact that they allowed the state to provide a positive explanation of its functions and legitimacy, and they hardened the state against more intrusively universalized constructs of law.

Natural law and the positivization of law

This correlation between ius-naturalism, legal positivization and the consolidation of state power also formed the horizon in which prominent philosophers of natural law during the early German Enlightenment approached legal analysis, and philosophical debate on politics assimilated aspects of the anti-universalism of this era. Pufendorf's practical philosophy, for example, also contains teachings about law that emphasized the necessity of closure and unity in law and the state. Underlying Pufendorf's philosophy is the argument that in the act of creation God added moral entities, *entia moralia,* to the physical world, and so established a realm of moral value distinct from the purely material universe. These moral entities can be construed as the moral values and judgements of individual persons, or as the moral norms connecting people in a state or society. Generally, however, these entities refer to normative contents in the world, which restrict the arbitrary use of human freedom, which provide norms for the regulation of actions, and which help establish moral value in human affairs.[125] These entities were first created by God to bring order into human life; God originally endowed humankind with moral entities and he created humankind as moral animals, destined, unlike other animals, to have knowledge of their maker and to follow the will of their maker.[126] In addition, however, human beings can create moral entities in independence of God, so that a secondary realm of moral entities can evolve, which also serves to institute moral order, but is not derived directly from God's will.[127] Human beings are uniquely created with the free power of the will through which they can determine their actions by an 'extrinsic principle' or a 'notional norm', and so constitute moral entities as an autonomous realm of moral liberty, or of natural law.[128]

For Pufendorf, therefore, the world was created as a moral world by God's will, and certain natural or moral laws exist in this world. Once the world has been created, however, human beings cannot have metaphysical knowledge of God's will or God's law.[129] Indeed, Pufendorf claimed that it is inappropriate for humans to speculate on God's will; human speculation on God's will implies a belief that this will is bound by a rational plan or by universal ends or rules, in which reason independently participates. Such speculation degrades the majesty of God by indicating that God's will is compliant with some 'absolute necessity', existing divisibly from God himself.[130] To assume that God's will exists in conformity with universal contents or principles is, in fact, tantamount to imposing an external norm on God's will, which in turn undervalues God's position as the author and creator of the world through a spontaneous act of volition.[131] Natural law is simply manifest in the fact that, as God willed human beings to exist as free, rational and social animals, humans must be equipped to deduce natural laws, or to 'govern through laws' that allow them to live freely, rationally and socially.[132] Pufendorf thus concluded that the foundation of morality and natural law resides in human nature, as created by God. Natural law can be divined through 'the contemplation of the human condition',[133] and such contemplation leads to the insight that the human being, as a moral entity, tends to live by laws, and, above all, that human beings are bound by the 'law of sociality':[134] they tend to organize their actions around the need to coexist with others, and they even show a pronounced 'proclivity' for forming societies and entering social commerce with others.[135] Laws are valid as natural law, consequently, where they uphold the conditions of sociality to which human beings are naturally oriented.

Central to Pufendorf's anthropological account of natural law is a separation of law from rational metaphysics and from moral theology and an insistence that legislation must be conceived as a consistently positive function.[136] Legislation, he argued, is not validated by speculative reason, and it cannot exist in demonstrable conformity with divine reason; legislation, rather, is a constitutive element in human society, positively embedded in and authenticated by the moral dispositions of human character. He consequently defined legislation as a constitutively positive element of human activity, through which human beings create a legal reality for themselves which is both founded in, yet also distinct from, God's own originary creative will. As the order of the world was first created by God, the order of the polity is created by the legislator, and the laws promulgated by this legislator are human laws containing a certain positivized distinction against God's own laws. For this reason, Pufendorf stated that the rule of law depends on the volitional act of the law-giver and that the formation of law is always the concrete corollary of a legislative will. Law demands obedience because of its volitional origin. It demands obedience because it expresses the 'command of a superior':[137] indeed, law is a decree 'through which a superior obliges someone who is subject to him' to do or not to do a certain thing.[138] The 'human laws' of the human polity are consequently nothing more than the 'decrees' issued by the state, which 'subjects have to observe for the well-being of the state'.[139] Following this voluntaristic principle, Pufendorf also concluded that where there is no positive law the contents of human actions are 'indifferent', that there is no universal or absolute standard of law for evaluating the moral worth of actions and, thus, that all operative law is law that has been positively constituted through the volitional acts of legislators.[140]

None of this should be taken to mean that Pufendorf was an advocate of moral arbitrariness in government or that he viewed unrestricted princely voluntarism as the essence of public authority. On the contrary, he stated clearly that legislative authority in the state originates in a set of covenants through which members of a society establish consensus about the necessity and the exact form of their government.[141] Moreover, he argued that good government has its origins in the human law of sociality and that sociality provides the 'foundation' for the principles of natural law by which government should be guided. Everything which is 'necessary for this sociality' is prescribed under natural law, and everything which disrupts sociality is prohibited under natural law.[142] The index of natural law, accordingly, is that it serves the stability, utility and harmony of a society. The 'supreme law' of a polity is that all who exercise power should act so as to serve the well-being and interests of the people,[143] and they accomplish this where they create conditions conducive to social coexistence and harmony.[144]

Despite this, however, although at times close to an early utilitarian approach to legal order, Pufendorf's accounts of legislation and natural law also at times reflected the wider anti-universalist tendencies of early modern political theory, and they viewed the political order most likely to create reliable conditions of governance as one in which legal diversity and externality are eliminated. Governments likely to enjoy and promote social stability, he claimed, are those in which the wills of the many are effectively 'directed and moderated' by the will embodied in the state, and where the origin of positive law is identified with one cohesive will.[145] Such governments are governed by one spirit: one will unites all parts of the state, and the highest exercise of power is 'undivided'.[146] For Pufendorf, therefore, monarchy has the specific advantage over other regimes that it stimulates the highest attainable degree of unity and security in the state and that it facilitates quick and effective reactions to all factors that endanger this security.[147] For this reason, Pufendorf concluded that there is no constitutional difference between the real and personal majesty of the state: the state has its highest dignity in the unity conferred upon it by the personal power of the monarch.[148] Similarly, there are no formal or external constraints on the power of the prince; once the founding covenants of state have been agreed, the prince is governed or 'obliged' by natural law alone, and the prince alone is responsible for transforming the general constructs of natural law into positive law.[149] The exercise of 'absolute power', Pufendorf consequently argued, does not 'involve anything iniquitous or intolerable'. Absolute power is, in fact, a necessary precondition of the stability of the republic, and it is profoundly compliant with natural law. The rule of law, or of natural law, is, therefore, both the foundation and the corollary of undivided sovereignty, and the state of natural law is likely to be unsettled if it is restricted by specific or particular compacts between monarch and subjects, where distinct commissarial obligations are imposed upon the king, or where there are fundamental laws to which the monarch is held in obligation.[150]

It is notable that in his more direct political interventions Pufendorf did not unequivocally take the side of territorial power against the empire, and he did not fully oppose the constitution of the empire. In discussing the empire, he lamented the uncertainty in the division of power and law between emperors and princes; he bemoaned the 'monstrous' lack of clarity in its account of sovereignty and statehood, which allowed different and rival accounts of political power and sovereignty to confuse and dilute each other.[151] He also complained bitterly that the ruling dynasty of the Habsburgs used its power in the empire for the pursuit of private motives, and it undermined the unity required by any sovereign body politic. In principle, therefore, Pufendorf declared his general preference for regular forms of state in which the entire polity is unified in an ordered, ideally monarchical, structure. However, he also recognized that, realistically, the empire could not be reformed to comply with this model without a full transformation of the 'entire state'.[152] The most pressing structural weaknesses of the empire could be rectified, however, through a clarification of its existing constitutional form and through its acceptance as an irregular constitution, with monarchical and estate-based elements, constructed as a system of quasi-sovereign confederated states. This conclusion does not imply that Pufendorf viewed shared sovereignty or federal government as an ideal model of statehood. On the contrary, he indicated that the empire actually prevented the foundation of a regular state in Germany: that is, a state governed by a cohesive and uniform will, capable of imposing positive-legal principles on all those subject to it. However, his commitment to a positive analysis of legal application also ensured that he pursued a realistic analysis of the empire and that he endeavoured, despite his reservations, to contribute to the stability of the imperial system as a legal order.[153]

Like Pufendorf, Thomasius also constructed his practical and political philosophy around the attempt to create a unified state on positive legal foundations. Indeed, to a greater extent even than Pufendorf, Thomasius argued that discourses on law and power should be placed on resolutely secular/utilitarian premises, and no principles should be admitted in such debate that might corrupt legal thought with metaphysical reflection or non-rational demands. He protested against the introduction of 'metaphysical distinctions' in practical discourse,[154] and he suggested that the realm of political doctrine should exclude contents which burden law with problems which cannot be resolved through secular discourse.[155] Central to the philosophy of Thomasius, therefore, was the claim that human reason cannot have knowledge of 'God's secrets', and that reason is nothing more than a positive faculty intended to help the human being 'using his natural forces' to further the interests of the 'temporal life'.[156] This argument was not always consistently articulated, and Thomasius did not always propose an entirely anthropological doctrine of rational self-sufficiency. He indicated, for instance, that there exists a certain 'harmony between natural light and supernatural light', and that the postulates of human reason need not contradict religious dogma.[157] At times he even suggested that God's will is positively revealed in the world, that God confers an original order on the universe, which is manifest as natural law.[158] Indeed, there are also moments in Thomasius' work where creationist legal ideas rather unnervingly invaded his analysis. In his earlier works, for instance, he claimed that the 'invisible essence of God' is positively 'revealed' in works and creation.[159] At a more fundamental level, however, Thomasius was intent on drawing a clear distinction between the practical science of law and the speculative science of theology. Law, he explained, is a science whose purpose is to show the 'ways and means to further external political peace and order', whereas religion is a field of inquiry referring only to the 'inner tranquillity of souls'.[160] If religion has a practical virtue, it is simply that it contributes to civic order, because people with tranquil souls are unlikely to threaten civic stability.[161] The laws of nature guiding human legislation, in consequence, have no metaphysical or divine origin; they are merely practical guidelines for the organization of human behaviour, and they can only be derived from considerations of social utility.[162] Knowledge of truth, in consequence, cannot be a knowledge of facts that might upset human stability. It is constitutive of true knowledge that it serves the 'utility of people' and prevents anything that is detrimental to this utility.[163] Laws of nature thus prescribe that no actions should be committed by which 'human society is disturbed'.[164] For this reason, Thomasius concluded, political authority has its justification through its ability 'to protect its subjects from internal and external violence', and it is entitled to use 'means of violence' to obtain this result. Thomasius consequently followed Pufendorf in identifying *legislation* as the most essential and constitutive act of human reason: legislation is the activity in which human reason sets itself apart from metaphysical controversy and in which it constitutes a realm of existence marked by distinct human interests and cares.[165] The contents of this legislation are entirely positive, and they require no external addition to ensure their validity.

This account of political order contains two quite distinct implications. First, Thomasius gestured in the direction of early social-contractarian principles, as he argued that authority could not exist without a constitutive element of rational 'consensus'.[166] Like Pufendorf, he avoided the extremes of Hobbesian voluntarism by explaining that human societies are born out of an innate human inclination towards sociality, which recognizes social union and community as the most natural and adequate mode of human existence. Because of this, rational people understand that *affection* is the natural precondition of social order, and they are predisposed rationally to love their fellow members of society and to act in a manner serving common interests. Rational people in fact love 'other people more than themselves', and they accept the necessity of subordinating their own individual wills to the wills of others in order to pursue common objectives of security, stability and peace.[167] The most enduring, harmonious or *natural* legal orders are, consequently, based in rationally sublimated love.[168]

Second, however, Thomasius also occasionally sympathized with arguments that placed less emphasis on consensus in government. The rational affection underlying a stable polity, he argued, is not egalitarian affection, but affection that gives stability to princely rule. Indeed, where love exceeds its rational limits and urges equality, commonality or even shared ownership of goods, it becomes a degenerate form of love.[169] Rational affection, therefore, is most effectively maintained in a polity in which the prince ensures that power is not used irresponsibly or with brutality, and in which the prince is careful not to erode the love in which the state's stability is based.[170] The law of affection, in consequence, is a natural law, which the representatives of the state are expected to apply to themselves. This natural law is not derived from or imposed by any external source.

Because of this, Thomasius also followed Pufendorf in arguing that the will is the foundation of the law. All morality and all law, he explained, have their 'source' in the will of particular people.[171] Law requires the volitional acts of the legislator in order to assume positive applicability; it cannot be derived from categorically given universal norms; and the extent of law's validity is defined by the will positing law. Subjects, he argued, are consequently bound to structure their external actions 'in accordance with the will' of their 'superiors', and, where civic stability is in question, even 'inequitable laws' have to be accepted and obeyed.[172] In this voluntaristic argument, in fact, Thomasius also expressed scepticism about the deduction of binding natural laws. Pure natural laws, he concluded, constitute at most the founding 'norm of positive law', and ideas of natural law might provide guidance on questions relating to the application of law.[173] However, there are many issues that cannot be regulated by natural law, and where natural law gives no reference for legal application. To a greater degree than Pufendorf, therefore, Thomasius saw positive law as possessing autonomy against all perennial normative standards,[174] and, crucially, he claimed that natural law only becomes law through the technical process of its positivization, which occurs as it is spoken as a norm by the legislator.[175] Indeed, Thomasius lastly conceded that civil law and natural law are two substantively distinct academic disciplines, that universal ethical reflection is not a necessary condition of legal validity and that civil law is not necessarily underscored by natural law.[176] After Thomasius, this positivizing approach became increasingly influential and his students, most notably Johann Jacob Schmauß, extended his ideas to concentrate a doctrine of civil law around the natural or instinctual dispositions of the human being, not around formal elements of natural law.[177]

Thomasius, in consequence, construed the ideal polity as one whose laws are ordered by a princely legislator, who is obliged to pass laws that preserve the well-being of his subjects and maintain the relations of affection underlying civil society, and whose legal findings are expressly not guided by metaphysical norms. He understood his political doctrine at once as a thorough critique and as the culmination of the evolution of post-Reformation political thought. He saw his anti-metaphysical approach to law as clearly opposed to the princely confessional states that had evolved through the Reformation and as excluding from law's positive structure all religious and metaphysical distractions. However, he also indicated that his anti-metaphysical view was rooted in Luther's own anti-theocratic stance. He noted, for example, that Luther had found scholastic philosophy detestable, especially because it confused 'divine law, common law, Mosaic law and particular human laws'.[178] He thus saw the conflation of human and divine laws as deeply conflicting with Lutheran beliefs, and he saw his own teaching as contributing to the formation of a state that might finally give consistent expression to the original Evangelical attack on theocratic politics and to the original Evangelical demands for freedom under own laws.[179] Above all, therefore, Thomasius saw his own doctrine as resolving the problems of positivization arising from the Reformation, and as finally instituting a reliable order of positive law within a horizon determined by Evangelical laws. The problem of positivization, he intimated, could only be resolved if divine reason and the human will were segregated from each other and if the practically guided moral will was acknowledged as the source of legal order. Like Pufendorf before him, therefore, Thomasius saw the legislative will as the cornerstone of the world emerging from the Reformation, and he saw the moral decisions enforced by this will as the only guarantor of order in the post-metaphysical universe. It is only positive acts of legislation that can lead the world away from the exceptionality induced by the end of metaphysics, and this highest calling of legislation is undermined wherever the will is disturbed by excessively formalized ideals of natural law.

Natural law and the return of metaphysics

If, in the early German Enlightenment, Thomasius and Pufendorf were theorists of the quasi-secular state, seeking to neutralize all legal principles likely to undermine the consistent order of state, Gottfried Wilhelm Leibniz was the most prominent opponent of voluntaristic conceptions of law and state power and the most prominent adherent of metaphysical deductions of natural law. The controversies between Leibniz, Thomasius and Pufendorf formed the crux of the theoretical rivalries underlying the politics of state-building and legal construction in early modern Germany, and the debates between these theorists touched on the primary issues of law's authority: they addressed the origin of law, the limits of territorial power, the status of the Holy Roman Empire and the position of the church in the empire. At the foundation of these controversies, however, was a seminal and theoretically divisive debate about the metaphysical body of the law and about the positive origins of state power. It was around these debates that the battle lines of early Enlightenment practical philosophy were drawn.

Leibniz shared the fundamental conviction of Pufendorf and Thomasius that natural law must be derived from considerations of utility. Just law or natural law, he argued, serves 'public well-being',[180] and the 'highest rule of law' is that it must 'direct all things to the greatest general good'.[181] However, whilst his rivals defined the general good as a good stipulated by a particular legislative will and distilled from human dispositions, Leibniz asserted that the good underlying natural law is defined by teleological reference to an ideal political order or to a condition of human perfection: to the City of God. Law deserving to be called natural, he explained, is not based in anthropological observation, but is law that is identical with the 'laws of the best republic', and that guides human society towards the 'idea' of unity with God's own law: that is, with laws which God might freely give to himself.[182] Leibniz thus saw natural law as constitutive of and deducible from a condition of human perfectibility, and he saw human perfectibility as a condition of possible likeness between humanity and God.

In seeking a metaphysical or divine-natural foundation for the laws of the good polity, Leibniz did not abandon all anthropological considerations. On the contrary, he argued that natural law contains certain principles of utility that aid social coexistence and induce harmony in human relations: indeed, it is essential to natural law that, as it guides society towards perfection, it must serve practical human interests.[183] Likewise, he also emphasized that natural law does not exist independently of human reason. Natural laws are expressly rational laws, and they cannot be extracted from any positive theology or revealed divine-positive law.[184] Knowledge of natural law can, in fact, only result from the employment of 'formal reason',[185] which moderates the human will and organizes actions in compliance with the principles of human utility and harmony. Reason used in this manner is the 'science of charity' or the 'charity of the wise'.[186] The charity of the wise culminates in the maxim that people ought not to act in a manner that which they might find loathsome in others, and in the knowledge that actions conforming to this maxim will help establish and maintain harmony in human society.[187] Nonetheless, at the heart of Leibnizian legal philosophy was a reintegration of metaphysics into practical philosophy and an essentialist account of the sources of legal validity. This attitude was deeply tied up with a rejection of early positivist accounts of law, which saw the law as contingent on a coercive will. For example, in his commentaries on Pufendorf he denounced the deduction of law from voluntaristic structures of human superiority and command, and he claimed that such positivist tendencies lead to a paradoxical arbitrariness in law's content and to an eradication of legitimate obligation in its application.[188] Leibniz did not deny in this that laws are positively enforced by states, or that the state has the character of an institution applying power. However, he argued that all transmission of power through law must be validated by metaphysical-rational principles of harmony, and necessity, and that power alone cannot be taken as the 'formal reason of justice'.[189] It is, he stated, 'abhorrent to reason' that law should be simply founded in prerogative.[190] Leibniz's thinking was thus shaped by an intense hostility towards the rupture between law and morality or reason and will in the more positivistic accounts of legal force, which sought to neutralize metaphysical elements in legal doctrine. The legitimate obligation of law can, he asserted, only be derived from law's irreducible justice: law's justice, in turn, can only be determined through a rational assessment of law's conformity with the highest metaphysical principles of reasonable harmony in the universe. He, therefore, concluded that 'natural law' does not 'differ from divine moral law',[191] and the task of human reason is to deduce laws which are, of their own essence, metaphysically *necessary*. Unlike other practical philosophers of the early Enlightenment, therefore, Leibniz also insisted that there is no necessary disjuncture between what is just for humans and for human wills and what is just for God and for the divine will. God might have a greater facility than humans in acting in accordance with moral laws, he acknowledged; indeed, the divine will, as a perfect will, must be perfectly compliant with natural law. However, the rationally necessary content of justice is identical for both human and divine beings: justice, in fact, is external to both human and divine minds, and all creation can be held accountable to the principles that rational justice contains.[192] In an inversion of the formative principles of post-Reformation philosophy, therefore, he claimed that God's freedom to will justice is defined by the necessary content of justice, and God is only free where the content of his freedom is also rationally necessary.

Leibniz argued that there exists a three-tiered hierarchy of natural law, with each lower level leading to and finding its perfection in the higher level. The most rudimentary level of natural law is defined by the first precept of Ulpian's formulation of Roman law: *neminem laedere* (hurt no one). This, for Leibniz, is the principle of private law or commutative justice, and it underpins the law pertaining to property and ownership: it, therefore, expresses natural law as it applies to the state of nature.[193] This principle leads to the second level of natural law, defined by the second principle of Roman law, the principle of equity: *suum cuique tribuere* (render to each his or her due). This, for Leibniz, is the principle of public law or distributive justice, and it constitutes the moral conditions for the laws pertaining to human social coexistence: it gives rational-ethical substance to ownership, it transforms mere relations of property into the foundation of human commonality and mutual assistance, and it gives moral structure to human relationships. The highest level of natural law is defined by the third precept of Ulpian's law: *honeste vivere* (live honestly or piously). This represents the law of piety, of universally necessary justice, and of 'natural obligation towards God', and it directs all human affairs towards the 'perfection of the soul':[194] a truly moral society requires this principle as its ethical centre. The highest level of natural law, consequently, has the two inferior levels as its own precondition, but these lower levels are not sufficient independently to guarantee justice and well-being in a polity. Indeed, Leibniz argued that models of political order that separate principles of legal obligation from metaphysically necessary ethical substrates remain at a low level of natural law, and they explain political order merely as the functional maintenance of ownership and the coercive suppression of natural antagonism. Such accounts (exemplified by Hobbes) fail to grasp the necessary universality of natural law; they fail to account for the multi-level process of rational legal evolution through which stable and just societies construct themselves; and they fail to appreciate the fundamentally rational foundations of enduring social stability.[195] Indeed, the transition from the state of nature to the well-regulated polity, Leibniz suggested, cannot be accomplished through simple acts of will, reflected in possessive contracts between citizens or acts of legislation imposed from above. The formation of a just polity always requires a metaphysical-universal addition to these acts of will, and through this addition the human mind must replicate in its laws the legal unity and harmony of God's universe, and it must make human wills compliant with the principles of this unity and harmony. The state of unity and harmony incorporates relations of property and the need for political stability, but it also incorporates universal piety and compliance with categorically binding laws. The good polity, for Leibniz in short, is always a metaphysical or rationally necessary polity and it can only be derived from a will whose freedom is exercised in uniformity with supra-positive legal norms.

Leibniz's attack on legal voluntarism was not restricted to human volition, but it also extended to God's own will. Pufendorf and other voluntarists argued that the principles of natural law are derived originally from God's creative will, and that these principles are good because they were first ordained by God. These principles are now applied by human wills, and they obtain a certain positive distinction against the first form of their creation. In contrast to this, Leibniz asserted that natural-law principles have priority to God's will, and, by consequence, to all other wills. God's justice is just because it conforms to rationally necessary and invariable principles of justice, not merely because God, in his freedom and contingency, willed justice to be just. In fact, if justice were defined simply as the arbitrary outcome of God's will, Leibniz reasoned, it would be impossible conclusively to define the content of justice, and God himself might even be free to act unjustly. If justice were merely an act of God's will, God might unjustly 'condemn the innocent or beatify the evil', he might pass other laws contravening natural justice, and he might act as a tyrant, ruling through fear not love.[196] This, he argued, is inconceivable: it is essential to divinity that it is determined by universally demonstrable ideas of justice, applying formally to all wills.[197] It is consequently constitutive of God, Leibniz concluded, that he exercises his will and his freedom in conformity with prior rational or natural laws. God himself, thus, is not the volitional origin of laws, but is necessarily bound by law, and he has no supreme power or absolute freedom that transcends rationally binding normative constraints.[198] In consequence, law, whether human or divine, can never be a 'command of the creator'; instead, it is 'a command of supreme reason', which pre-exists and determines all creative wills. Natural law has its origin not in the legislative *will* or *freedom* of God, but in God's natural-legal *essence,* which, as *reason* and *necessity,* is originally distinct from, prior to, and obligatory for God himself.[199]

If the will of God is bound by the rational principles of the law, this also applies to the state, which, in certain respects, Leibniz saw as the *genus proximum* of God. The state, for Leibniz, is inviolable in so far as it shows wisdom in fostering the cause of harmony, justice and perfection in the world. However, where it corrupts these principles by abandoning wisdom and applying power as a will exercised outside the parameters of universal law, it forfeits its quality as a legitimate state, and it becomes tyranny.

Wisdom and law are, therefore, closely correlated at the core of Leibniz's conception of the human polity. Wisdom is a charitable mental disposition which understands the essence of the 'most perfect being', which is God, which knows that God's perfection consists in compliance with essential law, and which seeks the institution of legal-political orders continuous with God's perfect law and with the 'sovereign wisdom' of God's perfect plan.[200] Where wisdom informs the polity, therefore, all human society is oriented towards a condition of shared perfection in the city of God, and this condition takes the shape of a universal legal state, in which all power is bound by wise, necessary and ultimately harmonious *natural laws.*

In opposing the proto-positivistic tendencies of the early Enlightenment, Leibniz also denounced more common ideas of the territorial state as a location of sovereignty, and he argued that these ideas evolved from a false separation of power and law. This was evident not only in his metaphysical writings, but also in his more concrete political interventions. In his writings on ecclesiastical law, for instance, he advocated the creation of an Episcopalian constitution, based on the 'most ancient hierarchy' of the Roman Catholic Church.[201] He justified this position by following the English 'no bishop – no King' maxim, and claimed that a monarch could only assume legitimacy if crowned by a bishop, conferring divine-legal justification on political authority. In addition, Leibniz also pleaded for the resurrection of a 'universal church', fusing Roman Catholicism and the main Protestant confessions in order to promote love, unity and universality amongst the Christian peoples, and overriding particular states.[202] In his works on the constitution of the empire, similarly, he claimed that the powers of the territorial princes constituted, in most instances, what he defined as the *Suprematus:* that is, the princes had (or might obtain) control over their own courts and the right to administer their own territories, and, like the princes of the Italian states, they had the right (the *jus legationis*) to send envoys to foreign states and to participate in the formation of international laws and agreements.[203] However, he also argued that they did not possess entirely unlimited or exclusively sovereign powers; their authority was bound by the imperial constitution,[204] and they owed 'special service to the Emperor'.[205] Even at this most practical level, consequently, Leibniz was reluctant to see political authority detached from its overarching legal framework, and he opposed the recognition of territorial power as the primary site of statehood.

Leibniz's treatises on the imperial constitution were not designed to depreciate the political claims or independence of the German princes. Rather, his main claim in these works was that a state can possess powers of sovereign statehood without exercising total or undivided territorial dominion. In fact, he described the empire as a state or republic that comprised 'many sovereignties' in the form of a federal state, and in which a centralized monopoly of power was not necessary.[206] This federal division of administrative power in the empire, he concluded, was not in conflict with the idea of sovereignty; in the good polity, sovereignty is always a condition in which power is defined by law and by the compliance of government with universal legal obligations. Sovereignty, therefore, can never be a condition in which one prince or one legislator is exempt from all legal constraint, and the majesty of power does not reside in the personal will of the sovereign, but in the many necessary laws by which the polity is determined.[207] For Leibniz, in consequence, theorists seeking to exclude all external law from territorial power misinterpreted the nature of sovereignty, and they confused sovereignty with voluntaristic absolutism.

The dialectics of positive law

It is important to remember when comparing Leibniz with the more eclectic philosophers of natural law that Leibniz did not see his work as a simple return to metaphysical constructions of the law, and he understood his interventions in legal philosophy, like those of Pufendorf and Thomasius, as attempts to generate secure preconditions for the authority and autonomy of human law. Evidently, his work was attached to residually pre-modern and even Thomist conceptions of natural law, as it argues that the content of justice is prior to all specific intelligence and is essentially deducible from the necessary overarching harmony of the world. Central to his philosophy was the insistence that law cannot be authorized by one will, but assumes authority as it is united with absolute reason: the modern severance of metaphysical reason and law is consequently invalid. His work thus invoked again, on new preconditions, the medieval ideas of the universal state, represented by the Holy Roman Empire, and the universal church.[208] Indeed, he even returned to quasi-Thomist arguments about the relation between divine intellect and divine freedom or divine will. However, Leibniz also viewed his legal theory as an attack on pure-metaphysical accounts of the law and on doctrines of statehood defining the state in theological terms. As mentioned, Leibniz denied that law and theology are directly cognate disciplines. In fact, he specifically argued that faith and reason should not be conflated, and he clearly implied that the deduction of law occurs independently of faith and provides categories of law which override faith.[209] Moreover, by implying that the necessity of law depends on its conformity with rational wisdom, he sought to explain the foundations of politics as distinct from all fully heteronomous metaphysical concepts or beliefs: valid law, he explained, is an invariable entelechy of reason, and both humans and Gods can obtain knowledge of this law. Underlying this argument, in fact, is the intimation that Leibniz considered his own philosophy as better able to account for the autonomy of law and the humanity of politics than Pufendorf, Hobbes and his other more voluntarist, functionalist or utilitarian adversaries. For Leibniz, the voluntarist theorists of law and state made the law falsely dependent on the will, be this the will of God or the will of the legislator, and, for voluntarist theory, all law retains a finally transcendent contingency at its core: the source of law is, thus, in the last analysis, ultimately unaccountably metaphysical. Leibniz, however, argued that what is legally just is what accords with the criteria of human reason and what serves the harmony of human coexistence. Natural justice is, therefore, always rational, and rational justice is always a human justice, which bears no trace of metaphysical contingency. The just state, consequently, is a rational state, and this state represents principles which, although metaphysically deduced, are also constitutively human.

In this respect, Leibniz's legal-political thought was most fundamentally determined by a rejection of the notion that the freedom of the divine will transcends all reason, or that God's essence is entirely external to human wisdom and human law, and that laws have their original source in an unaccountable locus of transcendence. God's will, for Leibniz, is not separable from rational law: the divine will both creates and is created by the rational-legal principles of necessary harmony, and it has no free externality to those principles. Similarly, the just state is constituted in analogy to God and is inseparable from and co-emergent with the law: the will of the state cannot freely place itself outside or above the law, either as its author or executor. In consequence, only those states that are not legal states, or those states unable to secure harmony, preserve the conviction that the will of power is separate from and prior to law, and these states transpose the false metaphysical myth of God's transcendence into the worldly form of the polity. The myth of God's metaphysical transcendence or absolute freedom is, consequently, the foundation of tyranny, and the legal form of the legal state is always the medium in which God abdicates transcendence or irrational freedom, and, in according with necessary norms of reason, becomes a *human God.* If Pufendorf saw God's freedom as will, therefore, Leibniz saw reason as the form of God's freedom, and this freedom is also the form of human freedom.

As a result of this, Leibniz and Pufendorf might easily be viewed as two methodologically opposed theorists, each of which hoped to explain the autonomy and positivity of law's foundation, each of which accused the other of maintaining falsely metaphysical preconditions in this endeavour, and each of which saw the other as imputing a false idea of divinity and freedom as the basis of statehood. Leibniz sought to found the state on God's non-transcendent *essence,* manifest in rationally deduced human law. Pufendorf, in contrast, sought to found the state on the human will, which interprets the divine will as a set of positive norms embodied in human society, and which applies these norms as it considers appropriate. For Pufendorf, Leibniz accounted insufficiently for the practical variability and the concrete/positive origin of law, and his theory remained wedded to rationalized ideas of metaphysical harmony. He thus constrained the state to act as a rational God, bound by the paradoxical myth of God's legal union of intellect and will. For Leibniz, in turn, Pufendorf's work was shadowed by a belief in the voluntaristic transcendence of God, which depreciated both the absoluteness of justice and the constitutive role of human reason in obtaining justice. He thus allowed the state to exist as a free God, inappropriately exercising its will without full justification.

In consequence, although Leibniz was clearly closer to metaphysical or anti-positivist traditions of practical philosophy, the divide between him and Pufendorf might be seen, in essence, as a divide between alternative paths of legal formation, one of which defined the will and one of which defined reason as the source of law's post-metaphysical validity. Indeed, both Leibniz and Pufendorf might be viewed as theorists who recognized the paradoxical positivity of the law as a central factual problem of social reality as they encountered it, and who tried to explain or overcome this paradox in distinct manner. Leibniz explained law's paradox by arguing that the human mind can recreate as law the ancient interwovenness of law and divine reason. The laws that the human mind creates are, thus, absolute laws, analogous to divine laws, but they are also human laws, which the mind rationally constructs as its own laws, and which can be applied as positive laws. Pufendorf referred to this same paradox in arguing that the human will was created by the divine will, and it can now authentically create the law as both distinct from and analogous to the divine will. The laws that the human will creates are absolute laws, referring to God's original volitional acts, but they are also human laws, which the will freely constructs for itself and applies to other humans. Both Pufendorf and Leibniz, in short, recognized that the law is not metaphysical and that laws originate in human acts of deduction and prescription. Both theories thus sought to create positive preconditions for the assertion of law's validity. In this, however, both still expressed a trace of law's paradox and exception, for both invoked God, either as reason or as will, as the originating guarantor of this law: of law, that is, which is not God's law. They invoked God, not as the originator of legislation, but as the originating paradox that both legislates and is absolutely different from the ground of its laws. In the works of both Pufendorf and Leibniz, distinct elements in the metaphysical corpus of law – God's reason and God's freedom, as contrary aspects of God split personality – were dramatized to authorize laws, after metaphysics, as human laws, and so as laws able to assume positive form. Both these philosophies thus marked advanced stages in two distinct lines of legal analysis, both of which sought to transform legal ideas originating in theistic metaphysics into secular or even positive accounts of law's validity. In this, both referred to the metaphysical trace in the law as a means of authenticating laws that are not metaphysical.

After Leibniz and Pufendorf

After Leibniz, the political works of Christian Wolff extended and elaborated aspects of his rational metaphysical conception of the legal state, and his partial revival of neo-Thomist ideas.[210] Like Leibniz, Wolff argued that a just society is founded in natural-law principles that serve interests of universal harmony and utility. He defined 'common welfare' as the 'highest or ultimate law of society', and he argued that the ethical content of all human actions can be deduced from the extent to which they uphold common security and welfare.[211] The legitimacy of political order, he therefore claimed, depends on the state's compliance with natural law,[212] and authority 'has no freedom to command' actions contrary to natural law.[213] Moreover, he followed Leibniz in placing God's reason over God's freedom, and he concluded that natural law reflects God's own law but does 'not emanate from God's will'.[214] Instead, the justice of natural law exists independently of God, and the laws of nature cannot be prescribed or altered by God. Wolff thus duplicated the Leibnizian claim that there exists a juridical order in the world that pre-forms and determines all wills, even that of God, and that the will becomes moral in so far as it exists in conformity with this juridical order. This order reflects the necessary orientation towards perfection which inheres in the universe: it is an order that guides God's own choices, and it ensures that, as the most perfect being, God's choices – including his decision to create the world and humanity – are always good. Because it exists independently of God, the laws of this order can be deduced by human reason and, crucially, those who act in compliance with it become *laws unto themselves:*[215] that is, they elevate themselves to a condition in which their wills accord with the principle of universal perfectibility and so they become distantly participant in God's own order.

If natural laws reflect the underlying order and perfectibility of the universe, Wolff concluded, the most virtuous states must necessarily be ordered states: they must be states in which the interests of subjects are balanced against the interests of regents and in which those who apply power and those who obey power form a legally cohesive and ordered whole, each with their own ground and justification in the other.[216] In human societies as in natural processes, consequently, there is always 'more truth where there is greater order',[217] and the highest degree of truth exists in a society where the intentions of all particular agents are 'associated with each other in such a way that no one of them runs counter to the other, and each one is in fact a means for reaching the other'.[218] The task of human reason is to deduce and prescribe laws that help direct human society towards absolute order. Laws serving the machine-like order of society are *natural laws,* and a state obtains legitimacy and commands obedience where it replicates the metaphysical order of natural law.

Although sharing aspects of Leibniz's anti-voluntarism, Wolff's political theory also reflected more obviously voluntaristic doctrines of state power. Wolff clearly saw the legitimate state as a state of law, whose will, committed to the overarching objective of social perfectibility, perfectly reflected natural law. However, he also claimed that a state compliant with natural law has binding power in all areas of the law; like Pufendorf, he defined specific laws as the 'command of superior', and he imputed a high degree of coercive authority to the princely legislator. Valid law, he concluded, is determined by absolute principles of reason, but it can only be deduced and enforced by the positive 'will of a rational being', and this will can only exist in the sovereign legislator, who is uniquely empowered to interpret and apply laws within the constraints of natural law.[219] The legislator, he argued, is charged with the duty constantly to write new and 'more perfect laws', to strive for ever greater unity in 'law books for common usage',[220] and to obtain a maximum of legal power over his territories.[221] As contractually bound or covenanted members of society, then, subjects are forced to 'allow the will of those in authority to be their own will' and to subordinate their interests to the overarching purposes of the state.[222] Unlike Leibniz, consequently, Wolff was prepared to endorse a concept of absolute political majesty or sovereignty, which ascribed to princes 'the unrestricted power to promote common well-being and security'.[223] Despite this enthusiasm for absolutism, the universal aspect of Wolff's concept of legal order also meant that he saw non-compliance with the law as acceptable where laws promulgated by princes contravene natural law,[224] and he also argued that princes themselves are bound by the fundamental laws of state, originating in the covenants which stipulate the form of state.[225] Lastly, therefore, Wolff acknowledged that supra-positive or rationally necessary law always possesses a certain primacy over positive law and its bearers. However, he saw the ideal and legitimate state as a state in which positive and natural law are united in the overarching pursuit of order and perfectibility. Where the state acquires this characteristic, subjects have no sphere of freedom outside the state, and they have no claim to any liberty that might entail transgression against positive law. Their freedom is, in fact, expressed through necessary adherence to law.

Following Leibniz, Wolff concluded that in a legitimate state there can be no conflict between freedom and necessity, and that a legitimate state recreates the unity of free will and necessary reason which God himself first incorporated. Human beings, he argued, are naturally free where they comply with the moral necessity contained in natural laws, and, where they accord with these laws, they seek perfection: both of these conditions exist in a legitimate state. However, Wolff gave rather greater emphasis than Leibniz to the specific human origin of state power, and he sought to escape formally deterministic interpretations of legal validity. He thus claimed, like Kant after him, that the legitimate state has a determinate anthropological foundation – namely, in human rational autonomy or in a condition of human personality derived from autonomy.[226] This means that he saw the authentic form of the human being as a condition of *legal personality*, in which the person exercises the faculty of reason in order to define morally necessary purposes and then makes his or her will transparent to these purposes in order to pursue objectives whose content is recognized as generally imperative. A legitimate state, by extension, also exists as a legal personality, and it obtains this status by regulating itself in accordance with morally necessary laws. Where a state possesses such legal personality, those among its subjects who adequately exercise their rational faculties will not experience its laws as heteronomous, but as rational and natural; they will know themselves addressed as bearers of legal relations endowed with a legal personality; and they will, for this reason, obey the laws.[227] The anthropological precondition of the legitimate polity, consequently, is that both the author of laws and the addressees of laws exist in the condition of legal subjectivity or legal personality. The state misuses its authority wherever it abandons the condition of legal personality, or wherever it fails to acknowledge that it is bound to recognize the legal subjectivity of its addressees.[228] The rationalist-metaphysical doctrines of the early Enlightenment thus finally culminated in a definition of the human being as a *legal subject,* and in a definition of the legitimate state as a legal subject or as a legal state. In setting out this theory, Wolff rearticulated earlier voluntarist theories by placing the source of legitimate law in the state itself and by insisting that the attribute of legal subjectivity is guaranteed by primary acts of the state. However, closer to Leibniz, he also saw the personality of the state as formed by laws that pre-exist the state and that are deducible by legal subjects, and he thus saw the state as unable to act independently of rational-universal legal principles. Legality, in short, is here the precondition of legitimacy, and necessity in law binds the freedom of the legitimate state. Under such a state, both state and person must act as the *subjects of law:* that is, as bearers of necessary legal relations within an already given moral-legal universe. Wolff's work, therefore, defined the bearers of law, as subjects, as the genetic source of law's rational unity and necessity. The human subject under law internalizes the metaphysical order of law, and, as a legal subject, the human subject acts as the primary reference for law's positive validity. In this, Wolff's work marked a step beyond Leibniz in the positive-rational analysis of law, as Wolff, unlike Leibniz, saw the origin of law's legitimacy as fully integrated into the legal autonomy of human persons, as they are positively defined under law.

The antinomy between political thinkers influenced by Leibniz and those influenced by Pufendorf also stimulated a number of attempts to reconcile or steer a middle course between their divergent views. For instance, Johann Gottlieb Heineccius proposed a doctrine of natural law that accepted Leibniz's view that natural law reflects an invariably self-identical set of norms, or an 'eternal law' by which God himself is bound.[229] However, he also accepted the Pufendorfian claim that law results from God's will, and that this will is the 'principle of all justice' and the 'sole norm of human actions'.[230] Like Leibniz, therefore, he defined the science of natural law as the rational interpretation of legal necessity – or as 'divine jurisprudence'. However, like Pufendorf, he also defined this science as a 'practical' facility for interpreting the content of the 'will of the supreme legislator'.[231] Buddeus, analogously, followed Pufendorf and Thomasius in placing volitional constructions of security and order at the foundation of good government.[232] He rejected divided constructs of sovereignty,[233] and he saw the integrity of state as hinging on the obligatory force provided by the 'will of a superior', which confers moral necessity on law.[234] However, he also advocated a more obvious religious foundation for the natural law of state than either Pufendorf or Leibniz, and he saw the 'cause of natural law' in God himself.[235] He, therefore, also resisted the separation of law and religious ethics in more widespread types of legal voluntarism.[236] Christian August Crusius also moved between voluntaristic and deterministic constructs of state, law and political ethics. Like Wolff and Leibniz, he argued that 'God's perfection, and that of our own essence' is the guiding principle of natural law, likely to create a society based in universal love, and he claimed that considerations of perfection must give the foundation for all civil law.[237] He also argued that where a state complies with natural laws furthering harmony and perfection, it becomes a 'moral person' and it is bound by general laws and obligations, which also determine the status of other moral persons – especially its subjects.[238] Crusius thus set out an account of the legal state which reproduced elements of the Wolffian account of legal personality; indeed, he claimed that it is only as a moral person that the state obtains 'majesty' or sovereignty and is entitled to exercise power, as law, throughout society.[239] Unlike Leibniz and Wolff, however, Crusius argued that the moral-legal person of the state is not formed by the state's harmony with metaphysical principles. Rather, this personality derives from the recognition enshrined in law that all subjects of the state have their own unique dignity as created by God. As Kant later agreed, Crusius concluded that the hallmark of a legal state is that it does not utilize its subjects to obtain ends to which they would not freely and rationally accede, as legal subjects. The state only secures legitimacy where it recognizes its subjects as subjects under law, with their legal entitlements justified by the fact that they are the absolute 'final purposes of God', and where it ensures that its laws serve the preservation of its subjects in their status as final purposes.[240] Like Leibniz, Crusius arrived at an early concept of the universal legal state. In so doing, however, he denied that knowledge of perfect law could be founded in rational deduction, and he sought instead to place the more anthropological idea of personal ethical recognition at the origin of the good polity.[241]

Early positivism and the end of natural law

If political voluntarism and ideas of universal natural law constructed the antinomical horizon for the defining debates of the early German Enlightenment, the end of this period saw the evolution of certain new, and quite distinct, orientations in legal-political discourse. These orientations opposed both pure ius-naturalism and voluntarism. Indeed, they saw both ius-naturalism and voluntarism as related signs of the inability of legal analysis to constitute a positive field of inquiry, independent of residually religious and metaphysical preconditions. The later works of Johann Heinrich Gottlob von Justi, for example, revived Epicurean ideas of governance and set out an early liberal theory of social freedom and responsible government. He argued that the 'final purpose' or 'highest law' of government is to ensure 'common happiness' throughout society and that laws of government are justified by the extent to which they reflect and promote this purpose.[242] Justi supported a mixed theory of the constitution, centred on a royal executive.[243] However, he also argued that the origin of the state is not the will of the sovereign but the 'unification of many wills',[244] and the unity of wills underlying the state expresses itself in the 'basic laws' that form the customary form of the state. The regent of the state is thus bound by these laws, and he is not permitted to place his own personal will above the 'will of the state', represented and transmitted through the laws.[245] Slightly later, the historian August Ludwig Schlözer provided a more strictly anthropological account of government. This account condemned abuse of privilege under political absolutism; it insisted on the legal circumscription of power as the source of legitimate government;[246] and it argued that the natural or meta-political dispositions of human beings engender social rights, which states are obliged to respect.[247]

At the same time, the era of the later Enlightenment also saw the emergence of a positivist tendency in legal thought, and at this time positivism gradually assumed a central role in legal analysis and teaching. The first evolution of positivism as a distinct field of legal analysis is usually associated with Johann Jacob Moser, who published some of the most influential commentaries on imperial law in the eighteenth century. Moser's approach to legal questions was in certain respects deeply connected with pietism, and he was not a consciously secularist thinker. His work reflected the common pietist conviction that Christianity is an ethic of civil obedience, and that 'true Christians' accept the regimes, secular and ecclesiastical, of the states under which they live.[248] Similarly, he shared the customary hostility to religious associations propagating ideas of legal obligation against the state, and he defined jurisdiction in religious matters both as a necessary centrepiece of territorial power,[249] and as the necessary political consequence of Evangelical church law.[250] At a methodological level, however, Moser's ambition was to effect a full separation of legal inquiry from the religious, metaphysical, extra-legal and formal-normative burdens placed upon it before and during the Enlightenment and to determine questions of legal validity exclusively through reference to constitutional sources.[251] He, therefore, rejected both historical interpretation of the law, which he saw as tending to obscure legal facts,[252] and ius-natural analysis. Abstract criteria of natural law, he argued, are of little use in interpreting acceptable constitutional law, and they should under no circumstances be viewed as prior to the legal facts that they are supposed to regulate.[253] The conditions of legal justice, consequently, must be derived solely from correct interpretation of positive laws and from adequate analysis of the agreements and historical compromises around which public law has evolved. This early positivist turn was designed to free law from ambiguity and from moral/religious expectation and to delineate an order of public law to which religious and metaphysical concerns had little immediate relevance. Indeed, if the longer trajectory of legal thought between Reformation and Enlightenment ran through a number of stages of positivization, from the internalization of religious law in the confessional state to the neutralization of religion in the absolutist state, positivism instituted a new era of legal positivity, in which law, as a self-explanatory set of terms, finally reflected itself as the centre and author of its own validity. Above all, Moser's intention was to ensure that courts of law, at both territorial and imperial level, could dispense justice reliably and without bias, and that these courts could apply law without consideration for the confessional affiliations of the parties in dispute.[254]

This immanent approach to the law was also central to Moser's understanding of territorial sovereignty and imperial law. His views on points of constitutional dispute were largely based in the interpretation of accepted legal precedents in different territories, and in a reconstruction of the agreements enshrined in the Religious Peace of 1555 and the treaties of the Peace of Westphalia. In his assessments of imperial law, he accepted that the validity of the law always presupposes a unified centre of authority, and this cannot be instituted where authority is split by confessional elements that contradict the unity of the law.[255] On this level, he defended the integrity of territorial state forms, and he saw the emergence of territorial power as a positively formed and irreversible legal fact. However, Moser's positivism was also deeply hostile to territorial absolutism and to the uncurtailed concentration of princely power. Moser was a proto-liberal constitutionalist, and he interpreted the public law of the empire as a balanced constitution, founded in a multilateral 'contract', connecting, on one side, the Emperor and the imperial estates and, on the other side, the territorial sovereigns and the regional estates or parliaments (*Landstände*) in the territories.[256] He consequently argued for a rejuvenation of the Holy Roman Empire as a three-tiered constitutional structure in which the power of the imperial executive might be counterbalanced by the imperial princes, and the imperial princes might be bound by constitutional agreements with both the Emperor and regional interests.[257] He refused to glorify the 'servants of sovereignty', who pledged themselves to limitless territorial power,[258] and he argued against the assumption that princely powers necessarily reflected 'divine right of majesty and privilege'. Instead, he defined the exercise of princely power as constitutionally reliant on 'a mass' of constitutional agreements that confer irreducibly consensual form on territorial sovereignty. Sovereignty, he thus concluded, was always divided, and it hinged on a constitutional equilibrium between princes and estates in which 'territorial supremacy and regional freedoms' are codependent.[259] Unlike many other pietists, therefore, Moser's work contained a clear anticipation of the main liberal themes of 1848: it envisaged the formation of a constitutional legal state; it rejected princely absolutism; and it endorsed an all-German idea of statehood, albeit here still under the constitutional apparatus of the empire. Above all, Moser's work implied that non-positive (metaphysical) analysis of the law was inclined to exaggerate and dramatize the power of the princely state, and the source and extent of the state's power could only be reliably deduced from within the terms of the law itself.

This move towards constitutional positivism was then extended in the constitutional-theoretical works of Johann Stephan Pütter. Pütter also argued that the sovereignty of the German territories had evolved through laws regulating confessional questions, and that princely powers of ecclesiastical jurisdiction were the foundation of sovereignty in the territories.[260] In this respect, he abandoned Moser's claim that there existed a uniform constitution for all German states, and he ascribed greater importance to the legal particularity of each state within the empire.[261] Nonetheless, he also accentuated the importance of positive laws that placed restrictions on the exercise of territorial sovereignty, and he insisted that the form of the empire was a constitutional monarchy.[262] Like Moser before him, Pütter concluded that princely power was not entitled to 'exceed the limits' prescribed by imperial laws,[263] that its justification required guarantees for the 'common welfare', and that it was bound to offer protection for the 'liberty and property' of all its subjects.[264]

Pütter's work had particular importance in the emergence of German public law as it marked an attempt to combine the practical ambitions of historicist and early positivist theory with the more universalist claims of natural-law doctrines. Central to his work was the argument that all members of a society possess 'customary rights' and socially constructed freedoms, which must be acknowledged as inviolable by a legitimate state.[265] As expressions of these rights, he saw regional legislative deputations (*Landstände*) as possessing rights of participation in government, and he insisted that all legislation must be supported by some degree of delegatory consensus.[266] In this argument, Pütter's work converged in part with the ideas of more classical natural-law theorists, who deduced the necessity of social rights from principles influenced by philosophical formalism. Indeed, Pütter collaborated with Gottfried Achenwall, who combined positivist and formalist methods to argue that the state is bound by a 'fundamental constitution' and is circumscribed by a sphere of inalienable social rights.[267] Although occasionally close to such ideas, however, Pütter rejected all metaphysical personalization of the state, and he claimed that legal rights can only be founded as law and that all law is nothing but positive law.

In sum, therefore, the debates of the early German Enlightenment, across all theoretical divisions, were focused on accounting for the integrity of the state and the conditions of law's validity. At the centre of these debates was a primary division in the analysis of which natural law, voluntaristic or abstract-universal, offered the most effective foundation for law's validity and for freedom in the state. These debates often re-enacted, in constitutional terms, the anti-metaphysical reaction emanating from the first era of the Reformation, and at their centre were rival views on how the state might make good the lost unity of scholastic law and create a reliable basis for legal order. In the period of high Enlightenment, however, the question about the law's validity was increasingly posed from an altogether different perspective: as a matter of *positivist* analysis. The earlier constitutional positivists had some common ground with the different lines of ius-natural philosophy. They too sought to construct a model of legal validity that would explain both state and law as post-metaphysical facts. However, whilst the exponents of different natural-law traditions only moved uncertainly and paradoxically into a post-metaphysical analysis of law's origin, the positivists paved the way for an account of legality and legitimacy as constructs of the law itself, interpretable solely by and within the law.

3 German idealism

The Enlightenment and the reconstruction of legal metaphysics

In many respects, the political works of Immanuel Kant formed the defining turning point in the history of modern political philosophy, and, more specifically, in the history of political thought challenged by the legacies of early Protestantism. The first element in Kant's epoch-making importance is that he called into question the antinomy between voluntaristic or anthropological thinking and universally normative or metaphysical thinking that had shaped political debate from the Reformation to the early Enlightenment. Following more voluntaristic impulses, he argued that human legislation is the centre of the human world and that the human will has responsibility for instituting positive norms for an ordered human society. However, closer to more metaphysical theories, he also argued that the legislator can and must ensure that laws meet the criterion of rational universality, so that the human world is determined by unconditioned contents. Kant thus asserted that valid law has a distinction against purely positive law, and that reason deduces a realm of moral laws to which the sphere of positively applied law must be adapted. However, human reason has sole responsibility for deducing valid law, and the rational will is able to transform valid law into positively applied form. He consequently argued that the deduction of universally applicable norms need not necessarily entail a diminution of the free human will as the centre of legislation and accountability, and that reason and will are conjoined in the deduction of laws. Indeed, his practical philosophy marked an attempt to explain how laws can be proposed that express rationally *necessary* metaphysical principles and, at the same time, allow the exercise, in *freedom,* of constitutive human faculties: the laws of Kantian philosophy are thus conceived as laws in which the primary distinction between reason (necessity) and will (freedom) is overcome.

In this respect, furthermore, Kant's philosophy stands as a response to the collapse of metaphysical law and the problems of positivization arising from the Reformation. The salient implication of his philosophy is that law, as deduced by human reason, can be at one and the same time *positive* and *universal, human* and *metaphysical:* that the freedom of laws does not mean that such laws are detached from universal foundations, and it does not mean that they have only restricted validity. Underlying Kant's work is an insistence that the rupture in the legal order caused by the Evangelical inversion of scholastic normativity need not be seen as a permanent condition, and that the freedoms obtained by the Reformation can be experienced as components of a rationally ordered political universe. Whilst early Evangelical thought revolved around the claim that laws cannot be derived, except paradoxically, from a rationally interpreted divine will, Kant indicated that the human will itself can be made transparent to absolutely binding and necessary laws. Indeed, at the centre of Kantian thought is an endeavour to transpose the will of the rationally free God onto the human will, to allow the human will to reintegrate the unity of intellect and freedom originally possessed by God and, so, to propose the rational human will as the source of valid positive law. Kant, therefore, transferred the metaphysical paradox of God's legal originality in scholasticism into a metaphysics of the human will, and he argued that the freely exercised human will is both spontaneously constrained by law and acts to institute absolute laws for all members of human society. In this light, Kant appears as a Protestant Aquinas, reconstituting the lost metaphysical unity of law and reason under the structure of a rationally and positively humanized metaphysics,[1] and seeking in this way to resolve the classical aporia of Evangelical politics. Communities exercising freedom under *own laws,* he concluded, need not be without law, or with exceptional laws: their freedom must, in fact, have an integral and mandatory legal structure. God's freedom can be a meaningfully human freedom, and this freedom can be captured in the form of free laws.

Autonomy and metaphysics

Kant's philosophy, in both its cognitive and its ethical implications, was centred on a reconstruction of metaphysics as a science, not of essences or laws which are external to human reason, but of human reason itself. Metaphysics, he argued, can only exist as the culminating moment in the 'culture of human reason':[2] that is, as an account of the possibilities, preconditions and extent of valid and rationally sustainable human knowledge, not as a science of transcendent contents. The limits of human knowledge are consequently restricted to the intelligible realm of the temporal and the spatial, and reason cannot provide answers to metaphysical or speculative questions relating to objects outside this realm. For this reason, Kant centred his account of reason on the claim that *autonomy* is the distinctive characteristic of reason, that reason's scope is restricted to knowledge of objects for which it can autonomously account, and that reason, consequently, is a *juridical* organ, whose integral function is to generate, by itself, categories of consistent synthesis and self-determination. In his purely cognitive doctrine, therefore, Kant described the functions of reason as 'legislatory' operations,[3] oriented to the production of an internally consistent account of its insights and syntheses, and responsible for legislating, without external addition, the categories through which synthetic knowledge is made possible. As in its pure-cognitive acts, then, in its practical and ethical operations reason is also constituted as a faculty of 'legislation',[4] or as an 'a priori legislative' organ.[5] Practical reason is a faculty of reason that has responsibility for legislating over human action and over the conditions under which human action can consistently and autonomously justify itself. The function of practical reason is to legislate maxims for volitional action under which action becomes independent of all material and sensory stimulus, and so authorizes itself as internally consistent, justifiable and, consequently, *free*. Practical reason is thus a faculty of rational spontaneity which exercises itself in the deduction of universal laws or maxims, in which reason recognizes its own absolute or transcendental *idea of freedom*, and it then prescribes these maxims to the human will, so that the will becomes free as it acts in conformity with these principles.[6] Although in principle defining ethics and cognition as quite distinct operations of reason, Kant implicitly placed a practical doctrine of autonomy at the heart of his whole philosophy, and he pronounced at various points in his work that practical reason obtains a certain primacy over pure reason, and that the legislation of moral maxims and purposes constituting freedom is the highest duty and realization of human rational life.[7] The central focus of Kant's idea of reason is, thus, the delineation of the human being as an agent endowed with legislative faculties of self-causality, which allow it to constitute itself as free.

Human freedom, Kant concluded, is a condition in which the human will is not guided by particular purposes of self-interest or happiness, but where reason prescribes ideas to the will giving formal conditions for its universally valid and morally necessary exercise. The free human will, therefore, is a will that makes itself transparent to an 'unconditioned law', obtained by human reason and possessing no reality outside reason and the rationally regulated will.[8] Where the human will allows itself to be determined by this law, the bearer of the will demonstrates that he or she is free of all external determinacy and motivated solely by principles by which all people, if correctly exercising their rational faculties, *ought* to be obligated. In this condition of universality, then, the human being becomes freely self-causing: it becomes its own author, it forms itself as the freely constitutive centre of its own reality, and it exercises its will at once as *free* and *necessary*. For Kant, in fact, the human being only approaches a full realization of its innate faculties as a human being where it is self-creating, and it is self-creating where it freely legislates transcendentally or universally necessary maxims, or categorical imperatives, and where it freely recognizes these as the conditions of freedom for its own will. The human being is only truly a 'person' where it is the 'subject of moral-practical reason'. It only fully elaborates itself as such where it makes its will transparent to self-given *laws*,[9] where it is 'self-legislating',[10] and where it spontaneously creates itself through the deduction of moral laws. The truly human being is, thus, the human being whose will is entirely co-original with the law. And the truly human world, in consequence, is a legal world, a world whose will is determined by the universal laws of practical reason. In this fully human world, each person is the author of his or her own freedom, and the will of the human person is exclusively determined by universal maxims. In this world, moreover, each person, in so far as he or she follows these universal maxims, recognizes each other person as a bearer of rights and freedoms which cannot be legitimately restricted, and each person recognizes each other person as possessing an innate and rationally demonstrable dignity. Each person recognizes that he or she is not entitled to use other persons to pursue arbitrary purposes, and that each other person, as a rationally self-causing will, in fact constitutes a realized rational purpose, which requires recognition as a focus of rights. In this legally humanized world, therefore, the antinomy between voluntarism and normativity or between anthropology and metaphysics is suspended: the true human being, for Kant, realizes its will as a metaphysical norm and its anthropological freedom as a rationally necessary metaphysical content.

In this analysis of the human being, Kant argued that human freedom and legislative self-authorship rely on metaphysics. Indeed, he specifically claimed that it is only where reason abstracts from all objective elements or interests – from all 'matter of the will' – and where it determines the will in accordance with metaphysical ideas of reason that human freedom becomes possible.[11] Human freedom is consequently an *intelligible* condition, which cannot be deduced from any material or experiential sources, but which results exclusively from the metaphysically binding legislations of practical reason as it constructs an ideal account of universally prescribed and therefore *necessary* action. Indeed, the subject of the genuinely free human being exists, for Kant, not as a substantial or material will, but as a *homo noumenon:* as a person, that is, whose actions are determined by the necessary maxims of practical reason and form an abstracted reality of instituted necessity or duty, distinct from all contents of material volition.[12] The moral person of freedom is, thus, the dutifully free or metaphysical shadow of the *homo phaenomenon,* who is still driven by material, physical, affectual and sensory interests. The actions of the moral person are internally virtuous and dutiful, and they construct a secondary reality of necessity above the phenomena operations of humanity in its unfree (material, sensory, affectual, historical) expressions. Indeed, to be free (that is, to be truly human), Kant implied, is also to be metaphysical: it is, to legislate rationally necessary maxims and to determine the will in accordance with these noumenal maxims.

At the same time, however, Kant's account of metaphysics differed fundamentally from classical-metaphysical arguments, and his notion of human freedom might also be seen to contain a resolutely anti-metaphysical set of postulates. It is fundamental to the philosophical Enlightenment, he argued, that it explains how the conditions of human freedom are autonomously legislated by human beings themselves, using only their innate resources. The intelligible realm of freedom, although not founded in material or sensory life, is an enlightened human realm, constructed solely by the rational faculties of human beings and justified by human beings to each other through the public exercise of reason. Kant's metaphysics of the will is, therefore, also a fully autonomist account of the will, which insists that the will is unfree if it is not determined by laws legislated by practical reason. The realm of freedom is a realm where human beings exercise rationally demonstrable causality over their willed actions and where they terminate the influence of laws or prescriptions obtained from external, or heteronomous, metaphysical sources. Indeed, Kant argued quite plainly (almost blasphemously) that where human beings deduce laws that compel them 'a priori and unconditionally', human reason assumes for itself the role originally ascribed to God: that is, to the 'highest legislator', whose 'will is the law for all people'.[13] He thus negated the original scholastic idea that there is an already-existing unity of necessary or divinely ordained law in the world, or that the world is created with a unitary legal substructure, which reason must merely observe and interpret. The human being, for Kant, categorically does not require 'the idea of a being above itself' in order to 'recognize its duty'.[14] As a self-creating moral person, the human being dispenses with the idea of God the law-giver, it dispenses with all sense of an instituted order in the universe, and it institutes its own inviolable moral prescriptions as the centre of the human world. The free human being is, thus, also free of God, and, in fact, the human being supplants God as the spontaneous cause and arbiter of moral necessity. For Kant, in consequence, moral freedom relies on a metaphysics of the self-causing will. Yet this metaphysics is a thoroughly human metaphysics, which opposes all classical metaphysical ideals or traditional constructs of natural law and seeks to organize the universe around principles legislated by humans (or by human reason) for humans (or for human reason).

If classical metaphysics was, in its practical implications, centred in the idea that there is a necessary normative or intellectual order in the created world and that human beings are bound to adhere to this order, Kant, like other Protestant theorists, experienced this claim as paradoxical. He accepted the Protestant belief that there is freedom in the world and that both God and humans have a degree of freedom against external accounts of their necessary order, and he concluded that the necessary normative order in the world must now be legislated by humans, and it must be an eminently autonomous and human order. The human being must now assume 'causality of its own will', and it must accept as its own the functions of rational-legal authorship once imputed to God.[15] In this respect, Kant's philosophy responded directly to the loss of metaphysics and to the loss of overarching natural laws experienced through the end of metaphysics. Indeed, underlying Kant's practical philosophy is the intimation that the loss of metaphysical certainty has placed a heavy and constitutive charge on human reason: reason must now recognize that it exists in a condition of transcendental exceptionality, and that it alone has the metaphysical power to produce laws to give necessary structure to human freedom. After metaphysics, therefore, reason must become the self-causing author of its integrity, and it must reunite law and freedom through its own strenuous deductions; only through such self-authorship is it able to overcome the exceptionality of a universe experienced without metaphysics and without an external horizon of absolute or unconditioned laws. Kant's metaphysics of the will thus documents a most profound experience of metaphysical loss and the deepest sense of a universe that has lost its metaphysical foundations. It is the metaphysics of the Protestant universe: it is an *exceptional metaphysics,* which accepts and reflects the fact of metaphysical fragmentation at the legal centre of the modern world, and which then seeks to rebuild the legal order in this world, not through a reunion of reason and freedom in God, but through a union of reason and freedom in human laws. In its deepest impulse, therefore, Kant's philosophy sought to convert the loss of scholastic metaphysics into a post-metaphysical metaphysics, or a human metaphysics, in which human reason spontaneously acts to reunite necessity in law and freedom of will. This metaphysics produces laws, not, as in scholasticism, as an imposed reality of heteronomy, but as a spontaneously autonomous reality of new laws. If early Protestantism, in sum, dissolved the originating paradox in the scholastic unity of reason and will by placing freedom over reason, Kant sought to show that the union of reason and will need not be paradoxical, and that freedom, united with reason, can be a freedom under human laws. Kant's philosophy, in consequence, is the most systematic attempt both to accept the post-metaphysical reality of Protestantism, and yet also to translate Protestantism into an account of reliable legal order.

In reconstructing classical metaphysics as a human or Protestant metaphysics, Kant also argued that elements of religion should not be seen as external to humanity, but as integrated elements of humanity itself. Practical reason, he explained, is a faculty that transforms the religious idea of God into a rational 'idea of the human being', or into an 'idea of legislative reason':[16] that is, into an internal regulative function, under which human reason elevates itself to virtuous life and moral self-creation. Indeed, close to the centre of this argument is the implication that justice is not done to God if God is viewed as an external legislator over humanity and creation, or if God's reason and freedom are perceived as external to human reason and human freedom. Instead, justice is done to God where human beings, through their moral autonomy and self-causality, realize themselves as the manifest form of God's reason and God's freedom. Kant stated clearly that the ethical community exists in an analogy to 'God's people', and he saw the community of moral self-legislators as a community existing in objective likeness to the divine will.[17] The truth of religion, therefore, is not obtained in metaphysical legislation: it is obtained where religious laws are transmuted into human laws and where divine freedom is enacted as human freedom. For this reason, like earlier Protestants, Kant attacked religion based in fetishistic or rationally non-accountable principles, especially in 'statutory commandments, rules of belief and observances',[18] and he saw the realization of God's will and freedom by human beings as impeded by all positively instituted or symbolic religious forms. He thus indicated that only Protestantism allows for a doctrine of human self-reliance and existence under own laws and that only Protestantism allows for God's justice to be converted into human justice, and so for justice to be done to God. Rationally necessary laws, consequently, are the genuine realization, not only of human freedom, but also of God's freedom, and this realization can only occur under Protestantism, where laws are recognized as new laws or own laws, not falsely heteronomous or ritualized laws. Whilst Protestantism first appeared as an exceptionalist faith that destroyed the legal order of classical metaphysics, therefore, it is in fact, if seen as the source of a human metaphysics, a faith that gives perfect foundation for reliable laws and for a fully realized unity of reason and freedom.

A new natural law and the autonomy of liberalism

Underpinning Kant's moral universe, therefore, is a reflected inversion of the moral universe of scholasticism. Whereas scholastic metaphysics had posited a moral order in the universe originating in God's will and discernible as a continuous order of natural law, Kant argued that there is no positively manifest law in the world, and the suggestion that law can be extracted from natural/material processes belittles the human capacity for self-legislation. The moral order of the universe must consequently be separate from pre-ordained law. Despite this, however, there remains a moral order in the universe: this order is spontaneously legislated by self-reliant and autonomous human beings, who rationally generate independent and absolutely valid ideas of freedom. Indeed, if the legal and theoretical crisis of Protestantism arose from the fact that the first Evangelical theologians first discredited natural law by dismantling the laws connecting God's reason and the human will, Kant responded to this crisis by arguing for a reconception of natural law as laws expressing the unity of reason and will which is constitutive of authentic human nature.

At times, manifestly, Kant was close to classical paradigms of ius-naturalism. In his attempt to institute an ethical order of perennial and universal moral principles, he shared many common preconditions of natural-law theory. His argument that practical reason is the faculty for deducing and agreeing on moral principles was clearly indebted to Aristotelian ideas of *phronesis* and practical agreement as the source of law-finding. Likewise, in his assertion that there inheres a moral *telos* in human history, so that human action is progressively inclined towards a state of greater universality and greater moral-political freedom, he also replicated more classical-metaphysical ideas of natural law. However, whilst non-idealist theorists of natural law amongst his contemporaries, such as Carl Friedrich Bahrdt, still attempted to distil moral axioms from nature itself,[19] Kant saw the belief in positively disclosed natural law as a sign of the persistence of moral convictions which originate outside human reason and are burdened with heteronomy. He consequently set out a thoroughly rationalized analysis of natural law, which argued that human reason accounts for valid law only where it extracts itself from all material nature and natural determinacy and focuses its account of legal necessity on the internal principles of reason. In fact, as far as he actually referred to natural conditions as a foundation for legal necessity, Kant argued that there are two quite distinct types of natural law, or two types of human nature, which produce very distinct legal principles. There is, he claimed, the state of first nature or material nature, whose law is that described by Hobbes: the law of private prerogative or of irreconcilable antagonism, or of the 'war of each person with each person'.[20] However, he also claimed that there is a state of second nature, a condition into which human beings elevate themselves as they leave the state of first nature and as they allow their wills to be regulated by universal maxims. This condition is characterized by laws of second nature or by rationalized natural laws, in which the human being suspends particular natural-material interests and prerogatives. The condition of second nature is one in which the human being fulfils its own most authentic nature as a *homo noumenon* – as a rational and self-legislating agent. The condition of natural law, therefore, is precisely *not* natural in a physical or material sense. It is formed when the human will applies universal maxims to itself and, through this, becomes *other than mere nature.*[21] Natural law is, in fact, concretized in the idea of autonomy, and it is realized where human beings disconnect their actions from the sensory world of interest and stimulus and ensure that their actions form an intelligible realm, determined solely by universal duties and pure laws of practical reason.[22] Authentic natural law, in short, is in fact law *against* nature, not of nature, for it is only where humans divest themselves of the 'heteronomy' of (first) nature (i.e., influence by instincts, urges and impulses) that they institute universally binding laws, as autonomy, second nature, or 'rational nature'.[23] Kant consequently saw classical ius-naturalism as a doctrine that surreptitiously introduces principles of heteronomy into the human world and, so, diminishes the importance of rational autonomy. Real natural law is the law of autonomy or of genuine humanity: it is only obtained where natural law and human law become identical and where the autonomous will enacts moral maxims as elements of positive law.

The condition of second nature, on Kant's account, is also the condition of legal and political organization, and the doctrine of second nature also elucidates ways in which political orders legitimize themselves on human foundations. There is much controversy in scholarship on Kant as to whether he saw the conditions of the just rule of law as resulting directly from the moral maxims of reason.[24] At one level, he made a clear distinction between morality and law, and he vacillated when considering whether and to what degree politically enforced law must originate in binding moral norms. He argued that morality refers to the inner life of human beings, and it constitutes virtues requiring only human 'self-compulsion' for their fulfilment:[25] the inner maxims of practical reason, thus, create a community of virtuous people, united by the common faculties of self-causation. In contrast to this, law refers to the outer life and outer freedom of human beings, and it requires 'external compulsion' to be enforced:[26] legal principles thus create a community of law-abiding citizens, united in their adherence to rational legislation. Ethical duties, in consequence, are enforced by an inner law, and they have a higher status than legal duties, which must be guaranteed by an outer law.[27] Despite this distinction between 'juridical' and 'ethical' legislation, however, in Kant's philosophy there exists a close and necessary correlation between the inner maxims of virtue and externally necessary laws.[28] If ethical maxims with the power of obligation express duties by which all people adequately exercising their faculties of reason are bound, external laws possessing the power of obligation also express duties with the attribute of universality, to which all people adequately exercising their rational faculties must accede.[29] A justified legal-political condition is therefore one in which the 'highest legislator' is constrained to pass laws in accordance with the 'true duties' resulting from ethical maxims,[30] which reflect the rational and ethical will of the entire people. This is only possible where laws and duties have the signature of rational universality.[31] Publicly enforced law to which categorical validity can be imputed, in short, is law that effects the 'restriction of the freedom of each person' so that one person's freedom does not exclude the freedom of others, and all freedom exists in conformity with a 'general law'.[32] Such law cannot but be distilled from the moral maxims of practical reason, and, as such, it reflects a collective condition of realized second nature.

It can, therefore, be concluded that in Kant's philosophy there exists both a relation of analogy and a relation of substance between the virtuous community under moral maxims and the political community under external laws, and that both conditions are measured by the criterion of universality. The ideal or legitimate political order is, consequently, a state in which citizens exist under a republican constitution in which the exercise of power is determined by the 'pure source of the concept of law'.[33] In this state, laws are natural laws, determined by absolute principles of reason, and they cannot contravene the noumenal conditions of freedom deduced by practical reason. The 'republican constitution' of the legitimate state is, therefore, the objective or external form of legal autonomy, in which reason gives generally imposed structure to the idea of its necessary freedom: constitutional rule under a legitimate state is a condition of 'highest agreement' between the objective laws regulating collective life and the categorical imperatives of practical reason. Where a state realizes this condition of constitutional rule, the state itself acquires 'autonomy', and it frees its laws from the force of non-universalizable prerogatives. A legitimate state thus exists in relation of direct analogy to the self-legislating human being: it constitutes itself as a state where it becomes autonomous, where it regulates its operations in accordance with formal 'laws of freedom' and avoids pursuing purposes (towards its citizens and towards other states) that it cannot reflect as compatible with principles of necessity.[34] The legitimate person and the legitimate state are, therefore, both spontaneous or self-causing conditions of *moral personality,* or personality formed under autonomous law. As such, they are conditions of realized *second nature,* in which the person is not driven by motives of private interest or first nature, and the state is not shaped by internal or external antagonism, but both are transparent to formally constituted laws of universal necessity. In both the legitimate person and the legitimate state, therefore, freedom and reason are unified, and person and state exercise their freedoms as rational freedoms. The will of the legitimate person and the will of the legitimate state, in sum, both rearticulate God's first union of freedom and reason as a human union, both in private ethics and public law.

The specifically political implication of this theory is that the legitimacy of a political order is measurable by the extent of its compliance with universalizable laws, derived from the ideas of practical reason, and that rational citizens of a polity enacting universal laws will recognize their ideas of freedom as contained and protected by the laws of this polity. Indeed, perhaps the culminating political claim in Kant's philosophy is that only a state reuniting reason and freedom can explain itself as fully legitimate and provide binding accounts of why its laws are necessary. In such a state, law is the prior foundation of political legitimacy, and politics is only justified as the technical or executive exercise of legally enshrined power. Under these terms, Kant concluded, the legitimate state is always a legal state or *Rechtsstaat.* A state assumes the quality of a *Rechtsstaat* where it defines itself as a moral personality under public law, where it recognizes itself and other moral persons as bound by practical and universal norms, and where it formalizes this recognition in a clear constitutional order. A patrimonial state, most especially, can never be a *Rechtsstaat,* and the instruments of government can never be defined as adjuncts to dynastic or inherited private interest;[35] indeed, on Kant's terms, a patrimonial state is not a state at all, for a state is an organ of public power or second nature, which is bound by common 'principles of law'.[36] A *Rechtsstaat,* moreover, will treat its subjects as citizens: that is, as bearers of inviolable rights and entitlements. The citizens of a *Rechtsstaat* are recognized as having rights of legal redress against other citizens where their innate freedoms are violated, as having subjective rights on which the state itself cannot encroach, and – most importantly – as having, in their quality as human beings, the right to be treated as ends in themselves under law. As such, they command respect and dignity, and they have the inalienable right not to be utilized by the state or by other persons to fulfil purposes to which they do not rationally accede.[37] Underlying the ideally constituted *Rechtsstaat* is thus a metaphysics of the purpose, in which law reflects its addressees as bearing rights deduced from maxims that every moral will would recognize as its own purpose.

Despite his opposition to the metaphysical elements of classical natural-law theory, however, Kant's doctrine, at least in its institutional structure, retained certain parallels with earlier accounts of the state under natural laws. In a legal state, Kant claimed, the general will of the people, and the generally willed freedoms, are the source of law. Laws are valid where it can be assumed that all people adequately exercising their rational faculties would approve them: that is, where they are universal. The constitutional legal state is, therefore, founded in an 'original contract', in which the content of the laws of the polity is agreed and universally accepted. Notably, however, this contract is not an actual document, reflecting a practical moment of consensus: instead, it is merely an 'idea of reason', which the state presupposes and represents, and by which it allows its laws to be guided. The contract articulates the rational-ethical foundation of the polity; it gives universal foundation to all laws of the polity; and it describes the ethical necessities contained in the human and social transition from first nature to second nature.[38] The contract does precisely not mean, however, that the general will of the people is reflected in the exercise of government through participation, or even through factual consent. In fact, Kant was quite clear that not all people can be integrated into the legislative process, and that pure democracy and popular sovereignty tend to undermine the legal fabric of the state and to lead to 'despotism'.[39] He, therefore, saw the general will of the people (and the freedoms pursued by this will) as a metaphysical will or a pure will, as the will of the people in so far as they adequately exercise their faculties of reason and deduce laws with categorically imperative status. The state, then, acts in compliance with the prescriptions of this will wherever its laws reflect universal principles. The will of the people, in short, is represented in government where the state, as a self-causing moral person, prescribes laws that accord with those laws which, as self-causing moral persons, people naturally legislate for themselves. Above all, the will of the people is represented in the state where the state acknowledges members of the people as legal subjects, with claims to invariable rights, and where it allocates rights to citizens and ensures that these are protected. As in earlier theories of natural law, therefore, the natural laws under which the state becomes legitimate are the state's own laws, created and applied by the state, and the state merely presupposes the popular will as an internal reference in its own self-justification. The state, in other words, formally unifies reason and freedom in itself and in the objectively binding laws that it promulgates, and it enshrines this unity in rights; these rights are then always formal limits on the exercise of power, and they have an invariable prescriptive status against the state's authority. However, the citizens of the state have little constitutive role in forming rights. In fact, the recognition of rights dualistically detaches citizens from the state; it stabilizes their freedoms around metaphysical norms; and it diminishes the politically formative significance of citizens. Rights, therefore, although enshrining negative limits on the state's authority, are generated and produced by the state itself, as aspects of its own moral personality.

Institutionally, Kant consequently concluded, the will of the people is represented most effectively under a republican constitution based in a separation of the powers. Under such a constitution, executive power remains in the hands of a legally accountable monarch. Legislative power, which is the actual material focus of 'sovereignty', and so manifests the 'unified will of the people', is vested in the hands of a small number of delegates and legislators. These delegates and legislators represent the body of the citizenry, and they qualify for legislative authority because of their social and intellectual status and their material independence.[40] The structural principle of the *Rechtsstaat* is, therefore, not public participation or commonly shaped freedom, but the separation of legislative from executive competence and the regulation of executive power by norms deduced by a legislative elite. Indeed, on Kant's account, the legitimate state does not consist in a factual relation between particular persons, but in an arrangement of legal facts, which together give concrete application to the ideas of practical reason: or to the 'will of the people, derived *a priori* from reason'.[41]

Although insisting on basic rights and constitutional order as preconditions of legitimacy in the state, therefore, the political aspect of Kant's Enlightenment was clearly not intended as a model of radical liberalism, revolutionary natural law, or active human liberation. Instead, set against its background as a response to the rapid processes of social transformation around the French Revolution, it sought to account for a possible rationalization of the state apparatus, and, crucially, it intended to show how a state, by shaping itself as a moral personality and by extirpating all patrimonial elements from its constitution, might adopt, through inner reforms, a constitutional order, which will then enable it to *avoid* revolution. In this, Kant's work was close to other late theorists of natural law in Germany after the French Revolution, who saw natural law as a doctrine that helped to stabilize and preserve the state, as a moral person, against revolution. Bahrdt, for example, argued that states governed by natural law assume a moral character which citizens respect, and so imbue people with 'obedience and respect' towards existing political authority.[42] Karl Heinrich Heydenreich also emphasized that natural-law theory tends to promote conditions of legal order and freedom, and he denied the 'moral possibility' of rebellion against a state under natural law.[43] From a more reactionary perspective, Theodor Schmalz even used the natural-law construction of the state as a moral person to argue that the rights of subjects can only be guaranteed by the state, that all 'actions and attitudes' must be made subject to the sovereignty of the state,[44] and that the sovereign under natural law is 'entirely independent' of all other political bodies.[45] Of these natural-law theorists, only Johann Benjamin Erhard argued unequivocally that 'revolution is in accordance with law' if the natural rights of citizens are jeopardized by the state.[46] Kant himself repeatedly explained that 'resistance against highest legislation' and 'rebellion' against executive authority are not morally justifiable.[47] The will of the people, as a legal will, must always be subject to law, and it cannot resort to extra-legal means to resist the law.[48] In accounting for the state as a human state, therefore, Kant clearly indicated that the condition of living under own laws must be concentrated in and administered by a state, that the rule of law becomes improbable where law is detached from the state, and that the state is the sole guarantor of the unity of law and freedom.

It is perhaps in the sphere of *private law* that Kant's doctrine of legal order most closely reflected early liberal ideas, and he placed himself most emphatically behind the processes of social and economic liberalization that determined his historical horizon. In this respect, he argued that the universally enshrined rule of law sanctions and provides conditions of stability for particular possession and relations of ownership and contract.[49] Indeed, as the rule of law marks the transition from first nature to second nature, it also marks the transformation of possessions produced through antagonism and violent expropriation in the state of nature into a universally and legally pacified system of ownership. Once stabilized under the rule of law, Kant argued, ownership is a morally justified and constitutive element of human society, and it contributes to the ethical constitution of second nature. As a commentary on the emerging property economy in Germany in the late eighteenth century, therefore, Kant's work indicated that undivided ownership of private goods is a basic precondition for the rule of law, both private and public. As owners of property, in fact, people develop a necessary interest in law and legally ordered virtue, for they recognize that it is only through law that their material goods are stabilized. Ownership is thus 'a condition of law', and the interactions is the sphere of private law are formative elements in a wider condition of legal humanization.[50]

Legal metaphysics after Kant

Kant evidently saw his philosophical Enlightenment as an attempt to show that political order can be authentically human and fully legitimate, and that human beings, without external addition, can deduce the necessary laws of their polities, recognize themselves as authors of the laws that structure their objective obligations and, yet, live in accordance with transcendentally valid ideas of freedom. He envisaged his theory as providing for a human universe and a human polity, at the centre of which is the human being qua legislator, who at once replaces and fulfils the conditions of divine legislation and who supplants metaphysical laws with human laws. Even as he was writing, however, the Kantian version of the Enlightenment fell under the suspicion that, in its dualistic formalism, it failed credibly to locate the human being at the legislative centre of the world, and it failed to move beyond a metaphysical analysis of law, leaving the human being factually bound by laws which it could not meaningfully identify as its own. Indeed, if Kant saw Enlightenment as effecting a destruction of metaphysics in the name of human freedom and accountable law, his contemporaries and immediate successors saw him, in many ways, as a metaphysician par excellence, whose Enlightenment was neither specifically concerned with humans nor able to provide an account of freedom, except through an experientially depleted equation of humanity with noumenal acts of legislation. Subsequent revisions of Kant were, therefore, motivated by the suspicion that the rational authorship of law proposed by Kant merely reformulated the paradoxical God of scholasticism as a fictitiously metaphysical act of self-causality, now relocated into the formal human will.

In general, the early critics of the Kantian Enlightenment sought to elaborate their accounts of freedom, law and politics through more substantial accounts of human subjectivity, through fuller accounts of human rights and through more determinate analyses of the historical and experiential processes in which human subjectivity senses and forms its freedom. As discussed below, early reactions to Kant stimulated the formation of philosophical outlooks that thoroughly repudiated the rationalism and formal ius-naturalism in Kantian thought. However, even philosophers who placed themselves directly in a Kantian lineage sought to correct his work by overcoming its puristic accounts of subjectivity and its metaphysical formalism in its analysis of law.

The reaction to Kant's transcendentalism in the works of Johann Gottlieb Fichte, for example, contained theoretical modifications to Kant's work that were intended to place Kantian ethical and political ideas on more concrete or substantial anthropological foundations, so that laws of freedom might be reflected as integrally human laws. To this end, Fichte extended Kant's very cautious privileging of practical reason over pure reason, and he argued that the exercise of reason is a process through which the human being actively and consciously causes itself to be. As it exercises reason, he claimed, the human subject freely and spontaneously 'posits itself as being', it becomes 'conscious of itself' through the act of its self-positing, and it then obtains knowledge of objects through this same act. everything the subject knows has its 'ground' in subjective self-causality or in the 'action of the I'. For Fichte, therefore, the human subject is not a static metaphysical presence, dualistically confronting the world of facts and phenomena: it is the autonomous, active and volitional source of itself and its objects, and the active self-positing of this subject is the constitutive source of all other things.[51] In the Fichtean subject, therefore, reason and freedom are always factually unified, and no act of transcendental deduction is required to bring about this unity. In exercising reason, the subject freely wills itself to be, and in freely exercising its will, the subject provides a rational account of itself, its contents and its freedoms. Through its self-positing as reason and will, therefore, the subject creates a human world, in which, in all aspects of their thinking, human beings express and recognize their own rational freedom.

On these grounds, Fichte also argued that the process of active self-positing (or thinking) always has a necessary legal dimension and that the rational self-positing of consciousness always involves moments of legislation and legal recognition. The human subject can only exercise its rationality and its freedom, he claimed, where it acknowledges that other subjects also posit themselves as equally possessing rationality and freedom, where it knows its rationality and freedom as formed and limited by others and where, in consequence, it enters a legally constitutive relationship to other subjects. All primary acts of reason, in consequence, have a legislative component and all have an integrally normative structure. The concept of law, Fichte concluded, is an 'original concept of pure reason', and in all its acts of self-positing reason recognizes its relation to other 'free beings' by forming laws.[52] Fichte thus categorically defined law as the primary term of human self-realization. He placed the unspoken intimation of Kant's practical philosophy – that is, namely, that to be human is to be legal, or to be self-legislating – squarely at the centre of his own philosophy. All rational and volitional actions engender laws, he claimed, and the human subject can only exist as an agency which produces laws, founded in reciprocal processes of legal-rational recognition with other subjects.

Fichte's attempt to provide an anthropologically concentrated account of law and moral normativity was centred in the conviction that the human subject can only posit itself and so obtain laws as an active and volitionally engaged member of a concrete and plurally formed community.[53] Laws, he argued, are deducible from the fact that the person is a person with others, that it encounters others in each act of its self-positing, and that its own freedom is only fully rational where it positively incorporates 'the freedom of the other'.[54] Rational laws, consequently, are not generated through the principle of formal autonomy or the pure will, but through the active recognition that subjective freedom is regulated by the objective existence of other wills seeking freedom. The legal unity of reason and freedom, consequently, is not, as for Kant, a subjective unity residing in a formal will, but an objectively present content, in which a number of existing wills rationally recognize each other as free. Indeed, whilst Fichte accepted Kant's assertion that autonomy is the source of the law, he defined autonomy, not as a static attribute nor as a formal moment of self-causality, but as a sphere of shared action, in which rational agents participate and which they progressively form through a dynamic/normative process of recognition. Because of this, moreover, whilst Kant saw human beings as bearers of formally subjective rights, deduced from statically rational ideas of freedom, Fichte tentatively intimated that that people under laws obtain rights as objective rights – through the recognition of these rights as rational by other wills seeking freedom. In contrast to Kant, therefore, Fichte saw the 'object of the concept of law' as the 'community between free beings',[55] not as the self-legislation of solitary subjects, and he saw the will of the objective community, not of the self-legislating subject, as the condition in which rational laws and free wills are unified, under a legitimate state.

The Fichtean notion of freedom was, in its stated terms, very similar to that proposed by Kant. Like Kant, Fichte viewed the highest idea of freedom as a moral imperative, stating that each person should found his or her own freedom in an awareness of the fact that freedom cannot be exercised as particular freedom.[56] Like Kant, he saw the state of freedom as a condition in which human beings recognize their objective laws as reflecting the foundations of their own self-reflection, and in which human wills consequently enact rationally universalizable principles. However, unlike Kant, he saw the moral idea and the objective reality of freedom, not as derived from the pure or formal will, but as derived from the situated person and the situated will, interacting with and reflected by a plurality of other wills. This also meant that there were important political differences between Kant and Fichte. In many respects, Kant's conception of the person was moulded to a minimal account of the state as a legal-moral person, whose legitimacy is defined by the existence of invariable universal laws, and which enacts a unity of law and freedom as its own function, in relative closure against the subjects that it incorporates and represents. In contrast to this, however, Fichte's construct of the legal person as an active and interactive agent was structured around a much more expansive account of the legal sources of legitimacy in politics, of the political content of the law, and of the elaboration of the freedoms that law communicates. He argued that each citizen of the state is communally and inevitably engaged in the free production of laws necessary for the legitimacy of the state. In fact, the practical self-fulfilment of each person relies on his or her engagement as a member of a political collective, within which the laws are actively constituted and enshrined. Fichte thus did not see law, legitimacy and freedom as deducible from the formal autonomy of subjects protected by overarching and pre-agreed laws applied by the state. Instead, he saw law, legitimacy and freedom as constituted by actively autonomous subjects, who are participants in shaping the laws and founding the state, and for whom the withdrawal into formal or purely subjective autonomy is not possible. Consequently, he did not offer a doctrine of a limited constitutional state, guaranteeing for its citizens a thin stratum of rights and a maximum of autonomy, so separating citizens out from the strictly political formation of the state and depoliticizing legislative and executive processes. On the contrary, he proposed a more Rousseauian doctrine of the state, which viewed the state as evolving ceaselessly and objectively from the concrete interactions and the claims to rights between many rational wills, and which saw the general will as present and concentrated in a close relation between legislature and executive.

Fichte's political doctrine construed the legitimate state, not as protecting formal-private interests, but as subordinating all private interactions to publicly acceded laws and as limiting the sphere of private or individual autonomy outside the political operations of the state.[57] At a public-legal level, Fichte argued for a concept of the social contract in which the rule of law is absolutely binding and admits no dissent.[58] Under the social contract, he argued, all legal judgement must be made subordinate to the 'judgement of the state',[59] formed by mediated agreements between rational citizens; the constitution of the state resides in the 'absolute unanimity' of the people and it allows no divergence from its prescriptions.[60] At an economic or private-legal level, Fichte, to be sure, still allowed for a concept of free ownership and autonomous disposition over goods; he argued that the social contract constitutes a 'protective contract', through which all members of society agree to protect and respect the property of others.[61] Notwithstanding this, Fichte was clearly wary of classical liberal and early capitalist accounts of ownership, economic autonomy and freedom of competition. Unlike Kant, he did not recognize ownership as an absolutely prior element of legal order, but as a right legitimized by objective political agreements, on the ground of a 'mutual recognition' between self-positing citizens.[62] He denied that there exists a sphere of property-owing autonomy outside wider processes of political discourse and consent, or that rights under private law might have an invariably formative role in the construction of public order. In his later works, in fact, Fichte modified more standard liberal conceptions of property as competitively justified ownership of static goods, and he claimed instead that rights of ownership should be derived from broader conceptions of collective needs, to be politically administered by the state. What constitutes the 'rational state', he concluded, is its ability to distribute resources necessary for collective – or, most especially, *national* – life, and to ensure that the centrifugal forces and interests generated in civil society by the economy do not destabilize the political order.[63] He therefore ascribed to the state extremely far-reaching powers of economic intervention and regulation, and he endorsed a model of the polity close in spirit to a neo-mercantilist state.

Both Kant and Fichte argued that human beings fulfil their innate capacities where they practically generate universalizable maxims and understand these as the contents of their freedom, and both saw the constitution of the legitimate state as the embodiment of these maxims and contents. Both thus sought to find a human form for the valid deduction and application of the law; both saw the constitutional state as a person, and both traced the origins of political legitimacy to certain primary dispositions of the rational and self-legislating human being, represented by the state. However, if Kant viewed the legitimate state as a formal distillation of the freely and rationally self-legislating moral person, Fichte viewed the legitimate state as the objective-collective form of the free and rational legal personality of the moral people. If Kant saw the state as embodying a unity of reason and freedom which it distilled, as formal rights, from the moral personality of its citizens, and which it then represented to these citizens as metaphysically abstracted reflections of their personalities under law, Fiche began to construe the state as embodying a unity of reason and freedom which is productively formed by its citizens, so that these fully acknowledge the laws of state as their *own laws,* not as laws imputing rights to them through metaphysically formalized imputation. Whilst working in broadly Kantian paradigms, therefore, Fichte sought an objective and anthropologically substantial account of the ways in which the legal life of the state reflects its citizens, of the ways in which the legal life of citizens is determined by the state, and of the conditions under which laws enjoy a fully human legitimacy. For all the vital importance of Kant's teachings on freedom, autonomy and universal law, Fichte saw the Kantian idea of the legitimate state as an insufficiently human state: as the unmediated metaphysical form of practical reason, distilled from a metaphysically under-evolved idea of human self-legislation and paradoxical self-causality. Underlying the state of human freedom, Fichte stated, is always the real active person with other real active persons. 'The person', he claimed, in fact, 'only becomes a person with other persons'.[64]

The early idealist work of Friedrich Wilhelm Joseph von Schelling, similarly, was also organized around a response to Kant's transcendentalism, which sought tentatively to renounce the static dualism of the Kantian subject, and which also raised questions about the legal elements of Kant's thought. At the heart of the practical philosophy of Schelling's early idealist period was a correction of Kant that asserted that binding moral and legal postulates are not obtained through acts of transcendental reason, but are ontologically embedded in the underlying or absolute form of the human subject: in the absolute I. The absolute I, he explained, is the potential for absolute freedom in the human subject, and this potential underpins and motivates the finite I of the subject in its everyday practical actions. The absolute I 'demands absolutely' that the 'finite I should become equal to it',[65] that the 'subjective forms' of human being should be elevated to 'the form of the absolute', and that the finite I should become identical with the absolute I.[66] The absolute I consequently articulates an absolute law or a 'natural law', which is processed out through human existence, whose force shapes all aspects of human life, and the realization of which marks a condition of genuinely instituted freedom.[67]

In contrast with Kant's purely rational account of natural law, therefore, Schelling set out a substantial doctrine of natural law, which saw the ontological structure of the human subject as the formative substructure of natural laws. The absolute I, he argued, incorporates the true nature, or the second, rational nature, of human existence, and all the operations of human reason are oriented towards the practical elaboration and consolidation of this second nature as a naturally manifest reality. Authentic law, he thus explained, should be viewed as a condition of factually realized human nature in which the rational nature and rational freedoms ingrained in the human constitution have formed themselves as manifest nature and where human beings now inhabit the materialized reality of their own absolute nature and absolute freedom. The condition of second nature is a condition where 'freedom is itself nature and nature is itself freedom', and where all laws fully articulate the rational freedom of human nature.[68]

At one level, the early Schelling intensified Kant's argument that integral human existence is centred on self-legislation and that freedom is a condition in which people recognize themselves as enacting, in laws, the highest ideas of their practical reason. Indeed, he articulated his own analysis of this insight in immediate reference to Kant's own dialectic of first and second nature. Like Kant, he viewed autonomy as the supreme principle of practical philosophy, and he saw idealism, in its entirety, as dedicated to the elucidation of the preconditions of autonomy and to the instantiation of humanity as a rationally free will.[69] Like Kant, also, he saw the formation of subjective autonomy as culminating in a categorical imperative that bans the objectification of other rational beings and prohibits the tendency to privilege one's own freedom over 'the freedom of other moral beings'.[70] Nonetheless, unlike Kant, he saw the condition of autonomy, not as an intelligible reality deduced through a spontaneous act of self-causality, but as a condition obtained through the concrete formation of the subject, or of the absolute I of the subject. In this respect, he sought to replace the formal 'moral law' of Kantian philosophy with the 'natural law of the I', and he envisaged autonomy, not as subjective self-legislation, but as a shared and manifest condition, in which the human subject knows that the absolute ethical contents of its consciousness concretely surround it as the objective (and objectively free) order of its life.[71] The self-elaboration of the absolute I in the state of autonomy, he claimed, is a natural material process in which the 'unchangeable self' of the absolute I seeks to realize its own natural laws, and to subordinate 'all heteronomous power' (that is, all outer nature) to its own law.[72] As heteronomy is banished, then, and as autonomous laws objectively unfold, this institutes a state of law in which laws appear as shared laws, in which rational laws are equally recognized by all wills, and in which common ideas of right and freedom are elaborated as material form. Unlike Kant, therefore, Schelling imputed a naturalized and shared objectivity to the condition of autonomy and second nature. Autonomy, he concluded, is experienced in a common legal expression of an 'absolute will',[73] which realizes the embedded potentials of the absolute I as an objective will, and in which all wills experience themselves as rationally and absolutely free. Unlike Kant, consequently, Schelling also concluded that, as rational ideas of freedom are elaborated, law itself becomes redundant. Where second nature is founded (that is, where the finite I and the absolute I have become identical), law 'necessarily destroys itself', and it forfeits all coercive or heteronomous force. Where the absolute I is instituted, law is no longer necessary as a distinct element of social structure, and human life is naturally ordered in relations of unconditioned self-obedience, self-identity or inner and outer autonomy.[74] The processual life of human consciousness, in short, is organized in its entirety around the formation of an order in which 'a second and higher nature' is 'put in place above first nature', as a result of which, ultimately, 'a natural law prevails'. This natural law, however, is 'very different from that in the visible nature'. It is 'a natural law in service of freedom',[75] and, as such, it fully reflects and objectivizes the rational ideas of freedom forming the absolute I of its addressees, and so ultimately acts as an inner element of a universally formed consciousness, not as a distinct prescriptive element.

Most immediately, Schelling might be seen as a thinker who, in part at least, reversed the Kantian achievement in moving beyond traditional metaphysics. In his account of autonomy and natural law, he reconstituted a metaphysics of nature and of natural process that integrated human subjectivity and rationality into a broader conception of metaphysical evolution. Indeed, he also argued that the natural-legal condition of autonomy, or of self-identity between inner nature and outer nature, will be marked by the positive *presence* of God in human life, not, in Kantian manner, by the mere *idea* of God. The natural law of self-identity, he claimed, will be God's personal law, a *new law,* and under this new law the objectivity of *fate* will be supplanted by the identity of freedom as a common human experience of self-obedience and self-recognition.[76] Despite these apparently regressive moments, however, Schelling also opposed Kant's philosophy because of its metaphysical formalism. He implied that Kantian philosophy resorted to chimerically metaphysical ideas in its attempt to account for the reality of human freedom, and, by analysing human freedom as a moment of transcendental self-causality, it detached freedom from its objective foundations and from the objective conditions of consciousness that make it possible. Like Kant, the early Schelling also hoped to see the emergence of a 'legal constitution', and even the institution of a 'constitution of universal citizenship', and, at times, he even suggested that law can steer humanity towards a state of harmony and perfectibility.[77] However, he argued that institutions ensuring freedom and harmony cannot be summoned from the noumenal air and immediately established as material forms in human society. Instead, he suggested that legal forms must be founded in an adequate condition of consciousness and naturalized freedom, and this consciousness must sustain these forms, it must allow them to flourish and it must create preconditions for their recognition. This consciousness, he argued, could only result from the natural 'progressivity' of historical life and could not be construed as an invariably given fact of all consciousness. He, therefore, saw his own work as philosophy that gave substance to the formal-subjective metaphysics of Kantian idealism and that refused to construe rationally valid law as transcendentally disembedded from natural/historical consciousness or imposed across human life as a mere 'supplement to visible nature'.[78] Schelling's response to Kant was thus marked by the simultaneous sense that Kantian philosophy was too metaphysical (that it stabilized moral and legal ideas at a purely normative level and so struggled to explain why laws should be accepted as objectively legitimate) and that it was insufficiently metaphysical (that it failed to account for the position of human laws within the total conditions of natural evolution and objective consciousness, and it fictitiously assumed that laws could command obedience as mere positive facts).

Hegel: the state and the objectivity of the will

The legal philosophy of Georg Wilhelm Friedrich Hegel expanded aspects of these early idealist critiques of the Kantian Enlightenment, and it sought to show that both Kantian idealism and early positivism were founded in falsely constructed ideas of human reason and falsely metaphysical accounts of the human will. Like earlier idealists, Hegel sought to account for legitimate law as the metaphysical 'realm of realized freedom',[79] where original ideas of freedom become positively manifest. Moreover, he sought to illuminate the condition of legitimate political order as a condition of rational-natural law or of *second nature,* in which people recognize themselves as the free and ideal-rational authors of their own laws, and in which they recognize the rational-legal form of their freedom as both restricted and constituted by that of others. However, Hegel was distinct from earlier idealists in that he argued that this condition can only exist on the foundation of an objective or fully mediated conception of the human will: rational freedom under law is not elaborated by simple or transcendental persons, but through shared processes of human interaction, recognition and limitation, in which the will is gradually formed as a rational will and learns to recognize its freedom as freedom including other rational wills. Underlying Hegel's philosophy of law, in consequence, was an attempt to break with static ideas of the legal person promulgated by both early positivism and by idealism and to comprehend both law and state as articulations of an objectively evolved rational will and an objectively evolved rational person. This was guided by the sense that the unity of reason and freedom in the Kantian legal state is a false unity, distilled from metaphysical acts of a metaphysical personality, and the Kantian legal state, in consequence, is not able objectively to explain to real persons why the laws of a legitimate state should be recognized as legitimate. For the state to be legitimate, the Kantian state and the Kantian subject must be reconstructed as substantial personalities whose freedoms are recognized in substantial laws.

In his mature political philosophy, therefore, Hegel claimed that reason and free will evolve together through socially determinate processes of formation, and that reason and freedom, in their conjunction, constantly work to shape a condition of *objective law,* in which rationality and freedom are progressively conjoined as manifest contents of the worldly order. In the formation of reason and freedom as law, he argued, reason and the will are organized on three distinct terrains, some of which are determined by more reflected and enduring principles of rational freedom than others, and that different types of law, some more valid (more natural or more rational) than others, emerge from different forms of the will and different experiences of freedom.[80] Aspects of this theory closely reflected Leibniz's earlier analysis of the triadic structure of freedom under natural law. The crudest level of freedom, for Hegel, is the level of immediacy or of abstract particularity, where human beings act as *legal persons:* that is, where they construe themselves as atomized bearers of rights and freedoms, and assert their wills through the singular and exclusive claim to dominion over things. This level of freedom is characterized by the law of property or by *abstract right,* and the legal personality that determines this level of law enshrines the rights of individual wills in their claims to ownership and in their desire to pursue particular freedoms and subjective purposes. Although reflecting a limited mode of legal formation, Hegel argued that the legal personality of abstract right has the epoch-making and deeply liberating significance that it allows people to operate not only as proprietorial individuals, but as individuals who *own themselves* (who are not slaves), who dispose freely over their own interests and purposes and who obtain legal entitlements of possessive autonomy and material self-reliance. Nonetheless, the legal personality under abstract right, Hegel stated, cannot generate substantial or universally rational forms of law, and it cannot exceed unilateral and cognitively unformed demands for freedom. In his earlier work, he was quite clear that models of public order residing in the models of legal personality derived from Roman law and early positivism promulgated alienated laws based in formal atomism, in 'autonomy without spirit' and 'empty generality', and that, as legal persons, agents under law encounter themselves and each other only as bearers of an 'alien content' imposed upon them by an irrationally generalized will.[81] Abstract right is the foundation of law in its most 'formal' and non-universal structure, which incorporates only a highly inchoate unity of reason of freedom, and it inevitably raises substantive dilemmas that can only be reconciled at a higher or more reflected level of legal universality and rational freedom.[82] Central to this aspect of Hegel's philosophy was thus, following Leibniz, a critique of more positivist types of early liberalism, which assumed that the distillation of the legal person from the property law of Roman law can provide a basis for substantial legal and political freedoms. Hegel certainly did not deny the right of free private property. However, he argued that it is only where the will of the person recognizes the limits of its own freedom as a possessive agent, where it begins to abstract from its own proprietary particularity and where it acknowledges that ownership requires a higher moral sanction that it reflects and produces more substantial freedoms in law. The legal person of Roman law, in consequence, must be carried over, as one subordinate element, into higher and more mediated spheres of legal freedom, and ownership only acquires its justification where it is enshrined as a necessary but subsidiary component in the objective form of a more generally mediated and more substantially rational common will. Throughout Hegel's work, therefore, private law pertains to an inferior level of human organization, and the freedoms peculiar to private law can only be fully enjoyed where they are secured and applied by a higher and more rational collective will, comprising a higher idea of freedom – that is, by the state.[83]

The second level of freedom, then, is a condition where human beings act as *subjects:* that is, where they recognize that their wills are restricted by those of other persons, who have equally legitimate legal claims, and that the realm of human freedom must be regulated by universal moral standards and duties. The legal expression of this level of freedom is *morality:* the 'law of the subjective will'.[84] The moral subject is the specifically modern condition of the human being in which individual people exercise reason to determine their freedoms and duties and to produce autonomous ideas of what is right.[85] This condition finds its highest expression in Kantian doctrines of practical autonomy, duty and the pure will, in which people determine their actions in accordance with independently stipulated necessity. However, if the level of abstract right is marked and limited by the particularity of the legal purposes that it sanctions, the level of morality is marked and limited by the generality of the purposes that it sanctions. Under morality, people perpetrate moral actions as dutiful purposes, as actions whose value is externally prescribed and ultimately heteronomous to their own freedom and reason, and their legal life is consequently regulated by oppressively hypostatic moral norms.[86] At this point in the evolution of the law, therefore, Hegel turned against Kant's moral liberalism, which he saw as vainly intent on deducing the terms of ethical life, both particular and political, from noumenal ideas of duty. Under such terms, he argued, human freedom cannot be realized as anything but formal heteronomy, in which ethical choices are determined by external principles. Like abstract right, therefore, morality also engenders legal antinomies that cannot be resolved or reconciled at the level of generality and it necessitates an idea of freedom in which the will sees its freedom neither in particularized purposes nor in generalized duties, but in a third condition of freedom, reconciling particularity and generality. It is only where they are underscored by a substantially free and objectively rational will that law and state become a genuinely human and genuinely free order, and that the laws and purposes regulating human life become something other than naively particularized or heteronomously imposed metaphysical norms.

The highest level of freedom, consequently, is a condition of the human will in which the will spontaneously pursues universal purposes and where it recognizes its own freedom as one mediated element of the objective conditions that surround it.[87] The realization of this freedom occurs as the outcome of the progressive mediation of the wills of many people: it is a condition of *ethical life* (*Sittlichkeit*), in which, over long periods of time, many wills have shaped themselves, through complex processes of conflict and recognition, into an overarching rational will, containing objective sanction for universal ideas of freedom. Other conceptions of the free will – especially the proprietorial will of Roman law and the pure will of transcendental idealism – fail, for Hegel, fully to reflect the freedom of the will in its objective situatedness, and they mistakenly deduce ideas of freedom under law from an incomplete or hypostatic account of reason and will. Above all, these conceptions stabilize the will at a position prior to its concrete determinacy – before it has engaged with other wills, and before it has incorporated the ideas of freedom asserted by other wills. Other accounts of the will and freedom are, thus, still caught in the preconditions of formal metaphysics, and their analysis of human freedom (as ownership or normative self-regulation) does not describe truly rational freedom, and it does not account for the laws of freedom as laws that are fully and integrally authorized by their addressees. Other accounts of the will and of freedom are, consequently, only valuable as subordinate aspects of a substantial interpretation of human freedom as self-reflection in shared law.

The highest realization of the idea of human freedom, Hegel argued, is the objectively formed state: it is only through the 'association of a people in the form of a state' that conditions of objective freedom can be elaborated, and that the pursuit of freedom can be shaped by genuinely rational and universal laws.[88] Substantial experiences of freedom are also found in the family and in the economy, he explained, but these experiences are ultimately limited by their inherent commitment to 'subjective particularity' and, in the economy, to the latently antagonistic pursuit of unilateral interests and purposes.[89] In consequence, he concluded that only a fully evolved and substantially integrative state is equipped to ensure that universal law is applied through society and only the state is capable of regulating the imbalances in legal recognition found at the level of ownership and morality by transmitting higher and more substantial definitions of freedom as the content of laws. The state is the 'reality of the substantial will', which is responsible for integrating other areas of legal life into its overarching structure and for ensuring that all areas are determined by universalizable legal ideas.[90] The state allows free ownership of property, and it supports universal moral codes and duties. However, it also creates a horizon in which these freedoms and duties are experienced as subsidiary aspects of a universal self-consciousness or a universal idea of freedom, and the state might even – under certain conditions – intervene in other spheres of activity and determine these in accordance with the idea of freedom that it embodies. The legitimate state is, as for Kant, a state in which people reflect themselves as the subjective authors of the laws that bind them objectively and in which their laws and their freedoms are rationally recognized as identical. This legitimate state, however, is founded in a substantial will or a fully objectivized idea of human freedom in which all people experience themselves, subjectively, as free, but where they also know their freedom, objectively, to be rationally reflected in the wills of others. Against Kant, therefore, Hegel intimated that reason's unity with freedom cannot be resolved at the level of pure will, as a moment of self-causality in the moral personality of the citizen or of the state; this unity of reason and freedom is only obtained through a long course of historical and rational formation, through which freedom, articulated and desired in many ways by many wills, gradually evolves in the form of rational law and culminates in the ideas of freedom represented by the state.

In his commentary on other ideas of law and freedom, Hegel's mature philosophy of law and state marked an attempt to reconstruct the more established ideas of private freedom and moral normativity characterizing early liberalism and to convert these into a doctrine of freedom that was emphatically centred in the state and in laws positively applied by the state. This doctrine, although accepting limited rights of private autonomy, normative regulation of power and some degree of political representation, was designed to avoid a condition in which *negative freedoms,* either as proprietary interests or moral norms, are allowed to dictate the principles by which the legitimacy of state power and the freedom of citizens are defined. Indeed, Hegel's philosophy of law might be viewed, implicitly, as a doctrine that claims that the constitutional rights and freedoms desired by liberals cannot be adequately protected by liberals subscribing to weak ideals of normative legal statehood and negative liberty, and that these freedoms can only be preserved within a rational state, strong enough to prevent one set of particular freedoms from obtaining exclusive primacy over others, and expressing universality in law as a condition of its own rationality, not as a norm placed as a limit upon it. The state, for Hegel, becomes legitimate to the extent that it is constitutionally founded in the concrete and evolving relations of the rational freedom of the human will: this freedom can only be formed if the will of the state is not stabilized around fully particularized or self-seeking purposes and if it is not dominated by abstractly imposed norms. As a commentary on early liberalism and early capitalism, therefore, Hegel argued that neither private freedoms nor moral norms can be seen as prior or invariable elements of political freedom or as prior or invariable conditions of political order, and that a state does not become legitimate because it integrates recognition of these freedoms or norms in a constitution. In fact, these freedoms and moral principles are only made possible by the prior existence of a substantial political will in the state, and rights and freedoms regulating the private sphere or moral duty in fact always presuppose the state as the positive guarantor of all freedoms. In questioning liberal ideas of freedom and legitimacy, therefore, Hegel, like Fichte before him, also suggested that the common liberal assumption that human or natural rights, based in property or morality, are prior elements of political order from whose prior recognition a state draws legitimacy, is deeply misguided. Rights, he claimed, are sanctioned as they are reflected as subsidiary elements of a common will and a common experience of freedom, centred in the state. It is not possible, on Hegel's account, to imagine subjective rights as invariable elements of law or freedom determined prior to the formation of the state, or to articulate rights as formal constructs of freedom against the state's overarching rational will. This does not mean that

Hegel refused to see the state as providing guarantees over rights, or that he saw rights as thoroughly independent of individual wills. On the contrary, he clearly stressed that all political relations, even those reflecting extreme imbalances of power and interest, incorporate an acknowledgement that all members of the polity obtain a recognized sphere of social rights that no stable political order can afford to ignore.[91] However, in his mature work he argued that the state is the formed will that gives objective recognition to rights; it is only as they are recognized by the state that rights have legal purchase. The attempt to disarticulate rights from the wider will supporting their free exercise is thus an example of metaphysical reductivism, which is in fact liable to weaken the state and undermine the rights and freedom that it advocates. The state itself, in sum, is the condition of *second nature,* and ideas of right and freedom inscribed in natural law by liberal theorists can only be realized and enforced through the objective and integrative order of the state.

It is important to note, however, that for all his critique of liberal preconditions, Hegel did not abandon the ambitions of early liberal politics. Instead, he saw his own philosophy of right as allowing for the evolution of socio-economic autonomy and for the constitutional regulation of political authority, albeit within the overarching framework of a traditionally formed monarchical state. Throughout his work, Hegel placed himself resolutely against all reactionary or restorative theorists, especially Karl Ludwig von Haller, who claimed that all power is founded in patrimonial structures and personal relations of ownership and that rational accounts of rights and freedoms have no role in the elaboration of the terms of constitutional order.[92] Against such ideas, he asserted that all political orders evolve from the knowledge of those bearing power that those subject to power possess social entitlements and freedoms, and these shape the conditions under which power can be exercised.[93] Hegel's theory thus concurred deeply with Kant in its hostility to patrimonial rule, and, like other liberal theories, he saw the end of private control over the means of government as an essential and inalienable attribute of the state guaranteeing rational freedom. Indeed, following Kant, Hegel's entire political philosophy was, not lastly, an attempt to show that states that do not integrate elements of socio-economic pluralism and rational representation into their constitutions are likely to suffer overthrow and revolution. He thus saw the rights of self-ownership and autonomy proclaimed in the French Revolution as necessary elements of modern consciousness, which must be incorporated in the constitutional fabrics of modern states.[94] Against both pure liberal and pure patrimonial ideas, however, he argued that all freedom (both economic and political) is validated only where it is reflected by a common rational will, and where it is objectively enacted by the rational will of the state. Freedoms that are dislocated from the will of the state and statically concentrated in particularized expressions of will place true freedom in jeopardy.

The new metaphysics and the state of freedom

One particularly salient point in Hegel's political argument was that he considered both Kantians and positivists to be *formalist metaphysicians.* These metaphysicians, he implied, sought to distil substantial freedoms from the examination of an as-yet-unformed subjective will, and they failed to explain the unity of rationality and liberty in anything but abstract or rather gratuitously paradoxical categories. As a corrective to this, Hegel intended his philosophy as a commentary on the human will in the concrete contexts of its formation, and he sought to illuminate how increasingly universalized elements of constitutional right and freedom are elaborated in the diverse locations of human activity. In this respect, Hegel's philosophy might be interpreted as an attempt to transfer originally Kantian ideas of the self-legislating person and the legitimate state onto anthropologically determinate foundations, and so to elaborate the ideas of Kantian metaphysics in a more determinate structure. At the same time, however, whilst turning against metaphysical subjectivism, Hegel's doctrine of autonomy also proposes a metaphysics of historical process, which tries to overcome the formal ideation of Kant's practical reason by interpreting historical foundation and evolution as constitutive elements in the refinement of concrete ideas of human freedom. In his attitudes towards early liberalism, therefore, his thought, like that of Schelling before him, was shaped by the view that liberal Kantian ideas are at once *too metaphysical* and *insufficiently metaphysical.* On the first point, he implied that liberal ideas are inattentive to historical activity and to the social formation of ideas; they fictitiously conceive of freedom as a formal and abstracted property of particular subjects and particular self-causing wills; and they fictitiously derive the condition of free laws in the state from such wills. On the second point, he argued that liberals fail to understand freedom in its fully mediated and elaborated content; they do not appreciate how the evolution of freedom expresses a broader unfolding of the human spirit; and they reduce freedom to a number of limited positive facts, existing in a constitutional form that is placed prior to or negatively against the total reality of political order. In the final analysis, then, Kant's philosophy appeared to Hegel as a doctrine that stabilized a thin metaphysics of freedom in the constitution, but which was unable to grasp the deeper metaphysics of process and self-consciousness that elaborates genuine rational freedom in the state. Like Kant before him, Hegel saw the rational freedom of humanity as God's freedom, and he intimated that the self-determination of humanity under rationally free laws is the necessary form for the freedom of God, as God's necessary otherness to himself. Like Schelling, however, he argued that human freedom could not, in a sequence of spontaneous rational acts, create itself in likeness of God's freedom, but must integrate all areas of historical life and consciousness in this freedom.

The central idea in Hegel's legal and political thought, in consequence, is that the outlooks of his major theoretical rivals failed to account for the conditions of rational freedom because they undervalued the role of the state and because they failed fully to comprehend the state as the place where the metaphysical unity of law and freedom must be redeemed. Liberal conceptions of the legal state, he claimed, describe only the legal (either private-legal or the moral-legal) element in this state, they are not able adequately to reflect the objective structure of the will underscoring the unity of law and freedom in a free state, and their idea of freedom in the state can only fictitiously account for laws of freedom. Hegel thus argued that Kantian theory fails to accomplish its desired resolution of the antinomy between universal normativity and voluntarism. Kantian theory in fact, for Hegel, deduces the unity of reason and freedom from a paradoxically self-generated idea of the pure will, refracted then in the laws of the legal state. This analysis, however, is not able to offer anything but a paradoxically inconclusive account of human freedom and the human will. The authentic reconciliation of reason and freedom can only be effected without paradox, he suggested, on the ground of a doctrine of the objective will, which sees the antinomy of freedom and necessity as resolved in the historically rationalized state, in which reason and will gradually coalesce through objectively mediated processes of reconciliation. Hegel's work was, therefore, organized around a transposition of the subjective-idealist metaphysics of the will in Kantianism into an objective-idealist metaphysics of the will, through which the original Kantian vision of the community of self-legislators is reconstructed as a metaphysically formed state.

In this respect, more generally, Hegel's doctrine of the state as the realm of ethical freedom and rational will contains a reflection on the entire history of European political life. This doctrine defines the rational state as an arena of essentially modern liberty, and it resolves the insufficiencies of the ideas of freedom in its immediate environment. At the same time, however, Hegel saw his account of the state as also correctively transforming the ideas of freedom informing all earlier eras of European political formation. Underlying Hegel's thought is the sense that European political culture in its entirety has integrated two distinct ideas and experiences of common freedom, that it has been shaped by two great attempts to unify reason and freedom in the political arena, and that these attempts now form the foundation, the intellectual fabric and the *metaphysical memory* of contemporary political reasoning. Modern freedom, thus, is founded in a recollection of ideas of freedom elaborated in ancient Greece and in an internalization of ideas of freedom reflected in Christianity. Hegel intended his own work to show that modern freedom must both incorporate and surpass both these antecedent ideas of freedom, and the rational state is the arena that accomplishes this.

First, Hegel argued that classical Greek society produced a legal order that gave concrete expression to a general idea of freedom, and which, at least in part, realized a rational community under own laws. The Greek city-states ordered human action around substantial laws in whose formation human beings knew themselves as freely participant, and which, as immediate expressions of local culture, were not experienced as external or coercive norms. However, Hegel claimed that the substantial legal freedom of Greek society ultimately proved ephemeral and insufficiently refined, and it was soon superseded. This freedom was brought to crisis by the emergence of modern reason as a critical element in the laws, and by the liberation of 'inner life' and 'subjectivity' from the polis as a demand for more particular freedoms.[95] The freedom guaranteed under Greek law, he concluded, was ultimately doomed to *positivity:* it lost its vital bond with the intellectual freedom of citizens, and it was therefore finally experienced as *heteronomy.* Greek freedom gave initial expression to the idea of freedom, but the critical pulse of this idea required new and more subjectively refined expressions than could be guaranteed in the local cultures of the ancient city-states.

Analogously, then, in his earlier works Hegel also saw early Christianity as inaugurating an idea of freedom and a distinct vision of the community under own laws. He viewed the first Christian communities as examples of legal organization in which the human subject reacted against falsely objectivized law (both as Jewish theocratic law and formal morality), and in which participants in commonly shaped life forms were bound together by affectual legal ties.[96] The community instituted by Jesus Christ, therefore, overcame heteronomy in law, and it spontaneously reconciled law and its addressees through *love.*[97] In the first Christian community of affection, or the *Gemeinde,* Hegel argued, people were willing to recognize others as legally entitled and equal and to commit no action that might undermine the legal status of others, and thus they naturally created a condition of freedom under laws. It is specific to early Christian law, however, that it was law founded in inclination, so that Christianity in fact engendered a community integrated without law, which existed in parallel to other legally formed communities, but did not form objectively valid laws.[98] Whereas Greek society had produced an experience of legal freedom based in objective law, therefore, Hegel saw the experience of autonomy in Christianity as suffering from a counterposed deficiency. Christian communities, he concluded, contained a lack of 'objectivity'; the *new laws* of the *Gemeinde* were merely laws that bound people together in an affective experience of freedom, and these laws only *appeared* to efface heteronomy.[99] In fact, early Christianity lacked sufficient objectivity to constitute laws of its own,[100] and so it allowed existing objective laws to persist as an external reality of 'positivity'.[101]

For Hegel, in consequence, Athens and Jerusalem both failed finally to produce enduring conditions of real and substantial freedom, and the spirit of both these political cultures remained, for different reasons, beset and plagued by the spirit of objective heteronomy. Greece suffered from an excess of materiality or externality, and it was brought to crisis by particular, inner or rational ideas of freedom. Christianity suffered from a lack of materiality or externality, and it could only project freedom as an inner vision of redemption, *without law*. Neither, however, was able to give stable or rationally adequate shape to the idea of freedom.

Underlying Hegel's political philosophy is thus the intimation that the evolution of the idea of freedom has, at different times, generated different societies that have been convinced that they experienced a condition of freedom under own laws. These societies were also the societies that produced the most enduring metaphysical doctrines and that most pervasively shaped the cognitive memory and the intellectual formation of Europe: they produced Aristotelian communitarianism on one hand and Christian interiority and eschatology on the other. On Hegel's account, however, neither of these experiences of freedom was fully adequate to the rational idea of freedom. Indeed, Hegel's work might legitimately be viewed as an attempt to bind together the commonly realized unity of the Greek polis and the inner life, particularity and the future-oriented redemptive vision of Christianity, and so to outline a progressive model of human politics in which the particular demand for inner freedom is gradually reconciled to the manifest moral life and laws of the objective polity or state.[102] In this light, Hegel's philosophy can be seen as evolving from a constructive confrontation of the two original metaphysical experiences at the core of Western intellectual culture and from an attempt to obtain the truth of both of these visions through their fusion with each other.

The most important element in his reflections on the metaphysical foundations of modern politics, however, is the claim that the two original cultures of freedom did not produce a condition of reliable statehood, and they did not produce a legal order providing an objective account of the necessary contents of human freedom. Hegel's mature philosophy, therefore, insisted that the rational concretion of freedom and the general removal of heteronomy requires the existence of *a state:* only a state giving constitutional sanction for objective rights and instituting a universally controlled legal order can save the contents of past metaphysics and produce a fully adequate idea of freedom. The state, he concluded, is at once the substantial order of the political community in which common conceptions of freedom are accepted, and it is the rational form of human life, in which individual and internally reflected claims can be represented and recognized. People integrated into legal states as citizens thus escape false law more reliably than the Greeks and the early Christians. Indeed, citizens integrated into legal states experience both the natural order promised by Greek metaphysics and the inner liberty promised by Christian metaphysics. The state, in sum, is the practical condition under which people positively obtain the freedom intimated metaphysically in earlier philosophical and political epochs. The state is the reliably human form of metaphysics; indeed, it is the form that enables freedom to become an eminently human freedom.

On these grounds, it might be concluded that Hegel identified four falsely metaphysical doctrines of legal freedom, and he sought to correct and redeem all of them in his own work. In his own intellectual context, he saw the Roman-law personalism of early positivism and the subjective transcendentalism of Kantian idealism as offering profoundly epochal and important, yet also decidedly limited accounts of the human foundations of freedom and political order. In a wider context, he also saw Greece and Christianity as embodying rival ideas of human freedom, which were of intensely formative, yet also finally restricted, importance in the evolution of modern political life and liberty. The resolution of the aporia in all these ideas of freedom was, he implied, to be found in the rational human state, and it is only in the objective metaphysics of the rational state that the highest implications of other analyses of freedom can be fully appreciated.

4 Historicism and romanticism
Against liberalism as metaphysics

As discussed above, the Kantian Enlightenment viewed itself as an intellectual movement that followed an anti-metaphysical course in its attempt to deduce rationally independent foundations for legal validity and political legitimacy. However, to many of its contemporaries and to the next theoretical generation, the Kantian Enlightenment appeared merely to replicate the most pernicious aspects of the metaphysical traditions that it reconstructed and opposed. Post-Enlightenment political thought in Germany was, therefore, dominated by the belief that the early liberal ideals of contractually bound legal statehood and private-legal autonomy in the Enlightenment lead to an atomistic and impoverished analysis of political life, and they diminish political freedoms by projecting unreliable and disruptive ideas of liberty onto the complexly structured organ of the state. Central to this reaction against Kant's Enlightenment was the sense, first, that the deduction of liberty from individual persons fails to understand how persons are both shaped and fulfilled in commonly structured historical situations and, second, that the deduction of freedom from formal norms fails to recognize how people can live freely under norms that evolve gradually and without abstract compulsion. Both these reservations culminated in the claim, which was widespread after Kant, that the unification of rational law and political freedom in early idealism remains paradoxical, and idealism obtains its concept of rational freedom only by insinuating an impossibly depleted rational subject as the self-causing origin of freedom and law. This conception of the rational subject, it was argued, in fact obstructs the true experiences of freedom under law, which is already positively given in most customarily formed societies.

In consequence, the aftermath of idealism was marked by theoretical attempts, of varying character, to reconfigure liberalism and idealism on new foundations. At the heart of this endeavour was the belief that law should be disarticulated from all prior or metaphysical principles: private law should not be viewed as a system of static or negative elements against the state, and public laws should not be viewed as a set of formal norms imposed upon the state by the self-proclaimed authority of reason. The Enlightenment, it was argued, had signally failed in its attempt to reconcile law and power and to obtain conditions of personal freedom under legitimate states. Instead, it had dualistically segregated individual people from the wider settings of their liberty, it had disconnected the state from its organic origins in tradition, custom and acknowledged privilege and it paradoxically imagined freedom under laws as an act of spontaneous moral auto-genesis in citizens and in states. Theories responding to the Enlightenment thus sought to examine the law as a fully incorporated element of the community, as a living interpretation of the community's ongoing form, reflecting not prior norms or atomized articles of reason but the existing cohesive historical spirit of the community itself. These ideas formed the theoretical foundation of the movements widely known as historicism and romanticism, both of which remained influential intellectual forces throughout the entire nineteenth century and, indeed, beyond.

Providing a definition of romantic and historicist political thought is not always easy. Historicism in fact shared many common features with romanticism, and both historicism and romanticism shared common features with other political perspectives; historicism, for example, cannot always be securely differentiated from positivism, and aspects of romanticism often merged with organic theory. Indeed, there are certain thinkers who fall into the interstices between these categories and who cannot be classified without ambiguity. This is particularly the case with Gustav Hugo and Friedrich Carl von Savigny, the major earlier historicist legal thinkers, who might in certain respects be viewed as the precursors of both historicism and positivism. For the sake of uncomplicated categorization, however, it will be argued here that historicist thinking, in legal and political debate, evolved as an intellectual outlook that hoped to counteract the universal or metaphysical ius-natural accounts of legal validity in the Enlightenment by claiming that the origin of valid law is the historical form of a particular national culture, and that this culture is deeply shaped by religious impulses. Similarly, it will be argued here that romanticism was a broad theoretical tradition which, like historicism, rejected the assumption that legal values or laws can be reliably deduced from universal preconditions, and so accentuated the experiential and religious sources of law in historically formed communities. Unlike historicism, however, romantics often placed emphasis on the universal elements of Christian culture. Whereas historicism emphasized national particularity and hoped to recuperate liberal ideas of freedom on the ground of national culture, romanticism sought to derive from religion a new universality in law, to oppose the rational universalism of the Enlightenment. However, historicism and romanticism had a common origin in their opposition to rational metaphysics and in their belief that the freedoms of Enlightenment can only be false freedoms.

As discussed in Chapter 2, eclectic and historical approaches to legal and political questions were generally characteristic of German intellectual life from the early Enlightenment onwards, and historicist concepts of law and legitimacy were already well consolidated before historicism was established as a compactly defined set of outlooks. However, the emergence of historicism as a broad intellectual stance is commonly associated with the works of Johann Gottfried von Herder. Herder reacted against the universalizing ethical approaches of the Kantian Enlightenment by examining historical uniqueness and diversity as the central element of human social formation, and he rejected as simplistic and crudely metaphysical rationalized ethical positions claiming to represent universal moral or legal certainties.[1] After Herder, then, historicism developed as a number of pervasive political and philosophical perspectives, concentrated initially amongst eminent historians at German universities. Historicist thinking was not wedded to one particular political standpoint, and its representatives obtained influence in quite distinct political camps during the formative events of the nineteenth century – especially the failed liberal revolutions of 1848–49 and the unification of Germany by Bismarck in 1870–71. However, underlying the politics of historicism was the assumption that historical knowledge has a constitutive role in political life, that historical research reinforces historical and cultural unity, which in turn acts as the precondition of reliable political order, and that the nation is the defining form of human organization. All historicists, therefore, posed legal and political questions from a nationally inflected perspective; they all tended to argue that the resolution of political problems should be guided by considerations of national and cultural integrity; and they saw engaged national belonging as the highest attitude of all intellectual culture. All, moreover, were hostile to universalist views in ethical and political analysis, and they argued that legal principles should be determined on the foundation of national cohesiveness, not of rational necessity. For this reason, historicism, in its political ramifications, tended to produce an attitude of progressive-conservative nationalism, usually opposed to classical liberal ideas about constitutional order and tending to criticize conceptions of natural law.

Hugo, Savigny and the Historical School

The original application of historicist methodology to legal questions is usually traced to the works of Gustav Hugo. Hugo's work was shaped by a critical attitude towards Kantian-rationalist accounts of legal validity, and he argued that the 'legal truths' of a particular people cannot be derived *a priori* as 'pure, general, or necessary'. Instead, he explained, valid laws can only 'be learned historically, from facts': they are 'empirical', and they are 'different depending on time and place'.[2] Hugo, therefore, rejected the 'strict science' of law; he argued that all law 'rests on human statutes',[3] and on the 'spirit of positive law',[4] and that the positive structure of law is subject to distortion wherever it is assessed in rationalized natural-law categories. Legal decisions, he concluded, cannot be founded in any categorically valid or invariable principles: the validity of a law always presupposes that there are other laws to which this law refers and is related, and legal dilemmas can only be resolved (in fact, they can only be posed) where a formal 'legal condition', transmitted through the culture of a particular legal tradition, already exists.[5] Human freedom itself, moreover, cannot be derived from immutable or supra-positive legal principles, but depends on the 'particular constitution' of positive law.[6]

In arguing that legal validity depends on law and that questions pertaining to law are soluble only through reference to other law, Hugo, building on Moser's earlier views, moved between historicist and positivist ideas. In fact, his work contains several dimensions in which historicism and the more historical branch of positivism intersect. His analysis of positive law, for example, concentrates especially on Roman private law, and he saw Roman law as a system of laws facilitating the organization of laws governing property, exchange and contract and providing secure principles of legal autonomy and personality for agents operating in the private economy. In this respect, his work formed one of the major attempts to give a more systematic legal structure to the realm of contractual liberty evolving outside the control of the state in Germany around 1800, and it anticipated later positivist endeavours to clarify legal principles determining legal exchange in the early capitalist private economy. Most importantly, however, he also used analysis of Roman law to elaborate a doctrine of the state and the constitution of the state, and he claimed, anticipating later positivists, that private law provides the legal forms in which the constitutional state evolves and which determine the legal conditions of the state's legitimacy. In this doctrine, he asserted that the state is an analogue to the individual person under private law.[7] Like the individual, the state should be construed as a legal person or a *juridical person,* which is entitled to pursue certain legal purposes, and which possesses certain rights and entitlements, yet which is also bound by certain legal constraints: these constraints are represented by the state's constitution, which mirrors the legal or juridical personality obtained by the person under private law. This conception of the state provided a model that enabled the state to operate as a legal agent in the changing environment of early capitalist modernity, to respond positively yet with some reliability to the legal demands emerging from this environment, and to assert itself within a socio-legal terrain increasingly dominated by privatist principle of contractual autonomy. However, crucial to this idea of legal personality was also the implication that a state endowed with legal personality is not a patrimonial state, and it cannot apply power as a private attribute of a dynasty, but must recognize itself as bound to the legal recognition of other persons. Against the metaphysical strategies of the Kantian Enlightenment, therefore, Hugo argued that the constitutional personality of the state should be construed, in positivist terms, as a *legal or juridical personality,* not, in ethical-universalist terms, as a *moral personality.* The constraints imposed by the constitution on the state should therefore be obtained from the historical form of law, and the ideas of personality are already ingrained in law reflecting the 'healthy reason' embodied in national culture.[8] These constraints cannot reliably be derived from the paradoxical contents of purely rational legislation.

If Hugo's work fell into a region between historicism and positivism, Savigny, the founder of the Historical School of legal science, placed historicist ideas still more firmly in the foreground of theoretical debate, and he especially accentuated the 'organic connection of the law with the essence and character of the people'. He claimed that valid law, or law guaranteeing freedom, is law that proceeds 'from the innermost essence of the nation itself and its history',[9] and he saw in the reception of Roman law in the German states a vital and organic reflection of the traditions and customs of the German people.[10] Consequently, he defined the 'production of law' as a process of natural-historical self-interpretation, in which the 'natural whole' or the integral spirit of the people externalizes its defining characteristics and its specific rationality in the form of law.[11]

On a practical level, Savigny's work focused on the most pressing legal problems of the early nineteenth century, and it formed part of the broad fabric of debate prior to the major political and agrarian reforms in Prussia beginning in 1806, which, under the influence of Napoleonic legislation, saw the gradual implementation of capitalist law in this state. In this respect, Savigny formulated his ideas as a response to the theoretical legacy of post-1789 liberalism, to its demands for political and economic reform, and to the formal principles of legal and economic uniformity which early liberalism employed to advocate reform. On this point, Savigny's work obtained perhaps its greatest prominence as a response to the increasingly widespread demand that the German states should by regulated by a uniform civil code on the model of the Napoleonic *Code Civile,* or even that these states should be subject to a uniform constitution. In this, he resolutely defended the piecemeal form of civil law in the German states, and he saw the function of legal analysis as residing, not in uniform codification of law, but in clarification of individual points of law from historical sources, especially from the sources of Roman law. He thus espoused a course of gradual evolution in the law, rather than a sudden modernization of all legal application. In addition, however, Savigny's gradualist historical approach was also evident in his extensive writings on questions relating to the legal regulation of freely held property, to the guaranteeing of contract, to the dissolution of class barriers in the reformist era, and to the emancipation of the tenured peasants, which was accomplished in the German states, in various steps, after 1807. Addressing these questions in his deeply influential work *The Right of Possession* (first published in 1803), he sought to provide a theoretical foundation for examining the relations of ownership in the capitalist economy emerging through the demise of feudalism and through the resultant termination of jointly or commonly held properties and tenures. He employed principles of Roman law to assert that the human will is the source of legal order, that legal order evolves as it reflects the purposes of the human will, and that legally valid ownership is constituted by the exercise of the will over an object.[12] He therefore concluded that the right to free ownership is deducible from the human will itself, and that the subjective will of the person claiming property – the *animus possendi* – is sufficient to justify ownership.[13] Ownership, consequently, is not attached to moral considerations; it is a positive legal fact, sanctioned through existing proprietorial relations, which are shaped by effective human wills. He restricted this claim by acknowledging that the will exercising ownership must be constantly demonstrated, so that where the owned object is neglected or not put to use its ownership can become void.[14] However, central to his analysis at this point was the view that the human being invariably exists as a possessive volitional agent, that property, enshrined by Roman law, is validated by this original positive fact of human personality, and that legal principles of ownership are already ingrained in existing sources of civil law.

Placed against its historical background, this argument contains two important practical implications. First, reflecting on the agrarian reforms and the abolition of serfdom in the early 1800s, Savigny claimed that the changes in social relationships and relative status caused by the dissolution of feudal tenures need not necessarily result in a full transformation of the social order, and they need not mean that property owned by the aristocracy under feudal tenure must be renounced. On the contrary, he suggested, Roman law provides a device to clarify principles of possession and to allow socio-economic changes to be integrated at a legal and political level without any fundamental destabilization. The application of Roman law to these questions in fact shows that the aristocracy did not have to forfeit property obtained under feudal law simply because it had been acquired under a legal order whose foundations were now being dissolved. On the contrary, Savigny saw possession as justified wherever the will to own things is sustained and exercised by particular people. Second, however, this analysis also implied that the rights of ownership acquired through feudal tenures were only tenable if these were constantly restated and their use-value constantly reasserted; ownership could, in sum, be invalidated by desuetude. Underlying this view on agrarian reform was, at one level, a desire to avoid anti-aristocratic revolutionary upheavals and to justify the security of the aristocracy as an independent class. Yet, at a secondary level, Savigny also wished to see the evolution of a legal system allowing for capitalist principles of exchange, contractual autonomy and for the possible organic transformation of classes. He hoped to show that the aristocracy should utilize the pending reforms to transform itself into a high bourgeoisie and so gradually to evolve into a new elite order, with its status based, not on tenured lands, but on the active usage of inherited property, formerly held under seigneurial law. Savigny was, therefore, a spokesperson for a slow capitalization of the German economy, for the resolute avoidance of the immediate abolition of the aristocracy, yet also for a cautiously progressive endorsement of social and economic reform.

In these practical questions, Savigny used historical analysis of law at once to eliminate the radically transformative aspects of the processes of legal and economic reform that marked his historical horizon and to show how different sectors of society could be assimilated to a broadly conciliatory and cautiously progressive course. He saw the evolution of capitalism, and the resultant alteration of inherited social structures and legal principles, as an inevitability, which, with certain reservations, should be welcomed. However, he also wished, in large measure at least, to preserve the existing order of society and to integrate into this state the newly evolving modes of social independence without unduly jeopardizing the position of established social and political elites. Underlying Savigny's thinking was the intimation that where it is permitted to articulate its legal functions in purely formal-contractual or uniform modes of obligation, capitalism is a corrosive and disaggregating force. The implementation of capitalist law in the form of universal codes, for Savigny, is born of a metaphysical spirit, which disregards social formation, seeks to level all historical forms to a standard shape, and consequently brings great disorder and unhappiness. Codified capitalist law is thus close to classical natural-law theory, it disruptively distils universal principles of contract, personality and obligation from chimerical or insubstantial legal sources, and it imposes these violently across all cultural and national distinctions. Where capitalist legal preconditions can be integrated into the historical evolution of legal cultures, however, this has liberating, progressive-dynamic, yet unthreatening consequences. At the centre of Savigny's thinking is thus the sense that the laws of modern society must be allowed to form themselves from the existing corpus of law and that, in fact, freedom under law depends on a slow reconciliation of old and new laws.

In relation to this, Savigny's doctrine also taught that law cannot be deduced from categorical ethical imperatives. The normative force of law is shaped by custom and organically formed expectations, and its foundation is sustained and constructed by the historically active human will, especially that of the property-owning person. Valid law, consequently, is the aggregate of legal relations as they exist at any moment in the historical evolution of a society and a people, as they are infused by common volitional impulses, and as they reflect the historical freedom of a people and allow this people to interpret its freedoms as realized in the structure of its historical life. For Savigny, in short, a people encounters itself and its freedoms in its living laws, and the political shape and future of a nation is formed through an interpretation of the existing normative apparatus of the law. Where law is defined through abstract norms of reason, however, the substance and content of freedom in law are corrupted and obscured. The Enlightenment claim that rational law creates conditions of autonomy is illusory, therefore: it merely replicates metaphysical heteronomy in new form. Free law, Savigny asserted, is the objectively experienced and interpreted 'life of people themselves', and such law cannot be distilled from any theoretical postulates or from any principles that formalize the life and freedom of the people in normatively perennial precepts.[15]

In its political-theoretical content, therefore, Savigny's doctrine placed itself against the ideas of state and law widespread in the early liberalism of the Enlightenment. The law, he concluded, is essentially a locus of national or common self-interpretation, not formal legal prescription. The legitimate state, in consequence, is a public order that is formed through common self-interpretation under laws, and freedom in the state, under laws, is an expression of common historical self-interpretation. The legitimacy of the state cannot be derived from the normative and atomistic privatist legal principles characterizing metaphysical liberalism. Political freedom is not freedom normatively or negatively secured against the state, but freedom realized and interpreted in the state. In consequence, whereas early liberal thinkers deduced legitimacy in politics as an inner reflex of the moral personality of the state, Savigny saw legitimacy in the state as the evolutionary result of common and organic, not particular and rational, processes of formation.[16] In this respect, to be sure, Savigny did not oppose all ideas of legal statehood, and he did not see the state as outside or above the law. On the contrary, he saw the state as a legitimate state where it is formed with some kind of constitution or at least embedded in a context of legal agreement: where it expresses the historically interpreted nation as its own legal corpus. The state, he explained, is the historically shaped 'appearance of the people in a particular legal form',[17] and, as such, it represents the 'true personality' of the people who are subject to it.[18] He thus did not relinquish the construction of the state as a person under the law, and his conception of state power still incorporates basic notions (albeit with a strongly conservative inflection) of legal constraint and representation. However, he insisted that the legal body of the state is not reliably accounted for by any abstract principle – either rational-metaphysical or formal-juridical. The true state must be one founded in the life of a national community, self-interpreting in law. It is to this corpus, then, and not to any formal-constitutional circumscription or any set of abstract freedoms, that the state, as a legitimate state, is accountable and obligated. The unity of law and freedom in the legitimate state is always present in the life of the community, and this is overlooked and dismembered by views that see law and freedom in the acts of solitary metaphysical minds.

In addition to its critique of the Enlightenment and ius-naturalism, Savigny's historical methodology was also opposed to some of the theoretical elements that later dominated positivist constitutional thinking. He argued that the positivist attempt to construct the constitutional personality of the state from paradigms of private law serves lastly, like the idealism of the Enlightenment itself, to impose a thin idea of legal order on the state, and it fails to account for the substantial content of the state. Rather than following the private-legal path towards a deduction of the state's constitutional form, therefore, he argued that private law is subordinate to the state, and it cannot be legally formative of the state's power or the state's constitution. Private law, he asserted, contains the legal relations that address individual people. State law or public law, however, stands above the purely atomistic or personal interests refracted in private law, and it incorporates and regulates the organic people in its entirety. Such law is the 'physical shape of the spiritual popular community', and it guides this community towards greater, yet peaceful, knowledge of its historical freedoms.[19] The law of state is, therefore, not produced directly out of private-legal agreements or compacts,[20] and the state cannot be reduced to an organ translating private-legal ideas of personhood into public-legal form: the state has a substantial historical content, generated from the manifold customs and the legal inscriptions of a unique historical people.

Underlying the works of the early legal historicists, in conclusion, is an endeavour to account for the power of the state as organically founded in the customary laws of the people, and so to propose alternatives to the ius-natural and formally privatist accounts of law's validity underpinning early liberalism. At the heart of early legal historicism was the sense that political thinking dominated by ius-naturalism and universal contractualism is not able adequately to comprehend human freedom, or the place of human freedom in a political order, and it only fictitiously secures conditions of rational freedom under law. Indeed, for the historicists the claim of ius-naturalists that they propose reliable foundations for positive legal validity is fallacious. Ius-natural thinking destroys the self-interpreting freedoms of independent communities by seeking to impose like laws across all cultural and historical boundaries, and it undermines the political orders of free communities by questioning their legitimacy in light of universally distilled normative principles. Indeed, the early historicists saw the French Revolution as a corroboration of this view: they saw the revolution as the malign triumph of natural law, or even as the triumph of rationalized metaphysics, over more gradually unfolding experiences of legal freedom. Legal historicism consequently subscribed to a conception of *historical freedom* against *enlightened autonomy,* and it hoped to disclose the constitutively human sources of legitimate statehood in the organically and traditionally connected collective, not in the self-legislating moral/metaphysical person. The Enlightenment accounted for the legitimacy of the state as a moral personality, distilled from the obligation of the state to certain perennial norms and then written into a constitution of freedom. Historicism, however, argued that the legitimacy of the state is tied to the historical unity of its constituents, and it can only provide freedom under law through reference to the historical shape of this freedom and to the formative bed of national traditions. The antinomy between law and power that the theories of legitimacy in the Enlightenment sought to resolve is in fact, for Savigny at least, an antinomy which does not exist. Law and power, he indicated, are always factually united in the common ground of the historical tradition, and the question of power's legitimacy is simply theory's own question: it is a metaphysical query that need not be raised except where theoreticians need theories.

Historicism, liberalism and the freedom from law

In the first stage of their evolution after Herder, historicist ideas often fused with more common idealist arguments, and they were frequently aligned to more clearly or early liberal idealist political doctrines. For example, the works of Wilhelm von Humboldt combine elements of historicism with aspects of idealism, and they formed an important reconfiguration of liberal humanist doctrine. In certain respects, Humboldt's educational humanism is often close to more idealist perspectives. He argued, for instance, that human education involves the formation of ideas, which cannot be reduced to history, or explained in accordance with any natural or material law.[21] Humanity, although realized in history, is thus a bearer of ideas that only 'unfold' in history or 'obtain reality' in history, but are not of themselves internally historical. All history, in fact, is ultimately the 'fulfilment of an idea'.[22] At the same time, however, he also observed critically that the idealist separation of the human being from its historical context fails to provide a substantial analysis of human self-realization and personality, and that, although purporting to be humanists, the pure idealists had ultimately offered only a rather thin and spurious account of humanity and free human character. He therefore emphasized the importance of historical life as a context and condition of human spontaneity, unique self-fulfilment.[23] Humanity, he argued, can only evolve in a historical situation, and human freedom can only be realized in historically localized personalities under distinct objective conditions and life horizons.[24] Humboldt's humanism thus clearly accentuates the necessary interchange between historical life and human accomplishment, and he saw historical creativity as a vital element in the evolution of the 'concept of humanity'.[25]

His position between historicism and idealism means that Humboldt's political ideas contain quite disparate elements. Certain historicist motifs are squarely at the heart of his political thought. For example, he defined the nation as an irreducible historical accretion, and he concluded that all German states were bound together as an inseparable whole; this sense of wholeness resided both in common language and literature, but also in the 'recollection of commonly shared rights and freedoms'.[26] He then employed this analysis to argue against formal constitutional systems, claiming that durable political constitutions are expressions of a particular time, a particular culture and a particular sense of unity and order. Constitutions emanating directly from the era of French Revolution, he claimed especially, were marked by 'poverty and fragility'; that is, they were founded in unstable and abstract ideas of right, with little conception of historical appropriateness.[27] Even in his very early writings on the French Revolution, he rejected the attempt to construct an entirely new state in accordance with 'principles of reason': a nation, he concluded, can never be 'mature enough' for a fully rational constitution, and it can never act entirely in compliance with rational-legal ideals.[28] In his later constitutional works, this critical impulse was intensified, and, before and after the Congress of Vienna, he endorsed the formation of estate-based constitutions as an alternative to pure-republican models of state law. Nonetheless, Humboldt's organic constitutional ideal was still, in its context, a highly progressive proposal; it placed weight on the legislative influence of the estates and the subjective rights of citizens and it affirmed the ideals of legal universality and procedural compliance characterizing more standard liberal systems.[29] Like other theorists in his environments, therefore, Humboldt used historicist ideas to correct and transform liberal principles and objectives, but he nonetheless remained genuinely committed to a modified form of early liberal politics.

As historicism was gradually delineated as a distinct body of thought, however, it began to intensify its earlier aversion to ius-naturalism and liberal constitutionalism, and it began to formulate its objectives through a much more critical reconstruction of the methods of idealism and early liberalism. This is evident in the few direct political pronouncements made by the great historian of nineteenth-century Germany, Leopold von Ranke. Ranke argued that political reflection should concentrate on practically viable objectives, and it should limit the importance of ideas that have not grown organically from a particular historical situation. Metaphysical ideas of right, he claimed, are likely to 'prove delusory' and to provoke tumult.[30] Metaphysics ignores the 'supreme need' of political communities, the maintenance of 'security, of right and law', which is only feasible where the historical shape and traditions of society are acknowledged.[31] Ranke thus took up a position against democratic governance, which, he suggested, seeks the violent overthrow of the past. However, he also opposed pure aristocratic governance, which clings unnecessarily to the past. He claimed instead that a 'regular development' of the political order, based in the knowledge that the 'present requires the past and the future' was most likely to ensure conditions of liberty for the most people.[32]

Responding to the everyday questions of the early nineteenth century, Ranke recognized the need for some kind of procedural-constitutional order in the state and for a rational mediation between the increasing demand for private autonomy and the public order of the state.[33] However, like Savigny, he was unwilling to take principles of private law as a model for constructing the legal personality of public power. He dismissed all contractual attempts to provide a constitutional foundation for the exercise of state power,[34] and he described the state instead as the articulated historical personality of the 'original life' of a national community.[35] A progressive state offering conditions of freedom, therefore, would be based in historical unity and in the 'homogeneity of national existence',[36] and this homogeneity, more than any constitutional guarantee of private independence under constitutional government, would act as the condition of freedom in the state. These conceptions also reflect an attitude of anti-rationalism in Ranke's work, as he claimed that human reason alone cannot deduce the foundations of law and state, independently of all historical circumstance. Human rational consciousness, Ranke argued, is itself historically formed and pre-formed, and it cannot assume normative or prescriptive dignity against the manifest facts and traditions of historical life. Each 'people has its own politics', he explained, and the imposition of ideal orders irrespective of the organic contents of particular nations invariably stimulates disorder.[37] When ideas are crudely imposed on the finely meshed fabric of historical life, the 'realm of ideas' becomes a 'location of struggle', and this metaphysical disorder is always likely to become a real disorder in human society and in human politics.[38] Ranke thus urged for an anti-theoretical and entirely non-metaphysical definition of law and state, in which the conditions of legitimate rule are allowed to evolve historically, free of universal prescription. The terror of the French Revolution, most obviously, stood as a stark reminder of the metaphysical strife that can occur when people are 'chained to ideas', and when 'rational' constructions prescribe the coercive form of 'legality'.[39]

Although anti-liberal, Ranke's thought remained resonant through subsequent, more avowedly reformist and pro-constitutional movements. Johann Gustav Droysen, the great liberal historian and liberal delegate in the Frankfurt Parliament of 1848–49, also claimed that each nation contains distinct ideas of freedom, and that these ideas are brought to crisis by universalistic legal tendencies. The political culture of Germany, he argued, was marked by an idea of freedom under law that was incompatible with formal or privatist constitutionalism,[40] and which defined the state as an integrating and evolving whole, capable of incorporating principles of 'bourgeois freedom' without dismantling the traditional edifice of statehood.[41] Droysen, despite his liberal affiliation, remained hostile to all conceptions of political obligation that tie the state to a 'contract', that offer 'the people guarantees against the state and the ruler of the state', or that see the constitution as a contractually mediated expression of 'organized distrust' towards the state.[42] Like Ranke, therefore, Droysen saw the constitution of state as a token of the state's integrative self-organization on the foundation of national unity, not as a rationally stabilized check on its operations. The state, he implied, is the integrated form of the non-metaphysical community under own laws.

The attempt to free national politics from false law that informed Ranke's conservative reformism and Droysen's more committed national liberalism ultimately found its apotheosis in the national liberalism of Heinrich von Treitschke, the most influential nationalist historian of the Bismarck era. Indeed, Treitschke's works underline the increasingly nationalistic transformation of historicist ideas and ideals throughout the nineteenth century, and they demonstrate how historicism progressively reconceived liberal values and ideas, in order to define liberty under law, not as a condition of formal right, but as an experience of nationally integrative principles.

Like earlier historicists, Treitschke shared many ambitions of liberalism. He supported the relative liberalization of economy and society in Germany, and he endorsed the establishment of a socio-political order in which the freedoms of capitalism might be guaranteed without excessive reform of the traditional national-political apparatus of state. Like more orthodox liberals, therefore, he argued for freedom of belief and worship and for freedom of economic activity, and he demanded a restriction of 'state interference' in the economy and the guarantee of 'freedom of labour' without state control.[43] Like other historicists, however, he was also hostile to pure democratic government; he rejected classical constitutional principles;[44] and he opposed formal-liberal or negative ideas of the legal state.[45] As an alternative to such ideas, he argued that the state is the concrete expression of the people in its independence and freedom, and that the state cements conditions under which citizens might exercise their freedoms. The state, therefore, is the basis of national freedom, and its constitution cannot contain laws that restrict or undermine this freedom. The legitimate state, accordingly, is neither an 'organism' (in the sense implied by romantic state theory), nor a 'fictitious will' (in the sense implied by positivist state theory):[46] it is the 'total personality' of all those who belong to it as members of the national community,[47] and, as such, it forms the horizon in which personal freedoms can be obtained and enacted.

To obtain legitimacy as the total personality of the nation, Treitschke argued, the state must express an entirely free political will. The will of the legitimate state must be determined only by the internal contents of the nation, and it cannot be obligated to natural or revealed law of any kind. The will of the legitimate state must detach itself from all vestigial metaphysical principles, and it must produce laws solely as expressions of the personality of the nation. The will of the legitimate state, therefore, is a national will, and as a national will it replaces all metaphysical law: the national will assumes absolute power and absolute responsibility for the form and the order of the state, and it contains no principle of order derived from any source outside this will.[48] Underlying this argument is the idea, first, that human freedom is experienced in concrete historical forms, and it is liable to be corrupted by all universal or formal accounts of its preconditions. The national state, therefore, is the concrete form and the primary guarantee of freedom. This claim is tied, second, to the assertion that powerful national states are founded in Protestantism, that only Protestant culture can produce free states and only Protestantism allows states to form themselves as organs of free volition, manifest in free laws. Protestant states, Treitschke argued, have an eminent quality of freedom. These states produce their laws by excluding all external laws, and the foundation for their laws is a constant experience of unity, integration and shared national freedom. The national state, therefore, is the arena in which the resources of historical formation and liberty, first unbridled by Protestantism, have their most pointed expression and defining self-interpretation, and the supreme form of human liberty is the united Protestant nation. All attempts to underscore politics with formal principles – either internally, through Roman Catholic or liberal ius-naturalism, or externally, through universal international law – can only lead to the destruction of 'this world of freedom'.[49] For Treitschke, in short, the nation is the integrated body of the people under its own laws, and the freedom of the nation ends wherever it is subject to laws that are not its own. If liberalism is to engender an authentic experience of freedom, self-determination and self-realization, therefore, liberalism must be a *national liberalism,* and liberal law must be law that expresses the concrete liberty of the nation.

Political romanticism

Political historicism was thus, in most of its expressions, an attempt to explain the politics of the national state as the supreme locus of human freedom and shared self-realization, and so to liberate the state and human freedom from all formally imposed laws – that is, from law founded in metaphysics. The most important historicist theorists all endeavoured to provide an account of the community under its own laws, in which the entire body of the nation, not distracted by privatist or normative elements, acts as the originating person of the law. As mentioned above, in the early stages of its evolution, historicism was closely related to romanticism, and the main exponents of political romanticism also articulated arguments found in common historicist perspectives. Like historicism, romanticism had its source in a critical response to the Enlightenment and the French Revolution. Like historicism, romanticism sought to revoke the rationalized ius-naturalism and formal constitutionalism supporting the Enlightenment, and it sought to elucidate the vital, integrating and cultural-experiential origins of law and state. Moreover, romantics, like historicists, argued that social transformation should take place organically and gradually, and that human historical existence, if not regulated by abstractly formalized ideas, tends to shape itself into legal customs and conventions likely, on their own, to reflect and guarantee deep-rooted freedoms.

In one key respect, however, romanticism was markedly different from historicism. Many, although not all, romantics were either Roman Catholics or had a measured sympathy for Roman Catholic political ideas; in many cases they looked with nostalgia at the institutional order of Europe and the *ancien régime* before 1789, or even before the Reformation, and they generally invoked religious universalism, not national freedom, as the most potent corrective to the Enlightenment. Most historicists, in contrast, saw German history as a specifically evolved expression of Protestantism; they saw national freedom as the secular corollary of Protestantism; and they saw the atrophy of historical freedom under natural laws or the laws of the

Enlightenment as originally caused by the legal metaphysics of Roman Catholicism. Indeed, many historicists tended to see the Enlightenment and liberalism as newly reconstituted derivates of Roman Catholic legalism and theocracy. Ranke, for instance, described the Jesuit movement as the forerunner of the liberal and radical ideals of popular sovereignty that he opposed.[50] Droysen, although for quite different reasons, saw the Reformation as a moment of national-historical consolidation, in which the 'waking call of Evangelical freedom' rang out from 'the middle of the German people'.[51] Treitschke denounced all natural-legal conceptions as 'entirely unhistorical',[52] and he described the Lutheran Reformation as a movement that freed political life from ius-naturalism and theocratism, so facilitating the ultimate 'unity of the German state'.[53] Treitschke also detected in Roman Catholicism an antecedent of formal liberalism, or even of socialism, and he saw Catholicism as a creed that compresses all social life into a 'firmly ordered unity' dominated by fixed 'moral laws', so that all national freedom is suppressed.[54] Historicism thus fervently rejected the burdening of the state with externally deduced religious law; it construed cultural-religious freedom as a precondition of the strong and independent polity; and it saw Protestantism as distinguished precisely by the fact that it produces laws that are positive and free. Historicism, in consequence, at its deepest level, contained a secularist or even positivist set of outlooks, which accepted religious culture as a precondition of national cohesion but which negated all aspects of religion threatening to split the legally united body of the nation. Despite its similarities with romanticism, therefore, historicism divorced itself from romanticism on central philosophical points, and it specifically argued that the national state is the source of freedom under law, and that the law is legitimized by the extent to which it consolidates national freedom.

Although romanticism did not appear as a fully distinct theoretical orientation until the beginning of the nineteenth century, romantic legal and political ideas had in some respects already become visible in the late eighteenth century, especially in the works of Justus Möser. Möser was first and foremost a supporter of organic monarchy. He argued that the 'happiest constitution' is one that descends in finely graded steps from the throne to the subject and in which each echelon in this hierarchy is accorded and willingly accepts its own distinction and honour.[55] He saw the ancient constitutions of the German cities, based in guilds and corporations, as the ideal socio-political order, and he condemned both the 'territorial supremacy' of absolutist governance and the uniform laws and 'common-law books' of the Enlightenment as related results of corrupted and dualistically abstracted models of government. Möser, in fact, saw both pre-Enlightenment absolutism and post-Enlightenment legal uniformity as closely associated – and comparably malign – products of an increasing abandonment of historical legal sources, and of a general move away from customary models of law and state towards ius-natural conceptions of legal and political authority.[56] Opposing all systematic accounts of legal validity, therefore, he argued that societies offering the greatest freedom are those that accept 'richness' and 'manifoldness' in law, which do not bind the law either to princely prerogatives or to theoretically inspired formal codes,[57] and which see laws guaranteeing freedom as the 'result of experience'.[58] The rationalization of law, he claimed, actually has its origin in military culture, and rational law leads directly to despotism: the more rational or 'simple' laws are, the more 'despotic' and 'impoverished' the state will be.[59] Elements of Möser's theory anticipated later, more socially progressive expressions of organic theory; indeed, his assertion that rational-legal uniformity leads to absolutism might easily be seen to anticipate the organic-democratic works of the Germanists of the late nineteenth century. However, Möser also set out certain vehemently reactionary claims. He insisted that rights under law should not be perceived as originating in natural or universal entitlements and that enjoyment of legal protection and privilege must depend upon local belonging and enfranchisement.[60] Moreover, he also argued that the full exercise of legal rights must depend on stakeholding or property ownership. Rights, he concluded, do not accrue to a person simply because they possess a formal quality of 'humanity', but because the person holds a 'share' in the material basis and purpose of a society.[61]

Ideas with some similarities to these then also appeared in the works of the seminal romantic philosopher, Friedrich von Schlegel. In his political publications, at least those of his later period, Schlegel expressed a highly critical attitude towards the legal principles of the Enlightenment, and he attempted to imagine conditions of political order not derived from formal law. In his first writings, this critique took a politically radical form, as he lamented the historical and experiential deficiency in Kantian politics, and he argued that only a more Fichtean 'universal republicanism' could secure genuine freedom.[62] During the era of Napoleonic occupation, however, Schlegel, like most other romantics, turned much more sharply against political rationalism, and he began to demonstrate a nostalgic attitude towards the institutions of pre-Napoleonic Europe. As in the works of Novalis at the same time,[63] this nostalgia focused in part on the Holy Roman Empire. He celebrated the Carolingian origins of the empire as a 'Christian union of all Western countries', in which political life was suffused with religious ideas, and in which, he noted affirmatively, the aristocracy was the 'basic force of the state'.[64] He consequently denounced Napoleon's influence over Europe as the triumph of 'false theory' and 'destructive principles' over the historical, personal, hierarchical and local institutions of old Europe.[65] The tyranny of the rational over the traditional, he concluded, brings about a shallow positivization of law, in which the richly structured foundations of traditional governance is hollowed out by rational argument and reduced 'to factual and crudely material positivity'. Such positivization is especially evident in the historically depleted form of written constitutions, of modern-style liberal legal states, and of modern – that is, Napoleonic – codifications of civil law. Modern constitutions, he concluded, are nothing but a formal 'piece of paper', consisting of 'abstractions' and 'formalities' which have no living relation to the actual life of the state or those governed by the state.[66]

Against rational and ius-natural processes of legal positivization, therefore, Schlegel advocated a path into modern society in which 'relations of state' are allowed to develop in a historically gradual manner. The legal source of the state's legitimacy, he suggested, should be located in 'historically positive' forms, or in local agreements growing out of long historical traditions.[67] The state form likely to reflect such laws is an 'organically ordered and vitally composed monarchy', in which the state, placed between the family and the church, forms the living and integrating centre of society.[68] Under a corporate constitution of this kind, legal relations are likely to evolve organically, historically and, above all, *peacefully.* Indeed, Schlegel specifically claimed that religious corporatism produces peace, whereas liberalism, as a rationalized articulation of metaphysics, attempts to compensate for its loss of God by violently imposing paradoxical terms of order and correctness on anciently constructed historical forms. Like all metaphysics, therefore, liberalism, although purporting to provide for peace and justice, is always latently violent, and it is inclined to produce volatile and unstable political forms.

The political writings of Adam Müller also exemplify the main tendencies in romantic political thought. As a converted Roman Catholic, Müller lamented the loss of the 'unity of church and state' in modern society, and he saw the secularization of political institutions and laws as a source of deep malaise in modern politics.[69] Consequently, he rejected the constitutional ideas of the Enlightenment, arguing that constitutionalists fail to understand the historically formed character of the law, and they erode the substance of the law by expecting it to be pure, mechanical and compliant with abstractly normative concepts.[70] He also opposed the proto-democratic impulses expressed in the constitutional movement in the era of reform after 1806, and he urged a return to organic or estate-based governance, in which organs of popular deputation can only assume 'subordinate importance'.[71] Likewise, he denounced contractarian and formal-constitutional concepts of political obligation, claiming that the social contract, as a distillation of interests enshrined in *private law,* is unable to found an authentically representative, integrative or *political* state.[72]

Müller thus construed the emergence of private law as a political force as an element of acute degeneration and secularization in modern politics, and he saw standard liberal ideas of property as corrosive components in the harmonious body politic. Property, he argued, is indeed necessary and inviolable in any state; however, the liberal assumption that property pre-exists the state or that ownership is justified by abstract entitlements attaching to particular persons misunderstands the relation between property and the state. Property is inviolable, he stated, because it is sanctioned as such by the state, and it is only where the subject claiming ownership of property is a member of the state that this subject can legitimately bind property to him or herself. The precondition of all law, consequently, is the state, and legal principles that attempt to vindicate rights and entitlements as principles of subjective and private-subjective law always contribute to an erosion of the very institutions on which such entitlements are founded. Even in 'the middle of civil life', Müller explained, the human being is 'interwoven with the state on all sides'.[73] Those who wish to protect civil freedoms should, therefore, not detach these from the state or define them in opposition to the state. Rather, they should seek to reinforce the state and to reinforce the classes that uphold the power of the state; that is, the aristocracy – the 'only necessary institution of state law in the state' – and the 'ruling, sovereign person' of the monarch.[74]

At the centre of this organic vision is an account of the state as an endlessly evolving order, which can only be impoverished by attempts to render it accountable to static constitutional forms, to principles of natural law, or to private rights.[75] The mobility and dynamism of the political order, Müller emphasized, has its origins in the ongoing *conflict* between different constituent organs and different members of the state. The 'conflict of freedom with freedom', he claimed, is the foundation of a vital political life, and it is only through conflict that the integrity and strength of the political order reproduces itself and can be maintained.[76] Embedded in liberal political thinking, however, is the cardinal error that it assumes that the natural condition of politics is 'absolute peace', and that all society can be ruled by laws and rights deduced from an imaginary construct of the person as an agent invariably seeking peace. In making this assumption, liberalism enchains political order to false laws, and it weakens the creative elements in the process of political formation.[77] For Müller, there can be no 'private right of the human being' that can be extracted from the process of social conflict; all rights and entitlements are generated out of conflict and momentary balance, and they represent moments in the organic/conflictual evolution of society.[78] As the supreme organ in this society, the state represents the 'totality of human affairs', and it presides over and unifies all disparate and antagonistic elements of society as a 'living whole',[79] or as an 'eternally living idea'.[80] Legal ideas, especially those of liberalism, which assume that laws of state can be enunciated in absolute and permanent categories, impose false criteria on the state, and they deprive the state of its spontaneous ability to integrate and articulate meaningful ideas of freedom.

At much the same time, Franz von Baader also sought to counteract liberalism with an explicitly Roman Catholic theory of social and political formation. Rather than fully rejecting the liberal ideal of a state based in law, Baader argued that the mistake of liberalism is that it seeks to derive laws from individualist or rationalist principles, whereas laws of an authentic legal state should be derived from the common experiences of all humanity – especially from the bonds of love and affection that bind human beings together in so far as they are devoted to God.[81] Love, he concluded, is the sole ground of authentic law and legal statehood. Love, Baader stressed, does not demand formal equality or shared entitlement as the basis of right, and states that assume that they become legitimate through their simple compliance with laws of equality and prescribed entitlement fail to understand the complex nature of the affective bonds shaping the laws. On the contrary, states founded in love are likely to take the form of an 'organic hierarchy', based in 'authority and subordination',[82] and ordered in estates, corporations and guilds.[83] However, he also asserted that true authority is not exercised as the attribute of personal, patrimonial or absolute power; rather, the legitimate exercise of power is always limited by the legal constraints which are derived from the organic bonds of love that bind the community. As a theology of love, therefore, Christianity provides the foundation for a harmonious and organically substantial legal state, which is centred in the 'principle of civil freedom'.[84] Christian political ideas, consequently, culminate in a peaceful constitutional order that does not 'violently overthrow' existing social and political relations, but expresses 'mediation and balance' between its members.[85] A genuine legal state, Baader thus concluded, is close to 'true theocracy'.[86]

The most encompassing formulation of the concerns of political romanticism is found in the works of Schelling, or at least in the works of the middle and the later periods of his trajectory, after he had, to a large extent at least, abandoned the post-Kantian idealist tradition that shaped his early thought. As he first moved away from Kantian ideas, his work retained some elements of idealist philosophy, albeit now heavily coloured by romantic impulses, and it continued to uphold the post-Kantian claim that state and law are areas in which people seek self-realization and perfection. In his first steps towards romanticism, therefore, he opted, first, for an organic variant on Kantian ideas, and he explained that a state possesses legitimacy if it allows each 'particular member' to act as a 'purpose in itself', with fully recognized dignity and moral freedom.[87] States whose constituents are recognized as purposes in themselves, he explained, generate organic freedom and cohesion throughout all society, and their laws are justified and accepted as expressions of both universal norms and individual freedoms. At this point, Schelling defined the legitimate state as an organic unity of pure purposes. Indeed, like Kant, he argued that the legitimate state is one which is 'formed after the original image of the world of ideas' and which allows each person to exist in ideal liberty and dignity.[88]

As he distanced himself further from Kantian idealism, however, Schelling's philosophy also began to reflect the influence of more common romantic ideas. At this time, he rejected liberal principles of atomism and formal rationality, and he showed an increasing tendency to subordinate law and politics to religious concerns. He thus gradually renounced his earlier belief that members of states can determine the conditions under which states are justified, that states can adequately guarantee conditions of human freedom, and even that the state is intended to serve specifically human interests. Instead, he argued that the ideal order of politics is a condition of organic integrity or identity in which the unity of the people is sustained by *absolute ideas*: that is, where people are united by the highest ideas of their cultural and metaphysical purpose, and where the laws of state represent these external purposes. The absolute ideas reflected in the state in the integral polity, thus, are not ideas obtained in Kantian style as principles of rationally deduced necessity; rather, they are the metaphysical ends of the polity, and they are originally derived from God. These ideas are preserved and represented through cultural traditions and the high artistic endeavour of the most dignified representatives of these traditions, and they serve to unite all members of the polity as a vital and inspired whole. Modern societies, Schelling claimed, which are ordered around a materialized and atomistic 'civil society',[89] and which are dominated by the tendency to found political ideas and institutions in conceptions of the 'merely useful', dissolve the unifying metaphysical ideas of the polity.[90] Most particularly, the individualistic separation of 'private life and private law' from public existence has a deeply corrosive effect on the ideal life of the polity. Under the separation of public law and private law, individual life loses its connection with the ideas of the organic whole and it chains itself to the pursuit of 'mechanical' principles that have only limited and particular value.[91] The freedoms which such privatized societies define as their own can never be organic or metaphysically unifying freedoms, and they can never produce metaphysically valid law; in fact, freedom under private law sanctions oppressive and antagonistically utilitarian prerogatives or purposes, and it leads directly to a 'confusion of freedom and slavery'.[92] The reality of modern politics, Schelling thus concluded, is marked by a fragmentation of the organic-metaphysical order of the state, by an absence of unifying ideas, and so by the impossibility of laws that guarantee freedom. The legal ideas of liberalism, in short, derive valid law, at a private level as at a public level, from the 'murky source' of 'self-interest and antagonism'.[93] These ideas are consequently inimical to the 'absolute organism' of the true state.[94]

Throughout Schelling's later trajectory, he also increasingly mourned the demise of religious and metaphysical substance in modern society, and he sought to correct this by developing a philosophy of religious *personalism*. In this, he argued that human history is a process that elaborates a positive disclosure of God's personality, and that elements of God's personality and God's personal will are manifest throughout the stages of human history. 'God's person', Schelling claimed, is the 'general law' of all history. This law organically suffuses and guides all creation, and the positive 'personality of God' is the driving force both of natural process and human action, revealed in the progressively articulated condition of human freedom.[95] Human history, in fact, *is* the freedom of God's personality, and all authentic human freedom has its origin in this source. In their political extension, these personalist ideas led Schelling to conclude, first, that rationalist ideals of government reflect a depleted or thinly paradoxical account of legitimate order, and they fail to recognize that legitimate politics must represent, in human form, a revelation of a divine/personal will, as the precondition of human freedom. Rights and freedoms obtained in the legitimate state are thus not rational or negative freedoms, detached from personality or fixed against the personality of the state. Instead, they are a positive expression of personality, both individual and divine, and they express the contents of freedom in the state as elements of a positive metaphysical will. The personalism of the universe, Schelling concluded, is most aptly reflected in *personal* systems of governance, founded in one authoritative personal will, giving personal representation to political ideals and positively articulating the contents of human freedom in its own will. Second, then, these ideas also led him to argue for a religious founding of the polity: he viewed the retreat of religious mystery from public life as the token of a loss of 'unity' between the ideal-metaphysical and the objective-natural components of human existence.[96] Indeed, he ultimately concluded that the state is an 'exoteric' order, unable legitimately to exist without the 'esoteric' element of religion and liable to lapse into tyranny wherever it forfeits its bond with personal or metaphysical ideas.[97] Only 'metaphysics', he argued, can make 'states organic' and permit 'a group of people to be united in their hearts and minds – that is to become a people'. Metaphysics, therefore, is the necessary foundation of the truly organic and truly free polity. Personalist metaphysics is 'the antithesis' of all atomistic or mechanistic construction of human interest and human law: 'It is an organic way of feeling, thinking and acting', which provides a vital and integrating foundation for the substantial political order.[98] The modern world, Schelling claimed however, is 'the world of mixture': it is a world in which organic ideas coexist with atomistic or individualistic ideas, in which metaphysical ideas are weakened by materialist and utilitarian notions,[99] and in which the positive freedom and formation of the person is impeded. Government under the private-legal and rationalist doctrine of liberalism, consequently, is nothing less than the 'destruction of all metaphysics', and liberalism produces deeply 'unmetaphysical', 'mechanical' and unfree orders of state.[100]

In his later works, therefore, Schelling clearly adopted a conservative political stance, and he opposed the conviction that politics is a distinctly – or even supremely – human place, where constitutively human freedoms are enacted and interpreted through the laws. Politics, he claimed, must be seen as a subordinate element in a transcendent metaphysical order, with no independent claim to dignity or constitutive freedom. In this stage in his evolution, he enthused for monarchical states, in which philosophers and intellectuals of genius assist in public life.[101] In such states, the 'constitution of state', obtained through historical evolution and philosophical counsel, forms an image of 'the realm of ideas', and absolute ideas take concrete form in the absolute person of the monarch.[102] States of this kind, he claimed, have nothing in common with the political reality emerging in nineteenth-century Germany, where 'kings are even ashamed to be kings', where philosophy can 'never be of use', and all metaphysical content is expelled from the state.[103] In parallel to this, in fact, Schelling increasingly devalued the role of the state in the formation and realization of the human being. The state is never an 'absolute unity' through which people reflect their relation to the unconditioned ideas of their existence: often, in fact, it is nothing less than a 'curse resting on humanity'.[104] The realization of the most authentic human ideas must consequently be sought outside politics and law – in 'genuine religion' or in the 'mythology, the poetry and the art of a nation'.[105]

It would be inappropriate to give the impression that all representatives of political romanticism were committed to monarchical conservatism, or that all consistently opposed political reform. The political writings of Joseph Görres, for example, clearly show that the opposite is the case, and that early romantic opinion also accommodated more progressive theoretical ambitions within its wider critique of Enlightenment rationalism. Görres began his theoretical career as a revolutionary enthusiast in the 1790s and he ended it in the reactionary Catholic milieux in Bavaria in the 1840s. Between these points, however, his most important political works revolved around the attempt to combine a Roman Catholic outlook, demanding the integrity of the church as a principle of political order, with a critical approach both to Napoleonic policies and to the processes of reactionary restoration after Napoleon and the Congress of Vienna. In these works, then, he followed romantic ideas in criticizing standard liberal ideas of statehood. Liberalism, he argued, fails to construct reliable or integrative political orders, and it usually creates highly formalized states, with little internal spirit or cohesion. One reason for this, he explained, is that liberal polities eliminate all religious elements from political life and they even seek to subjugate the church beneath a secular apparatus. However, unlike most romantics, he argued that an effectively integrated state would be a state based in a balanced constitution, combining the 'authority' of a stable sovereign government and the 'freedom' of the people, channelled through the institutions of state and public opinion.[106] He also passionately lamented the failure of the proto-constitutional reforms in the German states in the Napoleonic era, and he advocated the establishment of a relatively advanced constitutional order with a strong chamber of elected delegates.[107]

Despite such cases, however, underlying the characteristic views of romanticism is a lament that the formal law of the Enlightenment has eroded the unity of law and substance in the world and a tendency to see organic monarchy as the solution to this loss. Far from securing reliable conditions of peace and legitimacy, therefore, both historicists and romantics were joined in claiming that the Enlightenment has allowed the terms of freedom to be dictated by fatally abstracted and paradoxical constructs of the human person. Indeed, at the centre of historicism and romanticism was the belief that the liberal politics of the Enlightenment have robbed human society of the grounds of its freedom and have ensnared humanity in a formalized and rationally self-generated set of metaphysical laws and ideas. Both historicism and romanticism, consequently, sought to explain laws supporting political freedom as embedded contents of a personal will, not as negative elements against this will, and they imagined the unity of law and power underlying the legitimacy of state as a reflection of the presence of a positive will in the laws and customs of thc community. Whilst seeking to engender a unity of law and power in the state, therefore, the Enlightenment, for both historicists and romantics, destroyed the given form of this unity, and rendered it paradoxical and violent. Nonetheless, although historicism and romanticism converged in many points, they diverged quite fundamentally on the question of metaphysics. At the heart of historicism is an intensified critique of metaphysics in politics, which denounces Enlightenment ideas as too metaphysical. Historicism thus sought to separate the volitional body of the nation from metaphysical law and to allow the nation to form itself as the community of freedom, as a will under its own laws. Romanticism, in contrast, opposed the Enlightenment for other motives, and it expressed nostalgia for the metaphysical polity and for political order representing transcendent forces and ideas. On these grounds, in fact, although both romanticism and historicism were closely configured responses to the Enlightenment, they ultimately viewed each other as reflecting new articulations of liberal ideas, and so as unable to propose persuasive alternatives to the rationalism of the Enlightenment. Implicit in romanticism is the claim that pure historicism is a corruptly secularizing body of work, which is often indistinguishable from liberal or republican theories. At the same time, implicit in historicism is the sense that romanticism is an endeavour to reconstitute the metaphysical universalism of Christian natural law, and so to revitalize the theocratic intellectual sources of both liberalism and the Enlightenment. The historicists were clearly sympathetic to religion and religious culture: indeed, they viewed German culture as God's own cultural nation, and the German nation as the place of God's freedom. However, they refused to see religion as an ideal world outside national culture, and they saw the nation as the human form of religious freedom. The romantics, likewise, saw culture and politics as the place of God's freedom. However, they saw this freedom as a personal freedom, not as a rational freedom, in the sense proposed by Hegel, nor as a collective freedom, in the historicist sense. They, therefore, stressed the relative independence of God against the contents of human freedom, and they saw freedom and culture not suffused with God's personal will as fallen culture. The main reason for this was that, in most cases, the romantics were deeply marked by the influence of Roman Catholicism and were unwilling to dislocate the nation from metaphysical personality as the site of national foundation and interpretation.

Schleiermacher: between historicism and romanticism

Despite these differences, however, historicist and romantic legal and political ideas converge, and find perhaps their most important articulation, in the writings of Friedrich Daniel Ernst Schleiermacher. Like most historicists, Schleiermacher rejected the 'abstraction' of natural law,[108] he refused to accept formal universality in law as a necessary precondition of legitimate order,[109] and his work reflects the wider historicist claim that the state exists prior to and as the precondition of legal application. The 'natural evolution of a state', he argued, produces modes of political freedom and legitimacy that cannot be fully comprehended by contractarian or natural-legal conceptions, and the 'basis of the state' resides, not in formally deduced laws, but in the 'common peculiarity' of the people which it incorporates.[110] Like most romantics, however, Schleiermacher's political vision is rooted in the idea of a vital and richly sentient community bound together, not in law, but in emotional, affective or religiously inspirited unity. It is on this foundation that Schleiermacher developed his 'theology of feeling' (*Gefühlstheologie*). This doctrine defined the true community as a 'pious community', whose members are linked to one another by outwardly realized feelings of piety. The 'positive laws' of this community are not formed by prior norms, but they express in practical form the inner 'pious feeling' or the 'feeling of dependence', which animates the soul of all members of the community.[111] In defining feeling as the foundation and manifestation of faith, Schleiermacher enunciated an intense critique of all metaphysical religious ideas and so relegated rational deduction or theological speculation to a position of religious irrelevance. In addition, however, in defining feeling as the uniting source of the worldly community, he also expressed an intense critique of all metaphysical legal and political ideas, and he projected a vision of law and politics founded in the free unity of the inspired community.

Central to Schleiermacher's work is the belief that the most genuine communities need no laws and that laws petrify the organic or affective modes of association that bind such communities. These ideas were especially formative in his writings on religion, and especially in those concerning the church constitution and the union of the Lutheran and Calvinist churches in Prussia, which began in 1817, and which Schleiermacher strongly encouraged. Reflecting on these questions, he argued that the 'highest ideal of the Evangelical church' is that a condition might be instituted in which 'everything would run on its own without any law'.[112] He consequently proposed for the united Prussian church a constitution based on a Presbyterian model, opposing all hierarchical methods of dogmatic prescription and seeking to reduce the legal or administrative aspect of the church. Under such a constitution, he explained, priests would be 'elected by the commune', laypeople would 'take part in legislative and consultative assemblies',[113] the church would be largely independent of the state,[114] and the community would be founded directly in 'freedom of scriptural interpretation'.[115] The truly religious community, Schleiermacher concluded, is formed and united by the hermeneutical and interpretive activity of religious observance, and all constitutional or legal forms that obstruct this are detrimental to the life of the community. The true church, he claimed, is not bound by 'law of majesty and sovereignty',[116] and it can never exist as a 'petrifying institute',[117] or as a 'fixed letter' with powers of 'sanction'.[118] The clear advantage of Protestantism over Roman Catholicism, therefore, resides in its 'minimization of the church constitution', and, more generally, in its minimization of all statutory or mandatory forms of law.[119] The true church can only exist as a pneumatically inspired and internally unified community of believers and interpreters. Whereas it is constitutive of the Catholic church that 'it has the law' and that it knows God through the law,[120] it is constitutive of Protestantism that it views community with God as a 'mobile whole', which is 'able to progress and develop' through 'more correct understanding and more perfect appropriation of what is instituted in Christ'. Protestantism consequently has an inner knowledge of God which cannot be fixed in law, but which endlessly inspirits and unifies the community and endlessly shapes itself in the life of the community.[121] For this reason, Schleiermacher lamented the fact that the Reformation had not led to the formation of a fully independent church and still placed religious observance under temporal or political control.[122] Indeed, he implicitly saw his own theology of feeling as a conclusion of the work begun in the Reformation and as a final liberation of the church from legal codification, political captivity or metaphysical doctrine.

Schleiermacher did not view the religious community as an immediately transferable model for the political community. He explained that the civil community, unlike the religious community, cannot be formed without law and hierarchical organization, for 'civil conditions are based essentially on the contrast between authority and subject'.[123] There is, consequently, always a certain tension between religious life and the state, and the state cannot be viewed as an immediate organic 'product of Christian life'.[124] However, his religious ideals are, at the very least, a potent influence on his political thought, and they coloured the central impulses in his wider political outlooks. For example, he accentuated the significant 'analogy' between the church organization and 'civil conditions',[125] and, at one juncture, he claimed that the democratic religious assemblies envisaged in his draft for a Presbyterian constitution might also provide 'examples' for 'civil assemblies'.[126] In more general terms, then, as he defined the church, not as a formal legal institute, but as the people united in faith and piety, he also saw political communities as formed by a 'feeling' of 'popular unity' and historical cohesion;[127] he defined the state as the 'form of the people'; and he saw the laws and obligations of the legitimate state as evolving directly from the historically interpreted 'ethics and habits' of the people. He thus claimed that the people always exists as a historical body, before the state and before the law: 'without a people' there is 'no state'.[128] The people is defined by an experience of 'national determinacy',[129] which, prior to all law, binds individuals into their communities and gives organic substance to the state. The existence of a state presupposes the 'consciousness of the unity of the whole' within the historically formed people, and the state obtains its legitimacy as the outer articulation of the spirit of this community.[130] Against more standard liberal arguments, therefore, Schleiermacher claimed, referring to both religion and politics, that the community is the inspiring source of political order, and it is only where the community already possesses an inner cohesiveness that its law can become legitimate.

Schleiermacher elaborated this idea of the spiritually unified community as the basis for a critique both of the ethics and legal ideals of the Kantian Enlightenment. He opposed Kantian moral ideas because, he claimed, they neglect historical and natural experiences, because they view moral contents as entirely rational and, so, dualistically counterposed to the realm of historical and natural experience, and, most especially, because their fixation on formal moral laws distorts and suppresses the spiritual and experienced origins of ethical life. Opposing Kant's concept of the categorical imperative as the supreme moral regulative, therefore, he argued that transcendentally universalized precepts, which are not embedded in natural or historical reality or historical experiences, have only spurious and reductive claim to legal validity.[131] Against Kant, he claimed that moral subjectivity and moral personality are not ahistorically determined, and they do not act as the rationally prior preconditions of a moral community. Instead, moral subjectivity and moral personality are only formed through the 'appropriation' by persons of moral contents already incorporated in the existing community, and the moral persons of both subjects and states which are constituted by these moral contents are the active interpreters of historically inspirited laws: they are not merely formal agents shaped by prior invisibly deduced legal norms.[132] The moral imperative founding valid law is therefore founded not in abstract subjectivity, but in the processes of ethical and, importantly, *linguistic* integration and interpretation which constitute communal life. Law obtains binding validity not because of its rational/universal content, but because it expresses the ethical substance of the formed and inspired community. True ethical life is only possible, consequently, where the person enters a community and where it interpretively internalizes and participates in the realized life of this community.[133] Underlying these ethics, therefore, is a *political hermeneutics,* which sees ethical recognition and law-production as elements in the self-interpretation of the community.

To draw these points together, therefore, in Schleiermacher's practical-political work, the idea of free interpretation in Protestantism – that is, the claim that the spiritual contents of human life are not enshrined in perennial laws and dogma, but are interpretively and locally disclosed – gives rise both to an ideal of religious life based in free interpretation and in inner and outward piety, and to an ideal of political life based in free commonality and national/historical unity. In both religion and politics, therefore,

Schleiermacher's work revolves around a critique of metaphysics: he imagined pious life and national life as conditions that are not dependent on categorical doctrine or overarching metaphysical principles. He thus saw the community, in faith as in politics, as a *hermeneutical* – not *metaphysical* – community, and this hermeneutical community replaces the metaphysical or legal basis imputed to the community in Roman Catholicism and in doctrines related to Roman Catholicism. The Protestant community, Schleiermacher concluded, is bound neither by doctrinal nor by hierarchical laws, but by language. The 'highest interest' of human being, he stated, is always formed and interpreted 'through language', and communication is the primary medium for the external formation of ethical and spiritual life.[134] Indeed, Schleiermacher's idea of the Protestant community (both religious and political) culminates in the argument that free religion creates societies that have refined experiences of public life (*Öffentlichkeit*). True Christianity, he explained, is always 'reliant on communication through speech', and Reformation theology, centred in free common exegesis, has its political corollary in public life and public exchange, in which the contents of piety become discursively manifest. The legitimate 'formation of state', consequently, always has a constitutively linguistic element, and free states are always those that give maximum latitude to communication.[135] Only Roman Catholics seek 'to restrict the freedom of religious communication' by proposing unalterable dogmatic forms for faith, and they are, consequently, unable to form free states.[136]

Schleiermacher's work stands alongside Hegel's philosophy as a most strenuous endeavour to transform early liberal thinking into a non-metaphysical account of the political community. To be sure, Schleiermacher was no democrat. He argued that the contrast between 'government and subject' is the 'essential scheme of the state' and the basic determinant of politics.[137] He claimed that only monarchical government is able to rule large states and societies,[138] and he described the fully constituted form of the state as a 'national monarchy'.[139] However, he also supported many views held by early liberal thinkers, and he conceived his communitarian ethics as an attempt, not to abandon, but to redeem, on new foundations, the original ideas of freedom in liberalism. In consequence, he was clearly hostile to all patrimonial, privatist or absolutist conceptions of the state; states affected or dominated by pure 'private interest' are, he stated, unable to produce stability, and they are likely to be undone by revolution.[140] More importantly, he viewed 'the most perfect state' as one that permits the 'unfettered enjoyment of freedom',[141] which respects the social rights of citizens and avoids 'despised' intervention in their private lives and private economic activities,[142] which maintains universal law and legal protection for all,[143] and which also guarantees the material subsistence of all its citizens.[144] Although opposed to contractarian and formal-normative accounts of legitimacy, therefore, Schleiermacher argued that law is the central element of the state; he claimed that 'law conditions the state'; and he argued that a separation of powers in the state is required to ensure that independent legislators retain control over the state executive. Indeed, although claiming that politics is founded in the distinction between those who govern and those who are governed, he argued that those who are governed are always implicated in legislation;[145] the governed are entitled to communicate opposition when 'law is bad' and to provide impulses for the establishment of 'better law'.[146] The people, in fact, are the generic origin of law, and their legal interests are constitutive of the terms of for just rule.[147] In apparent paradox, therefore, Schleiermacher depreciated the role of formal law in politics (as in religion), yet he nonetheless proposed a doctrine of the constitutional state or *Rechtsstaat,* intent on determining the limits of political power and on accentuating the constitutive role of public discourse. The 'state is', he thus concluded, 'where law is'.[148]

Like other historicists and romantics, Schleiermacher suggested that the formal-metaphysical and rationalist elements in the legal states of the Enlightenment create false laws that have no source in their communities and fail to establish conditions of meaningful freedom. Rational autonomy is thus not a source of free laws, but of new heteronomy. However, he used communitarian and organic paradigms to develop an alternative theory of the legal state and of the free community under laws. The true state, he argued, is always a state under law and under a constitution. Yet the state does not assume a constitution through formal decree or formal imposition; rather, the legitimate state has an interpretive constitution whose laws are not 'formal' and invariable, but substantial, 'material', and endlessly alterable through the changing self-interpretation of the united people.[149] In Schleiermacher's work, consequently, the historicist vision of the community as before the law converges with the early-liberal demand for accountability, participation and legal universality as the cornerstones of the modern state. Together, these views articulate an idea of the legal state in which the internally integrated community is substantially and positively present, not negatively or rationally reflected, in the laws of state. In this theory, the liberal ideals of constitutional normativity and inviolability in property ownership are transformed into a doctrine that sees norms of the constitution and rights of property as free expressions of the ethical spirit of the community, not as suspiciously prescribed against the state,[150] and that sees the laws of state as the interpreted freedom of the pious community.

Kant's philosophy, to conclude, marks perhaps the epochal theoretical moment in post-Reformation political reflection. One reason for this is that it strategically corrects original Protestant ideas of the invisible community by adding to these an externally binding account of legal universality and legal statehood. On this ground, Kant's philosophy transforms the exceptional freedoms of Protestantism into a legally ordered system of liberalism. Schleiermacher's work marks an opposed, yet not incomparable, moment in theoretical history in that it seeks to construct a model of necessary legal order from within the dynamic foundation of Evangelical thought; it takes the inspirited community of the *Gemeinde* as a genetic locus of legal-political organization; and it attempts to interpret the *Gemeinde* as the source of a different type of liberalism and a different type of legal order. For Schleiermacher, the community of the *Gemeinde*, where it freely interprets and articulates its inner piety, is always a reliable source of positive laws, producing conditions of freedom in all areas of moral life. These laws, however, are destroyed wherever they are stratified against the *Gemeinde* in the form of perennially rationalized institutes. Against Kant, therefore, Schleiermacher's work is a renewed attempt to imagine a progressive human politics, guaranteeing freedom, participation and legal protection, founded solely in the non-metaphysical community of the Protestant believers, without any metaphysical or formal-legal dependence. Like other historicists, in fact, Schleiermacher saw the antinomy of power and law preoccupying the Enlightenment as a false paradox, which deflects attention from the existing source of valid positive law, and which, in any case, is always factually resolved in the moral life of the pious community.

5 The Young Hegelians and Karl Marx

Stahl and positive philosophy

The decades after the French Revolution in Germany were generally characterized by critical attitudes to the constitutional ideals arising from the Revolution. These attitudes at times expressed a full rejection of liberal ideas, but more generally they were marked by tentatively progressive attempts to incorporate these ideas within a gradually evolving state apparatus. Almost universal in the aftermath of the French Revolution, however, was a broad aversion to formal ius-naturalism and to the rational and individualistic concepts emerging from ius-natural political philosophy. The more conservative elements in this set of responses to the Revolution were reinforced during the period of political restoration after the end of the Congress of Vienna, which saw both the reconsolidation of monarchical government in the German territories that had been controlled by Napoleon, and the termination of the reforms that had been stimulated by Napoleonic ideas. As discussed, the post-Napoleonic backlash against reform and revolution found varied articulation in different romantic outlooks, but it reached perhaps its most exemplary status in the *personalism* of Schelling's positive philosophy.

Apart from Schelling, the most important representative of positive philosophy in political debate was Friedrich Julius Stahl, whose work both captured and pervasively influenced the spirit of reactionary consensus between 1820 and the revolutionary years of 1848–49. Like other conservatives, Stahl criticized political doctrines based in natural law,[1] he rejected contractarian political conceptions,[2] he wrote polemics against atomistic or individualistic ideas of legal entitlement,[3] and he took a stance against institutional analyses that limited the personal authority of monarchs.[4] Above all, Stahl reserved his most envenomed invectives for Hegelian ideas of legitimate statehood, and, like Schelling, he denounced what he viewed as an alleged *depersonalizing* tendency in Hegel's political thought: that is, a tendency to view processes of social formation and evolution as shaped by an overarching rationalism, not as the results of absolute personal decisions or absolute personal wills.[5] For this reason, he rejected Hegel's claim that the legal origins of political order evolve from a socially embedded rationality or from an 'impersonal substantial will', rather than from a personal centre of power, and he saw Hegel's rationalist ideas of freedom as responsible for a devaluation of personal authority in the state.[6] Hegel's misinterpretation of political evolution, he in fact concluded, was caused by Hegel's insistence that God is a rational entity, not a personal will, and that God's freedom is a freedom of the rational will, not of the absolute will. Against Hegel, therefore, Stahl argued that the personal God is the unifying foundation of human life and human politics, and God's absolute will, not God's reason, is the origin of legitimate and enduring political orders. For Stahl, in other words, Hegelian rationalism disturbs the personal-metaphysical fundament of the world: it removes God from his position as an originating and positively revealed force in the world, and it consequently erodes the stable basis of will, character and personality upon which legitimate states are dependent. Stahl advocated a *personal polity,* united around a monarch representing God's personal will. The 'monarchical principle', he claimed, is the 'foundation of all German state law',[7] and the monarch obtains legitimacy by enacting a 'personification' of divine will in the state.[8] The 'basic structure' of the state is its division into 'authority and people', and this hierarchy is immediately founded in the personalist principles of Christian dogma: the state possesses its greatest legitimacy where it represents the absolute personality of God and where this personality acts as the cause or first mover of the freedom of the subjects living under the state.[9] Indeed, Stahl argued that the church itself should be organized in an episcopal constitution, enabling the monarch to exercise 'external power over the church',[10] and to cement an 'autocratic principle' at the centre of religious representation.[11]

Despite this authoritarian attitude, however, if viewed against its contemporary background, Stahl's work also contains an intentionally moderating account of monarchical rule. At the core of his thought is an idea of 'limited monarchy',[12] which seeks, albeit cautiously, to combine personalist monarchism with elements of constitutional legal statism. Unlike the ultra-reactionary theorists around Haller, for instance, he insisted that a personal state must always necessarily be 'a legal state', in contrast to the 'patriarchal, patrimonial' state, and he was insistent that pure absolutism cannot produce a reliable state form.[13] Stahl's personalism in fact revolves around a reiteration of the classical Evangelical attempt to fuse elements of personal voluntarism and universal normativism, and so to derive laws in the state, not from principles of human reason, but from the state's analogy to the divine will. He argued that personal states, united under Christian monarchies, are representatives of God's own personality, which is, necessarily, a moral personality. In consequence, such states always have the natural propensity to institute rule by universal moral laws, both for their subjects and for their own administrators, and they are naturally inclined to institute laws under which both state and subject are recognized as personalities, as agents endowed with wills, freedoms and entitlements.[14] A polity concentrated in princely personality in fact contributes to the formation of the 'human personality', and it elevates 'the human community' towards a condition of personal unity and freedom, under one will and one law.[15] The prince is, therefore, bound simultaneously by laws that are deduced from God's personality and laws that are deduced from the ideal personality of the subjects; these laws confer a universal legal fabric on the state, whose origin – dialectically – is in the prince's own representative personality. The prince who exercises personal rule, consequently, can under no circumstances own the state, and he cannot act independently of the state's laws. He is obliged by laws originally deducible from his own personality not to 'contravene the law',[16] and to ensure that laws are communicated in procedurally correct manner.[17] He must also provide for a condition in which all subjects are treated as equals (as persons) before the law, endowed with social rights and a 'firmly delineated and assured legal position'.[18]

Stahl's work, therefore, undoubtedly formed a conservative response to the constitutional and liberationist movements stimulated in both church and state by the French Revolution. Nonetheless, he did not deny that legally secured freedom is a necessary element of legitimate statehood, and he did not wish categorically to reverse the processes of legal positivization and structural liberation that he identified in post-1789 societies. On the contrary, implicit in Stahl's political theology is the claim that the legal basis of the personally constituted state is always, in an eminent sense, *free,* and that divine personality in politics manifests itself in processes of representation, which do not preclude 'reform', change and legal transformation.[19] Indeed, it is constitutive of princely power, as a personal will, that, like God's will, it is positively free, that it enacts new principles of order, and that it cannot be bound by immutable constraints. He consequently did not conceive the representative personality of the prince as a theocratic body tied to immutable metaphysical ideas.[20] Instead, he saw the state founded in personality as a dynamically representative will, which is able to allow modification and flux into law and state without relinquishing all stable foundation. The positive alteration of the law's foundation, Stahl thus concluded, is inevitable and desirable; alterations in the law constitute the dynamic element of freedom in the polity. It is, however, necessary to ensure that law does not become entirely positivized, and that it does not forfeit all foundation in substantial principles; it is necessary to ensure, in other words, that the ongoing reformulation of law – its 'positive formation' – remains connected to 'God's world order', and is not severed from substantial ideas.[21] This balance between positivization and order, for Stahl, can only be preserved through the origination of law in the princely will: the role of the prince is to ensure that processes of social change and legal positivization take place within certain guiding parameters and within an orderly representative structure. Indeed, one implication in Stahl's work is that the principles of formal natural law, which have stimulated legal positivization through the Enlightenment, the French Revolution and early capitalism, do not constitute reliable foundations for the free socio-political order, but in fact tie common life to static principles of unfreedom. The personal prince, however, embodies an alternative idea of natural law, whose originating personality is bound in two directions to God and to the people, and this idea contains stronger, more flexible and ultimately more enduring ideas of natural law and legal positivity than the static and intractable prescriptions of human rationality. Freedom in the state, in short, is obtained through God's absolute freedom embodied in the human will, and the personal will is always one element in God's own freedom.

For this reason, Stahl, who was in fact of Jewish origin, saw Protestantism as a distinctively modern theological-political doctrine, producing modern ideas of freedom inside and outside the state. Protestantism, he argued, is the religion of free personality, founded in a belief in God as a free and spontaneously creative person,[22] and it is able to institute a genuine ethic of personality in the state. As a consequence, only Protestantism can meet the challenges of modern politics by establishing state forms that are not only positively free but also structured and ordered. Protestant states, Stahl explained, have the particular advantage that their monarchs are not bound by perennial legal or theocratic prescriptions; they can develop their personal rule in relative independence; and they can freely alter the conditions of governance for their subjects – but they also remain bound to the orderly representation of overarching ideas of divine-natural law.[23] Only Protestantism, therefore, can give substance to the progressive conservative state, which Stahl viewed as the necessary antidote to excessive reformism and revolutionary zeal.

Heteronomy and the personal God

Reactionary thought in the period 1820–48, exemplified primarily by Schelling and Stahl, was thus shaped by the belief that God's personality exists as a unique, distinct and transcendent metaphysical subject and that the legitimate human polity is the personal state that positively represents this prior metaphysical subject in laws. These reactionary views saw the legitimate will of the state as a metaphysical or absolute will, and they saw the laws defining political legitimacy as derived, not from a human will or human needs, but from the divine personality represented in the state, which allocates certain rights and freedoms to citizens as (at most) externally imposed formal attributes. The metaphysical conception of the state as an absolute person had its corollary in a construction of individual subjects as absolute persons: that is, as formal bearers of positive wills, whose claims to rights and entitlements are contingent on their recognition by the person of the state, but who are invariably positioned outside the state. These views consequently supported a state centred in a monarchical executive, coupled with certain minimal constitutional constraints, sanctioning subjects as free in the exercise of private rights and entitlements.

For this reason, critics of monarchical legitimism in Germany often expressed their opposition to government in the era of restoration in theological categories, and dissenting political views were sustained by a metaphysical critique of personalism.[24] Indeed, the increasing groundswell of hostility to monarchical restoration which became vocal in the 1830s, and which ultimately led to the quasi-revolutionary upheavals of 1848, enunciated many of its guiding ideas in the form of an anti-metaphysical argument, and it explained its political content as a revolt against the presence of positive metaphysics in politics, law and religion. This was particularly characteristic of the works of the Young Hegelians, a group of intellectuals who took an emancipatory interpretation of Hegel's dialectics as the basis for an attack on absolute personalism in religion and politics, and who saw the critical transformation of metaphysics in religion as a constitutive precondition of human liberty in politics.

The major Young Hegelians, Bruno Bauer, David Friedrich Strauss and Ludwig Feuerbach, all organized their work, albeit in highly diverse manner, around an attempt to elucidate the contents of religion through anthropological categories, as accounts of human freedom. In this, all criticized the metaphysical foundations of positive philosophy, and all sought to provide a view on religion that might allow human beings to free their laws from religious ideas, and to interpret law, not as an emanation of absolute or divine personality, but as an expression of human essence and human freedom. Central to the work of all Young Hegelians was thus the insistence that positive philosophy stands in the way of legal positivization and human freedom under law. Positive philosophy, they claimed, is in fact a fully heteronomous legal doctrine, under which laws are detached from human freedom, and so inflict a condition of alienation throughout society. To develop these perspectives, the Young Hegelians proposed a reconception of Hegel's ideas in which they sought to separate the idea of rational freedom in Hegel's philosophy from its metaphysical substructure and from all attachment to political authoritarianism. Central to this, in fact, was the claim that Hegel had not developed his own philosophy as a doctrine of radical freedom because his thought had not liberated itself from metaphysics. Despite their metaphysical suspicion of Hegel, however, they drew extensively on his theory of the rational state, and they also called extensively on his philosophy of religion; especially in its insistence that ideas of freedom in religion are ideas of human freedom, imagining a 'unity of divine and human nature', and that human reason is operative in fulfilling these ideas.[25] This view gave a foundation on which the Young Hegelians were able to construe religious concepts as moments in a course of human formation and self-liberation, to convert religious narratives into signifiers of reason's own freedom and, most importantly, to divert religious and political thinking away from monadically substantial or pure-metaphysical accounts of truth as divine essence or personality.[26] Young Hegelian philosophy was thus centred on a reaction against positive philosophy and religious personalism and on a critical move towards a philosophical *anthropology*, whose main principles were applied particularly to religion. Through this anthropological turn, they argued that the rational freedom of human personality, not the absolute will of the metaphysical personality, is the centre of religious analysis, and they claimed that the freedom of God is falsely reflected wherever it is identified as a will that is external or superior to human freedoms. Human freedom, they argued, is the only possible content of God's freedom, in its necessary difference to itself, and all objective obstruction of human freedom is an objective obstruction of God's freedom.

The early writings of Bruno Bauer, for instance, used religious analysis, scriptural exegesis and religious historiography to set out a critique of the religious-metaphysical and politically authoritarian ideas underlying positive philosophy and to transform religious reflection into an anthropological analysis of the ideas of human freedom. Bauer's earliest works still show a proximity to the more conservative or at least moderate wing of post-Hegelian religious-political philosophers. During his formative period, he did not formulate religious questions in exclusively anthropological terms, and he retained the belief that documents of religion have a real historical content.[27] In some respects, in his very early works Bauer was close to the post-Hegelian theology of Philipp Marheineke. Marheineke opposed Schelling's static personalism in religious inquiry,[28] and he negated all suggestions that human reason is indifferent in religion, or that there might exist a 'dualism between philosophy and religion'.[29] Nonetheless, he also asserted that reason accounts for its foundation when it recognizes its 'dependence' on God, that God has a personality prior to humanity, and that revelation, not reason, is the 'original source' of truth.[30] Despite this, however, even in his early works Bauer differed from more orthodox Christian Hegelians; he rejected the claim, exemplified by Marheineke, that the truthful content of human 'self-consciousness and worldly consciousness' is in fact the 'consciousness of God', whose personality is above that of humanity.[31] In fact, even in his early works he described religious contents and revelations as moments in the formation of human self-consciousness, in which reason reflects the stages of its own ideas of 'freedom'.[32] Human religious reflection, on Bauer's early account, is thus 'God's relation to himself', in which humanity progressively recognises God as the ground of its freedom.[33] In consequence, the early Bauer viewed religious reflection as a process of conscious formation in which the metaphysical 'strangeness' of God to humanity, and – in consequence – the 'otherness' of humanity to its own freedom is overcome. In religious reflection, the 'self-consciousness of God' is reflected in the human being, and, through this, God's freedom is formed as a human idea, or as humanity's consciousness of its own ideal form.[34] Consequently, he interpreted God's revelations as stages in a particular human course of human self-possession and realization, and he saw the contents of the scriptures as reflected ideas of human freedom. On this foundation, then, Bauer ultimately proposed a strategy of religious hermeneutics and critique, claiming that the Christian scriptures should be interpreted as historical figures of human self-consciousness, in which the human spirit describes for itself the different stages of its self-alienation, renewal and ultimate free self-fulfilment.[35] He described the narratives of the New Testament as enacting a rebellion of human self-consciousness against the conditions of its first alienation and underdevelopment, symbolized by the purely metaphysical or theocratic God of the Old Testament. The revelation and incarnation of Christ in the New Testament, he then explained, marks a moment of reconciliation in self-consciousness, in which 'subjective spirit' unites itself with 'divinity', in which the human and the divine self-consciousness are reconciled, and in which human reason concretely reflects its own idea of freedom.[36] In this critical hermeneutical approach, Bauer began to interpret religious contents for their ideal-anthropological foundations and to construe these contents as real moments in the ideal evolution of the human being towards a realization of itself as free, in likeness to God.

Of great importance in this, moreover, is the fact that the early Bauer also interpreted religious narratives as *legal narratives,* and he saw stages in the ideal relationship between human and divine self-consciousness as articulated stages in the formation of human freedom *under law.*[37] He consequently saw Christian religion as enacting an overcoming of pure metaphysical (theocratic) law and as narratively figuring a legal realization of self-conscious human freedom, in which freedom is rationally reconciled with its laws. This process of reconciliation, he explained, began with the emergence of a subjective spirit of self-legislation, which sought to overcome the oppressive heteronomy of Old Testament theocracy;[38] Bauer saw the laws of the Old Testament as the laws of the absolute 'person', in which legal entitlement is determined statically and heteronomously, and in which human consciousness has no role in founding the conditions of entitlement and obligation.[39] This process of reconciliation is then completed in the 'revealed religion' of the New Testament, in which people encounter revealed law (the new law) as their *own law,* or law in their own likeness.[40] Biblical scriptures thus describe the formation of self-consciousness as a human liberation from the yoke of heteronomous or pure-metaphysical laws. Indeed, God's revelation in Christ contradicts all objective or authoritarian law, for it represents a condition in which humanity is reflexively reconciled with its absolute essence, and where, consequently, it is no longer determined by law as an external or heteronomous edict.[41] The telos of human self-consciousness, therefore, is to move away from theocratic or metaphysical legal orders, exemplified by the personal Jewish state of the Old Testament, and to elaborate a condition of non-metaphysical self-consciousness under own laws.[42]

After the late 1830s, Bauer ceased to define himself as a theologian, and he came to the conclusion that only 'materialism' can provide for a plausible 'philosophy of self-consciousness'.[43] At this point, Bauer asserted that religion cannot express ideas of freedom or account for a condition after heteronomy: all religion, he claimed, *is* heteronomy, and religion invariably subjugates humanity to an 'alien, tyrannical law'.[44] In his works of this period, he concluded that only the ultimate overcoming of religion could bring about the act of liberation from false law, which he had once seen as the function of religion. Human freedom, he concluded, is not God's freedom – it is merely human freedom, and it can only be freedom in so far as it is exclusively human freedom. Even after his anti-religious turn, Bauer did not wholly abandon his earlier scriptural hermeneutics, and he still argued that certain moments in Christianity describe an anthropologically constitutive negation of false law.[45] However, he asserted that religion can play no meaningful role in instituting the 'moral world', and all burdening of human existence with religious ideas can only impede the realization of human freedom.[46] The state, not religion, he in fact concluded, is the 'sole form' in which the 'infinity of reason' can be represented, and the institutions of religion can never be more than a subordinate element in the constitution of the state.[47] Religion has no 'legal existence' outside the state, he now argued, and it cannot generate reliable conditions of freedom and entitlement.[48] Authentic law, consequently, can only be instituted by a strong republican state, and it is only in the state that fully self-conscious ideas of freedom under law can be put into effect. Close to Fichte, then, he argued that a state guaranteeing freedom subordinates all spheres of intellectual exchange (including religion) to the sovereign will, and that this state is formed by a republican constitution that generates ideas of right and entitlement, not as metaphysical norms, but as commonly elaborated claims.

Bauer intended his earlier religious writings to salvage religious contents from the claims of theological metaphysics and positive philosophy. His later writings both transformed and extended this approach and sought to rescue human consciousness from *all* metaphysics, including religion itself. His later works therefore articulated an intense aversion to all metaphysical thinking, which he construed as a dragging and debilitating force in politics, philosophy and – above all – in *law*. The motives for this change of mind are expressed most evidently in Bauer's later political writings, after the failure of the revolution of 1848–49. After 1849, he argued that the inability of the liberal revolutionaries in the Frankfurt Parliament to create a sustainable constitutional order had been 'internally connected' with the persistence of metaphysical ideas in philosophy.[49] The enduring influence of metaphysical constructions and intellectual schematism in this period, he claimed, testified to a pervasive weakness in human politics and to an under-evolution of human powers of rational self-assertion in the political domain. This made human political life highly susceptible to absolutism, both in intellectual life and in political organization. Metaphysics, he concluded, imposes intractable order on creative and personal life; it depreciates local or immanent expressions of freedom and reason; it makes human existence accountable to chimerical and abstracted concepts of right, concentrated in reduced ideas of personality; and it leaves society reliant on absolute and universal descriptions of its own foundations. Societies which are not fully liberated from metaphysical universalism and which have not elaborated rational, anthropological and fully positive foundations for their own administration tend, therefore, to promote abstractly personalized ideas of legal and constitutional life and abstractly personalized models of governance, which give little opportunity for the genuine realization of freedom.[50] Above all, he argued, metaphysics tends to stimulate a legal hypertrophy throughout society, as metaphysical attitudes derive the values of political life from insubstantial, yet oppressively applied abstract laws. The failure of the republicans and the constitutionalists around 1848 to emancipate themselves from metaphysics was manifest, above all, in their inability to interpret law as a terrain of freedom and the rational will. Instead, they remained obsessed with 'the cult of law', which, with its 'paragraphing' of all vital aspects of political existence, did little more than replicate the 'mania of earlier absolutism' and to 'dominate every sign of life with its regulations'.[51] The positivist orientation in constitutional theory, Bauer indicated, was primarily responsible for disseminating a conception of rights that failed to understand rights as anything more than formally allocated adjuncts to monadic persons, and that simply transposed the fiction of personality from the metaphysical God to the personalities of state and subjects. Because of this, the rational will behind the revolution had been inhibited, and it had fatally compromised with metaphysical ideas of legal personality and freedom. Bauer's later political view thus culminated in the claim that the survival of strong political cultures requires a constant critique of religion and metaphysics,[52] and a ceaseless endeavour to separate political freedom and rational spontaneity from their domination by false – and falsely metaphysical – laws. Indeed, one guiding impulse throughout Bauer's work is the claim that the dominant areas of human activity – religion, politics and philosophy – allow metaphysics to prevail over humanity and that in each of these areas humanity must reflect and assert its freedom as other than metaphysics. The outcome of this, if successful, will be a reliably human system of rational law.

Species-being and the law

David Friedrich Strauss moved towards still more resolutely anthropological perspectives in his reflections on politics and theology, and he placed himself at the left of the intellectual milieu around the Young Hegelians.[53] Unlike the early Bauer, Strauss denied the historical factuality of divine revelation,[54] and he was prepared to see the scriptures only as mythical forms or as ideal reflections or projections of human self-consciousness,[55] requiring rigorous analytical critique for their true content to be illuminated.[56] The stories of the birth and resurrection of Christ, he claimed, above all, should not be approached as truthful historical narratives, but as myths in which human consciousness constructs and expresses *an idea* of its own essence and its own freedom. In Christ, therefore, the human mind interprets its own 'divine-human life' and, in consequence, it invigorates 'the idea of humanity' within itself. The figure of Christ is not one unique historical personality; it is an 'idea', symbolically embedded in historical form, through which the human mind configures the possibilities of humanity and freedom that are common to all human beings, as a species (*Gattung*).[57] Christ is the symbolic or ideal encompassing personality (*Allpersönlichkeit*) of the entire human species, and Christ's characteristics belong, not to one, but to an infinite number of persons.[58] Each person is, therefore, charged with responsibility for interpreting Christ's attributes of humanity and freedom as the attributes of all persons, binding all persons to all other persons.

Strauss did not see the revelation of Christ as an accomplished realization of human essence. Instead, he argued that religious figures of humanity always refract a disjuncture between human existence and its highest possibilities. Like Bauer, in fact, Strauss saw Christian dogma and church history as describing the gradual evolution of human species into a state of legal self-consciousness and freedom, and, at the same time, as perpetuating a complex 'alienation' of human beings from their own essence.[59] The contents of religion, he argued, are merely human contents, and these contents are alienated through their construction as divine or sacred. Humans are consequently called upon to reclaim or 'take back' the human ideas that have been objectivized as the contents and commands of religion.[60] It is the task of rational religious interpretation to transform religious symbols into human freedoms and to translate the externality of revealed commands into indices of human self-legislation. Religion is only fully understood and complete where its contents have been interpreted, through a critical hermeneutic, as mythical figurations of freedoms inherent in human species, not as external or metaphysical substances. It is, in consequence, only through the 'evolution of Christianity into pure humanism' that the true implications of religion can be redeemed.[61]

Amongst the Young Hegelians, the works of Ludwig Feuerbach contain the most critical analysis of religion. In his writings of the early 1840s, Feuerbach intensified the views of Strauss on religion and human species, and he argued that orthodox conceptions of divinity are merely distortions of the needs, desires and the possibilities of freedom, which are constitutive of the human species. God, in fact, is nothing more than a falsely alienated objectivization of the ideal and constitutive attributes of humanity: its species-being (*Gattungswesen*). God is a fictitious site onto which human beings are coerced into projecting the founding contents of their own nature, and in which they admire and fear attributes that are nothing but externally transformed elements of their own primary ideal nature and dispositions. God, consequently, is perceived as absolute freedom or an 'absolute essence'. Yet this essence is factually humanity's 'own essence' or species-being, distortedly transmuted into a personality outside humanity and withholding from humanity the possibility of its personal freedom and self-possession.[62] To a greater extent than Strauss, therefore, Feuerbach concluded that religion is a violation of human life and its originary dispositions. Religious constructs prevent human beings from accomplishing and fulfilling their own basic dispositions. Religion is a 'negation' of all that the human being truthfully is, and the symbols of species-being, which humanity encounters in religion, are sustained only because, in religion, humanity wilfully and paradoxically allows itself to be alienated from the conditions of its self-fulfilment and permits an alien God to stand in for the condition of its freedom and self-legislation.[63] The task of religious analysis is thus to conduct an anthropological or humanist reappropriation of theological ideas for human society, to understand the symbolic forms of religion as external and falsified indices of human essence, freedom and possibility, and to recuperate the elements of humanity objectivized as God for the self-formation of humanity itself.[64] For these reasons, Feuerbach's philosophy of religion contains a most vehement attack on theological personalism and on the doctrine of God's metaphysical personality.[65] God's absolute personality, Feuerbach argued, represents nothing less than the total alienation of humanity from itself; God's personality is the alienated essence of the human species, which has been violently 'transformed into a person' and removed from humanity as a set of formal predicates attached to a fictitiously projected divinity.[66] God's personality, therefore, is an expropriated form of the human personality, of the personality of the species, distortedly reflected as a metaphysical person. This metaphysical personality, then, is the paradox at the centre of the human universe; it is a personality that is abstracted without reality from human existence, yet prevails over the human will and controls human life with its commands and its regime of moral self-suppression. It is only where the metaphysical personality of God is recognized as paradoxical and where it is interpreted as the residue of a human personality or of many human personalities that the self-alienation of human species occurring as religion can be terminated.[67]

Feuerbach also gave clear articulation to the political implications of anti-personalist theological reflection. His philosophy of religion is pervaded by a Promethean impulse, which suggests that the final recuperation of human attributes from their metaphysical externality in religion will result in a utopian political condition. In this condition, human beings will be reunited with their common essence, and so freed from the life-denying tyranny of metaphysics and false personalism. This condition, moreover, will be one in which people are free authors and interpreters of *their own laws,* and where their laws reflect primary human orientations and needs. In this condition, metaphysical laws will be transformed into a 'personally living law, a law become flesh, a human law'.[68] More clearly still than other Young Hegelians, therefore, Feuerbach's view on religion provided for an emancipatory political vision, which saw the overcoming of personalist metaphysics as the end of false laws and the beginning of shared freedom under laws.

At the heart of Feuerbach's philosophy, additionally, is a quasi-hermeneutical theoretical turn, which also contains distinctive implications for his legal and political ideas. Human beings understand each other, he argued, because they have a common species-being. Wherever a human being speaks, he or she speaks with another person as a member of the species, and the speech-acts occurring between these persons always mark an inter-subjective elaboration and disclosure of capacities for commonality and shared insights which all people, as members of the species, possess.[69] Speech, consequently, is a process in which human beings gain greater understanding of each other, of themselves and, at the same time, of their ideal selves as bearers of species-being. On these grounds, Feuerbach indicated that the absolute human person – species-being – is falsely construed where it is seen as one solitary or monadic person, incorporating a stable and finally invariable set of qualities. Instead, the truly human person is a collective person, founded in shared dialogical processes of free elaboration and interpretation, in a constant process of evolution and self-formation. In this respect, therefore, Feuerbach's account of human essence fundamentally denounce the personalism of the religious thought and religious politics that surrounded him, and, similarly, it deeply undermine the legal and political preconditions distilled from such thought. His essential motive in this was to show that human personality is not only distorted where it is projected onto a metaphysical God, but that the metaphysical God, in turn, has led to a distortion of how human beings think of themselves as personalities, and of how they think of other human beings as personalities. The habitude in which people construe and presuppose the absolute subject of the metaphysical God as the supreme locus of truth, contained in itself and distinct from other subjects, has conditioned people to think of themselves and others as absolute subjects, fully self-contained and eternally distinct from other subjects. Because of this, human subjects ignore their constitutive relationships with other people; they tend to construct objectifying and purposive images both of themselves and of others; and they tend to accept social and political structures founded in absolute constructs of personality. Feuerbach's critical reading of religion was, therefore, most manifestly, intended to reclaim the metaphysical person of God as humanity's own person. But the hermeneutical aspect of this approach was also intended to redeem the human subject from its metaphysically deluded self-construction as an absolute person and to allow a reinterpretation of this subject as social, changeable and contingent on formative dialogue. Underlying this idea is the intimation that the end of humanity's fixation on God's absolute person will also permit people to see their own persons in conditions of reciprocity, shared freedom and commonality. The liberation of humanity from metaphysics will, in other words, be a collective liberation, and in this condition of liberation people will not live under the laws of solitary subjects, but they will form laws as common laws, in which one person's freedom acts as the condition of the freedom of others. In this respect, Feuerbach's anti-personalism in religious critique clearly intersects with an anti-personalism in legal critique, which construes the abrogation of personalism as a new law, founded in a common, not a personal, will.

As an extension of this, Feuerbach also asserted that the metaphysical personalism of positive philosophy promoted dualistic or authoritarian conceptions of the state. Like Bauer, he saw personalism as the metaphysical basis of absolutism. In the same manner that personalism in religion effects a division between the absolute subject of God and the absolute subjects of self-alienated people, who are separated as creators and created, personalism in politics, he argued, effects a division between the absolute subject of the state and the formally purposive subjects of civil society, who are separated as legislators and legal addressees. Personalism thus creates an intellectual disposition that allows the state to stratify its functions above society and to disaggregate society and economy into a plurality of antagonistic and self-seeking individuals; that is, into a set of competitive economic agents, endowed with fixed rights of ownership, committed, as absolute persons, only to exercising rights of acquisition and self-furtherance.[70] In this, Feuerbach indicated that the political reality of pre-1848 Germany, structured around a late-absolutist political order and an early capitalist economy with little representative or organic mediation between them, was the material substrate of metaphysical personalism. The contemporary foundations of private law and public law, he concluded, have their origins in a falsely metaphysical view of God's personality and in the retraction of rational freedom that this enacts; the abstractly personalized state of public law and the abstractly personalized agents of private law are both derived, in equal measure, from an insufficiently human understanding of personality. Like Bauer, therefore, Feuerbach also came to the conclusion that the weakness and alienating intractability of German political life was induced by a persistence of metaphysics, which obstructed the evolution of a political culture permitting the positive production of free and rational laws.

Hegelians on the Left and Right: the schismatic personality

It is around the questions of personality and metaphysics that the religious and political doctrines of the Hegelian thinkers in the 1830s and 1840s were most sharply divided, and these questions formed the fault line separating more conservative Hegelians from the more radical younger generations of theorists. The most conservative Hegelians such as, first, Karl Friedrich Göschel and, later, Julius Schaller opposed all anthropological theories of God's personality. They argued instead that God should be viewed as a transcendent personality or 'highest personality' – or, in Hegelian terms, as the personal form of the 'absolute spirit'. God's personality, they claimed, is absolutely prior to all the members of the human species and it is manifest in the historically unique revelation of Christ.[71] Göschel especially insisted that 'the absolute personality of God' is the constant and positive 'condition of creation' and of the 'created personality' of all finite beings.[72] Only revelation, not human reflection, can disclose God's personality.[73] Analogously, Schaller protested against the mythological interpretive approach pioneered by Strauss, and he insisted that the formal personality of Christ should be viewed as a historically unique figure,[74] and that the 'real revelation' of 'absolute personality' is the sole form of absolute human self-knowledge.[75]

More moderate, or moderate conservative, Hegelians, such as Marheineke, Karl Ludwig Michelet and Karl Rosenkranz, also rejected the mythological and anthropological ideas of the left wing of the Young Hegelians. Marheineke accepted that God's historical revelation results in part from an 'idea of God' in human consciousness, and that human consciousness has a specific 'receptivity' for revelation; revelation is thus a distinctive event of human consciousness.[76] However, he also claimed that Christ's incarnation should only be seen as an incarnation of a prior personality, never 'anthropologically'.[77] Rosenkranz also defined God as an absolute subject or 'transcendent creator', albeit as a creator who remains present and active in the world and in human consciousness.[78] Michelet mediated between different post-Hegelian intellectual tendencies. He shared with Bauer, Feuerbach and Strauss the conviction that God's personality should not be viewed as metaphysical essence, but as God's own formative humanity.[79] Like Bauer, he concluded that the 'eternal personality of the spirit' is not God in abstraction or difference from humanity and creation, but 'God's self-consciousness', which can only be realized in the 'human spirit'.[80] He therefore sought at once to preserve the categorical distinction of divinity and humanity, yet also to construe divine personality, not as static essence, but as God's evolution *in* and *as* humanity. However, unlike the left-leaning Hegelians, Michelet opposed anthropological theories that defined God as a condensation of common human attributes. He saw in this, first, both a denial of the 'absolute objectivity of divine substance',[81] and, second, a depreciation of the role of individual human subjectivity as the particular location and expression of divine substance.[82] Michelet therefore never renounced the claim that God is metaphysically prior to humanity, and that human personality, either individual or collective, only assumes its greatest dignity as a necessary moment 'in the life of the absolute',[83] or in a relation of 'conscious unity' with the 'general divine personality'.[84] Although politically closer to the Hegelian left than Michelet, August Cieszkowski also occupied a mediating position between anthropological and transcendent personalist arguments. Cieszkowski saw human historical process as a divine/material elaboration of God's 'absolute personality'.[85]

The different views on the divine personality in post-Hegelian thought were closely bound up with the different political attitudes of these philosophers. The more conservative Hegelians adapted their emphasis on God's absolute personality to endorse authoritarian political attitudes, defining the personal executive as the focus of state authority. Göschel's personalism, for instance, led him to claim that monarchical systems are most likely to foster a climate of 'real personality' and personal freedom and formation.[86] Other conservatives argued that the ideal state is one that is both closely integrated with the church, and in which princely power enjoys divine sanction.[87] These theorists thus tended to deny that the state is an arena of independent will-formation and self-realization, and they founded the personality of the state in its constitutional unity with God's own personality. The more moderate personalists tended to support monarchical political systems in which the personality of the state is expressed in socially accountable constitutions.[88] These views construed the constitution as the human element of state's personality. Michelet's moderate personalism, for example, led him to support a constitutional state, in which the 'personal freedom' of individual citizens is secured by a 'representative constitution'.[89] He thus endorsed a progressive 'constitutional monarchy, surrounded by democratic institutions'.[90] In addition, then, the three major thinkers to the left of the Young Hegelian milieu developed their anti-personalism to insist that the substantial and self-interpreting personality of humanity must form the constitutive basis of all political authority. Strauss supported a progressive constitutional system. Bauer opted for an actionistic republicanism, framed within a strong representative monarchy.[91] Feuerbach was close to aspects of early socialist thought, and he saw liberation from God's metaphysical personality as the precondition for an emancipatory or republican politics.

The post-personal state

The left-leaning Young Hegelians construed the political sphere as the sole sphere of society in which human beings, if liberated from false ideas of personality, can express their ideas of freedom. They condemned all contamination of politics by religious ideas as the persistence of false metaphysics in a region of activity properly determined only by human reason and human laws. They consequently demanded either, as in the case of Strauss, that church and state should be completely separated,[92] or, more vehemently, as in the case of Bauer, they argued that only a fully secular community can form a legitimate state,[93] and that the 'personal existence' of human freedom can only be safeguarded by the state.[94]

The secular-republican and anti-metaphysical idea of the state was most pronounced, however, in the works of Arnold Ruge, a radical delegate in the 1848 parliament, who stood some distance to the political left of other Young Hegelians. Ruge argued that the free 'unfolding of the spirit' could only occur only in the state,[95] and was currently impeded in its formation by quasi-theocratic influences, and especially by the 'political pope' in the figure of the Prussian monarch.[96] Like earlier Young Hegelians, therefore, Ruge saw his objective as the liberation of the state and the sphere of political freedom from falsely metaphysical ideas. However, whilst other Young Hegelians saw the political liberation of humanity as a critical-theoretical or interpretive process, Ruge argued that human liberty can only be secured through collective *action,* and that *praxis* is the sole medium of emancipation. In fact, whilst other Young Hegelians identified the anthropological critique of religion as the path beyond metaphysics, Ruge saw these approaches as still ensnared in metaphysical analysis, and as failing to appreciate the emancipatory primacy of *praxis.* The theory of *praxis,* he thus argued, marks a 'radical reform of consciousness' and only such reform can free humanity from false determinacy.[97] *Theoretical* reflection that has not yet become *practical,* and that does not seek to validate itself in praxis, is nothing other than a renewal of metaphysics, and it cannot contribute meaningfully to the task of human liberation.[98] As an extension of this, then, Ruge viewed the constitutionalist liberalism of 1848 as a theoretically overburdened or residually metaphysical political perspective that was still focused on abstractly personal ideas of legal statehood. This perspective failed adequately to acknowledge the active-practical aspect of political foundation, and, instead of recognizing full popular sovereignty and active participation as the source of legitimate order, it falsely assumed that a weak fabric of possessive legal rights and formal constraints could provide a sufficient bedrock for an enduring polity.[99] In consequence, it is only where liberalism is replaced by a radical democratic outlook, sustained by an actively enfranchised 'public sphere', that the metaphysical formalism and theoretical ponderousness of liberalism might be superseded.[100] Like Cieszkowski, therefore, Ruge viewed active political foundation – 'post-theoretical praxis' – as the highest condition of human self-realization, and he argued that actively formed political orders are the supreme expression of human personality.[101]

This anti-liberal element in the works of the more radical Young Hegelians was also articulated in the works of Max Stirner. The theoretical centre of Stirner's work was the assertion that liberalism effected a false overcoming of religion and metaphysics, and it founded its political ideals in false constructs of human personality. Liberalism, based in universal humanism, proclaimed the category of the human being as the foundation for its post-metaphysical theories and post-metaphysical politics, and it sought to justify its politics through reference to universal ideas of human need and interest. The humanism of this liberalism, however, succeeded only in reconstituting the false freedoms of religion on new and newly distorted foundations. In assuming that a unitary human personality could be posited as the source of all politics, liberalism formed a 'human religion' in which 'God has had to make way for the human being', but in which individual – or authentically *personal* – human needs are subsumed under universally personalized categories and not fully addressed.[102] Moreover, as it assumed that the state alone is able to provide for the universal interests of the human being (perhaps by granting 'human rights' or 'natural rights' to individual citizens), liberalism enchained human life to falsely universalized laws derived from falsely abstracted ideas of the person, and it narrowed human freedom to a sequence of formal guarantees of universal rights before the law. This freedom, as a consequence, lacks all substantial content. The religion of humanism and liberalism, in short, is a 'state religion', founded in a derivatively metaphysical notion of the human being as an absolute person, and in formalized accounts of the laws adequate to this human being.[103] All 'existing law' of this state can only be metaphysical law: it is 'alien law'.[104] Whereas Ruge proposed a radical-republican path beyond the metaphysics of liberalism, therefore, Stirner supported a voluntaristic praxis of radical self-authorization and individual self-legislation. The authentic person, he argued, is the originator of its own law – this person expresses itself, not in the residual category of 'human being', but as an intensely particularized individual, and it recognizes 'no other source of law' but itself.[105] Underlying this analysis was the belief that all universalized outlooks generate heteronomy or false freedom. Liberalism and humanism, therefore, are simply new expressions of abstract personalism, and they cannot lead to experiences of genuinely realized emancipation or self-legislation.

Despite these differences, however, these Young Hegelian views converged in two central claims. First, they argued that politics is the site where human species frees itself from metaphysical form. In contemporary society, however, political institutions are burdened by the personalist or absolutist residues of metaphysical reflection (of which positive philosophy is the most salient example), and these decelerate the process of human self-liberation. In politics, therefore, humanity is charged with responsibility for disencumbering itself of personalism and metaphysics and for forming societies reflecting fully human interests and commitments. Second, then, the more theoretically refined Young Hegelians also indicated that metaphysics also intertwines with the rationality of liberalism early capitalism and early capitalist law, and that the rationality of early capitalism extends and exacerbates the pernicious illusions of metaphysics. On this view, the legal paradigms underpinning capitalism – the legal subject, the possessive individual and the contract-forming juridical agent – are themselves outgrowths of a mental attitude formed around false and paradoxical constructs of personality, originally deriving from theological metaphysics, but lacking all substantial or human foundation. Indeed, the legal idea underlying much Young Hegelian doctrine is that division of society into a set of purposive legal subjects reflects a dispersal of the originary paradox of God's personality, so that all society, although interpreting itself as secular, orders itself around chimerically auto-generated, yet also universally coercive, principles of right and obligation. Personalism, in short, creates heteronomy at a religious, a political and a legal level. The unifying legal-political project of the Young Hegelians was thus an attempt to free human life and human agency from all theocratic or metaphysical heteronomy, and, in relation to this, to free human life and human agency from all domination by falsely metaphysical determinations of itself as a formally purposive proprietorial agent under the state and under law.

Marx, metaphysics and capitalism

It has been widely documented that the young Karl Marx was greatly influenced by certain tendencies of left-Hegelian thinking in the late 1830s and early 1840s, and it is equally well known that he also did much to distance himself from the Young Hegelian milieu. The following discussion does not intend to document all aspects of Marx's appropriation of left-Hegelian thought. However, it seeks to show that the political principles of Marx's theory, and especially of his earlier work, were not discontinuous with the anti-metaphysical critiques of the Young Hegelians. Marx in fact both rearticulated and reconfigured certain underlying impulses in the critiques of metaphysics and in the anti-personalism of the Young Hegelians.

Most obviously, Marx's early works borrowed and modified from Feuerbach a universal-anthropological concept of human essence or species-being, whose elaboration he saw as the precondition of human freedom. Marx's definition of species-being was centred on the claim that the essence of the human species resides in its active orientation towards sociality and commonality. Human beings are essentially social in nature; they realize themselves in relations of commonality with others and, where they interact naturally with each other, they form societies based in shared freedoms and reciprocally contingent self-realization. In addition, where human beings follow the impetus of sociality and commonality, they create historically enriching and enduring social conditions, so that common actions build the bedrock for a wider socio-political reality that people recognize as their own, and in which their actions contribute to the utility and well-being of different generations across time. Elaborated species-being, therefore, institutes social orders characterized by non-instrumental interactions between human beings, by the employment of natural goods in the service of shared self-realization, and by common experiences of freedom and historical authorship. Societies underpinned by elaborated species-being are thus founded in the *second nature* of the human species. These are societies in which humanism and naturalism have become inseparable; they are societies where the founding potentials of human nature and species are unified with external nature to constitute an overarching condition where nature is moulded to human needs and human needs reflect underlying natural dispositions.[106]

In this modified reading of Feuerbach, Marx argued that species-being is not an object that can be liberated or fulfilled through interpretive processes of moral self-recuperation or religious critique or that inheres abstractly in each individual exemplar of the species. In fact, he viewed human essence as an active content, which naturally unites all members of the species, and is manifestly enacted in collective human *praxis.*[107] The natural medium for the externalization of species-being is consequently *labour:* labour is the activity through which human beings manifest and relate to their particular and collective essence and create historical conditions approximating to common human freedom. In free labour, human beings shape and alter the 'inorganic body' of the natural world, they enact a vital process of transformative interaction with external nature, and they form first nature as a humanly realized and inhabitable environment.[108] In freely labouring, likewise, human beings construct an 'objective world' of useful things, which contribute to the evolution of human society and produce a commonly humanized historical world, in which, even across lengthy periods of time, people can encounter and recognize each other as equal and equally participant species-members.[109] The 'object of labour' is, therefore, the 'objectivization of the species-life of humanity'. In societies dominated by the capitalist organization of labour, however, labour is impeded, divided, or *unfree.* In consequence, the free manifestation of species-being is impossible and other more revolutionary modes of self-realization become necessary in order to adjust social conditions to the needs incorporated in species-being.[110]

In capitalist societies, Marx explained, the realization of species-being is obstructed by a number of different factors. Human beings are prevented from elaborating their species-being because their labour is divided in the process of industrial production, and because it is expropriated and alienated from them and formally transmuted into *exchange value.* Through this expropriation, the commodities produced by human labour are integrated into nexi of financial exchange and technical regulation, over which individual producers have no determinate control, and labourers are allowed to encounter their labour only as a content which is entirely 'independent' of their labour and so 'alien' to them.[111] Consequently, under capitalism, human labour does not act as a medium of self-realization, and it does not contribute freely to the evolution and benefit of human societies. Instead, individual labourers are prevented from gaining any understanding of themselves as formed and expressed by the products of labour and all manifest experiences of self-formation are denied to them, as their labour appears only in the falsely externalized medium of exchange or prices, which have no integral connection to the labour originally invested. As a result, capitalist societies are fragmented through labour, and members of modern society are alienated from each other through the alienation of their labour. Similarly, in modern societies, labourers lose all vital connection with the natural world, as their labouring transformation of this world is pursued to obtain ends that they cannot determine. Their liberty to form nature as their own second nature, or as the material base of a shared society, is foreclosed. The humanization of nature that is central to an authentic society is consequently obstructed, and society evolves, not as the 'essential unity of humanity and nature',[112] but as an abstract system of alienated forms. In high capitalism, in short, labour is alienated from the producer of commodities, and the society that the producer inhabits is transformed into a set of objectively alienated relations. All modern society and all social relations within this society are, therefore, structurally determined by the alienation of labour, and this alienation thwarts all possibilities for particular and collective self-realization or freedom. The alienation of labour and the private interests served by this alienation then also form the basis for the objective structures that regulate human activity; the objective conditions of human life in capitalist societies are shaped by entirely heteronomous and coercive laws that exclusively serve the interests of private property and exchange and so compound the universal experience of alienation. The material reality of modern society is thus underscored by a corrupt construction of the law, which at once evolves from and perpetuates an intense alienation of the social, natural and material basis of human life.[113]

At the centre of Marx's early analyses was an attempt to adapt left-Hegelian anthropological critiques to a socially determinate account of the reality and the causes of alienation. Marx restated Feuerbach's assertion that modern society is founded in heteronomy, formed by the distortion of constitutively human qualities and emphases, so that integral experiences of freedom and self-encounter are rendered impossible. Moreover, he also argued that the critical analysis of alienation is a precondition of human freedom and self-realization, and that human freedom is obtained through a recuperation of conditions allowing the elaboration of species-being. His earliest accounts of class-conflict and materialist dialectics thus originated in the humanist idea that authentic history is driven by the dynamic evolution of species-being and that human activity has its gravitational centre in the realization of species-being. In contrast to the Young Hegelians, however, Marx clearly saw capitalism, not religion, as the source of human alienation, and he interpreted alienation as a primarily material, not spiritual, condition. Self-evidently, Marx saw the fact that the Young Hegelians still organized their work around speculative critique and religious inquiry as indicating that the social/material origins of human alienation and the social/material basis of human society remained hidden to them. Equally, he saw the fact that they structured their theories around historically invariable accounts of human essence and socially indeterminate analyses of human consciousness as demonstrating that their naturalist or natural-anthropological turn had only been incompletely fulfilled, and that they had not fully concentrated their analysis on determinately human conditions and experiences. Moreover, he saw the fact that they deduced the false laws of modern society, not from economic processes, but from prevalent ideas of personality as implying that they were unable to think in genuinely non-metaphysical terms, and they imputed excessive causal influence to the ideal and intellectual elements of human life.

Marx believed, in other words, that common Young Hegelian ideas of humanity and human freedom still remained at a metaphysical or ideological level of refinement and were tainted by attachment to the principles of static personalism that they purported to negate. In defining the human being as an invariable personal substrate of all social formation and in presupposing that the alienation of human beings could be terminated through a simple recuperation of this substrate, the Young Hegelians failed, on Marx's account, to see the human being, and its alienation, as the determinate result of material and evolutionary forces, and they failed to recognize how human personality, and its alienation, are constituted by processes of determinately material causation.[114] A genuine analysis of human alienation, Marx concluded, must be a material-historical or material-causal analysis, which examines the forms of human consciousness and self-experience as produced by economic relationships, which rejects hypostatic anthropological accounts of human essence, and which recognizes that only a transformation in the material forces bearing on human life can lead to its emancipation. In interpreting the history of capitalist economic exploitation as the causal centre of alienation, therefore, Marx sought to translate the analysis of the corruption of species-being proposed by the Young Hegelians into a thoroughly material and, so, resolutely post-metaphysical and post-personalist analysis. This analysis was designed to consolidate both the primary object of Young Hegelian analysis (human nature) and the processes bearing on this object (capitalist production and exchange) as fully post-metaphysical contents, and so to organize the critique of the conditions of species-being around accountably non-metaphysical objectives.

Despite his sense that the Young Hegelians had not fully moved beyond metaphysical interpretation, however, Marx's account of alienation always reflected its origins in the metaphysical critiques set out by Feuerbach and others. Although stressing the material determinacy of capitalist alienation and the necessary materialism of all inquiry into the process of capitalist commodity production, Marx also indicated that the capitalist production process acts as an analogue to the modes of tyranny and oppression associated with metaphysics. The capitalist production process performs an assimilation of human life and labour into an abstract system of exchange relations, in which producers lose all integral anthropological connection with the products of their labour, and in which commodities are magically altered and distorted through their transformation into objects of exchange.[115] As a consequence of this, Marx claimed, under social conditions created by capitalism human existence can only encounter itself as paradoxically or metaphysically dislocated and it can only experience itself and the objective forms of its life as determined by metaphysically untransparent processes. For this reason, human life under capitalism struggles to recognize itself as able independently to bring about its truthful self-realization, and human agents are prevented from recognizing other people as like, equal and reciprocally implicated in the process of human self-realization.

Moreover, human life under capitalism is also unable to act politically or construct legal-political orders which place human freedom at their centre, and it can only envision its laws and natural rights as *unnatural laws*, distilling human existence into a false account of its naturally necessary form and detaching human beings from the original natural commonality enshrined in species-being.[116] The objective or normative structures of capitalism, Marx thus explained, are 'ideological forms', in which human beings believe to find reflections of their thoughts and liberties, but which in fact merely distil and refract economic antagonisms.[117] At the heart of Marx's thought, consequently, was the sense that the alienation caused by capitalism is at once a material and a metaphysical fact, which, although caused by dynamics of material expropriation, nonetheless replicates (in materialized form) the ancient order of metaphysics by disseminating coercive laws through state and society and by sustaining itself through deeply fraudulent and abstracted explanations of its origin and validity. The vocabulary of metaphysical critique was therefore not wholly alien to Marx's analysis of the real and material conditions of capitalism, and his account of capitalism as a system of material paradoxes, ideological alienation and *false laws* is not completely outside the tradition of earlier critical metaphysical commentary.

What troubled Marx in the social theories of the Young Hegelians, therefore, was not necessarily that they condemned alienation and heteronomy as a metaphysical condition, but rather that they failed to see the heteronomy of metaphysics in its fully materialized substructure. Because of this false analysis, they also failed to identify the correct material antidote for alienation and heteronomy, and they failed to identify the necessarily materialist path beyond metaphysics. For Marx, simply, the form of alienation (and of metaphysics) is not religion, but capitalism. In Marx's analysis, capitalism takes the place of metaphysics as the cause of human impoverishment. However, this does not mean that Marx did not see capitalism as obtaining metaphysical features or as possessing the nihilistic consequences originally imputed to metaphysics. On the contrary, his work might be seen to hinge on the intimation that the adequately modern critique of metaphysics must either be a critique of capitalism or it must resign itself to remaining metaphysical.

Marx, law and metaphysics

The point over which Marx disagreed most decisively with Young Hegelian perspectives was his view on politics and law. The most influential Young Hegelians saw the persistence of metaphysical or personalist ideas in the law as the most damaging problem of modern political life, and they sought to constitute the state as a republican political order, freed from all obligation to laws which are not rationally accountable. It is for this reason, primarily, that they placed themselves to the left of Hegel; they saw Hegel's partial conservativism as a result of the fact that he had not fully accounted for the state as a place of human reason, action and freedom, and still reflected the state as embodying paradoxical and metaphysically realized ideas of freedom. In fact, Bauer and Ruge both concurred in claiming that failure in the practical quest for political and legal liberation around 1848 had been the concrete result of the residues of political metaphysics in the law.

In contrast to this, Marx, ostensibly at least, denied that politics and law are locations of particular emancipatory significance.[118] Indeed, as the Young Hegelians saw the Hegelian state of freedom as a paradoxical state of freedom, the young Marx derided all claims that the political state is a distinctive or privileged arena of human liberty as the outcome of naive or metaphysically unformed analysis, and he saw all assertions that the state can practically guarantee freedom under law as illusory. He consequently described Hegel's philosophy of state, for example, as a 'mystical abstraction', incapable of accounting for the factual material origins of political power.[119] The conviction that the state gives realized legal form to the idea of freedom, he argued, obscures the foundation of political power in bureaucratic regulation and private property, and it draws a veil over the determination of laws in the state by powerful private and economic purposes and over the insidious modes of social coercion exercised by these purposes. He therefore denounced Hegel's political philosophy as a doctrine that idealizes *political* freedoms in the state but that sustains its account of these freedoms only by placing them in a fetishistic relation of abstract dualism against the factual material or the *social* unfreedom of the human beings, whom the state and its laws are intended to represent and liberate. This abstracted or falsely dualistic account of the state was then, for Marx, not effectively surmounted by theorists who declared political opposition to Hegel, and it remained a persistent feature of political reflection amongst the Young Hegelians. He saw Bauer's republicanism, for example, not as a repudiation of Hegelian political metaphysics, but as a doctrine still ensnared in metaphysical fallacy and deluded by the 'illusion' that laws of state are founded in 'the *free* will' of citizens. He thus viewed Bauer's strong-state republicanism as evidence that Bauer had not fully renounced his earlier religious ideas, and that he had simply transposed his original belief in 'religious authority' into a parallel belief in 'political authority'.[120] Underlying the statist tendencies of the Young Hegelians, therefore, Marx discerned a residual trace of political personalism and metaphysics. This personalism allowed the state, as notionally rational and secular, to supersede the free personality of God in earlier variants on personalism, and it transferred the elements of religious personalism onto the belief that the state is the sole centre of human dignity and liberty, and that the state, detached from its social and material determinacy, is uniquely able to represent and fulfil the free personality of citizens.[121]

For Marx, in short, the modern state has its centre in the metaphysical or ideological myth that it serves and represents the politically liberated human being, defined as a 'sovereign' or as a 'highest being'.[122] This myth is reinforced by all theories, including those of the Young Hegelians, that see the state as an agent of liberty. Factually, however, the modern state is founded in the 'unfree person', living in a condition of 'realized alienation',[123] and the state, in its public paradox of freedom, can do nothing to alter this unfreedom and alienation. Alienation, in fact, is the precondition of the state, for the modern state is always a capitalist state, and its laws refract the primary functional necessities of the capitalist economy. Whereas the Young Hegelians saw alienation and the paradoxicality as attributes of the dominion of the false metaphysical God, therefore, Marx saw the state as a new metaphysical fiction, to which the Young Hegelians themselves helped to give credence and substance. For Marx, in fact, the state is the contemporary form of the false God. As a false God, the state claims to sanction and give general form to human freedom, but it sustains this claim only by imposing and accepting manifest conditions of unfreedom throughout civil society. At the heart of the state is a duality between the apparent freedom that it claims to guarantee and the factual unfreedom that it necessitates, and in this duality it immediately replicates the metaphysical duality between God's freedom and humanity's imperfection originally stabilized by religious personalist ideas of divinity.[124]

To understand the role of politics and law in contemporary societies, Marx argued, the political apparatus must be thoroughly demystified and made transparent to the economic interests that it serves and stabilizes. The state can never offer liberties that contradict the interests of the ruling groups in civil society, who use the state as their instrument, and its primary function is to maintain conditions of contractual stability and legal security for interactions in the economic base. Even the rational and centralized states of emerging liberal or constitutional democracies, he asserted, do not offer conditions for human fulfilment and freedom. The apparent guarantees of freedom or autonomy contained in the public laws of seemingly rational and legitimate modern states are, in fact, highly illusory or metaphysical fixtures, allocated to citizens as formal or possessive rights in order to preserve the interests vested in the state, but impeding the elaboration of full rights of citizenship. The main function of these constitutional or natural rights, in fact, is to engender a contractual underpinning for the circulation of commodities and the exploitative engagement of labour, and they are simply the apparatus of private egotism. Likewise, the formulae of freedom enshrined in capitalist private law – particularly the legal subject or the legal personality of Roman law – are not genuine tokens of liberty and autonomy.[125] Instead, they are malign fictions of personality that the economy imposes on human wills as the false form of their freedom: they are coercive constructs of legal personality which focus human subjective life on minimally prescribed freedoms of contractual interaction, exchange, and monetary disposition over resources and labour. The 'character of the laws' of modern states, Marx therefore argued, is 'cruelty', 'cowardice' and 'inhumanity', and these laws generate ideas of freedom and personality only insofar as these sustain the idea of the person as a schematic bearer of economic interests, supported by the legal apparatus of the state.[126] Laws, consequently, can only *appear* to enable the exercise of a free will in the state, or to ensure citizenship and political participation. Law obtains this appearance where it is 'torn away from its real base' in relations of property and exploitation, and where it is counter-factually proposed to its addressees as a universal medium of equality and justice.[127] Behind and beneath the laws, however, there is always a profound condition of estrangement and denaturation, in which human existence suffers a metaphysical violation and experiences the form of its objective life as wholly bereft of real freedom and real personality.

This anti-legal attitude, however, does not mean that Marx dismissed law per se, that he viewed the fulfilment of species-being as a legally irrelevant condition, or that he saw legal critique as marginal to the course of human liberation. In fact, the contrary is the case. In his earliest writings, for example, he denounced historicist deductions of legal validity based solely in positivist conceptions of validity,[128] and he wrote long invectives against the exclusion of moral contents from laws and against the application of laws as pure 'material instruments of private interest'.[129] In these early works, he argued that modern legal states, which reduce laws to devices for stabilizing private interests, are not legal states at all: they are merely coercive organs, founded in an 'exception from the law', and they cannot claim validity for their laws.[130] He thus saw the reduction of state and law to formal utensils of capital as an exceptional betrayal of true law and of the universal potentials of the law, and he clearly intimated that the law could, if authentically formed, act to ensure common justice. More generally, in fact, Marx's early concept of species-being also contained certain primary notions of justice, legal personality and common entitlement, which remained pervasive influences throughout his work. Labour not regulated by exchange, he argued, tends to produce substantial laws, which give a juridical expression to species-being and which have greater moral validity than all 'general law'. The organic 'customs of the impoverished class', which have evolved through common labour on nature, he explained, show an 'instinctual legal sense',[131] and they articulate a relationship between human beings and the natural world which produces distinctively legitimate (that is, anthropologically integral) legal claims. Above all, human labour on nature generates natural rights of entitlement and common property, and it shapes human agency into collective forms of legal recognition.[132] Human custom, historically cemented through interaction between humans and nature, contains a legal expression of species-being, and, as such, it is a source of authentic natural law, against which the laws of abstracted private interest are merely metaphysical or exceptional.

These early legal arguments expressed the sense that the organic labour on nature through which species-being is articulated contains a legal orientation which is suppressed by the juridical apparatus of modern states. It is specific to capitalist states, Marx asserted, that they found their legal orders in concepts of right which are distilled from anthropologically depleted ideas of human integrity, and they construe the subjectivity or the personality of social and legal agents around an 'isolated and withdrawn monad'. The modern (or capitalist) foundation of right thus depends on the exclusion of all interpersonal, collective or eminently *social* aspects of human existence: it defines right solely as the 'right of the limited individual' (of the individual seeking only private purposes), without any 'relation to other people'.[133] If the monadic subject is the false form of subjectivity, however, the human being engaged in the active and authentic elaboration of species-being is formed as an eminently 'social being' and its individual or subjective life is inseparable from the 'totality' of all conditions of human social freedom.[134] The natural emphases of species-being thus allow the human subject to evolve as the subject of society or as a social subject, and subjects are created as social as they recognize that they *need* other human beings as the integrally constitutive conditions of their own natural self-realization.[135] If the monadic or asocial subject is the source and form of false (or capitalist) law, then, it can be assumed that the social subject gives rise to legal claims, entitlements and expectations, which are very distinct from those borne by the purposive or monadic legal subjects of capitalist law. Indeed, it can be presupposed that, if human subjects abandon their self-concentration on ownership and if they freely interact with the natural world and with other people in the natural world, they will, according to Marx, arrive at ideas of obligation which deduce law, not from the proprietorial interests of private-legal subjects, but from more communal modes of human interaction and collective needs. Where individuals realize themselves as species-being, and where, because of this, they abdicate their position as purposive and self-seeking individuals, Marx intimated, they will emancipate themselves from their self-reflection in merely abstract or formal laws, and they will elaborate fully emancipatory rights, founded in the practical-moral inclusion of shared material needs.[136] In this respect, rather than finally contradicting Young Hegelian ideas on law, Marx intensified the earlier notion of the Young Hegelians that modern capitalist law (especially the private law of Roman law) creates metaphysical subjects, and it fragments common subjectivity into atomized and narrowly purposive constructions of rights, freedom and integrity. Human freedom, therefore, is not a condition in which law plays no role, but rather one which emerges through the destruction of the metaphysical laws of capitalism.

Marx's work was, therefore, deeply committed to articulating new ideas of legal validity and legal personality, and the law occupied a central, though at times unfocused, position in his work. His critique of the legal personality of capitalism was particularly influenced by Eduard Gans, who also used modified Hegelian ideas to oppose the influence of economically derived concepts of legal validity and legal subjectivity. Gans turned with particular vehemence against Savigny, whose positivist and volitional approach to law foundation he saw as neglecting the ethical dimension in human legal agreements, especially of those pertaining to property. The legal subject, he claimed, cannot be constructed from factually existing legal relations and cannot be presupposed as a morally neutral basis for ownership, but must be construed as a manifestation of the historically operative and socially recognized moral will.[137] Valid law, therefore, should not be viewed as a system of purely positive norms protecting the possessive rights of solitary legal agents, but as a substantial order enshrining socially and consensually mediated rights. All legal formation, he concluded, is the result of the self-elaboration of the moral will of the human person in the originally 'unfree and lawless' realm of nature.[138] The self-elaboration of the moral will leads to the objectivization of natural right in the world as a moment in a common will and to the formation of legal subjects as agents of universally acceptable moral laws, not as solitary subjects or solitary self-seeking personalities. The justification of a legal right, consequently, resides in the fact that a shared moral will views this right as necessary and as contributing to wider conditions of personal freedom and self-realization. Gans therefore defined the free ownership of property as a right, for he construed property as an essential precondition and expression of human freedom.[139] Marx clearly did not share Gans's belief that property could be legitimately held as an extension of the substantial moral will. However, the legal elements of Marx's concept of species-being incorporated a constructive appropriation of Gans's view that the legal person must be defined as a person actively engaged in the formation of rights, not as a person to whom prior or formal rights are positively imputed. Indeed, close to other Young Hegelians, Gans viewed elaborated freedom as a condition of commonly formed and recognized natural rights. For Marx, however, the full elaboration of species-being necessarily creates a condition in which entitlements are fully separated from the possessive will and from the possessive personality.

Marx claimed, to conclude, that modern laws offer at most an illusion of freedom and participatory enfranchisement, and they ideologically obscure the extent to which political reality is founded in universal unfreedom, resulting from the alienation of labour in the capitalist production process. The assertion that politics, law or the state might provide an arena for the freedom of species-being demonstrates, in consequence, a wilfully paradoxical approach to theoretical analysis, which abstracts a coercive apparatus from the material processes of its evolution and proclaims then that it is an organ of human self-liberation. Where capitalism remains the pervasive mode of production, for Marx, all appearance of political liberation must have an ideological or metaphysical character. The state under capitalism can only ever be a dualistically split expression of species-being, in which the free human person, as a citizen, encounters its freedom as a formally meaningless experience, to which its factual unfreedom as an economic agent appears as an irreducible 'contradiction'. Under the rule of the capitalist state, the citizen only obtains its freedom in that section of his or her life that is not legally determined by material and economic compulsion and not subject to private laws of exchange and exploitation, whilst the material life of the citizens remains in absolute heteronomy, under laws reflecting a private-legal rationality of divided labour and economic expropriation.[140] The state's claim to uphold the freedom of citizens thus merely reflects an ideological/metaphysical form, in which the factual unfreedom of these citizens is perpetuated and intensified. Unlike the Young Hegelians, therefore, Marx had no faith in the ability of a modified or constitutionally formed political apparatus to construct a socio-economic order founded in the realization of common needs and the abolition of the unjust scarcity of natural goods. To obtain a politics of authentic and integral freedom, he indicated, it is necessary to free human thinking from all traces of metaphysical ideology: in fact, it is necessary to free human thinking from the state itself, and from the falsely metaphysical laws of the state. The politics that Marx envisaged in this instance would be a *post-state* politics, founded in a thoroughly post-personal elaboration of species-being. This condition would be a condition of natural commonality, integrating a goods economy based in shared utility, and a social order in which commonly evolving natural/human essence, not norms or values abstracted from statically purposive or possessive persons, shape the material structure of human existence.

Marx's account of elaborated species-being, however, need not be viewed as a *post-legal* condition. On the contrary, the idea of species-being always contains an echo of the claim that surfaced intermittently in Young Hegelian thought – that the realization of human substance will form a condition in which human law will lose all traces of objectivity, purposive coercion and metaphysical force. Such effortlessly universal law will, for Marx, not be the law of state, but of society, as the formed natural/human reality of species-life. Marx was thus clearly far removed from the religious or essential anthropological conceptions of the Young Hegelians. However, he duplicated certain aspects of their argument that the elaboration of human essence can only occur as a revolt against heteronomy, as a revolt against all existing legal forms and the traces of alienation which infiltrate these, and so as a revolt *against metaphysics*.

6 Positivism and organic theory

The two faces of early German liberalism

Positivism: a definition

It is notoriously difficult to define legal positivism and to determine exactly which legal theorists might be classified as positivists and which not. This difficulty is partly due to the fact that positivism contains a number of quite distinct, and often rival outlooks, and partly also to the fact that its methods and aims changed markedly through the nineteenth century. As discussed, though, this difficulty also results from the fact that positivist accounts of law and state often had much in common with other legal-theoretical orthodoxies.

For the sake of intellectual coherence, however, this chapter defines positivism as a method of legal analysis primarily – or at least originally – specialized on clarifying the legal relations of private law, and usually marked by the following characteristics. First, positivist analysis tends to presuppose that questions of legal validity can only be posed within a frame of reference produced by the law itself and that no extra-legal principles (such as metaphysical or ius-natural ideas) can be invoked to rule over disputes of jurisdiction. Second, positivism claims that the evolution of the law occurs, not through the principled or normatively guided transformation of legal objectives, but through the quasi-naturalistic self-reproduction of the legal system. External direction of the law can only occur, if at all, through the reinterpretation of legal sources, especially the pandects of Roman private law, not through purposive intervention. Third, positivism assumes that the relationship between law and politics is not of primary constitutive importance for the law, and that, to a large extent, the evolution of law takes place independently of political control. Fourth, however, positivism also argues that the principles of private law provided the foundations for deducing the legal basis of the state, and that a state defines itself as legitimate by acting as a legal person and by assuming a legal character analogous to that of the person under private law. Positivism thus asserts that the state is a person under law; it is distinguished as a formal legal personality; and, as it possesses a personality, it must also have some kind of constitution: the constitution is the legal form of the state's personality. The state, therefore, might possess extensive privileges and rights as a purposive person of law, but it is not absolutely above the law, and its legal personality (its constitution) presupposes some recognition of other legal personalities, whose rights cannot be ignored. The formation of the state as a legal order is, thus, a self-originating act of the state itself, in which the state is obliged by the constitutional personality which it gives to itself to exercise its freedoms in a form constrained by rational law. Although bound by law, however, the state is also responsible for passing and for enforcing laws, and it is the final guarantor of legal order throughout society. As an analogue to the person of Roman law, in short, the state exists as a purposive agent constrained by law, but it also stands apart from the other legal persons in the rest of society, and it exercises its particular purposive will in acts of legislation. Indeed, the personality of the state is distinguished precisely by the fact that it contains specific legislative functions that are the exclusive property of the state, and which cannot be transferred to other persons.

In these respects, positivism shared much ground with historicism, and positivism and historicism formed related perspectives on legal statehood and constitutional formation in nineteenth-century Germany. There were, of course, certain irreconcilable differences between historicism and positivism in these debates, and these were at times expressed in polemics between positivist and historicist theorists. Unlike the historicists, positivists saw the importing of cultural and national objectives into legal analysis as an inappropriate juridical method, and it did not share the historicist assertion that states are constituted as centres of national-cultural integration. On the contrary, positivists tended to opt for a thin construct of state power, and they deduced the state's personality through formal-legal analysis, not from wider cultural or anthropological preconditions. In this respect, positivism at times moved close to a morally reduced variant on Kantian-formalist ideas, insisting that the form of the legitimate state can be produced by the law alone, through an act of self-causality in the state, and that legitimacy cannot be derived from any external source. Whilst historicists defined national-historical evolution as the evolving substructure of the law, therefore, the positivists favoured systematic and universal codifications of legal order, extracted from constant constructs of the legal personality of the state. Nonetheless, if the above broad characterization of legal positivism is accepted, certain jurists more commonly linked to historicism, especially Hugo and Savigny, might also be categorized as early positivists.[1] The historicists and the positivists shared the crucial conviction that the law itself, as it is currently applied, contains the solutions to legal and political problems. They argued that all radical transformation of law and politics, guided by principles external to law in its existing form, should be avoided, and that a legally bound constitutional order is obtainable without a total rationalization or a metaphysically motivated upheaval of the order of state. Both argued that rationalized and natural-legal attempts to explain legitimate statehood in the Enlightenment and in early liberalism operated on false preconditions, and so tended to create insubstantial or precariously imbalanced states. Both approaches consequently described the legal foundations of state power in ways that, though not resolutely anti-progressive, sought to express alternatives to classical Enlightenment models of the legal state and to account for the origins of legitimate statehood without positing metaphysical legal values. Both movements, in other words, enunciated overlapping, yet ultimately opposed, perspectives in the broad climate of post-Napoleonic politics in Germany, which supported limited liberalization of law and state and a protection of economic freedoms from encroachment by the state, but which remained alarmed at the memory of rationalized disorder and legal upheaval caused by the ideas of 1789. To a greater extent even than historicism, positivism captured the spirit of cautious progressivism and reserved commitment to formal-constitutional rule which dominated established lines of German political theory, in different variants, through most of the nineteenth century, and which shaped constitutional debate around 1848, and, most especially, in the aftermath of 1848. Indeed, in this era, the positivist derivation of the legal personality of the state from the paradigms of private law formed the central or consensual ground in the divergent accounts of how the German state should be formed as a determinately constitutional order, or as a *Rechtsstaat.*

Positivism: for and against liberalism

Positivist theory was clearly not the sole foundation for liberal politics in the early and middle decades of nineteenth-century Germany. In fact, the contrary is clearly the case, and there are many diverse examples of influential liberal doctrines prior to and after 1848 that had little to do with positivism. As discussed, in the aftermath of the French Revolution, Wilhelm von Humboldt proposed an early and highly regarded configuration of liberal ideas, in which he took a humanist approach to the questions of how and to what extent the state should be founded as a constitutional state. Humboldt's central argument was that the state's power must be restricted to the preservation of security and 'positive welfare' amongst its citizens and to ensuring that 'legal freedom' is preserved for all citizens.[2] He therefore insisted that the state has no power to regulate education, debate and opinion, and he argued that political control of private liberties is especially deleterious for human evolution and personality.[3] Paul Johann Anselm von Feuerbach also set out a doctrine which developed and altered Kantian ideas to insist on the necessary limits and moral content of state power, and which sought to transform classical natural-legal principles into a positive conception of the state's personality and will.[4] In this, Feuerbach argued that the content of laws cannot be deduced from the metaphysics of moral law, and he claimed that the state is the source of law and that there is no natural law outside or opposed to the state.[5] However, he argued that the representatives of the state are only entitled to regulate society if they comply with laws implied in the contractual origins of the state, and if regents transgress against laws of state they are subject to legal sanction.[6] Moreover, he also argued that each person, as an addressee of law, is a positive legal subject, obtaining rights and dignities under law, which place formal limits on the state's power.[7] A legitimate state, he concluded, recognizes people as positive centres of legal entitlement, and it also recognizes the integrity of the sphere of private-legal interaction, and it upholds conditions of mutually acknowledged freedom between citizens.[8] At the same time, Karl Salomo Zachariä also expanded Kantian ideas to argue for a strictly constituted *Rechtsstaat,* whose laws, enshrined in a universal code, represent principles of reason,[9] and elevate all addressees of law into a realm of moral autonomy.[10]

In the years leading up to 1848, subsequently, Karl von Rotteck and Karl Welcker edited a political encyclopaedia that provided staple reading for the liberal and progressive elements of the South West German bourgeoisie. This encyclopaedia also contained a distinct liberal outlook, close to conventional Kantian and ius-natural accounts of legal validity and political accountability. Unlike the positivists, Rotteck and Welcker argued that positive law must be made transparent to rational law, and they insisted that a rational law provides the most reliable basis for a constitutional state, ensuring social rights and freedoms.[11] They therefore defined the legitimate state not as a formal person under law, but as a bearer of rationally constituted sovereignty: as a 'free social association of a people', governed by a 'common constitutional law', with a freely constituted constitutional assembly.[12] During and after 1848, similarly, other models of the legal state also assumed great importance. For example, Friedrich Christoph Dahlmann, a liberal delegate in 1848, claimed that organic republicanism was the political outlook most appropriate to German constitutional politics. Central to this view was the claim that that the traditional estate-based system in Germany could, without revolutionary upheaval, constitute the foundation for a state employing more modern techniques of delegation and representation, and that a constitutional state could be formed organically on the foundation of German political culture.[13] Dahlmann thus advocated the establishment of a state based in a constitutional balance between monarchy and delegation, and he stressed the importance of the monarchical aspect of the constitution, which he saw as an element of 'custom' or 'conviction', serving to confer stability on the entire political order.[14] Similarly, Robert von Mohl, also a delegate in 1848, added important elements to emerging positivist preconceptions. Whilst following the positivist argument that law depends on a 'commanding will' in the state, in his later works he rejected the construction of the state as an ideal personality, and he insisted that strict constitutional limits should be placed on the legislative power of the monarch.[15] He also ascribed extensive social and distributive responsibilities to the state, which far exceeded the minimalist ideas of statehood characteristic of positivism.[16] After 1848, then, Lorenz von Stein analysed the socio-economic and political situation in Germany and concluded that only a fusion of welfarist, conservative and liberal political ideals could bring longer-term stability to the political order. Although certainly out of step with more classical liberal ideas, Stein's work argued that the liberal-capitalist economic order could only be defended and perpetuated if its beneficiaries accepted the necessity of state regulation and if its latent antagonisms were softened by palliative policies of 'social reform'.[17]

Despite the influence of non-positivist views, however, liberal or republican constitutional ideals became increasingly cautious through the course of the nineteenth century, and the expression of liberal ideals was increasingly couched within broadly conformist or, at most, proceduralist political attitudes. Through the periods of constitutional formation and national unification around 1866–67 and 1870–71, therefore, liberal ideas were usually articulated in socially compliant manner, and they reflected a widespread aquiescence in the limited constitutional system which was stabilized at this time and which underpinned the political structure of Imperial Germany. For this reason, consequently, positivist doctrine largely set the parameters for broadly liberal debates on constitutionalism after 1848, and it ultimately provided the main vocabulary in which the political order implemented under Bismarck was debated and justified.

Positivism began to take the shape of a distinct orthodoxy during the debates about legal codification stimulated by the introduction of the Code Napoléon after 1804. The Code stimulated controversies between the leading German lawyers, and it provoked intense debate over the necessity of universal legislation and over the appropriateness of borrowing French law for German civil organization. Most especially, however, it generated debate over the origins of law's validity, and over the processes of its positivization. These controversies culminated in the famous polemic between Savigny and Anton Friedrich Justus Thibaut on these questions. In this debate, Thibaut argued that the most reliable source of law's validity is a fully positivized code, and he pleaded for the institution of a generalized legal system throughout the German states. In contrast to this, Savigny defended the existing patchwork of laws in the different German regions, which he saw as expressing the national spirit of the German people. Thibaut did not reject all aspects of Savigny's historicism. Like Savigny, he opposed the unaltered implementation of French civil law in Germany and he insisted that a German code should reflect the 'strength and activity' of German culture and German legal ideals.[18] However, he justified his demand for a universal civil code by claiming that a code was necessary to remove legislation and jurisdiction from the 'arbitrariness of particular governments',[19] and he saw systematically positivized codification as a civil constitution, acting to protect liberal political interests in the sphere of civil law. Central to Thibaut's work, consequently, was an insistence that uniformity and stabilized positivity in the law is the cornerstone of progressive politics, secured against princely encroachment. Pure ius-naturalism and pure historicism, he indicated, are equally unable to provide foundations for a politically and economically liberated society: this can only be accomplished by reliably organized legal texts.

Thibaut cannot in all respects be seen as an exemplary representative of the political aspirations of early legal positivism. In his insistence on the systematic purity and uniformity of the law, his work certainly cleared the terrain for the later evolution of positivist methodologies. Similarly, he did much for the cause of legal convergence between the German states, which remained one of the most pressing areas of positivist debate throughout the nineteenth century. Moreover, in defining civil law and private law as obtaining quasi-constitutional power he reinforced the central belief of positivism that the clarification of private-legal relations is the most effective way to limit the prerogative power of the state. However, Thibaut also deviated from more common templates of positivist doctrine. First, he was obviously close to the more progressive liberal factions of post-Napoleonic Germany, and this distanced him from later positivist thinkers. His analysis of private law was marked by the express insistence that the rights and obligations of the person under private law have a constitutive political role: the determination of private-legal personality, he claimed, also imposes clear restrictions on the exercise of public power, and whoever exercises public power is always, as a private person, 'subject to his own laws' and accountable to judicial procedure.[20] His writings were thus shaped by a conception of the law as a potent transmitter of political ideals, and as an ethically influential constraint on political authority, and his construction of private law provided the foundation for a comprehensive critique of late absolutism and for an advanced account of a modern *Rechtsstaat*. Second, moreover, he was strongly attached to more consolidated Kantian ideas about natural law as the necessary substrate of all law. Although insistent on the positivity of law as the precondition of its validity, he argued that legal interpretation must be guided by moral considerations and that valid positive law can only be discerned by 'philosophical reason'.[21]

Despite his reintroduction of ius-natural conceptions into post-Enlightenment debate, however, Thibaut claimed that ius-natural ideals should not be viewed as extra-legal principles, but rather as ethical ideas intrinsic to law's positively evolved form. Opposed simultaneously to pure natural-legal and to exclusively historicist methods, therefore, he argued that the correct application of positive law depends on the committed exegesis of the 'philosophical interpreter', who must allow the application of law to be guided by the moral content which the law, in its positive shape, already contains.[22] The 'dry analysis of a metaphysical principle', consequently, will not on its own create 'foundations of positive law'. Instead, the interpreter must always show 'thorough historical knowledge', and interpretation must avoid applying 'philosophical insights' to the law, if these are not commensurate with law's historical content.[23] Underlying Thibaut's moral-hermeneutical approach to the law, therefore, was always a distinction between positive laws and natural laws.[24] Only positive laws, he claimed, are relevant to legal application, and natural law does not provide 'necessary' rules of interpretation independently of the given corpus of the law.[25] However, he also indicated that philosophical interpretation of the law can refine the body of positive law so that it can, through interpretation, be gradually adjusted to the condition of natural law.

The defining principles of positivism were articulated in most quintessential form in the works of Georg Friedrich Puchta. Puchta's intellectual formation was deeply influenced by Savigny's methodology, and his work gave emphatic expression to the conviction in the Historical School that valid law cannot be deduced from formal reason. Methods 'proceeding from the concept of reason' or seeking to generate universal precepts for legal application are not, he argued, able to constitute stable foundations for the law.[26] Law, instead, must be allowed to evolve organically through tradition and through interpretation: valid law is based in the 'popular convictions' of the nation, and it serves to unite 'the members of a national whole'.[27] To a greater extent than Savigny, however, Puchta emphasized, in his later works at least, that law is essentially a positive set of rules, and that expert academic interpretation, not cultural understanding, holds the key to elucidating its guiding concepts.[28] In this respect, in fact, he began to renounce historicist views on law's genesis, and he sought to place law on purely positive, conceptual foundations and to deduce points of legal principle from the inner-juridical preconditions of the law itself. In this respect, his work revolved around the claim that the rules constituting the body of law are deducible from the idea of the legal subject or legal person, derived from the private law of Roman law, which underlies all assumptions of legal necessity. At the centre of legal order, consequently, is the idea that law is a set of relations referring to legal persons or subjects. These persons all have like qualities, they are all engaged in the free exercise of wills to obtain certain purposes (especially possession of property), and they are all entitled to objective legal security as they pursue these purposes. Where the law can construct the legal person as its form of reference, then, law can explain its validity in coherent and consistent terms, it can provide rules to resolve legal grievance and it can create a reality of legal regularity through society. Where legal subjects are construed as persons, they are constructed as bearers of certain interests, which the law objectively protects, and they are reflected by the law as claimants to legal goods objectively provided by the legal system, and the rulings over specific cases are determined by considerations of the rights and entitlements which these subjects, as legal subjects, possess. It is central to the law, on this account, that it refers to persons, and that it dispenses justice and ensures equality as required by the persons which, in an act of primary causality, it has freely constructed. The law has no content exceeding the objectives of its own construction, and it cannot be rendered transparent to constitutive human or national interests and dispositions. Law, in fact, is nothing but a medium giving positively generalized form for the freedoms and entitlements that people seek as legal subjects. Law, Puchta concluded, constructs 'the human being as a person', it refers to people exclusively in this quality, and the analysis of law has solely to do with the legal relations between juridified persons, not between people in any intimately integral or culturally cohesive sense.[29]

At the heart of Puchta's work is, thus, the assumption that law is a set of relations between persons as created by law. As far as he was prepared to attribute any anthropological substance to these persons, he argued that persons under law are determined as persons by the fact that they exercise *wills*. Extrapolating from the construct of the person in Savigny's account of Roman law, he claimed that people obtain the status of legal personality, first, through their volitional demand that rights should be attributed to them, and then, second, through the volitional demand that recognition should be granted for the possessive claims which they assert over other objects: over objects which they claim as possessions.[30] All law, consequently, 'consists in the recognition of the freedom which the human being obtains by being the subject of a will', and all legal relations have as their constitutive source the claims made by the will of legal persons and communicated as relevant to law.[31] The legal person, therefore, is the social form of human freedom; it is the form under which the human will can exercise itself in appropriate manner, and under which this exercise of the will can be protected. At the same time, however, where the freedoms of legal persons are recognized by laws, these freedoms also undergo a certain rational transformation, as freedom of the will only obtains legal sanction as universal freedom: as a universal freedom which all wills can exercise. The legal person is, therefore, constructed by law as both *free* and *rational,* and where it exercises its will under law it necessarily exercises its will in rational and necessarily sanctioned manner. The unity of reason and freedom at the heart of legal and political legitimation, therefore, is reflected here as a form which law generates spontaneously within itself, so that the original source of legitimacy under law is autonomously constituted by the law and for the law. By extrapolating the legal person as the focus of rational freedom, in short, law creates a reference in which it can always explain itself as permitting rationality and freedom, and it thus becomes the author of its own positive validity.

Underlying Puchta's concentration of socio-legal reality on the subject of Roman law was a further theoretical move, which also influenced later theoretical innovations in the positivist line. By constructing law as the medium of rational human freedom and the legal subject or the legal personality as the bearer of the concrete conditions of reasonable freedom, Puchta implied that legal analysis, and perhaps all social analysis, need concern itself exclusively with social facts as they appear or are transmitted through the law. The facts behind or beneath the legal facts and the persons behind or beneath the legal persons are of no importance for understanding the law, he claimed, and all processes of social formation which have not been transformed into legal processes are not of primary importance. He thus conceived of the law in quasi-naturalistic or biological manner, as a 'living organism' composed of dynamically related legal facts, which, in their ongoing interpenetration, produce new and constantly altered legal facts, each of which autonomously produces conditions for its validity.[32] Social or moral facts outside this complex of organic wills cannot contribute to the examination of law's validity or to the positive explanation of the conditions of human freedom. Indeed, all attempts to integrate social or moral considerations into the analysis of law serve only to blur the view of the basic units of legal analysis and to restrict the freedoms which law, on its own, safeguards.

Given his focus on the pure person as the centre of law, it is not surprising that Puchta opposed the proto-democratic movements in German society prior to 1848. Instead, he declared sympathy for monarchical forms of governance, in which political authority is founded, like other possessions, in possessive personality: as 'the right of a person'.[33] In this respect, the Roman-law construct of the personality in positivism supported a political stance analogous to that contained in Stahl's construct of absolute personality. Like Stahl, Puchta argued that the personality of the state is distinct from other legal persons, and it exercises its will over these persons as a formal and static centre of authority. However, like other positivists, he tempered his pro-monarchical stance by insisting that the construction of the monarchy as a legal person necessarily means that the use of power is procedurally and constitutionally limited, and that the state must never be viewed in patrimonial categories. Both the state and its subjects are persons under public law, and the bearers of public-legal authority cannot arrogate to themselves 'private-legal' rights over public power.[34] In this, clearly, Puchta did not see the state as bound by socially evolved limits or constraints. In fact, he saw the person of the state as a direct analogue to persons under private law and as restricted only by the very general laws implicit in the formal sanction of personal freedoms. The person of the state, he claimed, is in fact a juridical person or a juridical 'fiction' which the law presupposes in order consistently to construct stable points of agency and imputation under public law,[35] but which is factually and legally indifferent to the social agents or natural persons which it incorporates and represents. Like all other persons, in short, the state is nothing more than a construct of law, and it can only actively exist as a person recognized by law, with no contents attributable to it from outside the law. Because of this, however, the state must only exist as a legal state: as a state whose operations are both defined and controlled by law, and the limits of whose power are determined by the normative or procedural structure which it necessarily obtains as a legal person.[36] The state, therefore, might exist as a distinct or even privileged element in the law, or even as a 'necessary complement' to the law, executing law through its own apparatic organization.[37] However, the state invariably 'presupposes the law' and the 'consciousness of law', and it can only exercise its will in passing laws if law frames the application of its power.[38] It cannot, in other words, contravene the conditions of its own legal personality, which stipulate a basic recognition of other legal persons.

In this respect, Puchta's work forms a key intervention in the history of theoretical reflection on reason and freedom, and on legality and legitimacy, in the state. He concluded that the personality of the state, in analogy to the legal person under Roman law, is a will that exercises its freedom as it makes and enforces laws. As a will constructed as the will of a legal person, however, this legislative will is not merely an indeterminate sequence of volitional acts or decisions, but it is bound by elements of its own laws, and it must recognize other persons as bearing legal rights and entitlements. The origin of law is, therefore, *at one and the same time* the free will of the legislator and a rational normative order: the free will of the legislator can, *paradoxically,* only be exercised in and as an overarching normative system, and the freedom to make laws can only be enacted with the knowledge that freedom is bound by other freedoms, and is, therefore, rational. The free rationality of law, in consequence, necessarily constructs the state in which it originates as a legal state. Most importantly, however, the unity of rationality and freedom in the state is a unity that the state, as an agent under laws, creates for itself, in a primary act of self-causality: the state is always the author of itself as a state under law. In its practical implications, Puchta used this doctrine to imply that the law, on its own, creates conditions of legal rule and accountability more effectively than more socially embodied or normatively committed campaigns. Indeed, he intimated that natural-legal or ethical attempts to provide a constitutional foundation for the state are deeply self-deluding in their interpretation of the relation between law and politics. Politics, for Puchta, can never be more than law: the state has law as its own self-generated precondition, and it is only as a person created by the law that the state can be understood. Correct interpretation and application of the state's law, in consequence, will always create conditions of legal statehood.

Positivism and the constitutional legal state

The example of Puchta shows how early positivists used the ideas of personality in Roman private law to construct a model of the legal state. Underlying this account of state and law was a rejection both of the moral-rational personality imputed to the state in the Enlightenment, and of the substantial personality imputed to the state by historicists. The positivists dismissed both of these accounts as insufficiently legal, and so beset by fantasy and likely to induce problems of application. Indeed, the positivists clearly viewed their own juridical construction of the state as an ultimately more effective means of defining and limiting the state than rival natural-law or covertly metaphysical doctrines. The law itself, they argued, is the source of law, and the law, cleansed of all metaphysical adjuncts, ensures that law is applied rationally by the state.

These ideas obtained defining expression, around 1848, in the works of Carl Friedrich von Gerber. Gerber's major early work was a highly influential analysis of private law. In this work, he argued that the primary duty of legal science is to establish a 'unity of private law' and, employing methods derived from Roman law, to deduce and clarify legal principles for organizing economic relations.[39] Gerber saw himself, in part at least, as a lawyer with a specific interest in Germanic law, and so as distinct from positivists who saw Roman law alone as the source of private-legal concepts.[40] Consequently, he claimed that Germany had its own integral legal culture, and that German law, productively fused with the methods of Roman law,[41] must play a dynamic role in the gradual transformation of Germany into a nation-state with a unitary national order.[42] He also protested against the exclusive construction of legal paradigms and persons around positivist fictions and abstractions; private law, he claimed, is always rooted in concrete 'legal facts' and socially constitutive relationships, and is, therefore, embedded in a particular legal-political culture.[43] However, unlike later Germanists, he rejected the claim that law is independently formed by 'associations' existing in society, and he argued that legal research should exclude from its inquiries all extra-legal principles, and so restrict itself to the elucidation of the 'particular laws' of private law.[44] Gerber's thought thus moved on a fine line between pure positivist analysis and a more anthropological consideration of the relation between law and power. However, the overriding claim of his work is that legal questions relate only to the law, and that the scientific treatment of these questions should not be excessively burdened with normative or directly politicized objectives.

In his writings on public law, Gerber also moved between classical positivist and more typically Germanist perspectives. Like other positivists, his doctrine provided for a limited model of the constitutional legal state, reflecting the widespread conservative outlook after 1848, but not entirely hostile towards liberal demands for economic autonomy and a basic system of political delegation. In his later political writings, he argued that the state must necessarily be a monarchy, for it is only in a monarch that the 'abstract personality of the state' can be incorporated. However, he also followed earlier positivists in insisting that the exercise of monarchical power must be subject to constitutional constraints; the power of the monarch cannot be exercised as 'a right of individual human personality', but rather as the 'the highest organ of the will of the state'.[45] The state, he concluded moreover, can only possess a 'minimum of influence' in private-legal and economic issues, and the personality of the state must accept itself as limited by the other personalities imputed under private law.[46] At the same time, however, Gerber contradicted conventional positivist views in that he interpreted the will of the state in partly organic terms: that is, as constituted through its social and material relations with those whom it incorporates. The state, he concluded, cannot be seen solely as a juridically abstracted person or as a 'mechanical concentration of many individual wills': it is also an embodiment of the 'ethical organism' of the German people.[47] The state, consequently, has a personality which is higher than that of other legal persons, and this personality is formed through the organic integration of a plurality of human wills. As a result of this, Gerber argued that the wills incorporated into the state become legal elements in the state, so that the state can never exercise its will without some degree of determinate accountability towards those whose wills constitute the state.[48] For all his basic positivist orientation, therefore, he argued that public law has its origins in the organically evolved will of the state and it is only when authenticated directly by this will that the 'abstract norms' of the law have validity.[49]

The early writings on law and state of Rudolf Jhering also employed similar vocabulary and methods, although ultimately reaching rather different political-theoretical conclusions. Jhering's early publications formed perhaps the most extreme example of an ultra-positivist, quasi-biological conception of law. In these works, he defined law as the 'objective organism of human freedom',[50] in which legal forms and concepts have an autonomous 'productive' power to 'conceive' new elements and principles out of their existing inner unity,[51] and he denounced all assumptions that law is susceptible to external guidance. Like earlier positivists, Jhering also took the 'idea of the personality' as the genetic origin of all law,[52] and he too interpreted the law as a medium which articulates and protects the purposive freedoms contained in the 'subjective will' or in the 'personal active force' imputed by the law to the human subject.[53] On this basis, he reiterated the earlier argument that the state is formed as a juridical person, as an organ which is 'distinct from and superior to natural persons',[54] which is bound by the laws through which its personality is constructed, and which enacts its freedom as freedom under laws. To a greater extent than the first positivists, however, he accentuated the fact that the derivation of the legal person from private law places precise restrictions on the public-legal authority of the state. He argued that the conception of law as originating in the 'autonomy of the individual' precludes solely state-centred models of the political community, and he claimed that the contractual obligations characteristic of private law provide the basis for public law, and so for legitimate political order.[55] The contract, he argued, is the binding principle of private law under Roman law and it is through this idea that the 'guarantee of law by the state' first evolved.[56] The state, he therefore concluded, is 'constituted according to the principles of private law', and private law possesses an 'original independence' against the state.[57]

By the 1860s, however, Jhering largely abandoned the pure-positivist methodology of his earlier work. In his later writings, he adopted an approach that saw valid law as determined by concrete-objective interests and by considerations of societal utility.[58] Strongly influenced by British utilitarianism,[59] he asserted that the objective 'question of interest', not the subjective will, should be taken as the underlying principle in considerations of legal validity.[60] The clearest illustration of this, he explained, is the question of property. The right of property does not exist, he concluded, because – as Savigny imagined – a subjective will makes exclusive claim to objects and so produces subjective freedoms and entitlements for itself, nor – as Hegel and Gans suggested – because human wills interact with each other to engender an overarching volitional and ethical order which sanctions property rights. Instead, property rights exist under law because ownership and economic utilization of property serve the practical and objective interests of modern society, and the law accordingly provides a concrete normative structure in which the interest in property can be secured. The ground of the law, therefore, is *objective interest:* interest is prior to law and it conditions both the formation and application of law.[61]

Jhering's later methodological volte-face reflects a fundamental reconsideration of the status of the person under law. He now rejected the belief that the source of law can be distilled from the subjective purposes or the subjective will of the legal person. Law, to be sure, has a purposive structure, and it always enacts an underlying will. However, the purposes underlying valid law are common purposes, refracting the interests of all society, and the will enacting law is an objective will, seeking to implement these purposes throughout society.[62] The origin of law, thus, resides in the concrete ethical and utilitarian purposes of human consciousness,[63] and the person under law is not the formally free person of positivism, but the actively purposive person whose purposes enter common associations with the purposes of other persons and reflect common conceptions of utility and necessity.[64] Law, consequently, does not evolve as a set of legal relations between socially abstracted or chimerical persons; rather, it is the expression of concrete interests growing out of associations between objectively purpose-seeking legal agents.

The later Jhering also disclaimed his earlier view on the state as a self-limiting formal-juridical person. Even in his earlier publications, he underlined his belief that the personality of the state incorporates wide-ranging social responsibilities. The state, he explained at this point, possesses a 'positive will' which creates conditions for the freedom and improvement of all persons throughout society;[65] indeed, the state can even be viewed as the 'organism of freedom' which assists the purposive fulfilment of individual members of society.[66] In his later works, he expanded this approach to include the claim that legitimate public authority should be defined as the 'culmination' and 'organization' of all common social purposes.[67] The legitimate state, on this account, is a 'purposive subject' that incorporates and pursues the common 'purposes of society',[68] and secures and upholds the necessary 'living conditions of society'.[69] As in his earlier work, Jhering remained committed to accounting for the state as a *Rechtsstaat*. The state, he explained, must always bind itself 'by the norms which it has established', and it cannot pursue purposes not reflected and shared throughout society.[70] However, he concluded that the evolution of the state as a legal state occurs, not because of the absolute juridical personality of the state, but because the state requires law to fulfil and secure its purposes; in using law to pursue purposes shared through society, the state binds itself objectively to a normative structure, and it exercises its power in a legally imposed set of moral objectives. The legal state is instituted where the state acts as the 'purposive subject' of law and where it uses law as the medium for reflecting and stabilizing common purposes and interests.[71] Central to the works of the later Jhering was, thus, the sense that positivism was correct in suggesting that law can be invoked as a medium that forms the state as a simultaneously free and rational person, but it was misguided in thinking that the legitimate personality of the *Rechtsstaat* can be derived from the formal principles of private law. The state does indeed have a purposive personality, through which it forms itself as a *Rechtsstaat.* This, however, is an objective and intrinsically political personality, which is formed by the state's obligation to deduce and enforce, through objective law, the optimal conditions of social utility. Although he began as a positivist, therefore, Jhering's construct of the purpose as an objectively applied social interest finally initiated a line of anti-positivist thinking, which construed positivist models of the legal state and legal state as shadowy, metaphysical ideas, based in the externalized paradoxes of the state's self-causation as a legal state. These positivist ideas, he concluded, cannot explain either the substantial evolutionary body of the state or the necessary contents of the law transmitted throughout society. They cannot, in short, explain how power is objectively constituted, how power assumes objective legal form, and – most importantly – why and to what ends power exists.

Late positivism and public law

In the latter part of the nineteenth century, the private-legal foundations of positivism reached their highest refinement in the works of Bernhard Windscheid. Windscheid saw academic law as a simple conceptual science whose task is to elucidate principles of Roman law and to provide reliable categories to assist in legislation and judicial procedure.[72] At much the same time, however, other later positivists, most notably Paul Laband, began to recast positivist theory and to harden it against the accusations of lapsed positivists such as Jhering that it was methodologically ill-equipped to offer a substantial account of the state. Laband thus devoted himself to transforming positivist doctrine into a consistent system of public or constitutional law, and he used this system as a model for clarifying and defending the constitutional apparatus under Bismarck's chancellorship, in the first two decades of Imperial Germany.

At the centre of Laband's work is the claim that private and public law are both based in the fiction of the 'juridical person' or legal person, and the legal position of the state is most accurately construed as the supreme legal person: as the 'juridical person of public law'.[73] The core paradigms of private law thus play a central role in articulating the legal structure of the state. On one hand, Laband followed earlier positivist arguments in claiming that the state's personality is best reflected in personal rule. Indeed, he was quite clear that in the imperial constitution, the kaiser was the centre of personal authority or sovereignty in the state,[74] and the final point of sanction for new laws.[75] Moreover, he also replicated earlier views that the state is the precondition of all law, and that law reflects the purposive will of the state. Nonetheless, he also argued that, as a legal person, the state must necessarily be a *Rechtsstaat:* the state is subject to the same legal restrictions as other legal persons, and it cannot be used to assert private rights or private prerogatives.[76] He therefore saw the personality of the imperial state as incorporating a number of distinct institutional organs and as determined by quite precise constitutional norms: its legislative power was divided between the Kaiser and organs outside the imperial executive, notably the parliament and the Federal Council (an organ of delegates from different federal states),[77] and it was obliged to acknowledge rules of procedural compliance in all legislative processes.

Laband's work contains a more concentrated expansion of the paradoxical claim underlying earlier positivist political theory. Central to his theory is the argument that the state, as a person under public law, is necessarily a legal state: the state is invariably bound by laws and norms of procedure and it invariably gives to itself a constitutional order to ensure that these norms are fulfilled. These laws, however, originate in the state itself; they are laws that the state, as a legal person, makes for itself, in which it permits itself to be bound by a constitution, and which it alone, as the supreme legal person of public law, is authorized to enforce and, where necessary, to alter. At one level, therefore, the state is a volitional legislator and it exists prior to law: it is the institutional source of law and there can be no law without the authorizing and enforcing will of the state. The state is therefore *positively free* to make laws. At the same time, however, wherever the state legislates, it ceaselessly posits a constitutional fabric for itself, and it necessarily becomes a constitutionally formed legal person, bound to acknowledge the laws that are enunciated in its own personality. In this respect, Laband's positivism once again rearticulated the antinomy between free will and rational law in the state, and his solution to this antinomy was once again paradoxical: it was to claim that the state's personality is both free and transcendent, but that the state always freely causes, contains and articulates its legitimacy as freedom under laws.

Laband's work marked both the apotheosis and the incipient dissolution of positivism, for after Laband the paradoxical account of the positivist *Rechtsstaat* was increasingly subject to scathing criticism. From the last decades of nineteenth century onwards, even those theorists whose approaches and ideals had initially been shaped by positivism also made fundamental alterations to its core principles. The most striking example of this was Georg Jellinek. Like earlier positivists, Jellinek opposed all accounts of law's origins that see law as evolving from concrete human interactions or associations.[78] Like Laband, he also insisted that public law is the precondition of all legal application validity, and that the legal status and the entitlements of legal persons in society originate in the laws stabilized by the state.[79] 'The state', he concluded, is the personality that 'creates the personality', and it is only because the state upholds a legal order that recognizes people as possessing legal personality that legal claims can be pursued and authorized.[80] Similarly, Jellinek also supported the wider claim that the personality of the modern state must take the form of a *Rechtsstaat* and that the sovereignty of the modern state can only be defined as 'legal power', which is always 'bound by law'.[81] Where the state passes law, in short, it necessarily accepts laws and binds itself to laws; every legal statute is born from the 'self-subjugation of the state' beneath its own law.[82] The entire stability of the modern legal system consequently depends on the state's construction of itself as a 'legal subject', not as a 'power subject'.[83] Even the supreme bearer of political authority only exists as an 'organ of the state' or as an element of the wider legal personality of the state,[84] not as its personal incorporation.

Whilst sharing the wider personalist preconditions of positivism, however, Jellinek also subjected the political preconditions of positivism to a thorough critical revision, and he introduced important sociological elements into his interpretation of the state. Against pure-positivist concepts of the state's personality, he claimed that the state always exists in two dimensions: both as a 'social appearance' and as a 'legal appearance'.[85] The state, consequently, cannot be construed solely as a fact of law, but must also be viewed as an objective aggregate of 'social phenomena'.[86] Purely juridical interpretations of the state only have a restricted validity; they cannot comprehend all aspects of state power; and, most significantly, they cannot fully understand the formative relation between state and law. Attempts to obtain purely 'juridical knowledge of the state' fail to appreciate the state's 'real essence', and they fail to understand the objective processes of formation underlying its legal personality.[87]

Jellinek therefore argued that the positivist construct of the state as legal person is – at most – a convenient and simplifying semantic form that compresses the enormous complexity of the state's sociological origins into a useful, yet infinitely paradoxical term for expressing its legal structure. In fact, the legal personality of the state evolves because the state is an objective organ that pursues and protects human objectives and 'human purposes',[88] and that takes responsibility for the 'solidaristic manifestations of human life'.[89] Because it pursues concrete purposes, the state participates in a rich complex of social relations, and in order effectively to engage in these relations it must incorporate legal recognition of other social agents as persons, or as legal persons, and it must acknowledge its subjects as addressees of rational law or as bearers of rights and entitlements. The state, therefore, is the primary concrete foundation of all private- and public-legal order, and it sets purposes that are applied throughout all society. However, it cannot fulfil this role if it does not reflect itself as a legal person, bound to recognize others as legal persons, and, in consequence, if it does not reflect itself as a legal state.[90] The legal personality of the state, consequently, is certainly a juridical fact, and this fact is the founding source of all law in a given society. However, this personality is also a socially constituted and elaborated fact. For this reason, the legitimacy of the state is not only determined by its legal functions, but by its sociological origins. The legitimacy of the state is therefore measurable, not in categories that it constructs from its own self-causality, but by the value of the common 'purposes' which it pursues and obtains.[91]

The main philosophical implication of Jellinek's doctrine is that positivism was incapable of providing a sustainable account of political order. In implying that law exists independently of determinate social processes and that the personality of the state is deducible from pure legal principles, positivism, for Jellinek, fails to explain how law and power are formed, and it is unable to account concretely for how law and power command obedience or explain themselves as legitimate in their constitutional forms. Positivism thus fails to move beyond the metaphysics of the Enlightenment, which it originally opposed, and it constructs its unity of state and law and projects freedom under law in the state as mere fictions or paradoxes of self-causality. In the case of Laband, this results in the quintessential tautological claim that the power of the state originates in generalized law and generalized law originates in the volitional force of the state, and that the co-genetic relation of law and state is expressed in the state's inevitable codification of its own personality as a constitution. Against this, Jellinek conceived his work as an attempt to show that the unity of law and power cannot be derived from socially disembedded ideas of law. Rather, law and state emerge together through an interplay of simultaneously factical and normative processes, in which the sociologically formed body of the state gradually generalizes itself as a universally normative order. Law evolves as a check and counterweight to pure political force, he argued, because prevailing social conditions are normally inclined, however gradually, to assume normative features and because 'existing institutions' inevitably undergo a process of legal 'rationalization' through which they adjust to, and permit themselves to be structured by, prevailing social expectations.[92] The idea of the *Rechtsstaat* is, thus, an essential and definitive component of modern social orders: indeed, all social orders gravitate towards the form of the *Rechtstaat.* Yet the normative element in the *Rechtsstaat,* Jellinek explained, is not deducible from abstract law and from the state's abstract personality: it is only ever a factical norm (both in its genesis and application), and it is imposed on the state through the functional and evolutionary dynamics through which states are formed. The state evolves specifically as a *Rechtsstaat,* in sum, because of the 'normative force of the factical'.[93]

Positivism as metaphysics

One salient intimation in Jellinek's revision of positivism is that positivism conceives itself as an anti-metaphysical doctrine of legal statehood but fails to locate the power of the state on non-metaphysical foundations and to overcome the aporia of metaphysical or ius-natural doctrine. Jellinek was not alone in accusing positivism of a miscarried attack on metaphysics. By the early twentieth century, in fact, most opponents of positivism expressed similar suspicions and criticisms. After 1900, for example, representatives of the Free Law Movement, primarily Eugen Ehrlich, Hermann Kantorowicz and (in part, at least) the young Gustav Radbruch, argued that positivism should be replaced with a more historical and spontaneously interpretive approach to the law and that legal application should not concentrate on formal legal facts, but should be guided by 'subjectively valid legal ideals',[94] in which the personal value decisions of the judge assume a constitutive role.[95] The Free Lawyers denounced the 'rigid dogma' of Roman law and the 'rigid immobility' of the private-law principles used by positivism to elucidate legal and political problems.[96] Positivism, they explained, is a surrogate for formal ius-naturalism, which, in positing invariable formal principles as the basis of legal finding, remains a covertly metaphysical doctrine.[97] They therefore argued, in different ways, that a free-hermeneutical approach to jurisdiction can detach law from all metaphysical fixity,[98] and concentrate law on fully human or personalized accounts of justice and moral content.[99] Positivism, therefore, should give way to creative moral humanism in the law, based in the moral commitment of interpreters who are prepared to use law as a substantial medium for obtaining and imparting justice.[100]

Before its rapid critical dissolution after 1900, however, positivism had already been confronted with a rival account of the state, which also accused the positivists of entering a covert alliance with metaphysical ideas of law and state. This alternative account of statehood was based in the Germanic School of legal history and the main exponents of this approach argued that the principles of Roman law are unable to give anything but a depleted and formally paradoxical explanation of the origins of state and law. The science of Roman law, they argued, examines the law as a small number of unreal constructs and principles, and it does not have the theoretical resources to understand either the full concrete plurality of law's social evolution or, consequently, the binding reasons for law's acceptance and recognition throughout society. Under Roman law, consequently, law can only give a fictionalized account of itself as rational and deserving compliance. Because of this, moreover, the Germanists saw Roman-law personalism as tending to foster authoritarian ideas of statehood in which the personality of the state endows formal rights on its subjects, yet remains fixed and dualistically counterposed to these subjects as isolated agents in civil society. This, they claimed, is primarily due to the fact that Roman law cannot grasp the deep social, associational or organic sources of legal formation, and it is not equipped to determine how law emerges and obtains its content from the embedded processes of agreement and associational consensus. The theorists associated with the Germanic School of legal theory thus responded to positivism by seeking to establish more socially integrative and formative concepts of the state and the legal person and by expanding legal analysis to incorporate all spheres of social exchange as implicitly legislative operations.

Early representatives of the Germanists included the liberal politician and private and criminal lawyer, Carl Joseph Anton Mittermaier, who argued that there existed a 'unity of unwritten laws' in Germany, and that these provided a more sustainable guarantee of social freedom than Roman law.[101] Jacob Grimm also belonged to this school. Grimm argued that the 'encroachment of Roman law' had led to a degeneration of popular legal and political culture in Germany, and he saw research on 'the history of German law' as a vital contribution to cultural/political rejuvenation.[102] It was also from within the Germanist camp that one of the most potent early-liberal analyses of the *Rechtsstaat,* set out by Wilhelm Eduard Albrecht, was enunciated. Albrecht was a prominent liberal constitutionalist, and, with Grimm, one of the seven professors (the *Göttinger Sieben*) expelled from Göttingen University in 1837 for their protests over the abolition of the Hanoverian constitution, instituted in 1833. Albrecht argued that any construction of the state as a 'juridical person' implies that the state is a responsible organ of public law, firmly bound by its own laws to serve the 'total interest' of the people, and so categorically distinct from the personal will of the monarch. The state construed as a bearer of personality, he concluded, marks a final break with the 'private-legal colour' of older patrimonial or estate-based political conceptions, which continued to influence political life in the German states.[103] Legal analysis of the state must, therefore, emphasize the distinction of the state from all private-legal rights, and it must recognize that the state has a real personality, which includes a concrete accountability to those bound by its laws.

The platform on which this tradition developed, however, was originally established by Karl Friedrich Eichhorn, who first formed the Germanic branch of the Historical School. At the heart of Eichhorn's work is the claim, *contra* Savigny, that before the reception of Roman law in Germany there already existed a unified corpus of Germanic law, expressing specifically German legal and political ideals. The reception of Roman law was, therefore, not a natural expression of German legal culture, but in fact only reflected the interests of an elite academic legal establishment, and it led to the alienation of law from its original cultural setting.[104] Eichhorn also argued that German society before the introduction of Roman law had been bound together as a 'truly organic whole',[105] and that German law formed an overarching set of bonds integrating all elements of society into a quasi-corporate unity. For this reason, he was especially scathing about the influence of canon law on medieval German law. He saw canon law as responsible for promulgating a 'system of hierarchy' in German society and for disrupting the complex organic relations of indigenous law.[106] He denounced dualistic ideas of political sovereignty as outgrowths of Roman law and he argued that indigenous German legal thought favoured models of shared or integrated sovereignty.[107] Most significantly, he also claimed that the medieval social order had provided only for limited rights of private law, as all ownership had been derived through shared feudal entitlements.[108] He therefore suggested a corporatist or organic model of the legal person under private law as an alternative to that pioneered by the early positivists and the historians of Roman law.

After Eichhorn, the Germanic branch of the Historical School underwent a process of politicization and conceptual refinement, through which its major representatives gradually associated themselves with liberal-progressive, or at least socially oriented tendencies in German society, especially in the period prior to 1848. For example, Georg Beseler, a liberal delegate in the Frankfurt parliament, saw Roman law as the cause of a fateful process of abstraction and formalization running through modern German cultural life. During the years of its reception, he argued, Roman law had stimulated a momentum of early absolutist political centralization and legal codification. This, in turn, had placed legal power in the hands of an independent bureaucratic judiciary, it had eroded the 'popular law' that had previously applied, and it had abstracted the law from its sources in the popular community.[109] Like other opponents of positivism, Beseler also argued that positivist conceptions of the 'juridical person' are not able to elucidate the origins and the legal form of the state. The 'legal foundation' of the state and its constitution, he explained, cannot be distilled from formal principles of the private law of Roman law: such analysis leads to insubstantial and falsely dualist accounts of sovereignty. The constitutional personality of the state should in fact be viewed as drawing legal substance from the 'associational spirit' of a real political community and as shaped, not as the will of one formal subject, but as the living unity of many wills.[110] Against positivism, therefore, Beseler claimed that Germanic law construed the state as a legal order generated by 'fellowship' (*Genossenschaft*): that is, by the interactions between enfranchised members of local and national associations. The state based in fellowship, consequently, is not a formal fiction, but the concrete form of evolving agreements between social associations,[111] and the laws of this state are recognized as legitimate or reasonable because they reflect the concrete freedom of many particular wills.

In establishing this model of fellowship, Beseler moved close to quite standard aspects of liberal theory, as he claimed that the state has its origins in the principles of private law, and in the legal personality of private persons. At the same time, however, he also proposed a thorough reconception of more standard liberal ideas, as he argued that Germanic private law is not centred in the concept of the purposive, possessive and contract-forming legal subject, and that states evolving from Germanic private law obtain an integrative, not a formal, legal personality. Germanic private law, he claimed, has its fundament in a social conception of the legal person: this conception sees the agent of private law as interacting consensually and forming legal associations with other agents; it concludes that the validity of private law is derived, not from narrowly atomized or proprietorial interests, but from entitlements which are formative of common experiences of freedom and unity. The model of legal subjectivity or personality underlying the Germanic idea of the state thus defies classical ideas of private-legal autonomy, and it insists that both the subject of private law and the subject of the state should be construed as *transpersonal subjects,* constructed from the plural memberships of organic associations.[112] On these grounds, then, Beseler concluded that the formal Roman private law of property is foreign to the organic private law of Germany. Roman private law fails to provide legal principles reflecting German ideas of shared freedom and it is always likely to stimulate absolutist expressions of power, both in political and economic processes.[113] Roman law, he in fact claimed, structures the human personality as an *absolute person.* Persons under Roman private law exclude organic recognition of others and association with others from their activities; they construct themselves in absolute legal distinction from all other agents; and they identify other persons under law only as legally protected adversaries or competitors, not as participants in common rights. Similarly, then, Roman law also constructs the person under public law (the state) as an absolute person, separating itself dualistically from its subjects and reflecting these subjects in its constitution as nothing more than formally entitled bearers of rights or as applicants for legal protection or redress. In contrast to this, Beseler sought to outline a Germanic interpretation of law in which, under private law, legal agents would cooperate organically in forming law and, under public law, the state would integrate its constituent subjects and derive its legal/constitutional structure from the agreements organically obtained by these subjects. The authentic state, he argued, evolves by integrating a number of corporations or associations into its general structure, and it obtains a constitutional form – a legal personality – not by imposing formal norms upon itself and by metaphysically causing itself as a legal apparatus, but by articulating laws which these corporations already, albeit inchoately, contain. Like other more radical theorists of the *Vormärz,* therefore, Beseler claimed that Roman law and its outgrowth in positivism are essentially metaphysical legal systems. As it constructs the person under law as an absolute person, Roman law transforms people and states into absolute essences, preformed and legally independent of all social reality, and it ostracizes from the law all reality which is external to these abstracted essences. Positivism, based in Roman law, might therefore claim to provide a fully post-metaphysical account of government and legal validity and it might purport to advocate government under laws in the form of a *Rechtsstaat.* In fact, however, Roman law is invariably in league with metaphysical absolutism: it is a system of law that orders social life around invariable principles, that separates the source of law from the living bonds of human communities and fractures these communities into atomized persons, and that stratifies law over social existence as a virtual and authoritarian second reality. Roman law, in short, constructs the person in legal analogy to the transcendent God, and underscoring Roman law is always a close and constitutive collusion between metaphysics and absolutism.

The Germanic constitution

Similar perspectives on private law, the legal person and the state informed the writings of the Swiss historian and politician, Johann Caspar Bluntschli, who also used an interpretation of German law to elaborate a substantial anthropological foundation for the state. In his writings on public law or state law, Bluntschli argued for the institution of fully constitutional monarchy in Germany.[114] He justified this by defining the legitimate state as the 'human legal community in person', generated from and restricted by the organic legal connections integrating all constituents of social order.[115] He also associated Roman law with the formation of 'absolute power' in the state, in contrast to Germanic law of fellowship, which he saw as guaranteeing 'personality and freedom' under organic law.[116] The Germanic legal state, he concluded, is a 'moral-intellectual organism' or a 'moral-organic personality', whose personality is produced by the subjects which it integrates, and whose laws recognize these subjects as the originating authors of laws.[117]

In the later evolution of liberal theory, then, Germanic conceptions of law continued to form the preconditions for constitutional doctrine. This was evident, for example, in the works of Albert Hänel, an influential left-liberal politician of the middle period of Imperial Germany, whose account of the constitutional state fused elements of positivist and elements of organic theories of the state. Close to the positivists, he argued that the state occupies the 'supreme leading position' in society, and is charged with shaping the law in accordance with its 'common purpose'.[118] However, he rejected positivist claims that the state can be reduced to a 'uniform legal subject' or a formal person. Rather, he argued, the state is founded in a 'corporate association', which factually underlies and constantly regenerates its constitution.[119] The state, thus, is certainly endowed with a 'juridical personality', for this is essential for determining the legal position of the state. However, the state, viewed in its sociological origins, is not a static construct of law, but an 'organisational form', in whose corporate constitution and whose laws the entirety of society is present.[120]

The principles of Germanist legal theory were expressed most clearly in the works of Otto von Gierke. Like other organic theorists, Gierke claimed that the reception of Roman law in Germany, culminating in positivism, had produced a tradition of statehood in which the state, dualistically positioned against the rest of society, was formed as a formally 'authoritarian idea' of legal personality.[121] Moreover, although purporting to consolidate the liberties of private agents outside the state, Roman law succeeded in establishing private freedoms only in the most spurious form: as a formal sphere of private autonomy outside the state, where social agents interact as competitors and adversaries, and where these agents are denied all constitutive role in the formation of law and state. As a result of this, German cultural life in the nineteenth century, Gierke stated, was marked by a thorough disaggregation of private and public existence, and in each sphere social agents experienced only highly reduced opportunities for freedom and self-enrichment. The root cause of this dualism between the formal freedom of private law and the abstract authority of the state was the fact that Roman law is unable to derive its concepts of the legal person and the legal subject from substantial or organic ideas of personhood, and it consequently stabilizes persons under law, both private and public, as absolutely atomized legal forms.[122] The person under Roman law, he argued, relies on a metaphysical process of 'abstraction', which reduces the complexities of legal status, entitlement and formation to a narrowly 'uniform concept'.[123] This concept lacks all content, and it restricts agents under law to a statically prescribed series of solitary and purposive rights and freedoms. The notion of a monadic legal subject or legal person, however, is entirely foreign to Germanic legal culture, and the deduction of common obligations from solitary atomized subjects belongs to an imposed legal and political tradition.[124] Under Germanic law, the person from which laws originate is not construed as a subject endowed with an 'unlimited absolute power of will', or as a 'will without relations'. On the contrary, Germanic law views persons of private law and persons of public law as associational or corporate persons: that is, as persons who form laws and entitlements under law through interaction with other persons, who freely exercise their wills as persons through this same interaction, and who consequently form and consolidate their subjective freedoms as detached from purely private motives.[125] Underscoring Gierke's thinking in this point is in fact the anthropological argument that the human being assumes its truest form and realizes its highest level of freedom, not as a formally self-legislating or juridical subject, but as a corporate legal subject, whose freedom of will is bound to and constituted by other legal subjects. 'All that the human being is', he explained, 'is due to the association of one person with another person'.[126] Legal ideas that petrify the freedom of subjects around static and absolute attributes merely project metaphysical ideas of absolute personality onto human agents and they fail to incorporate the formative and relational aspects of human experience in their concepts of freedom. The 'membership of a fellowship' is, therefore, the condition of genuine human freedom, and any legal order guaranteeing human freedom must have its foundation in the organically constructed personality of a fellowship.[127] The fellowship (*Genossenschaft*), in sum, is the irreducible source of legal personality under Germanic law.[128] Unlike the chimera of the subject under Roman law, this subject is an 'actual, not merely fabricated person'.[129]

In centring law and state on the corporate person, therefore, Gierke indicated that Germanic law does not fully differentiate between public and private law. The private rights and freedoms pursued by members of a fellowship are not in any strict way 'private', for they are founded in commonality, and the pursuit of freedoms in fellowship serves to reinforce shared freedoms and to invigorate the 'organic community' of the people, not to serve unilaterally purposive or individual interests.[130] In societies founded in fellowship, therefore, the freedom of one person is always constitutive of that of another person, and the private exercise of freedom is inseparable from the common or public exercise of freedom. For this reason, Gierke implied that the entire formation of the private law of modern capitalism, depending on the abstraction of the person as a self-seeking will and the resultant fragmentation of the legal order into laws relating solely to individual persons (private law) and laws relating solely to the state (public law), has exercised a deeply corrosive influence on social and political existence. Through this process, in fact, human life has wilfully chained itself to abstracted and pernicious constructs of social liberty, and it has depleted its resources for genuine private and public liberty.[131] The private law of pure capitalism deprives human beings of the full experience of commonality and sociality which, as true associational agents, is their anthropological destiny. Rights and guarantees of property necessitated by the modern economy should, Gierke thus suggested, not be deduced from abstract constructs of the person as a naturally possessive will, but from a morally constitutive 'sphere of personality', which deduces proprietary rights, not from subjective interests, but from the function of property in shaping and reinforcing associational life and liberty.[132]

In its political implications, the most important point in Gierke's work is the claim that Roman-law constructs of the personality, represented by positivism, do not understand the condition of legitimate statehood. On one level, he praised in positivism the attempt to interpret the state as a *Rechtsstaat:* that is, as an apparatus defined by legal principles.[133] However, he argued that positivism misses the opportunity to construe the state as a fully elaborated and substantial order of freedom under laws, and, by deriving its legal principles through formal private-legal method, it fails to account either for the social origins of the laws of state, or for the conditions of law's factual legitimacy.[134] Roman law theory, he claimed, arrives at an account of the legal state only by defining law as an abstract medium, which distils from private law a fictitious constitutional form for the exercise of power, but which makes only minimal stipulation about the formation and necessary content of this constitution.[135] The positivist idea of the legal state, therefore, dualistically severs society and state from each other as two formal and static quantities, and it allows the constitution fictitiously to stand in for all the manifold and concrete interests of society.[136] In so doing, Roman law merely imposes a thin surface of private-legal order (personality) on the state, but this has no foundation in social interaction or agreement, and it cannot account for the freedom that it defends or explain why this freedom is constitutive of legitimacy. Underlying this argument is the assertion, then, that positivism fails to account for the state as a positively constituted *public* or authentically *political* will, and it simply cements political order around a set of unreflected, unmediated private prerogatives. Underlying this argument, moreover, is the sill deeper assertion that the state of Roman law is a metaphysical state, which circumvents the need to explain its laws as guaranteeing freedom through a simple *ex nihilo* act of self-creation as an order of freedom under law.

Under Germanic law, in contrast, the constitutional order of the state evolves as an extension of socially embedded organic personalities. Public authority obtains a legal-constitutional personality by integrating all its components and by reflecting the legal agreements between these as consolidated elements of its internal structure. In so doing, the state assumes the character of a 'general personality' (*Allgemeinpersönlichkeit*),[137] or 'living total personality' (*lebendige Gesammtpersönlichkeit*),[138] constituted by a plurality of consensual wills and consensual laws. One example of such a public person, Gierke stated, is the governmental order of late medieval Germany, when Germanic law was most refined and least corrupted. At this time, the Holy Roman Empire existed as a legal person by integrating the legal persons of the imperial estates, and beneath this level the towns also formed themselves as legal persons by integrating the legal persons of the enfranchised burghers and the members of the guilds.[139] Only the Germanic legal tradition, in sum, is capable of understanding social and political reality in a genuinely democratic/constitutional perspective: only the Germanic legal tradition is fundamentally inclined towards the promotion of the *Rechtsstaat* as a naturally evolving legal form, in which freedoms are articulated which obtain natural consensus and reasoned compliance.[140] Where it constructs itself integratively as a total personality, the state assimilates the legally binding agreements that exist between its organic constituents, and it accepts these agreements as irreducible elements of its own constitutional fabric: indeed, the state has no constitutional reality that could be distinguished from these agreements – these agreements *are* its constitution. Thus, whereas the Roman-law ideas in positivism lead the state, through the pure form of law, to assume a negative or *external* constitution as a limit placed on its power, the Germanic-law ideas in organic theory see a constitutional state as positively formed and *internally* bound by the legally constitutive acts of its members. Germanic legal states, consequently, are reliable and enduring constitutional legal states, which allow a plurality of wills to live in freedom, and the laws of such a state are accepted as legitimate because, in their original formation, they are authorized by the citizens themselves. States based in Roman law, in contrast, are precarious, dualistic and founded in one fictitious will. As a result, they are always likely to subside into neo-absolutist forms.

In its deeper theoretical consequence, Gierke's work contains a threefold theoretical critique that touches the heart of the common preconditions of European political thought. First and most obviously, he opposed the construct of the person under Roman law and the resultant fact that modern law (public and private) is distilled from abstracted ideas of how people coexist with one another and how public systems of authority are engendered and reproduced. Like others before him, he rejected Roman law because he considered that it promoted a metaphysical idea of the *legal person* and so enchained all social reality to latently authoritarian and anthropologically evacuated accounts of human freedom. In this, Gierke derided as insubstantial, unstable and deeply paradoxical the types of liberal politics resulting from Roman-law ideas of private autonomy, legal subjectivity and legal statehood. Second, then, Gierke also rejected all common natural-law accounts of statehood, which define the state, after Kant, as a *moral person.* Such perspectives, he asserts, are still ensnared in the dualistic 'scheme' of the Roman-law model of abstract statehood;[141] they assume that legitimacy in the state can be instituted through the imposition of external norms on the state; and they are incapable of understanding, except in metaphysical paradox, the organically co-genetic relation between the state and the law. Indeed, he argued that ius-natural ideas are in part to blame for bringing about the death of the corporation-based idea of the state, as in their first emergence they imposed abstract-dualistic norms and sanctions upon this state, and so undermined its self-regenerative consistency.[142] Natural law and positivism, therefore, are closely related and only superficially antagonistic analyses of political order. Third, then, underlying both these points was also the claim that all non-organic theory is inevitably caught in an antinomy between voluntaristic and normative accounts of the state, and it can only overcome this antinomy through paradoxical projections of law and power. As a doctrine that sees the legal state as an *organic person,* however, organic theory is able to reconcile this antinomy on a substantial anthropological substructure.

On all these counts, Gierke's critique is sharpened against what he saw as metaphysical notions of law and the state, and against all dualist or formalized constructions of human moral freedom or integrity. He consequently sought to place modern political thinking on new foundations by proposing a non-dualistic, non-atomistic conception of the fellowship as the source of law. A political doctrine derived from this foundation, he claimed, would not ultimately dismiss all elements of ius-natural argument: at the very least, it would uphold a moral 'idea of law', and it would protect law from its possible 'dissolution' through prerogatives of 'utility and power'.[143] However, a corporatist doctrine of law and state would insist that the moral power of law cannot be distilled from or into any one source, person or principle, but must be viewed as an organic resource contained and generated by a great plurality of associations throughout all society. An organically pluralized account of law's source and location can help to divest law of all traces of dualist abstraction and paradox; it emphasizes the concrete and social formation of law; and it proposes a committed liberal model of the constitutional state, which finally abandons the customary metaphysical preconditions of liberalism – either in its positivist or ius-natural variation.

The second stage of organic theory: Hugo Preuß and the Weimar Constitution

The Germanist attempt to explain the organic social origins of law and power reached its most politically influential expression in the works of Hugo Preuß, the constitutional lawyer who was primarily responsible for drafting the provisional constitutional documents for the Weimar Republic in the winter of 1918–19. Preuß's work contains a series of arguments characteristic of all organic theory, albeit expressed with a more engaged democratic commitment. He argued, first, that the modern absolutist or authoritarian state is closely correlated with the construction of the 'absolute person' of Roman law, and that the absolute sovereignty of this state sustains itself by generating an illusory foundation of legal regularity, based in the fiction of the formal-legal subject of Roman private law.[144] Second, he claimed that legal-political ideas derived from the concept of the person in Roman law cannot explain the social origins of the state and the laws, and it cannot comprehend the 'real persons', formed from a commonly elaborated organic will, which constitute these legal and political institutions.[145] Third, then, he stated that the principles of Roman law cannot truly account for the *political* or *public* character of the state, but reduce the exercise of power to the operations of a person in endless pursuit of private motives and private purposes.[146] Fourth, he asserted that Roman law cannot provide a reliable conception of the legal state, that it impoverishes democratic-political culture and that it cannot account for the laws of a legal state as legitimate expressions of human freedoms. Fifth, he concluded that the distillation of the legal subject or the legal person as a purposive agent, requiring legal authority and protection for individual self-realization, simplifies and violates the complexity of human social interaction, and it examines the contents of human freedom, both at a public and at a private level, in exclusive and reductive terms.[147] Consequently, it is only where the state is viewed as a corporation or as an organic personality formed by concretely interacting persons, he argued, that the intimate and mutually constitutive relation between power and law can be understood, and that laws can articulate genuine and encompassing freedoms.[148] Like other Germanists, he thus advocated a shift of legal and anthropological paradigm away from atomized ideas of legal-political personality. The 'identification' of the person 'with the individual', he explained, is a lamentable 'peculiarity of private law'.[149] Doctrines seeking to account for the personality of the legitimate legal state must dispense with the Romanist paradigm of the 'fictionalized individual',[150] and replace this with the 'living reality of the total personality',[151] which produces laws through common interactions.

To a greater extent than earlier organic theorists, however, Preuß expressed these perspectives as elements of a committed democratic constitutional argument, and he insisted that Germanic legal ideas have their necessary corollary in an organic-democratic and legislatively inclusive legal state. A state formed under Germanic law, he explained, would derive its legal structure from the many corporate wills of civil society, not from the fictitious will of the legal person. A state of this kind would accept the positive form of a written constitution, yet it would also give maximum legislative power to organs of 'self-administration' amongst groups of citizens in civil society, and it would allow its legal form to be shaped by interactive associations in different spheres of social production.[152] In this argument, he moved much further to the party-political left than his precursors in organic theory, and he argued that an organic constitution would sanction the abandonment of the 'purely individual law' of Roman private law and of its outgrowth in capitalist law. Instead of enshrining rights as the legal properties of particular purposive wills or absolute subjects, an organic constitution would place emphasis on collective subjects (for example, on citizens' groups, trade unions or other labour delegations) as bearers of rights, and it would construe rights as evolving expressions of collective personal interests, assuming stable form in an organic constitution. He consequently concluded that a true legal state would not be merely a state of law, sanctioning formally equal rights of property, contract, opinion and labour. Instead, a legitimate legal state must be founded in 'organic social law', in which the rights of citizens can be negotiated to incorporate material entitlements and rights of distribution.[153] Like other Germanists, consequently, he saw Germanic law as overcoming the duality between private and public law and as allowing publicly binding legal principles to be formed out of collective interactions in the economy. The institutions of Germanic law, he intimated, mark the final renunication of law's metaphysical paradox or formality, and they allow law to evolve as a medium forming a *material personality* in the state, constituting conditions of *material citizenship* throughout society and so permitting citizens to recognize themselves as the originating authors of law in all spheres of human agency.

In his later writings, Preuß at times moved away from his commitment to organic self-administration as the ideal of legal integration and democratic formation. Like most liberal theorists of his era, he periodically fell under the influence of Max Weber, and his theory ultimately accommodated the more obviously positivist Weberian conception of democracy as a technique for producing political elites.[154] Elements of his drafts for the Weimar Constitution were consequently coloured in part by Weberian ideals, which were originally foreign to Preuß's organic perspective. However, after the foundation of the Weimar Republic, Preuß's account of the democratic legal state as an organic unity based in the associative interactions of citizens, in which authority is derived from the 'community of comrades, of citizens',[155] remained one of the most refined attempts to provide a model for cross-class cooperation and collective will-formation in the fractured political landscape of the Weimar Republic. At the heart of this model is the argument that the constitution of a legal state is legitimate where it makes possible an integrative and politically constitutive relation between people from all class backgrounds and economic groups,[156] and where it allows a 'community based in fellowship' to evolve on the foundation of this state. Such constitutions, Preuß concluded, provide a durable basis for democratic legal states, especially states such as the Weimar Republic, struggling to stabilize themselves against economic depression and political insurrection.[157]

Two responses to the metaphysical state

As the two rival orthodoxies in German legal-political debate in the second part of the nineteenth century, positivism and organic theory competed with one another over related objectives. Both theories analysed the relation between private freedom and public order in modern societies, and both sought to fashion a transformation of statehood in Germany from a late-absolutist to a liberal-capitalist representative order. Both theories, moreover, attempted to account for the evolution and necessary constitutional form of the *Rechtsstaat,* to explain the personal-anthropological origins of law and power, and, like historicism, to give a relatively consistent foundation to the often disparate and inconsistent ideologies of German liberalism. In this latter respect, both doctrines converged as attempts to explain the state as a person under law, to elucidate the relation of mutual contingency between power and law, yet, against the metaphysical natural-law theories of the Enlightenment and early liberalism, to demonstrate that the legal form of legitimate power does not result from external normative prescription and that legitimate states take the form of law through fully immanent processes of legal formation. The positivist argument that law is a sequence of pure norms and that the state becomes a legal state by adopting a personal structure already implicit in law's form was designed to put an end to the presumption that legitimacy in the state is derived from universal rational principles. The organic account of the state as an endlessly developing natural-organic legal person was also intended to supplant metaphysical or rationalized descriptions of the theoretical justification of power. Nonetheless, the two doctrines also differed fundamentally in their construction of the state's constitution. The positivists claimed that the state's personality results from its formal self-definition as an analogue to the legal person of private law: in this form, they claimed, the state recognizes persons outside itself as legal persons and it enshrines this recognition in a constitution that constrains the powers it can deploy in its relation to these other persons. For the organic theorists, in contrast, the state evolves as a concrete total person, integrating all legal agreements between the corporations of civil society, and it culminates in a constitution which gives positive, yet changing form to these agreements. In other words, positivism moved beyond ius-natural ideas by minimizing the sphere of legal relevance in society and by restricting law (private and constitutional) to a set of formal or procedural codes derived from Roman law. Underlying positivism was, thus, a thin theory of law, which, whilst accepting as necessary a limited constitution, restricted law to a narrow set of constraints on state power. Organic theory, in contrast, moved beyond ius-natural theory by maximizing the sphere of legal relevance, and it saw the law (private and constitutional) as materially produced by all interactions in society. Underlying organic theory was, thus, an expansion of the law, which saw all elements of society as implicated in constitutional formation.

The debate between positivism and organic theory hinged, at its most fundamental level, on the question of metaphysics. Both doctrines tried to understand the legal personality of the state in terms distinct from the purely normative analyses of ius-naturalism, yet, at the same time, both refused to see the state as independent of all normative circumscription, and both insisted that the idealist definition of legitimacy as a condition where laws enshrine rational freedoms should be upheld. Both, therefore, sought to explain the origins of the state on contingent, positive grounds, with no external addition or rationalized substructure, but also to insist that the state must be a *Rechtsstaat,* allowing no direct contradiction between reason and will. Positivism saw reason and will as reconciled in the state's self-production as legal person. Organic theory saw reason and will as reconciled in the state's evolution through the accommodation of many wills in an overarching personality. Both doctrines were ultimately separated from each other, however, by the fact that each one accused the other of still being metaphysical, of introducing inadmissible principles into the description of the state's legal corpus, and of failing, except through metaphysical recourse, to resolve the antinomy between free will and rational law. Organic theory reproached positivism with the claim, first, that its fictions of legal subjectivity and juridical personality do not effectively correct the doctrines of natural-legal universality that positivism purports to reject, and it stabilizes political order, once more, around a flimsy metaphysical or quasi-transcendent account of the state's subjection to its own law. At the same time, however, positivism also intimated that organic theory still laboured under romantic illusions about the formation of power and law, and that it constructed its inclusive model of the legal state only by counterfactually presupposing that all human interactions are oriented towards agreement, that these agreements (through some unspecified process) can be inscribed as law, and that all of society is integrated under a unitary personality. For the positivists, therefore, organic theory was ultimately nothing more than a fancifully totalizing or metaphysical theory of society, founded in aestheticized constructs of human interaction, which, in hard points of dispute, was not able to produce reliable norms to regulate the interpretation of law and the application of power. Whilst organicists saw positivists as stabilizing a paradoxical construct of law and power in the formal constitution of the state, positivists saw organicists as resolving this paradox only by naively and improbably disseminating legislative power through all spheres of social formation.

7 The vitalist interlude

Depersonalization and the law

The critical response to the metaphysical ideals of natural law in the Enlightenment did not only form the background of the legal and political orthodoxies of nineteenth-century Germany. In fact, the hostility to juridical metaphysics acted as a pervasive intellectual stimulus in many areas of intellectual inquiry, including areas of philosophical debate not primarily concentrated on law, and even early sociology. The migration of legal and political problems into other areas of philosophy and sociology is reflected most clearly in the works of Friedrich Nietzsche and Wilhelm Dilthey and by the constructive transformation that Nietzsche's ideas experienced in the works of Georg Simmel and Max Weber.

Nietzsche: law, metaphysics and violence

The defining assumption in Nietzsche's philosophy is that modern Western thought is, in its entirety, corrupted by metaphysics. In Nietzsche's judgement, metaphysics is an overarching intellectual attitude, which is marked by the conviction that the truth of being does not reside in natural or temporal being itself, but rather, originally, in absolute and perennial essences, or values, which are considered external and superior to being. These values might, on Nietzsche's account, be contested and debated over long periods of theoretical evolution, and different outlooks or philosophies might promote one set of values over another. However, the existence of abstracted and rationally defined and defended values is the 'fundamental belief of metaphysicians'.[1] As a consequence, metaphysical thought patterns are necessarily *normative* and *explanatory:* they are based in the claim that values provide judgemental criteria by which natural and temporal being can be evaluated, elucidated and regulated. Common to all metaphysical views, therefore, is a *depreciation* of being or of life itself and an assumption that being only becomes meaningful where it exists in conformity with transcendent norms or where it is made transparent to underlying intelligible laws or patterns of regularity. For this reason, all metaphysical views, for Nietzsche, have a pronounced juridical element: all assume that it is possible to deduce norms or values above the manifold phenomena of being, and all assume that these norms provide a matrix through which the factual reality of being can be explained and judged.[2] All metaphysical views, consequently, allow their understanding of the objects of the natural and the temporal world to be obstructed by causal and normative schemes; they construct their intellectual world around the suppression and domination of the actual contents of natural things; and they effect a separation of human life from the vital and natural sources of its creativity and energy.

Nietzsche argued that Plato was initially responsible for allowing metaphysical attitudes to pervade human thought. However, he saw all the seismic shifts in Western thinking – the evolution of Christianity, medieval scholasticism, the moral teachings of the Enlightenment, the emergence of the natural sciences, and, in nineteenth-century Germany, the formation of historical research as an analytical science – as reformulating, in new constellations, the original attitudes and presuppositions of metaphysics. Consequently, whilst Platonist metaphysics originally devalued being by insinuating the existence of absolute essences distinct from the world of nature and history, Christianity reinforced this approach by examining the world as the result of an external creator and as subject to an order of law that had been externally ordained by this creator. Christianity is thus founded in an 'instinctive hatred for all reality',[3] and it derives from this hatred an 'abstract' set of moral codes, which it resentfully places in 'contradiction to life', and through which it tries to regulate all the vital aspects of human life.[4] The Enlightenment, then, which only erroneously construed itself as a secularizing or anti-Christian set of philosophies, continued the instinctively anti-natural tendency of metaphysics by identifying human reason as the legislative centre and arbiter of all reality and by deducing allegedly unshakeable norms from reason, in order both to measure and to guide the evolution of society.[5] Subsequently, the natural sciences and the technological innovations of the nineteenth century reinstituted the metaphysical principle that reality can be explained through positively deducible laws of 'cause and effect', and that all phenomena can be explained as acting in correspondence with these laws.[6] Similarly, the historicist orthodoxy of the nineteenth century, although initially conceived as a reaction against the tyranny of uniform moral norms, also, for Nietzsche, restated the metaphysical conviction that the factual reality of history can be explained through rationalized analysis and that the truth of historical phenomena is necessarily located outside these phenomena themselves.[7] In addition, the universal laws of equality and equal entitlement in modern democratic legal states, Nietzsche argued, are also based in the legacies of metaphysics, and these values express a metaphysical 'form of degradation' of the human being.[8]

For all the divergence between these stages in the evolution of European thought, Nietzsche argued, all share the overlapping belief that an abiding order either underpins or inheres in the world, that this order is external to the merely contingent (natural and temporal) facts of life, and that human reason has a privileged capacity either for divining and legislating the conditions of order in the world. The metaphysical lineage thus constructs reason or 'science' as the constitutive link between the world and the truth of the world, and it culminates in the autonomist claim of the Enlightenment – namely, that reason itself is the origin of the order of the world and that the world has its highest reality, not in itself, but in reason. In the metaphysical lineage, therefore, reason initially evolved as a capacity for *interpreting* the order of the world as created by laws or entities above human reason. In the Enlightenment, however, reason was recast as a capacity for *creating* the order of the world and for stipulating binding laws by which all things can be guided and explained. In all its manifestations, however, metaphysics is an attitude that imputes a fixed juridical order to phenomenal reality, and it invariably construes reason as the attribute of human beings, which allows them to comprehend this order.

The practical result of the metaphysical traces in human thinking, Nietzsche argued, is that human agents internalize as elements of their own existence the principles of order which they either believe to exist in the world, or which they prescribe as preconditions for the order of the world. Under the influence of metaphysics, consequently, human beings construct themselves as rationalized or *regularized* centres of moral calculation: they see themselves as accountable to perennial norms and as bound to the fulfilment of overarching moral objectives and prescriptions. Through this process of metaphysical internalization, then, human beings become alienated from the spontaneous and the naturally creative aspects of their lives, and they organize their actions around norms that suppress their unregulated natural inclinations and shape their behaviour in accordance with universalized precepts or abstracted purposes. As metaphysically self-constructed agents, therefore, human beings form themselves as reliable, constricted and experientially impoverished social beings, concentrated on their obligation to laws, values and purposes which are not naturally or integrally their own. Metaphysics, therefore, is not only a cognitive attitude, giving reason primacy over being. It is also a necessary precondition of societal formation. As an intellectual order which instils uniformity in the human mind and shapes human values and purposes around consistent laws, metaphysics facilitates the socialization of human instincts and desires, and it leads to the organization of society in its entirety as a legally ordered unity.[9]

Nietzsche connected his critical analysis of metaphysics with a quasi-psychological analysis of the value structures of modern society, in which he argued that the metaphysical attitudes of legal conformity, rational regularity and experiential suppression in modern societies are products of originary human weaknesses and anxieties. The metaphysical mentality, he claimed, has its psychological cause in the terror felt by human beings when they are confronted with their original naturalness or nothingness: metaphysics originates in the *horror vacui* of the human mind when it senses itself bound into natural cycles of birth and decay. Human beings react to this primary nihilistic terror by subordinating themselves to long-term *purposes,* and by elevating themselves above nature by imagining themselves to be determined by higher laws, principles or ideals.[10] Fear, therefore, stimulates the formation of laws: fear confers meaning on existence by imposing explanatory schemes on the natural world, by forming value systems that attach absolute value to certain select human actions and by thus legislating rational or moral purposes for humans to pursue, so that they are distracted from their naturalness. Laws and values produced in this manner serve to *humanize* the world. These laws create a 'functional security' in the world inhabited by human beings;[11] they allow human beings to feel that their actions in the world meaningfully serve constitutively human goals; and they allow human beings to live, at least, in an illusion of human justification and moral purpose. Laws, Nietzsche argued above all, serve to *create time:* by imposing moral or legal purposes upon itself, the human mind interprets itself as bound to generalized sequences of obligation, and these sequences differentiate human life from the cyclical temporal processes of mere nature or from the chaotic temporal events of historical contingency. Moral or rational law, in consequence, is a mechanism through which human time – the time of past, present and future – becomes distinct from the unstructured and terrible time of nature, and it permits human beings to envision their actions as occurring in regular sequences and oriented towards valid purposive objectives.[12]

Whilst possessing the obvious psychological utility that they protect people from knowledge of their own naturalness, however, Nietzsche argued that the laws created by reason form highly coercive and dominatory intellectual structures, which, in seeking to suppress fear, fixate human reason on the acquisition of power. The resentful attitude of human beings towards the natural world expresses itself, not only in a desire to regiment the world, but also in a desire for domination over the world and over the threatening traces of naturalness in the world. At the origin of the laws of modern society, in consequence, is a *will to power:* a desire not only to suppress and organize nature but also to take possession of it and to render it harmless. Metaphysical thinking deduces laws of morality or regularity and seeks to prescribe these laws as mechanisms of explanation and control because it reflects a fearful will to obtain power, a power that can only be secured through the extirpation of whatever is residually *natural* – including the residues of nature in reason itself. As a product of fear, however, Nietzsche argued that this will to power is invariably the will to power of weak people. It is power resentfully desired by those who cannot contentedly tolerate the naturalness and spontaneous futility of life, who require order and self-suppression to convince themselves of their own worth, and who, unlike stronger, less nihilistic natures, produce sense for their lives only through the pursuit of obligatory, yet ultimately illusory laws and purposes.[13] The laws of the metaphysical mind, in short, are laws derived from the will to power of the weak.

Nietzsche's reflections on reason, nature and law contain two implications of particular importance for legal thinking. First, he implied that the law is a sequence of norms that refract contentions and controversies over values, and the values proclaimed as legally, rationally or morally binding originate in psychological strategies of subterfuge and anxious control. Laws, therefore, have no neutral or autonomous value, and all claims that certain laws are absolutely justified or that certain purposes must have a rationally sanctioned priority over others are fictitious expressions of the underlying instincts and struggles for power that the law articulates. Legal order, in short, always contains and suppresses an element of exceptionality – for all order only emerges through the 'conflict of power complexes', in which one will seeks to project an ideal account of necessity, which enables it to exert dominion over other accounts and other wills.[14] For this reason, Nietzsche also argued that, contrary to the progressive and legal-emancipatory visions of thinkers and politicians attached to German liberalism, the rule of law under the *Rechtsstaat* does not reflect a condition of progress or reasoned pacification in modern society. Instead, the ordered relation between law and power always discloses an exceptionality at the normative centre of legal order, and even the most liberal and refined legal apparatus transmits barely suppressed elements of violence through society. 'States of law', in consequence, are always 'states of exception'. The relatively pacified rule of law is only obtained by means of a vigilant domination and restriction of human existence by one particular will, and the normative conditions of legal domination exercised as the rule of law can never be viewed as final or finally instituted.[15] The legal organization of power thus still manifests a fervent contest over power, and alternative manifestations of power can at any time rupture the fabric of legal order. Thinkers claiming to evade and dilute the exceptionality of power by proposing positive legal forms for the good polity are themselves still, in consequence, *exceptional* theorists. These theorists seek both to impose norms and order on the acute complexity and arbitrariness of natural life and to assert their own wills as the necessary fundament of legal structure. The laws of seemingly rational states, in short, do not efface or neutralize the exceptionality of power; they merely relocate, displace and perpetuate the fact that law is founded in violence and exception.

Second, Nietzsche also claimed that, as a device for instilling regularity in society, law causes a deep degradation of the innermost potentials of human personality and society, and its apparent humanization of natural and social existence obscures and betrays a deeply cruel subjection of human freedom. The cruelty of law is refracted, most especially, in the fact of human *memory*. Memory, he argued, is particularly important for the formation of the normative horizon in which social agents order their actions in accordance with law. Law can only evolve where it refers its addressees to stable recollections of pledges or promises which they have made in the past, where it can expect and insist that its addressees bind their future actions by these pledges and promises, and where it can presuppose the existence of subjects who are relatively static and consistent *across time:* who order themselves and their actions through the faculty of moral memory. Law thus is a medium that ties human past to human future, that imposes on its addressees (human subjects) an insistent experience of uniformity between the otherwise disconnected moments of human life-history, and that constructs subjects as ordered centres of stability and predictable self-control.[16] However, Nietzsche claimed, it is not natural to the human mind to live outside the present, to memorize things or to accept memories (in the past) as containing purposes or legal obligations (for the future). On the contrary, the natural mind is full of 'forgetfulness'. The natural mind is spontaneous and active, and memory is instituted in it only by regimentation and by the use of violent sanctions against it to ensure that it commits itself to promises and maintains conditions of regularity throughout its actions.[17] Memory evolves through the imprint on the subject of the punishments that it has suffered in instances where it has failed to keep promises – where it has committed the cardinal social sin of *forgetting* the promises that it had previously made, and so of diminishing the regularity imposed on subjects by law. The purposes prescribed by the law to the human subject, then, are the objective form of the coercive force of memory, and, by creating a linear sequence of obligations across time, these purposes act as a constant reminder of the violence and punishment that human subjects have experienced as the attribute of memory and social 'responsibility' was inculcated into them. Law, in short, obtains compliance, not because it is authentically rational, but because it makes people recall cruelty, and the humanity of law in modern states is the humanity instilled in people by prohibition and violence. At the very deepest level of modern human subjectivity, in consequence, there is always a constitutive configuration of law and memory, which, sedimented in the metaphysical form of reason, imposes uniform sense on the otherwise alarmingly contingent realities of time and nature and transforms human beings into legally self-obligating agents.[18] The human subject or person is itself, in fact, a fearfully unnatural aspect – an 'imaginary idea' (*Einbildung*) – of modern social life,[19] which individuates itself as a subject only in order to police its actions and to distil itself, in malign fiction, as the controlling centre of all natural and temporal being. The human subject, therefore, is itself a *legal construct,* emerging from the experiences of painful recollection, natural suppression and mandatory purposiveness that make social formation possible. The human subject, therefore, is also a *metaphysical construct,* which organizes itself as an absolute person by imposing laws on the timelessness and lawlessness of inner and outer nature and by imagining itself as an agent under laws of rational necessity. In this self-construction, however, the subject is also a mere *fiction of personality,* generated through the exigencies of socio-legal control and bound to purposes that are stratified against the authentic liberties of human life. Like the Young Hegelians and Karl Marx, therefore,

Nietzsche saw the modern form of personality as distilled from the purposes of false law, and he saw the laws imposed by this purposive personality as paradoxical laws. In modern society, human life subordinates itself to laws that it accepts as rational and necessary, but the factual source of these laws is in metaphysical deceit and rational autogenesis.

In this argument, Nietzsche also asserted that the metaphysical form of law is closely bound up with the legal institute of the monetary contract. In fact, he argued that the evolution of modern subjects as metaphysically burdened by memory and committed to long-term moral purposes is deeply tied to the reliance of modern society on contracts and to its need to ensure that contracts can be valorized across time and place. The 'moral conceptual world' of duty and conscience, he claimed, has one of its primary origins in the 'obligation rights' of property and contract, which have been imposed over centuries to ensure that relations of proprietorial predictability operate through society.[20] As a faculty for prescribing and accepting legal and normative purposes, therefore, the human subject is not only formed as a stable moral agent, but also as a stable economic agent, which engenders reliable conditions for contractual predictability and monetary exchange: indeed, the human subject first actually emerged as an internal reproduction of external monetary relations. Monetary calculations, Nietzche claimed, 'preoccupied the first thinking of human beings' to such an extent that human thinking cannot be fully distinguished from the logic of the money economy; the human being in its social form is created by the 'contractual relationship' of monetary exchange and obligation, and its rationality is suffused by the necessities of 'purchase and sale'.[21] The punishments that reason has suffered in order to become reasonable and law-abiding, in consequence, are also the punishments required for the subject to uphold the contractual foundations of exchange, investment and profit. It is for this reason that the modern social order is formed on the paradigm of the *legal person* or the *legal subject.* The modern legal subject or legal person is a condition of subjectivity in which the human being confronts other persons as persons, in which it recognizes other persons as obtaining dignity and as sharing in a common legal/moral world, and in which it obtains legal sanction and protection for the free exercise of the will and the free pursuit of purposes. The conditions of this legal personality, however, are entirely determined by a rationality focused on 'prices', on 'values', and on 'equivalences', and the person constructs itself as a person and others as persons only because this construction forms a legal order in which the performances of the economy can be effectively accomplished.[22] As a subject or person of law, therefore, the human being is not, as Kantians and positivists argue, the social form of freedom: it is a concentrated and fictitious focus of the wider economic dynamics that law reflects and perpetuates, and it incorporates paradoxical values of accountable entitlement, regularity and predictability which permeate all societal exchanges. In its experiential foundations, moreover, this person is always a depersonalized person, paradoxically abstracted from monetary functions. The law, in short, is the negation, not the rational precondition, of human freedom, and it is the negation of humanity itself.

In this last respect, Nietzsche turned with bitter irony against the preconditions of the Enlightenment and of liberalism, in its different forms. Nietzsche responded to the legal claims of the Kantian Enlightenment, and later of liberalism and historicism, by arguing that the laws of 'impersonality and general validity' endorsed by the Enlightenment do not mark the elaboration, but rather the suppression, of authentic human nature: the laws mark the 'final weakening of life'.[23] Similarly, the moral universalism of Kantian ethics and the legal subjectivism of positivism do not mark a liberation of humanity and the human will, but a subjugation of humanity beneath the paradoxical laws and purposes of a malign will to power. The metaphysics of the Enlightenment, consequently, does not constitute a fully independent inquiry into the conditions of freedom. This metaphysics condenses and reflects wider processes of social formation and economic change, and it forms one moment in a far broader intellectual genealogy, devoted to the metaphysical enslavement of the vital aspects of human life. Like other metaphysical views, therefore, this metaphysics arranges human reality around a fiction of rational freedom and inviolable law, but this freedom and this law are mere self-generated paradoxes, purchasing freedom at the price of a deep alienation and denaturation of human existence.

At the very centre of Nietzsche's interpretation of modern society, in sum, is an account of human subjectivity that, like the one proposed by Marx a few decades earlier, identifies a profound collusion between *metaphysics* and *capitalism* which influences human life at a number of different levels. At one level, he implied, the self-organization of the modern human subject as a rational-legal subject manifests a general determination of reason by the legacies of metaphysics and an invariable tendency in reason to confront its place in the natural world by seeking comfort in metaphysical laws outside its own spontaneous experience. However, at a different level, the legal form of human reason and subjectivity also upholds quite determinate conditions of societal regularity. Indeed, it helps to preserve social reality as a distinctively capitalist reality and, as a primary guarantor of contract and exchange, the purposive shape of the subject as a legal subject acts as the basis for the continual self-replication of society as a capitalist society. The metaphysical fictions at the heart of society are, therefore, generated by, or at least intimately correlated with, capitalism: the human subject, as a fictional person, is the distilled form of capitalism, and the laws that this subject projects and enforces are originally deducible from the exigencies of capitalism. Both as the refraction of capitalism and as the refraction of metaphysics, however, the legal form of the human subject manifests a deep malaise in human experience, a deep paradox at the centre of the human world and a deep alienation of human life from its vital and natural creative origins. Human subjectivity might only experience itself in more authentic manner, Nietzsche concluded, if it overthrows the legal/subjective form imposed on it under the banner of social regularity. This, in turn, might only occur if the subject is able spontaneously and heroically to accept its own naturalness, or if it recollects the primary natural sources of its humanity. Only a renaturalized subjectivity, Nietzsche indicated (again echoing Marx), might invert the metaphysical corrosion to which the human subject is commonly exposed and so allow humanity to live as its own revitalized purpose – that is, as its own spontaneous or non-metaphysical law. As a non-metaphysical subject, the human being might invent its own laws, and it might live in accordance with 'its own virtue, its own categorical imperative', determined solely by its own present instincts.[24] As for Marx, however, the subject's recollection and reintegration of nature would necessitate an entirely different objective structure and an entirely different objective law for human experience.

Dilthey: metaphysics and historical reason

An analogous and at times overlapping critique of metaphysics also informed the culminating theories of the historicist tradition, expressed in the works of Wilhelm Dilthey. Whereas Nietzsche saw metaphysics as forming a rationalized juridical superstructure, suppressing in human life all spontaneity and creative *naturality,* Dilthey opposed metaphysics because he saw metaphysical concepts as corrupting and obstructing the spontaneity and vital freedoms of human *historicality.* Like Nietzsche, therefore, Dilthey's thinking revolved around the argument that the evolution of modern reason and modern society has suffered greatly from the corruption of human thought by metaphysics. Under the influence of the metaphysical legacy, modern human reason seeks to account for itself and the society that it inhabits by postulating abstract and general *laws* to examine human experience.[25] It then uses these laws to construct a reductively explanatory model of itself and its social environment as a regularized and calculable whole, determined by underlying simple or monadic causes and intelligible in universal categories. Constitutive of modern thinking, therefore, is the fact that thought thinks of itself as an amalgamation of legal functions, and it constructs itself as a source of explanatory or prescriptive laws; this juridical self-construction of reason as a universal legislator is the result of the ubiquitous influence of metaphysical principles on human intellect. For Dilthey, as for Nietzsche, the metaphysical domination of reason and society began with Plato, who claimed that there exist perennial ideas outside worldly life, from which ideal laws about events in the world could be distilled. This reductively metaphysical approach to worldly experience was later perpetuated by scholastic natural law, and then by the Kantian Enlightenment, whose rationalist universalism and formal ius-naturalism Dilthey viewed as a re-enactment of earlier metaphysical impulses.[26] Equally, though, Dilthey also saw the causal systems of the natural sciences in the nineteenth century as a new form of metaphysics. He described these sciences, like all metaphysical analyses, as explanatory sciences, deducing highly generalized 'laws of intellectual life', which make sense of human experience and existence only by reducing the plurality and freedom of historical and cultural events to narrow and easily explained sequences of cause and effect.[27] These sciences, most particularly, are unable to comprehend the human freedoms residing in *culture,* and their imposition of generalized laws on historical phenomena undermines the spontaneous potentials embedded in the distinctively human sphere of cultural action. Dilthey concluded that the legacy of conventional metaphysics prevents human beings gaining knowledge of themselves, their societies, and their cultural-political possibilities. This, he argued, is because metaphysically determined reason is only able to propose reductive techniques of explanation for the analysis of the socio-historical world. Because of this, reason limits the appreciation and understanding that human beings might obtain of those spheres of their existence, which cannot be explained in normative or causal terms, and it excludes all creativity and freedom from human life: it prevents human life from being fully and freely human. The underlying causal unity that metaphysics imputes to the world is thus not only theoretically untenable, it has an intensely damaging role in human existence, and it obstructs human life in its attempts to understand itself in its constitutively human freedoms.

As a corrective to this, Dilthey, in his earlier works at least, proposed that classical-metaphysical or rational analysis should be transformed into a 'metaphysics of spiritual facts'. In so arguing, he indicated that genuine human understanding occurs, not where people seek to construct law-bound images of themselves and their historical world, but where they approach the cultural forms constituting historical reality as expressing formative and authentic cultural and personal experiences, and so as disclosing an inner-worldly metaphysics of human freedom.[28] The later Dilthey then replaced this metaphysics of personal experience with a descriptive method, supported by a doctrine of *historical reason* and *historical experience,* which also placed itself against formal-rational or natural-scientific methods.[29] The human world, comprising both people and things, can only be understood through fully immanent historical *interpretation,* which captures the historical essence of interpreted forms by referring them to the historical experiences of the interpreter and by assuming a shared foundation of experience connecting those who interpret and the forms and the people which are interpreted.[30] Human beings, he claimed, are able to interpret themselves, other human beings and things created by other human beings, because they are all *historical,* and because, as historical agents, all human beings share certain common experiences, which provide an interpretive structure in which knowledge of people and objects can be obtained. He thus hoped to overcome the rationalist constructions of the Enlightenment by accounting for human knowledge as arising from historically embedded processes of interpretation, self-interpretation and cultural retrieval, not through formal or legal prescription and deduction. Where they interpret themselves and other people on the ground of common historical experiences, human beings place themselves fully in their own history; they allow themselves to contribute freely and spontaneously to shaping the history that they make their own; and, in this way, they fully authenticate themselves as *human.* Humanity and historicality thus fall very close together in Dilthey's work. Where human beings approach each other metaphysically or legislatively, however, they occlude their imaginations against historical spontaneity and freedom; they forfeit the liberty of historical (self-)authorship; and they undermine their own resources of humanity.

In its directly political implications, Dilthey's concept of historical reason has two crucial implications. First, Dilthey sought resolutely to centre human society, and its account of itself, on human freedom – that is, on the human being as a freely post-metaphysical agent, whose freedoms are not quantifiable or measurable in metaphysical categories, but are historically self-interpreting in cultural, social and political forms. Indeed, Dilthey's notion of historical reason was directly conceived as a means of correcting the construct of formal autonomy in the Kantian Enlightenment. As discussed, Kant saw the human being as obtaining freedom in the moment of practical self-legislation, and as creating legitimate political forms through a political externalization of this freedom. Dilthey, in contrast, suggested that the human being is only free, and only truly human, where it admits its historicality, and freely interprets itself as a historical agent or subject. As a historical subject, then, the human being participates in and productively transfigures the historical tradition in which it exists, and it creates freedom, both personal and political, as it shapes and revitalizes the freedoms already given in tradition; freedoms destroy both tradition and, ultimately, freedom itself, however, if they are imposed as externally deduced laws upon tradition, or if they are expressed as abstract universal contents. For this reason, Dilthey was strongly opposed to all ideals of natural law, which he condemned as a 'metaphysics of society', and he imagined valid laws as created by common experiences of interpretive freedom.[31] Second, therefore, like earlier historicists, Dilthey also suggested that liberalism, as a doctrine of freedom, cannot be reliably based in metaphysical constructions of right and legality. If liberalism is genuinely a doctrine of human freedom and human self-realization, he explained, this doctrine can only be formulated as a hermeneutical theory of historical life, which interprets and reinforces freedom in its historically immanent shapes, and which abstains from the attempt to condense all historical life into simple legal forms. Like earlier historicists, therefore, he implicitly viewed legitimacy in the state as an interpretive, not legislative, condition, and he saw truthful politics as the highest expression of interpretive culture, allowing the fragile capacities for self-realization and self-creation inherent in culture to develop and assume concrete articulation. On both counts, Dilthey indicated that freedom is necessarily *post-metaphysical:* it cannot be determined by any abstract standards or laws, and it is founded only in a legacy of interpreted cultural knowledge.

Simmel: law, rationality and depersonalization

In many respects, the works of both Nietzsche and Dilthey had their theoretical centre in a radicalization of the critique of metaphysics and rational law in historicism. In Dilthey's case, this resulted in a fully hermeneutical account of humanity and human freedom as an interpretive historical condition, which rejects the subordination of historical life to metaphysical laws. In Nietzsche's case, this resulted in a naturalistic account of human authenticity as a willing acceptance of naturalness, and as a refusal to subjugate nature under metaphysical laws. Both these outlooks saw humanity as critically disrupted by the paradoxical chimera of metaphysics and metaphysical laws. After Nietzsche and Dilthey, then, these arguments began to find resonance in more expressly political debate, and Georg Simmel's sociology marked the first major step on the path towards a reconstruction of vitalist philosophy, especially that of Nietzsche, for more obviously political and social-scientific analysis.

Simmel's work contains certain elements of Kantian reflection, which moved him away from more standard vitalist ideas. He was resolved to preserve certain elements of the legacy of the Kantian Enlightenment, and he accepted, against Nietzsche's naturalism, the defining assumptions of Kantian epistemology: namely, that human subjects are rational and independent centres of cognition, and they are endowed with certain capacities for self-legislation and responsible liberty. Additionally, he was far less sceptical about the outcomes of the rational self-construction of society than Nietzsche. He in fact saw modern society as driven by an evolutionary momentum of differentiation and rationalization, which, in certain respects, guarantees new experiences of human freedom in different social spheres, and which cannot, in Nietzsche's sense, be seen solely as a process that erodes vital possibilities and experiences.

In other respects, however, Simmel also remained in the terrain of Nietzschean thought. First, he echoed Nietzsche's view that modern society has witnessed a far-reaching process of metaphysical formalization and intellectualization, as a consequence of which the authentic and distinctive elements of human personality and experience have been diminished, whilst more uniform or symbolic social identities have become prominent. Indeed, Simmel concurred with Nietzsche in arguing that in modern society human consciousness has been subject to a process of *monetarization.* Underlying the emergence of modern society, he claimed, is a process of rationalization, as a consequence of which the human mind increasingly abstracts from determinate contents, and places itself in a more generalized relation to itself, and to the objects and the contents of its reflection. This process of rationalization is intimately correlated with the distillation of money as a uniform and dominant medium of social exchange, and with the increasing formalization of human interaction as a result of money's pervasive influence. A society dominated by monetary exchange, he explained, generates certain widespread experiences of liberty: it permits high levels of particular social and geographical mobility; it expands freedom of individual choice in different spheres of life; it allows social exchanges to reach over large geographical and temporal zones; it integrates more and more people in social communication; and it enables individual persons to pursue a greatly widened spectrum of purposes and to construct a very broad range of objects as objects of their own wills.[32] However, a society dominated by monetary exchange also imposes generality on the actions and freedoms that it incorporates, and it homogenizes originally distinctive experiences of relationship, ownership and self-formation into relatively uniform types.[33] Indeed, it is also characteristic of a monetarized society that the human mind becomes increasingly indifferent towards its objects, its actions and its temporal locations, and that the person no longer appreciates its purposes or its actions as vitally bound to its own needs and character.[34] The ownership of money, for example, permits a person to purchase one commodity, which can then be transacted for a given sum of money, which then facilitates the purchase of a different commodity, which can in turn be transacted for different sums of money, so that other objects and other purposes can be pursued and purchased. In principle, therefore, actions facilitated by money can be endlessly re-enacted, and each action merely acts as a link in a distended chain of purposes, actions and transactions, in which the objects pursued by actions possess only an attenuated relation to the person who pursues the object and conducts the action. Money, consequently, creates a social order in which human beings can entertain an almost limitless number of purposes and act in pursuit of an almost limitless number of objects. However, in view of the number of purposes that people can pursue, and of objects that people can obtain, purposes and objects and actions conducted in pursuit of them, lose their particular character, and the visceral attachment of the human being to its purposes, objects and actions is dissolved. Like Nietzsche, therefore, Simmel saw the capitalist economy as marking the final triumph of the human being as a formally purposive agent, and he also saw the purposive rationality of capitalism as weakening or neutralizing the relation between people and the purposes or objects of their possession, and even between people and their own actions. Under the generalized rationality of capitalism, therefore, the purposes of economically constructed persons assume a heteronomous primacy over human life itself. Whilst positivism and Roman law saw the purposive human being as a free human being, acting in accordance with its essential social freedoms, Simmel saw the purposiveness embedded in the structure of modern monetary subjects as the originating source of alienation in a modern society. As an agent seeking purposes, he argued, the modern subject alienates itself from the experiential sources of genuine subjectivity, and it constructs itself as a thinly neutralized set of contents and objectives. The monetary alienation of the human subject from its purposes and actions, then, also leads to a weakening or dissipation of the relation between people and other people,[35] and ultimately, to a weakening or dissipation of the person itself – to a lack of 'definite substance in the centre of the soul', or to a diffuse experience of *depersonalization.* The rationalization of society under capitalism permits, in short, an increment of freedom and a definite expansion of the sphere and the purposes of human experience. Yet it also lessens the intensity and particularity of the freedoms that it permits, and it flattens originally vital attachments into experiences of 'momentary satisfaction' or superficial 'sensations'.[36]

In addition, Simmel also concurred with Nietzsche's claim that the changes in modern human experience are linked to the relation between human subjectivity and human law. In modern societies, he argued, law evolves in homology with money, and it follows the wider process of generalization most eminently reflected by money. Modern law, in fact, constitutes a system of wholly positive or 'autonomous norms', which are marked by 'indifference to individual characteristics' amongst legal subjects, and which condense social relations into universalized ideas of personality, obligation and entitlement.[37] As a result of this, subjects under modern law clearly enjoy certain basic rights and generalized modes of legal recognition. However, they also lose connection with the legal imperatives that structure their lives, and their actions are ordered through disembodied and opaque sequences of legal expectation. Simmel extended this argument to incorporate a moderate critique of modern legal states and liberal institutions, which he viewed as the political expression of depersonalization. He argued that in modern democracies more and more people are integrated under law and state, and power and law are transmitted as equalizing and enfranchising media to all realms of social exchange. This, however, does not solely signify a process of emancipation. The organization of society around principles of 'equality in the law' also reflects a wider reality of anonymity and disengagement, for the equality and universality of law are only sustained because law becomes indifferent to individual facts, cases and persons, and it constructs people as equal only by assimilating them to reductive ideas of universal personality.[38] Under modern law, in consequence, the relation of the person to the law loses integrity and singularity, and the reasons for law's validity are accepted only in general and relatively indifferent manner. The person under law, in other words, is not the real person, recognizing itself as free and vitally obligated under law, but the general person, the chimerical shadow of the real person.

The generalized idea of personality underpinning modern law, Simmel thus concluded, is undoubtedly the source of an increase in social freedom, for it allows laws to be passed uniformly, and it permits all actions and exchanges to enjoy legal sanction and protection. However, this personality is a personality in a condition of extreme generality, shaped by the attenuation of authentic purpose, substantial experience and *real personality*, which the wider monetarization of consciousness induces. The personality of the person under modern law is a personality pursuing purposes that are not fully its own, enjoying freedoms that are equal but not integral, disposing over objects and other persons as things of relatively indifferent significance, and so hollow and fragile in its own essential structure. At the heart of the modern legal order, in short, is a personality in a state of metaphysical degeneration, alienated from the genuinely constitutive relationships of human life and from authentic experiences of self-formation. The democratic legal state and its laws, consequently, are not founded in an experience of personal freedom and self-legislation, but in a vacuity, where integral personality is (almost imperceptibly) relinquished. Closely echoing Nietzsche, therefore, Simmel concluded that the universalized and autonomist legal doctrines of the Kantian Enlightenment closely refract the depersonalization of human experience under capitalism. Underlying modern society, he indicated, is a constitutive nexus between metaphysics, money and law, and the metaphysical universalization of law promoted by Kant does not stand outside this process; it is merely one moment in the wider dialectic between these elements.

Simmel's response to the metaphysical state of the law was to develop a quasi-existential or decisionistic perspective on questions of legal content and subjectivity. He argued that it is possible for human subjects to break with their general formalization by deriving laws and legally reflected purposes from impulses shaped by their historical and vital experiences, and so to proclaim legitimacy for their actions on the ground of an *individual law*.[39] In this, Simmel sought, without abandoning law to simple relativity, to transpose the origin of authentic law from the abstraction of post-Enlightenment metaphysics and capitalist depersonalization towards vital human experience and historical self-authorization. At the heart of this conception is a metaphysics of *particular personality*, which sees certain persons as capable of condensing their own character and experience into absolutely valid imperatives, and so of proclaiming their own personality as the necessary origin of law.

Weber: the metaphysics of capitalism

It is in the legal theories of Max Weber that Nietzsche's insights came to play their most influential political role. The central thesis in Weber's work is a theory of rationalization. Modern society, he explained in this theory, has evolved through a process of positivization or rational differentiation, in which different spheres of social practice have regularized themselves in accordance with independent and distinct functions, and in which all actions within each realm of social practice have rationalized themselves as means of obtaining stipulated *purposes*. Through this process of rationalization, he concluded, human life in modern society is oriented towards purposes that increasingly acquire relative primacy over life itself, and for whose validity human beings can no longer integrally account. This is especially the case in the economy and the law, in which human action routinely structures itself around purposes that it internalizes from the generalized mode of practice that surrounds it. In this analysis, Weber was not only influenced by Nietzsche, but also by Ferdinand Tönnies. Tönnies argued that the evolution of modern societies, distinct from pre-modern communities, is underpinned by a process of atomization, through which the organic whole of common existence is dissolved into distinct spheres of exchange between rational, purposive and self-seeking *persons.*[40] These persons, he claimed, are originally distilled from the principles of Roman law; Roman law generates the idea of the 'abstract human being', determined by its pursuit of unilateral purposes of self-interest, and it transmits these principles through all society as the basis of social and legal interaction.[41] As a result of this, modern society dismembers itself into a series of independent functional realms, dominated by formally purposive agents. It develops, for example, a legal system in which all 'individuals are fully independent of each other', and all organic or commonly evolved purposes are eradicated.[42] It forms an economy, based in the formally purposive interactions of proprietorial agents. Similarly, it also institutes a political order, which is organized around 'the absolute person' of a dualistically formed state. This state is separated from its constituents, and it explains its legitimacy solely through reference to its own distinct formal purposes.[43] Modern society thus loses all organic cohesion, and the bonds between people lose their integral character, and human agency is translated into an infinite set of isolated actions.

Close to both Nietzsche and Tönnies, therefore, Weber claimed modern society in its entirety is determined by a structure of purposive rationality (*Zweckrationalität*). This rationality manifests itself in a mental attitude that proportions human action to the accomplishment of long-term generalized objectives or rational purposes. It therefore limits affective or traditional influence on human action, and it restricts the impact of 'value-rationality' – that is, of ethically modulated considerations of value – on human behaviour.[44] Famously, Weber argued that the evolution of purposive rationality was first conditioned by the ethics of self-denial, 'systematic self-control',[45] deferral and 'ascetic conduct', which he identified as emerging from the religious ethics of Calvinist Puritanism.[46] The purposive form of modern reason, he claimed, was engendered through a secularization or positivization of originally religious outlooks, through which religious mental forms were adapted to worldly necessity, and came to form the basis of prevalent worldly attitudes and institutions. The attitudes shaped by Calvinism, then, formed the origin of the mental apparatus of capitalism, and of the attitudes that have allowed capitalism to evolve as the dominant mode of economic practice.[47] Purposive rationality imposes a strict order of predictability on human behaviour; it orders human action around purposes of monetary obligation, investment and contract arising under capitalism; and it ultimately instils in human rationality an irreducibly purposive and instrumental attitude towards objects and other people. Although centred in the economy, this attitude also conditions other social spheres; law, especially, is a crucial and pervasive site of such rationalization, which immediately internalizes the spirit of purposive regimentation. Weber insisted that modern society is driven by a dynamic of differentiated evolution, so that law and the economy cannot be seen as fully coupled. Nonetheless, he also argued that law is closely linked to the evolving rationality of the economy, and it is charged with responsibility for generating a framework of 'rational rules' and 'calculable functioning', in order to stabilize the autonomous processes of capitalist production, circulation and – above all – 'contractual freedom'.[48] Modern law, founded in the construction of human beings as purposive agents endowed with formal guarantees of 'individualistic freedom', thus provides normative foundations for operations in the economy; it articulates principles of validity that allow the economy to explain and justify its functions, and it serves to organize all social interaction around the purposive dispositions necessary for capitalism.[49]

Modern society, Weber concluded, is structured around the causally linked processes of rationalization, juridification and monetarization, and these processes mesh together to produce and determine the alienated conditions of secular modernity. In secular modernity, human thinking and acting are dominated by a climate of rational-legal regulation through which law transforms economic motives into a formal-coercive order of generalized norms. As they act in compliance with such laws, people are alienated from their factual social relationships; they are forced to renounce their own natural enjoyments; and they abandon all purposes that they can accountably define as their own. Modern law, a 'rational, technical apparatus', which is 'devoid of all sanctity in its content' and explains its validity 'only in purposive-rational manner', thus weighs down on modern humanity as its metaphysical 'fate'.[50] In a nightmarish inversion of Kant's post-metaphysical dream of purposive autonomy, therefore, modern society has formed itself as a realm of purposes in which individual social and legal agents are unable to propose and pursue their own inclinations and are forcibly compliant with purposes produced by the overarching frames of action in which they operate. Far from delineating a sphere of human freedom, the purposive construction of the person has turned the person paradoxically against itself and against its constitutive freedoms. The person now appears as pursuing solely false yet universally imposed purposes and as a self-alienated reflex within an invisible yet coercive set of legal-economic directives. Under capitalism, in short, the legal person is not its own autonomy, but its own heteronomy.

On these grounds, Weber's work can be seen to bring together elements of Marxist analysis and elements of the socio-cultural and metaphysical critique proposed by Nietzsche and Simmel. The underlying claim in Weber's account of modern/secular society is that the positivization of social forms and practices, transmitted primarily through the law, has not formed modern society as a place of post-metaphysical legal freedom, and it has not lessened the impact of unaccountable power or non-rational coercion. On the contrary, the rational positivization of social life forms is driven by and endlessly refracts the purposive logic of capitalism. In consequence, the process of positivization has served only to produce new experiences of heteronomy and legal paradox, and human life now remains metaphysically entrapped in an objective reality over which it has no control, whose preconditions it cannot shape, but which proclaims itself as internally rational and free.

Power and legal exceptionality

In this respect, Weber also echoed elements of Nietzsche's argument that the liberal *Rechtsstaat* is a metaphysical or paradoxical state. Weber surely considered himself a liberal. He attached himself throughout his life to the political representatives of the German middle class,[51] he pledged himself to the main causes of the left-leaning liberal parties in the political landscape of later Imperial Germany, and he especially supported the demand of the liberal factions for the institution of a more democratic constitution and for an expansion of parliamentary authority in the imperial state. Indeed, Weber's work formed one of the defining positions in the reconsolidation of liberal theory around 1900; his ideas concerning the legal state and the relation between state and economy offered one of the main alternatives to pure positivism, and they contributed in crucial ways to the evolution of a distinctively German strong-state liberalism at this time. Nonetheless, Weber followed Nietzsche in defining the main political achievement of post-Enlightenment liberalism – the *Rechtsstaat,* with its claim that legal compliance and the imposition of checks on the dissemination of power leads to legitimate order – as a fictitious and often self-deluding accomplishment. He saw the *Rechtsstaat,* especially in its positivist formation, not as an institution in which power is constrained by agreed norms, or in which rationalized ideas of freedom are communicated through society, but as a particularly malign mode of governance: as 'an impersonal order' of 'formal legality',[52] whose 'cosmos' of abstract rules diminishes the distinctive features of the persons and objects to which law is applied,[53] and whose appearance of regularity hides the fact that laws of legal states bind human beings to anonymous legal principles and alienate human beings from their own authentic purposes. The law of the *Rechtsstaat,* he consequently asserted, is a medium of purposive rationality, whose intrinsic content is secondary to its formal function of stabilizing human action and expectations around stipulated purposes: these purposes, to some extent at least, originate in the economy, and they maintain a regime of economic tyranny over human life. Legal states, for this reason, are invariably highly bureaucratic. Indeed, bureaucracy is the 'purest type' of the *Rechtsstaat.*[54] Indeed, legal states are bureaucratic precisely because they are determined by economic purposes. Bureaucracy acts as a transformer in which economic imperatives are given legal form and in which economically derived purposes are transmitted through society as universally valid principles. Bureaucracy, in short, is the place where the paradoxical unity of law and power, on which the *Rechtsstaat* is founded, is articulated, and where laws obtain the *appearance* of rationally constructed rule-conformity and procedural correctness. At all times, however, Weber was clear that the legally prescribed purposes of bureaucratic regulation are false purposes, which entrap human beings within false orientations and alienate them from the conditions of their freedom. The *Rechtsstaat* is primarily a technically rule-determined system of government, which evolves, first, from law's assumption of a stabilizing function in the economy and, second, from the fact that modern institutions tend to obtain recognition and legitimacy by promoting assurances of rule-compliance and purposive order. The *Rechtsstaat,* therefore, is a paradoxical state, which propagates an impression of universal law and procedural compliance, but which in fact derives its substance from highly oppressive and depersonalized purposes and imperatives. In the *Rechtsstaat,* as in other states, Weber concluded, power remains exceptional, founded in violence.[55] The appearance of legal normalcy and rationality does nothing to eradicate power's exceptionality. Law in the legal state, in fact, is a metaphysical illusion of rational freedom, which in fact perpetuates a domination of human life by inhuman purposes and norms.

Weber's famous typology of legitimacy also refers to this discourse of legal exceptionality. Political systems, he argued, tend to legitimize themselves in one of three ways. Some systems obtain legitimacy because they have existed for a long time and they are embedded in the historical fabric of a society: these systems enjoy *traditional* legitimacy and their laws are accepted for customary motives. Some systems obtain legitimacy because they are perceived as complying with rule-determined prescriptions and as serving the pursuit of long-term goals: these systems enjoy *rational* legitimacy, and their laws are accepted because they appear rational and reliably normative. He associated this type of legitimacy with predominantly bureaucratic regimes, and so also with parliamentary legal states under advanced capitalism. Some systems, then, obtain legitimacy because they have little formalized law; they are not determined by immediate economic rationality; and they are sustained by the distinctive personal – or 'extra-quotidian' – qualities of their figureheads: these systems enjoy *charismatic* legitimacy, and their laws are accepted for affective reasons.[56] Weber also characterized this type of legitimacy as *revolutionary* legitimacy, and he saw this as a type of legitimacy that helps to stabilize political systems in exceptional or violent periods of transition or upheaval.[57] In each instance, Weber emphasized his conviction that a system does not possess legitimacy because it communicates power in the service of human ideals or because its laws have the measurable quality of universal validity. Rather, legitimacy is nothing more than the ability of a political system to generate motivations for obedience or 'compliance'.[58]

Weber stressed that none of these models of legitimacy exist in pure or ideal-typical form and that most political systems combine elements of all these models. However, he also indicated that regimes that rely exclusively on *rational* legitimacy are unlikely to fulfil the integrative tasks of statehood in modern mass democracies, which incorporate highly varied class structures, divergent social interests and a fluctuating and restless electorate. In modern mass democracies, he suggested, the foundation of political order is inevitably unstable and conflictual, and it lacks traditional or inherited solidity. It is consequently naïve to assume that the rule of law alone, concentrated in the hands of a bureaucratic apparatus, will be strong enough to draw all the disparate components of this society into one cohesive unity and to make all people believe that the laws determining their lives are valid. He therefore argued that an element of charisma is an essential ingredient of political stability in a mass democracy. In fact, mass democracies must be unified by powerful leaders, who impose order, discipline and common purposiveness on society by exercising a specifically *political* will: a personal will that stands above the technical rationality of the bureaucracy and formal law and that cannot be reduced to technical or formal-purposive motives. Politicians exercising such a will are likely to be distinguished by demagogic or Caesaristic attributes.[59]

For this reason, in his contributions to constitutional debates during the collapse of the Hohenzollern monarchy in 1918 and prior to the foundation of the Weimar Republic in 1919, Weber endorsed the institution of a mixed-democratic system, including a chamber of parliamentary delegates, whose members were to be elected by general election, and a president, to be elected by plebiscite.[60] Central to his objectives at this time was the desire, echoing the earlier influential ideas of Rudolf von Gneist, to place legal controls on the infamously non-accountable executive or ministerial bureaucracy of the imperial state and to extend parliamentary competence so that delegates elected to parliament could assume ministerial positions.[61] Weber thus sought to design for Germany an integrative *Rechtstaat* in which political authority could be founded in an authentically democratic political will, not in a technical bureaucratic apparatus. At the same time, however, he also argued that parliament should not be allowed to act as the bearer of unlimited legislative sovereignty, and that laws derived from parliament are not sufficient to consolidate order and legitimacy in the state. Parliament, he argued, is lastly a bureaucratic component of the political system, which is incapable of exercising integrative force through society, and which must, in decisive points of policy, remain subordinate to the president. Only a president incorporating charismatic authority has the capacity to unify all the disparate classes and parties of the nation and, consequently, to enact policies supporting the national interests and consolidating the vitality of the nation. The essential role of parliament in a democracy, he concluded, is to provide a breeding ground for the production of potential elite candidates, bearers of *charisma,* who, once trained in parliament, might compete with each other for the dignity of presidential office and ultimately bind the nation together through their charismatic appeal.[62] In this point of theory, Weber borrowed deeply from the analysis of law and law's personality set out by the historian of ecclesiastical law and the prominent liberal intellectual of Imperial Germany, Rudolf Sohm. Sohm had argued earlier that the pneumatic or charismatic community of the early church represents the most authentic human community. Early Christian communities, he claimed, were not bound by or integrated in law,[63] but were held together by the immediate charismatic authority of spiritual teachers,[64] and all attempts to stratify a hierarchical, metaphysical or rational legal order across the community contradict their originary spirit.[65] Weber derived from this account an idea of the nation as a vital community, which is liable to erupt into uncontrollable and revolutionary demands for power where its spirit is not captured in intense experiences of unity and integrity. Following Sohm, thus, he concluded that rule-bound or purely legal order will not pacify modern societies or reflect the legitimacy of these societies. Systems seeking to construct themselves as legitimate and warranting obedience also require an adjunct of charisma. Modern societies, above all, cannot be fully integrated by law, they must also be integrated by charisma, and it is only where they obtain a charismatic integrity that they are responsive to laws, and that they can be made to comply with legally prescribed purposes. Law, in short, is a metaphysical form of order that presupposes more integral forms of identity and unity as the precondition of its full validity.

This does not mean that Weber envisaged a constitutional order in which the charismatic leader would be permitted to exercise unlimited authority, or to apply power entirely without law. On the contrary, he viewed the charismatic leader as a figure able to confer a vital legal form upon the community and to make laws serving more authentic purposes than those sanctioned by the impersonal rationality of procedure or bureaucracy. The charismatic leader, he thus argued, is defined not only by unique attributes of character, but also by a profound ethical distinction. Genuine leaders are motivated, not by formal moral considerations nor by arbitrary personal goals, but by an 'ethic of responsibility' (*Verantwortungsethik*).[66] This ethic is the attitude of politicians whose actions concentrate a resolutely particular decisiveness, and who propose purposes for the political order which are motivated by absolutely committed personal responsibility. Such decisive responsibility, for Weber, need not exclude moral generalized concerns: on the contrary, the ethic of responsibility and its moral correlative – the ethic of principled conviction (*Gesinnungsethik*) – are not necessarily 'in absolute contradiction'. However, the ethic of responsibility has a particular distinction amongst other moral forms and attitudes: this is an attitude that forms binding and morally valid purposes, that integrates diverse social groups into the pursuit of these purposes, but that authorizes its purposes without any recourse to formal or transcendent presuppositions. The ethic of responsibility is, thus, the highest attitude of human personality in its historical and secular location. Responsibility manifests a 'humanly genuine' ethic; it constitutes the ethical form of 'the genuine person'; and the political decisions produced by the bearers of such rationality are the ultimate foundation of legitimate governance. Parliaments and legal states cannot on their own produce such responsibility, and it is only where the apparatus of the legal state is guided by responsibility that its laws become genuine, substantial and integrative.[67]

Only responsibility, Weber consequently concluded, can provide a human foundation for politics and law, and only responsibility can release government under law from the suspicion of a coercively metaphysical paradox. As discussed, Weber argued that all politics is founded in the contest over the means of violence, and political orders marked by the universal rule of law do not evade this characteristic. Instead, they channel power and violence in new ways through society, their appearance of rule-based uniformity merely transforms economic prerogatives into public dictates, and they are sustained by an erosion of the most integral resources of human personality. The humanization of law of power in such systems is only ever chimerical, depersonalized and paradoxical, and the universality of such law can only acquire dubious and precarious validity. Responsibility exercised by rational-charismatic leaders, however, is an attitude that counteracts the insubstantial generalization of law, and that recognizes that power is most legitimate where it is bound to common objectives and expresses the shared purposes of stability, unity and order. Responsibility, thus, is the sole source of *human law,* of a human unity of freedom and reason, and only those societies held together by responsibility obtain laws whose value is manifestly derived from human commitments. At a practical level, this idea of charismatic responsibility was intended to provide a new grounding for German liberalism as a political outlook and, also, for a liberal political society in Germany. It sought to provide a model for a society enjoying full enfranchisement, an independent parliament, constitutional guarantees of social freedom and economic dynamism. Yet Weber's liberalism also sought both to correct and surpass what he perceived as the personally and nationally impoverishing foundations of traditional liberal institutions and theories. He hoped to accomplish this by reflecting the origin of law, not – following the positivists – in law itself, nor – following the romantics or organicists – in the corporations of civil society, but in personal responsibility. By placing the responsible and genuinely *personal* will at the centre of politics and law, Weber in fact attempted to construct a viable model of liberalism *without metaphysics.*

8 Neo-Kantianism and its aftermaths

The rebirth of Kantian philosophy

In the latter part of the nineteenth century, opposition to the metaphysical elements of Kantian theory was not exclusively the province of strictly anti-Kantian philosophy. On the contrary, this period also saw the emergence of a school of political philosophy that defined itself expressly as neo-Kantian, but that also endeavoured to eliminate the metaphysical elements from Kant's philosophy and to provide a fully post-metaphysical account of human determinacy and human politics. The resurgence of Kantian theory at this time was exemplified by Friedrich Adolf Trendelenburg, who followed Kantian political ideas in defining legitimacy in the state as a condition of 'rational legislation', serving the natural-legal 'realization' of the rational and ethical dispositions of the people.[1] Close to the same time, Karl David August Röder also expanded Kantian ius-naturalism to argue that legitimate law creates enabling conditions for the fulfilment of 'human destiny' and collective moral life.[2] By the 1890s, neo-Kantianism, however, was the dominant academic philosophy in Germany and, with historicism, it constituted the intellectual background for most political theory in the early twentieth century. Neo-Kantianism was concentrated around Hermann Cohen in the Marburg School, at Marburg University, and around Heinrich Rickert in the Southwest German School, at Heidelberg University and Freiburg University.

The major theorists of the neo-Kantian movement sought to eliminate from Kant's works all traces of metaphysical reflection and to reconstruct Kantian ethics as a strictly anthropological doctrine of rational human autonomy, self-realization and legal statehood. At the centre of neo-Kantian theory in the Marburg School is an amplification of the philosophical-anthropological argument, which is expressed rather more elusively in Kant's own writings. This argument, namely, is that the human being is only truly human if it is *autonomous:* that is, if, without external addition, it can account for its cognitive and practical operations as an internally consistent and necessary unity of consciousness, and if it can independently produce necessary laws to govern these cognitive and practical operations. This anthropological reading of Kant was guided by the intention to account for all elements of Kantian thought as contributing to an analysis of consciousness as fully independent and self-legislating. It consequently aimed to transform all aspects of Kantianism that appeared residually attached to metaphysical or dualist conceptions, and it interpreted the autonomist claims of practical reason as the constitutive centre of Kant's theoretical objectives. Cohen, for instance, was emphatic in claiming that Kant gave 'primacy' to practical reason over pure reason, and that the regulation of inner-worldly ethical life is the main intention of Kantian philosophy.[3] He therefore rejected Kant's doctrine of the thing in itself, and he reconstructed the transcendental ideas of pure reason, not as metaphysical limits of reason, but as moral elements in reason, marking reason's attempt to determine the extent of its autonomy.[4] This privileging of practical reason over pure reason was expressed most clearly by Paul Natorp, an early theoretical associate of Cohen. Natorp claimed that the 'basic law' of all human consciousness is that it contains an inalienable 'tendency to unity', and it is oriented towards the production of universally necessary laws of reason to organize the manifold phenomena of practical and cognitive life.[5] Where consciousness obtains this unity and universality, this forms the basis for a conscious condition of ethical integrity in which human reason explains itself as a self-causing and self-justifying agency. The highest condition of human being is, thus, a condition of autonomy, in which reason legislates its own terms without any external directive, and its knowledge and action obtain the quality of universal validity. Rickert also argued that human reason is primarily guided by practical impulses; he too asserted that practical reason has 'primacy' in the Kantian system; and he claimed that even purely cognitive processes contain an evaluative-normative element, which refers objects to 'normative-general values',[6] and so moves 'theoretical behaviour close to ethical behaviour'.[7] Pure knowledge, therefore, runs 'parallel' to the subject's construction of itself as ethically autonomous, and each correct act of cognitive judgement presupposes the existence of an autonomous ethical will.[8]

In their emphasis on practical reason, the neo-Kantians, and most especially those based in Marburg, organized their works around principles of *legal humanism,* and they defined autonomy both as a state of constitutively human self-causality and rational freedom, and also as a practical precondition for social and political life under valid and authentically human laws. Cohen, for instance, stated that his philosophy was concentrated on the primary question of anthropological self-realization, and he intended it to provide an essential 'doctrine of the human being'.[9] The doctrine of the human being, he then added, must necessarily be a doctrine of *law.* Law, he argued, is the medium in which human reason charts the extent and limits of its capacities and in which it gives to itself an account of the conditions of its own authentic freedoms: law, consequently, is 'the foundation of the self', and the human being becomes fully human where it explains its freedom through the autonomous deduction of rationally justified laws.[10] For

Cohen, human beings dispose in law over a medium in which they can detach themselves from all traces of heteronomy (which Cohen termed 'pathology'), and in which they can form themselves, in freedoms, as pure wills or as purely self-legislating wills, not stimulated by 'any other content' except the purpose which they rationally prescribe to themselves.[11] Cohen's legal humanism culminated in the claim that it is in the form of a 'legal subject', as a bearer of certain universally valid rights, freedoms and obligations, that the human being becomes most human, and that the faculties of the rational human being obtain their most perfect unity and autonomy.[12] Whereas the positivists argued that the legal subject is a social form of freedom that law constructs for itself, therefore, the neo-Kantians set out a much fuller account of the legal subject, which explained legal subjectivity as a condition produced by the subject itself, in which the subject autonomously deduces the human preconditions of the law and transmits integral accounts of its freedom into law.[13] The condition of legal subjectivity, on this account, is one where the human being has fully elaborated its rational faculties and has freed itself from determination by motives that are not rationally accountable. The legal subject is a subject which has become autonomous and rationally free: it has become *its own law,* and it pursues purposes that are integrally its own, covered by universal rational sanction. As a legal subject, the subject both produces and accepts universal laws, and it constructs itself as the centre of an entirely *humanized* world, as the fulcrum of a world bound by laws reflecting universally binding and non-instrumental human norms. The *autonomy* of legal subjects thus allows the world to evolve from human capacities of moral self-creation and self-legislation, and it generates binding criteria to determine the validity of both subjective and objective laws. Kantian notions of autonomy, Cohen concluded, mark a profound break between the integrally humanized world of law and the non-human world of metaphysics, and it is only through pure acts of self-legislation (not freedom) that human beings create the world as their own world.[14]

Rudolf Stammler, an early, rather marginal associate of the Marburg School, gave a rather different accent to these arguments.[15] Stammler followed Kant in claiming that the ideal of 'unconditioned unity' is fundamental to human consciousness, and that consciousness produces unity for itself where it abstracts from particularized interests or inclinations.[16] Likewise, he argued that consciousness which is internally consistent and autonomous reflects itself as a purity of will: that is, as an orientation towards practical purposes, whose content can be sanctioned by all rational members of a society. This purity of the will, like Kant's realm of purposes, then forms a regulative idea that guides human consciousness towards a state of harmonious coexistence and co-operation.[17] In this, however, Stammler did not fully share Cohen's claim that law gives immediate expression to the internal unity of human consciousness or the purity of the human will, or that the conditions of ethical autonomy can be fully applied as objective law. On the contrary, he remained closer to the initial separation of ethics and law in Kant's philosophy, and he interpreted law as an objective medium, which acts as a 'form for ordering the human will',[18] and organizes external life in the pursuit of rationally sanctioned purposes'.[19] This, in fact, was the major point of contention in the Marburg School. Cohen argued that ethics and law are homologous, and that morally autonomously people spontaneously form and adhere to universal objective laws.[20] Stammler, in contrast, ascribed a necessary objective or coercive function to law, he argued that there exists a necessary 'contrast' between 'morality and external law',[21] and he accentuated the necessity of 'legal coercion' as a condition for 'social compliance' with the highest norms of reason.[22] He therefore concluded that validity in law is determined by the objective unity and necessity of the law, and by its objective ability to ensure conditions of societal harmony, not by the fact that it originates in a specific condition of the will or a substantial moral disposition. Natorp took up a mediating position in this controversy, although he also finally supported Cohen's view, and denied that objectively valid law cannot be viewed as resulting from any form of 'heteronomy', or from any objective demand for obedience, and must therefore be seen as originating in primary acts of self-legislation.[23] All 'heteronomous law', Natorp concluded, is 'incorrect (*unrichtiges*) law', and valid law must be immediately founded in the condition of human ethical autonomy.[24] Despite these disagreements, however, Stammler still echoed Cohen's claim that objective law must reflect the founding regulative ideas of consciousness, and that the application of law can lead human society towards a condition of necessary collective non-instrumentality.[25] For Stammler, therefore, valid law remains law which gives manifest form to the 'formal unity' of human consciousness,[26] and it provides the form for the self-articulation of the innermost possibilities of human existence and coexistence. Right law is law whose norms guide human action towards correspondence with the 'social ideal' of an objective unity of purposes.[27] Stammler's theory, moreover, was also anchored in a conception of the legal subject. He viewed the legal person as the objective form of the pure will, or as an 'end in itself', defined by the possession of inviolable rights and by the recognition of those rights in others. The principles underpinning the entire legal community, he claimed, are deducible from this subject.[28]

The *Rechtsstaat* as the human state

The theorists of the Marburg School also placed particular emphasis on Kant's original claim that the adequate exercise of human reason as autonomy will lead to the evolution of a legal state ensuring conditions of rational legal freedom and rational-subjective rights for all citizens, and that the *Rechtsstaat* is the appropriate objective order for the world of human autonomy. To a greater extent than Kant himself, in fact, these philosophers accentuated the universal-anthropological personality of the state, and they defined the legitimate state, the *Rechtsstaat,* as the objectively formed corpus of the ideal and autonomous human being.

Natorp's doctrine of personal autonomy, for example, also incorporates an account of legitimate socio-political forms, and he saw the particular autonomy of the human being as a substructure for a society based in collective autonomy, self-realization and non-coercive law.[29] In this, Natorp argued that legitimate legal order is underpinned by and constantly refers to the fully autonomous human person as a legal subject: the *Rechtsstaat* is the ideal material form of the legal subject, and wherever the state is correlated with the legal subject it ensures governance under human laws. Stammler also argued that the legitimate state has no independence of the law, and it evolves as its transports into law the rationally unifying characteristics of its constituents, and it maintains legitimacy only as it acts a subject of these laws.[30] The state, therefore, represents the collective form of the ideal and objectively harmonious person, and it forfeits this representative function wherever it acts in contravention of the laws of the pure will. Cohen also concluded that the realized legal state represents the 'immediate model of the ethical personality'.[31] He saw the 'unity of state' as the form in which the human being reflects objectively the unity and consistency of its consciousness,[32] and in which it gives manifest form to the human self as a pure will.[33] The legitimate state, consequently, is the perfect manifestation of the defining human quality of ethical autonomy, in which each person is recognized as a fully realized purpose, subject to no coercive laws.[34]

Unusually amongst the prominent intellectuals of the late nineteenth century, many philosophers associated with the Marburg School were inclined to feel theoretical sympathy for aspects of the early socialist movement, even at a time when this movement was still, in principle, illegal. In many ways, their models of the legal state acted as ethical and legal-philosophical supplements to the political programmes of the revisionist movement on the right wing of the SPD around 1900, which, led by Eduard Bernstein, sought to eradicate from Marxism the deterministic, positivist and revolutionary components and to consolidate Marxist theory as a progressive legal and ethical humanism.[35] Cohen, for instance, attempted to introduce elements of Kantian legal humanism into Marxist theory, and to develop a moral-egalitarian doctrine of collective self-realization through law, defining law and the legal state as the constitutive forms of social reconciliation and self-realization, as well as ethical integrity. This doctrine shared the socialist view that progressive emancipation and increasing human equality are necessary and inevitable elements of human history. However, it viewed social progress and improvement as consequences of a legal rationalization of human relations and of an increasing realization of human potentials under law – not as the result of class conflict or material need-satisfaction. A socialist society, Cohen claimed, should be envisioned as a material extension of a Kantian legal state in which 'each person is defined as an end in him or herself', and in which laws represent and protect the ideas of a morally autonomous community, including ethical and material equality and freedom.[36] Similarly, Stammler, although much less sympathetic to socialist ideals, also set out an anti-determinist revision of Marxist theory. Whilst endorsing the 'social striving' for equality as a dynamic component of human society, he argued that a just, free and equal society can only emerge on the basis of a legal state founded in 'a harmony of all contents of the will', guided by the regulative idea of the 'purity of the will', and so establishing justice through morally directed legislation.[37] The Marxist ideal of a society based in collective ownership of the means of production, he argued, fails to see that an enduring socialist society cannot be established without certain ethical and legal preconditions, and it fails to appreciate the constitutive role of law in shaping conditions of social justice.[38] Natorp also questioned the deterministic elements of dialectical materialism, and he saw the evolution of a society guaranteeing social justice as a process of human self-realization, which can only be accomplished 'in juridical manner'.[39] Central to these reconstructions of Marxism was the critical claim that, owing to its deterministic account of law's functions, Marxism is generally no more successful than its conservative adversaries in interpreting a genuinely human state, and it falls behind its declared objective of human liberation. In its common deterministic form, in fact, Marxism permits the human being to subside into a secondary position, and it gives priority to material and heteronomous laws of causality over the human being and over laws deduced by the human being. It is only where Marxism is reconstructed as an ethical/legal doctrine, centred in the idea of the human being as a universal legislator and as rational author of itself and of its historical and material conditions, that the substantial humanist content of Marxism can be elaborated. This, then, can only occur under a legal state.

A number of thinkers more peripherally attached to the Marburg School were still more emphatic about the necessary link between neo-Kantian legal statism and socialism. Franz Staudinger, for example, argued that the common realization of the pure will is the essential ground and ideal of socialist politics,[40] and he insisted that class struggle should be redefined as a struggle for 'moral liberation', not for class supremacy.[41] Karl Vorländer also proposed a fusion of Kantian ethics and socialist ideals.[42] The primary Austro-Marxist theorists, most especially Max Adler,[43] claimed that Marxist theory should be reinterpreted as an ethically prescriptive doctrine, and they emphasized the normative content in Marxist accounts of evolution and social transformation. These ideas elicited a caustic response from more orthodox theorists in the Social Democratic mainstream, most notably from Karl Kautsky. Kautsky rejected abstract or universalist conceptions of freedom, and he fundamentally opposed the post-Kantian claim that moral principles could be dislocated from their historical class determinacy and presented as legal imperatives, with an 'independent existence', capable of steering society towards a universally valid goal.[44]

Kant after metaphysics

In defining the legal state as the objectivized form of the autonomous human person or human consciousness, the Marburg neo-Kantians also attached the greatest importance to defining the legal state as a non-metaphysical state, whose preconditions are deducible without any recourse to ideas, and whose evolution reflects an underlying substantial formation of the human personality. This, crucially, involved a critique of the residual elements of metaphysical transcendentalism and natural law in Kant's philosophy, and, against both Kant and the positivists, it called upon an anthropologically intensified analysis of the formation of the human subject as a legal person and as a source of law. Implicit in this analysis, consequently, is an intimation that Kantian accounts of the legal state remain paradoxical, and that, in reflecting valid law as concentrated in the state and relatively indifferent to those addressed by law, Kant finally failed to place the state and law on authentically human preconditions or to account for freedom under law as a human freedom.

Stammler, for example, centred his legal philosophy on an anti-transcendental reconstruction of Kant's doctrine of ideas. He accepted Kant's arguments that ideated moral maxims should assume a regulative role towards practice and that ethical action depends on rational-legal ideation. However, he argued that ideas guiding human actions should not be conceived as 'transcendent', but as 'immanent to particular knowledge' and as practically articulated in the objective processes of human ethical life.[45] Indeed, he denied that any rational or legal deductions could be validated by postulates of reason 'abstracted from all experience', and he defined the role of reason in engendering right law as limited to the production of 'regulative principles' to bring law into accord with a realm of objectively harmonious purposes.[46] An ethical law is normatively necessary, he concluded, not when it corresponds to a transcendental idea or when it reflects an abstract natural law, but when it 'provides an indispensable condition' for human harmony, and for engendering 'unity and order in our consciousness'.[47] The signature of ideal necessity, consequently, resides in reason's consistent unity and order, not in any ideal ground outside thought itself. In his doctrine of the legal state, by extension, Stammler transformed Kant's idea of necessary freedom into an objective 'idea of pure community',[48] and he argued that an objectively valid law is defined as such by the extent to which it facilitates objective freedom, unity and order in the form of the state.[49] He thus saw the idea of objective unity as the key regulative of human reason, and he saw law regulated by this idea as consolidated in the legal state. Natorp also argued that the autonomy of reason relies on a critique of all 'metaphysicism' in the deduction of ideas, and so in a dislocation of Kantian laws from their transcendental externality.[50] More emphatically, Cohen expressed an 'insuperable suspicion towards truth which resides in justifications other than those of reason'.[51] He therefore argued that ethical ideas cannot be construed as external or prior elements of consciousness, but should be viewed and articulated as manifest elements in the ethical self-legislation of citizens.[52] On all these accounts, therefore, true law is a constitutively human law: this law must be both reflexively and objectively disarticulated from metaphysics, and a state under such law is a state whose legal personality is the objectively reflected personality of autonomous citizens. Outside Marburg, Rickert denied that metaphysics can have 'any place' in epistemology and ethics.[53] Emil Lask, the main legal philosopher of the South West German school of neo-Kantianism, also asserted that 'all metaphysics' obstructs the normative functions of reason and stands in the way of reliable legislative deduction.[54]

This neo-Kantian critique of metaphysical residues in Kant's theory of the legal state found its most theoretically resonant expression in its attempt to move Kantian ideas away from purely monadic conceptions of the autonomous human subject. Indeed, all neo-Kantian thought articulated the suspicion (expressed in varying degrees of intensity) that Kant's distillation of the solitary human subject as the exclusive origin of cognitive and political legitimacy marks a reduction of social reality and tends to concentrate purportedly *human* legislation on a metaphysically or dualistically abstracted source. In this respect, the main neo-Kantians all hinted at an unresolved metaphysical paradox underlying the unity of reason and will and law and power as postulated by Kant, and all implicitly lamented the absence of a fully evolved person at the centre of the legal state. For this reason, the neo-Kantians sought to explain valid law as resulting from an anthropologically consolidated person, to see rational freedom in the state as evolving from objectively elaborated forms of reason, and to see the legal state as the objective form of an anthropologically integrative human subject. This was clearly the motive for Stammler's deduction of necessary law from the objective idea of a free community.[55] More significantly, however, Cohen also sought to detach Kantian thinking from its centration on the atomized subject and on abstracted accounts of the subject's self-formation as autonomous. He accomplished this by imputing an inter-subjective structure to the concept of the pure will or the autonomous legal subject, and by explaining the content of rationally valid law as the determinate outcome of interaction between a number of rational human wills. The autonomy of the pure will, he thus explained, articulates itself in the acknowledgement of one rational subject that one human consciousness cannot construct the conditions of human practical freedom without another human consciousness, and, thus, that one person's freedom, and the laws expressing and protecting this freedom, must necessarily incorporate the freedom of another. The will, therefore, can only reflect itself as a pure purpose or a pure norm, and so as the will of an authentic person, where it makes itself identical to the purposes and norms of other wills – where the will becomes one part of a congruent community of purposes. As a result, Cohen concluded, 'the other, the *alter ego,* is the origin of the I', and the ideal form of the I cannot be imagined without its limitation and constitution by another.[56] The pure will is thus elaborated as a communicative structure which 'unifies you and me', and, in establishing this unity, it gives perfect objective form to the necessary norms of self-consciousness.[57] The laws expressing essential human character and demanding binding obligation (both in ethics and in politics) are, consequently, laws that are reflected as rational and necessary by a plurality of wills, which form the person as a person under shared laws, and which cannot be reduced to metaphysically simplified causes. It is only where laws reflect the unity of many wills that they become fully human laws and that human wills acknowledge themselves as necessarily or rationally bound by them. Moreover, only states applying such laws are recognized as genuinely human and legitimate states.

In this theory, Cohen attached his theory of the legal person to the corporate theory of law around Gierke, and he argued that the form of the state cannot be deduced either from the rational principles of the state on its own or from the rational principles of solitary minds throughout society. Only legal states founded in corporate, rather than formal-monadic, notions of the legal person offer the intersubjective content and the 'genuine unity of the will', that legitimate statehood, with generally free laws, presupposes.[58] Like Kant before him, therefore, Cohen saw the legitimate state as the material form of human consciousness as it comes to reflexive clarity about its own necessary constitution as a subject of law.[59] However, against Kant, he argued that this clarity can only occur on the foundation of an overarching dialogue between one legal subject and other legal subjects, and the universal basis of political legitimacy cannot be obtained through the monological exercise of reason. If the legal state is genuinely to be a human state, he concluded, it must be a state whose personality is objectively formed by many human wills, not by one formal will, and it must reflect the anthropological genesis of rationally free law in interactions between these human wills.[60]

After neo-Kantianism: metaphysics and the end of legal formalism

Although distinct from positivism in its commitment to humanist analysis and to moral egalitarianism, neo-Kantianism was often seen by its opponents as related to positivism; its analytical formalism and its systematic rejection of metaphysics were often taken as signs of a methodological proximity between neo-Kantianism and positivism. Like positivism, therefore, neo-Kantianism increasingly became an object of theoretical hostility in the years around the First World War. Indeed, through the war and after 1918, both neo-Kantianism and positivism were widely attacked by newly influential lines of analysis, and the philosophical contours of the early Weimar Republic were in many ways formed by a critical reaction against both positivism and neo-Kantian formalism.

The anti-Kantian views of late Imperial Germany and the early Weimar Republic were expressed from a number of theoretical backgrounds, and they reflected a number of distinct theoretical concerns. Julius Binder, for instance, called upon neo-Hegelian ideas to argue that law should not be derived from the formal will of autonomous subjects, but rather from the objectively formed will of the national-historical community. The precondition of legal validity, Binder claimed, should not be placed in the formal legal subject, but in the objective horizon of national life, and the legal rights and principles that Kantian theory saw as prior subjective contents of the law should be viewed as contingent on the existence of a historically enriched legal order.[61] Binder concluded that Kantian ideas remained founded in 'metaphysics', and in formally normative ideas of natural law.[62] At the same time, anti-Kantian views also emanated from late-historicist perspectives. In his writings of the Weimar era, for example, Friedrich Meinecke expanded his earlier insistence that democratic culture necessarily resides in the 'powerful life-communities' of nation states,[63] sustained by a richly formed national personality and a strong political culture. A legitimate democratic state, he concluded, requires an interpretively structured historical base, consolidated by moral education and historical culture. States of this kind support an enduring democracy far more effectively than the 'heteronomous morality' and technical culture derived from Kantian politics.[64]

The works of the legal philosopher Erich Kaufmann were perhaps more exemplary of the wider tendencies in the reorientation in political and legal thought after 1918, and they also refracted an altered and slightly more affirmative approach to metaphysics, which influenced political theory during the fragmentation of neo-Kantianism. Kaufmann criticized neo-Kantian legal thought for its 'abstract formalism and transcendental rationalism'.[65] Because it has these characteristics, he concluded, neo-Kantianism reduces interpretation of the law to the analysis of 'purely static' legal and cognitive forms,[66] and it is unable to appreciate how laws are engendered by 'legal communities', and how they help concretely to organize these communities.[67] Kaufmann then added to this argument by claiming that the neo-Kantian conception of autonomy in law does not provide for a genuine understanding of autonomy. By focusing reason and rational self-legislation on particular acts of individual subjects, he claimed, Kantian thought narrows autonomy to an abstracted experience of formal self-regulation, which excludes all real content from law. This experience, for Kaufmann, is always ultimately 'heteronomous': genuine autonomy is not a solitary experience, but an experience of living under the laws and life forms of the community, in which laws have obligatory force because they integrate ideas of freedom formed in particular communities.[68] In this critique, Kaufmann differentiated himself from other anti-Kantian views by seeking to reintroduce metaphysical contents into legal debate and by articulating a more sympathetic recuperation of the metaphysical ideas excluded from law and the state under the Kantian banner of autonomy. Kaufmann, in fact, saw the inability of Kantian ideas to envision substantial conditions of freedom, not as resulting from the attachment of Kantianism to metaphysics, but as the outcome of the fact that it 'fundamentally rejects all metaphysics', and that it extirpates all vital and transcendent contents from human communities.[69] The 'demetaphysicization and formalization of Kant' perpetrated by the neo-Kantians, Kaufmann concluded, imposes perennially reductive values on the richly layered vitality of common political life, and it can only engender the most sterile forms of political order.[70] Because of this, most importantly, neo-Kantianism, in its fixation on *autonomy*, erodes the substantial grounds of *freedom*. The expulsion of metaphysics from human law and human politics entails, for Kaufmann, an exclusion of all living and evolving contents from the horizon of legal and political existence, and it destroys the spontaneous and local foundations of freedom in politics. It is, in consequence, only where reason abdicates the dream of its legislative autonomy that politics can offer freedom as its source and content.

Similar ideas also shaped the legal and political works of Max Scheler. Opposing Kant and the neo-Kantians, Scheler also attacked the autonomist assumption that the formal subject and the formal will can be posited as the foundation of ethics and judgement. Instead, he claimed that authentic ethical judgements are founded in a substratum of common being and personality – in the 'total person' – which forms an ontological realm of shared ideas or 'modalities of value', which are implied and realized in all social forms and particular personal acts of a community.[71] The 'sphere of the "I"', Scheler explained, is derived from a realm of common existence and attributes, and it does not exist as a monadic form or an absolute person that is fully distinct from other forms and persons.[72] Indeed, the human person does not exist as a static person at all, and it has no prior absolute unity of consciousness and no prior personal structure. On the contrary, the human being is nothing more than an 'ordered structure of actions' which 'constantly enacts itself' within a phenomenological horizon,[73] and whose moral attitudes are experiences shaped by an underlying realm of transpersonal values.[74] The highest forms of human social life, in consequence, are the forms that give full expression to personal commonality: Scheler, therefore, favoured social orders based in shared personality, or in affectual and loving experiences of 'solidarity' and sympathy, over atomized orders such as 'the mass' or simple 'society'.[75] Like earlier romantic theorists, in fact, Scheler concluded that love is the origin of all true community,[76] and a community of love is most reliably realized, not in a formal legal state, but in corporate organizations, centred around a 'determinate hierarchy of estates'.[77]

Scheler's invectives against the autonomism of Kantian theory were driven by the belief that Kant, in detaching freedom from the communities that shape the experience of freedom, demonstrated an inability to understand freedom. Scheler accentuated the constitutive role of the community in human authenticity; he dissociated human freedom from all Kantian-anthropological notions of the human being as a particular self-legislating agent; and he claimed that freedom of the person is freedom within the organic corpus of the community in which it is integrated.[78] Subjective life, in short, is not the 'private property' of a subject, but the outgrowth of a common organic-historical life, and the freedom of this life is directly obstructed wherever it is misidentified as freedom to choose oneself or to legislate for oneself as a rationally circumscribed or legally regulated entity. Like Kaufmann, moreover, Scheler argued that genuine 'forms of community' always incorporate elements of metaphysical experience, as the community constitutes the vital horizon and the source of all meaning for those who interpret their lives on its foundation: the community is thus the metaphysical origin of all meaning and all life.[79] Kantian philosophy, however, destroys this metaphysical source with its formal subjectivism, and it petrifies all vital freedoms and experiences.

This more sympathetic attitude to metaphysics after 1918 was not exclusive to anti-Kantian theoretical perspectives. At this time, Heinz Heimsoeth initiated an alternative interpretation of neo-Kantianism, which rejected standard neo-Kantian readings of Kant's philosophy as a rationalized account of formal autonomy. Heimsoeth reaccentuated the pure-metaphysical and dualist aspects of Kantian thinking,[80] and he sought to elaborate Kantian philosophy as the basis for a metaphysics of the person and personal self-experience.[81] Karl Jaspers also offered a sympathetic reconstruction of Kant, which strongly opposed the anti-metaphysical or purely juridical readings of his work amongst the mainstream neo-Kantians. Jaspers argued that Kantian accounts of synthetic regress and the unconditioned should be recast as a doctrine of metaphysical liberty or as 'an activity of self-realization'.[82] He thus asserted that human consciousness, which merely regulates its cognitive and practical operations on the ground of its autonomous unity, invalidates and excludes its most vital experiences, and it limits itself against the possibility of its authentic formation and freedom.[83] In its political implications, Jaspers took his philosophy as the basis for a liberal-conservative outlook, which bemoaned the formal and technical character of parliamentary governance, and which argued, in Weberian style, for a politics of decisive *responsibility,* of cultural freedom and of existential self-interpretation.[84]

Perhaps the most striking reconfiguration of neo-Kantianism after 1918, however, came from the heart of neo-Kantian orthodoxy itself, in the late works of Paul Natorp. As discussed, before 1914, Natorp endorsed the autonomist, anti-metaphysical claims of the Marburg School. After 1918, however, his work underwent a fundamental modification, and he abandoned his own earlier conviction that rational autonomy is the cornerstone of a vital polity and a binding legal state. He claimed at this point that the ideas that determine the authentic political order are not only derived from reason, but are also manifest in political realities and shared national and cultural experiences. 'Germanness', he argued, for example, is *an idea,* and this idea can act as a vital guide for political practice. Likewise, 'the *Volk*' and 'leadership' are incarnated ideas, which shape political reality and strive for full elaboration through this reality. Natorp thus proposed an existential-metaphysical conception of political being, which argued that true politics is driven by lived and culturally produced ideas, that such ideation occurs in local and existentially distinct horizons, and that these ideas have greater political validity than the universal ideas of rational autonomy and volitional purity. The ideas of true politics, therefore, must renounce 'all support in the merely rational', and they must aim to institute, especially in the Germany of the 1920s, the earliest metaphysical notions of the state as a divine order.[85] Natorp proposed for Weimar Germany that the constitution of state should be founded on three ideal pillars: on economic regulation, legal universality, and – most importantly – on the education of its citizens.[86] Legal order and legal universality without ideal-cultural enrichment and substance, he stressed, however, are not able to form a vital and integrative political order. Law on its own, he concluded, is 'heteronomy', or 'empty autonomy',[87] and it can only sustain political life where it is invigorated by ideal cultural and educational experiences. For this reason, although never abandoning the claim that legitimate states must show a 'fundamental renunciation of violence' in their exercise of power,[88] in the 1920s Natorp opposed the institutional form of the democratic system of the Weimar Republic,[89] and he approved governments based in the 'corporate ordering' of economic activity.[90] He also turned against pure legal-state models of democracy, and he claimed that politics must possess a vital or spontaneous element that is distinct from law, and that creates unique forms of expression for the national will.[91] True politics, therefore, is not a politics of formal self-legislation or autonomy, but a politics of spontaneous *creation, self-creation* and 'self-production (autopoiesis)', emerging through the decisive will of genius that guides and gives content to the founding ideas of human politics.[92] It is only, he claimed, on the ground of a living metaphysics of community that the political order can evolve as something other than the factual unfreedom of life under a technical-technological apparatus or a thin order of formal norms.

After neo-Kantianism: the end of metaphysics and the birth of the new law

These arguments between the neo-Kantians and the anti-Kantian theorists of the Weimar era focused on the specific relation between metaphysics, humanism and law. The neo-Kantians argued that humans become human in so far as they are autonomous and as they detach themselves from all vestiges of natural or metaphysical heteronomy. The later critics of neo-Kantianism contested, however, that the distillation of human being around autonomy falsifies human freedom, and it occludes human self-experience against vital and historical contents. Furthermore, these critics also claimed that in its attempt to overcome metaphysics, neo-Kantianism institutes an impoverished *secondary metaphysics* of formal laws, stratified invariably across the more vital arenas of life. Against this legal metaphysics, they proposed that politics should be refounded in the spontaneous experiences of shared life, and that this communal life should be viewed as an originating site of innerworldly ideas and locally binding laws.

These controversies over metaphysics, humanism and law in neo-Kantian philosophy also formed the background for the two most influential philosophical projects of the 1920s: that is, for the early writings of Martin Heidegger and Georg Lukács. Like other theorists around them, Lukács, the communist, and Heidegger, the ultra-conservative, both reacted against the formalist and antinomical structure of neo-Kantian philosophy, and both organized their work around a correction of what they perceived to be the historical vacuity in Kantian thought. Both, moreover, sought to provide a new account of human formation and freedom, attentive to the constitutive historicality of human life, and they tried to supplant more formalized ideas of human freedom as the action of human agents in their quality as abstract legal subjects. However, whilst other post-Kantian theorists after 1918 proposed a metaphysics of culture or personal experience to correct neo-Kantian formalism, Lukács and Heidegger shared the conviction that the weakness of Kantian philosophy was caused by the fact that it was insufficiently rigorous in its attempt to think in post-metaphysical categories, and its inability to understand freedom was caused, not by the fact that it excluded all metaphysics, but by the persistence of its metaphysics in its inner structure. Above all, they argued that the Kantian construction of human subjectivity as a legislative agency failed to overcome metaphysics: this construct merely compressed human freedoms into a series of thinly abstracted normative functions; it distilled human life around a depleted sphere of legislative personality; and, like all metaphysics, it generated its claims to truth and validity only through the self-referring and paradoxical assertion that the truth is law, and the source of law is auto-genetically removed from all historical determinacy and freedom. Lukács and Heidegger, thus, both shared the original Kantian and neo-Kantian belief that human freedom evolves at the end of metaphysics. Yet both claimed, equally, that Kantianism and neo-Kantianism had not been able to point beyond metaphysics, and their cult of autonomy had simply resulted in a new and newly paradoxical metaphysics of law.

In opposing Kant, Lukács and Heidegger did not seek to invalidate all intentions of Kantian idealism. In certain respects, in fact, Heidegger in particular placed his philosophy on a continuum with Kant's original position, and he might well have construed his own philosophy as one that corrected and radicalized, yet also continued some of Kant's proposals. Manifestly, Heidegger centred his entire philosophy on the claim that *temporality* is the horizon of all being and that the metaphysically composed systems of Western philosophy have failed to approach the truth of being because they have proved incapable of understanding the ways in which human thought is ontologically structured through temporal factuality and historical being-in-the-world.[93] On this central point, Heidegger directly attached himself to Kant's argument that all thought is determined and constituted by temporality. Likewise, his phenomenological attempt to account for human cognitive and practical operations as producing validity without any external addition or reliance on metaphysical principles marked a strategic affirmation of Kant's original anti-metaphysical reflex. Indeed, Heidegger's separation of *Dasein,* as a realm of practical and interpersonal meanings, from Being itself (*Sein*), as a realm of non-intelligible contents, replicated in modified form Kant's own separation of the phenomenal and noumenal realms, and it expanded Kant's insight that the sphere of human knowledge is defined as being *different* from the realm of metaphysics, and concentrated on practically knowable positive facts.[94]

In many fundamental respects, however, Heidegger's philosophy, even in its entirety, is also framed by an intense critique of Kant, and especially of the Kantian model of the formal juridical subject. Central to this critique is the claim that, owing to his attachment to post-Cartesian subjective ontology, Kant was not able to make good his intention of placing philosophy on post-metaphysical or fully temporal foundations. Crucially, Heidegger believed that Kant's organization of ethical functions around the self-legislative acts of one subject, instead of the inner-worldly linguistic-interpretive subject of *Dasein,* prevented him from understanding human existence and authority as entirely temporal contents. In consequence, Kantian thought remained caught within the ancient legacy of metaphysics, which placed truth *outside time,*[95] and it was only able to comprehend the laws of human ethical life in paradoxical or metaphysical terms. For this reason, Heidegger claimed, Kant was not able to accomplish his main objective of deducing a *human law* for truly human persons and states. Instead, he concluded, Kantian ethics consolidated its idea of the human person by postulating a rationalized concept of the 'moral I' or the 'idea of a moral law' as distinct from, and ontologically prior to, all being, and then by extrapolating an account of authentic personality from this construct. Kantian ethical thought, Heidegger suggested, then placed this absolutely prior rational personality at the origin of laws, and it construed all worldly being as regulated by laws derived by the human person from itself, through original rational acts of self-legislation and self-causation. This person thus legislated its laws only by evacuating all determinate content and freedom from human self-experience and by transmitting laws through the world that no humans could recognize as meaningfully their own.[96] In other words, Kantian ethics, for Heidegger, defined the human being as human only where it participates in rational acts of self-legislation and where it translocates itself into the intelligible ethical realm, which it constructs as its own. Such humanity, on Heidegger's account, is not yet authentically human; it is a condition of humanity petrified in the duality between subjective time and objective time, between universal truth and worldly facticity, between ethical autonomy and worldly unfreedom. Consequently, the laws, of this humanity are not human laws but metaphysical laws, reflecting, not autonomy, but the ancient heteronomy of metaphysics in a new disguise. In its endeavour to see humanity as a rational condition of post-metaphysical autonomy and legislation, Kantian philosophy, for Heidegger, had thus chronically failed to understand the constitutive temporality of humanity, and, as a result of this, it mistakenly crystallized human being around *secondary metaphysical laws,* in a state of secondary heteronomy. For Heidegger, rational-subjective law is always a token of false humanity, and the world humanized by such law is, in fact, always a residually inhuman world.

Heidegger thus indicated that, even as the greatest attempt to construe law and ethics in non-metaphysical terms, Kant's philosophy had succeeded, not in placing law on human grounds, nor in explaining valid law as a unity of reason and freedom, but merely in displacing law's metaphysical paradox and in reintegrating the original legal order of metaphysics into the prior structure of human subjectivity. At the heart of Heidegger's debate with Kant was the telling claim that Kant saw the human subject as constituting itself, as becoming a subject, only through an original act of 'self-obedience' or 'self-subjugation':[97] that is, through an act in which the subject makes itself compliant with laws and imperatives which it, in its originating self-causality, deduces and enunciates, and which it then accepts as the founding norm of its own will. Kant's entire concept of the human person,[98] therefore, hinges – for Heidegger – on the tautology that, in their quality as humans, human beings can, in acts of originary ideation, produce the law through which they become humans. This tautology, however, merely obscures the fact that Kant's posited idea of humanity still relies on the metaphysical assumption that law has priority to life, and, paradoxically, it sees human autonomy as a condition in which law, although self-caused, is a necessary *prior* foundation for personality and human self-becoming. For this reason, Heidegger indicated that the unity of reason and freedom in Kant's thought cannot be sustained: the idea of law as law legislated by a rationally pure will reflects the fact that this law is actually a metaphysically prior law, which is unable to account for itself as a genuine law of freedom. This unity is purchased, on one hand, through a paradoxical act of legal-subjective autogenesis and, on the other hand, through a persistent obligation to a prior order of metaphysical law. For Heidegger, therefore, Kant did not have the full courage to face the question of human freedom; he did not think about human freedom with sufficiently post-metaphysical resolve to admit the temporal contingency of human freedom or autonomy, and, in the moment of thinking autonomy as ethical self-causality, he fearfully retreated from freedom and sought to enshrine this autonomy in immutable (and dubiously humanized) laws. Legally constructed ideas of humanity and the human person, he thus concluded, could only arrive at an idea of the human being as bound to and produced by static norms, as a *metaphysical person,* and so as re-enacting the ancient tyranny of metaphysics over temporal being. Indeed, central to Heidegger's critique of

Kant is the claim that, owing to his fixation of law, Kant's work merely reorganized metaphysics as 'anthropology'. In this, he refocused the original questions of metaphysics as questions about the primary and essential characteristics of the human person, and he identified the distinctiveness of the human being in its invariable capacity for producing and acknowledging laws.[99] For Heidegger, in any case, Kant failed to overcome metaphysics, and his philosophy merely oversaw a rebirth of metaphysics as *legal humanism,* which derived the composition of humanity from absolute laws and which paradoxically derived laws from the eternal composition of humanity.

In consequence, Heidegger saw his own work as an attempt, after Kant, to reimagine the possibilities of fully post-metaphysical reflection and fully post-metaphysical ethics. Central to his philosophy was an attempt to free cognitive and ethical validity from their identification with monadic thinking subjects and to construe valid meaning as a process of practical disclosure between communicative agents, situated fully in the plural 'co-being' of *time,* and producing communicative and interpretive meanings on the ground of this historically structured temporality.[100] In his earliest writings, Heidegger still acknowledged a metaphysical element in human experience. He restricted such metaphysics to a concrete hermeneutic of human being in its historical location, to a 'metaphysics of practical being (*Dasein*)', and he sought to concentrate his philosophical analysis, not on theoretical postulates, but on the ontological or pre-metaphysical conditions of human existence and self-interpretation: that is, on the temporality of being itself. However, he viewed metaphysics as an inevitable constituent of the 'factic existence' of human being, and he argued that all existential truth-seeking contains a metaphysical dimension.[101] Through the 1930s, though, Heidegger broke much more decisively with the metaphysical legacy, and, from this time, he criticized all rationalist, ethical or scientific metaphysics as disrupting the unity of human existence with its temporal and historical foundations,[102] and as falsely conflating truth – or the 'openness of being' – with more monadic processes of rational deduction, reduction and self-empowerment.[103] He ultimately concluded, then, that metaphysics is an insignia of an original instrumental violence performed by the human mind upon being, it prevents human being from finding its home, in being, with other objects of the natural and temporal world. Against the Kantian tradition, therefore, Heidegger construed the realm of the human, not as the realm of the law, but as the realm of the historical or the fully temporal, where human life is *in freedom* with its historical forms, and is not distracted from historical life by normative consciousness or atemporal moral postulates. The truly human realm, he suggested, is a realm where human consciousness accepts itself beyond metaphysics and as plurally and contingently formed by the historical realities of its being. It is, in consequence, only where life accepts the full contingency of its being and forswears the desire to hide its contingency in paradoxical or rationalized accounts of moral necessity, that it obtains a disclosed understanding of its authentic being and of its authentic laws.

On these grounds, Heidegger concluded that the post-metaphysical condition of human freedom cannot be expressed in universal laws or formal ideas of legal personality. The freedom of human being, in fact, occurs at *the end of law.* Freedom is a condition where human beings interact with each other on the foundation of a collectively shaped historical reality, where laws are not deduced through rational postulations, and where persons do not generate validity for themselves through solitary acts of legislation, but through participation in tradition and through practical encounters in everyday historical situations. Indeed, for Heidegger, neither one of the classical accounts of freedom is adequate. Freedom is neither freedom to exercise will nor freedom to exercise reason and comply with law. Both these concepts bind freedom to metaphysically atomized ideas of personhood. Freedom is, in fact, the freedom to be historical, at one with temporal being. For this reason, Heidegger conceived his idea of post-metaphysical freedom as an idea of post-humanist freedom. Underlying Heidegger's work is an attempt to separate the human being from the juridical and the volitional apparatus imposed upon it in the metaphysical legacy and to account for freedom and humanity as a condition in which the content of freedom is not deduced by necessary laws or enacted by particular wills, but experienced as a gift of a historically contingent world. Kantian humanism, he argued in particular, commonly derives its notions of humanity through an analysis of prior laws, and it only imagines humanity and human freedom as a condition of personality deduced from paradoxical legal principles. Such humanism, however, is not human, and its freedoms are not human freedoms. They are metaphysical freedoms; humanism, in the Kantian tradition, 'is either founded in metaphysics or it makes itself the foundation of metaphysics'.[104] Post-metaphysical freedom, thus, is a condition where the human being detaches itself from all normative self-conceptions, where it accepts itself as fully delivered unto the objective reality of its historical being, and where it abandons all sense of its humanity as a specific set of legislative functions. Indeed, the freedom of humanity, for Heidegger, is factually a freedom *from* humanity, from both reason and will, and this condition arises only as human beings renounce the principles of their specific self-construction as *human.*

As far as an element of legal-political prescription can be deduced from Heidegger's practical philosophy, therefore, he indicated that authentic obligations (perhaps expressed as laws) do not evolve through the reasoning powers of one person or one group of people; indeed, there is no isolated legislative aspect of human reason which might empower it to make valid or *necessary* laws. Similarly, there is no form of state that can legitimize itself in legally invariable manner without stabilizing itself through paradoxical references. He therefore argued that necessity in the law, if not a mere paradox, only emerges as a sporadic expression of the historical form which a people or a nation has assumed, and this law has its binding force only as it ties the members of this people or nation together in an objective community. Such law is always transcendentally contingent and unfounded; it is a law without self-analysis and justification, and it cannot provide rational accounts of why it should be accepted. In its contingency, this law might appear as an expression of historical being, or it might appear as a moment of grace or revelation or as the historical shape of fate, as fate exposes this community to its shared destiny. The origin of necessity in law, however, can never be a single, formal or universal act of legislation: law can only be a historically fateful event, in which a people are bound by fate to act in a particular way, and in which the people *decisively* and *resolutely* accepts this fate.[105] Invoking both Luther and St Paul, Heidegger intimated that such law exists as *the new law,* in which a community knows itself unmistakably addressed by fate.[106] Heidegger, thus, also saw the end of metaphysics as leading to a life under own laws; for Heidegger, however, the community under own laws is a community under laws that no longer recognize human beings as the authors or the addressees of law, and that place a far heavier burden of obligation on human communities than any merely human laws. The community under post-metaphysical laws, therefore, is a community under post-human laws.

If Heidegger, on the political right, viewed the authentic form of the human being as a post-legal, post-subjective condition of *historical consciousness,* Lukács, on the political left, saw authentic human being as a post-legal, post-subjective form of *class consciousness.* In simultaneous agreement and deep antagonism with Heidegger, in fact, Lukács argued that human consciousness, as defined in the idealist and neo-Kantian traditions, exists in an antinomical condition or a 'contemplative duality', in which it is abstracted from the contexts of its historical being and reduced to a sequence of subjective-categorial functions. In their abstracted form, then, both subject and object are divided into distinct and mutually indifferent monads,[107] and the subject loses its ability to obtain truthful knowledge of the objective conditions that surround it.[108] For this reason, Lukács argued that human consciousness, as formed under Kantianism, can only ever be a consciousness *of nothing.* Subjective consciousness is a *false consciousness:* it is consciousness that posits itself as in possession of absolute truths through its categorical unity and its historical invariability, but which in fact possesses its truths as empty reflections of its own form and actually obstructs its access to the objective truths of historical life and temporal process. Like Heidegger, therefore, Lukács argued that human consciousness is habitually afflicted by the legacy of metaphysics, especially in the dualist form of post-Kantian idealism. False consciousness is metaphysical consciousness, which constructs itself within a duality between subject and object, between truth and history, between norms and facticity, and which consolidates its cognitive truth-claims only extracting these from time and from the objective reality of history. Unlike Heidegger, however, Lukács argued that the conditions of false consciousness are causally enmeshed with capitalism, and he explained the antinomical or metaphysical structure of reason as a particular form of *bourgeois reason*. Reason, he claimed, determines itself and its objects as static monads for certain quite specific strategic reasons: that is, because it wishes to leave both itself and the material conditions of its objects unaltered, and because it desires to consolidate objective reality in an appearance of naturalness and perennial order or necessity. It wishes to do this because it wishes to stabilize and preserve this reality as it encounters it – and, above all, because it wishes to preserve the property relations that characterize this reality. The rational form of metaphysics, or false consciousness, is, thus, consciousness formed as *ideology*. Ideology is an order of consciousness that determines its truths as distinct from and perennial against historical-material existence, and that confers an unchanging, a reified, or a quasi-natural, form upon itself and on the material objects and processes about which it thinks.[109] Like Marx before him, therefore, Lukács argued that metaphysics and capitalism enter a constitutive relation in modern society. However, whereas Marx saw the relation between metaphysics and capitalism as sedimented solely in a condition of material and natural alienation, Lukács saw the metaphysics of capitalism as leading to an abstracted cognitive condition – to a condition in which reason, refracted through relationships of abstract ownership and material domination, distils its knowledge from a self-alienated and paradoxical fiction of itself as the source of all truth. The falsehood of antinomical consciousness can, consequently, only be overcome on the ground of a distinctively *proletarian* form of consciousness, which recognizes its objects as materially produced and determined, which reflects itself as *mediated* through the totality of objective historical conditions in society and which comprehends how changes in material process determine subjective consciousness and how changes in subjective consciousness can alter material processes. Proletarian consciousness is, thus, the sole form of non-metaphysical consciousness: it is consciousness that recognizes the material determinacy of both subject and object, which overcomes its *reification* towards material contents and processes, and which, consequently, obtains a degree of constitutive freedom in its relation both to itself and its objects.[110]

Lukács's attack on bourgeois reason also contained an attack on the ethical and the juridical/political foundations of metaphysical thinking, especially in their Kantian formation. In this, he argued that bourgeois false consciousness has a specific juridical structure, and this colludes deeply with the objective reality of capitalism. Capitalist societies, he argued, are experienced by their members as a totality of heteronomous laws, whose quasi-natural appearance obscures a condition of total objective compulsion. The laws of capitalism, expressed in cycles of exchange and production, are deeply dehumanizing; they 'take possession' of the individual human being; they prevent each human being from 'becoming a person'; and they enslave the person in the service of strategies of material expropriation.[111] In its internal cognitive forms, however, bourgeois consciousness creates a mental apparatus that directly supports the heteronomy of the capitalist world. In its explanatory approach to material and social phenomena, bourgeois consciousness, especially as positivism or neo-Kantianism, explains the world to itself through universalized laws of causality; it assumes that laws determining social processes are natural and necessary; and it examines human phenomena under the aspect of invariable moral norms. In all of these respects, false consciousness has the function that it transforms the outer reality of compulsion into an inner reality of necessity, and it thus stabilizes the outer reality in an inner metaphysical image of itself as invariably ordained and unchangeable. In its ethical forms, then, false consciousness performs a similar function: it deduces legal validity from invariable and formalistic principles, based in formal or quasi-naturalized constructs of moral necessity and necessary order. It consequently refuses to recognize how laws are produced by objective processes, or how laws claiming universal validity reflect specific economic interests, and it again translates objective patterns of compulsion into a system of metaphysical necessity. The tendency in Kantianism and in positivism to provide entirely formalized accounts of legal necessity, most particularly, is an example of a mental attitude that internalizes outer necessity, and so serves to legitimize both inner and outer reality as perennial and natural. The laws of false consciousness endlessly reproduce and reinforce the 'intellectual forms of bourgeois society'.[112] Kantian consciousness and the primacy of bourgeois law, both centred in the paradigm of the absolute person, are thus linked by a common cause: namely, by their determination by a mode of production that atomizes human beings, that segregates them from the material/historical foundations of their unity and truthful knowledge and that prevents them from evolving either a cognitive or a legal structure to permit them concretely to alter the laws that institute heteronomy in their lives. The overcoming of the cognitive conditions of bourgeois consciousness must therefore, for Lukács, also involve an overcoming of the legal relations evolving from bourgeois consciousness, and these processes of cognitive and legal transformation can only be effected by a collective proletarian consciousness: by a consciousness that knows itself thoroughly determined by material forces, and which is prepared to deploy objective revolutionary means to end this determinacy. Proletarian consciousness, Lukács concluded, will ultimately give rise to a socio-political or genuinely human condition, in which legal principles are not construed as invariable or fixed in spurious naturality against human historical needs, but in which consciousness, mediated with its objective conditions, will give rise to law (a *new law*) as a materially formed expression of its own ideal character.[113]

Across the great divide between the far left and the far right of political debate in inter-war Germany, the philosophies of Lukács and Heidegger thus converged in the argument that modern reason has failed to disentangle itself from the history of metaphysics. Because of this, human reason shapes human persons and human communities in distorted and falsely personalized forms. Both Lukács and Heidegger accepted, in consequence, that human persons and human communities bear the imprint of a deep and traumatic alienation, resulting directly from their misformed cognitive structure. For Heidegger, this alienation was an alienation of humanity from the historical sources of being itself, and it could only be overcome on the foundation of national-collective unity, or the *community of the nation.* For Lukács, this alienation was an alienation of humanity from the material and cognitive basis of human self-realization, and it could only be overcome on the foundation of economic-collective unity, or the *community of the class.* The tyranny exercised over the human being in capitalism, he suggested, is not solely the tyranny of capital over labour. It is also the tyranny of metaphysics over humanity, and true humanity, in which humanity forms the centre of its historical existence and is not distracted by elements of false consciousness, can only emerge at the end of metaphysics: the end of metaphysics is, therefore, also be the end of capitalism. Both Lukács and Heidegger concluded, moreover, that the end of metaphysics must also bring a reconfiguration of law. Post-metaphysical life, both indicated, will not be characterized by law in any formal or antinomical sense, for post-metaphysical reason will no longer separate itself out from historical process in order to enunciate points of law possessing universal validity or false normativity against history. After metaphysics, law will evolve, in history, as the reflex of a common historical consciousness (of nation or class), adequately shaped into its objective forms.

9 Theories of state in the Weimar Republic

The anti-formalist tendency that shaped the contours of philosophical debate during the last years of Imperial Germany and the early years of the Weimar Republic also extended beyond philosophy, and it set the parameters for the main legal-theoretical and constitutional controversies of the 1920s. During the first years of the Weimar Republic, therefore, legal-political orthodoxy was sharply divided between two rival lines of analysis. On one side were late-positivist and neo-Kantian theorists, most notably Hans Kelsen, the Austrian constitutionalist and main founder of the democratic Austrian constitution of 1920. On the other side, although greatly divided amongst themselves, were prominent opponents of positivism, including Carl Schmitt, Hermann Heller and Rudolf Smend. The arguments between positivism and its adversaries set the tone and context for much legal discourse of the Weimar period, and the majority of legal analysis positioned itself around this divide.

Hans Kelsen: politics after personalism

Like other positivists, Kelsen's theory contains the central claim that the legitimate state has no existence independently of law, that the 'order' of the state invariably takes the form of a 'legal order',[1] and that power necessarily communicates itself as *legal power,* enshrined in a constitution. The state, therefore, does not make law, and it has no material or personal agency prior to law: the state is merely one objective legal fact amongst many other legal facts. He consequently opposed all legal doctrines that view the state as a decisive location of sovereignty or that view sovereignty as a personal or exclusive attribute. Sovereignty, he argued, does not have its foundation in the subjective will of the state or of individual persons representing the state. Rather, sovereignty resides in the law, in the *original norm* contained in the constitution of the state, and the constitution is the 'final source' of all legal power in the state,[2] and all aspects of political decision-making are regulated by the highest norms of law, which the constitution codifies.[3] A legitimate state, consequently, can never be other than a legal state, and it has no personality and no independent volitional attributes that can be dualistically differentiated from the legal norms formulated in the constitution and applied by a constitutional court. A legitimate state, in short, is a state that fully unites law and power, and that sanctions no exercise of will, either by the state or by other subjects of law, which is not determined by law.

At one level, Kelsen's theory marked the final refinement and consummation of positivist political ideas. It clearly accentuated the classical positivist claim that sociological, personal and historical analysis of law's origins is not relevant to questions pertaining to legal validity and political legitimacy. Law is simply *pure law:* it is a 'logically closed complex of norms', and these norms regulate legal questions and dilemmas without any external direction.[4] In consequence, Kelsen explained, 'juridical knowledge' need concern itself with 'legal norms' and nothing else.[5] Like the earlier positivists, therefore, Kelsen's sought to effect a thorough depoliticization of the law and to define law as a strictly *objective* normative order. Even the terms of the constitution, he claimed, should not be construed as value-rational principles or as volitionally committed decisions about the order of state. Rather, the constitution, although authorizing law, is itself (paradoxically) nothing but an objective fact or reference of the law, which law creates for itself: it is an original norm, or a 'point of departure for a procedure', and its sole function is to create a normative frame of reference, in which legal questions can be formally processed, and in which law can refer to objective principles to regulate the exercise of power.[6] Laws are, thus, applied to the phenomena of social life as a set of pure norms, and both the phenomena and the norms applied to them are constructed by law simply as legal facts, without any consideration for external principles or broader questions of right. In this respect, Kelsen also gave a clearly Kantian inflection to his positivism. He argued that the law forms a unitary and virtual sphere serving the normative resolution of legal problems. This sphere is categorically distinct from the 'world of being', which is characterized by natural facts and by relationships between voluntaristically empowered agents.[7]

At the same time, however, Kelsen also broke with some of the main principles of positivism. For instance, he argued that the central precondition of positivism, namely the construction of both the person under private law and the state under public law as *juridical persons,* is illusory. To be sure, he acknowledged that the juridical person or the legal person might be necessary fictions, conferring consistency and cohesion on the application of legal norms.[8] Indeed, he suggested that the self-reflection of the state as a legal person may have a convenience value in that it shows that the state is subject to law in the same way that all other legal addressees exist under law.[9] Nonetheless, Kelsen saw the introduction of the concept of the juridical person into private law and public law as serving to initiate a falsely subjectivistic or anthropomorphic account of law's origin, which falsely ties law's application to conceptions of subjective-personal purposes or needs.

Law, he argued, is neither deduced by nor attached to *wills* or *persons,* either to sovereign persons applying law from above in the form of power or to private persons utilizing law from below to obtain or seek recognitions for rights or entitlements.[10] Law is derived from the objective order of law which is established, by law, in the constitution, and this objective order is the universal source of law's validity. The state, therefore, has no distinct personality; its legal character is determined by the fact that it is part of the overarching 'unity' of all legal facts, and it has no privilege or distinction against any other element in this unity as a source or focus of legal volition or application.[11] In this, Kelsen denounced positivist personalism as a miscarried attempt to place the state on neutral legal foundations, and as one further example of a general dualist inability in legal thinking adequately to comprehend the indistinctness of law and state.

The main reason for Kelsen's attack on the personalization of law and state is that he considered personalism to be inevitably close to voluntarism, and to infect legal analysis with the conception that law's application is shaped by wills. Personalizing conceptions of law, he claimed, are only able to perceive the law and the state as *heteronomous* institutions: that is, as institutions originating in non-universal conceptions of power and monopolized by the wills of determinate subjects or social groups for specific social purposes.[12] It is only where law is viewed as an overarching normative system, not concentrated in any one place, will or person, that reliable conditions of legal (and, most probably, *democratic*) order can be established, and that law effectively fulfils its most function: namely, that it satisfies the wide societal need for legal stability, pacification and reasonable freedom. Paradoxically, therefore, it is only where law is thoroughly depersonalized that it becomes adequate to a distinctively human society. It is, in other words, only where law is construed as an internally consistent and fully autonomous order of norms that it is able to reflect the conditions of autonomy and inclusion characteristic of modern societies and normally desired by the constituents of these societies. In consequence, whilst rival theories of law saw the depersonalization of the law as a token of its alienation, Kelsen saw the demise of personality in law as a precondition of societal freedom and democratic rule, for human persons.

Underlying this critique of personalistic voluntarism was a broader philosophical undertaking. In rejecting the deduction of law from persons endowed with a will or from volitionally constructed social phenomena, Kelsen's primary critique was directed against legal doctrines that make law's validity contingent on purposes imported into law from sources external to law's own norms. He saw the assumption that law might have a subjective/purposive origin or that it might respond to subjectively articulated claims and demands as distorting the consistency of law's own self-reference, and likely to lead to a misuse of the law. In addition to his critique of legal personalism, therefore, Kelsen also condemned all natural-legal modes of justification, all value-rational models of legal formation and all contractual explanations of law's origin.[13] All external normative perspectives on law, he claimed, share (in diverse manner) the fundamentally erroneous conviction that the ground of legal validity can be dualistically detached from the law itself, and they consequently make law vulnerable to interventions that law cannot control. Natural-law arguments, for example, seek to bind the law to a realm of ontological facts or subjective values; they thus originate in a 'solipsistic epistemology', which mistakenly believes that particular value-deductions can form a reliable foundation for objective legal norms.[14] Similarly, contractarian claims that the law forms agreements of principle, which then provide a scheme for the 'legitimation of the state', make both the law and the state dependent on external values or moral notions, which the law cannot produce or regulate.[15] Legal security, both in law and state, is only reliably obtained if law is viewed as a neutral condition of objective unity, not if it is determined by substantive prescriptions.

In short, therefore, Kelsen pleaded for a methodological approach to the law which defines law as an entirely autonomous science, and for a practical approach to the law, which construes law as an entirely objective normative order. All sociological, ethical or voluntaristic notions of legal derivation, he concluded, introduce inadmissible contents into law. These notions in fact conflate law with *metaphysics:* that is, they make law contingent on the will and on subjectivistic principles which are not internally legal; they misunderstand the limits of legal debate and procedure; and they undermine the objective order of norms which law, as an autonomous order, institutes for itself. Most notably, however, these views show their attachment to metaphysical ideas because they assume that laws are created by persons or by wills, often represented in the state, which are not part of law, and have an originating or authorizing relation to law. The most fateful result of such metaphysical corruption of law, therefore, is that it leads to a 'meta-legal' notion of the state, which claims that the state 'transcends the law', and that the state freely determines the content of the law.[16] Kelsen therefore viewed the sovereign state claiming 'exclusivity' in the exercise of legal power as the malignant outgrowth of legal constructs affected by the residues of metaphysical or subjectivist conceptions.[17] 'All great metaphysicians', he argued, 'have opposed democracy and favoured autocracy'. Metaphysics opposes democracy, he claimed, because it seeks to recreate the absolute personality of God in an authoritative and absolute political order, and, accordingly, metaphysical views struggle to accept the objective neutrality of law, on which democratic law depends.[18] At the heart of all metaphysics, he claimed, is the belief that all reality can be explained by absolute causes, usually attached to absolute persons, and that these absolute causes determine the contents of absolute laws. This belief is invariably hostile to democratic ideas of law, state and freedom under law.

Kelsen extended this critique of political metaphysics to argue that dualistic or personalist ideas of state and law have not yet constructed fully positive foundations for themselves, and still rely on quasi-theological paradigms to support their arguments. The claim that the origin of law resides in the subjective will of the state or the sovereign is, he explained, nothing more than a secular trace of religious ideology, originating in the idea that the transcendent God stands above creation and exercises purposive freedom or volitional power over it, in laws. Like Carl Schmitt after him, therefore, Kelsen claimed that legal thinking exists in a relation of 'analogy' to theology, and that there exists an 'extraordinary relatedness' between the 'logical structure of the concept of God and the concept of the state'.[19] However, unlike Schmitt, he insisted that theories of the state should resolutely abdicate their theological preconditions. This is only possible where state theory renounces the 'systemic dualism' of personalism, where it accepts the objective/democratic co-originality of law and the state,[20] and where it analyses the state as a fact of law with no priority over other facts of law. Even classical positivists, who sought to ensure that the originally 'meta-legal' state 'submits itself' to law and acts 'as a legal subject' bound by law, were still afflicted by theological myths of divine freedom and originary transcendence, and their ideas of legal personhood betrayed the belief that the will is the origin of law. It is for this reason that they failed to provide a reliable account of the state as a purely normative order.[21]

Kelsen thus clearly viewed his theory of pure law as marking a decisive step beyond metaphysical accounts of law and state, and as uniquely equipped to construct the state as a democratic unity of law and power, on positive and genuinely post-metaphysical foundations. Rather than viewing the end of metaphysics as a distinctively human political reality, however, he argued that law and power can only be understood *post-metaphysically* if they are viewed *post-personally:* if law and power are separated from all anthropological principles and objectives. The idea of personality in law and state, he suggested, always enacts a malicious transposition into law of God's original authoritative purposes and metaphysical personality, and the freedom of this personality obstructs the actual social freedom of human persons under law. His own theory, espousing a model of the purely legal state and conceiving legal application as an entirely inner-juridical process, sought to show that power has no externally founding source, and it is not informed by any 'absolute value' or absolute person.[22] Where power is detached from persons, he concluded, power becomes universal and, at least in tendency, democratic, for it is shaped only by its unity with law, and it has no metaphysical source or cause that ties it to monolithic or exclusive conceptions of its purpose or derivation. In this respect, Kelsen gave most advanced expression to the displacement of legal paradox in post-metaphysical argument. Those who accept that law has no origin in God, he explained, must cleanse their outlooks of all metaphysical beliefs, and they must accept that the origin of law is simply law, and that law hides its paradoxicality in a constitution, which refers law and state to the fact that they are merely law. It is only where law is entirely positive, in short, that it can reinstitute the unity of reason and will that it first forfeited as it began to positivize itself, as other than God.

The Weimar Constitution: between positivism and the material citizen

Kelsen's contemporaries in the Weimar era did not share his belief that his work provided a path beyond political metaphysics. In fact, many of his critics held a directly contrary opinion of his work, and they saw it as nothing more than a new type of juridical metaphysics.[23] To his contemporaries, in fact, Kelsen's pure theory of law appeared as a doctrine that sought to organize all social reality around formally abstracted normative principles and that eliminated the decisive role of human agency and freedom in legal and political foundation. It therefore appeared, contrary to its most express intentions, as a doctrine whose anti-personalism replicated and exacerbated the errors of both formal ius-natural thinking and of positivism – as a doctrine, that is, that located the origin of law and state in an indeterminate transpersonal source, that imagined legitimacy in law and state only as a paradoxical act of legal self-causality and that consequently derived the legal order of the state from ethereal metaphysical norms. Critical responses to Kelsen's work, therefore, condemned the formality of his legal doctrine, they re-emphasized the necessary volitional foundations of strong democracies, and they generally asserted that states without volitional or anthropological foundations are metaphysical states. Common to most influential opponents of Kelsen, moreover, was the belief that purely normative and quasi-metaphysical theories of state were not equal to the concrete tasks of political life after World War I, and they could not reliably safeguard the freedoms of the fragile political democracies of inter-war Europe.

Kelsen's main constitutional intervention was the writing of the drafts for the Austrian constitution of 1920, which contained many features of a fully positivist document. Opposition to his work in Germany, however, was also bound up with controversies about the Weimar Constitution, and critical debate with Kelsen acted, throughout the 1920s, as a framework for criticizing the positivist or allegedly formalist aspects of the Weimar Constitution and for suggesting amendments to the legal order of the Weimar state. This was particularly the case in the periods of most intense political instability, notably 1919–23 and 1930–33. In some respects, it is no coincidence that criticism of Kelsen and criticism of the Weimar Constitution fell together. The constitutional fathers of the Weimar Republic created a document for German democracy that was, in part, marked by the conventional ideas of positivism. For instance, the constitution established a central state with separated powers and a limited parliamentary chamber; it defined its laws as a system of mandatory restrictions on state authority; it incorporated a distinct catalogue of rights; and it construed the constitution in its entirety as a procedural-administrative order, dictating to the state how its functions should be fulfilled. It therefore viewied the state, in classical positivist manner, as an agent under law, whose competences must be exercised in conformity with the prescriptions of the law. Despite this, however, the constitutional fathers of 1919 in Weimar also drew on a variety of anti-positivist theoretical sources, which meant that certain aspects of the Weimar Constitution deviated from more standard positivist ideals, and they actually reflected a counter-constitution to Kelsen's pure-positivist documents for the First Austrian Republic. Amongst the constitutional fathers, for example, Weber called upon elite-democratic ideals and he argued for a personally integrative constitutional apparatus, centred in a presidential executive. The drafts for the constitution set out by Hugo Preuß were shaped by the ideals of organic theory, and they rejected static and purely normative accounts of statehood. Friedrich Naumann, who presided over the commission responsible for the catalogue of basic rights in the constitution, had his theoretical origins in the broad terrain of Cultural Protestantism, the liberal nationalist Protestant movement around Adolf von Harnack and Ernst Troeltsch which claimed that German culture and politics were formed and united by the distinctive values of loyalty, inwardness and anti-revolutionary progressivism implicit in Lutheranism.[24] In his earlier works, Naumann had tried to reconstitute German democratic theory as 'religious liberalism', sustained by historically formed Protestant values.[25] On this foundation, he urged the establishment of a constitutional system that would accept the formal principles of liberalism, but that would also allow a socially integrative political order to evolve, combining welfare policies and a strong executive leadership.[26] In his contributions to the Weimar Constitution, then, Naumann used this outlook to propose a catalogue of basic rights that were intended not, in the classical liberal or positivist style, as guarantees of individual liberty and personal legal sanctity against the state, but as programmatic principles of identity and integration around which cohesive ideas of cross-class unity could be promulgated. Naumann's favoured project in 1918–19 was, in fact, to transcribe the basic rights into a vernacular catechism, to reinforce the democratic identity of the new republic.[27]

At the centre of constitutional reality in the Weimar Republic was, thus, a clear opposition to pure positivism and an attempt to construct the constitution as a focus of social integration. Also of great importance in the debates regarding the form of the Weimar Constitution were the left-oriented organic models of Hugo Sinzheimer. Sinzheimer employed the corporate elements in the Austro-Marxist legal theory set out by Karl Renner to propose an idea of constitutional foundation that fervently contradicted formal-positivist accounts of legal personality and legal statehood.[28] Sinzheimer argued that the origin of law and state should not be identified in exclusively legal terms, but should be viewed as residing in the plural associations of civil society, especially in those representing the material-political interests of the labour movement. He thus proposed that in late-capitalist societies delegates of unions and representatives of business should be allowed, in full legal autonomy, to negotiate conditions of labour, employment and distribution, and that agreements over these matters between the negotiating parties should obtain binding legal force. If allowed to act as legislative organs, he assumed, delegates of labour and representatives of business are likely to produce organic foundations for the legal administration of society, and, over long periods of time, they will bring whole sectors of social and economic administration under the jurisdiction of an organically formed cross-class consensus. *Labour law,* transmitting agreements between workers and management, can thus act as a powerful medium in the resolution of social conflicts, and it can even assume a central role in forming the legal preconditions of the state itself. Sinzheimer especially identified the collective wage agreement (the *Tarifvertrag*) as an element of organic law, which, reflecting a cross-class 'spirit of self-organization', can produce consensual legal arrangements from the heart of civil society and integrate an idea of *distributive citizenship* in the political order.[29] He did not entirely abandon the notion that the constitution of the state should retain a certain dignity over and against the groups of civil society.[30] Nonetheless, he identified industrial relations as a source of autonomous organic will formation, which might ultimately guide the state and its constitution towards a more egalitarian or common-economic political order, and he saw the ideal state as one centred, not in formal persons, but in the organic persons of economic bargaining franchises. For this reason, in his interventions in the debates on the Weimar Constitution, Sinzheimer ensured that the constitution contained a council clause, Article 165, which provided for rights of collective bargaining and – in principle – for the consensual/collective organization of the economy.

The Weimar Constitution, therefore, reflected a number of diverse and often contradictory legal ideas and ideals. It did not mark a full break with the basic principles of positivism. However, it based its idea of legitimacy in the state on a fuller and more integrative conception of state power and citizenship than that normally countenanced by positivism, and it defined itself as a programmatic document enabling the state to act as an agent of social unity, collaboration and community. Under the Weimar Constitution, the state obtained powers enabling it to intervene in processes of economic distribution and dispute, to regulate questions of ownership, to draw disparate sectors of society together in bargaining processes or in plebiscites and to integrate citizens into experiences of constitutional identity through a popular catalogue of rights. Indeed, the constitution enunciated the rights that it enshrined as programmatic rights, not as formal rights, and these rights contained active socio-economic provisions and prescriptions. In these respects, the Weimar Constitution clearly hoped to found itself, albeit in rather confused and tentative manner, in a paradigm of the integrated citizen, of the citizen not (in Kelsen's sense) as a fictional person under law, nor (in Laband's sense) as a formal person under law, but as an actively constitutive agent, both in civil society and the state.

Heller: the material will of the state

Despite these ambitions, however, the Weimar Constitution soon came under fire from critics at various points in the political spectrum, and it was widely argued that it did not break thoroughly enough with positivist political conceptions. Naturally, not all influential political theorists in the Weimar Republic sought to overthrow or fundamentally to correct the constitution of the republic. Its authors, predictably, remained pledged to its defence, although Naumann and Weber did not survive long enough to see the problems that the constitution created, and Preuß also died, in 1925, long before the final crises of the republic and of its constitutional apparatus. Eminent liberal lawyers, such as Gerhard Anschütz, also wrote favourably of its importance in the broader evolution of statehood in Germany, and so promoted its widespread acceptance.[31] However, after the ratification of the constitution in 1919, political theorists on both right and left rapidly began to denounce the constitution as a compromise document that failed to give effective foundation and integrity to the new political order, and that remained tied to outmoded conceptions of formal-legal rule. These attacks on the constitution were, naturally, flanked by a wider critique of the more general preconditions of positivism, and especially of Kelsen's constitutional theory.

The most sustained organicist attacks on positivism emanated from the German-Jewish Social Democratic theorist, Hermann Heller, who followed Sinzheimer in linking revisionist Marxist social analysis to a conception of the state as an organically structured life form. Heller's organicism was distinct from more conventional lines of left-leaning corporatism as it was underpinned by a cultural-anthropological theory of legal production. Following the late-historicist and early phenomenological works of Dilthey and Theodor Litt,[32] he argued that the legal and political institutions of modern society form themselves from a 'reality of experience' that unifies all members of a national or cultural order, and they endlessly regenerate themselves as new articulations of the vital experiences embedded in culture.[33] More generally, however, at the centre of this work is the common anthropological claim of organic theory: namely, that the human being is a naturally organizational creature, and that the human being fulfils its innate dispositions by forming associations and organizations with other humans. The state, accordingly, is the highest organization, and it is the highest expression of these originary human dispositions. The state, Heller consequently explained, is an 'organized' – and, if necessary, 'authoritarian' – 'life-form', giving sovereign legal expression to the agreements established between voluntary organizations of persons in civil society, on the foundation of a national-historical unity of culture and experience.[34]

Heller's theory was shaped by the conviction that positivism, especially as set out by Kelsen, constructs a purely 'depersonalized' legal state, deriving its authority from the false presumption that there exists an invariable order of law, which can be neutrally imposed onto the complex, emergent and, at times, antagonistic reality of social evolution.[35] Tellingly, he saw in such theory the residue of an outmoded liberal ius-naturalism, reflecting a 'bourgeois ideal of security', which is not sustainable in complex and sociologically divided societies. He therefore opposed all accounts of political legitimacy and order that derive the conditions of legal rule from generalized norms or legal facts, and he denounced as wittingly paradoxical the claim that the legitimacy of the state can be derived from the laws of a constitution with no volitional content or purpose.[36] Plausible political and legal analysis, he claimed, must always proceed from the human will as the irreducible focus of political constitution and order, and it must always identify the will of the state as the guarantor of legal order, in the form of sovereignty. Both natural-law and positivist analysis, he asserted, have the corrupting weakness that they secondarize the human will, and they depreciate decisive 'responsibility', both of leaders and citizens, as the formative source of order.[37] Law, he concluded, is necessarily centred on sovereign wills, who 'give binding commands' and 'make binding decisions'.[38] Law, consequently, is always 'established, sustained and destroyed by the processes of the human will',[39] and the 'establishment of law' always has its origin in the 'command of state'.[40] A state based in the human will, moreover, always takes the form of a sovereign state, whose decisions are not subject to any other higher power or universal legal regulation.[41] Indeed, Heller claimed repeatedly that the positivization of law only occurs because, through the evolution of modern states, political executives have assumed legislative authority, and so detached the law from its original religious foundations. The human will is therefore the origin of legal positivity, and there are no laws independent of human will: the 'unity of the legal system' originates exclusively in a 'unity of wills exercising domination'.[42]

On these grounds, Heller's theory of state was intended, after Kelsen, to *repersonalize* the state and, once more, to locate the state on the anthropological foundations of will and decisive freedom. In this, however, Heller did not offer an entirely voluntaristic model of governance; he did not renounce the idea that moral or supra-positive constraints apply to the exercise of political power; and he clearly insisted that legitimate statehood must develop in the form of a *legal state*. It is illusory, he claimed, to view the state as one solitary personal will or as an 'individual subject', crystallized in an all-powerful sovereign executive and acting without legal restriction. Instead, the personality of the sovereign state should be viewed as evolving from voluntary agreements between associations in civil society, and as the form in which the freedoms pursued by these associations culminate. The state, construed in this way, is founded in an organic 'unification of wills':[43] it is the organization in which these wills are reconciled and in which their freedoms are expressed in a socially adequate manner. The state thus evolves by integrating the many wills and the many persons incorporated in the associations throughout society. Once formed as an amalgamation of these associations, the state exercises supreme personal power over all those whom it incorporates. Nonetheless, Heller emphasized that the state, as an integrative organ, has no abstract dignity against the associations from which it evolves. On the contrary, the state only exists because it integrates other associations and because it provides a structure in which the freedoms pursued by these associations can be reflected, protected and generalized. The state, therefore, cannot separate itself from these associations in the exercise of its power; it is internally accountable to the normative elements inherent in the freedoms pursued and moderated by these associations; and – crucially – its integrity is threatened wherever it disregards the freedoms that it contains. The associations whose freedoms are ordered in the state thus form the state's constitution, and the volitional unity underlying the state constitutes at once the objective power exercised by the state and the legal form in which this power is to be exercised. The concrete evolution of a state as a centre of territorial sovereignty occurs because the state grows out of the normatively weighted interactions – that is, the 'normative associations of will' – existing between particular groups of people in a particular place, and these interactions necessarily lead to agreements over rights and freedoms that assume some degree of constitutional universality in the state and so determine the conditions under which the state can pass laws.[44] For this reason, Heller concluded that the formation of power is always insolubly bound up with the formation of law, and the state obtains its legitimacy only as the highest integrative representative of the organically structured general will of the people that it integrates. The 'volitional power of the state which positivizes law', consequently, is always 'dependent on norms', and the state cannot operate in distinction from the 'power-building character of law'. Law, Heller consequently concluded, is certainly positivized by the will of the state – but, as it is positivized, it also produces 'supra-positive foundations for its validity', and it binds the state to its own inner constitution.[45] Indeed, the state develops and regenerates itself by integrating citizens in highly diverse social and economic life contexts, and it can only fulfil this function by generating rights and laws to which all of its citizens are likely freely to accede and in which, in Kantian manner, they recognize an element of their own freedom, integrity and authorship.

In these analyses, Heller set out a new variant on the wider claim, originating in Kantian doctrines, that a legitimate state is one that unites law and freedom, or reason and will, and communicates its laws as laws of rational freedom. The organic state, he argued, must be a legal state in which the power of the state is internally formed and bound by generally accepted norms in a constitution. In this, he rejected the idea that a constitution might be external to the state, that it might prescribe terms of procedural compliance to the state, or that it might enshrine formal norms or rights against the state. Instead, he argued that the constitution of the state is the integrated yet evolving legal form of the wills that interact in civil society and create common forms for their freedoms, thus articulating norms and rights as aspects of their participation in legal and political formation. As such, the constitution can assume a written or codified structure, but it does not fulfil its essential function by fixing normative or procedural prescriptions or universalized principles of right as *limits* on the exercise of state power.[46] Rather, the most authentic function of the constitution is to integrate and express the complexly formed will of the people, to recognize and to stabilize the freedoms pursued and elaborated by this will, and, above all, to consolidate this will as the state's own will.

An organic constitution thus unites power and law and freedom and reason in the state by producing consensual laws that positively reinforce, not negatively restrict, the will of the state, and by sanctioning rights that are fully enacted as elements of a positive will in the state. The organic constitution, in other words, is a human constitution, which disarticulates rights from their normative or metaphysical stasis against the will and which fuses freedom and reason in the state by producing laws as the stabilized articles of associative agreements concluded through society, but culminating in the state.[47] The authentic constitution is an active, experiential component of society in which all constituents of society feel and know themselves constitutively implicated.[48] As such, however, it also contains a universally normative structure, and a state that contravenes its *laws* or that neglects *rights* inevitably weakens its legal personality and so gradually also suffers a loss of *power*. The strong state, in sum, is always a legal state: the stronger the state, the stronger and more universal are its laws and the stronger and more participatory are the rights attributed to its citizens. In this, Heller gave perhaps most exemplary expression to the wider organicist conviction that the antinomical conception of the relation between freedom and reason, and power and law, is misplaced, and that law and power in fact presuppose and sustain each other. Only metaphysically abstracted analyses of law and the legal state fail, for Heller, to understand the constitutive reciprocity between law and power.

In addition to this, Heller asserted that the organic production of binding norms in civil society also contains a material or materialist dimension. Like Sinzheimer, he claimed that the formation of a state in a mass democracy must lead, not only to the formation of a *legal state,* but also to the formation of a *social-legal state.* Organic agreements in a pluralized mass society, inevitably, do not focus solely on areas of interaction regulated by formal-political laws, but they also address questions of production and economic administration. An organic state thus incorporates laws ruling consensually over questions of distribution and employment. A constitution adequate to a mass-democratic society, in consequence, is a constitution in which relations of industrial production, usually seen to pertain to private law, are brought under the public-legal will of the state, and in which the economy is made to conform, under the public rule of law, to universal material norms.[49] Fundamental to this notion of the material-organic constitution is the belief that formal-positivist constitutions not only fail to constitute the state as a living personality, but they also allow the constitution of the state to be restricted, and often eroded, by the unregulated private law of capitalism and by bodies that are guaranteed autonomy under such law. The weak constitutions of positivist doctrine are especially designed, Heller indicated, to allow economically powerful groups to assume legally relevant power and to permit the principles of private law and private personal autonomy to prevail over the political decisions and the public personality of the state. Because of this, under positivist constitutions citizens are excluded from legal participation in the most vital areas of social exchange (that is, in those relating to production, employment and material entitlement), and their rights are hollowed out to mere formal rights of private ownership, electoral enfranchisement and contractual compliance. It is only an organic constitution, which construes legal rulings over production as politically constitutive and which is sufficiently powerful to enforce these rulings through society that can protect its citizens from the corrosive influence of private-legal freedoms in the economy and so stabilize an authentically universal legal state. Positivist constitutions recognizing the formal autonomy of private law, Heller concluded, replicate – in new form – the intrusion of external metaphysical ideas on the political order; they distract from the cohesion and legitimacy of the organically constructed constitutional state; and they order political life around principles that erode the associational bases of human life. Control of the economy, in sum, is always a 'political matter', and a politically legitimate state must ensure that all areas of social and economic exchange are regulated by one plurally uniform and sovereign will.[50]

Integration theory between anthropology and religion

One underlying implication in Heller's theory is that the legitimate state both integrates and represents the culturally united people, and it guides the body of the people towards constantly increasing levels of material and legal integration and freedom. In this doctrine, the legal principles that the state *represents* are identical with the substantial realities that it *integrates:* all disjuncture between the representative and the integrative character of the state is superseded. The positive or experiential substructure of the legitimate state is national culture, and culture forms the generic precondition of the associationally embedded norms and agreements that organize the state in legal form. The formation of reliable order is directly impeded by all modes of legal analysis, whether pure positivist, pure private-legal, classical ius-natural or rational ius-natural, which force the state onto the Procrustean bed of an empty metaphysical 'science of norms', and so dissolve the vital process of organic association and of cultural transmission between state and society.[51]

In certain respects, the cultural and integrative turn in democratic thought in the 1920s was closely tied to religious debate and tended to see effective integration as a specific feature of Protestant states. Before Heller, for example, Radbruch argued that democracy should not be viewed solely as a legal or political condition, but also as a condition of cultural unity, in which the personality of citizens is detached from pure 'individualism' and 'arbitrariness', and formed around objectively integrating values.[52] In this, Radbruch extended the earlier hostility to legal formality amongst representatives of the Free Law Movement; he argued that political cultures formed by Roman law do not promote integrative values, whereas Germanic law and specifically German religious views tend to create collectivistic and integrated political cultures.[53] He ultimately elaborated these claims to conclude that ideas of legal personality and legal subjectivity underlying modern conceptions of valid law should be placed on new anthropological premises, and should be connected to wider objective values. The personal origin of the law, he explained, should not be conceived as an atomized individual corresponding to 'an abstract scheme of freedom, self-interest and cleverness'.[54] On the contrary, law should be viewed as a series of values and duties embedded in objective culture, and the constitutional state founded in the atomized legal subject should be replaced by a state representing the legally 'organized community'.[55] In this, he stressed that the 'transpersonal values' of authentic law are closely connected to religious values, and he ascribed a primary role to religiously formed culture in constituting this legal community and in reinforcing the values in which its unity is rooted.[56]

Further to the political right, then, Rudolf Smend argued that it is a peculiar feature of Protestant states that that they rely on *positive* processes of integration. Such states are forced to provide positivized accounts of their legitimacy and legal integrity, and – unlike Roman Catholic states – they cannot presuppose unshakeable foundations for the exercise of power. For this reason, he claimed, the legitimacy of Protestant states tends to presuppose a cultural and interpretive unity of experience; it tends to be variable and subject to constant evolution; and, most importantly, it ceaselessly enacts itself through internal processes of *integration.* Indeed, whilst Roman Catholic states obtain legitimacy through the external-metaphysical attribute of *representation,* in which the state refers its power to an invariable sequence of legal norms, Protestant states internalize this originary reference and derive legitimacy through integration, in which they internally articulate experiences of freedom and of cultural unity.[57] Lutheran states, most especially, have no external or perennial legal structure and they only sustain themselves through culturally unifying mechanisms of integration.[58] States without external representative foundations legitimize themselves primarily, Smend asserted, by referring to culturally cohesive *values,* and in so doing they generate experiences of objective identity in which laws and decisions are likely to be met with compliance and recognized as legitimate. A Protestant state is therefore legitimate, he concluded, where it can presuppose a constituency united by common 'objective values', and where it can interpret and reflect these values in its legislation.[59]

On this basis, Smend also set out a distinctive theory of the constitution and of the personality of the state. He claimed that the role of the constitution is not to secure a set of rights or norms against the state, or in distinction from everyday human existence. Instead, the constitution of a legitimate state is the 'integrating reality' or the 'living reality' of the state, which gives public shape to the values and identities around which citizens organize their lives. Where the constitution expresses a set of objectively held values, citizens feel themselves personally and objectively bound to the state, and the constitution integrates the citizens in support of the state. The rights enshrined in the constitution, he thus concluded, are not formal, ius-natural or inviolable norms by which state is formally bound, or that impose external entitlements on the fabric of the state. On the contrary, constitutional rights are active-objective elements in the interpretive culture and the objective order of value formed around the constitution, and they help provide legitimacy for the 'order of state and the order of law' because they frame value concepts that citizens share with the state and that engage citizens in interaction with the state.[60] The state thus obtains its legitimacy as a 'total event', or as an 'everyday plebiscite', in which all functions of the state participate in the unceasing task of integrating the diverse sectors of the population. Basic rights and other elements of the constitution, consequently, are not metaphysical principles that place limits on the integrative plebiscitary authority of the state. On the contrary, they are dynamic components of the state, and they contribute directly to ensuring that the everyday plebiscite will be successful.[61]

Smend's integration theory differed from that set out by Heller in that he emphasized the objective role of the constitution in integrating citizens, and he claimed that the constitution binds people into an already formed apparatus of state. Indeed, in this respect, Smend allowed a high degree of latitude in his interpretation of which values might obtain broader social recognition and contribute to the legitimacy of the state. One central implication of his theory is that the content of integrative values cannot be stipulated, but is derived and tested through ongoing processes of common interpretation. For this reason, he was willing to recognize a number of different political systems, from monarchies to republics, as capable of providing conditions of political cohesion. Nonetheless, like Schmitt at the same time, he suggested that purely liberal or parliamentary systems lack the symbolic devices to promote cohesive cultural unity: they consequently struggle to elaborate potent mechanisms of integration, and they commonly suffer from legitimatory deficits.[62] Monarchies and pure democracies are more likely to stimulate unitary declarations of support and integrity, for it is specific to such systems that they deploy symbolic resources and refer legal addressees to overarching experiences of unity in their attempts to gain consensus.[63] However, Protestant monarchies, he concluded, are the states that have the greatest chance of maintaining political integrity in modern society. Such states are specifically suited to the production of objective values and objective sources of integration under socio-political conditions where the validating foundations of the law have become contestable.[64]

Such stances also intersected with influential positions at the extreme reactionary fringe of legal theory in the Weimar Republic. Hans Gerber, for instance, denounced the Weimar Constitution as a document that undermined the 'force of its legitimacy' through its attachment to the 'formal principle of legality', and that was ultimately incapable of sustaining an integrative ethic or sense of cultural-political identity. He therefore concluded, following Smend, that the integrative weakness of the constitutional and parliamentary order could only be offset by a strong state rooted in the most fundamental religious values of the German people: '*Auctoritas*', he explained, 'can only come from faith'.[65] He thus announced a programmatic plan to found a specifically 'Evangelical theory of state', defining law as an 'unconditional obligation' born from an objective legal community of a historical people, and so 'rejecting natural law in any form'.[66] The young Otto Koellreutter, later a prominent National Socialist legal theorist, also defined the 'idea of the Christian state' as one of the 'living' elements of the modern political order.[67]

Carl Schmitt: exceptionalism, representation and integration

The critique of positivism, in sum, crossed many political boundaries and it was reflected in many distinct political attitudes. It was central to the social-integrationist ideas on the left of the political spectrum in the Weimar Republic, yet it also clearly coalesced with extremely conservative doctrines of Protestant political substance. The rejection of positivism obtained its most dramatic and influential expression, however, in the works of Carl Schmitt.

Schmitt's first writings, before the foundation of the Weimar Republic, were close to neo-Kantian ideas. At this early stage in his thought, he argued for the 'primacy of law' over the power of the state, and he referred to Roman Catholic teachings to explain the existence of supra-positive legal norms applying to all legal frameworks and used to measure all exercise of power.[68] After the collapse of the Hohenzollern monarchy in 1918, however, Schmitt renounced normative analysis of political order, and he identified the purpose of his work in more strategic terms, as an attempt to consolidate the stability of the political orders under which he lived.[69] Most of his most influential theoretical interventions were, therefore, shaped by the desire to give substance to the political order of the Weimar Republic and to explain in concrete terms how the state might defend itself against the manifold threats (Bolshevism, foreign annexation, internal sabotage) which he saw as afflicting it. After 1919, therefore, he turned against positivism, neo-Kantianism and all types of liberalism influenced by these doctrines, and he set himself against all stances that he considered incapable, especially in the context of the weak democratic tradition in Germany, of contributing to the stability of political institutions.

Central to Schmitt's work through the 1920s was the claim that the spirit of depersonalization in liberalism and positivism had led to the evolution of a weak state in Germany, which was fraught with internal divisions, lacked cohesive foundations and was inclined to extreme indecisiveness. Most particularly, he viewed the positivist assumption that law is a *neutral* or purely normative medium of social communication that is not subject to political interference and that the legitimate state is a state bound by neutral law as an absurd and perilous fallacy of liberal political thought, whose consequences for Germany were only too visible in the acute instability of the governmental system of the Weimar Republic. This assumption, perhaps more than any other, was, Schmitt claimed, the reason why liberal political doctrines struggle to form strong states and why they are vulnerable to internal and external destabilization. The relation between law and power should in fact be examined as a site of entrenched conflict between rival organs of political interest, and legitimate political systems are those that can voluntaristically exert power and channel concrete interests through the law. Legitimate political orders must therefore be founded in one uniform, sovereign and often *personal* will, and this will must provide the precondition for all decisions of state and all laws of the state. In this, Schmitt concurred with Kelsen's claim that there always exists a 'methodological relationship' between 'theology and jurisprudence',[70] and he asserted that all aspects of political theory are 'secularized theological concepts'.[71] Like Kelsen, in fact, he also argued that the transition from sacral to secular constructs of order is a necessary and inevitable aspect of modern political life. However, unlike Kelsen, Schmitt saw legitimacy as residing in the state as the decisive will of the sovereign, not in the regulation of power by law. He thus followed Hobbes in arguing that sovereign decisions assume their legitimacy by their analogy to the primary freedom of God's will or to the primary revelation or 'miracle' of God's will. Unlike the liberal *Rechtsstaat,* which derives its idea of legitimacy from the rationally constrained God of theism, the truly sovereign state derives its form from its reference to the willing God or the God of freedom, not to the intellectual God or the God of reason.[72] The edicts of the sovereign will are not contaminated by prior constraints or norms, and they appear as secular reflections of God's originary will. Indeed, where states seek to be both rational and free, or where they allow the terms of freedom to be stipulated by universal ideas of reason, they run the acute risk of losing both their rationality and their freedom.

Schmitt consequently concluded that law on its own, defined as a neutral system of formal norms, can under no circumstances constitute the legitimate foundation of the state. The positivist or neo-Kantian claim that the state is invariably bound by an impersonal constitutional order serves only to dissipate the power of the state, and it fails to reflect the necessarily voluntaristic origin of power. Likewise, the standard liberal assumption that law is a medium of political administration that can be employed to palliate social antagonisms, manufacture compromises between rival social groups and, so, create conditions of operative consensus for the state can only secure the most chimerical forms legitimacy for the state. These arguments, for Schmitt, entirely misunderstand the relation between law and power and between law and legitimacy. For Schmitt, the 'metaphysical system of liberalism', imputing natural harmony and neutrality as law's inalienable precondition, is not appropriate to analysing state forms under the conditions of social plurality and intense material antagonism that define modern societies.[73] In such societies, a unitary foundation of legitimacy must be established *before* law is applied, and law must resolutely transmit the principles originally constitutive of this legitimacy. If this is not the case, and if law is applied as a neutral or universal medium, law insinuates principles into the state that erode the legitimacy of the state, and it thus dismantles the basis of order on which the state is founded.

In addition to his critique of positivist ideas of legal neutrality, Schmitt was also intensely hostile to the role of political parties in the modern state; indeed, he saw party democracy as closely connected with positivism. The fact that government is conducted by political parties, and usually by coalitions between different (often naturally antagonistic) parties, he argued, means that the exercise of power is conducted by technical 'compromises and coalitions' between different associations, not by a uniform or homogenous political will.[74] Political parties allow democracy to subside into a fragmented or materially parcellated set of interests, and, in seeking to mediate balances between their diverse constituencies, they in fact impede the emergence of a substantial general will, which might give a cohesive substructure to government.[75] Moreover, the fact that modern mass-democracies permit any party to gain access to power, regardless of whether this party supports the principles of democratic rule, clearly underlines the weakness of such party democracies, and it shows that these systems are unable to express clear principles of order – or even clearly to define a 'form of state'.[76] Party democracy, in consequence, ties the political system to an uncontrolled party-political pluralism and to an uncontrolled plurality of divergent interests, many of which either actually or latently oppose the existing political order. Central to Schmitt's critique of party-democratic pluralism is, thus, the conviction that parliamentary democracy, in its customary forms, cannot be genuinely democratic.[77] Rather than enabling a condition of popular government, parliament, based in the delegations of parties, precludes the emergence of precisely that general and unifying will which all democracy requires. For this reason, he argued, 'dictatorship' itself might be more democratic than parliamentary governance.[78]

In the broadest terms, Schmitt claimed that the evolution of modern political systems has brought about the demise of the form-giving or voluntaristic element of politics, and, in consequence, it has led to a fundamental neutralization of politics and a fragmentation of the original legitimatory resources in politics. This neutralization, he argued, began with the formation of liberal political movements in the nineteenth century and the ensuing establishment of early parliamentary-democratic systems. Through the evolution of liberalism and its doctrines of natural law and private-legal positivism, diverse private interests were admitted – as 'organizations' of 'individual freedom' – into the fabric of the state.[79] The state then became determined by a plurality of distinct legal principles reflecting the objectives of distinct social groups, and it became difficult for the state to act in accordance with one uniform will or set of prerogatives. Early liberalism nonetheless had the particular strength that its adherents, as property owners, formed a relatively closed franchise with a small active public sphere; they were thus unified by a relatively homogenous group of material interests, and they channelled consistent interests into the state and avoided taxing it with impossible regulatory burdens. However, through the subsequent expansion of the franchise to include different classes with directly opposed class interests, and then through the resultant institution of fully evolved mass democracies and welfare democracies in the twentieth century, the state has gradually been forced to internalize an amalgamation of acutely antagonistic prerogatives, the reconciliation of which in the form of one governing will is not possible. As a result, the state has been refashioned as a battleground in which interest groups (both inside and outside parliament) compete, in barely pacified manner, for a portion of political power and a share of material goods. The modern state has, thus, necessarily assumed the function of an 'instrument of social and political technology', whose primary legislative objective is simply to palliate the pluralized associations that have obtained a stake in it and that ceaselessly vie for increased power.[80] A state of this kind, Schmitt argued, is incapable of determining the actual concrete principles of government or the content of laws for its citizens, and, because of the compromises and barely obscured antagonisms in which it founds itself, it is incapable of maintaining long-term conditions of legitimacy. A state of this kind, in short, can never be *political:* underlying the transformation of the modern state is a process of materialization, through which all elements of the public will are supplanted by precariously balanced material interests, and politics is replaced by highly technical and materialized systems of command.[81] The natural-legal rationalism of liberalism and the private-legal normativism of positivism have thus acted in the course of modern history, Schmitt concluded, as politically debilitating masks for the grasping self-interest of a series of newly powerful social groups. Indeed, liberal ideas have used the shadow of metaphysical universality to impose a set of highly instrumental private purposes on the apparatus of public order, and to empty the state of the resolve necessary for underwriting political stability. Liberal doctrines, consequently, have contributed to the creation of a helpless state, whose constituents, even where they most require it, cannot rely on the state for protection – even for protection *from themselves* and from the fateful consequences of their own self-interest.[82] A structural precondition of a legitimate state is that it must be different from the interest groups in society, and that it must be able to impose principles of order across all different sectors of society.

In many of his diagnostic writings on the Weimar Republic, Schmitt's works were marked by the (albeit at times wilfully self-contradictory) insistence that democratic government, if it is to survive, must divest itself both of its Kelsenian fictions of legal neutrality and of its interest-based pluralism, its *polycracy,* and it must refound itself in a constitution embodying a uniform and decisive will. In his major works of this period, then, he positioned himself as a conservative defender of the constitution, insisting that constitutional order is only sustained where the constitution is stated as the expression of one positive will and where this will is hardened against the 'pluralism of concepts of legality', which is promoted by liberalism and which 'destroys respect for the constitution' and erodes the fabric of democratic order.[83] The actual nature and origin of the uniform will embodied in the constitution appeared to Schmitt in different ways at different times, depending on historical context. In his first writings after the foundation of the republic, especially in *Dictatorship,* he argued that, at least in periods of crisis, commissarial dictatorship might be the governmental form that can most effectively 'protect' the constitutional will of the state.[84] At different junctures in the 1920s and early 1930s, he also set out a defence of government by presidential prerogative, and he argued that the exceptional powers embedded in the Weimar Constitution – especially those incorporated under the infamous Article 48 – should be utilized to concentrate powers in the president or in the executive around the president, in order to preserve the basic constitutional structure of the republic. In these works, he showed enthusiasm for the weakening of the legislative procedures of parliamentary governance and for the consolidation of all power around a semi-accountable presidential executive, which, he claimed, could demonstrate its foundation in a united will by garnering popular *acclamation* in one-issue plebiscites.[85] This was particularly the case in the last years of the Weimar Republic, when Germany was governed by a succession of chancellors, Heinrich Brüning, Franz von Papen and Kurt von Schleicher, who had little support in parliament and who were placed in office through presidential appointment under the powers accorded to the president in Article 48. At other points in the Weimar era, however, Schmitt was intermittently prepared to support a more broad-based constitutional rule, and he advocated increased presidial and executive power only in so far as this served to protect the democratically formed constitution of the republic. This latter view was especially pronounced in Schmitt's writings during the years of relative stability in the Weimar Republic, 1924–28. In this period, he began to adopt the view that the constitutional reality of the republic might in fact possess a degree of internal security and legitimacy, and it might indeed give form to the unified will of the German people.[86] At this time, in consequence, he set himself the task of showing how the constitution could be reformed or redevised in order to place the state on more reliable foundations. He thus argued that constitutional forms evolving out of liberal or positivist political ideals – i.e., the guarantees for a separation of legislature, executive and judiciary and the catalogue of basic rights limiting the competence of the state and satisfying social and economic expectations outside the state – lead only to the 'relativization of state power', and they weaken the structural unity of the state.[87] Such examples of liberal divisiveness in the Weimar Constitution, he therefore claimed, should be abandoned, and they should be replaced with a constitutional form in which all institutional components of the state are integrated elements of one decisively positive will. Indeed, even at the end of the Weimar era, Schmitt did not finally throw his weight behind those agitating for a complete overthrow of the republic. During the years of the presidial regime, he saw the power of the president as a bastion against the collapse of the republic,[88] and he also sought to institute different constitutional provisions to ensure that parties intending completely to dismantle the republic (especially the Nationalist Socialist Party [NSDAP]) should be kept out of power.[89]

Because of his association with the late-Weimar presidential system, Schmitt is often associated with the so-called conservative revolutionaries of the Weimar Republic. These were a group of literary philosophers around Ernst Jünger and Oswald Spengler, who encouraged the supplanting of Weimar democracy with an authoritarian non-parliamentary government and who saw the ideal political order as one based in a militarized society, integrated by mythical symbols of national unity and order and governed by a technologically empowered aristocracy.[90] Schmitt's association with this group, however, does not capture the full range of his thinking, and, at times, it aligns him to views that are directly inimical to his own. Although he shared with Jünger and Spengler a highly sceptical approach to the parliamentary order, he did not unequivocally endorse their extreme enthusiasm for technology, and he did not sympathize with their vehemently anti-Christian attitude, their post-Nietzschean naturalism or their mythomanic construction of human authenticity. Nonetheless, Schmitt did move close to these theories in that, like the conservative revolutionaries, he claimed that legitimate government is founded in *decisions,* and that these decisions usually involve adversarial conflict over the means of political coercion.

One key aspect of Schmitt's theory, consequently, is the claim that liberal governments erroneously assume that *peace* is the natural condition of human coexistence, and they naïvely presuppose that the normative foundation of law can be derived from naturally manifest or easily moderated compromises between all members of the polity. On Schmitt's view, however, the opposite is factually the case, and the liberal belief in 'social harmony' is in fact an element of liberal metaphysics.[91] Modern polities are, in fact, marked by extremely high levels of antagonism between extremely pluralistic social groups, and the state cannot produce for itself a normative foundation from agreements between these groups. In the final analysis, therefore, the state must assert its power, not normatively, but *exceptionally.* Only the 'state of exception', Schmitt claimed, 'reveals the core of the state in its concrete character',[92] and it is only where it demonstrates that it can produce unifying principles of order in deeply unstable social settings that a state can claim to be legitimate.[93] In this respect, therefore, Schmitt dramatized the original paradox of modern state foundation, and he fixed his theory on the defining problem of politics after the disintegration of universal order. He argued that, originally, the source of political legitimacy is the contingent will: it is the will which creates itself *ex nihilo,* without any prior, necessary or intellectualized legal circumscription and without any support in underlying natural or social dispositions. The source of legitimacy, Schmitt argued, if 'viewed in normative terms' is 'born from nothing'.[94] Once created, then, this will is the sole guarantor of political legitimacy – without the exercise of a will there is no legitimacy in the state, and the state has no recourse to principles outside the will to underwrite its legitimacy. Parliamentary legal states, however, especially those regulated by positivist or neo-Kantian constitutions, cannot establish the will to uphold legitimacy, and their claim to derive legitimacy from their essential normativity remains an index of their internal lack of legitimacy and of their reliance on pious fictions of normative harmony. Accounts of political order, such as that set out by Kelsen, which view power and law as mutually constitutive, remain entrapped in the falsehoods of metaphysical thinking, and they use paradoxical feint to transpose the original metaphysical notion of universal natural law onto the secular form of the state. Such outlooks, however, fail to grasp the basic facts of modern politics: namely, that there is no benign legal, anthropological or metaphysical power in the universe which might give support to government, that government is acutely accountable for producing and enforcing the conditions of its own stability, and that law on its own will not protect the state. Classical natural-law theories might have believed in an overarching order of norms, created and presided over by God, to which the state must refer. In a secular society where God is not an agent in history, however, the rule of law has no external substructure, and it either stands or falls with the effective presence of a sovereign will.

The philosophical motif connecting Schmitt's work of the Weimar era was, thus, an inversion of the Kelsenian equation of metaphysics and personalism. Whereas Kelsen saw a persistence of metaphysics in personalism, Schmitt saw a persistence of metaphysics in pure normativism. For Schmitt, the state is legitimate where it is founded in *decisions,* not *norms,* and – consequently – where it is *personal,* not *metaphysical:* where it accepts the radical contingency of its foundations and refuses to obscure this contingency in a paradoxical reinvocation of the lost metaphysical unity of law and power. The 'legal order', Schmitt concluded, 'is based on a decision, not on a norm', and the normative power of law is inseparable from the decisions that uphold it.[95] The voluntaristic decision underpinning political order is, therefore, emphatically not a token of a metaphysical residue in politics. The decision might exist in analogy to God's own free creative will, and it might shadow a reference to metaphysics. Factually, however, the decision is the freedom of a polity to decide, positively, to exist in a particular way and to take a particular constitutional form and so to be other than metaphysical and to accept the paradox of its contingency and variability. The decision is the moment in which an order of state reflects its contingency and absolute positivity and where it produces reliable foundations for itself, without any reference external to itself. A state that cannot institute decisive and voluntaristic foundations for itself is necessarily *metaphysical:* it legitimizes itself through references to principles that it has not positively constituted for itself; it presupposes helpful legal norms outside its own will; and it is consequently unable to underwrite the preconditions of its own survival and it opens itself to invasion by heterogenous ideological components. This, Schmitt claimed, is especially the case with Kelsen's theory, but he saw similar metaphysical traces afflicting all examples of liberalism. Kelsen's theory, he argued, is founded in a false 'metaphysics', which identifies 'normative legality with natural legality' and which erroneously concludes that power must inevitably – for either natural or metaphysical reasons – take the form of law.[96] Therefore, whilst Kelsen saw himself as a positivist and viewed the positivization of law as a neutral and abstractly normative process of legal application, Schmitt intimated that Kelsen did not understand the meaning of legal positivity. In fact, Kelsen (on Schmitt's account) allowed law to operate as a set of metaphysical paradoxes that enable potent social interests to manipulate the law and dismantle the state's political form. It is only when it is founded in the contingent decision of one will, in consequence, that law can assume a reliable enforceable positive status.

Schmitt did not insist that the decision upholding legal and political order must be an expression of dictatorial sovereignty. The decision might, he conceded, be a decision of a historically united people, or it might be a constitutional decision, or, equally, it might be the decision of a president or a commissarial dictator. Whatever its source, however, the decision is an element of unity and integrity that communicates principles of order – 'power and authority' – through the political system.[97] Where all aspects of the political order are informed and determined by a decision, politics obtains foundation in a will that separates itself from all insubstantially abstracted, universalized or transcendental laws and that claims undiluted self-originating authority for the principles it imposes. A polity ordered by a decisive will is always an *exceptional* polity, and an exceptional polity must justify itself by absolutely positive means.

Schmitt between Protestantism and Roman Catholicism

In his assertion that the sovereign decision is the source and guarantor of order, Schmitt appeared, in certain respects, to move towards quite standard positions in the history of Protestant political doctrine. Indeed, in opposing ideas of universal law and political metaphysics in favour of a dramatic and anti-metaphysical exceptionalism, he, surely deliberately, placed his work on the classical terrain of Protestant politics. Despite this, however, Schmitt was in fact a Roman Catholic, albeit a lapsed one, and much of his work was organized around a dialectical interchange between Protestant and Catholic ideas of political form.

The influence of Roman Catholic ideas on Schmitt's thought was evident, first, in the fact that he refused to eliminate all representative elements from the state, and he insisted that the legitimate state possess a certain structural dignity over and against the material interests and exchanges of civil society. To be sure, Schmitt did not argue (except in his very earliest works) that the state must represent supra-positive or metaphysical principles independent of particular societies or particular histories, and he did not believe that the conditions of legitimacy in the state must comply with one exclusive normative or hierarchical model. For this reason, unlike certain ultra-conservative Catholic contemporaries in the 1920s, he was willing to accept a number of different state forms as possessing legitimacy. In the context of political debate in the Weimar era, he was consequently closer to moderate Catholic thinkers such as Konrad Beyerle, Joseph Mausbach and Peter Tischleder, who attempted to promote Roman Catholic support for the constitution of the Weimar Republic, than to those such as Franz Xaver Kiefl, who denied that a non-monarchical republic could ever obtain representative dignity.[98] However, throughout his work, Schmitt insisted that the state could not be reduced to a simple form of integration and that the positive origins of legitimacy cannot be understood without a non-material or transcendent adjunct.

In his major theoretical work, *Constitutional Theory* (1928), Schmitt set out a concept of political representation that, in complex and deliberately paradoxical manner, placed itself outside the classical outlooks of Protestant political thought and that strategically fused elements of standard Evangelical theory with concepts more characteristic of common Catholic political ideas. Central to this work is an analysis of the political principles of *representation* and *identity,* which Schmitt described as the two primary and original principles of political structure, which give rise to and characterize very different forms of state. Typically, he explained, the principles of representation and identity exist only as *antinomies.* Representation, he argued, is the structural principle of pre-democratic states. It is the principle of states based in hierarchy, in supra-positive or transcendent norms. States founding themselves in this principle claim to obtain legitimacy through the metaphysical representation of 'something existential' or of 'an invisible Being', which is higher than the state itself and which is reflected in the form of hierarchy or authority.[99] In his earlier works, Schmitt in fact stressed that *representation* is the structural principle of the Roman Catholic church: the church is determined by an 'essentially representative attitude', and representation characterizes states that internalize the representative hierarchy of the papacy.[100] Representation, therefore, is the structural principle of metaphysical states, whose source of legitimacy is outside their integrally positive legal structure. Modern society, Schmitt argued, however, is marked by a decline of representation and by the emergence of state forms founded in either real or illusory conditions of *identity.* These are state forms whose legitimacy is derived from a source internal to their own order and which have no external reference by which they can explain themselves as legitimate. Identity, consequently, is the principle of democratic states, and also – perhaps – of Protestant states, which are forced, often under exceptional circumstances, to produce the conditions of their own legitimacy. In modern mass democracies, however, the structural division between identity and representation tends to become uncertain, and most contemporary states require elements of both principles to secure their stability and legitimacy. The legitimacy of mass democracies cannot in fact be produced by identity alone, but depends on representation: it depends on the deployment of symbolic resources by the state executive and by the projection of a hierarchical dignity onto the state, over and above the rest of society. Mass democracy, therefore, cannot be constituted or sustained as legitimate if it does not contain a manifest element of representative hierarchy or *non-identity;* this representative element creates a focus of identification in the state, and it instils unity and identity amongst even deeply polarized and pluralistic groups of citizens. Mass democracies, thus, always presuppose a 'representative' or a 'non-democratic' element in order to perpetuate themselves as founded in democratic identity. Indeed, it is only this non-democratic element that allows these mass democracies to operate as democracies.[101]

Central to this aspect of Schmitt's work is a productive fusion of principles of Roman Catholic politics with principles of Evangelical political doctrine. At one level, Schmitt insisted echoing Roman Catholic political orthodoxy, that the legitimate state requires a hierarchical or metaphysical source of order and legitimate order cannot be entirely and irreducibly positive, but it must represent symbolic or intellectual principles that are originally external to its own positive form. At a different level, however, he also insisted, close to the structural principles of Evangelical political thought, that order is founded in freedom of political will, in historical unity and in positive – or even exceptional – decisions. For Schmitt, therefore, a state is legitimate if it is free; if it positively and exceptionally authorizes the internal foundations of its laws and if it integrates its citizens through its positive decisions, which have no source in metaphysical law. However, the state's decisive and positive freedom depends, paradoxically, on its ability to reflect within itself a reference to intellectual substances or metaphysical norms that it does not contain, and so to construct itself as a representative state. As a representative state, Schmitt stressed, the state need not factually represent supra-positive or transcendent legal ideas; indeed, it need not represent any particular content. Nonetheless, representation remains, for Schmitt, a necessary symbolic trace in the state, in which the state formally shadows a metaphysical idea of its content and dignity, and it is only where a state can dramatize this representative function that it actually becomes free and self-authorizing in its legislative functions. Representation, therefore, is a necessary paradox in the state, which allows the state to project itself as united with originary metaphysical essences, yet which at all times serves the state's positive legislative freedom. Schmitt clearly recommended this use of paradox, and he saw the witting deployment of metaphysical references as a useful tool in the state's quest for positive freedom and contingent power.

Central to Schmitt's work, in sum, is the recurrent allegation that the rationalized metaphysics of the Enlightenment and the formalized metaphysics of positivism are unable to constitute a reliable and sovereign state form. For this reason, Schmitt argued that reliable and legitimate state forms are those that accept their post-metaphysical *exceptionality* and so abandon all legal and normative preconditions external to their own volitional or functional fabric. Close to the surface of Schmitt's theory is the intimation that modern post-metaphysical politics is integrally Protestant: it is the politics of identity, free positivization and exceptional contingency. In his dialectical theory of representation, however, Schmitt deliberately used a Catholic idea to aid a Protestant cause. He indicated that the construction of legitimacy as a positive fact still relies on the secular traces of Roman Catholic politics – that is, on representation. In fact, it is only where they refer to the traces of (Catholic) transcendence that secular (Protestant) states obtain the unitary legitimacy that allows them to operate as secular states. The condition of post-metaphysical politics and legitimacy, thus, still requires a metaphysical dialectic.

Hitler's lawyers: the state as metaphysics

Schmitt, provoking surprise and despair amongst those who knew him or had been taught by him, became a high-profile spokesperson for the regime of the NSDAP in the years of its consolidation, until 1936. During this time, he abandoned many of the exceptionalist and representative elements of his earlier doctrine, and instead he set out a late-historicist doctrine of concrete order to support Hitler's dictatorship. This period in his work was shaped by the belief that a political system is legitimate and commands obedience whenever it can consolidate the concrete order of a people at a given moment in its objective evolution. He therefore described Hitler as a figure supremely equipped to enforce laws likely to maintain conditions of concrete order, and he saw the origin of law as the popular national community, interpreted by the leaders of the Nazi party.[102] At this stage, therefore, the radically voluntaristic aspect of his earlier decisionism faded into the background of Schmitt's thinking, and the statist/representative element was – at least in part – replaced by a more obviously positivist approach to the law, which construed valid law as the interpretable will of a historical people.

In altering his stance to suit the new regime, however, Schmitt did not successfully secure favour for very long. Other theorists also sought to ingratiate themselves with the Nazi elite, and these theorists soon identified weaknesses in his position that made him susceptible to damaging and dangerous criticism. Koellreutter, for example, proposed a theory of the constitution which criticized Schmitt's concentration of politics on the state, and which defined law and state as legitimized by their foundation in the objective national community. He therefore described the political apparatus under Hitler as the most perfect example of 'a legal state', in which the 'idea of state' and the 'idea of law' were perfectly unified as expressions of the same underlying will.[103] Koellreutter tied this idea of the national legal state to a distinctively Evangelical political theology. He claimed, for example, that Protestant national culture is always a 'bearer of political and religious values', and that political order obtains legitimacy through its cohesion with the values embedded in this culture.[104] In this, he specifically sought to champion the principle of integration in Protestantism in order to gain capital over the principle of representation in Roman Catholicism, and so to use his theological perspective to discredit Schmitt. He argued that Roman Catholic political theology necessarily detracts from national identity and from the national sources of political authority, as it centres political life on ideas and institutions claiming representative distinction from the people and introducing universalist principles into the united body of the nation. All representative elements in political theology are, he consequently concluded, 'irreconcilable with the claim to totality made by National Socialism'.[105] In fact, Koellreutter argued that political order is always falsely construed where it is imagined as an institutional or representative hierarchy segregated from the constituents of an objectively unified nation. The representative idea of the state itself, therefore, constitutes an element of illegitimately personal hierarchy in the organic life of the national collective, and this threatens the cohesion of the community and its life as a legal state. The party, not the state, is in fact the legitimate coordinating organ in German society, and unity, not representation, is the absolute precondition of effective political power: the state, in other words, is a distant but damaging residue of political metaphysics which corrupts the life of the national community, and in a truly German community the representative state must give way to the integrative party.

Other legal and political adherents or apologists of the NSDAP also tended to propose historicist or objective-interpretive accounts of the state and its relation to law. In the early 1930s, for instance, Julius Binder intensified his earlier conservative-Hegelian approach, and he argued that law should be viewed as the objective form of a collective will, so that law contains the 'ground of its validity' entirely within itself, and cannot be criticized or steered by any 'idea of law' outside law's objective dominion.[106] Like Binder, Karl Larenz also argued that valid law results from the 'immanent structure and order' of the national community, and that 'community and law can never be separated from each other'.[107] In his pre-1933 works, Larenz espoused a hermeneutical conception of right law, inflected by nationalist Hegelian ideas. He had thus claimed that correct application of the law hinges on the creative role of the judge in legal finding, and that the judge operates within an objective legal order that must determine questions of legal doubt.[108] This theory implied that the rights and entitlements of bearers of the law are not to be derived from universal principles, but from the wider objective exigencies of the political community. Rights are therefore sanctioned under law because the exercise of these rights contributes to the consolidation of national unity, not because they are presupposed as neutral or invariable manifestations of human dignity. Law, on this account, can never be viewed as an apolitical or abstract element in human life, but must constantly be constructed as a positive component in the reinforcement of national order. After 1933, then, Larenz extended this approach to pursue a thorough modification of liberal ideas of legal entitlement and subjectivity. The liberal-subjective or universalist construct of the legal subject must be supplanted, he argued, by a national-objective or historicist construct of the 'legal comrade' (*Rechtsgenosse*) as the bearer of rights and legal claims. Participation in the rights afforded by the law, on this perspective, must not be viewed as a universal or quasi-natural entitlement, but as depending rather on whether the person belongs to and serves the concrete purposes of a 'popular community'.[109] The person under law, therefore, is not a 'subjective will', but a 'concretion of objective law, of the order of community', tied to the 'ethical and religious life of the community',[110] and the rights of this person are fully defined and circumscribed by the needs of this community.[111] In the works of Larenz, therefore, the objectively materialized order of the community replaced all metaphysical-universal ideas of legal and political personality, and this order became the sole ground for regulating issues of legal validity. This redefinition of legal entitlement and purpose even fed into judicial practice of Hitler era, as Roland Freisler, ultimately head of the high court under Hitler, also argued that legal application should only be informed by the 'National Socialist moral order of Germany'. The judges of the National Socialist regime, he concluded, should apply law, not to dispense justice, but to serve the stability of the regime and to uphold the principles of this concrete order.[112]

Ernst Rudolf Huber also emerged at this time as an influential theorist of National Socialist law. Huber was originally a member of the informally organized school of legal thinkers around Schmitt, and his early accounts of relation between state and law were strongly influenced by Schmittian ideas on representation and ecclesiastical law. In his first publications, he emphasized the legal integrity of the church against the state, and he insisted that both church and state obtained legal dignity through their 'supra-individual justification in a universal principle'.[113] After 1933, Huber's legal teachings still retained an element of statism, which distinguished him from other theorists of the NSDAP, and he insisted that under this regime the state had not simply been subsumed by the national community or the party. However, he also concluded that the state cannot be viewed as a location in which 'rights of sovereignty' are distilled in an institutional hierarchy, divorced from the popular legal forms of the community. The state should in fact be viewed as an organ of law that is 'formed in national comradeship', applying laws as the community's own laws.[114] Huber thus saw the legal administration of the NSDAP as finally overcoming the antinomy between strong-state absolutism evolving under Roman law, which construed the legal state as a distinct centre of legal power, and the more organic forms of law formed as Germanic common law, which viewed the state as the organic 'shape' of the historically formal people.[115]

Similarly, Ernst Forsthoff, also a student of Carl Schmitt, argued that the National Socialist movement had the particular legal advantage that it located the origin of law in the 'ordered life-relations of the members of the people' and so divested law of its pure formality and its concentration in formal-institutional hierarchies – in states.[116] National Socialism, he claimed, had its immediate foundation in Lutheranism, as both Lutheranism and National Socialism constituted legal order based in an 'invisible community', which cannot be stabilized in the 'normative security' of the formal legal state.[117] Like other theorists of the NSDAP, therefore, Forsthoff argued that valid law-finding is a process of national self-interpretation or a 'creative' process of cultural and linguistic formation.[118] This process, he concluded, should be seen as a methodological analogue to religious teaching, as both law-finding and pastoral activities depend on a constructive approach to originary texts: to national law and to the Bible.[119]

The legal teachings of the National Socialists therefore extended the anti-metaphysical perspectives that had coloured Weimar legal thought in general and that had exercised particular (but not exclusive) influence on the more conservative axis of Weimar political theory. The legal spokesmen of the NSDAP allowed the dream of a non-metaphysical law to culminate in a notion of the national community as a fully and internally united organ, suffering no separation into objectively distinct legal or institutional forms and coordinated by the party apparatus. Indeed, one theoretical element that allowed the doctrines of the NSDAP to act as a widely captivating ideology was the fact that it constructed an extreme conservative ideology whilst actually relinquishing what had traditionally been the ideological centrepiece of extreme conservatism – namely, the state. Whilst earlier conservative outlooks had tended to view the personal state as the source of law and order, National Socialist thinkers derided this conception of law's origin as a quasi-transcendental example of political metaphysics. Instead, as Schmitt had warned might ultimately be the case, these theorists used originally liberal ideas of legislative freedom and autonomy outside the state to construct a radically new type of violent conservatism, in which neither state nor law could be separately extrapolated from the national-racial community.

10 Critical theory and the law

The legal divide in critical theory

Perspectives on law in critical theory evolved, primarily, through a series of debates between associates of the Institute for Social Research in New York in the 1930s concerning the nature and the formation of fascism. These debates made manifest certain differences of approach between members of the institute, and they illustrated certain fundamental distinctions in their understandings of politics and law. In their analyses of the political apparatus evolving under Hitler, for instance, the most prominent members of the Frankfurt School, Max Horkheimer, Theodor W. Adorno and Friedrich Pollock, all concluded that National Socialism should most accurately be categorized as *authoritarian state capitalism*. They saw Hitler's regime as a system in which the privatist features of liberal capitalism had been eradicated from the economy, the autonomous economic groups of the private economy had been replaced by state-supported economic coordinators, and the state had begun to bring the originally private processes of commodity exchange and monetary circulation and distribution under direct political control. Pollock's interpretation was most pointed in this respect. Building on the earlier analyses of late capitalism set out by the Austro-Marxist Rudolf Hilferding, he described the political order of the NSDAP as a coercive apparatus, which had assumed central regulatory responsibility for all functions normally pertaining, in free or liberal market systems, to the private economy.[1] The state, in consequence, had become accountable for controlling credit supply via the banks, for regulating the supply and demand of commodities in the private economy, for setting prices and for allocating excess capital. In the state of the NSDAP, political power and economic power had become indivisible, all previously economic interaction was now subject to mandatory constraint,[2] and the state effectively replaced the market (in the conventional sense of a system of economic exchange outside the state) with a sphere of centralized bureaucratic planning and regulation. The state, in short, had brought about the 'demise' of competitive or liberal capitalism.[3]

This analysis led Pollock to conclude that under National Socialism a new kind of state had emerged, one whose functions extended far beyond all liberal concepts of legitimate state activity, which abandoned all protective conceptions of rights and freedoms enshrined in liberal constitutions and in which political elites and economic elites were united in a single hegemonic apparatus. Pollock saw this state as evolving directly from the earlier forms of the liberal state. Indeed, he identified the 'monopolistic institutions of private capitalism', and especially the highly cartellized organization of the economy of the Weimar Republic, as preconditions for the formation of the political apparatus of the NSDAP.[4] Nonetheless, he also viewed the state of state capitalism as marking a qualitative leap against earlier forms of liberal statehood. The distinctive characteristic of this state resided in the fact that the organs of political direction had obtained total *primacy* over economic factors in the overall organization of society: state and society under the NSDAP were thus marked by a *primacy of the political.* Under this system, in consequence, economic autonomy had disappeared and all legal divisions and all traditional checks on the power of the state had also been eroded. Law now operated solely as a prerogative medium for regulating production, for maintaining conditions of obedience and for securing the fulfilment of the preferences of the political leadership.

Amongst other associates of the institute, Herbert Marcuse, whilst not accepting all aspects of Pollock's interpretation of National Socialism as state capitalism, also viewed the authoritarian regimes of the 1930s as political systems in which the state had taken responsibility for the 'political integration of society' and had instituted an unprecedented level of 'political organization' throughout society.[5] Similarly, Horkheimer also viewed the 'authoritarian state of the present' as an example of 'state capitalism',[6] in which the spontaneous reflexes of the free market were subject to far-reaching regulation, in which 'private capitalists' – that is, capitalists not using the apparatus of state to organize production and regulate demand – had been 'abolished', and the political impact of organizations representing private capital was greatly reduced.[7] Underlying the different variants on the theory of state capitalism were two underlying assumptions. First, exponents of this theory assumed, simply, that the state is factually able to assimilate the market to its political functions and that the expanded public economy emerging through total state control still functions as a distinctively capitalist economy. Second, then, they also assumed that the state has no distinction against economic processes and that, even in non-fascist societies, the state is, at least latently, a concentrated organ of coercion or an 'instrument of domination', closely fused with the prerogatives of powerful economic groups.[8]

Although promoted as orthodoxy by Pollock and Horkheimer, the theory of state capitalism was strongly opposed by other associates of the Institute of Social Research. Indeed, debates around this theory became one of the most important political fault-lines in the early evolution of critical theory, and it separated those who took a purely instrumental view of politics, law and state from those, such as Franz Neumann and Otto Kirchheimer, who refused to see the law and politics exclusively as an adjunct to economic interests. In their interpretations of Hitler's regime, these theorists consequently resisted Pollock's concept of the primacy of the political and they sought to modify the more established concept of state capitalism.

Kirchheimer accounted for National Socialism as an authoritarian order in which a ceaselessly shrinking 'proprietary class' has obtained ceaselessly increasing leverage on the organs of political control, and in which the state had lost all autonomy against high-level economic groups.[9] In its legal consequences, he argued that this process was marked by a dissolution of the structural elements of the constitutional state; standard legal entitlements had come to depend on personal relationships to and within different 'ruling groups', and individual rights had either been eliminated entirely or subsumed under 'group rights', which were reliant on personal patronage or membership of associations supported by the regime.[10] At the heart of this account was the argument that the governmental apparatus of Hitler's regime had relinquished all autonomous legal structure to the economic class that administered it, and it could, in consequence, no longer properly be described as a state. Kirchheimer's analysis thus contained a powerful critique of Pollock's concept of state capitalism. Indeed, it implied that the idea of state capitalism is a contradiction in terms, that it is not possible for a state to dominate a capitalist economy without subordinating itself to the exigencies of the economy, and that a state entirely dominated by the interests of economic groups renounces the legal features of statehood. Franz Neumann's response to Pollock's thesis was marked by a still higher level of disagreement. Underpinning his analysis of Hitler's regime, set out in his *Behemoth,* is the assertion that this regime was not *political* at all, and that it merely comprised a loosely correlated set of institutions, under the coordination of the 'party hierarchs' of the NSDAP, serving the interests of dominant economic groups.[11] The formative precondition of statehood, for Neumann, is the existence of a publicly constituted centre of authority, empowered to stabilize itself against the pluralistic and self-seeking interests of economy and society. Under the regime of the NSDAP, however, the state had lost its institutional distinction, and it had been disaggregated into a number of organs whose primary function was to transform distinct economic prerogatives into executive policy.[12]

The implicit claim in both these analyses is that the legally formed state of liberal societies contains ideal and normative elements that cannot be reduced to purely instrumental or coercive strategies, and it is precisely these elements of statehood that were suspended by the regime of the NSDAP. At different points in their trajectory, Neumann and Kirchheimer were, although surely highly critical of liberalism in its practical embodiments, even prepared to accommodate their analyses to ethical and natural-legal ideas regarding the rule of law and the formation of the state. Kirchheimer implicitly declared an attachment to the ethical idea of highest justice underpinning liberal legal thought, and he interpreted Hitler's system as one in which individual rights were thoroughly eroded and a condition of profound 'alienation between law and morality' had been reached.[13] Likewise, although deriding common natural-legal ideas as ideological abstractions, Neumann also concluded that ideals of natural law must be invoked to criticize 'authoritarian theory and practice',[14] and even that natural law, in its insistence on a distinction between positive law and valid law, can found the normative basis of critical theory.[15]

Liberalism and rationalization

Despite these fundamental differences, however, there were also deep continuities in the accounts of law, power and statehood set out by the different theoretical factions in the Frankfurt School. The similarities in these accounts are generally found in their critiques of liberalism. All theorists linked with the Frankfurt School were connected by the argument that liberalism had put in place the economic and the cognitive preconditions on which fascism eventually evolved. In addition, moreover, all these theorists saw fascism as a system whose evolution had been assisted by the legal structures, the legal concepts and the principles of legal rationality that liberalism promotes.

Pollock for example argued that the 'liberal phase' of capitalism, although sustained by rhetorical ideas of free trade and private-legal autonomy, was in fact dominated by a process of intensifying capital concentration and monopoly formation. Because of this, the liberal era paved the way for the emergence of a heavily cartelized economic order, in which political and economic control was divided between members of a small number of monopolies and cartels who had little commitment to democratic rule. The illusion of freedom under early liberal private law, therefore, was in fact an important stage in a complex pre-history of authoritarian state capitalism.[16] Marcuse also claimed that the fascist system had its origins in liberal capitalism and especially in the autonomous system of private law on which liberal capitalism relied.[17] Horkheimer also subscribed to an evolutionary theory of capitalism, which identified the origins of monopoly capitalism and state capitalism in the legal and economic apparatus of liberal capitalism.[18] The 'real consequence of liberal economics', he argued, was not liberal democracy, which was a mere fleeting expression of liberal interests, but the 'totalitarian conception of the state'.[19]

Kirchheimer argued, in similar terms, that the evolution of capitalism has been marked, first, by a progression from the state of liberal democracy to the state of mass democracy, and, ultimately, from the state of mass democracy to the state of fascism. Each of these phases is characterized by a distinctive set of technical compromises and material bargains between the political apparatus (the state) and the representatives of powerful economic lobbies. Fascism is the last stage in a process through which the bargains on which government is founded have become increasingly restricted and instrumental, as a result of which the instruments of national governance are finally placed in the hands of one tightly delineated hegemonic bloc. Fascism is distinguished from earlier modes of political direction by the fact that under fascism economic groups obtain full powers of direction over the state, and they eliminate its independent legal structure.[20] However, there is always a continuum between different stages of capitalist evolution, and fascism cannot be explained without an analysis of the preceding stages. Indeed, Kirchheimer argued that liberal-capitalist states always tend to evolve legal systems that make them susceptible to overthrow. This is because liberal constitutional states invariably presuppose and accord the status of inviolability to *private law,* and to the ideas of ownership and autonomy embedded in the legal subjects of private law. This means that the normative constitutional form of the liberal democratic state is always undermined by the securities offered to independent economic interests protected under private law, and that the constitutional bedrock of democracies can be overridden or even rescinded where powerful economic interests wish to introduce laws serving their interests.[21] Indeed, the very fact that in liberal democracies private law is recognized as an autonomous legal sphere means that liberal democracies are always unstable, for it is structural to liberal democracies that democratically founded laws and institutions exist in conjunction with laws serving an independent bloc of powerful and narrowly privatized interests. In liberal democracies, consequently, the most important areas of social exchange are not regulated by democratically founded law, and free reign is given to interests that are either indifferent or hostile to the conditions of democratic rule enunciated in the constitution.[22] Fundamental to liberal democracy is, thus, the fact that it lacks substantial foundations of legitimacy; it founds its legitimacy in the technical 'form of legality' derived from insubstantial compromises and thin formulae of equality and freedom; and it can easily, especially in periods of economic contraction, be transformed into an instrument of economic hegemony.[23] Indeed, at the heart of Kirchheimer's analysis is the claim that liberal democracy only promises government by universal law and by consensual or legitimate agreement. Factually, however, it acts as a mechanism for ensuring that political order has little or no basis in consensual agreement, and that government can be conducted without consensual legitimacy. In this respect, above all others, liberalism, with its cult of private law, facilitates the formation of radically non-consensual types of authority. Fascism, in short, simultaneously incorporates, preserves and *reinforces* the legal and political institutes inherent in pre-fascist political economy, and the fascist economy, now conjoined with a highly authoritarian party apparatus, is sustained by the same principles of contractual and private-legal autonomy that liberalism first pioneered.

Analogously, Neumann also asserted that the essential function of liberal law is to generate a series of masks or ideological chimera that obscure the origins of law in relations of economic antagonism. He saw liberal law as a distillation of the patterns of coercion and expropriation inherent in the relations between wage labourers and entrepreneurs, and he argued that the primary function of state and law under liberalism is to facilitate the fulfilment of contracts, and so to stabilize the existing political-economic order, based in 'ownership of the means of production'.[24] At one level, he claimed, liberal law purports to protect concepts of social equality and freedom: it contains certain legal principles – basic guarantees of rights and entitlements, due process, parity before the law – which are equally and universally applied to all interests and all legal claims throughout society. The very fact of its universality, however, means that liberal law instils a spurious *pluralism* in the political order: under liberal law, the state is forced to reflect all legal claims as equally valid and as equally protected by legal process, and it is consequently unable to impose substantial norms throughout society or to select whether certain legal or economic interests warrant greater protection than others. The liberal state is, therefore, prevented by its legal apparatus from ensuring that social groups are protected that favour democracy or from denying equal recognition to groups that seek to overthrow democracy. The pluralism fostered by law's own formal even-handedness ultimately has highly detrimental repercussions for the democratic state. This pluralism destroys the sovereignty of the state; it means that constitutionally circumscribed parliaments invariably struggle to enforce the principles of their constitutional order through society, that many areas of social activity simply escape the application of constitutional law and that powerful economic groups can freely use the law to reinforce their own position and even to influence the state.[25] The consequence of this, Neumann concluded, is that modern democracies are subject to a number of crisis tendencies. These include the undermining of parliament by pluralistic or quasi-corporate lobbies situated at the fringes of parliament, the restriction of political decision-making competence by the judiciary, the emergence of centrifugal or federal tendencies in the institutional order of the state, the relative autonomy of the state administration against the democratic principles of the constitution, and the curtailment of parliamentary authority in crucial spheres of legislation.[26] Like Schmitt, therefore, Neumann concluded that liberal constitutional orders are victims of their pluralistic conceptions, and they are incapable of defining themselves as categorically and decisively committed to one idea of necessary democratic order. Both Neumann and Kirchheimer in fact ultimately accepted the Schmittian argument that democracy presupposes the existence of a constitutional order that is applied programmatically to all civil society and that is capable of transmitting one will and one uniform set of ideals and objectives throughout all society. Most particularly, they argued, a constitutional order supporting a genuine democracy must eradicate, or at least place strict limits on, the formal autonomy of private and contract law. The liberal vision of constitutional democracy, both Neumann and Kirchheimer implied, can only be fulfilled if the liberal insistence on the sanctity of private law is overcome and if the constitution is allowed to act as the sole source of legal order in society. Neumann, in particular, was always clear that the principles of universality, legal personality and due process in liberal law do indeed serve to preserve certain basic conditions of freedom, and that democracy without a constitutional system is not thinkable. However, both he and Kirchheimer also emphasized that purely liberal societies can never be democratic, and that the principles of law by which liberals seek to uphold democracy also imperil democracy, in its specifically liberal institutional form.

The legal subject and false secularity

All the political-sociological analyses attached to critical theory claimed that liberalism, in its most fundamental principles, institutes a political apparatus which is underpinned by contractual and latently exploitative calculations of self-interest and self-satisfaction that threaten to cause the collapse of democratic government. All these analyses, moreover, saw the exploitative disposition of liberalism as crystallized most perfectly in the form of the *legal subject*. Indeed, they saw this disposition as reflected most especially in the idea of the legal subject extracted from positivist readings of Roman private law: in the idea of the legal subject, that is, that recognizes that each person is a bearer of rights of freedom and ownership, that each person is surrounded by a sphere of formal-legal autonomy, that personal rights pertain to social agents as atomized units, and that the political order, as a legal state, is bound to the formal recognition and the protection of these autonomous rights. The theorists of the Frankfurt School all viewed the idea of the legal subject as the ideological centre of liberal capitalism and as the ideological bridge linking liberal capitalism to more authoritarian types of capitalism. By referring to the paradigm of the legal subject, they argued, liberal law can rationalize itself as a fully valid normative system, offering its citizens equal treatment before the law and sanction for individual freedoms and entitlements, and it can purport to provide universal recognition of each person as a rationally accounted purpose of the law, endowed with a sphere of liberty upon which no other legal agent can legitimately encroach. By referring to the legal subject, moreover, liberal law can also construct legal states, which justify themselves by giving rational recognition to their subjects as legal subjects, with rights of freedom, property and redress, and which appear to guarantee conditions of harmony, equality and justice throughout society. This process of rational recognition, however, enabled liberal law to perpetuate, under law, the most manifest experiences of inequality and exploitation. In assuming, as a principle of universal rationality, that all persons under law are equally equipped to avail themselves of their formal rights as legal subjects, that all legal subjects require protection for the same proprietary rights and the same proprietary freedoms, and that all legal subjects only wish to possess those rights inscribed in their formal autonomy as possessive legal subjects, liberal law succeeds only in ostracizing all substantial freedoms from the law. Liberal law, in fact, allows freedom under law to emerge as a highly diminished, and even irrational, construct – as the freedom of a person seeking freedom as nothing but autonomy and desiring self-enrichment as nothing but ownership and material supremacy. Likewise, in assuming that liberal states are legitimate where they recognize legal subjects, liberalism accepts as legitimate a variety of state forms which in fact possess only the most superficial legitimacy; it excludes more substantial ideas of legitimacy from the sphere of legal and political relevance; and it always incorporates the seeds of more authoritarian governance. For exponents of critical theory, in short, the paradigm of the legal subject demonstrates that classical liberalism was based in a false unity of law and power, that it falsely explained itself as a system guaranteeing conditions of rational freedom, and that it was factually unable to place power on fully consensual or legitimate foundations. They viewed the legal subject, therefore, as the *metaphysical paradox* of liberalism, as the term to which both liberal law and liberal state refer for their own rational self-explanation as just and legitimate, but which in fact sustains itself only through technical duplicity and false reflection.

As an example of such analysis, Neumann claimed that the legal rights attached to legal subjects under liberal capitalism restrict individual freedom to a thin sphere of rights and entitlements, which can only be exercised by agents or 'economic subjects' in the private economy.[27] At the heart of the legal subjectivity of liberalism, therefore, is a concentration of law around contractual autonomy and proprietary dispositions, and a consequent distillation of ideas of freedom from a depleted construct of the legal agent as private person.[28] These rights construct human persons, as legal subjects, in a relation of 'closure' against each other, and, by privileging economic freedoms above other freedoms, they create a propensity even in allegedly liberal societies for instrumental and latently authoritarian attitudes.[29] It is only where the law admits an 'actionistic element' of political engagement, which elaborates and gives intensified substance to the thin rights and legal guarantees underscoring more standard liberal models of democracy, that law and the democratic state can escape their pure liberal formality, and that the rationality underlying law and state can liberate itself from its narrowly purposive or private structure.[30] Like Neumann, Kirchheimer also saw the rights of the legal subject under the liberal *Rechtsstaat* as rights that restrict human freedom to a set of depoliticized freedoms and heteronomously sanctioned purposes.[31] Similarly, he also argued that a legitimate state depends on the willingness of citizens to deploy the formal-democratic apparatus of the state to found a substantially and volitionally unified order. Fundamental to a fully legitimate state, most particularly, is that citizens expand the content of the rights enshrined in liberal constitutions and that they actively articulate these rights as elements of popular democratic action. A legitimate democratic constitution, he thus explained, must be infused with the actively reclaimed and exercised contents of human political freedom, and it must decisively elevate human life above the insubstantial ideas of apolitical freedom condensed into the liberal formulae of the legal subject and the legal state, into a condition of political unity and 'unrestricted will formation'.[32] In parallel to this, Marcuse also focused his analysis of the continuities between liberalism and fascism on the concept of the legal subject. The liberal legal subject, he argued, rationalizes human life and human action by conferring legal form on human beings so that they become identifiable as stable and calculable centres of autonomy and entitled interest. In so doing, the legal subject enacts a reductive transformation of human freedom, and it limits rights and freedoms to legal forms that consolidate the individual person as an 'economic subject', and so serve the overarching 'direction of the economy'.[33] At a later stage in the evolution of critical theory, then, Adorno argued that the legal subject of early liberalism is nothing other than the original 'dark secret of bourgeois society', which falsely suggests that human freedom is a 'function of regularity' and so disseminates falsely rationalized ideas of freedom and entitlement through society. This dark secret of the legal subject masks a reality in which, under liberal capitalism, 'the formal freedom' of persons under laws creates a climate of coercive economic order and, ultimately, models human subjectivity around the false freedom of the solitary economic agent and the self-preserving property owner.[34] Although the idea of the legal subject was originally shaped by Enlightenment ideas of rational autonomy and self-liberation, Adorno argued, the freedoms imputed to the legal subject under liberalism concealed a 'heteronomous and authoritarian' reality of unfreedom,[35] and they instilled a spirit of embittered purposiveness in all human relations.[36] Horkheimer also described the construction of the modern subject around the idea of formal-legal autonomy as the essential foundation of modern 'bourgeois' reason, and he saw the primary function of this subject as residing in its regularization of reason around a sequence of economically prescribed purposes.[37] Both Adorno and Horkheimer saw liberalism, in consequence, as fundamentally determined by an exploitative subject, which offers and withdraws freedom simultaneously, which transmits spurious and paradoxical ideals of equality throughout society, and which stimulates attitudes of atomized instrumentality throughout all spheres of social exchange.

These inquiries into the formation of the legal subject were closely connected with an inquiry into the processes of secularization underpinning modern society and modern rationality. In different configurations, all analyses associated with critical theory claimed that the conditions of modern society have been shaped by the emergence of specifically secular forms of reason. These forms of reason first sought to free human life and human thought from natural, religious and metaphysical determinacy, but, as Enlightenment, they have now stabilized themselves as the dominatory centres of modern social reality. Each perspective within critical theory, then, also identified the legal subject as the fulcrum of these processes of secular rationalization, and each perspective used the paradigm of the legal subject to argue that the Enlightenment of secular reason has not produced the freedom which it first promised, and that this Enlightenment has ultimately become a false Enlightenment.

From a purely legal perspective, for example, Neumann argued that the legal subject and its political corollary in the legal state have evolved through a particular process of formalistic rationalization, which is integrally connected with *positivism.* The positivist constructions of the legal subject and the legal state, he argued, have reduced law to a formally 'immanent' and self-referring system of rules, which excludes all external moral or sociological contents in the deduction of validity and entitlement under law. As a consequence of this, liberal law has acted to create a climate of formal regularity around the functions of government and economy, and it now stabilizes all life under conditions of rule-determined order and factual unfreedom. The positivist legal subject describes the central point in a wider culture of secular reason, which concentrates human life in highly technical and curtailed accounts of its freedom and legitimacy and which forecloses all possibilities of freedom and critique that cannot be posed within the terms of formal order.[38] The experience of liberalism consolidated under legal positivism thus appeared to Neumann as the result of a particular sterile and ideological course of positivization. If modern thinking, he intimated, was first driven by the great dream of rational self-legislation and Enlightenment, which imagined that, as legal subjects, human beings might legislate conditions in which the laws of state structuring their life would be their *own laws,* then the advent and triumph of liberal positivism, directly underscored by powerful economic prerogatives organized as private law, had fatally corrupted this process. The course of legal positivization conducted by positivism had only in fact led to extremely depleted experiences of legal and political freedom, and it had provided the most formulaic and reduced account of what the conditions of freedom and legitimacy might be. Indeed, positivism had reconstructed the enlightened human person as an abstract formula of chimerical freedom, as a paradox legislating minimal conditions of order throughout society, but unable to institute conditions of authentic freedom and authentic legitimacy. The secularization of reason in the positivist paradigm of the legal subject, in short, had simply redesigned human freedom in a secondary metaphysics – it had centred all social reality on the thin paradoxical form of the legal person as economic agent, but, in so doing, it offered less substantial liberty than the original order of heteronomy, which the laws of the Enlightenment sought to supersede.

Like Neumann, Marcuse also insisted that the rationality underscoring the liberal-capitalist legal subject is a deeply impoverished rationality, representing a depletion of the authentic scope and content of human reason. Such rationality in fact reflects a broad *privatization* of rationality; in focusing its rational analysis on narrow spheres of private interest and exchange, the rationality of legal subjects prevents subjects from reflecting on the social constellations in which they might articulate and experience their most genuine freedoms, and it truncates the actual constitutive foundations of reason. It is fundamental to the private rationality of liberal legal subjects, Marcuse argued, that it has not yet become fully rational, that it restricts itself to self-centred constructs of necessity and that it cannot give itself a rational account of the wider socio-economic conditions in which it operates. The rationality of liberalism is in fact lastly *irrational,* and it contributes directly to the persistence of ideological and oppressive modes of political and economic governance. It is for this reason that the private-legal rationality of liberalism is the genetic source of totalitarianism.[39]

Although less manifestly concerned with legal questions than their more institutionally minded counterparts, Adorno and Horkheimer also expressed the view that the form of modern law reflects a malaise at the core of modern reason, and they argued that miscarried rationalization and positivist legal formation are closely conjoined causes of the pathological tendencies of modern society. In *Dialectic of Enlightenment,* for example, they argued that modern reason and modern law have emerged simultaneously and in close relation to each other, that each plays a crucial role in the consolidation of the economic relations in modern society, and that each stabilizes a malignantly instrumental attitude at the centre of all social interaction. Modern reason, they claimed, has formed itself through a course of Enlightenment and demystification in which human thinking has gradually engendered explanatory concepts for itself that free it from natural, mythical or metaphysical-theological determinacy and allow it to underwrite its own position as the organizing centre of social reality. Through its self-assertion as the free centre of the universe, however, reason has forfeited the ability to obtain genuine knowledge of its objects; it has emptied itself of all organic, natural or sensory contents; and it now obtains knowledge *of* objects as an exercise of falsely taxonomic dominion *over* them. In this instrumental attitude, the falsely free and falsely knowing subjects of Enlightenment constitute the cognitive foundation for the evolution and the organization of late capitalism, as the late-capitalist economy replicates the cognitive dispositions of modern reason in its administration of people and goods as formal objects of exchange: the economy in fact constitutes a supra-subject, originating in and ultimately also over-layering the instrumental dispositions inscribed in human subjectivity. In addition, however, the falsely knowing subject of secular reason also forms itself as a specifically *legal subject* and it contains juridical elements that both internalize and perpetuate the wider dynamics of capitalist oppression. The subject of false knowledge, Adorno and Horkheimer thus argued, is always a juridical or legislatory subject, able to obtain knowledge of objects only by legislating for itself the conditions of their intelligibility and by aligning them and rendering them *identical* to categories which it has autonomously formed for itself to serve the purposes of its own dominion.

The subject thus imposes 'legal titles' or categories upon the objects of its knowledge, and it disposes over these objects, cognitively, as sets of 'abstract material'.[40]

Like other exponents of critical theory, therefore, Adorno and Horkheimer asserted that through the course of rationalization and Enlightenment the human mind has shaped itself into a juridical form, and, in this form, it exercises power over other objects and other people, it contributes to the processes of domination sustaining capitalism, and it disseminates false laws through society. The juridical form of this subject, Adorno later explained, sustains itself by claiming *autonomy:* by claiming to act as a focus of self-legislation, providing necessary laws for all society.[41] In fact, however, the autonomy of this subject is always paradoxical. The subject engenders its autonomy through illusory acts of self-constitution; it assumes prescriptive and normative centrality in all social exchange whilst in fact reducing its content to sequences of formal abstraction and self-regulation; and it rationalizes itself as a source of freedom whilst supporting a reality of full heteronomy. The autonomy of modern rationality, in other words, is not autonomy at all, but heteronomy: the modern rational subject converts itself into a metaphysical subject, which distils social reality around abstracted laws and causes and so fully alienates itself from the grounds of its freedom and genuine self-realization.[42] Through this configuration of the modern subject as a paradoxical device, then, the impulse of freedom that originally stimulated the formation of the rational human subject is lost. The subject now closes itself into a metaphysically fictitious account of itself as an agent of self-legislation, and it perpetuates, in exacerbated form, the reality of oppression against which, in seeking Enlightenment, it first reacted.

On these grounds, Adorno concluded that reason can only overcome the 'metaphysical despair' or the 'radically metaphysical alienation', in which it constructs itself as a legal subject if it opens itself to objects that challenge its formal self-certainty and that contain contents which, as a centre of juridical authority, it does not produce for itself.[43] Horkheimer, similarly, also concluded that the human subject can only place itself beyond the formalism and false rationality of positivism if it exposes itself to objects which it does not derive from its own formal structure, and which subvert reason's claim to jurisdiction over all things.[44] For both Adorno and Horkheimer, therefore, overcoming the false metaphysics of liberalism might require that human reason disposes itself in new ways to the original metaphysical legacy which reason, as Enlightenment, first suppressed.[45] The dream of humanity at once demanded and undermined by post-Enlightenment liberalism can only be redeemed, on this account, if reason abdicates its claims to absolute jurisdiction in the world, and if it begins, at least dialectically, to recuperate the contents banned from reason in its original quest for autonomy.

11 The dialectics of refoundation

The politics of humanism and anti-humanism

The return of natural law

The immediate aftermath of the Second World War and the collapse of National Socialism saw a widespread rejuvenation of political humanism in Germany, often with a strongly existentialist intonation. This re-emergence of humanist thinking also fed into legal debate, and it stimulated a rebirth of natural-law theory. The natural-law principles of post-1945 theory were usually articulated as part of an attempt to cleanse legal thinking of all elements which (really or allegedly) had contributed to the moral vacuity of law under the Hitler regime and, above all, to erase the traces of positivism from legal discourse.[1] Underlying this transformation in legal thinking in post-war Germany, therefore, was a renewed attempt to link legal theory and humanism and to construe legitimacy in law as integrally correlated with ideal human attributes and ideal human values.

This shift towards humanistic legal thought was especially characteristic of those theorists who reappeared after 1945 and who had not been acutely contaminated by association with National Socialist party. One important example of such thinking is Julius Ebbinghaus, whose revitalization of Kantian ideas of practical reason had enduring influence on the evolution of political theory in the Federal Republic of Germany.[2] From a more phenomenological tradition, Gerhart Husserl also contributed, at a slightly later stage, to the re-emergence of humanistic legal ideas. Husserl attempted particularly to construct the law of justice as a principle of historical, not metaphysical, validity, embedded in a particular set of legal facts and a particular legal community. He thus argued that authentic law is ontologically enmeshed with the conditions of human temporal and historical being, and it demonstrates its naturalness or validity as it consolidates conditions of peaceful coexistence and stability.[3] These arguments were also echoed by the early Werner Maihofer, who argued that natural law, far from evolving from metaphysically abstracted norms, is a historically necessary phenomenon, in which human beings articulate, in their historical lives, the conditions of their most authentic 'self-being'.[4] Later, Ernst Bloch contributed to debates on natural law from a Marxist perspective, and he insisted that

Marxist analysis should not conflate itself with ideological or systemic analysis, but should also recognize the aspects of normative humanism and radical ius-naturalism in Marxist theory.[5]

Perhaps the most influential position amongst the theories of natural law in this era was expressed in the works of Karl Jaspers. As outlined above, Jaspers had been an important figure in the fragmentation of neo-Kantianism in the 1920s, and he had occupied a position in the conservative fringes of democratic discourse in the Weimar Republic. After 1945 and into the 1950s, however, Jaspers emerged for a short span as the most influential advocate of committed democratic foundation in the Federal Republic of Germany and as the major spokesperson for the democratic integrity of the new republic.

Jaspers was an unlikely intellectual figurehead for the democratic system implemented in the Federal Republic in 1949. Even in the altered configurations of post-1945 Germany, he retained many of the more conservative political predilections which marked his thought in the Weimar era: he remained committed to elite-democratic views; he was sceptical about the role of political parties in public will-formation; and he was scrupulously cautious in his approach to the 'wild, dark and fanatical' idea of full popular sovereignty and pure democracy.[6] Nonetheless, he also set out a series of ideas, derived at times from Kant and at times from Hannah Arendt, which both crystallized the most pressing preoccupations of the immediate post-war era and set the parameters for later innovations in political theory. In his writings of this time, most importantly, he used Arendtian arguments to demand the foundation in Germany of a republican order, based in the 'unlimited public discussion' or in the 'freedom of mutual communication', and he argued that communication between citizens can only take place in a public sphere which is not subject to technical regulation or controlled by administrative prerogatives.[7] He thus echoed Arendt's anthropological approach to political foundation, and he claimed that legitimate political order must have its substructure in the essential active resources of the human being. In more Kantian spirit, however, he added to this the claim that democratic life depends upon the establishment of a constitutional system, incorporating legally protected basic rights and codified principles of universal or natural law to regulate the exercise of power and give shape to the general will of the people.[8] Anticipating later doctrines of constitutional patriotism, therefore, he concluded that constitutions articulating ethical decisions and sanctioning basic rights are the preconditions of all legitimate political order. The constitution, he concluded, must act as the formative horizon of political identity, and the principles enshrined in the constitution should form the basis of active democratic life and common 'self-education'.[9] Like Kant, therefore, Jaspers saw the constitution of state as a document reflecting the ideal or natural personality of the citizen, and as enunciating the 'inner' ethical conditions of ideal human self-realization.[10] Like Arendt, however, he also argued that legitimacy in politics cannot be stabilized in formally normative postulates, but must be enacted in integral processes of political communication.

Politics against technology

Following Arendt, therefore, Jaspers centred his post-1945 work on the belief that the existence of a legitimate political order is disrupted by the functions of *technology,* and that the integrally human state is one which gives legal form to political ideals that elevate the people above technical, functional or formally purposive considerations. Where the state becomes a primarily technical or technological agent, he claimed, the state concentrates its power on prerogatives of technical regulation, administration and *planning,* and it erodes its foundation in the enactment and the representation of integral human interests. He consequently saw the organization of public power around planning activities as a *denaturation* of political life, which reduces human being to an object of 'technical' disposition and ties it to purposes that are not integrally its own.[11] Indeed, he concluded that where technology becomes a dominant and independent force in human society and where technical interests shape the laws of the constitution, this tends to produce coercive and latently violent political regimes.[12] Technological governance, he concluded, is an invariable feature of totalitarianism, and the attempt to eradicate technology from the foundations of the polity is the most potent and most necessary bulwark against subsidence into renewed oppression. Technology, for Jaspers, is the manifest form of an end-oriented or metaphysical rationality that has detached itself from human interests and consolidated itself in pernicious heteronomy against the human sources of life. Humanity, in consequence, is the 'limit of the technical'.[13] It is a quality of existence that can serve no other end than itself and that does not endlessly distract from itself in pursuit of purposes.

In this critique of technology, Jaspers called upon earlier hermeneutical accounts of human reason, and in this he was also joined by Heidegger. At this stage in his trajectory, Heidegger also elaborated elements of Dilthey's initial hermeneutical doctrine, arguing that the technical superstructure of modern society has shaped itself from metaphysical forms of reason, and that this superstructure has sedimented itself over and against the authentic freedoms of human life. Heidegger consequently described technology – or *Technik* – as reflecting an irreducibly instrumental quality in human rationality,[14] as imposing tyrannical purposes on material things and human beings to fulfil the abstract prescriptions of the human will, and so as incompatible with the 'essence of freedom'.[15] Technology, he concluded, represents a 'perfected metaphysics', in which the disposition of modern reason towards formal and instrumental accounts of worldly phenomena reaches its 'highest form'.[16] Under the metaphysical dominion of technology, consequently, the 'truth of being' is foreclosed to the human mind and the mind cements itself in a dominatory or proprietorial relation to the world that it inhabits. Like Jaspers, therefore, Heidegger argued that the 'devastation of the earth' experienced in the course of the early twentieth century is an event that 'results from metaphysics'.[17]

Jaspers, Heidegger and Arendt all agreed that the deduction of meaning and value from *purposes* or from the projections of *the will* marks a violent corruption of freedom, and they all saw metaphysics, especially as embodied in technology, as the rational or material form of the purposive will. Jaspers particularly criticized technology because he viewed it as a falsely purposive order in which the 'means' of human life (that is, the material apparatus which supports it) present themselves as the 'ends' of human life, and in which all existence is subjugated beneath falsely imposed purposes.[18] The true condition of human life, they suggested, is always obscured by the will, and by the metaphysical structures emanating from this will. In its political implications, this argument imagined a true politics as one without technology and without rationalist metaphysics, and it saw true political existence as a condition where human life uninhibitedly inhabits its own historical location and is not severed from its historical essence by technical or abstracted principles and purposes. These theories were consequently deeply hostile to all types of technocratic government, which they saw as government by false purposes, obliterating the sites of human freedom and constraining humanity by false projections of the will.

In this joint attack on metaphysics in politics, however, certain clear differences appeared between Jaspers, Arendt and Heidegger. Heidegger and Arendt indicated that the freedom of politics must also involve an attack on natural law; indeed, they saw natural law, like technology, as a distension of a falsely self-authorizing moral will. Heidegger's ontology, as discussed, clearly opposed all non-historical ideas of rights Arendt also saw the condition of authentic politics as founded not in laws, but in *actions, promises* and *remembrance:* in spontaneous yet binding agreements between political agents and in the recollection of earlier words, existence and actions.[19] Like Heidegger, she concluded that genuine politics is politics without metaphysics: it is politics in which human spontaneity segregates itself from direct end-subordination (either technical or ethical) and spontaneously enacts the conditions of a world of freedom. She therefore eliminated all universal or perennial purposes from political order, and she saw the order of freedom as a radically and spontaneously reshaped horizon of action. Unlike Heidegger and Arendt, Jaspers did not fully share the vision of the entirely self-creating human polity, and he was reluctant to identify the human being, liberated from all transcendental or natural-legal principles, as the creative origin of politics. Indeed, his critique of technology was always guided by the assumption that the ideas of humanity which are eroded and debased by technology are in fact metaphysical elements of human being: he suggested in consequence that an authentically human polity cannot be founded entirely *without metaphysics* or without 'transcendence'.[20] The legitimacy of the polity ultimately relies, he concluded, on its representation of *supra-political* principles of reason, in which citizens confront the ideated forms of their integrity and authenticity.[21] This representation can only be accomplished by rational statesmen who project binding ideas of moral and natural correctness and by the ethical precepts embedded in constitutional orders. The constitution, therefore, is a document that both binds the polity to metaphysical ideas of ethical commitment, yet which also engages human beings in active political discourse and objectively formed identities.

The political views that shaped the formative period of post-1945 German politics, therefore, moved between anthropological and metaphysical accounts of the sources of political legitimacy. Nonetheless, all converged in the demand that human life should be saved from its technological reduction to an object of 'utilitarian functions'.[22] All, moreover, indicated that the true polity is a spontaneously human polity, not one dominated by abstracted or formally metaphysical objectives of the will.

Technology, the legal state and the functional state

The argument that technology erodes the 'anthropological precondition' of political legitimacy was also widely taken up by more mainstream institutional theorists and political scientists, especially by those addressing the problems of the legal state in the early Federal Republic.[23] Critical reflection on technology at this time coincided, most particularly, with the broad expression of concern about the rapidly evolving welfare state and the corporate techniques of governance that accompanied the evolution of the social-market economy pioneered by Konrad Adenauer and Ludwig Erhard. It was widely argued in the 1950s that under the welfare state the political system had been transformed into a technical apparatus of planning and regulation, which was founded, not in democratic consensus, but in pragmatic bargains between parties and interest groups. As a result of this, it was claimed, the state forfeited its original representative – or truly *political* – character; it lost connection with the vital and ideal (or human) orientations of its citizens; and it obtained its legitimacy by technical means – through the strategic allocation of resources and the palliation of material imbalances in society.[24] It was thus asserted, at different points in the political spectrum, that the evolution of welfare state after 1949 led to a thorough *materialization* or *privatization* of politics, in which constitutive political power was transferred from citizens to civil or economic associations and lobbies, which then assumed a dominant position in the process of legitimization and legislation.[25] As a consequence, it was argued, the original idea of democracy – namely, that public power represents a united public body of citizens and that public laws communicate public interests through society – was supplanted by a technical system of social management, in which government was held in thrall to rival private interests. This, in turn, prevented the emergence of a founding consensus about the problems and objects of governance, and it transformed legislation into a series of technical or technological processes of disposition and administration.

Underlying these analyses of the welfare state in the 1950s was the claim that welfare democracy also caused a transformation in the role and the character of the citizen and in the personal preconditions of political life. Owing to the increasing concentration of laws and policies on material welfare, the citizen, ideally the subject of legitimate democratic power and law, was allowed to degenerate into a mere passive object of material allocation, administration and technical assignation. Underlying this claim, in turn, was the more fundamental argument that the democratic state must have a determinate anthropological foundation. It must have its legal origins in human 'self-determination':[26] that is, in the idea of the person as an active legal agent who requires self-expression in universally applied laws and whose needs are not reducible to functional exigencies and cannot be satisfied by purely technical administrative operations. Only where democracy has this human foundation, consequently, is it a truly legitimate or truly *political* order.[27] The technical apparatus of modern governmental systems obscures the integral origin of democratic law, and it only acknowledges the presence of humanity in the political process as a unit of primary material needs, to be satisfied through private acts of planning, allocation and satisfaction. Technically oriented political systems, consequently, cannot found themselves or their laws in a representation of the full character of the human person, and they can therefore only purchase their legitimacy through the material application of law, and so by spuriously *technical* means.

Despite this humanist orientation in philosophy and political science in the early Federal Republic of Germany, however, many of the most theoretically influential social and political doctrines of this time were not opposed to the influence of technology in democratic life, and they were deeply sceptical about the humanist accent in liberal and left-liberal examinations of democracy. For example, Heidegger's own view on technology and on the role of technology in politics contained certain ambiguities, which at times moved him away from an unequivocal rejection of technology. At one level, clearly, Heidegger argued for a hermeneutical or late-historicist notion of human determinacy, which indicated that the original historical location of human worldliness is threatened by the instrumental or metaphysical imperatives of technology.[28] At the same time, however, he also denounced the humanist concepts used by theoretical stances hostile to technology, and he saw the normatively inflected constructions of human agency in humanism as products of the same metaphysical legacy that produced technology. He consequently argued that both the preponderance of technology and the humanistic anthropologies of its adversaries are related expressions of a metaphysical worldview that construes all life as centred in human purposes and makes all life accountable to norms and objectives deduced from these purposes. Humanism, he concluded, is not an acceptable alternative to technology: humanistic thinking cannot counteract the pervasive influence of metaphysics in technology, and it can only reorient the critique of metaphysics into alternative metaphysical attitudes.[29]

The critical relation between humanity and technology, Heidegger consequently indicated, is an argument between two moments within the same metaphysical constellation, and he saw the belief that human beings might be able to deduce values or laws which immediately place their polities on discernibly human foundations as no less disruptive than the metaphysical system of technology. It is only through a more acquiescent acceptance of the objective conditions of being under technology, he thus suggested, that the real end of metaphysics can be imagined or experienced. For this reason, he ultimately opted for an attitude of indifference to technology, and he finally construed technology as nothing more than a neutral condition of modern being in which the specific historical form of modern life is objectively expressed. He in fact described technology, like other forms of historical and quotidian existence, as a 'region [{.. .}] where truth occurs'.[30] Although he claimed that it obstructs the human historical domain, therefore, Heidegger saw in technology a particular objective form of historicity, and he implied that resistance to this form could not be proposed without recourse to rather crudely schematic accounts of humanity as a universal propensity for moral agreement and legislative autonomy. In Heidegger's later work, therefore, the hermeneutical critique of metaphysics as technology and natural science gradually fused with his wider critique of metaphysics as Kantian moral universalism and naïve humanism, and it produced an outlook which saw the adequate approach to *techne* as one based in resolute acceptance. Indeed, although commencing as a hermeneutical commentary on metaphysics, Heidegger's work also cleared the terrain for a more functionalist attitude, which dismissed moral-anthropological critiques of technology and which finally affirmed technology as the modern shape of *fate*.

This Heideggerain ambiguity was intensified in the works of Hans Freyer, who derided all attempts to focus theories of government around humanist paradigms. In his writings of the early 1930s, Freyer had argued that modern political systems are inevitably structured around bureaucratic decisions or plans, and the legitimacy of these decisions is not founded in any anthropological facts of human character or interest.[31] After 1945, he expanded this earlier argument, emphasizing that the political institutions of modern society cannot be viewed as corresponding to integral needs or rational prescriptions of human beings. Definitions of legitimate government as an 'essential order', which reflects constitutive needs of human life are, he claimed, not relevant to modern institutions, and it is anachronistic to presuppose that the institutions of the political system might give form to or be bound by laws that human beings, following their natural emphases, might prescribe or deduce for themselves.[32] The human being, in short, is not the subjective source of law and power in modern society; the human being is, in fact, entirely 'functionalized',[33] and it becomes relevant to socio-political institutions only as a highly 'reduced' object of technological administration and material allocation.[34] This *dehumanization* of power and law, Freyer concluded, is especially characteristic of the modern welfare state. The welfare state is a system that transforms the human being into a 'bearer of a determinate, schematizable and organizable interest',[35] and it legitimizes itself, not by facilitating conditions of human self-legislation, but as it deploys its technological resources to offer goods and material compensations to citizens as 'surrogate forms of individual freedom'.[36] Underlying Freyer's approach was the conviction, close to Heidegger, that the imputation of a distinctively human substructure to political institutions is a remnant of archaic interpretations of society, which imagine social order as according with moral-metaphysical or teleological constructions of progress and right.[37] Such constructions, however, cannot be applied to modern complex societies, and they succeed only in misinterpreting the factual and technical sources of modern legitimacy.

Similar ideas also appeared in the works of Arnold Gehlen who, like Freyer and Heidegger, had also been badly contaminated by his proximity to certain aspects of National Socialist ideology. Gehlen echoed Freyer's argument that modern social institutions are not transparent to the human being as a centre of subjective agency and moral prescription. In fact, he expanded this claim to state that modern institutions form accretions of order *against* human beings and they replace human beings as the structural determinants of social life.[38] In modern societies, therefore, concrete human beings recede into contingent areas outside the spheres of direct institutional relevance, and they do not and cannot provide a legislative foundation for political power. The basis of modern institutions resides, in fact, not in the human being, but in *technology* and in technological instruments of regulation and management; technology thus assumes the role originally fulfilled by the human being, as a force that shapes and structures the objective conditions of social life.[39] As a result of this, government is not the public representation of human needs or character, but an 'aggregate of manifold modes of function',[40] which demonstrates its legitimacy solely through administrative competence.

In contrast to Freyer, who, close to Schmitt, still saw modern society as shaped by the decisions of powerful figures and suggested that the means of technology remain subject to volitional control by political leaders,[41] Gehlen argued that modern society, especially under the welfare state, is increasingly inclined to pluralistic or polyarchical techniques of governance. Personal 'macro-decisions', he thus explained, play a rapidly diminishing role in social organization, and the function of state power is gradually minimized as social action is regulated by corporate strategies for balancing interests and for ensuring technical stability between social groups.[42] Despite these differences, however, the approaches of Gehlen and Freyer converged in the fact that they described modern society as essentially *post-personal* and that they minimized the role of consensual legislation or shared volition in the ordering of socio-political institutions. Government by technology, both suggested, is the inevitable condition of modern social order. It is a condition that has freed itself from normative processes and anthropological fixity and where laws have been dislocated from all human foundations. Indeed, both intimated that recourse to humanist foundations in sociological or political analysis merely reflects a desperate tendency to cling to counterfactual or essentialist paradigms. To be a humanist in modern society, in fact, is to be a metaphysician; it is to resort to factually invalidated ideas of founding essence and to assume, in deep self-delusion, that the great complexity of modern institutions can be directed in accordance with norms deduced by human reason and articulating constitutive human interests or needs.

These arguments culminated in the writings of Helmut Schelsky. In his earlier works, Schelsky described modern society as characterized by the increasing power of technology and by the evolution of the 'technological state'.[43] Under the governance of this state, he explained, politics 'in the sense of normative will-formation' becomes impossible, and power is applied merely through the functional disposition over scientific and administrative resources.[44] Societies governed by such states, Schelsky explained, are not necessarily 'anti-democratic'. However, in such societies, the state forfeits its classical legal-democratic 'substance',[45] and it generates legitimacy for itself through technical processes, as it demonstrates its adeptness in responding to administrative challenges. Schelsky was even more emphatic than Freyer and Gehlen that the invocation of humanist preconditions in the explanation of political and institutional legitimacy reflects a retrograde 'metaphysical longing', to which no objective reality corresponds.[46] Like Gehlen and Freyer, therefore, he viewed technology as the realized form of human existence, and he saw all attempts critically to re-centre this reality on the human being as reliant on archaic perspectives, which simplify and distort the actual nature of social being.

Metaphysics and the constitution

The battle lines of political debate in the early Federal Republic were therefore drawn between humanists and technocrats. At the centre of the rivalry between these two camps was, once again, a debate over metaphysics, and both camps justified their own position by accusing each other of distorting the authentic nature of political order by deploying metaphysical categories of analysis and prescription. The humanist political outlooks of this time founded their claims in earlier hermeneutical or moral anthropological theories, and they argued that modern government has integrated the originally purposive and metaphysical features of technology, and it has consequently alienated itself from the constitutive characteristics of human political life.

In contrast to such humanist thinking, however, the social theorists of the early Federal Republic who were more enthusiastic about the role of technology in modern life also claimed that their opponents relied on simplified ethical humanist accounts of modern society and had not separated their analysis from the residues of metaphysics. These theorists viewed the hope that society might, in its entirety, be reconsolidated around legal or moral norms or the authentic orientations of human beings as reflecting an outmoded commentary on how modern societies operate. This hope could only be sustained by nostalgic reference to invalidated philosophical traditions, which view the political apparatus as an essential person, and which fail to appreciate the functional complexity and contingency of modern political institutions.

The antagonism between these divergent views on politics, metaphysics and humanism culminated in the rivalry between distinct analyses of the role of the constitution in the early Federal Republic. As discussed above, Jaspers' influential writings on constitutional reality claimed that the constitution of the republic must articulate a 'basic decision', placing the republic on entirely moral and fully evolved human foundations.[47] At the same time, Dolf Sternberger gave further substance to the emerging doctrine of constitutional patriotism, and he argued that the constitution should form an interpretive horizon in which the political identities of all citizens of the new republic might be shaped and elaborated.[48] At the most left-leaning extreme of political discourse in the early Federal Republic, Wolfgang Abendroth proposed a Marxist-humanist model of the constitution which argued that legitimate constitutional documents should enshrine the rightful equality of the human being in all aspects of its life – in its social, political and economic activities.[49] Abendroth returned to earlier ideas of the material constitution and he claimed that political legitimacy can only be obtained through a system of constitutional order that expands the formal constitutional rights of equality and justice to all spheres of social exchange, and that integrates the human being into constitutional life as a citizen possessing political and material rights of participation or co-possession (*Teilhabe*). Similar arguments in fact extended across the divide between the early Federal Republic and the German Democratic Republic. Early legal and constitutional doctrines in the Democratic Republic also often viewed legitimate constitutions as documents that place the state on determinately human ground and incorporate the 'entire person' and all 'qualities of human personality' in their construction of the legal person and the legal addressee.[50] These socialist-humanist doctrines argued that only socialist constitutions, with formalized rights of material equality and provisions for the abolition of private ownership of the means of production, can ensure that the state integrates and represents the personality of its citizens in all its dimensions.[51] All of these views, whether supporting a liberal or a socialist constitution, construed the constitution as a specific site of human agency and moral self-realization, where a particular image of authentic humanity is cast as the founding source for all laws of the legitimate republic.

In contrast to these perspectives, the functionalist social theorists of the early Federal Republic denied that the constitution of the state has its function in representing any distinctively human contents or universal human rights in the state or in the laws of the state. The assumption that the constitution is a bearer of human rights or interests is in fact, they argued, one of the more unfortunate legacies of the unreflected humanism of nineteenth-century liberalism. In response to such constructions, Freyer argued that constitutions could not be drafted in 'accordance with conceptual principles'; in fact, the attempt to tie constitutional legitimacy to prior norms tends to undermine the perceived legitimacy of the constitution and to erode its technical power.[52] The constitution should be viewed at most, he explained, as a regulatory or prescriptive document, ordering and sanctioning certain types of behaviour and so underpinning the stability of the state.[53] Schelsky also set out a functional account of constitutional operations. The role of the constitution, he claimed, is to confer a formal and irreversible structure on the functions of state and to alleviate political institutions of their need for constant self-justification and self-explication.[54] It is erroneous to assume, he claimed, that a constitution expresses 'democratic' human interests, which are articulated as binding norms and imposed on the state in the form of rights.[55] Instead, constitutions obtaining legitimacy serve and reflect a need for stability,[56] and they instigate stability both in the people, who rely upon the objective administrative reliability of the state, and also in the state, which protects itself through its constitution from the excessive demands of the population.[57] The function of the constitution, in short, is that it neutralizes debates on certain principles; it gives enduring form to the state; and it creates functional conditions throughout society that are likely to serve the stability of the state.

Such anti-normative approaches to the constitution found their culminating expression in the works of Schmitt's old pupil, Ernst Forsthoff, who applied arguments of clearly Schmittian derivation to the legal-political contours of the early Federal Republic. Forsthoff's primary concern was to show that through its construction as a welfare state the state has been subject to a process of socialization and corporate control that undermines its ability to act as a legal state or as a genuine democratic state. As a welfare state, the state is 'instrumentalized' by the social groups that seek a share of the resources that it distributes,[58] and the social groups obtaining a stake in the state assume the status of 'privileged legal classes', who obtain direct influence on policy and legislation. The privileged position of these groups then undermines the basic conditions of legal freedom and equality guaranteed by democratic constitutions, and it deprives the state of its authentic character as a neutral representative and legislator, as it means that some social agents have greater opportunity to receive favourable treatment by law than others.[59] For this reason, Forsthoff concluded that the overriding function of the constitution of a democratic legal state is to protect the preconditions of legal application from colonization by political factions inside and outside the state.[60] The constitution is not an integrative system serving to facilitate full social inclusion or 'unity', or a normative embodiment of a human vision underlying all of society.[61] In fact, the constitution has its greatest justification as a functional device for placing limits on the extent to which the state integrates persons and personal interests and for ensuring that laws are implemented in like manner throughout society. The function of the constitution in the legal order of the state, Forsthoff concluded, is rendered deeply precarious and problematic in welfare democracies. Where law is used programmatically to regulate social problems and allocate material goods, he claimed, this tends to erode the legal foundations of the democratic constitution, and to transform the democratic legal state into an 'administrative state', which applies law as an objective medium of control and integration, not as a neutral and formal guarantee of democratic rights and procedures.[62] Unlike other technocrats, Forsthoff did not argue that the state should expand its technological structure;[63] this, in fact, would be to exceed the proper limits of state action. However, he evidently viewed the state as an apparatus with neutral or 'technical' character, whose efficacy depends on its liberation from excessive material, moral or human burdens.[64] Indeed, the ability of the state to represent the interests of humanity and to secure conditions of individual liberty is at its greatest precisely where it is not defined as the omnipresent defender and protector of human interests and liberties.[65]

The constitutional debates of the early Federal Republic thus revolved around the humanity of the state and its capacity for representing human laws in the form of a constitution. Representatives of the left-leaning or liberal-democratic side argued that legitimate democracy could only be secured as a human democracy, through a humanization of state and law, an integration of human beings as free participants in political process and political identity, and a rejection of the technological metaphysics dominating the state. Representatives of the more conservative side claimed that government (even, or especially, democratic government) is only stabilized through its dehumanization and through the resultant expulsion of all elements of normative metaphysics from the state.

12 Jürgen Habermas and Niklas Luhmann

Two rival critiques of metaphysics

Habermas: a new legal humanism

The works of Jürgen Habermas and Niklas Luhmann formed the two most salient and influential political outlooks of late twentieth-century Germany. Indeed, the works of these two theorists, together with those of Habermas's US-American interlocutor, John Rawls, set the basic contours for international debate in political theory in the last three decades of the twentieth century. At the heart of the works of Habermas and Luhmann are two sharply divergent analyses of the relations between law, politics, reason and metaphysics, and of the legal sources of legitimate political power. Both Habermas and Luhmann developed their theories as conflicting accounts of the positivization of law in modern society and of the necessary conditions of legal obligation, equality and constitutional rule characterizing democratic legitimacy. Central to the works of both these theorists is the claim that law and power are co-evolutionary, that the increasing positivization of law in modern societies inevitably shapes and rationalizes the exercise of power and that the most legitimate form of governance in modern society is a legal state under positive law. Central to both these theories, moreover, is an attempt, in starkly different terms, to account for rational freedom and political legitimacy as attributes of a free society, without any dependence on metaphysical concepts.

Habermas's early writings, especially *Structural Transformation of the Public Sphere* (1962), sought to provide a new analysis of the founding conditions of political legitimacy and, specifically, to define and describe the human dispositions that enable the emergence of a legitimate governmental apparatus. These early writings revolved around the claim that the legitimacy of a political system depends upon the existence of a public sphere in which citizens, freely exercising their powers of reason in debate and open communication, arrive at insights and agreements by which the state can be critically held to account.[1] The public sphere, consequently, is the genetic origin of legitimate law, which shapes the exercise of legitimate power. In the public sphere, agreements forming public opinion serve to elaborate consensus on major points of political debate, to provide legal criteria under which power can and must explain and justify itself,[2] and so ultimately to found power in transparent and rationally generalized agreements.[3] In accounting for the normative functions of the public sphere, however, Habermas argued that it can only elaborate legal-rational agreements where it is not annexed from above by immediately politicized prerogatives, where it is not determined from below by a non-reconcilable set of private or material interests and where, in consequence, the freedom of discursive interaction between citizens is not burdened by external coercion or prior interest. The 'fundamental separation' of state and society is, thus, the precondition of a public sphere;[4] the historical emergence of a public sphere in fact coincided with the epoch in European social evolution when state and society began to separate at the end of the late-feudal or mercantilist era.[5] The public sphere, in other words, is a place where participants in debate suspend their purely private motives and where they allow a common will to be formed through discursive-rational or consensual mediation of opinions, renouncing all fully exclusive interests. This can only occur if the public sphere is authentically public: that is, if agents are freed from their purely economic or politically ascribed roles. Through its evolution as a space of free discourse, Habermas added, the public sphere conditioned and accelerated the emergence of the early Western European democracies, especially the early parliamentary system established in Britain. In these states, he argued, public agreements were produced through unrestricted public debate in salons, coffee houses and in early journalism, and participants in these debates comprised a relatively unified set of interests, so that public discourse was not disrupted, as in later mass democracies, by openly hostile and divergent concepts of necessity and legitimacy. The early formation of the public sphere constituted an epochal evolutionary event in which both the political and the religious determination of public interaction abated and human beings were freed from their purely materialized social roles in order to participate in processes of open communicative exchange, based in the free 'rational communication of a public of educated people'.[6] The early public sphere was, therefore, the space of Enlightenment, of *modernity,* or even of *humanity.* It was the realm of distinctively human interactions, which evolved as humans began to generate autonomous and post-traditional and post-metaphysical accounts of their own obligations, duties and constitutive freedoms and as they articulated these freedoms through a legal rejection of political heteronomy and 'coercion'.[7]

In his early writings, Habermas defined a legitimate political system as one whose laws evolve from or are at least rationalized by agreements between citizens interacting freely in the public sphere. In a state of this kind, he claimed, agents in the public sphere are the free subjects or authors of political power, and they recognize the will of the state and the laws that structure the objective conditions of their lives as originally derived from their own subjective/rational accounts of their freedoms and their rights. Under a legitimate state, thus, power is not experienced as an exceptional or coercive fact of domination, but as an accretion of communication whose evolution is inseparable from the common legal form of human reason. Underpinning the legitimate state, therefore, is an idea of a world in which law and power are positively reunited, and in which reason and freedom are mediated in speech. A free public sphere, in other words, gives rise to a legitimate state as a realm of freedom under rational laws, in which the human being discursively elaborates commonly acknowledged ideas of freedom and insists that positive public laws should be accountable to these ideas. Laws produced in a free public sphere are *positive,* and they can be applied through normal executive and judicial processes. Yet these laws also have a distinction against merely positive laws, as they channel anthropologically constitutive elements of consensus and value-rationality into the state. In his account of the public sphere, therefore, Habermas saw public communication as a medium that can overcome the distinction between positivity and natural legal or metaphysical necessity, and that can articulate positive laws which possess absolute necessity, as consensus, as their own positive content.

In the public sphere, therefore, human agents articulate the positive conditions of necessary freedom, and they construct a legal order that gives resolutely non-metaphysical form to the idea of necessary freedom.

In his account of the public sphere, however, Habermas asserted that modern political systems usually fall short of the normative ideals and the institutional realities of classical democracy, and they fail to generate reliable conditions of legitimacy. Modern democracies tend to forfeit their democratic legitimacy because, as mass democracies, they incorporate radically antagonistic economic interests in their franchises, and they are forced to use corporate and palliative techniques to pacify their constituents and to maintain an acceptable level of legal compliance throughout society. As a result of this, it is structural to modern political systems that they are unable to differentiate between private and political functions. On one hand, modern states allow lobbies and powerful associations to bid for material resources, to vie with each other for preference and status within the state apparatus, and so to assume quasi-legislative power at the fringes of government. They therefore directly *privatize* the public resources of the polity, and they permit private interests to be translated, without discursive mediation, into law. On the other hand, modern states act as primary distributors and contractors in the private economy,[8] and they colonize areas of private interaction in order to stabilize a passive social consensus, likely to provide approval for the continued exercise of power in its present form.[9] They therefore directly *politicize* areas of social interaction that are properly private, and they begin to show symptoms of *refeudalization* as they assume increasingly far-reaching directive powers in the private sphere. Modern political systems, in short, are no longer founded in the processes of consensus formation made possible by the existence of a free and unregulated public sphere. Instead, they have their foundations in fragile balances of private interest between political parties, unions and powerful lobbies, all of which ceaselessly compete for influence on the resources of government, and, importantly, they use technology as an increasingly pervasive medium of legislation, pacification and social management. As a result, the public sphere, initially the subject and origin of law and legitimate sovereignty, is transformed into an objective realm of conflicting interests, to which law is applied, from above, in order to underwrite private compromises between private associations and to maintain acceptable levels of socio-political stability and general compliance.[10] Owing to the change in the structure of the public sphere, the human foundation of democratic legitimacy – namely, that citizens freely exercise their faculties of reason in processes of communicative exchange and so authorize, subjectively, the laws that objectively form their obligations – is dissolved, and the consensual form of the legal state is replaced by a semi-authoritarian administrative apparatus. In this apparatus, legitimacy (as compliance) is purchased through the strategic use of law to effect material distribution, through effective socio-economic engineering and through symbolic processes for gathering acclamation: that is, through media, stage-managed elections and dramatized conflicts between interest groups. The public sphere, in short, becomes *manufactured:* it is transformed into an arena that is both technologically administered from above and reprivatized from below, as it is fragmented into a series of loosely atomized and competitive interest blocs. In modern mass democracies, the constitutive objectives of human life – the unification of reason and freedom, the production of states founded in the recognition of rationally mediated subjective freedoms – are betrayed. Instead, citizens confront the objective conditions of their lives as ideologically rationalized and technologically manufactured simulations of freedom.[11]

In setting out his early consensual-discursive model of democracy, Habermas honed his theory on a series of philosophical perspectives by which he was deeply influenced and in relation to which he sought to define his own work. First, in these arguments Habermas clearly elaborated a critical-reconstructive interpretation of Kant. At the most general level, the early Habermas was very close to Kant's account of reason as a faculty of autonomy. He concurred with Kant's claim that, once freed from religious or metaphysical determinacy, human reason organizes action and behaviour in accordance with generalized principles, or with 'validity claims', which are not based in factual reality but have their evidential support in reason alone.[12] For this reason, like Kant, he argued that human existence after the Enlightenment is marked by an increment of rational autonomy and by an increasing rationalization of human motivations. At a more specifically political level, then, throughout his career his work has also revolved around an affirmative response to the central claim of the Enlightenment: namely, that the free use of reason is the sole source of legitimate public authority, and political legitimacy depends upon the ability of the political system to universalize its legal foundations in accordance with rational ideas of freedom, as a *Rechtsstaat.* Following Kant, therefore, his work has also been shaped by the argument that the public exercise of reason has its primary objective legal form in the insistence on *basic rights,* and that the legitimate political order construes all addressees of its laws as entitled both to full rights of legal recognition and to rights of legislatory engagement and participation in the political process.[13] Rights, for both Kant and Habermas, are the moment in the legitimate political order where the subjective freedoms of citizens are formulated as articles of objective necessity.

Whilst approving Kantian objectives, however, the works of the early Habermas also indicated that Kant's theory of practical reason did not successfully consolidate the human sources of law and political power, and that his attempt to give rational form to human freedom in the state relied on falsely dualistic or paradoxical constructs of the ideal person as a metaphysical *noumenon.* He saw Kant's claim that practical reason is the source of law as serving, in its final implications, only to concentrate the law on solitary processes of transcendental deduction, as conflating the conditions of legitimacy in politics with formal-moral analysis and as failing thoroughly to account for the exercise of freedom as a necessary aspect in the formation of legitimacy. He consequently saw the Kantian legal state as providing only for a highly abstracted legal state, as offering only an 'intelligible' form for the unity of wills underlying valid law, as failing to reconcile positive and necessary laws, and, in consequence, as merely enshrining rights and freedoms as static principles externally allocated to law's addressees.[14] On the whole, he argued that Kantian legal ideas do not successfully reflect the element of free participation in legal formation and that they offer only a very curtailed description of human freedom under laws in the state. The rights and laws of a genuine legal state are obtained, he claimed, through the rational-communicative mediation of ideas of freedom pursued by different wills in the public sphere, and freedom, if exercised as a communicative freedom, has a directly constitutive role in the process of legitimate law-formation. The origin of legitimate law must, thus, always be sought, not in the solitary aspect of practical reason, nor in the determination of the contents of freedom by reason presiding over the will, but in the actively disclosed aspect of communicative reason and in the active-discursive exercise of freedom. Kant, consequently, saw the reconciliation of freedom and reason as reason's own achievement, and he saw rights enshrining the unity of freedom and reason as formal elements of the state's constitution, given by the state itself. Habermas, in contrast, saw the reconciliation of reason and freedom as a process in which reason and freedom are mutually constitutive, and he construed rights as actively and commonly elaborated expressions of freedom, integrated into the state through the participatory formation of a common will. For Habermas, in short, Kant's metaphysical transcendentalism prevented him from elaborating a fully conclusive account of legal foundation, and his work remained falsely centred on a construction of rational law as a law, lastly of unfreedom, produced by the state.

In these communicative alterations to Kantian legal theory, Habermas also moved closer towards a more evidently Hegelian account of realized natural law. Although he has generally attached himself much less explicitly to Hegelian than to Kantian ideas, his construct of the public sphere incorporates the claim that rational laws can only be formed through inclusive processes of recognition between concrete subjects. These laws must be constituted through an objective reconciliation of diverse wills and diverse ideas of freedom and through a rational reconciliation of interests which, at a purely material level, might appear extremely divergent and not susceptible to mediation. In this respect, Habermas echoed Hegel's earlier critique of Kant, and he insisted that legitimacy in the state should be conceived as the material form of a broad-based objective unity of wills, mediated through discourse, not of a formal or transcendental will, determined by abstract norms or ideas. Clearly, Habermas did not follow Hegel's suggestion that the objectively reconciled will is the result of the underlying formation of human spirit. On the contrary, he was adamant that reason has no teleological basis, but that, as communicative reason, it is guided only by an anthropologically formative orientation towards consensus and commonality. The objective unity of rational wills supporting a legitimate political system, therefore, is a unity of wills that unify themselves through rationally evidenced claims, not a unity of wills brought about by the metaphysical unfolding of spirit. Nonetheless, Habermas followed Hegel in denying that the conditions of legitimacy can be deduced in abstraction from all historical determinacy, and he clearly argued that the legislative functions of reason are only realized through the establishment of determinately historical concepts of freedom, to which many wills accede.

In his reflections on modern democracy, moreover, Habermas's work also set out a critical reconstruction of Marx, which involved a fusion of Marxist and Kantian ideas. In his first major works, Habermas integrated Marxist analysis of ideology into his critique of Kantian constitutional theory. He argued, for example, that the metaphysical minimalism of the Kantian legal state and Kantian ideas of political freedom were in part determined by the fact that the constitutional theorists of the Enlightenment based their accounts of legitimacy in the demands of a closed franchise, comprising only 'owners of private property' and 'competitive commodity owners'.[15] The main error of the early Enlightenment, thus, was that it assumed that all wills could be integrated in the state by simple ideas of reason, and that a minimal state apparatus suffices to guarantee reasonable freedom in society. The reason for this simplistic analysis was that the early Enlightenment assumed that politically relevant society would always be based in a narrow sector of material interests and that members of this society would easily agree on basic points of legal order. Habermas consequently indicated that early liberal legal states could only produce ideological accounts of their legitimacy, and their claims to universal validity were always undermined by their failure to reflect on how material disparities and social conflicts shape the law and by their inability to recognize that acute differences of interest cannot be reconciled through formal-monadic ideas of reason.

In his later works, then, Habermas expanded this perspective, now seconding Marx's claim that there always exists an inevitable conflict between capitalism and democracy, that capitalism undermines the content of democratic law and that genuine democratic or rational law cannot simply be imposed on the state as a uniform set of norms, but must reflect fully universal and socially deep-lying agreements. In the 1970s, his thought on these questions was strongly influenced by his collaborator, Claus Offe, who revised Marxist theories of class conflict to develop a neo-functionalist analysis of political legitimacy, examining the technical strategies of 'crisis management' and the 'pacifying functions', which modern welfare states deploy in order to obscure the absence of full consensus in their laws and to generate ongoing motivations for obedience.[16] At this point, Habermas argued that the states of modern democracies inevitably struggle to produce and maintain integral conditions of legitimacy, and they struggle to integrate their citizens under securely accepted laws. This is because, as late-capitalist states, they have acquired far-reaching responsibility for processes of investment, accumulation and distribution, located outside the state apparatus in liberal-capitalist democracies. Because of this, these states assume final accountability for engendering economic growth and promoting selective social enrichment; they organize their foundations around non-universalizable motives and prerogatives; and they cannot call upon integral rational consensus as the ground of their legitimacy. As a consequence of this, then, the state is forced constantly to regulate its relation to the economy by pursuing 'market-substituting or market-compensating' policies in order to maximize stability in politically sensitive sectors of the economy and to pacify social agents who are not the immediate beneficiaries of its economic policies.[17] Because of this, moreover, the state internalizes conflicts and antagonisms produced by the economy, and it is obliged ceaselessly to regulate and mollify these as a precondition of its own security. As a distributor and legislator, furthermore, the state repoliticizes these economic antagonisms, and it is forced to concentrate policy-making on their pacification. As a result of this, finally, the state burdens itself with an 'intensified need for legitimacy',[18] as it is constantly called upon to legitimize its functions to different social groups and, owing to its lack of substantial legitimatory foundations, to adjust its policies to sporadic challenges and imbalances in society. The late-capitalist state thus legitimizes itself, not through consensual foundation but through the application of palliative techniques. These techniques include, first, the administration of material goods as 'compensations' to interested or dissatisfied parties in society. Second, they include the preservation (through media and entertainment) of a 'de-politicized public sphere', so that underlying antagonisms are unlikely to threaten the stability of the system.[19] Third, they include the deployment of instrumental or technocratic policies, based in strategic consensus between appointed elites. The latent lack of legitimacy in the late-capitalist system becomes most problematically manifest, however, when the financial resources of the state are not sufficient for it to fulfil the demands for compensations addressed to it or when material expectations are expressed that cannot be satisfied through 'systemically conformist compensations' – through financial allocation.[20] In such times, especially during periods of economic recession, the state is always likely to suffer chronic crises of legitimacy. This can only be avoided, Habermas concluded, through the development of more substantial methods of producing legitimacy, in which the foundations of the polity are not derived from selective material interests or instrumental forms of systemic rationality but from 'rational consensus' between free participants in discourse.[21] Only such a consensus can provide a foundation for the passing of laws that reflect contents distinct from precariously balanced private interests and that command obedience (that is, obtain legitimacy) as reflections of demonstrable *human* interests.[22]

At this level, then, Habermas integrated aspects of Marxist analysis into a theory of political formation that, whilst wishing to preserve an underlying account of legitimacy, accepted Marx's view that the state's internalization of private prerogatives and private laws obstructs its evolution as a legal state. As the substructure for this theory, Habermas set out a typological account of human reason and human law in which he argued that there are two typically distinct kinds of law, reflecting typically different functions of human reason. First, he argued that there are *instrumental* modes of reason, based in 'technical rules'. The function of instrumental reason is to integrate external nature (that is, natural resources) into society – this rationality reflects the prerogatives of the *system* of society and it supports the social functions of political steering and economic administration. This rationality, moreover, generates technical or end-oriented laws, the purpose of which is to consolidate control over natural objects. At the same time, however, there are also dialogical or consensual modes of reason, whose task is to integrate internal nature (the nature of human beings) into society. Human beings can only be fully integrated through reason which acts as a 'medium of norms requiring justification' – that is, which provides and requires rationally sustained evidence as the foundation for consensus, identity formation and social integration. Internal nature, Habermas thus argued, is integrated into society in the *life-world,* which he defined as an arena of interaction constituted through reflected language and oriented towards communicative-rational consensus.[23] The rationality of the life-world thus also generates consensual or dialogical laws as it integrates human agents through free rational discourse and rationally acceded principles of obligation and free necessity. Habermas was clear that all societies require both life-world and system and that all societies need capacities for the technical disposition over natural resources. However, he also accentuated the fact that the rational and legal structure of the life-world is the eminently human aspect of rationality and law. Consensual laws produced in the life-world, above all, constitute the universal element of political legitimacy, and a genuinely legitimate state will always integrate citizens under laws originating in the life-world. In setting out this theory, however, Habermas followed Marx in concluding that late-capitalist states obstruct the integrative communications in the life-world, and they stabilize society around rational principles derived primarily from the sphere of systemic or technical administration. Indeed, in many instances, these states stabilize society around principles constitutively anchored in particular economic interests, and they apply laws as coercive norms in order to uphold compliance with the existing economic apparatus. Modern society, in consequence, is dominated by *inhuman* and *unnatural* laws, which are instrumentally stabilized against the life-world, which have their origins in technical/systemic acts of control and management and which suppress the freely consensual or fully human element of reason. In his writings of the late 1970s and early 1980s, in fact, Habermas concluded that contemporary social and political life is determined by a thorough *colonization* of the life-world by the system and by a thorough domination of the consensual/normative aspect of law by more instrumental legal imperatives.[24] He thus echoed earlier claims in critical theory that, under late capitalism, the law has a *dual function*. Where it represents agreements genetically derived from the life-world, law articulates the constitutive freedoms of humanity. Systemic laws, however, which translate private-material prerogatives into public obligation, reflect a misconstruction of human life in which the founding possibility of objective freedom is negated.

Whilst building on aspects of Marx's political economy, however, Habermas also thoroughly modified elements of Marxist political thought. First, he opposed the implicit depreciation of law in Marxist theory, and he refused to see law exclusively as a medium of economic or instrumental rationality. In fact, against Marx, he argued that, although undoubtedly serving instrumental interests, it is characteristic of law that it can act as a particular bearer of 'norm rationality' through society,[25] and that its 'generality' is subject to 'autonomous justification'. Law, therefore, is at once an instrumental device, and it is a crucial site for the autonomous rationalization of human social roles, for guiding the rational evolution of society and for the consolidation of 'generalizable interests' in the institutional systems of society. On these grounds, Habermas concluded that law gives highest expression to human practical rationality: human subjectivity is, in fact, centred on 'law-forming power', and the human subject is depleted wherever this power is abrogated.[26] He consequently arrived at the conclusion, against Marx, that Kant's insistence that the political institutions of society must organize themselves around principles of rational autonomy should be upheld and that law can constitute a genuinely legitimate political system, motivating obedience through rational recognition of freedom under law.

With Marx and against Kant, however, he also concluded that the condition of rational autonomy under human laws is not merely a condition of transcendental moral self-legislation, which is indifferent to the sociological determination of human reason. The condition of autonomy can only be obtained through a reconstruction of reason in all its functions, and autonomy realized in the state will apply law as a medium for implementing genuinely universal agreements throughout all areas of social exchange.

In insisting that human reason can deduce laws that give public form to its highest potentials for freedom, furthermore, Habermas passionately negated the deterministic aspects of Marxist materialism, and he denied that there exist processes of social transformation that evolve in absolute independence of human agency, reason and intervention. Indeed, the legal aspect of his work was especially designed to contradict the evolutionary or systemic implications of dialectical materialism. Human reason, he insisted, is always able to set itself above its determination by purely material process or by private prerogative, and it is fundamental to reason that it can form laws that reflect its capacity for non-technical, non-material and non-ideological freedom. The determinist claim that humanity is regulated by material laws over which it has no power drastically undervalues, for Habermas, the legislative dimension of reason, and it in fact places human life under new conditions of technical heteronomy.

Habermas's work, in short, evolved through a series of critical receptions of dominant perspectives in the history of German political thought. Indeed, he ultimately turned against all his major philosophical precursors for much the same reason: he ultimately viewed their transcendental, teleological or deterministic accounts of law, politics and social evolution as distracting from the role of the integral human being as the legislative source and centre of human order. Against the analyses of Kant and Marx, especially, Habermas's notion of the human agent in the public sphere – as an agent, that is, who interacts without coercive intentions with other people, who is not determined exclusively by non-negotiable private or technical interests and who is oriented towards the production and acceptance of consensus as a token of the evidence and validity of its claims – is designed decisively to locate the human person at the origin of law and to comprehend valid laws as reflections of integrally human freedoms. In response to Marx, Habermas placed particular emphasis on the claim that the human being is the author of laws and that it can establish through law objectively necessary conditions for its freedom. In response to Kant, then, Habermas's theory sought to redevelop the original task of Enlightenment, finally to imagine the conditions of human freedom without any metaphysical support and so to realize the Kantian unity of reason and freedom as a condition freely elaborated by human beings, not by insubstantial noumena.

Running through Habermas's work is in fact the suggestion that the Enlightenment, as originally proposed by Kant, was an incomplete

Enlightenment. This Enlightenment attempted to construct a model of legitimate political order as a condition of freedom legislated by human reason, suspending all metaphysical and theological heteronomy. Enlightenment, however, remained a metaphysical Enlightenment, for it remained ensnared in metaphysical-transcendental conceptions of human autonomy and volition, and it was incapable of fully accounting for the role of human freedom in creating the preconditions of objectively valid law. A genuine Enlightenment would be a spoken Enlightenment, not a transcendental Enlightenment. Speech, for Habermas, is the authentic legislative foundation of modern secular societies. As speaking agents, human beings freely construct their own subjectivities on a natural/interactive basis, without any metaphysical addition, and as post-metaphysical speaking subjects they freely arrive at agreements and insights that shape their objective reality as an entirely post-metaphysical condition.[27] The interface between speech and law is, thus, the constitutive centre of Habermas's vision of post-metaphysical freedom and unity, and it is only where laws originate in the spoken or communicative form of reason that they finally place the Enlightenment dream of a rationally free state on fully human foundations.

Liberalism or republicanism?

Habermas's critique of the metaphysical Enlightenment also contains an attempt to combine the theoretical strengths of, and ultimately to resolve, the two great antinomies of Western political reflection: Kantian liberalism and Aristotelian republicanism.

Habermas has repeatedly defined the central claim of Kantian liberalism – namely, that political systems obtain legitimacy by recognizing the status of citizens as legal subjects and so as bearers of immutable rights that cannot be infringed by the state – as a claim of the most constitutive importance for modern political theory. However, he also examined this claim as a view that is, lastly, politically deficient, and that serves, by implication at least, to prop up a thin and negative model of democracy. In the Kantian model of legitimacy, he indicated, the freely participatory or active element of democratic foundation is devalued, the freedoms constituting legitimacy are rationally formulaic and minimal in content, and most freedoms are secured and practised outside the state, in the 'privatism' of politically neutralized areas of interaction.[28] For this reason, he argued, the laws of liberal polities, in the Kantian paradigm, do not act as a foundation for full political freedom and integration; they fail to enshrine integrally experienced freedoms in the state, or to secure deep popular support for the state; and they sanction, de facto, the dislocation of the economy and the administration from popular democratic control. Liberalism, consequently, offers only a truncated realization of the human being as a rationally free citizen or as an agent in a rationally free state: reason outweighs freedom in liberalism and the Kantian polity is always dominated by rational laws that construe freedom and its exercise in deeply reduced terms. Against this, Habermas then argued, the republican model of democratic order has the great strength that it adopts a much more positive and constitutive approach to the state as a changing state of freedom; it views all citizens as freely and actively implicated in the formation of the state; and it integrates citizens as freely constituent and participatory members of politically relevant society.[29] However, he suggested, republicanism also has the disadvantage that it is heavily burdened by its association with the European nation-states and with the history of European nationalism, that it often prioritizes integrated group-freedoms over particular freedoms and that it even risks eliminating or relativizing the guarantees of basic rights, which all democratic states must contain.[30] Republicanism, in short, underplays the legal-universal element in human self-realization, and it sometimes confuses human reason with the contingent cultural or historical features that it assumes in its particular location: freedom outweighs reason in republicanism, and the republican polity offers only a spontaneous and localized analysis of reason's role in legislation.

For this reason, Habermas's discursive reflections on the origin of laws were intended to show that liberalism and republicanism need not be conceived as theoretical or practical antinomies, but that a fully emancipatory state requires both the *law* and *reason* of liberalism and the *power* and the *freedom* of republicanism. He therefore argued that the invariable rights-based or *liberal* component of democracy does not preclude popular participation in the shaping of political order, and it does not impede active and transformative processes of political integration and foundation. On the contrary, a liberal rights-based constitution both presupposes and is reinforced by the participatory and integrative moment in republicanism, and rights are most meaningful, not where they are petrified as thin guarantees of negative liberty, but where they are contested and expanded through constitutive participation. Similarly, political participation in the republican sense is not rendered unnecessary by the fact that a polity possesses rationally universalized rights enshrined in a constitution. On the contrary, authentic freedom is also shaped by the demand for inclusiveness and consensual universality, and it intensifies communicative rights as its own innermost expression. In seeking to overcome the dichotomy between liberalism and republicanism, therefore, Habermas argued that rights, expressing reason, and freedoms, expressing the will, are not necessarily in opposition to each other. On the contrary, where rights are exercised in discursive participation, they cease to be mere formal or static elements of political life, and they actively constitute conditions of generalized freedom and will formation. Likewise, where freedoms are inclusively justified in inter-subjective processes of discourse, they reinforce and enact rights as the structural foundation of the public will: rights and democratic freedoms are, thus, co-original elements of a legitimate polity. Rights, Habermas consequently asserted, should be disarticulated from the transcendental or metaphysical stasis which they assume in classical Kantian liberalism, and they should be enacted as freely articulated components of everyday human life-practice and self-expression. The legitimate state is, therefore, for Habermas as for Kant, a state which unites reason and freedom, and which provides conditions under which freedom and reason become jointly constitutive. This unity of reason and freedom, however, remains metaphysical unless these antinomies are actively unified in communication. Reason and will are in fact always latently unified in the everyday communicative interactions of the life-world, and it is only where this unity is abrogated by technical or privatist domination that human law is severed from the sources of its rational freedom.

In Habermas's earliest works, this analysis of the necessary correlation between liberal rights and republican participation was rather inchoate. At this stage, he simply claimed that the laws that legitimize power are not solely enshrined in the prior norms of practical reason, but evolve through discursive exchanges between citizens in the public sphere. However, in his later work, he expanded this argument to claim that political legitimacy is produced through *deliberative politics:* that is, that legitimacy evolves as members of a pluralized civil society discursively exercise their basic rights as *participatory rights,* and as they found a 'circuit of public communication' whose consensual outcomes are ultimately transmitted into the form of law.[31] In his major analysis of discursive democratic foundation in *Between Facts and Norms,* he further refined this perspective to claim that sustainable rights-conceptions depend on public discursive participation in democratic will formation, and they cannot be realized as formal-negative or private assertions of autonomy and entitlement. Rights are only fully valid where they are exercised as 'participatory rights and rights of communication'; as such, rights enact 'positive liberties', through which the organs of political authority are constituted as accountable to and representative of positively generalizable human freedoms.[32] Central to this argument is the claim that political power is legitimate where it is formed as 'communicative power': that is, where it is constituted by active public discourses originating in the exercise of rights in the life-world and conferring rationally sustainable form on discursive claims to freedom.[33] As communicative power, the state becomes a genuine legal state, whose laws are not formally imposed upon society but created by rational public discourse and founded in the freely communicative exercise of the human will.

This argument is also fundamental to Habermas's most widely influential intervention in more popular political debates, especially his theory of *constitutional patriotism.* He first developed this theory because he sought to show that, in rational post-Enlightenment societies, the identities within which human agents construe and enact their political freedoms only support genuine freedoms where they are detached from historical or traditional attachments and where they contain universalizable elements, compatible with basic rights. Identities permitting freedom, therefore, must necessarily be non-exclusive, and societies integrated through such identities obtain both a highly evolved experience of freedom and a necessary disposition towards peaceful coexistence both with the minorities or divergent 'life forms' that they might contain and with other societies under other rational states.[34] This construct of the rationally transparent identity ultimately became the basis for Habermas's more general view of the constitution and constitutional citizenship. He concluded that the concepts of political identity and citizenship in modern democracies, which comprise highly pluralized and historically heterogenous communities, must be disconnected from all ideas of cultural unity or tradition, and they can only form a reliable basis for democratic life where they refer to and are supported by rights-based constitutions, shaping inclusive modes of collective self-perception.[35] In this respect, Habermas's thought moved close to the constitutional arguments of Ulrich K. Preuß, who also viewed the constitution as an integrating semantic, providing an arena for the formation of participatory and integrative yet non-exclusive political identities.[36]

Habermas finally elaborated these concepts of rights-based republican identity and universal constitutionalism in his response to political issues arising from the process of *globalization.* Unlike most globalization theorists, his reflections on this theme are guided by the sense that globalization does not necessarily threaten the essential substance of democratic life. In fact, as a set of processes that erode the fabric of the nation-state and extricate political identities from their traditional historical setting, he has interpreted globalization as the correlative of a wider course of generalized or rationally transparent social integration, leading to the promulgation of post-national identities and perhaps culminating in a 'post-national democracy'.[37] The central point in this argument is the claim that, if democracies are centred on rights, not on exclusive identities, and if these rights are actively and freely exercised in public discourse, there is no reason why democracies cannot be extended beyond national boundaries and there is no reason why nationally embedded modes of integration and solidarity cannot be transformed into a transnational 'solidarity of citizens'.[38] The formation of the European Union, Habermas argued, is one key example of a process of transnational integration on the foundation of rights exercised as freedoms. In fact, after the devastating consequences of the traditional association of citizenship with the nation, the European Union and its constitution represent Europe's 'second chance'.[39]

It can be concluded that, at each juncture in Habermas's work, his intention has been to propose ways in which the fundamental intention of post-metaphysical thinking – the attempt to reflect a human unity of reason and freedom as a condition of legitimacy in the state – might be rearticulated on anthropologically enriched foundations. Underlying all Habermas's work is therefore a strong *legal humanism,* which aims to consolidate the claim of the Kantian Enlightenment that the human being is the source of determinately *human laws,* and that the human builds a universe of human freedom and human law through its acts of legislation. However, Habermas has also recurrently implied, like Heidegger, that the laws of the first Enlightenment were not yet fully human laws, and it is only where the legislative function imputed by Kant to practical reason is transposed from its transcendental or metaphysical focus into the plural and non-reified faculty of speech or communicative reason, that the legally humanized world might, as a world of spoken laws, become truly human, and so truly free. Where speech is construed as the centre of legislative reason, most importantly, the ancient and persistent antinomies which have affected the entire evolution of European political thought – that is, the antinomy between law and the will, between reason and freedom, between liberalism and republicanism and between legality and legitimacy – can be overcome. In the active freedom of speech, rights and laws are transformed from formal normative (or metaphysical) principles into the active precondition of democratic liberty and will-fulfilment. Where speech gives laws, law forfeits its metaphysical, its formal-positivist or its capitalist-instrumental abstraction from human interaction in the life-world, and it forms power as shared power or rationally free power.[40] Speech, in short, is the determinant of post-metaphysical life, and communicative power in the state is the collective form of human post-metaphysical freedom: it is specific to a 'post-metaphysical understanding of the world', Habermas argued, that it sees law as legitimate where it is formed in the 'language of law',[41] through the 'discursive opinion- and will-formation of equal citizens'.[42] In authentic communicative power, then, reason and freedom are themselves reflected as co-original, and legality and legitimacy both evolve, in a relation of necessary interdependence, on the foundation of communicatively mediated 'structures of recognition'.[43] Whereas Kant saw law's paradox as resolved in the autonomy of practical reason and in the state's legislation of rights, Habermas saw law's paradox as ending in speech: speech, in other words, is the real humanity of law and power.

Luhmann: a different autonomy

In certain respects Luhmann's work was, from his earliest publications on law, politics and public administration in the mid-1960s, conceived as a critical response to Habermas, whose *Structural Transformation of the Public Sphere* played a deeply influential role in early debates on legitimacy in the early Federal Republic. Most particularly, Luhmann's early work was designed as a critique of Habermas's plan for a reconstitution of Enlightenment under the aspect of communicative rationality and for the reconstruction of the Kantian legal state on anthropologically enriched foundations. His early work therefore mirrored Habermas's methodological focus on concepts of Enlightenment, rationality and legal statism, but it used these concepts to denounce Habermas's project as an ultimately simplistic reassertion of Kant's transcendental metaphysics. Indeed, at the heart of these two rival political and sociological outlooks was a rivalry over metaphysics, in which both Luhmann and Habermas pursued acutely divergent paths in their endeavour to account for how the institutions of modern society evolve, rationalize and legitimize themselves without metaphysics.

Throughout his early works, Luhmann argued that the Enlightenment, defined as an attempt to steer society towards a condition of greater emancipation, freedom and autonomy through the correct exercise of human reason, has, from the outset, been confused in its method and deeply misguided in its preconditions. This view was set out most systematically in his inaugural lecture of 1968, entitled *Sociological Enlightenment,* in which he sought to place his own perspective in critical relation to the original rational prescriptions and objectives of the Enlightenment. In this, Luhmann did not deny that the evolution of Western society has been determined by a process analogous to what is commonly viewed as Enlightenment. Western society, he reflected, has surely been marked by an evolutionary trajectory, through which society as a whole has moved away from metaphysical conceptual forms and non-accountable or superstitious belief patterns towards a condition in which rationality provides independent validity for itself. Most particularly, modern or enlightened societies are no longer ordered around monolithic or absolutely authoritative states, and the power of modern states is always counterbalanced by rationally reflected and generalized laws and by rational guarantees of freedom. Like Habermas, therefore, Luhmann argued that modern society is necessarily a *post-metaphysical* society in which freedoms are founded in wholly autonomous, *positivized* and consistently rationalized accounts of legal and political necessity. The positivization of law is, Luhmann insisted, the irreducible cornerstone of modern social existence, and the evolution in law of positive mechanisms for articulating legal validity is the foundation of all liberties characterizing modern societies.[44] To this extent, therefore, Luhmann agreed with Habermas that modernity and Enlightenment form a condition in which society provides a positive, autonomous and post-metaphysical accounts of its functions, and this condition is likely to promote a generalization of power in categories derived from law.

Nonetheless, in his juxtaposition of the terms 'sociological' and 'Enlightenment' to describe his own interpretive methodology, Luhmann argued that the process of Enlightenment is misconstrued by normative analysts who place *human rationality* at the centre of all modern social evolution and who see the Enlightenment of society as the result of rationally guided human choices and selections. In fact, he claimed, the rational evolution of modern society should not be viewed as an accomplishment of human rationality but as a condition of *society* itself and of the rationality conditioning the distinct social systems that this society comprises. The rational condition of social modernity, therefore, is not a human or humanly rational condition, it is in fact the result of quasi-organic or *autopoietic* processes of evolution, which occur independently of the prescriptions of human reason and which are shaped by an underlying systemic logic of *differentiation.* Modern society in its entirety, Luhmann argued, has emerged through the increasing specification of social systems on narrowly circumscribed functions and through the evolution within social systems of distinct types of *system rationality,* through which individual systems respond to and process the problems and functions that they construct as their own.[45] Modern society has thus been formed as a total reality of differentiation in which particular systems (for instance, the economy, politics, law, education, medicine, art) react to the increasing *complexity* of society by stabilizing themselves around internally differentiated codes, functions and references. With the evolution of modern society, therefore, politics has rationalized itself as a system that communicates exclusively about political problems; art has rationalized itself as a system that refers to aesthetic problems; law has rationalized itself as a system that refers to law; medicine as a system that refers to medicine and the economy as a system that refers to the economy. The result of this systemic differentiation is that modern or 'enlightened' society has rationalized itself as a thoroughly pluralistic and *de-centred* society, in which no one system of communication has primacy or measurable jurisdiction over any other system, and each system contains its own rationality which determines its continuing evolution. The rationality that guides the evolution and differentiation of society, however, is not a rationality exercised by particular people: it is a transpersonal rationality exercised by systems, independently of the people whose communications these systems contain. Through the differentiation of society, systems develop their own intelligence and *their own multiple standards of rationality* for communicating with and stabilizing themselves against other systems. A system is, therefore, rational wherever it consolidates itself as an 'intelligible world' of meaning communicating effectively with other systems,[46] and there are no criteria external to the system's self-organization to determine whether and in what measure it might be 'rational'. Modern societies in fact possess *many forms of reason.* Each of these forms of reason resides in a specific social system, and it allows this system to generate and communicate accounts of its necessity and its plausibility. If the reality of systemic differentiation, decentration and autonomy of modern society has a certain analogy to conditions usually viewed as Enlightenment, therefore, it is systems, not people, which act as the 'medium of Enlightenment'.[47]

Against Habermas and the entire post-Enlightenment tradition, therefore, Luhmann argued, first, that rationality has no normative dignity against the functional reality of social reproduction. Rationality, in fact, *is* this functional reality in the process of its reproduction. Second, then, he also argued that the idea of rationality has been falsely constructed by those who think that it is a specifically human feature and that it allows humans to make necessary statements or to prescribe 'immutable laws' to determine how and under what conditions they should live and how and under what conditions their societies, and the institutions contained in these, should be organized.[48] To assume that the human being is a bearer of rationality that transcends the differences between all social systems is, for Luhmann, simply to postulate a universal environment for all social systems. Such postulates falsely consolidate society around reductively monadic or fictitiously self-identical sources of value; they project an illusory ideal of society onto society's reality of multi-rational complexity; and, last, they prevent an accurate observation of how society actually rationalizes and explains its communications. Whilst the first Enlightenment sought to understand all things by studying the rational 'essence (the nature) of the human being', therefore, Luhmann's *sociological Enlightenment* denies that human reason offers privileged insights into social reality, and it argues that explanatory inquiry must accept that meaning is produced contingently, without necessity, and through multi-paradigmatic processes of communication.[49]

The idea of rationality as a uniquely or constitutively human characteristic is, in Luhmann's view, a residually metaphysical idea, counterfactually clinging to the certainty that invariable causes, norms and laws exist in the world and that these can be universalized beyond their particular systemic location. Likewise, the idea that one unchangingly self-identical rationality shapes all aspects of society is a metaphysical notion, counterfactually clinging to the certainty that there exist monadic epistemological centres that are able to construct universally valid accounts of what is true and correct. As a pluralistic and post-metaphysical society, however, Luhmann is adamant that modern society cannot be governed or explained by human laws or by metaphysical laws, and that both pure metaphysics, and metaphysics disguised as humanism, corrupt social analysis. Luhmann in fact saw his sociological Enlightenment as an Enlightenment that frees social analysis from metaphysical thinking and that, uniquely amongst theories of society, provides a multi-perspectival theoretical apparatus adequate to comprehending the factually enlightened nature of social modernity. He consequently defined his theoretical method as one that finally abandons the 'ontological metaphysics' of classical philosophy and that negates the idea that there might be an innate normative or causal order in the universe.[50] Similarly, he set his theory against the 'metaphysics of consciousness' and the 'metaphysics of reason' promoted by the first Enlightenment, which interprets human reason itself as a perennial or self-identical cause and arbiter of the moral and the political world.[51]

The paradox of law and power

Luhmann, quite evidently, did not see himself as a political philosopher. His conception of sociological Enlightenment was designed to undermine all general foundations of political philosophy and, indeed, of all normative political analysis. He viewed all normative theory as evolving from a false metaphysics of human consciousness and, as a result, from a conveniently manufactured account of rationality as a prescriptive agency. Abstract philosophical analysis of the conditions under which 'political domination is legally acceptable', he concluded, tends to present highly simplified, selective and often counter-productive accounts of legitimacy.[52] More specifically, in fact, Luhmann's political reflections contain a consistent attack on several main principles of normative political theory. First, he dismissed the standard normative idea that the state is a privileged system in modern society, that this system is placed dualistically against other systems, and that legitimacy – or, indeed, its absence – in the political system is of structural importance for all other systems.[53] Against this view, he argued that the political system is one system amongst many others, with no particular claim to dignity or centrality. Second, he attacked the belief that the political system is an apparatus constituted or steered by rational agreements and by moral norms, and that the legitimacy of the political system is measurable as a condition of compliance with external laws. The political system, he explained, is in fact a contingent system of communication; it is a system specialized on the application of *power* to make *collectively binding decisions,* and it perpetuates itself by restricting its communication solely to those issues that can be regulated by power. This means, primarily, that the political system does not obtain its legitimacy through universally necessary stipulations articulated as law or through norms or moral ideas transmitted into it through the medium of law. Politics is originally distinct from law; the contents of the political system cannot be engendered by law, and they are not dependent on invariable prescriptions. From the outset, therefore, Luhmann suggested that normative claims that power is necessarily regulated by laws applied '*ab extra*' are metaphysical, and they rely on the belief that law is a privileged bearer of universal rationality, which is located outside and independently of other systems.[54] Such claims are normally generated by theory for its own purposes, Luhmann explained, and the fact that questions are raised about the legitimacy of a political system need not mean that the system is factually lacking in legitimacy. Third, then, he intensified his attack on normative theory by defining legitimacy in the political system as a condition that has no necessary foundation, and that cannot be distilled into any universalized set of principles. Legitimacy in politics is *the formula of contingency* or the basic *self-reference* of the political system. Legitimacy is a resource that creates overarching conditions of plausibility for the political system and without which the political system cannot operate. However, legitimacy does not originate outside the political system; it is generated by the political system for itself; and the political system refers to a self-generated idea of legitimacy in order to reflect itself as a consistent and plausible set of communications and to transmit motivations through society that are likely to facilitate acceptance of its decisions.[55] Legitimacy, in consequence, has no determinate content. It is a semantic or paradoxical form which has no concrete or invariable essence and whose preconditions cannot be abstractly prescribed or explained in universally rational terms. Indeed, political systems are likely to obtain legitimacy precisely where they detach themselves from external principles, where they do not bind their claims to legitimacy to perennial accounts of their legal necessity and where their inner structures are able to engender a maximal number of options through which to underwrite policies and decisions. Legitimacy, in sum, is a reality of contingency in the political system, and all attempts to define legitimacy in invariable categories factually undermine the potential for flexible self-legitimization that the political system contains.

Despite this attack on normative theory, nonetheless, Luhmann also indicated that legitimacy in politics is not entirely independent of objective conditions, and that there are certain circumstances under which a political system is likely to forfeit its legitimacy. To this extent, although surely not setting out an ideal type of a legitimate political system, he suggested that some systems are more likely to obtain legitimacy than others and, thus, that some probable preconditions for legitimacy can be identified. Above all, he argued, a political system risks losing legitimacy wherever a system falls behind the de-centred and eminently *plural* reality of modern society – that is, wherever it *de-differentiates* itself from other systems by assuming regulatory functions outside its own sphere of communication or where it annexes other areas of communications (perhaps the economy, the law or the arts) to its own prerogatives. Wherever this happens, the political system is likely to impede its own operations by pursuing objectives that it cannot meaningfully fulfil, and by obstructing its ability to communicate with other systems – which it can only accomplish if it defines itself as fully different from these other systems.[56] It can consequently be inferred that Luhmann saw a legitimate political system (i.e. one reflecting itself as a plausible unity of communications and so generating motivations for obedience) as a relatively limited state.[57] Such a system is unlikely to take the form of a dictatorship or an excessively interventionist centre of power, and it is likely that it will maintain complex channels of communications with its systemic environments.[58]

Moreover, Luhmann's analysis of the danger of the *de-differentiation* of the political system was also motivated by the sense that a political system enjoying legitimacy in a modern society will probably be a *democracy.* It is probable, he suggested, that a political system able to legitimize itself will be one comprising a certain level of inner complexity and institutional differentiation, so that power is recursively communicated through the system and not concentrated at one personal or executive point in its operations.[59] Such a system will be likely to comprise a number of political parties communicating alternatives to present policies, and it will probably permit regular organized opposition. Parties divided into *government* and *opposition,* Luhmann argued, allow the political system to address problems in its environment in different ways, to generate flexible programmes for the management of complexity and – not lastly – to create policy options through which the system can secure compliance or acclamation in elections.[60] Most especially, however, a differentiated (and legitimate) political system will probably be one that reflects a difference between the executive (politics), the legislature (administration), and the public. This internal institutional division of the political system allows it to communicate with itself about the validity and adequacy of its policies and to ensure that it possesses sufficient internal complexity or 'alternatives' to respond to the plural issues that it faces.[61] A legitimate political system in modern society, in sum, is always likely to be a democracy with an internally formalized separation of powers.

In addition to this, then, Luhmann also arrived at the conclusion that modern political systems cannot operate without laws. Although power and law pertain to irreducibly different systems, in modern societies the exercise of political power can only be effected in a complex interdependence with law. At a manifest level, Luhmann saw the entire concept of the *Rechtstaat* as reflecting a 'grandiose tautology' or a false conflation of law and power.[62] However, he also argued that in differentiated democracies, power likely to be seen as legitimate requires a generalized and positively acceded form, provided by law, in order to transmit decisions through society, and the political system must consequently maintain a 'structural coupling' or a 'parasitic relation' with the legal system.[63] Through this coupling, law can transform the decisions of government into formulae likely to be met with compliance through society, and it offers 'alleviation' to the political system by stabilizing certain themes in organized or codified form.[64] In a differentiated society, therefore, there is no necessary unity between law and power; certainly, there can be no rational/metaphysical necessity by which law imposes inviolable principles upon power. However, the reality of differentiation is such that power is never wholly *without law,* and power cannot exist except as a *Rechtsstaat.* Indeed, in this aspect of his theory Luhmann also added that in modern societies it is likely that the relation between law and politics will be arranged in the form of a constitution. This constitution, in turn, will place a certain legal order on the political system, and it will most probably be centred in stipulations over basic rights. These rights will preserve the addressees of law from inappropriate political coercion and endow them with a plurality of liberties (such as freedom of speech, freedom of exchange, freedom of movement and freedom of contract), situated outside the central apparatus of the state. The constitutions of modern enlightened societies, therefore, necessarily reflect social agents as bearers of *subjective rights,* and the legal and political systems of such societies construct people as circumscribed by a sphere of inalienable entitlements.

Clearly, Luhmann's description of this relation between law and power does not mean that the legitimacy of the political system is somehow controlled by fixed rational criteria of legality. Luhmann in fact repeatedly stressed that the contrary is the case and that the legitimacy of a political system precedes the law and creates conditions in which its laws are likely to be regarded as deserving compliance. The coupling of power and law simply means that, in complex societies, power requires a general or iterable medium in order to communicate itself through society, and this medium is provided by law. Vertically applied power, in the form of a fiat or prerogative, is, Luhmann claimed, unlikely to be adequate to the complex shape of modern society, and law offers to politics a fluid and positive medium in which it can become 'effective power'.[65] Similarly, Luhmann's conception of legal statehood does not mean, in the classical sense of the *Rechtsstaat,* that in a legitimate state laws become transparent to the necessary freedoms of their addressees, or that legal addressees feel that they are freely and rationally implicated in legislation. On the contrary, Luhmann stated repeatedly that the positive legitimacy of law does not depend upon any rational motives or considerations and that, in most cases, laws are accepted as legitimate for reasons that are entirely contingent or manufactured. The most legitimate political system is, in fact, one in which 'an almost motiveless, unthinking acceptance of binding decisions' can be anticipated and presupposed.[66] The condition of legitimacy, consequently, does not mean that laws express a 'consensually founded legal relation' or are perceived as originating in rationally necessary agreements. On the contrary, the legitimacy of laws is 'to a large extent independent of the consensus of those affected by them'.[67]

Similarly, in his reflections on the constitution, Luhmann did not argue that democratic political systems assume constitutional form as a result of norms or agreements externally imposed upon the political apparatus or as the outcome of rational analyses of human dispositions and of the rights deducible from these. Instead, he explained, political systems take constitutional form because this form is adequate to the evolutionary intelligence of the political system itself. As a document that institutes a separation between legislative and executive power, for example, the constitution prevents the excessive concentration of administrative tasks on the limited resources of the executive, and it allows the political system to avoid overburdening one particular or personalized point within its communications.[68] As a document that sanctions rights of property, contract, belief and scientific inquiry, analogously, the constitution assists the political system in its self-differentiation from the systems that regulate questions of property and contract (the economy and, possibly, law), belief (religion) and scientific inquiry (science and, possibly, education). The origin of the constitution, therefore, is simply the political system itself: this system spontaneously creates a constitution for itself, and it endows its addressees with subjective rights because it requires the sanction of subjective rights enshrined in the constitution as preconditions of its own differentiation and self-reference.[69] Through its constitution, the political system produces a device through which it avoids exposing itself to over-taxation, de-differentiation or 'corruption' through communications that it cannot meaningfully regulate, and which deflect from its strictly political objectives.[70] Like earlier functional theorists, therefore, Luhmann concluded this line of analysis by arguing that the constitution should under no circumstances be seen, in Habermasian style, as a document legitimizing the discursive politicization of social problems or the employment of law and the rights established in law as expansive guarantees of political communication or participation. In fact, he concurred with Forsthoff in arguing that democratic legal states that seek to be more than democratic legal states – perhaps by inviting mass participation in decision-making, by sanctioning participatory rights or by channelling values into political institutions – tend to dismantle the legal-democratic fabric of the political system and to fix all competences of the political system on direct or mandatory power. The constitution has its essential function in its contribution to the *depoliticization* of social issues, to the *deflation* of political problems and to the separation of power and law – where it fulfils this deflationary role, it contributes to an 'increase in liberty', both in the political system and in the legal system.[71]

Luhmann's account of politics and law thus contains two conflicting implications. On one hand, it contains a recognition of the normative claim that a political system obtains legitimacy if it rationalizes its power and transmits this power as law. On the other hand, however, it insists that normative theory misconstructs the unity of law and power in the state and fails to account for this unity in authentically positive terms. The most essential implication of this is that, for Luhmann, power and law are entirely positive forms, and they enter relations of interdependence in modern society for entirely positive reasons: in fact, the unity of law and power is not a normatively deducible condition, but a paradoxical or evolutionary form, in which politics and law generate security for their communications by referring to each other under the paradox of legitimacy. In a legitimate state, there is no guarantee that either politics or law will be able to demonstrate why they become interdependent or obtain recognition.[72] In consequence, although normative theory correctly apprehends the probability of a rational relation between law and power, such theory, because it focuses its analysis on monadic constructs of human reason and human interest, cannot adequately interpret the contingent forms of law, power and legitimacy. Indeed, theory that stands outside law and politics and seeks universal causes for their functions often undermines the contingent processes of positivization on which law, politics and legitimacy depend.

Democracy after metaphysics

In describing the unity of law and politics in the legal state as fully positivized *contingency,* Luhmann returned to the original post-metaphysical questions about the relation between power and law, and freedom and reason, and he placed himself in a distinctive relation to his precursors in the German theoretical tradition. As discussed, most salient positions in German political theory have confronted the original paradoxicality of power's relation to law, and they have attempted to found legitimacy, after metaphysics, on non-metaphysical foundations; that is, they have attempted to demonstrate how the human being acts or might act as the source and centre of law, and to derive the origins of legitimate statehood from the constitutive freedoms of this human being. The defining moment in this tradition was Kant's attempt to reconcile both power and law and freedom and reason by positively founding both elements of this antinomy in the self-causality and self-legislation of the pure human will. Later, Habermas seconded this idea, suggesting that law and power and reason and freedom can be positively reconciled through the discursive activities of human legislative reason, in the form of communicative power. Luhmann added to this line of analysis by acknowledging that in modern societies power and law are fully post-metaphysical, or fully positive, and they justify themselves through wholly contingent and non-metaphysical forms of rationality. Luhmann, however, argued that analysis that seeks to provide rational evidence for the necessity of one type of political legitimacy or one type of legal order is marked by an inability to comprehend the absolute positivity and the absolutely contingent plurality of communicative meanings in modern society. Such analysis thus inevitably draws on outmoded theoretical outlooks, and it falls chronically behind the complexity of its object. Power, Luhmann claimed simply, is always paradoxical, and theoretical attempts to explain its necessity are in effect little more than acts of 'displacement', though which paradoxes of justification which have become strained or problematic are rendered less problematic and disruptive.[73] All attempts to posit final grounds of necessity in the unity of law and power in fact lastly mark a retrograde metaphysical recourse to the original fusion of freedom and reason in God's agency. To be sure, he suggested, the assumption of legal unity or rational freedom in the state might in many instances be a necessary self-reference or semantic, by means of which politics and law make their operations persuasive or plausible; indeed, political systems will often naturally arrange themselves around a unity of power and law. However, such ideas of legitimacy and necessity in politics are always produced by the political system for itself, *ex nihilo,* and they are simply paradoxes whose necessity and rationality ultimately derive from the political system's own intelligence and exigencies.[74] Law and power have no necessary founding origin and no necessary source of unity except in their contingency, or in their 'blind spot' – in the full contingency of their relation.[75] Therefore, if the political system claims to be founded in *legitimacy* and if it claims, as legitimate, to obtain sanction for its legitimacy from the legal system, this is in fact merely an autopoietic fiction of *self-reference* in politics, and this self-reference is highly likely to dissolve wherever a system that refers to it begins to thematize it as a material, human or value-rational content. The conjoined rationalization of power and law in modern society should, consequently, be viewed as an entirely positive arrangement in which the media shaping human life are placed on fully positive premisses. This condition does not mark a humanization of power or a triumph of human reason over power, and it does not mean that people are integrated under power because this power accords with any original human needs and absolutely rational insights. It simply means that power and law utilize each other under the conditions of societal differentiation, and power and law, for reasons of their own intelligence, enter a relation of contingent or paradoxical necessity to each other. The condition of social existence after metaphysics is, thus, existence in absolute positivity, in absolute contingency, or in absolute paradox, where neither laws nor political decisions are supported by any ultimate or unconditioned point of normative regress. All normative or humanistic attempts to go beyond the paradox of legitimacy can only ever disclose or refer to new paradoxes, and these paradoxes might easily dissolve the stability of the social forms presently underwritten by acknowledged paradoxes.

To be post-metaphysical and to obtain the post-metaphysical goods of freedom and legitimacy, for Luhmann, means to accept the contingency and paradoxicality of social communications. The original Kantian belief, replicated and reconstructed as a legal humanism by Habermas, that human beings possess rational faculties that allow them to deduce laws and to prescribe these to the political system, is insufficiently post-metaphysical and must be abandoned. Indeed, although Habermas expressly described his theories of reason and legislation as an extension of Enlightenment or as an attempt to place Enlightenment on fully human or positive foundations, Luhmann indicated that this humanistic approach was not in fact Enlightenment at all – it was still metaphysics. Habermas, for Luhmann, did little more than simply translate the original metaphysical fiction that the world contains an invariable juridical order or reflects the will of a prime mover into a humanistic or anthropological account of the world as determined by universal qualities of human reason and objectively necessary will-formation. He consequently viewed Habermas as a thinker who was not able to think about society in truly post-metaphysical terms and who still desperately sought to burden the evolving reality of society with unitary and essential ideals. Like Heidegger, therefore, Luhmann suggested that truly post-metaphysical analysis simply observes the contingency of claims for legitimacy and legal validity; it accepts the necessary contingency of legal forms; and, moreover, it abstains from probing these claims too intensely or incautiously, in case they collapse or give way to other, unforeseeable, paradoxes. Humanist visions of political order, which seek to reinflate the political system and to manipulate law as a transmitter of value-rational norms into the political system are, therefore, for Luhmann, guilty of great theoretical naïveté, as they erroneously impute a foundational structure to modern society.[76] Still worse, however, such political humanism also runs the risk of over-simplifying society, of reconstituting it around uniform rational ideas and, so, of *destroying* the fragile complexity, the freedom, the autonomy and the legitimacy that, as paradoxically realized post-metaphysical contingency, this society guarantees.

Perhaps predictably, Habermas responded to Luhmann's criticism by suggesting that outlooks that completely renounce humanism must also, once again, *become metaphysics,* for such thinking cannot avoid falling into alliance with doctrines sponsoring aggressive conservatism, and it invariably leads to an acute experience of alienation and heteronomy. Luhmann's theory, in fact, marked for Habermas an extreme reflection of the earlier metaphysical errors of positivism. Systems theory, he intimated, separates laws from human control; it insists that human agents, in the name of complexity and contingency, must relinquish all measurable jurisdiction over their life forms; and it allows the main institutions of society to persist as a merely coercive apparatus, with no foundation in human interest or reason.[77] Like the positivists, therefore, Luhmann (for Habermas) was a theorist who, in accepting the autogenesis of law and power, was prepared to accept coercion and non-accountability in government and law as semi-naturalized metaphysical necessities and to abandon humanity to this natural or metaphysical order. Habermas saw Luhmann's theory of systems, consequently, as marking an insidious return of pre-humanist metaphysics and a return of heteronomy, smuggled into political theory as a paradoxical and even quasi-biologistic analysis of positivity and autonomy.[78] Against Luhmann, therefore, he argued that the challenge for post-metaphysical thinking is not to accept positivity under law and state as a post-human reality but to ensure that the freedoms experienced at the end of metaphysics remain discernibly human freedoms, so that humanity, both objectively and conceptually, survives its disarticulation from metaphysics.

Conclusion

The main claim in this book is that German political philosophy has its origins in the Reformation and that its problems originate in a period of history that was marked by a fragmentation of the institutional apparatus applying law in the German territories and by a related, yet also distinct, fragmentation of metaphysical or invariable ideas supporting law's authority. At the inception of German political thought, therefore, is, at a practical as at a theoretical level, an exceptional experience of freedom from the law. As a legacy of this, this book claims that German political thought is abidingly characterized by the fact that it defines freedom under law as freedom in distinction from metaphysical norms, that it denounces as paradoxical the use of metaphysical principles to sustain legal validity, and that it also endeavours to preserve the freedoms obtained in its first exceptional reaction against law and to place these on more securely positive foundations. Indeed, German political philosophy in its entirety might be reconstructed as a sequence of positions in a history of legal humanism or legal anthropology, which attempts to conceive the positive structure of the law in such terms that it reflects the primary freedoms of the human being and permits the formation of political order which is not distracted by the formality of metaphysics. In all these respects, the element of exceptionalism at the genesis of German legal and political thought has retained a manifest structural importance: the transformation of law into a set of principles gaining relatively uncontroversial compliance and defining a state form obtaining widely accepted legitimacy has been a very slow process in Germany, and law has been recurrently called upon to address intermittent upheavals in the legal structure of the state and to refract a constant conflict of metaphysical and anti-metaphysical ideas about its necessary form.

Throughout the history of political philosophy in Germany, controversies between the defining theoretical schools of German political philosophy have normally revolved around an attempt in one school to indict members of a rival school as *metaphysicians*: as theorists, that is, who are only able to provide a metaphysically paradoxical, fictitious or depleted account of human law and the conditions of human freedom. Through the course of the controversies on this point many concepts and stances have fallen under the suspicion that they explain the human origin of law by sleight of hand, or by surreptitiously reinvoking metaphysical ideas. Generally, however, the suspicion of metaphysics has attached itself most heavily to ideas which are originally associated with, or which appear to rearticulate, legal ideas characteristic of *ius-naturalism*: that is, ideas that see law's validity as perennially deducible against positive law and the sources of its historical formation. Running through the history of German political philosophy, in consequence, is an endeavour to convert theoretical elements of ius-naturalism into positive outlooks, which guarantee freedom as a concerted and integrative exercise of the will, usually in the state, not as a static exercise of metaphysical rights and liberties. For this reason, German political thought has several distinctive characteristics, which it owes to its constitutive rejection of legal metaphysics. As discussed, for example, German political thought tends to be very historical, and it has often identified history and historical unity as the most valid sources of free law. Likewise, it has evolved distinctive conceptions of rights, which construe rights as practical extensions of the free will, either personal or collective, not as limits on the freedom of this will. Similarly, the anti-metaphysical perspective in Germany has also often, at different times and at different points in the political spectrum, denounced the principles of pure capitalist law as a particularly malign expression of metaphysics, which reduces social reality to formal and chimerical ideas of personhood and legal necessity. The distinctive positions in German political theory, thus, generally converge in a rejection of the claim that necessary laws (especially rights) can be defined prior to or against the active freedoms of the self-interpreting community, and they oppose the conviction that laws or rights are in some way prior to politics.

If the defining objective of German political philosophy has been to explain valid law as detached from a heteronomous metaphysical corpus, however, it is difficult to determine whether any position in this tradition has fully succeeded in overcoming legal metaphysics. Certainly, each view remains susceptible to the suggestion that it continues to work within metaphysical paradigms, and it does not ultimately provide an account of an integrally human or an integrally positive law, independent of all external derivation. The more obviously humanist theories of law, for example, reacted to the first loss of metaphysical law by attempting to reconstruct, as a human unity, the metaphysical or absolute unity of reason and freedom in law, which was first ascribed to God's personality in scholastic metaphysics. The insistence that legitimate law, and legitimate order, must include a balance or a union between reason and freedom in fact affects, in different ways, all major humanist political philosophies in Germany. In transposing the problem of God's unity into a human problem, however, the humanist impulse in thinking about law and the state is always susceptible to the accusation that it simply relocates the paradox of law's metaphysical source by deriving laws from a monadic structure of legislative reason which, in a primary paradoxical act, it imputes as the founding attribute of the human mind, and so by circumventing the need to give an account of the world as a place of real freedom and real freedom under laws. On this perspective, then, it can argued that, in its rational-humanist construction, human freedom under law is never a fully post-metaphysical freedom; it is freedom deduced by human faculties which are always privileged by theory as able to create laws of freedom.

This (arguable) inability of rational-humanistic analysis of the law to move decisively beyond metaphysical reflection has naturally been detected by theorists with less sympathy for humanistic or formally reasoned political ideals; these theorists have identified the paradoxes and subterfuges used by theory in its attempt to overcome metaphysics, and they have argued that rational humanists merely obtain law by assimilating God's authorship of law into the structure of human reason and by ascribing to this reason certain prior legislative faculties. Indeed, the most salient anti-humanist theories in the history of German political thought have generally concluded that all assumptions that the law can be traced to a constant self-identical origin (that is, to a rationally legislating human mind) are metaphysically fictionalized constructs, paradoxically close to, or displacements of, the original metaphysical reality which they purport to oppose. Despite their radical anti-metaphysical attitude, however, it is arguable that anti-humanist theories of law also fail in their attempt to construct law and power in terms that evade all traces of metaphysical content. Amongst the theorists of law and state who are less obviously indebted to humanist preconditions, the representatives of the different positivist schools, for example, ultimately concluded that the law should be seen as law's own construct; Schmitt argued that the law originates *ex nihilo*, as a paradoxical act of sovereign auto-causality; Marx privileged human nature as a primary legislative capacity; Heidegger privileged the contingency of national history as the reference for valid law; Lukács privileged class as the origin of legitimate obligation; Luhmann, in the most radical manifestation of anti-metaphysical positivism, defined valid law as law's consistent communication about itself, produced, as a knowing paradox, *ex nihilo*. Humanist theorists of law's positivity, therefore, have remained in the metaphysical terrain because they have integrated the paradoxical elements of metaphysics into human character and proposed freedom in law as the result of prior attributes of human reason. In opposing this, however, anti-humanist theorists have either simply relocated the legislative function away from reason onto another aspect of human existence (for instance, nature, history or class) or they have accepted law's paradox as a paradox, they have abandoned the idea that positive law might also be a determinately free or a determinately human law, and they have in fact allowed law to persist as an experience of heteronomy, and as an experience of metaphysics.

It might perhaps be concluded that law without metaphysics is not possible, and that law always remains the central repository for the metaphysical problems of human life and for the originating dilemmas in the self-projection of humanity as freely and positively human. Indeed, if law is intended to be the form of accountable freedom, it is not easy to imagine how legitimacy in law might avoid replicating or rearticulating some originary idea of an ordered universe; how it might not derive its theoretical impulse from the sense that law must have a dignified supra-positive origin; and how it might not, in short, always be the medium in which metaphysical questions are raised. A fully semantic analysis of law, as proposed by Luhmann, would surely indicate that all ideas in law that law gives shape to distinctive modes of rationality and freedom are merely law's own theories, designed to bring mobility into law's own communications or to obtain plausibility for law's own contingency. Outside such fully semantic analysis, however, it might be tentatively concluded that the assumption of a metaphysical burden, perhaps of a rebellion against metaphysics, or of a task to shape human freedom as positively other than the given structure of metaphysics, is more than just the blind spot or the endlessly relocated paradox of law. It might in fact be the unifying element in all legal philosophy, and the reactions against metaphysics in German political philosophy might be paradigmatic descriptions of law's reflection on its own founding problem. At the same, time, though, it might similarly be argued that the difficulty in law's being other than metaphysics is also an inevitable part of the law, and that law is always at once both the form of the human or humanist reaction against metaphysics, and the form in which metaphysics – dialectically – persists.

Notes

Introduction

1 Jan Werner Müller, 'Rawls and German Political Thought', *European Journal of Political Theory*, 2/1 (2002), pp. 163–79.
2 See Günter Vogler, *Absolutistische Herrschaft und ständische Gesellschaft. Reich und Territorien von 1648 bis 1790* (Stuttgart: Ulmer, 1996), p. 9.
3 On the aftermath of conciliarism, see Anthony Black, *Monarchy and Community: Political Ideas in the Later Conciliar Controversy 1430–1450* (Cambridge: Cambridge University Press, 1970), p. 80. On the basic ideas of the conciliar movement, see Brian Tierney, *Church Law and Constitutional Thought in the Middle Ages* (London: Variorum Reprints, 1979), p. 242.
4 See Peter Moraw, 'Versuch über die Entstehung des Reichstags', in Hermann Weber (ed.), *Politische Ordnungen und soziale Kräfte im alten Reich* (Wiesbaden: Franz Steiner, 1980), pp. 1–36; 15.
5 See Helmut Neuhaus, *Reichsständische Repräsentativformen im 16. Jahrhundert. Reichstag – Reichskreistag – Reichsdeputationstag* (Berlin: Duncker und Humblot, 1982), p. 26.
6 For a broader account, see Helmut Coing, *Römisches Recht im Mittelalter* in *Ius Romanum Medii Aevi*, V/6 (1964) esp. p. 10.
7 ibid., p. 6.
8 H. E. J. Cowdrey, *Pope Gregory VII. 1073–1085* (Oxford: Clarendon Press, 1998), pp. 261–62.
9 Colin Morris, *The Papal Monarchy. The Western Church from 1050 to 1250* (Oxford: Oxford University Press, 1989), p. 388.
10 ibid., pp. 402, 575.
11 Gerhard Ladner, *Theologie und Politik vor dem Investiturstreit. Abendmahlstreit, Cluni und Heinrich III* (Darmstadt: Wissenschaftliche Buchgesellschaft, 1968), pp. 46–47; Cowdrey, *Pope Gregory VII*, p. 76.
12 See Peter Classen, 'Das Wormser Konkordat in der deutschen Verfassungsgeschichte', in Josef Fleckenstein (ed.), *Investiturstreit und Reichsverfassung* (Sigmaringen: Jan Thorbecke, 1973), pp. 411–60; 454. Also useful is Edmund E. Stengel, 'Land- und lehnrechtliche Grundlagen des Reichsfürstenstandes', *Zeitschrift für Rechtsgeschichte*, 66 (1948), pp. 294–342; 299.
13 Morris, *The Papal Monarchy*, pp. 551–53.
14 Still noteworthy on this is Heinrich Mitteis, *Der Staat des hohen Mittelalters. Grundlinien einer vergleichenden Verfassungsgeschichte des Lehnzeitalters* (Weimar: Böhlau, 1944), p. 304. Very illuminating on differences between early-feudal and late-feudal law is Theodor Mayer, 'Die Ausbildung der Grundlagen des modernen deutschen Staates im hohen Mittelalter', in Hellmut Kämpf (ed.),

Herrschaft und Staat im Mittelalter (Darmstadt: Gentner, 1956), pp. 284–331; 310–11.

15 Exemplary for this interpretation is Gerhard Kallen, 'Friedrich Barbarossas Verfassungsreform und das Landrecht des Sachsenspiegels', in *Zeitschrift für Rechtsgeschichte*, 58 (1938), pp. 560–83; 566. In similar voice, see Tilman Struve, *Die Salier und das römische Recht. Aufsätze zur Entwicklung einer säkularen Herrschaftstheorie in der Zeit des Investiturstreites* (Stuttgart: Franz Steiner, 1999), p. 58. Likewise, Kenneth Pennington, *The Prince and the Law, 1200–1600: Sovereignty and Rights in the Western Legal Tradition* (Berkeley, Calif. and Oxford: University of California Press, 1993), p. 12, and Peter Moraw, 'Königliche Herrschaft und Verwaltung im spätmittelalterlichen Reich (ca. 1350–1450)', in Reinhard Schneider (ed.), *Das spätmittelalterliche Königtum im europäischen Vergleich* (Sigmaringen: Thorbecke, 1987), pp. 185–200; 190. For a dissenting perspective on these questions, see Heinrich Appelt, 'Friedrich Barbarossa und das Römische Recht', in Appelt, *Kaisertum, Königtum, Landesherrschaft. Gesammelte Studien zur mittelalterlichen Verfassungsgeschichte* (Vienna: Böhlau, 1988), pp. 61–80; 67. See also Gaines Post, 'Plena Potestas and Consent in Medieval Assemblies: A Study in Romano-Canonical Procedure and the Rise of Representation 1150–1325', in *Traditio*, I (1943), pp. 355–408. On the role of Roman law in reinforcing papal power within the church, see Ludwig Buisson, *Potestas und Caritas. Die päbstliche Gewalt im Spätmittelalter* (Cologne: Böhlau, 1958), p. 74. For a more personalized account of this process, see David Abulafia, *Frederick II. AMedieval Emperor* (London: Pimlico, 1992), pp. 33, 35.

16 Important on this is Dieter Wyduckel, *Princeps Legibus Solutus. Eine Untersuchung zur frühmodernen Rechts- und Staatslehre* (Berlin: Duncker und Humblot, 1979), p. 38. Wyduckel argues that the *lex regia* began to influence the structure of imperial authority earlier than is usually claimed (p. 42). Also important on this is Hermann Krause, *Kaiserrecht und Rezeption* (Heidelberg: Carl Winter, 1952), pp. 26, 31.

17 This is probably the best moment to admit my deep indebtedness to Harold Berman's research in my treatment of questions of law and secularization. I first read Berman's work about ten years ago, as I was first beginning to think about these issues. Although my overriding claims are rather different from his, his superb scholarship has shaped my thought in more ways than I can adequately recognize. On the point in the text here, see Harold J. Berman, *Law and Revolution. The Formation of the Western Legal Tradition* (Cambridge, Mass.: Harvard University Press, 1983), p. 113.

18 For example, Heinz Durchhardt, 'Das Reichskammergericht', in Bernhard Diestelkamp (ed.), *Oberste Gerichtsbarkeit und zentrale Gewalt im Europa der frühen Neuzeit* (Köln: Böhlau, 1996) pp. 1–14; 4. Heinz Angermeier, *Königtum und Landfriede im deutschen Mittelalter* (Munich: Beck 1966), pp. 489, 539; 253; Heinz Angermeier, *Die Reichsreform 1410–1555. Die Staatsproblematik in Deutschland zwischen Mittelalter und Gegenwart* (Munich: Beck, 1984), p. 253.

19 ibid., p. 69. Note the change against early periods, in which imperial power was more secure. See Erich Klingelhöfer, *Die Reichsgesetze von 1220, 1231/32 und 1235. Ihr Werden und ihre Wirkung im deutschen Staat Friedrichs II* (Weimar: Hermann Böhlau, 1955), p. 221.

20 Heinz Angermeier, *Königtum und Landfriede*, p. 436. Also: Heinz Angermeier, *Die Reichsreform 1410–1555*, p. 154.

21 Importantly, Georg Droege speaks of an increasing 'dualism between land law and feudal law' towards the end of the Middle Ages. See Georg Droege, *Landrecht und Lehnrecht im hohen Mittelater* (Bonn: Röhrscheid, 1969), p. 220.

22 Dietmar Willoweit explains the relations between the ownership of land and the demand for jurisdictional influence as the 'supporting foundations' of 'late medieval territorial power'. Dietmar Willoweit, 'Die Entwicklung und Verwaltung der spätmittelalterlichen Landesherrschaft', in Kurt G. A. Jeserich, Hans Pohl and Georg-Christophe von Unruh (eds), *Deutsche Verwaltungsgeschichte*, 6 vols. (Stuttgart: Deutsche Verlagsanstalt, 1983), Vol. I: *Vom Spätmittelalter bis zum Ende des Reiches*, pp. 66–176.

23 I refer here to Georg von Below's still deeply stimulating account of this process: Georg von Below, *Der deutsche Staat des Mittelaters. Eine Grundlegung der deutschen Verfassungsgeschichte*, 2nd edn (Leipzig: Quelle und Meyer, 1925), pp. 242–43, 301.

24 In support of this argument, see Karl-Friedrich Krieger, *Die Lehnshoheit der deutschen Könige im Spätmittelalter 1200–1437* (Aalen: Scientia Verlag, 1979), p. 341; see also Ernst Klebel, 'Territorialstaat und Lehen', in Theodor Mayer (ed.), *Studien zum mittelalterlichen Lehenswesen* (Lindau: Jan Thorbecke, 1960), pp. 195–228; 227. The epochal disjuncture between land ownership and the feudal law of the empire had in fact already been clear in the earlier legal documents of the empire, for instance the *Sachsenspiegel* (*The Saxon Mirror*). On a manifest level, the *Sachsenspiegel* expressed a classical medieval legal worldview. It defined human society as bound by a universal legal order, and it claimed that God inaugurates a legal framework in which obligations and entitlements are constituted by the Emperor, so that all legal relations are channeled through the supreme legal person of the Emperor (Eike von Repgow, *Der Sachsenspiegel*, edited by Clausdieter Schott, Zurich: Manesse, 1996, p. 29). At the same time, though, the *Sachsenspiegel*, almost unwittingly, also documented the erosion of this ideal overarching order of feudal law, for it demonstrated certain tensions between definitions of law based in *regalia* and those based in the ownership of land and it clearly acknowledged that land law had a formal independence from feudal law. Excellent on this point is Alexander Ignor, *Über das allgemeine Rechtsdenken Eikes von Repgow*, Paderborn: Schöningh, 1984, pp. 119, 197.

25 See, for instance, Ernst Schubert, *König und Reich. Studien zur spätmittelalterlichen deutschen Verfassungsgeschichte* (Göttingen: Vandenheock und Ruprecht, 1979), p. 139.

26 *Reformatio Sigismundi* (Augsburg: Lukas Zeissenmaier, 1497), p. 14. Although at times rather bizarrely construed as an ideological forerunner of the Peasant Wars of the 1520s, the *Reformatio Sigismundi* is quite clear in its demands for the universal introduction of Roman law and the imposition of *lex regia*. It does, however, still insist on the necessity of an overarching legal framework – a 'supra-positive legal order' – and in this respect it both looks back to medieval conceptions of order and anticipates some later debates. See Lothar Graf zu Dohna, *Reformatio Sigismundi. Beiträge zum Verständnis einer Reformschrift des fünfzehnten Jahrhunderts* (Göttingen: Vandenhoeck und Ruprecht, 1960), p. 87.

27 *Reformatio Sigismundi* p. 40.

28 ibid., p. 42.

29 ibid., p. 51.

30 See Reinhard Seyboth, 'Kaiser, König, Stände und Städte im Ringen um das Kammergericht 1486–95', in Bernhard Diestelkamp (ed.), *Das Reichskammergericht in der deutschen Geschichte. Stand der Forschung, Forschungsperspektiven* (Köln: Böhlau, 1990), pp. 5–24; 9. See also: Durchhardt, 'Das Reichskammergericht', p. 3.

31 Angermeier, *Die Reichsreform*, p. 224.

32 It is consequently no surprise that in the late medieval era both the free cities and peasants, both of whom depended on unwritten or participatory systems of

law-finding, were most obviously disadvantaged by Roman law. On the position of the towns during and after the Reformation, see Eberhard Isenmann, 'Reichsstadt und Reich an der Wende vom späten Mittelalter zur frühen Neuzeit', in Josef Engel (ed.), *Mittel und Wege früher Verfassungspolitik* (Stuttgart: Klett-Cotta, 1979) pp. 9–223; 141. An extremely important study of the decline of the towns and the urban constitutions at this time is Heinrich Richard Schmidt, *Reichsstädte, Reich und Reformation. Korporative Religionspolitik 1521–1529/30* (Wiesbaden: Franz Steiner, 1986). This book culminates in the claim that towns were the primary 'victims of the Reformation' (p. 333). On the legal position of the peasants, see Karl Siegfried Bader, 'Die Rechtsgeschichte der ländlichen Siedlung', in Karl Siegfried Bader and Gerhard Dilcher, *Deutsche Rechtsgeschichte. Land und Stadt – Bürger und Bauer im Alten Europa* (Berlin: Springer, 1999), pp. 3–250; esp. 177–78.

33 The most obvious example of such a pattern is England, where the process of post-feudal legal centralization was facilitated by the relative weakness of feudalism, and the early demise of purely feudal law. Naturally, no attempt is made here to suggest that in England the centralization of power and law was not contested. Self-evidently, English medieval history was marked by the early and at times violent negotiation of proto-constitutional settlements between the monarchy and aristocracy, in which the common law was manipulated to defend anti-monarchical interests (See the classic account of this in A. L. Poole, *From Domesday Book to Magna Carta*, 2nd edn, Oxford: Oxford University Press, 1993, pp. 468–82). Nonetheless, these settlements were normally structured around the acceptance of a centralized monarchical executive, and they served in many ways to integrate the aristocracy into the fabric of a tightly formed oligarchy around the monarchy. Fundamental to English constitutional history in the high medieval era was, therefore, the progressive formation of a relatively integrated monarchical government, with a relatively concentrated legal apparatus. As early as the twelfth century, Henry II began to systematize the common law and to reinforce the jurisdictional competence of the monarchy, not lastly because he wished to extend and clarify his authority in relation to the church in the wake of the dispute with Thomas Becket (see John Hudson, *The Formation of the English Common Law: Law and Society in England from the Norman Conquest to Magna Carta*, London: Longman, 1996, p. 150). In the late thirteenth century, then, Edward I significantly strengthened the monarchical executive by adding bodies of statutory law to the common law. At the end of the fifteenth century, Henry VII effected a rapid increase in the legislative and judicial authority of the crown. These processes finally culminated in the high level of judicial control obtained by the monarchy as a result of Thomas Cromwell's legal and administrative innovations of the 1530s, and in the increased employment of parliament as an adjunct of government at this time (See G. R. Elton, *Reform and Reformation. England 1509–1558*, London: Arnold, 1977, pp. 198–200; A. G. Dickens, *The English Reformation*, London: Batsford, 1964, p. 121; David L. Smith, *The Stuart Parliaments 1603–1689*, London: Arnold, 1999, p. 6). The English experience of feudalism paved the way for the relatively seamless emergence of an early modern state. Indeed, feudalism had a positively state-forming impact in English history, and the proclamation of national/territorial independence from the church in the Reformation occurred as one moment in a wider tendency towards monarchical sovereignty and legal and constitutional independence which had first evolved in conjunction with feudalism. During the early English Reformation, as a consequence, Christopher St German was able to stress that the 'customes of the Realm' and 'statutes made in Parliaments' have greater significance for legal finding than any other legal source (See Christopher St German, *The Dialogue*

in English, betweene a Doctor of Divinitie, and a Student in the Lawes of England, London: Printed for the Company of Stationers, 1613, p. 17). Importantly for the subsequent course of the English Reformation, St German also described parliament as the 'most high Court in this Realme before any other' (p. 88).

34 On the correlation between the Reformation and the establishment of the territorial state, see Karlheinz Blaschke, 'Wechselwirkungen zwischen der Reformation und dem Aufbau des Territorialstaates', in *Der Staat*, 9/3 (1970), pp. 347–64; 350. See also Angermeier, *Die Reichsreform*, p. 317. See also: Dieter Stievermann, 'Evangelische Territorien im Konfessionalisierungsprozeß', in Anton Schilling and Walter Ziegler (eds), *Die Territorien des Reichs im Zeitalter der Reformation und Konfessionalisierung. Land und Konfession 1500–1650*, 7 vols (Munster: Aschaffendorff, 1997), Vol. VII: 45–66; 55–56.

35 Ekkhart Fabian (ed.), *Die Schmalkaldischen Bundesabschiede 1530–1532* (Tubingen: Fabien Verlag, 1958), p. 37.

36 Heinz Angermeier's magnificent work on this period culminates in a superb account of the last attempts of Karl V to reassert central legal control in the late 1540s. See Angermeier, *Die Reichsreform*, pp. 308–9.

37 For an example of how this privilege worked, see Heinz Mohnhaupt, 'Organisation und Tätigkeit des Hohen Königlichen Tribunals zu Wismar', in Nils Jörn, Bernhard Diestelkamp and K. A. Modeer (eds), *Integration durch Recht. Das Wismarer Tribunal (1653–1806)* (Cologne: Böhlau, 2003), pp. 215–38.

38 On questions concerning the relation between the courts and confessional interests after 1555, see Bernhard Ruthmann, *Die Religionsprozesse am Reichskammergericht (1555–1648). Eine Analyse anhand ausgewählter Prozesse* (Cologne: Böhlau, 1996).

39 For a parallel account of the legal ideas of the Reformation, which has a rather more favourable view of the constitutive legal importance of the Reformation, see Gerald Strauss, *Law, Resistance and the State: The Opposition to Roman Law in Reformation Germany* (Princeton, NJ: Princeton University Press, 1986), esp. pp. 191–92, 271.

40 Thomas Aquinas, *Summa Theologiae*, edited and translated by D. Burke and A. Littledale, 61 vols. (London and New York: Blackfriars, in conjunction with Eyre and Spottiswoode, 1969), Vol. V: p. 21.

41 Aquinas, *Summa Theologiae*, Vol. XIV: p. 13.

42 ibid., p. 11.

43 See John L. Farthing, *Thomas Aquinas and Gabriel Biel: Interpretations of St. Thomas Aquinas in German Nominalism on the Eve of the Reformation* (Durham, NC and London: Duke University Press, 1988), p. 10.

44 Aquinas, *Summa Theologiae*, Vol. XXIX: p. 4.

45 Aquinas, *Summa Theologiae*, Vol. XXVIII: p. 20.

46 Aquinas, *Summa Theologiae*, Vol. XXIX: pp. 62, 42.

47 Aquinas, *Summa Theologiae*, Vol. XXVIII: p. 22.

48 ibid., p. 148.

49 Martin Luther, 'Vom Abdendmahl Christi', in *Weimarer Ausgabe* (hereafter given as *WA*), 120 vols. (Weimar: Böhlau, 1883–), 26: pp. 241–509; 506.

50 See, on this point, Burkhard von Bonin, *Die praktische Bedeutung des ius reformandi. Eine rechtsgeschichtliche Studie* (Stuttgart: Enke, 1902), p. 6.

51 Ernst Troeltsch argued famously that modern natural law, emphasizing individual rights and the imposition of strict legal limits on the exercise of political authority, evolved as a Protestant reconstruction of the ideas of natural law originally promulgated in the Roman Catholic church during the era of Gregorian reform. Owing to its acutely anti-legal dimension, however, and especially to its rejection of all claims that God is naturally manifest in law and that the community is bound together under law, the Lutheran Reformation, on this account,

produced a rather different account of natural law than its Calvinist, Anglo-Calvinist and Zwinglian rivals. Whereas other lines of Reformation theology developed principles of natural law into constitutional ideas or conceptions of political sovereignty, Lutheranism only produced a very curtailed account of natural law in the state. In fact, it tended to view natural law in minimal or even indifferent terms, and it usually identified the natural-legal order as an order preserving peace and maintaining stability. It was, thus, extremely circumspect in its discussion of individual rights in or against the body politic (See Ernst Troeltsch, 'Das stoisch-christliche Naturrecht und das moderne profane Naturrecht', in *Gesammelte Schriften*, edited by Hans Baron, 7 vols., Tubingen: J. C. B. Mohr, 1925, Vol. IV: pp. 166–91; 178).

52 Recent revisionist historians have argued that the legal aftermath of the Reformation was not entirely without constructive elements. See John Witte Jr., *Law and Protestantism: The Legal Teachings of the Lutheran Reformation* (Cambridge: Cambridge University Press, 2002, p. 184). Such historians claim above all that, having suspended the canon law, the Reformation set the foundations for a new corpus of civil law, expressing quite specifically Evangelical outlooks on issues of civil legislation. Nonetheless, at the level of state law (as far as this existed as a distinct legal sphere), the main doctrines of the early Reformation did little to elucidate the legal basis of the political orders to whose emergence they had contributed.

53 Peter Blickle, *Gemeindereformation. Die Menschen des 16. Jahrhunderts auf dem Weg zum Heil* (Munich: Oldenbourg, 1987), p. 205.

54 On this most important point, see K. B. Hundeshagen, *Beiträge zur Kirchenverfassungsgeschichte und Kirchenpolitik insbesondere des Protestantismus* (Wiesbaden: Julius Niedner, 1864), p. 86. In more recent accounts, see Blickle, *Gemeindereformation*, p. 205, and Martin Honecker, *Cura religionis Magistratus Christiani. Studien zum Kirchenrecht im Luthertum des 17. Jahrhunderts insbesondere bei Johann Gerhard* (Munich: Claudius, 1968), p. 39.

55 Most importantly, see Martin Heckel, 'Religionsbann und landesherrliches Kirchenregiment', in Hans-Christoph Rublack (ed.), *Die lutherische Konfessionalisierung in Deutschland* (Gütersloh: Mohn, 1992), pp. 130–62; 140. See also Udo Wolter, 'Die Fortgeltung des Kanonischen Rechts und die Haltung der protestantischen Juristen zum Kanonischen Recht in Deutschland bis in die Mitte des 18. Jahrhunderts', in Richard H. Helmholz (ed.), *Canon Law in Protestant Lands* (Berlin: Duncker und Humblot, 1992), pp. 13–48; 46; see also Ernst Walter Zeeden, *Konfessionsbildung. Studien zur Reformation, Gegenreformation und Katholischen Reform* (Stuttgart: Klett-Cotta, 1985), pp. 165, 186.

56 Joachim Stephani, *Institutiones iuris canonici* (Frankfurt am Main: Kopff, 1612), p. 7

57 See Martin Heckel, 'Staat und Kirche nach den Lehren der evangelischen Juristen Deutschlands in der ersten Hälfte des 17. Jahrhunderts', in *Zeitschrift für Rechtsgeschichte*, 73 (1956), pp. 117–247; 211. See also Johannes Heckel, 'Die Entstehung des brandenburgisch-preußischen Summepiskopats', in *Zeitschrift für Rechtsgeschichte*, 44 (1924), pp. 266–83; 272. See also Bernd Christian Schneider, *Ius Reformandi. Die Entwicklung eines Staatskirchenrechts von seinen Anfängen bis zum Ende des Alten Reiches* (Tubingen: Mohr, 2001), pp. 168, 318.

58 Ernst Benz, *Bischofsamt und apostolische Sukzession im deutschen Protestantismus* (Stuttgart: Evangelisches Verlagswerk, 1953), p. 15.

59 Philipp Melanchthon, *Vonn dem Ampt der Fürsten, und welcher gestalt Inen das auß Gottes befelch aufflegen thue die abstellung der Mißbräuch in den Kirchen* (Strasburg: Sigmund Bun, 1540), p. 14.

60 In these respects, the Lutheran Reformation was appreciably different from the slightly later Calvinist Reformation and from the Anglo-Calvinist reorganization

of the church, which ultimately took hold in England, and Lutheranism had to address questions of legal freedom and contingency in a manner that was distinct from other reformations. The first emergence of Calvinism was normally supported more by the urban patriciate than by the territorial princes, and its origins were not found, for the most part, in the revolt of landed power against imperial law, but in the historical constitutional freedoms of the wealthy cities of South West Germany and Switzerland. Like Lutheranism, Calvinism protested vehemently against the corruption of religious freedom through the excessive juridification of faith, and Calvin clearly mirrored Luther's anti-Thomist invectives against the presumption that compliance with law might bring salvation (See Jean Calvin, *Institution de la Religion Chrestienne*, 4 vols, Paris: Societé de Belles Lettres, 1939, Vol. IV: p. 150). However, Calvin gave more thought than Luther to the constitutional order of the church in its relation to the state, and his teachings contained a much more pervasive doctrine of natural law. His model of church government by presbyteries served to separate the church from the state and to confer on the church a more precisely constructed legal integrity against the state and a more constitutive role in forming public order. He argued that magistrates were entitled to insist, through constitutional forms, on the compliance of the prince or the state with the publicly acceded principles of the 'Christian polity' (see Calvin, *Institution de la Religion Chrestienne*, IV: pp. 216, 228–29; see also Emil Sehling, *Geschichte der protestantischen Kirchenverfassung*, in *Grundriß der Geschichtswissenschaft*, vol. II; section 8, Leipzig: B. G. Teubner, 1897, p. 43). He also stipulated that all functions of political institutions should be bound by the 'eternal rule' of divinely prescribed moral law (Calvin, *Institution de la Religion Chrestienne*, Vol. IV: p. 218). The orders of state which evolved in Calvinist territories were not marked by a less integrated relation with their churches than those under Lutheran supremacy; indeed, the contrary was often the case. However, the relation between church and state in Calvinist territories was normally construed as a relation under law, and where Calvinist princes exercised direct control over the church this power was commonly defined as an element of secular authority and necessity, not as a personal fusion of worldly and religious authority. The religious rights of Calvinist princes were therefore not derived, as in Lutheranism, as corollaries of the prince's own confessional status and authority. In contrast to Lutheranism, therefore, Calvinism provided a constitutional 'solidity' for the state and it offered a principled legal and moral matrix for organizing the relation between the church and the state (See Rudolf Smend, 'Protestantismus und Demokratie', in Smend, *Staatsrechtliche Abhandlungen und andere Aufsätze*, 2nd edn, Berlin: Duncker und Humblot, 1968, pp. 297–308; 297). Not all German states were Lutheran, of course. Indeed, recent historians have accentuated the importance of the so-called 'second Reformation' in the late sixteenth and early seventeenth century, which saw many states convert from Lutheranism to Calvinism, and they have concluded that the different epochs of reform did not necessarily produce classically distinct models of confessionalization (See, for example, Heinz Schilling, 'Die Zweite Reformation als Kategorie der Geschichtswissenschaft', in Schilling, *Ausgewählte Abhandlungen zur europäischen Reformations-und Konfessionsgeschichte*, edited by L. Schorn-Schütte and O. Mörke, Berlin: Duncker und Humblot, 2002, pp. 433–82; 468). After 1613, most notably, Calvinism was the state religion of Brandenburg, and later of Prussia itself. Nonetheless, the Calvinism of most German states was often a phenomenon largely restricted to the political elites and it commonly lacked the organic foundation in the parishes, communities and regional estates which had been characteristic of Lutheranism. The second Reformation, therefore, gave only rather attenuated expression to the democratic-constitutional implications of Calvin's political theology, and Lutheranism often remained the more pervasive influence, even in nominally Calvinist states. See Schilling, 'Die Zweite Reformation', pp. 472, 482; also Emil Sehling, *Geschichte der protestantischen Kirchenverfassung*, pp. 43–44. Owing to the principle of royal supremacy, Anglo-Calvinism evolved in a manner that Calvin could not have anticipated and would, in all probability, not have sanctioned. However, as it retained an episcopal order, the English church preserved a distinctive constitutional structure that was not fully integrated into the state, and, except under the fateful Laudian regime, the episcopate was accountable to parliament as well as to the crown, and could not be immediately absorbed into the prerogative order of government. On this, see Claire Cross, *Church and People. England 1450–1660*, Oxford: Blackwell, 1999, p. 200.

1 The Reformation

1 See Meyrick H. Carré, *Realists and Nominalists* (Oxford: Oxford University Press, 1946), p. 97.
2 Although it seems clear that some nominalists, especially Gabriel Biel, argued that ecclesiastical authority should prevail in questions of doctrinal doubt. See Heiko Augustinus Oberman, *The Harvest of Medieval Theology: Gabriel Biel and Late Medieval Nominalism*, Cambridge, Mass.: Harvard University Press, 1963, p. 403.
3 There is a good deal of debate on the extent to which Luther was influenced by Ockham. Wilhelm Link sees a direct connection between Luther and Ockham, and he examines Luther's doctrine of God's freedom as an extension of nominalist accounts of faith. See Wilhelm Link, *Das Ringen Luthers um die Freiheit der Theologie von der Philosophie*, edited by E. Wolf and M. Mezger (Munich: Chr. Kaiser, 1940), pp. 271–72. In his excellent and argumentative study, Graham White describes Luther straightforwardly as an 'Ockhamist' (Graham White, *Luther as Nominalist*, Helsinki: Luther-Agricola-Society, 1994, p. 73). Heiko Oberman also sees Luther in a nominalist tradition, but identifies a conflict between Lutheran ideas and nominalism, or at least with vulgar misconstructions of nominalism (Heiko Augustinus Oberman, *The Dawn of the Reformation: Essays in Late Medieval and Early Reformation Thought*, Edinburgh: Clark, 1986, pp. 107–8). For an informative discussion of whether Luther ever read Aquinas and of whether he was competently versed in nominalist doctrine, see John L. Farthing, *Thomas Aquinas and Gabriel Biel*, pp. 1–8.
4 Karl Holl famously saw Luther's lectures on *Romans* of 1515 as the first expression of his mature theology, especially in its doctrine of the 'Iustitia Dei', the passive reception of grace (Karl Holl, 'Die Rechtsfertigungslehre in Luthers Vorlesung über den Römerbrief mit besonderer Rücksicht auf die Frage der Heilsgewißheit', in *Gesammelte Aufsätze zur Kirchengeschichte*, 7th edn, 3 vols., Tubingen: J. C. B. Mohr, 1948, Vol. I: *Luther*, pp. 111–54; 114). Ernst Bizer argues that the discovery of the 'Iustitia Dei' actually occurred in 1518 (see Bizer, *Fides ex auditu: Eine Untersuchung über die Entdeckung der Gerechtigkeit Gottes durch Martin Luther*, 3rd edn, Neukirchen: Neukirchener Verlag, 1966, esp. pp. 23–52). Heinrich Bornkamm, in turn, differs from this view (see Heinrich Bornkamm, 'Zur Frage der Iustitia Dei beim jungen Luther', in *Archiv für Reformationsgeschichte*, 52 (1961), pp. 16–29; 17). Luther himself claimed that his early reading of Romans was the great revelation in his religious development (See Luther, 'Martinus Luther pio lectori', *WA*, 54, pp. 179–87; 185). For an important commentary on Luther's interpretation of Romans, see Dorothea Demmer, *Lutherus Interpres: Der theologische Neuansatz in seiner Römerbriefexegese unter*

besonderer Berücksichtigung Augustins (Witten: Luther-Verlag, 1968), esp. p. 207.
5 Martin Luther, *Vorlesung über den Römerbrief 1515/1516*, Latin-German edition (Weimar: Böhlau, 1960), p. 245.
6 ibid., pp. 167–249.
7 ibid., p. 380.
8 Martin Luther, 'Predigten über das 2. Buch Mose', *WA*, 16, p. 378.
9 ibid., pp. 99–103.
10 ibid., p. 43.
11 Troeltsch's commentary on the problem of natural law in Luther is still well worth considering. Troeltsch argues that Luther's doctrine revolves around a 'rejection of all legality' (Ernst Troeltsch, *Soziallehren der christlichen Kirchen und Gruppen*, in *Gesammelte Schriften*, Vol. I, p. 482). Yet he also sees in Luther a limited commitment to the Decalogue as a necessary expression of natural principles of order (pp. 611–12).
12 Luther's personal contempt for Aquinas has been well documented; he described him as the 'source and foundation of all heresy, error and obliteration of the Gospel' (see Denis R. Janz, *Luther on Thomas Aquinas: The Angelic Doctor in the Thought of the Reformer*, Stuttgart: Franz Steiner, 1989, p. 11). His main adversaries in the Roman Catholic camp were all strict Thomists, who accentuated the position of the church as a legal institution (see Gerhard Hennig, *Cajetan und Luther: Ein historischer Beitrag zur Begegnung von Thomismus und Reformation*, Stuttgart: Calwer, 1966, pp. 14–18).
13 See Jürgen Miethke, *De potestate papae. Die päbstliche Amtskompetenz im Widerstreit der politischen Theorie von Thomas von Aquin bis Wilhelm von Ockham* (Tubingen: J. C. B. Mohr, 2000), p. 41.
14 Martin Luther, 'Von der Freiheit eines Christenmenschen', *WA*, 7, pp. 20–38; 25–26.
15 Martin Luther, 'An den Christlichen Adel deutscher Nation', *WA*, 6, pp. 404–69; 445.
16 ibid., p. 430.
17 ibid., p. 414.
18 ibid., p. 433.
19 Martin Luther, 'Daß ein christliche Versammlung oder Gemeine Recht und Macht habe', *WA*, 11, pp. 408–16; 411.
20 ibid., p. 408.
21 ibid., p. 411.
22 ibid., p. 410.
23 Luther, *Vorlesung über den Römerbrief*, p. 47.
24 Luther, 'An den Christlichen Adel deutscher Nation', pp. 459–60.
25 Luther, 'Daß ein christliche Versammlung oder Gemeine Recht und Macht habe', p. 410.
26 ibid., p. 411.
27 ibid., p. 410.
28 Luther, 'An den Christlichen Adel deutscher Nation', p. 409.
29 Martin Luther, 'Von weltlicher Oberkeit', *WA*, 11, pp. 245–81; 247.
30 Martin Luther, 'Das Magnificat verdeutscht und ausgelegt', *WA*, 7, pp. 544–604; 590.
31 Luther, 'Von weltlicher Oberkeit' p. 252.
32 ibid., p. 262.
33 ibid., p. 265.
34 ibid., p. 271.
35 Martin Luther, 'Von den guten Werken', *WA*, 6, pp. 202–76; 259.
36 Luther, 'Von weltlicher Oberkeit' p. 251.

37 Luther, 'Eine treue Vermahnung zu allen Christen', *WA*, 8, pp. 676–87; 680.
38 Luther, 'Von weltlicher Oberkeit', p. 277.
39 Carlstadt, *Missive von der allerhochsten tugent gelassenheit* (Augsburg: Grim und Wirsung, 1520), p. 8.
40 See James S. Preus, *Carlstadt's Ordinaciones and Luther's Liberty: A Study of the Wittenberg Movement* (Cambridge: Harvard University Press, 1974) p. 82.
41 Important on these questions is Ulrich Bubenheimer, *Consonantia Theologiae et Iurisprudentiae: Andreas Bodenstein von Karlstadt als Theologe und Jurist zwischen Scholastik und Reformation* (Tubingen: J. C. B. Mohr, 1977), p. 286.
42 Carlstadt, *Berichtung dyesser red: Das reich gotis leydet gewaldt, und die gewaldtige nhemen oder rauben das selbig* (Wittenberg: Schirlentz, 1521), pp. 7, 17.
43 Carlstadt, *De legis sive carne et spiritu* (Wittenberg: Schirlentz, 1521), p. 4.
44 Carlstadt, *Von beiden gestaldten der heylige Messe. Von Czeichen in gemein was sie wirken und dewten. Sie seind nit Behemen oder Ketzer, die beide gestaldt nheme, sonder Ewangelische Christen* (Wittenberg: Schyrlentz, 1521), p. 20.
45 Carlstadt, *Von anbetung und eererbietung der zaychen des newen Testaments* (Wittenberg: Ramminger, 1521), p. 11.
46 Carlstadt, *Von dem Newen und Alten Testament* (Augsburg: Ulhart, 1525), p. 12.
47 Carlstadt, *Ob man mit heylicher Schrifft erweysen müge das Christus mit leyb und sele im Sacrament sey* (Basel: Wolff, 1524), p. 30.
48 Needless to say, Luther eventually extracted a series of humiliating apologies from Carlstadt, and Carlstadt was again, albeit temporarily, admitted to the Evangelical fold (see Carlstadt, *Von abtuhung der Bylder: Und das keyn Berdler unther den Christen seyn soll*, Wittenberg: Schyrlentz, 1522, p. 12).
49 See 'Ein bericht der handlung zwischen Doctor Martino Luthero unnd Doctor Andreas Bodenstein von Karlstadt', *WA*, 15, pp. 334–41.
50 Martin Luther, 'Von den himmlischen Propheten', *WA*, 18, pp. 62–214; 63.
51 ibid., p.115.
52 ibid., p. 204.
53 Luther, 'Eine treue Vermahnung zu allen Christen', p. 682.
54 Huldrych Zwingli, 'Von göttlicher und menschlicher Gerechtigkeit', in *Sämtliche Werke*, (hereafter *SW*) edited by E. Egli and G. Finsler, 14 vols. (Zurich: Theologischer Verlag, 1905–58), Vol. II, pp. 470–525; 486.
55 ibid., p. 496.
56 ibid., pp. 497–98.
57 Huldrych Zwingli, 'Auslegung der Artikel', in *SW*, Vol. II, pp. 1–457; 61, 68.
58 Zwingli, 'Von göttlicher und menschlicher Gerechtigkeit', p. 497.
59 Huldrych Zwingli, 'Die 67 Artikel' in *SW*, Vol. I, pp. 458–71; 463.
60 ibid., p. 463.
61 Zwingli, 'Auslegung der Artikel', p. 241.
62 ibid., p. 68.
63 ibid., p. 304.
64 ibid., p. 323.
65 ibid., p. 324.
66 ibid., p. 326.
67 ibid., p. 330.
68 ibid., p. 408.
69 ibid., p. 280.
70 Huldrych Zwingli, 'Aktion oder Brauch des Nachtmahls', *SW*, Vol. IV, pp. 1–24; 15.
71 Huldrych Zwingli, 'Eine klare Unterrichting vom Nachtmahl Christi', *SW*, Vol. IV, pp. 773–862; 791.
72 Johannes Oecolampadius also supported a commemorative doctrine of the Eucharist (see Oecolampadius, *Vom nachtmal Beweysug auß Evangelischen*

Schrifften, wer die seyen, so des Herren Nachtmals wort unrecht verstanden und außlegen, Augsburg, 1525, p. 55).

73 Caspar Schwenckfeld, the main Silesian Reformer, emphasized the politically compliant implications of Luther's conception of the Eucharist (see Caspar Schwenckfeld, *Vom Underscheyd der Schifftgelerten und Gottesgelerten: Was auch Schrifftgelerte und was Gottesgelerte heyssen*, (Gelger, 1558, p. 13). Indeed, Schwenckfeld implied that Luther, as a scholar of the scripture, used 'the preached word' as a surrogate for Roman Catholic law (see Caspar Schwenckfeld, *Von der heiligen Schrifft, irem Innhalt, Ampt, rechtem Nutz, Brauch und Mißbrauch*, Ulm: Varnier, 1551, p. 139).

74 See, for example, Karl Heinz Burmeister, 'Genossenschaftliche Rechtsfindung und herrschaftliche Rechtssetzung: Auf dem Wege zum Territorialstaat', in Peter Blickle (ed.), *Der deutsche Bauernkrieg von 1525* (Darmstadt: Wissenschaftliche Buchgesellschaft, 1985), pp. 237–52; 239.

75 See Günter Franz, *Der deutsche Bauernkrieg* (Darmstadt: Wissenschaftliche Buchgesellschaft, 1977), pp. 25, 42. For a view on these matters that is more cautious about the theocratic implications of the Peasants War, see Jürgen Brand, *Bibel und altes Recht im Bauerkrieg*, in *Leipziger Juristische Vorträge*, 17 (1996), esp. p. 22.

76 Thomas Müntzer, *Außgetrückte emplössung des falschen Glaubens der ungetrewen welt, durchs gezeugnus des Evangelions Luce* (Muhlhausen, 1524), p. 13.

77 Thomas Müntzer, *Hoch verursachte Schutzrede und antwwort, wider das Gaistlose sanfft lebende fleysch zu Wittenberg* (Nuremberg: Holtzel, 1524), p. 8.

78 ibid., p. 11.

79 ibid., p. 14.

80 This might not be viewed as particularly surprising, because after he was outlawed and his teaching prohibited under the Edict of Worms in 1521, Luther's survival depended on the protection of well-disposed princes, especially Friedrich the Wise of Saxony. Karl V considered that Friedrich was personally accountable for the spread of the Reformation and Luther could hardly afford to alienate his main protector (see Ingetraut Ludolphy, *Friedrich der Weise: Kurfürst von Sachsen 1463–1525*, Göttingen: Vandenhoeck und Ruprecht, 1984, p. 476).

81 Martin Luther, 'Ermahnung zum Frieden auf die zwölf Artikel der Bauerschaft in Schwaben', *WA*, 18, pp. 291–334; 292.

82 ibid., p. 315.

83 Müntzer, *Außgetrückte emplössung*, p. 6.

84 Johann Agricola, *Eyßlebens predig auff das Evangelion vom Phariseer und zolner* (Ulm: Gröner, 1526), p. 2.

85 Johann Agricola, *Confession und bekentnis Johan Agricolae Eislebens, vom Gesetze Gottes* (Berlin: Hans Weissen, 1540), pp. 4–5.

86 See Joachim Rogge, *Johann Agricolas Lutherverständnis. Unter besonderer Berücksichtigung des Antinomismus* (Berlin: Evangelische Verlagsanstalt, 1960), p. 160.

87 Johann Agricola, *Hundert und Dreissig gemeyner Fragestücke für die jungen Kinder ynn der Deutschen Meydlein Schule zu Eyssleben* (Wittenberg: Rhaw, 1528), pp. 6, 21.

88 Martin Luther, 'Die Thesen gegen die Antinomer', *WA*, 39, pp. 342–58; 347.

89 Luther, 'Von der Freiheit eines Christenmenschen', p. 24.

90 Luther, 'Die Thesen gegen die Antinomer', p. 348.

91 ibid., p. 346.

92 ibid., p. 349.

93 For this history of antinomianism after Luther, see Matthias Richter, *Gesetz und Heil: Eine Untersuchung zur Vorgeschichte und zum Verlauf des sogenannten*

Zweiten Antinomischen Streits (Göttingen: Vandenhoeck und Ruprecht, 1996), esp. pp. 17, 224–40.

94 On this see: Gustav Kawerau, *Johann Agricola von Eisleben: Ein Beitrag zur Reformationsgeschichte* (Berlin: Wilhelm Hertz, 1881), p. 291.

95 For examples of these debates, see Matthias Flacius Illyricus, *Widder ein recht heidnisch ja Epicurisch Burch der Adiaphoristen, darin das Leiptzische Interim verteidigt wird* (Magdeburg: Christian Rödinger, 1549), p. 17; Nicolaus Gallus, *Gegenbericht auf Dr. Pfeffingers und der Adiaphoristen gesuchte glosen oder ihr Leiptzigsch Interim, mit einer trewen warnung an alle Christen* (Magdeburg: Michael Lotther, 1550), p. 8.

96 Matthias Flacius Illyricus, *Von etlichen Artikeln der christlichen Lehr, und von seinem Leben, und endlich von den Adiaphorischen Handlungen, wider die falschen Geticht der Adiaphoristen* (1559), pp. 27–8.

97 For a wider account of the origins of this concept, see Ulrich Bubenheimer, 'Scandalum et ius divinum. Theologische und rechtstheologische Probleme der ersten reformatorischen Innovationen in Wittenberg 1521/22', in *Zeitschrift für Rechtsgeschichte*, 90 (1973), pp. 263–432; 290.

98 For the evolution of this doctrine, and its relation to Luther, see Wilfried Joest, *Gesetz und Freiheit: Das Problem des tertius usus legis bei Luther and die neutestamentliche Parainese*, 3rd edn (Göttigen: Vandenhoeck und Ruprecht, 1961), pp. 9–11.

99 On this, see, Lauri Haikola, *Gesetz und Evangelium bei Matthias Flacius Illyricus: Eine Untersuchung zur lutherischen Theologie vor der Konkordienformel* (Lund: C. W. K. Gleerup, 1952), p. 331.

100 *Deutsche Reichstagsakten unter Karl V*, 8 vols. (Gotha: Fr. A. Perthes, 1893–), Vol. II: p. 595.

101 Alfred Kohler (ed.), *Quellen zur Geschichte Karls V* (Darmstadt: Wissenschaftliche Buchgesellschaft, 1990), p. 437.

102 See, on this, Wolfgang Günter, *Martin Luthers Vorstellung von der Reichsverfassung* (Munster: Aschendorffsche Verlagsbuchhandlung, 1976), pp. 166, 173.

103 Luther, 'Von weltlicher Oberkeit', pp. 246–47.

104 See, for example, Philipp Melanchthon, *Vonn dem Ampt der Fürsten*, p. 16.

105 Philipp Melanchthon, *Apologia der Confession*, translated by J. Jonam (Wittenberg: G. Rhaw, 1531), p. 157.

106 Quoted from Walter Zimmermann, *Die Reformation als rechtlich-politisches Problem in den Jahren 1524–1530/31* (Göppingen: Kümmerle Verlag, 1978), p. 107.

107 It has been argued that Luther was reluctant to provide support for the princes by endorsing the principle of legitimate resistance, but that he did so on negative grounds, simply because the Gospel did not expressly forbid resistance in worldly law (see ibid., p. 132, and Diethelm Böttcher, *Ungehorsam oder Widerstand? Zum Fortleben des mittelalterlichen Widerstandsrechtes in der Reformationszeit (1529–1530)*, Berlin: Duncker und Humblot, 1991, p. 151).

108 Martin Luther, 'Warnung an seine lieben Deutschen', *WA*, 30, pp. 276–320; 278.

109 ibid., p. 282.

110 ibid., p. 283.

111 ibid., p. 282.

112 ibid., pp. 284, 291.

113 ibid., p. 299.

114 Lazarus Spengler, *Eyn kurtzer außzug auß dem Bebstlichen rechten der Decret und Decretalen* (Augsburg, 1530), p. 8.

115 Philipp Melanchthon, *Verzaichnung unnd kurtzliche anzaygung des rechten und aygentlichen verstands der Epistel, die S. Paulus zu den Rhömern geschriben hat* (Augsburg: Grimm, 1523), pp. 21–22.
116 Philipp Melanchthon, *Die haupt artickel und furnemsten punct der gatzen heyligen schrift* (Augsburg: Grimm, 1522), p. 13.
117 Melanchthon, *Verzaichnung und kurtzliche anzaygung*, pp. 51, 74.
118 ibid., p. 37. For a very good study of this concept, see Wilhelm Maurer, *Der junge Melanchthon zwischen Humanismus und Reformation*, 2 vols. (Göttingen: Vandenhoeck und Ruprecht, 1967), Vol. I, *Der Humanist*, p. 244.
119 Melanchthon, *Verzaichnung und kurtzliche anzaygung*, p. 96.
120 Melanchthon, *Die haupt artickel*, p. 63.
121 ibid., p. 211.
122 Melanchthon, *Apologia der Confession*, p. 285.
123 ibid., p. 164.
124 ibid., p. 157.
125 Melanchthon, *Verzaichnung und kurtzliche anzaygung*, p. 215.
126 Philipp Melanchthon, *Unterschidt zwischen weltlicher und christlicher Fromheyt* (Hagenau, 1524), p. 4.
127 Philipp Melanchthon, *Etliche Propositiones wider die lehr der Widerteuffer* (1535), p. 4.
128 Melanchthon, *Verzaichnung und kurtzliche anzaygung*, p. 77.
129 ibid., p. 93.
130 Philipp Melanchthon, *Ain klaine Außlegung uber das XX Capitel Exodi, der zehen gebot* (1525), p. 11.
131 Melanchthon, *Die haubt artickel*, p. 78.
132 *Concordia: Christliche widerholte einmütige Bekentnüs nachbenanter Churfürsten, Fürsten und Stende Augspurgischer Confession, und derselben Theologen Lere und Glaubens* (Magdeburg: J. Meißner und J. Walden Erben, 1580), p. 278.
133 Melanchthon, *Verzaichnung unnd kurtzliche anzaygung*, p. 58.
134 Melanchthon, *Die haubt artickel*, p. 83.
135 ibid., p. 211.
136 Melanchthon, *Apologia der Confession*, p. 45.
137 On the transformation in Melanchthon's position at this time, see: Adolf Sperl, *Melanchthon zwischen Humanismus und Reformation: Eine Untersuchung über den Wandel des Traditionsverständnisses bei Melanchthon und die damit zusammenhängenden Grundlagen seiner Theologie* (Munich: Kaiser, 1959), p. 141.
138 Philipp Melanchthon, 'Oratio de dignitate legum', in Guido Kisch (ed.), *Melanchthons Rechts- und Soziallehre* (Berlin: de Gruyter, 1967), pp. 234–40; 240.
139 Philipp Melanchthon, 'De dignitate legum oratio', in Kisch (ed.), *Melanchthons Rechts- und Soziallehre*, pp. 210–13; 224.
140 Melanchthon, *Die haubt artickel*, p. 54.
141 Melanchthon, 'De dignitate legum oration', p. 222.
142 Melanchthon, 'Oratio de legibus', in Kisch (ed.), *Melanchthons Rechts- und Soziallehre*, pp. 189–209; 202.
143 Philipp Melanchthon, *Ein christliche Ermanung an den hochgebornen König Ferdinandum, jetzt jungst zu Speyer geschriben* (Nurnberg: Peypus, 1529), p. 3.
144 Melanchthon, *Vonn dem Ampt der Fürsten*, p. 14.
145 ibid., p. 15.
146 Martin Bucer, 'Vom Ampt der Oberkait', in *Deutsche Schriften*, edited by G. Seebaß, 15 vols., (Gütersloh: Gerd Mohn, 1984), 6/2: *Zum Ius Reformationis: Obrigkeitsschriften aus dem Jahre 1535*, pp. 17–38; 36.
147 ibid., p. 28.
148 Martin Bucer, *Dialogi*, in *Deutsche Schriften*, 6/2, pp. 39–188; 49.
149 ibid., p. 165.

150 Johannes Oldendorp, 'De jure naturali gentium et civili', in *Tractatus ex variis juris interpretibus collecti*, 18 vols. (Lyon: Bertellus, 1549), Vol. I: fo. 87–105; 90.
151 Johannes Oldendorp, *Wat byllick und recht ys* (Rostock: Dietz, 1529), p. 20.
152 ibid., pp. 14, 16.
153 Oldendorp, 'De jure naturali gentium et civili', fo. 96.
154 Johannes Oldendorp, 'De jure et equitate disputatio forensis', in *Tractatus ex variis juris interpretibus collecti*, Vol. I, fo. 105–14; 110.
155 Martin Heckel, 'Religionsbann und landesherrliches Kirchenregiment', pp. 137–38. Schneider argues that *ius reformandi* was not formally cemented until 1648. See, Schneider, *Ius Reformandi*, p. 403.
156 Martin Luther, 'Ein Brief an die Fürsten zu Sachsen von dem aufrührischen Geist', *WA*, 15, pp. 210–21; 220.
157 Philipp Melanchthon, *Unterricht der Visitatorn an die Pfarherrn im Kurfürstenthumb zu Sachssen* (Wittenberg: Schirlentz, 1528), p. 42.
158 Otto Mejer, *Die Grundlagen des lutherischen Kirchenregimentes* (Rostock: Stiller'sche Hofbuchhandlung, 1864), pp. 111–12.
159 'Bedencken der Consistorien halben', reprinted in Ludwig Richter, *Geschichte der evangelischen Kirchenverfassung in Deutschland* (Leipzig: Tauchnitz, 1851), pp. 82–96.
160 ibid., p. 92.
161 Philipp Melanchthon, 'Iudicium de Episc. Naumb. 1. Nov. 1541', in K. Bretschneider (ed.), *Corpus Reformatorum*, 28 vols. (Halle: A. Schwetschke, 1836), Vol. IV, pp. 683–94; 684.
162 Philipp Melanchthon, 'Iudicium de Episcopo Naumb. 9. Nov. 1541', in *Corpus Reformatorum*, Vol. IV, pp. 697–99; 698.
163 Martin Luther, 'Exempel, einen rechten christlichen Bischof zu weihen', *WA*, 53, pp. 231–60; 254.
164 ibid., p. 258.
165 Martin Luther, 'Auslegung des ersten und zweiten Kapitels Johannis in Predigten', *WA*, 46, pp. 538–789; 736–37.
166 Luther, 'Exempel, einen rechten christlichen Bischof zu weihen', p. 255.

2 The early Enlightenment

1 As discussed, one important distinctive feature of the political order in early modern Germany was that several judicial frameworks, some territorial and some imperial, existed side by side, with one system often seeking to prevail over the other. Under these legal conditions, territorial states could only assume full jurisdictional (and, consequently, also fiscal) control over their territories by obtaining a special constitutional privilege from the empire (the *privilegium de non appellando illimitatum*). This privilege prevented legal addressees within the territory seeking rights of appeal in the imperial courts, and it directly consolidated the territorial judicial apparatus as the main source of legal coercion. Many territories did not obtain this privilege until the eighteenth century, and they consequently struggled to secure any independence from the constitution of the empire. For a full account of when different states obtained this privilege, see Ulrich Eisenhardt (ed.), *Die kaiserlichen Privilegia de non appellando* (Cologne: Böhlau, 1980). In view of the importance of this privilege, constitutional theorists in the territories were often deeply vexed by questions of jurisdictional supremacy and by anxieties over elements of external jurisdiction in the courts.
2 See Edward Coke, *Selected Writings*, edited by Steve Sheppard, 3. vols. (Indianapolis, Ind.: Liberty Fund, 2003), Vol. III, p. 1271. On this, see, for instance, the classic study on these themes: Margaret A. Judson, *The Crisis of the Constitution: An Essay in Constitutional and Political Thought in England,*

1603–1645 (London and New Brunswick, NJ: Rutgers University Press, 1949), pp. 191, 211; for recent analysis of this, see James S. Hart Jr, *The Rule of Law, 1603–1660: Crowns, Courts and Judges* (London: Longman, 2003), esp. p. 39; also J. P. Kenyon, *The Stuart Constitution: Documents and Commentary* (Cambridge: Cambridge University Press, 1966), p. 92.

3 Horst Dreitzel's work is exemplary in this respect. Horst Dreitzel, *Absolutismus und ständische Verfassung in Deutschland: Ein Beitrag zu Kontinuität und Diskontinuität der politischen Theorie in der frühen Neuzeit* (Mainz: Philipp von Zabern, 1992), pp. 139–40.

4 On the difficulties implicit in the employment of the term 'early Enlightenment' to describe to the eclectic philosophers of the seventeenth century, see Horst Dreitzel, 'The Reception of Hobbes in the Political Philosophy of the Early German Enlightenment', *History of European Ideas*, 29/3 (2003), pp. 255–89; 256. The account given here also subscribes to Dreitzel's claim that the term is applicable to the theorists discussed in this chapter.

5 Johannes Althusius, *Politica*, 3rd edn (Herborn: Corvinus, 1614), p. 174.

6 ibid., p. 177.

7 ibid., p. 169.

8 ibid., p. 286.

9 ibid., p. 277.

10 ibid., p. 585.

11 ibid., p. 894.

12 ibid., p. 296.

13 ibid., p. 307.

14 ibid., pp. 575, 596.

15 ibid., p. 575.

16 ibid., p. 885.

17 David Pareus, *Oratio de quaestione: Utrum leges Magistratus obligent in conscientia?* (Heidelberg: Rosa, 1616), p. 12.

18 David Pareus, *De jure regum et principum* (Amberg: Schönfeld, 1612), p. 77.

19 ibid., p. 60.

20 Reinhard König, 'Disputatio Politica', in Melchior Goldast (ed.), *Politica Imperialia* (Frankfurt am Main: Bringer, 1614), pp. 645–56; 646.

21 Matthias Stephani, *Tractatus de iurisdictione, qualemque habeant omnes iudices, tam seculares, quam ecclesiastici in imperio romano*, 3 vols (Frankfurt am Main: Kopff, 1611), Vol. II, p. 47.

22 Christophorus Besoldus, *Discursus Politici* (Strasburg: Zetzner, 1623), pp. 91–92.

23 Dominicus Arumaeus, *Commentarius juridico-historico-politicus de comitiis romano-germanici Imperij* (Jena: Lobenstein, 1630), p. 77.

24 Johannes Limnaeus, *Jus publicus imperii romano-germanici*, 3 vols (Strasburg: Spoor, 1699), Vol. I, pp. 7, 12.

25 See, on this, Rudolf Hoke, *Die Reichsstaatsrechtslehre des Johannes Limnaeus: Ein Beitrag zur deutschen Staatsrechtswissenschaft im 17. Jahrhundert* (Aalen: Scientia Verlag, 1968), pp. 106–17.

26 Benedict Carpzov, *Commentarius in Legem Regiam Germanorum* (Leipzig: Künnen, 1640), pp. 868–69.

27 Wilhelm Witzendorff, *De status et administrationis Imperij Romani forma hoderna Discursus* (Onolsbach: Lauer, 1643), p. 14.

28 Theodor Reinkingk, *Tractatus seculari et ecclesiastico*, 2nd edn (Marburg: Hampel und Genath, 1631), p. 38.

29 Veit Ludwig von Seckendorff, *Teutscher Fürsten-Stat*, 3rd edn (Frankfurt am Main: Götzen, 1665), p. 64.

30 ibid., pp. 69–70. The most eminent interpreters of Seckendorff define him both as an absolutist and as a theorist who recognized territorial sovereignty as

bound both by the empire and by obligations to regional estates (see Michael Stolleis, *Geschichte des öffentlichen Rechts in Deutschland*, in 3 vols. (Munich: Beck, 1988), Vol. I, p. 352).

31 Veit Ludwig von Seckendorff, *Jus publicum romano-germanicum* (Frankfurt am Main: Beyer, 1687), pp. 44.

32 ibid., p. 202.

33 Caspar Ziegler, *De juribus majestatis* (Wittenberg: 1681), p. 54.

34 ibid., p. 120.

35 Hermann Conring, 'Exercitatio octava de praecipuis negotiis in conventibus imperii Germanici ordinum', in *De finibus Imperii Germanici*, in 3 vols (Frankfurt am Main: J. Heinichen, 1693), pp. 398–462; 444.

36 ibid., p. 428.

37 ibid., p. 472.

38 Seckendorff, *Teutscher Fürsten-Stat*, p. 64.

39 Samuel Pufendorf, *De jure naturae et gentium*, in *Gesammelte Werke*, ed. W. Schmidt-Biggemann, planned for 9 vols (Berlin: Akademie Verlag, 1997–), Vol. IV, p. 669.

40 Herman Conring, 'Exercitatio Sexta de judiciis reipublicae Germanicae', in *De finibus*, pp. 214–324; 319.

41 Conring, *Propolitica*, p. 18.

42 For example, Conring, 'Exercitatio secunda de imperatore rom. Germanici', in *De finibus imperii Germanici*, pp. 32–72; 69.

43 Hermann Conring, *De origine iuris Germanici* (Helmstedt: Müller, 1649), pp. 194–95. On this, see Constantin Fasolt, 'A Question of Right: Hermann Conring's *New Discourse on the Roman-German Emperor*', *Sixteenth Century Journal*, 28/3 (1997), pp. 730–58; 740.

44 See Ziegler, *De juribus majestatis*, p. 488.

45 Samuel Strykius, *Quisquis Princeps est Imperator in suo territorio* (Wittenberg: 1690), p. 4.

46 Peter Johann Ludewig, *Germania Princeps* (Halle: Zeidler, 1711), pp. 111–12.

47 Burcard Gotthelf Struve, *Iurisprudentia feudalis* (Jena: Bielck, 1727), p. 242.

48 Nicolaus Gundling, *Ausführlicher und mit illustren Exemplen aus der Historie erläuterter Discours über J.F. Buddei Philosophiae practicae part III, die Politic* (Frankfurt am Main, 1733), p. 176.

49 On relations between Ludewig and Gundling and on Gundling's measured sympathy for the empire as a legal form, see Nokker Hammerstein, *Jus und Historie: Ein Beitrag zur Geschichte des historischen Denkens an deutschen Universitäten im späten 17. und im 18. Jahrhundert* (Göttingen: Vandenhoeck und Ruprecht, 1972), pp. 206, 223.

50 Gundling, *Discours*, p. 179.

51 ibid., pp. 189–90.

52 Johann Franz Buddeus, *Elementa Philosophiae Practicae*, new edn (Halle: Fritsch, 1727), pp. 357, 495–96.

53 The classification of certain constitutions in the church as 'episcopal' is something of an anachronism. It was not until the late eighteenth century that lawyers began systematically to differentiate between distinct types of constitution. This began with Daniel Nettelbladt, who initiated a more classificatory method in understanding ecclesiastical law (see Daniel Nettelbladt, *Systema elementare universae iurisprudentiae naturalis*, 5th edn, Halle: Renger, 1785, esp. pp. 376–78). This approach was then developed further by Friedrich Julius Stahl in the nineteenth century, who distinguished episcopal constitutions both from later 'territorial' models of church administration and from the 'collegial' models set out later by Christoph Matthäus Pfaff and Georg Ludwig Boehmer. See Christoph Matthäus Pfaff, *Origines juris ecclesiastici* (Tubingen: Schrammian, 1756),

p. 380, and Georg Ludwig Boehmer, *Principia iuris canonici* (Göttingen: Vandenhoeck, 1767), p. 11. More recently, it has been justifiably questioned whether any of the early constitutionalists can be unreservedly classed as 'episcopalists' (see Schneider, *Ius Reformandi*, pp. 310–11).

54 Stephani, *Institutiones iuris canonici*, pp. 16, 51–52.
55 Stephani, *Tractatus de jurisdictione*, Vol. II, p. 240.
56 Stephani, *Tractatus de jurisdictione*, Vol. III, p. 118.
57 Carpzov, *Jurisprudentia ecclesiastica*, pp. 5, 6.
58 Reinkingk, *Tractatus seculari et ecclesiastica*, p. 511.
59 Johann Valentin Andreä, *Freye Feder vom Ubelstand der Kirchen* (Frankfurt am Main: Zunner, 1678), p. 62.
60 Philipp Jacob Spener, *Pia Desideria: Oder herzliches Verlangen nach gottgefälliger Besserung der wahren Evangelischen Kirchen* (Frankfurt am Main: Zunner, 1676), p. 61.
61 ibid., p. 167.
62 Philipp Jacob Spener, *Letzte theologische Bedencken* (Halle: Verlegung des Waysenhauses, 1711), p. 580.
63 See Wolfgang Sommer, 'Johann Arndt im Amt des Generalsuperintenden in Braunschweig-Lüneburg', in Sommer (ed.), *Politik, Theologie und Frömmigkeit im Lutherthum der Frühen Neuzeit: Ausgewählte Aufsätze* (Göttigen: Vandenhoeck & Ruprecht, 1999), pp. 227–38; 233.
64 Johann Arndt, *Postilla, oder Auslegung des Sontags und aller Festen Evangelien durch das gantze Jahr* (Lüneburg: Johannes Stern, 1680), p. 457.
65 Johann Gerhard, *Loci Theologici*, 10 vols. (Berlin: Schlawitz, 1868), Vol. VI, p. 176.
66 ibid., p. 261.
67 See August Hermann Francke, *Schrift über eine Reform des Erziehungs-und Bildungswesens als Ausgangspunkt einer geistlichen und sozialen Neuordnung der Evangelischen Kirche des 18. Jahrhunderts. Der große Aufsatz*, edited by O. Podczeck (Berlin: Akademie Verlag, 1962), esp. pp. 74–75.
68 ibid., p. 110.
69 Important on this, although rather inclined to overstate its case, is Richard L. Gawthrop, *Pietism and the Making of Eighteenth-Century Prussia* (Cambridge: Cambridge University Press, 1993), pp. 120–21, 198–213.
70 Hermann Conring, 'Exercitatio septima de constitutione episcoporum Germaniae', in *De finibus Imperii Germaniae*, pp. 325–496; 403.
71 ibid., p. 479.
72 ibid., pp. 482–83.
73 Conring, 'Exercitatio sexta', p. 320.
74 Seckendorff, *Teutscher Fürsten-Stat*, p. 303.
75 ibid., pp. 304, 311.
76 Seckendorff, *Christen-Stat*, (Leipzig: J. F. Gleditsch, 1693), pp. 301–2.
77 ibid., p. 296.
78 ibid., pp. 689–90.
79 ibid., pp. 680–84.
80 ibid., pp. 688–90.
81 Nicolaus Gundling, *Allgemeines geistliches Recht der drey christlichen Haupt-Religionen* (Frankfurt am Main: Spring, 1743), p. 787.
82 ibid., p. 837.
83 ibid., p. 823.
84 For exemplary analysis of this, see Horst Dreitzel, 'Christliche Aufklärung durch fürstlichen Absolutismus: Thomasius und die Destruktion des frühneuzeitlichen Konfessionsstaates', in Friedrich Vollhardt (ed.), *Christian Thomasius (1655–1728): Neue Forschungen im Kontext der Frühaufklärung* (Tubingen: Niemeyer, 1997), pp. 17–50; 39.

85 Christian Thomasius and Enno Rudolph Brenneysen, *Das Recht evangelischer Fürsten in theologischen Streitigkeiten* (Halle: Salfeld, 1713), p. 53.
86 ibid., p. 26.
87 Christian Thomasius, *Vollständige Erläuterung der Kirchen-Rechts-Gelahrtheit*, in 2 vols (Frankfurt am Main: 1738), Vol. I, p. 16.
88 Thomasius and Brenneysen, *Das Recht evangelischer Fürsten*, p. 223.
89 Christian Thomasius, *Historia Contentionis inter Imperium et Sacerdotium* (Halle: Renger, 1722), p. xxxiv.
90 Ziegler, *De juribus majestatis*, p. 326.
91 Thomasius, *Vollständige Erläuterung der Kirchen-Rechts-Gelahrtheit*, Vol. I, p. 52.
92 See Christian Thomasius, *Monatsgespräche* (1688), p. 734.
93 Thomasius and Brenneysen, *Das Recht evangelischer Fürsten*, pp. 40–41.
94 ibid., p. 27.
95 ibid., p. 55.
96 ibid., p. 127.
97 Thomasius, *Vollständige Erläuterung der Kirchen-Rechts-Gelahrtheit*, Vol. I, p. 302.
98 Severinus de Monzambano [Samuel Pufendorf], *De statu imperii Germanici* (Geneva: Columesium, 1668), p. 200.
99 Samuel Pufendorf, *De habitu religionis christianae ad vitam civilem* (Bremen: Schwerdfeger, 1687), p. 101.
100 ibid., p. 150.
101 ibid., p. 168.
102 For an excellent and provocative example of this view, see David Saunders, *Anti-Lawyers: Religion and the Critics of Law and State* (London and New York: Routledge, 1997), p. 89; also Ian Hunter, *Rival Enlightenments: Civil and Metaphysical Philosophy in Early Modern Germany* (Cambridge: Cambridge University Press, 2001), pp. 90–91.
103 Here cited from Reinkingk, *Tractatus seculari et ecclesiastico*, p. 495. This principle was widespread in the ecclesiastical-constitutional documents of this time. See also, for example, Thomasius, *Historia Contentionis inter Imperium et Sacerdotium*, p. xxxii.
104 Balthasar Meisner, *De ecclesia* (Wittenberg: J. Hellwigh, 1630), pp. 239–40.
105 König, *Disputatio politica*, p. 645.
106 Limnaeus, *Jus publicus imperii*, p. 11.
107 Stephani, *Tractatus de jurisdictione*, p. 46.
108 Ziegler, *De juribus majestatis*, p. 18.
109 ibid., p. 19.
110 ibid., p. 126.
111 It is not necessary to share Christoph Link's perhaps slightly exaggerated belief that early German constitutional theory was *in toto* opposed to princely absolutism to accept that natural-law arguments played an important role in placing normative restrictions on princely authority and in propagating models of a representative or delegatory constitution. See Christoph Link, *Herrschaftsordnung und bürgerliche Freiheit: Grenzen der Staatsgewalt in der älteren deutschen Staatslehre* (Vienna: Böhlau, 1979), p. 89.
112 Matthias Stephani, *Tractatus de iurisdictione*, p. 46.
113 Seckendorff, *Fürsten-Stat*, pp. 62, 78.
114 Seckendorff, *Christen-Stat*, p. 275.
115 Heinrich Voß, *Dissertatio de ratione status* (Helmstedt: Müller, 1651), pp. 55–59. This dissertation was written by Voß. However, Conring, in the manner of the day, defended the thesis, and it is usually included in the list of works attributed to Conring himself.

116 Heinrich Cocceji, *Juris publici prudentia compendio exhibita* (Frankfurt am Main: Schrey, 1695), p. 21.
117 Heinrich Cocceji, *Autonomia juris gentium* (Frankfurt am Main: Conrad, 1720), pp. 78–81.
118 Samuelis de Cocceji, *Jus civile controversum*, new edn, 2 vols (Leipzig: Weidmann, 1791), Vol. I, p. 159.
119 Justus Henning Boehmer, *Introductio in ius publicum universale* (Frankfurt am Main: Trattner, 1758), p. 268.
120 ibid., p. 40.
121 ibid., p. 292.
122 ibid., p. 262.
123 ibid, p. 247.
124 Seckendorff, *Christen-Stat*, p. 320; Thomasius and Brenneysen, *Das Recht evangelischer Fürsten*, p. 65.
125 Pufendorf, *De jure naturae et gentium*, pp. 14–15.
126 ibid., p. 16.
127 For clarification on this point, I have consulted J. B. Schneewind, *The Invention of Autonomy: A History of Modern Moral Philosophy* (Cambridge: Cambridge University Press, 1998), p. 120.
128 Samuel Pufendorf, *Elementa jurisprudentiae universalis*, in Pufendorf, *Gesammelte Werke*, Vol. III, pp. 128–29.
129 Pufendorf, *De jure naturae et gentium*, p. 133.
130 ibid., p. 132.
131 ibid., p. 30.
132 ibid., p. 46.
133 ibid., p. 144.
134 ibid., p. 32.
135 ibid., p. 148.
136 There has been much interpretive controversy over Pufendorf's attitude to religiously founded doctrines of natural law. Some commentators have seen the voluntaristic aspect of his work as providing for, in principle, a full secularization of the law and a final positioning of the state on positive-legal foundations. (See, for example: Thomas Behme, *Samuel van Pufendorf: Naturrecht Und Staat*, Göttingen: Vandenhoeck 4 Ruprecht, 1995, p. 17) Others have proposed a diametrically opposed interpretation, namely, that his work hinges on the postulate of a 'vertical obligation' between God and humanity, and that natural law in human societies is always natural law willed by God. (See René Sève, *Leibniz et l'école moderne du droit naturel*, Paris: PUF, 1989, p. 59; also Leonard Krieger, *The Politics of Discretion: Pufendorf and the Acceptance of Natural Law*, Chicago, Ill.: Chicago University Press, 1965, p. 80).
137 Pufendorf, *De jure naturae et gentium* p. 30.
138 ibid., p. 71.
139 ibid., p. 697.
140 ibid., p. 132.
141 See Samuel Pufendorf, *De officio hominis et civis juxta legem naturalem*, in: *Gesammelte Werke*, Vol. II, pp. 71–72. For an interpretation of Pufendorf as a consensualist, see T. J. Hochstrasser, *Natural Law Theories in the Early Enlightenment* (Cambridge: Cambridge University Press, 2000), p. 101. For an interpretation that places him closer to absolutism, see Hans Medick, *Naturzustand und Naturgeschichte der bürgerlichen Gesellschaft: Die Ursprünge der bürgerlichen Sozialtheorie als Geschichtsphilosophie und Sozialwissenschaft bei Samuel Pufendorf, John Locke und Adam Smith* (Göttingen: Vandenhoeck und Ruprecht, 1973), p. 69; Behme, *Samuel von Pufendorf, p. 133.*

142 Pufendorf, *De officio*, p. 148.
143 ibid., p. 736.
144 ibid., p. 118.
145 ibid., p. 736.
146 ibid., p. 676.
147 ibid., p. 682.
148 ibid., p. 698.
149 ibid., p. 697.
150 ibid., pp. 705–6.
151 Severinus de Monzambano [Samuel Pufendorf], *De statu imperii Germanici* (Geneva: Columesium, 1668), p. 157.
152 ibid., p. 192.
153 I am indebted to Stolleis's excellent interpretation of the intentions behind this book (see Stolleis, *Geschichte des öffentlichen Rechts*, Vol. I, p. 23).
154 Thomasius, *Monatsgespräche*, pp. 785–86.
155 Christian Thomasius, *Einleitung zur Hoff-Philosophie* (Leipzig: Weidmann, 1712), p. 290.
156 Christian Thomasius, *Einleiting zu der Vernunfft-Lehre* (Halle: Salfeld, 1711), pp. 5–6.
157 Christian Thomasius, *Historia Juris Naturalis* (Halle: Salfeld, 1719), p. 6.
158 Christian Thomasius, *Von der Kunst vernünfftig und tugendhafft zu lieben* (Halle: Salfeld, 1710), pp. 41–42.
159 Christian Thomasius, *Summarischer Entwurf der Grundlehren, die einem studioso iuris zu wissen und auf universitäten zu lernen nötig sind* (Halle: Renger, 1699), p. 4.
160 ibid., pp. 35–36.
161 ibid., p. 36.
162 Thomasius, *Historia juris naturalis*, p. 4.
163 Thomasius, *Summarischer Entwurf*, p. 107.
164 ibid., p. 4.
165 ibid., p. 37.
166 Thomasius, *Monatsgespräche*, p. 762.
167 Thomasius, *Von der Kunst vernünfftig und tugendhafft zu lieben*, p. 92.
168 ibid., p. 310.
169 ibid., p. 325.
170 Thomasius, *Summarischer Entwurf*, p. 103.
171 Christian Thomasius, *Fundamenta juris naturae et gentium*, 4th edn (Halle: Salfeld, 1718), p. 44.
172 Christian Thomasius, *Ausübung der Vernunfft-Lehre* (Halle: Salfeld, 1710), pp. 43, 79.
173 ibid., p. 152.
174 ibid., p. 156.
175 ibid., p. 152.
176 See Hochstrasser, *Natural Law Theories*, p. 135.
177 Johann Jacob Schmauß, *Neues Systema des Rechts der Natur* (Göttigen: Vandenhoeck, 1754), p. 517.
178 Thomasius, *Historia juris naturae*, p. 67.
179 ibid., pp. 58–59.
180 Gottfried Wilhelm Leibniz, 'Initium institutionem juris perpetui', in Georg Mollat (ed.), *Rechtsphilosophisches aus Leibnizens ungedruckten Schriften* (Leipzig: Robolsky, 1885), pp. 1–7; 3.
181 Gottfried Wilhelm Leibniz, 'De tribus juris naturae et gentium gradibus', in: Georg Mollat (ed.), *Rechtsphilosophisches aus Leibnizens ungedruckten Schriften*, pp. 13–21; 14.

182 Leibniz, 'Initium institutionem juris perpetui', p. 6.
183 Gottfried Wilhelm Leibniz, *Codex Juris Gentium* (Hanover: S. Ammonus, 1693), p. 10.
184 Gottfried Wilhelm Leibniz, 'Von der Weisheit', in *Textes inédits*, edited by Gaston Grua (Paris: PUF, 1948), pp. 584–88; 585.
185 Gottfried Wilhelm Leibniz, 'Méditation sur la notion commune de la justice', in Georg Mollat (ed.), *Rechtsphilosophisches aus Leibnizens ungedruckten Schriften*, pp. 56–81; 59.
186 Leibniz, 'Initium institutionem juris perpetui', p. 13.
187 Leibniz, 'Méditation', p. 71.
188 Leibniz, 'Monita quaedam ad Samuelis Pufendorfii principia', in *Opera*, pp. 275–83; 279.
189 Leibniz, 'Méditation', p. 59.
190 Leibniz, 'Monita', p. 280.
191 Gottfried Wilhelm Leibniz, 'Observationes de principio juris', in Leibniz, *Opera Omnia*, edited by L. Dutens, 6 vols. (Geneva: de Tournes, 1763), Vol. IV/3, pp. 270–75; 270.
192 Leibniz, 'Méditation', p. 60.
193 Leibniz, 'De tribus juris naturae et gentium gradibus', p. 17. See also Leibniz, *Codex Juris Gentium*, p. 9.
194 ibid., pp. 20–21.
195 Leibniz, 'Méditation', p. 76.
196 Leibniz, 'Observationes', p. 272.
197 Leibniz, 'Méditation', pp. 56–57.
198 Gottfried Wilhem Leibniz, *Essais de la Theodiceé sur la bonté de Dieu, la liberté de l'homme et l'origine du mal* (Amsterdam: Isaac Treyel, 1712), p. 363.
199 ibid., pp. 272–73.
200 Leibniz, *Essais de la Theodicée*, pp. 175–76.
201 Johann Erhard Kappen (ed.), *Sammlung einiger Vertrauten Briefe welche zwischen dem weltberühmten Freyherrn Gottfried Wilhelm von Leibnitz und dem berühmten Berlinischen Hof-Prediger Herrn Daniel Ernst Jablonski* (Leipzig: Breitkopf, 1745), p. 247.
202 Gottfried Wilhelm Leibniz, 'Reunion der Kirchen', in Leibniz, *Sämtliche Schriften und Briefe*, edited by the Zentralinstitut für Philosophie an der Akademie der Wissenschaften der DDR, planned for over 80 vols (Berlin: Akademie-Verlag, 1923–), 4/3: pp. 260–98; 282. Paul Eisenkopf quotes Leibniz as stating that 'Protestants have to be prepared to re-enter the hierarchy of the universal church' (see Paul Eisenkopf, *Leibniz und die Einigung der Christenheit*, Munich: Ferdinand Schöningh, 1975, p. 195).
203 Gottfried Wilhelm Leibniz, *De jure suprematus ac legationis principium Germaniae*, in *Sämtliche Schriften und Briefe*, 4/2: pp. 3–270; 50, 90.
204 ibid., pp. 57, 64.
205 Gottfried Wilhelm Leibniz, 'Thesis', in: *Sämtliche Schriften*, 4/2, pp. 274–76; 275.
206 Gottfried Wilhelm Leibniz, *Entretien entre Philarete et d'Eugene*, in: *Sämtliche Schriften* 4/2, pp. 289–333; 303.
207 ibid., p. 291.
208 Compare Hartmut Schiedermaier, *Das Phänomen der Macht und die Idee des Rechts bei Gottfried Wilhelm Leibniz* (Wiesbaden: Franz Steiner, 1970), p. 98; also Erwin Ruck, *Die Leibniz'sche Staatsidee: Aus den Quellen dargestellt* (Tubingen: J. C. B. Mohr, 1909), pp. 10, 33. On the relation between Leibniz and Aquinas, see Patrick Riley, *Leibniz' Universal Jurisprudence: Justice as the Charity of the Wise* (Cambridge, Mass.: Harvard University Press, 1996), p. 226.

209 Leibniz, *Essais de la Theodicée*, pp. 2–3. See also: Sève, *Leibniz*, p. 126.
210 On the sympathetic reception of Wolff in Roman Catholic universities, see Michael Stolleis, *Geschichte öffentlichen Rechts*, Vol. I, p. 292.
211 Christian Wolff, *Vernünftige Gedanken von dem gesellschaftlichen Leben der Menschen und insonderheit dem gemeinen Wesen*, 2nd edn (Halle: Renger, 1756), p. 7.
212 ibid., p. 165.
213 ibid., p. 461.
214 Christian Wolff, *Vernünfftige Gedancken von der Menschen Thun und Lassen*, 5th edn (Frankfurt am Main: 1736), p. 27.
215 ibid., p. 28.
216 Christian Wolff, *Vernünfftige Gedanken von Gott der Welt und der Seele des Menschen,* 2nd edn (Halle: Renger, 1751), p. 105.
217 Wolff, *Vernünfftige Gedanken von Gott der Welt und der Seele des Menschen*, p. 81.
218 Christian Wolff, *Grundsätze des Natur- und Völckerrechts* (Halle: Renger, 1754), pp. 568–69.
219 ibid., p. 26. For the rivalry between more liberal and more absolutistic interpretations of Wolff, see Werner Frauendienst, *Christian Wolff als Staatsdenker* (Berlin: Ebering, 1927), p. 149 and Hanns-Martin Bachmann, *Die naturrechtliche Staatslehre Christian Wolffs* (Berlin: Duncker und Humblot, 1977), pp. 196–201. Frauendiest sees Wolff as an apologist for absolutistic territorial rule. Bachmann sees him as an early theorist of legal personality and rights against the state. In line with his general preference for the Pufendorfian tradition, Christoph Link also sees Wolff as a highly conservative thinker (see Link, *Herrschaftsordnung*, p. 55).
220 Wolff, *Vernünfftige Gedanken von Gott der Welt und der Seele des Menschen*, pp. 420, 427, 430.
221 Wolff, *Vernünftige Gedanken von dem gesellschaftlichen Leben der Menschen*, pp. 512–17.
222 ibid., p. 174.
223 ibid., pp. 485–86.
224 ibid., p. 461.
225 ibid., p. 466; also Wolff, *Grundsätze des Natur-und Völckerrechts*, pp. 700, 704–5.
226 See Christian Schröder, *Naturbegriff und Moralbegründung: Die Grundlegung der Ethik bei Christian Wolff und deren Kritik durch Immanuel Kant* (Stuttgart: Kohlhammer, 1988), p. 213.
227 Wolff, *Grundsätze des Natur-und Völckerrechts*, p. 47.
228 ibid., p. 59.
229 Johann Gottlieb Heineccius, *Elementa juris naturae et gentium* (Halle: Ophantroph, 1738), p. 14.
230 ibid., pp. 46–47.
231 ibid., p. 10.
232 Buddeus, *Elementa*, pp. 363–64.
233 ibid., p. 350.
234 ibid., p. 207.
235 Johann Franz Buddeus, *Selecta iuris naturae et gentium* (Halle: Orphanotroph, 1727), p. 66.
236 The main function of natural law, Buddeus argues, is 'subordinate to ethics', and it provides a norm by which humans regulate their actions. Those who act in accordance with this norm testify that they love God (ibid., p. 204).
237 Christian August Crusius, *Anweisung vernünftig zu leben* (Leipzig: J. F. Gleditsch, 1744), pp. 442, 447, 713–14.
238 ibid., p. 867.
239 ibid., p. 710.
240 ibid., pp. 411, 711.

241 ibid., p. 454.
242 Johann Heinrich Gottlob von Justi, *Die Natur und das Wesen der Staaten* (Berlin: J. H. Rüdiger, 1760), pp. 47, 60.
243 Johann Heinrich Gottlob von Justi, *Der Grundriß der guten Regierung* (Frankfurt am Main: Garve, 1759), p. 148.
244 Justi, *Die Natur und das Wesen der Staaten*, p. 45.
245 ibid., p. 251. For an account of changes in Justi's outlook, see Stolleis, *Geschichte des öffentlichen Rechts*, Vol. I, pp. 380–81.
246 August Ludwig Schlözer, *Allgemeines Staatsrecht und Statsverfassungslehre* (Göttingen: Vandenhoeck und Ruprecht, 1793), pp. 95, 114–15.
247 ibid., pp. 66, 158.
248 Johann Jacob Moser, *Rechtliches Bedencken von Privat-Versammlungen der Kinder Gottes* (Tubingen: J. Sigmund, 1734), p. 20.
249 Johann Jacob Moser, *Von der teutschen Religionsverfassung*, in *Neues deutsches Staatsrecht*, 20 vols (Stuttgart: Mezler, 1762–82), Vol. VII, p. 535.
250 Johann Jacob Moser, *Von der Landeshoheit derer teutschen Reichsstände überhaupt* in *Neues deutsches Straatscrecht* Vol. I, p. 63; also Moser, *Von der teutschen Religionsverfassung*, pp. 337–38.
251 Moser, *Von der Landeshoheit derer teutschen Reichsstände überhaupt*, p. 30.
252 Johann Jacob Moser, *Von Deutschland und dessen Staat-Verfassung*, in *Neues Deutsches Staatsrecht*, Vol. I, p. 213.
253 For an example of Moser's practical natural law, see Johann Jacob Moser, *Von der teutschen Reichs-Stände Landen, deren Landschaften, Unterthanen, Landes-Freyheiten, Beschwerden, Schulden und Zusammenkünften*, in *Neues Deutsches Staatsrecht*, Vol. XIII, p. 285.
254 Moser, *Von der teutschen Religionsverfassung*, p. 568.
255 Johann Jacob Moser, *Von der Landeshoheit im Geistlichen*, in *Neues deutsches Staatsrecht*, Vol. XV, p. 61.
256 Johann Jacob Moser, *Von denen deutschen Reichs-Tagen*, in *Neues deutsches Staatsrecht*, Vol. V, p. 540.
257 See on this: Reinhard Rürup, *Johann Jacob Moser: Pietismus und Reform* (Wiesbaden: Franz Steiner, 1965), p. 109.
258 Mosern, *Von der teutschen Reichs-Stände Landen*, p. 1146.
259 ibid., p. 1148.
260 Johann Stephan Pütter, *Geist des Westphälischen Friedens* (Göttigen: Vandenhoeck und Ruprecht, 1795), pp. 346, 398, 448.
261 Johann Stephan Pütter, *Beiträge zum teutschen Staats-und Fürsten-Rechte* (Göttingen: Vandenhoeck, 1777), p. 32.
262 ibid., pp. 42, 57.
263 ibid., p. 324.
264 ibid., pp. 319, 362.
265 Johann Stephan Pütter, *Kurzer Begriff des teutschen Staatsrechts* (Göttingen: Vandenhoeck, 1768), p. 50.
266 ibid., pp. 50–51, 94.
267 Gottfried Achenwall, *Die Staatsklugheit nach ihren ersten Grundsätzen* (Göttingen: Vandenhöck, 1774), pp. 21–24, 59.

3 German idealism

1 An analogous argument is made in far more critical terms by Reinhart Koselleck and the historians he has influenced. Koselleck has argued that the moral philosophy of the Kantian Enlightenment developed metaphysical ideas to assert a 'claim to domination' over the state, and that in so doing it destroyed the positive foundations of statehood that had emerged through the absolutism

of the early Enlightenment and that expressly limited the unsettling impact of moral metaphysics on politics (see Reinhart Koselleck, *Kritik und Krise. Ein Beitrag zur Pathogenese der burgerlichen Welt*, Freiburg: Alber, 1959, esp. p. 101). For a stronger version of this argument, see: Hunter, *Rival Enlightenments*, which accuses Kant of a returning to neoscholastic natural law (p. 323). Despite my great admiration for the work of these theorists, my view is that the Kantian Enlightenment should not be viewed as a re-entry of metaphysical abstraction into political debate or as a dismembering of the secularist achievements of the early Enlightenment. Rather, it should be viewed as a new stage in the attempt reliably to positivize law after the initial secular crisis of the Reformation.

2 Immanuel Kant, *Kritik der reinen Vernunft*, in *Werkausgabe*, edited by Wilhelm Weischedel, 12 vols. (Frankfurt am Main: Suhrkamp, 1976), Vol. I–II, p. 708.
3 ibid., p. 706.
4 Immanuel Kant, *Metaphysik der Sitten*, in *Werkausgabe*, Vol. VIII, pp. 309–634; 333.
5 Immanuel Kant, 'Über den Gemeinspruch: Das mag in der Theorie richtig sein, taugt aber nicht für die Praxis', in *Werkausgabe*, Vol. XI, pp. 127–72; 145.
6 Immanuel Kant, *Grundlegung zur Metaphysik der Sitten*, in *Werkausgabe*, Vol. VII, pp. 11–102; 84.
7 Kant, *Kritik der Urteilskraft*, in *Werkausgabe*, Vol. X, p. 412.
8 Kant, 'Über den Gemeinspruch', p. 137.
9 Kant, *Metaphysik der Sitten*, p. 569.
10 Kant, *Grundlegung zur Metaphysik der Sitten*, p. 65.
11 Kant, *Metaphysik der Sitten*, p. 505.
12 ibid., p. 550.
13 ibid., p. 334.
14 Immanuel Kant, *Die Religion innerhalb der Grenzen der bloßen Vernunft*, in *Werkausgabe*, Vol. VIII, pp. 645–879; 649.
15 Kant, *Grundlegung zur Metaphysik der Sitten*, p. 88.
16 Kant, *Die Religion* p. 714.
17 ibid., p. 758.
18 ibid., p. 852.
19 Carl Friedrich Bahrdt, *Würdigung der natürlichen Religion und des Naturalismus in Beziehung auf Staat und Menschenrechte* (Halle: Francke und Bispink, 1791), p. 7.
20 Kant, *Die Religion*, p. 755.
21 Immanuel Kant, *Grundlegung zur Metaphysik der Sitten*, p. 51.
22 ibid., p. 89.
23 ibid., p. 69.
24 See below, pp. 241–242.
25 Kant, *Metaphysik der Sitten*, p. 512.
26 ibid., p. 325.
27 ibid., p. 525.
28 ibid., p. 326.
29 Kant, 'Über den Gemeinspruch', p. 163.
30 Kant, *Die Religion*, p. 758.
31 Kant, 'Über den Gemeinspruch', p. 153.
32 ibid., p. 144.
33 Immanuel Kant, *Zum Ewigen Frieden*, in *Werkausgabe*, Vol. XI, pp. 195–251; 205.
34 Kant, *Metaphysik der Sitten*, p. 437.
35 Kant, *Zum ewigen Frieden*, p. 197.
36 Kant, *Metaphysik der Sitten*, p. 431.

37 ibid., p. 569.
38 Kant, 'Über den Gemeinspruch', p. 153.
39 Kant, *Zum ewigen Frieden*, p. 207.
40 Kant, *Metaphysik der Sitten*, pp. 430–31.
41 ibid., p. 461.
42 Bahrdt, *Würdigung der natürlichen Religion*, p. 237.
43 Karl Heinrich Heydenreich, *Grundsätze des natürlichen Staatsrechts* (Leipzig: Weygand, 1795), p. 15.
44 Theodor Schmalz, *Handbuch des römischen Privatrechts. Für Vorlesungen über Justinianische Institutionen*, 2nd edn (Königsberg: F. Nicolovius, 1801), p. 18.
45 Theodor Schmalz, *Das natürliche Staatsrecht* (Königsberg: Fr. Nicolovius, 1794), p. 61.
46 Johann Benjamin Erhard, *Ueber das Recht des Volks zu einer Revolution* (Jena: Gabler, 1795), pp. 92–93.
47 Kant, *Metaphysik der Sitte*n pp. 439–40.
48 ibid., p. 498.
49 ibid., p. 366.
50 ibid., p. 424.
51 Johann Gottlieb Fichte, *Grundlage des Naturrechts*, in *Werke*, edited by I. H. Fichte, 8 vols (Berlin: de Gruter, 1971), Vol. III, pp. 1–385; 2–3.
52 ibid., p. 8.
53 ibid., p. 39.
54 ibid., p. 120.
55 ibid., p. 9.
56 ibid., p. 10.
57 ibid., p. 151.
58 ibid., p. 185.
59 ibid., p. 166.
60 ibid., p. 16.
61 ibid., p. 197.
62 ibid., p. 129.
63 Johann Gottlieb Fichte, *Der geschlossene Handelsstaat*, in *Werke*, edited by I. H. Fichte, 8 vols (Berlin: de Gruter, 1971), Vol. III, pp. 387–513; 403.
64 Johann Gottlieb Fichte, *Grundlage des Naturrechts*, in Werke, Vol. III, pp. 1–385; 39.
65 Friedrich Wilhelm Joseph von Schelling, *Vom Ich als Prinzip der Philosophie oder über das Unbedingte im menschlichen Wissen*, in *Werke*, edited by Manfred Schröter, 12 vols (Munich: Beck and Oldenbourg, 1927–54), Vol. I, pp. 73–168; 122.
66 ibid., p. 123.
67 ibid., p. 122.
68 ibid., p. 165.
69 Friedrich Wilhelm Joseph von Schelling, *System des transcendentalen Idealismus*, in *Werke*, Vol. II, pp. 327–634; 535.
70 ibid., p. 177.
71 ibid., p. 165.
72 Friedrich Wilhelm Joseph von Schelling, *Neue Deduktion des Naturrechts*, in *Werke*, Vol. I, pp. 169–204; 172.
73 ibid., p. 184.
74 ibid., p. 203.
75 Schelling, *System des transcendentalen Idealismus*, p. 583.
76 ibid., p. 604.
77 ibid., p. 586. Very good on Schelling's early political thought is Alexander Hollerbach, *Der Rechtsgedanke bei Schelling: Quellenstudien zu seiner Rechts-und*

Staatsphilosophie (Frankfurt am Main: Klostermann, 1957). On this point, see especially p. 84.
78 Schelling, *System des transcendentalen Idealismus*, p. 583.
79 G. W. F. Hegel, *Grundlinien der Philosophie des Rechts*, in *Werke*, edited by E. Moldenhauer and K. M. Michel, 20 vols (Frankfurt am Main: Suhrkamp, 1969), Vol. VII, p. 46.
80 ibid., p. 83.
81 G. W. F. Hegel, *Phänomenologie des Geistes*, in *Werke*, Vol. III, pp. 356–58.
82 Hegel, *Grundlinien der Philosophie des Rechts*, p. 95.
83 ibid., p. 407.
84 ibid., p. 205.
85 ibid., p. 233.
86 ibid., p. 250.
87 ibid., p. 76.
88 Hegel, *Die Verfassung Deutschlands*, in *Werke*, Vol. I, pp. 461–581; 555.
89 Hegel, *Philosophie des Rechts*, p. 346.
90 Hegel, *Grundlinien der Philosophie des Rechts*, p. 399.
91 G. W. F. Hegel, *Die Phänomenologie des Geistes*, in *Werke*, Vol. III, pp. 147.
92 See, especially, Karl Ludwig von Haller, *Restauration der Staatswissenschaft*, 2nd edn, 6 vols (Winterthur: Steiner, 1821–25), Vol. III, p. 166.
93 Hegel, *Phänomenologie*, pp. 145–55.
94 See Joachim Ritter, *Hegel und die französische Revolution* (Frankfurt am Main: Suhrkamp, 1965), p. 69–70. I take this to be Ritter's intimation.
95 G. W. F. Hegel, *Vorlesungen über die Philosophie der Geschichte*, in *Werke*, Vol. XII, p. 326.
96 G. W. F. Hegel, *Der Geist des Christentums und sein Schicksal*, in *Werke*, Vol. I, pp. 274–418; 288, 299.
97 ibid., p. 331.
98 ibid., pp. 323–26.
99 ibid., p. 370.
100 ibid., p. 394.
101 ibid., p. 323.
102 See Michael Theunissen, *Hegels Lehre vom absoluten Geist als theologisch-politischer Traktat* (Berlin: de Gruyter, 1970), p. 380.

4 Historicism and romanticism

1 Johann Gottfried Herder, *Auch eine Philosophie der Geschichte zur Bildung der Menschheit*, in Herder, *Werke* in 5 vols. (Berlin and Weimar: Aufbau Verlag, 1978), Vol. IV, pp. 39–137; 65.
2 Gustav Hugo, *Lehrbuch eines Civilistischen Cursus*, 7th edn, 7 vols (Berlin: August Mylius, 1823), Vol. I, *Lehrbuch der juristischen Encyclopädie*, p. 19.
3 ibid., p. 55.
4 Gustav Hugo, *Lehrbuch eines Civilistischen Cursus* (Berlin: August Mylius, 1819), Vol. II, *Lehrbuch des Naturrechts als einer Philosophie des positiven Rechts, besonders des Privatrechts*, p. 36.
5 ibid., p. 487.
6 ibid., p. 189.
7 Hugo, *Lehrbuch eines Civilistischen Cursus*, Vol. I, p. 77.
8 ibid., p. 19.
9 Friedrich Carl von Savigny, *Vermischte Schriften* (Berlin: Veit und Comp, 1850), p. 113.
10 Friedrich Carl von Savigny, *Vom Beruf unserer Zeit für Gesetzgebung* (Heidelberg: J. C. B. Mohr, 1840), p. 11.

11 Friedrich Carl von Savigny, *System des heutigen Römischen Rechts*, 9 vols (Berlin: Veit und Comp, 1840), Vol. I, pp. 21–22.
12 Friedrich Carl von Savigny, *Das Recht des Besitzes: Eine civilistische Abhandlung*, 6th edn (Giessen: Georg Friedrich Meyer, 1837), p. 25.
13 ibid., p. 279.
14 ibid., p. 383.
15 Savigny, *Vom Beruf unserer Zeit für Gesetzgebung*, p. 30.
16 ibid., p. 30.
17 Savigny, *System des heutigen Römischen Rechts*, Vol. III, p. 311.
18 Savigny, *System des heutigen Römischen Rechts*, Vol. I, p. 23.
19 ibid., p. 22.
20 ibid., pp. 22–23.
21 Wilhelm Humboldt, 'Über die Aufgabe des Geschichtschreibers', in Humboldt, *Werke*, edited by A. Flitner and K. Giel, 5 vols (Stuttgart: Cotta, 1960), Vol. I, pp. 585–606; 599.
22 ibid., p. 605.
23 Wilhelm von Humboldt, 'Ideen über Staatsverfassung, durch die neue französische Constitution veranlasst', in *Werke*, Vol. I, pp. 33–42; 35–36.
24 Wilhelm von Humboldt, 'Über die Aufgabe des Geschichtsschreibers', p. 603.
25 Wilhelm von Humboldt, 'Theorie der Bildung des Menschen', in *Werke*, Vol. I, pp. 234–40; 240.
26 Wilhelm von Humboldt, 'Über die deutsche Staatsverfassung', in *Werke*, Vol. IV, pp. 302–22; 304.
27 ibid., p. 306.
28 Humboldt, 'Ideen über Staatsverfassung', pp. 34–36.
29 Wilhelm von Humboldt, 'Über Einrichtung landständischer Verfassungen', in *Werke*, Vol. IV: pp. 433–500; 434–36, 447.
30 Leopold von Ranke, 'Einleitung', in *Historisch-politische Zeitschrift*, Vol. I (1832), pp. 1–9; 2.
31 ibid., p. 5.
32 Leopold von Ranke, 'Frankreich und Deutschland', in *Historisch-politische Zeitschrift*, Vol. I (1832), pp. 77–93; 83–84.
33 Leopold von Ranke, 'Politisches Gespräch', in *Historisch-politische Zeitschrift*, Vol. II (1833), pp. 775–807; 789.
34 ibid., p. 806.
35 ibid., p. 794.
36 Ranke, 'Einleitung', p. 6.
37 Ranke, 'Frankreich und Deutschland', p. 91.
38 ibid., p. 86.
39 ibid., p. 86.
40 Johann Gustav Droysen, *Vorlesungen über die Freiheitskriege*, 2 vols (Kiel: Universitäts-Buchhandlung, 1846), Vol. I, p. 59.
41 Johann Gustav Droysen, *Vorlesungen über die Freiheitskriege*, Vol. II, p. 423.
42 ibid., p. 426.
43 Heinrich von Treitschke, 'Der Socialismus und seine Gönner', in Treitschke, *Zehn Jahre deutscher Kämpfe 1865–1874: Schriften zur Tagespolitik* (Berlin: Reimer, 1874), pp. 458–555; 494, 526.
44 Heinrich von Treitschke, *Politik*, 2 vols (Leipzig: Hirzel, 1898), Vol. II, pp. 15, 2.
45 Heinrich von Treitschke, *Die Freiheit* (Leipzig: Insel Verlag, 1912), p. 5.
46 Treitschke, *Politik*, Vol. I, pp. 26–28.
47 ibid., p. 28.
48 ibid., p. 103.
49 ibid., p. 8.

50 Leopold von Ranke, 'Die Idee der Volkssouveränität in den Schriften der Jesuiten', in *Historisch-politische Zeitschrift*, Vol. II (1833), pp. 606–16; 611.
51 Johann Gustav Droysen, *Geschichte der Preußischen Politik*, 5 parts, (Leipzig: Veit und Comp., 1859), Part II/2, p. 40.
52 Heinrich von Treitschke, *Politik*, Vol. I, p. 5.
53 Heinrich von Treitschke, *Luther und die deutsche Nation* (Berlin: G. Reimer, 1883), p. 20.
54 ibid., p. 16.
55 Justus Möser, *Patriotische Phantasien I*, in Möser, *Sämmtliche Werke*, edited by J. W. J. von Voigt, 10 vols, new edn (Berlin: Verlag der Nicolaischen Buchhandlung, 1842), Vol. I, p. 115.
56 ibid., p. 338, and Justus Möser, *Patriotische Phantasien II*, in *Sämmtliche Werke*, Vol. II, p. 10.
57 ibid., p. 21.
58 ibid., p. 213.
59 ibid., p. 22.
60 ibid., p. 9.
61 Justus Möser, *Kleinere, den Patriotischen Phantasien verwandte Stücke*, in *Sämmtliche Werke*, Vol. V, p. 191.
62 Friedrich Schlegel, 'Versuch über den Begriff des Republikanismus', in Schlegel, *Kritische Ausgabe*, 22 vols (Munich: Ferdinand Schöningh, 1966), Vol. VII, pp. 11–25; 22.
63 See Novalis, *Hymnen an die Nacht. Die Christenheit oder Europa* (Leipzig: Insel, 1912), esp. p. 38.
64 Friedrich Schlegel, 'Über die neuere Geschichte', in *Kritische Ausgabe*, Vol. VII, pp. 125–407; 202.
65 Friedrich Schlegel, 'Signatur des Zeitalters', in *Kritische Ausgabe*, Vol. VII, pp. 483–598; 485, 513.
66 ibid., pp. 525, 528.
67 ibid., p. 562.
68 ibid., p. 529.
69 Adam H. Müller, *Die Elemente der Staatskunst*, 3 vols (Berlin: J. D. Sander, 1809), Vol. II, pp. 122–24.
70 Adam H. Müller, *Die Elemente der Staatskunst*, Vol. I, p. xi.
71 ibid., p. 265.
72 ibid., p. 207.
73 ibid., p. 38.
74 ibid., pp. 264–65.
75 ibid., pp. 5–6.
76 ibid., p. 247.
77 ibid., p. 242.
78 ibid., p. 200.
79 ibid., p. 66.
80 ibid., p. 119.
81 Franz von Baader, *Grundzüge der Societätsphilosophie* (Wurzburg: Stahel, 1837), p 1.
82 ibid., p. 4.
83 ibid., pp. 16, 23.
84 ibid., p. 79.
85 ibid., p. 86.
86 Franz von Baader, *Über das durch die französische Revolution herbeigeführte Bedürfniß einer neuern und innigern Verbindung der Religion mit der Politik* (Nuremberg: Fr. Campe, 1815), p. 27.
87 F. W. J. Schelling, *Vorlesungen über die Methode des academischen Studiums* (Tubingen: Cotta, 1803), p. 44.

88 ibid., p. 154.
89 ibid., p. 51.
90 ibid., p. 107.
91 ibid., p. 228.
92 ibid., p. 231.
93 Schelling, 'Ueber das Wesen deutscher Wissenschaft', in *Werke*, Vol. IV, pp. 377–94; 387.
94 Schelling, *Vorlesungen über die Methode des academischen Studiums* p. 233–35.
95 F. W. J. Schelling, *Philosophische Untersuchungen über das Wesen der menschlichen Freiheit und die damit zusammenhängenden Gegenstände*, in *Werke*, Vol. IV, pp. 223–308; 288.
96 ibid., p. 230. See also F. W. J. Schelling, 'Ueber das Wesen deutscher Wissenschaft', 387.
97 F. W. J. Schelling, *Philosophie der Offenbarung*, in *Werke*, Vol. VI, p. 179.
98 ibid., p. 385.
99 Schelling, *Vorlesungen über die Methode des academischen Studiums*, p. 231.
100 Schelling, 'Ueber das Wesen deutscher Wissenschaft', pp. 386–88.
101 Schelling, *Vorlesungen über die Methode des academischen Studiums*, p. 316.
102 ibid., p. 110.
103 ibid., p. 109.
104 F. W. J. Schelling, *Stuttgarter Privatvorlesungen*, in *Werke*, Vol. IV, pp. 309–76; 353.
105 F. W. J. Schelling, *Philosophie und Religion* (Tubingen: Cotta, 1804), pp. 73–74.
106 Joseph Görres, *Teutschland und die Revolution*, 2nd edn (Koblenz: 1819), pp. 188–89.
107 ibid., p. 190.
108 Friedrich Schleiermacher, *Der christliche Glaube nach den Grundsätzen der evangelischen Kirche*, 2 vols (Berlin: G. Reimer, 1821), Vol. I, p. 94.
109 Friedrich Schleiermacher, *Entwurf eines Systems der Sittenlehre*, in Schleiermacher, *Sämmtliche Werke*, 32 vols (Berlin: Reimer, 1834–64), Vol. III/V, p. 145.
110 ibid., pp. 276–77.
111 Schleiermacher, *Der christliche Glaube,* pp. 35, 92–94.
112 Friedrich Schleiermacher, *Die praktische Theologie nach den Grundsätzen der evangelischen Kirche*, in *Sämmtliche Werke*, Vol. I/13, p. 525.
113 ibid., p. 553.
114 ibid., p. 668.
115 ibid., p. 626.
116 Friedrich Schleiermacher, 'Ueber das liturgische Recht evangelischer Fürsten', in *Sämmtliche Werke*, Vol. I/5, pp. 477–535; 500.
117 ibid., p. 503.
118 Friedrich Schleiermacher, *Geschichte der christlichen Kirche*, in *Sämmtliche Werke*, Vol. I/11, p. 12.
119 ibid., p. 600.
120 Friedrich Schleiermacher, *Die christliche Sitte nach den Grundsätzen der evangelischen Kirche im Zusammenhange dargestellt*, in *Sämmtliche Werke*, Vol. I/12, p. 99.
121 ibid., p. 72.
122 Schleiermacher, *Die praktische Theologie*, p. 531.
123 Schleiermacher, *Die christliche Sitte*, p. 128.
124 ibid., p. 217.
125 Schleiermacher, *Die praktische Theologie*, p. 521.
126 Friedrich Schleiermacher, 'Ueber die für die protestantische Kirche des Preußischen Staats einzurichtende Synodalverfassung', in *Sämmtliche Werke*, Vol. I/5, pp. 217–94; 263.
127 Schleiermacher, *Die christliche Sitte*, p. 455.

128 Friedrich Schleiermacher, 'Ueber die Begriffe der verschiedenenen Staatsformen', in *Sämmtliche Werke*, Vol. III/2, pp. 260–61.
129 Schleiermacher, *Die christliche Sitte*, p. 455.
130 ibid., p. 280.
131 Friedrich Schleiermacher, 'Ueber den Unterschied zwischen Naturgesetz und Sittengesetz', in *Sämmtliche Werke*, Vol. III/2, pp. 397–417; 409.
132 Schleiermacher, *Entwurf eines Systems der Sittenlehre*, p. 441.
133 ibid., p. 441.
134 Friedrich Schleiermacher, *Hermeneutik mit besonderer Bezug auf das Neue Testament*, in *Sämmtliche Werke*, Vol. I/7, p. 262.
135 Schleiermacher, *Entwurf eines Systems der Sittenlehre*, p. 296.
136 Schleiermacher, *Die christliche Sitte*, p. 455.
137 Schleiermacher, 'Ueber die Begriffe der verschiedenen Staatsformen', p. 261.
138 ibid., p. 268.
139 Friedrich Schleiermacher, *Lehre vom Staat*, in *Sämmtliche Werke*, Vol. III/6, p. 51.
140 Schleiermacher, 'Ueber die Begriffe der verschiedenen Staatsformen', p. 264; also, Schleiermacher, *Lehre vom Staat*, p. 65.
141 ibid., p. 76.
142 ibid., pp. 72, 105.
143 ibid., pp. 31, 88.
144 ibid., p. 88.
145 ibid., p. 19.
146 ibid., p. 62.
147 ibid., p. 166.
148 ibid., p. 21.
149 Schleiermacher, *Entwurf eines Systems der Sittenlehre*, p. 285.
150 ibid., p. 143.

5 The Young Hegelians and Karl Marx

1 Friedrich Julius Stahl, *Die Philosophie des Rechts nach geschichtlicher Ansicht*, 1st edn, 3 vols (Heidelberg: J. C. B. Mohr, 1830), Vol. I, *Die Genesis der gegenwärtigen Rechtsphilosophie*, p. 70.
2 ibid., p. 114.
3 ibid., pp. 104–6.
4 Friedrich Julius Stahl, *Die Philosophie des Rechts*, 3rd edn, in 3 vols (Heidelberg: J.C.B. Mohr, 1856), Vol. II/2, *Rechts-und Staatslehre auf der Grundlage christlicher Weltanschauung:Die Staatslehre und die Principien des Staatsrechts*, pp. 192–93.
5 Friedrich Julius Stahl, *Die Philosophie des Rechts nach geschichtlicher Ansicht*, Vol. I, p. 307.
6 ibid., p. 289.
7 Friedrich Julius Stahl, *Die Philosophie des Rechts*, Vol. II, p. 413.
8 ibid., p. 239.
9 Friedrich Julius Stahl, *Der christliche Staat und sein Verhältniß zu Deismus und Judenthum: Eine durch die Verhandlungen des Vereinigten Landtags hervorgerufene Abhandlung* (Berlin: Ludwig Oehmigke, 1847), p. 10.
10 Friedrich Julius Stahl, *Die Kirchenverfassung nach Lehre und Recht der Protestanten*, 2nd edn (Erlangen: Theodor Bläsing, 1862), p. 9.
11 ibid., pp. 225–29.
12 Friedrich Julius Stahl, *Die Philosophie des Rechts*, Vol. II/2, p. 258.
13 ibid., pp. 138–39.
14 ibid., p. 3.

15 Friedrich Julius Stahl, *Die Philosophie des Rechts*, 3rd edn, 3 vols (Heidelberg: J. C. B. Mohr, 1854), Vol. II, *Rechts-und Staatslehre auf der Grundlage christlicher Weltanschauung: Die allgemeinen Lehren und das Privatrecht*, p. 25.
16 Friedrich Julius Stahl, *Die Philosophie des Rechts*, Vol. II/1, p. 257.
17 ibid., p. 235.
18 Stahl, *Der christliche Staat*, p. 62.
19 ibid., pp. 25, 29.
20 Stahl deeply reviled all theocratic ideas. See Friedrich Julius Stahl, *Der Protestantismus als politisches Princip* (Berlin: Wilhelm Schultze, 1853), p. 16.
21 Stahl, *Die Philosophie des Rechts*, Vol. II/1, p. 219.
22 Stahl, *Die Kirchenverfassung nach Lehre und Recht der Protestanten*, p. 49.
23 Stahl, *Der Protestantismus als politisches Princip*, pp. 11–12.
24 For an excellent analysis of the rejection of personalism in the post-Hegelian philosophy of the *Vormärz*, see Warren Breckmann, *Marx, The Young Hegelians, and the Origins of Radical Social Theory* (Cambridge: Cambridge University Press, 1999), pp. 9–11.
25 G. W. F Hegel, *Vorlesungen über die Philosophie der Religion II*, in *Werke*, Vol. XVII, p. 273.
26 See David Friedrich Strauss, *Die christliche Glaubenslehre in ihrer geschichtlichen Entwicklung und im Kampfe mit der modernen Wissenschaft*, 2 vols (Tubingen: C. F. Osiander, 1840), Vol. I, p. 512.
27 Bruno Bauer, *Die Religion des Alten Testaments in der geschichtlichen Entwicklung ihrer Principien*, 2 vols (Berlin: F. Dümmler, 1838), Vol. I, p. xxii.
28 Philipp Marheineke, *Zur Kritik der Schellingschen Offenbarungsphilosophie* (Berlin: Enslin, 1843), p. 57.
29 ibid., p. 22.
30 Philipp Marheinecke, *Die Grundlehren der christlichen Dogmatik* (Berlin: Ferdinand Dümmler, 1819), pp. 148, 146.
31 Philipp Marheineke, *Entwurf der practischen Theologie* (Berlin: Duncker und Humblot, 1837), p. 36.
32 Bauer, *Die Religion des Alten Testaments*, p. xxii.
33 ibid., p. xlvii.
34 ibid., p. xlvii.
35 Bruno Bauer, 'Das Leben Jesu. Kritisch bearbeitet von David Friedrich Strauss', in *Jahrbücher für wissenschaftliche Kritik*, Vol. II (1835), pp. 879–911; 886.
36 Bruno Bauer, *Kritik der evangelischen Geschichte des Johannes* (Bremen: Carl Schünemann, 1840), p. 5.
37 Bauer, *Die Religion des Alten Testaments*, p. lix.
38 ibid., p. 145.
39 Bruno Bauer, 'Die Prinzipien der mosaischen Rechts-und Religions-Verfassung, nach ihrem inneren Zusammenhang entwickelt', in *Zeitschrift für speculative Theologie*, Vol. II/2 (1837), pp. 297–353; pp. 306, 308.
40 Bauer, *Die Religion des Alten Testaments*, p. lxvi.
41 Bruno Bauer, *Herr Dr Hengstenberg: Kritische Briefe über den Gegensatz des Gesetzes und des Evangelium* (Berlin: F. Dümmler, 1839), p. 13.
42 Bruno Bauer, 'Die Prinzipien der mosaischen Rechts-und Religions-Verfassung', p. 333.
43 Bruno Bauer, *Das Entdeckte Christentum: Eine Erinnerung an das achtzehnte Jahrhundert und ein Beitrag zur Krisis des neunzehnten* (Zurich: Verlag des literarischen Comptoirs, 1843), p. 113.
44 ibid., p. 12.

45 Note his consequent later enthusiasm for Gnosticism, in Bruno Bauer, *Christus und die Caesaren: Der Ursprung des Christentums aus dem römischen Griechenthum*, 2nd edn (Berlin: Eugen Grosser, 1879), p. 316.
46 Bruno Bauer, *Die Posaune des jüngsten Gerichts über Hegel den Atheisten und Antichristen: Ein Ultimatum* (Leipzig: Otto Wigand, 1841), p. 160.
47 Bruno Bauer, *Die evangelische Landeskirche Preussens und die Wissenschaft* (Leipzig: Otto Wigand, 1840), p. 104.
48 ibid., p. 100.
49 Bruno Bauer, *Rußland und das Germanenthum* (Charlottenburg: Egbert Bauer, 1853), p. 45.
50 ibid., p. 46.
51 ibid., p. 93.
52 Bauer also attributed the failure of the revolution of 1848 to the political weakness of the constitution caused by the religious affiliations of its authors. See Bruno Bauer, *Die bürgerliche Revolution in Deutschland seit dem Anfang der deutsch-katholischen Bewegung bis zur Gegenwart* (Berlin: Gustav Hempel, 1849), pp. 51, 260–62.
53 David Friedrich Strauss, *Streitschriften zur Vertheidigung meiner Schrift über das Leben Jesu und zur Charakteristik der gegenwärtigen Theologie*, 3 vols (Tubingen: Osiander, 1837), Vol. III, p. 126.
54 David Friedrich Strauss, *Das Leben Jesu*, 2 vols, 4th edn (Tubingen: Osiander, 1840), Vol. I, p. 186.
55 ibid., p. 87.
56 David Friedrich Strauss, *Das Leben Jesu*, Vol. II, p. 63.
57 ibid., pp. 709–10.
58 David Friedrich Strauss, *Die christliche Glaubenslehre in ihrer geschichtlichen Entwicklung und im Kampfe mit der modernen Wissenschaft*, 2 vols (Tubingen: C. F. Osiander, 1840), Vol. II, p. 75.
59 ibid., pp. 51, 53, 82, 256–57. For an account of the influence exercised by Strauss on Bauer, see Ernst Barnikol, 'Der Briefwechsel zwischen Strauß und Baur. Ein quellenmäßiger Beitrag zur Strauß-Baur-Forschung', in *Zeitschrift für Kirchengeschichte*, 4/73 (1962), pp. 74–125; 104–5.
60 Strauss, *Die christliche Glaubenslehre*, p. 355.
61 David Friedrich Strauss, *Der politische und der theologische Liberalismus* (Halle: Kümmel, 1848), p. 15.
62 Ludwig Feuerbach, *Das Wesen des Christentums*, 2 vols, edited by Werner Schuffenhauer (Berlin: Akademie-Verlag, 1956), Vol. I, p. 41.
63 ibid., pp. 71, 75.
64 ibid., p. 283.
65 Ludwig Feuerbach, 'Kritik der "christlichen Rechts-und Staatslehre" (Von Fr. J. Stahl, 1833)', in *Sämtliche Werke*, 10 vols (Leipzig: Otto Wigand, 1846), Vol. I, *Erläuterungen und Ergänzungen zum Wesen des Christenthums*, pp. 108–27; 109.
66 Feuerbach, *Das Wesen des Christentums*, p. 72.
67 ibid., p. 237.
68 ibid., pp. 228–29.
69 ibid., p. 36.
70 ibid., p. 124.
71 Karl Friedrich Göschel, *Beiträge zur spekulativen Philosophie von Gott und dem Menschen und von dem Gott-Menschen: Mit Rücksicht auf Dr D. F. Strauss Christologie* (Berlin: Duncker und Humblot, 1838), pp. 21–22, 62, 149.
72 Karl Friedrich Göschel, *Von den Beweisen für die Unsterblichkeit der menschlichen Seele im Lichte der spekulativen Philosophie: Eine Ostergabe* (Berlin: Duncker und Humblot, 1835), p. 126.

73 Karl Friedrich Göschel, *Aphorismen über Nichtwissen und absolutes Wissen im Verhältnisse zur christlichen Glaubensbekenntniß: Ein Beytrag zum Verständnisse der Philosophie unserer Zeit* (Berlin: E. Franklin, 1829), p. 150.
74 Julius Schaller, *Der historische Christus und die Philosophie: Kritik der Grundidee des Werks das Leben Jesu von Dr. D. F. Strauss* (Leipzig: Otto Wigand, 1838), p. 106.
75 Julius Schaller, *Die Philosophie unserer Zeit. Zur Apologie und Erläuterung des Hegelschen Systems* (Leipzig: J. C. Hinrichsche Buchhandlung, 1837), p. 319.
76 Marheineke, *Die Grundlehren der christlichen Dogmatik*, p. 83.
77 ibid., p. 205.
78 Karl Rosenkranz, *Kritik der Principien der Strauss'schen Glaubenslehre* (Leipzig: Gustav Brauns, 1845), p. 55.
79 Karl Ludwig Michelet, *Über die Persönlichkeit des Absoluten: Ein Gespräch* (Nuremberg: Theodor Cramer, 1844), p. 27.
80 Karl Ludwig Michelet, *Vorlesungen über die Persönlichkeit Gottes und die Unsterblichkeit der Seele oder die ewige Persönlichkeit des Geistes* (Berlin: Ferdinand Dümmler, 1841), p. 238.
81 Michelet, *Über die Persönlichkeit des Absoluten*, p. 35.
82 Karl Ludwig Michelet, *Entwickelungsgeschichte der neuesten deutschen Philosophie mit besonderer Rücksicht auf den gegenwörtigen Kampf Schellings mit der Hegelschen Schule* (Berlin: Dunker und Humblot, 1843), p. 314.
83 Michelet, *Über die Persönlichkeit des Absoluten*, p. 210.
84 Michelet, *Vorlesungen über die Persönlichkeit Gottes*, p. 196.
85 August Cieszkowski, *Gott und Palingenesie* (Berlin: Schroeder, 1842), pp. 58–59.
86 Göschel, *Beiträge zur spekulativen Philosophie von Gott und dem Menschen*, p. 61.
87 Marheineke advocated a consistorial constitution as the mediator between church and state (Phillip Marheineke, *Entwurf der practischen Theologie*, Berlin: Duncker und Humblot, 1837, p. 112). Göschel also supported a consistorial system; in fact, he was, for a time, head of the consistory in Saxony (see, on this, Karl Friedrich Göschel, *Der Dualismus evangelischer Kirchen-Verfassung*, Stettin: L. Weiß, 1852, p. 21). From a more moderate stance, Michelet pleaded for a more democratic synodal constitution (see Michelet, *Zur Verfassungsfrage*, p. 65).
88 See Karl Rosenkranz, *Meine Reform der Hegelschen Philosophie. Sendschreiben an Herrn. Dr. J. U. Wirth* (Konigsberg: Bornträger, 1852), p. 68; Michelet, *Vorlesungen über die Persönlichkeit Gottes*, p. 153.
89 Karl Ludwig Michelet, *Der historische Christus und das neue Christenthum* (Darmstadt: Carl Wilhelm Leske, 1847), p. 175.
90 Karl Ludwig Michelet, *Zur Verfassungsfrage* (Frankfurt an der Oder: Trowitsch und Sohn, 1848), p. 18.
91 For an excellent recent account of this, see Douglas Moggach, *The Philosophy and Politics of Bruno Bauer* (Cambridge: Cambridge University Press, 2003), p. 94.
92 David Friedrich Strauss, *Sechs theologisch-politische Volksreden* (Stuttgart: Cotta, 1848), p. 27. Strauss also saw the process of constitutional foundation in 1848 as imperilled by the religious interests of the delegates in the Constitutional Assembly in Frankfurt am Main (pp. 42–43).
93 Bruno Bauer, *Die Judenfrage* (Braunschweig: Friedrich Otto, 1843), p. 19.
94 Bauer, *Die evangelische Landeskirche*, p. 100.
95 Arnold Ruge, 'Der preußische Absolutismus und seine Entwicklung', in *Gesammelte Schriften*, 10 vols (Mannheim: Grohe, 1846), Vol. IV, pp. 1–59; 54.
96 ibid., p. 33.
97 Arnold Ruge, 'Selbstkritik des Liberalismus', in *Gesammelte Schriften*, Vol. III, pp. 76–116; 109.

98 Arnold Ruge, 'Das Verhältniß von Theorie und Praxis', in *Gesammelte Schriften*, Vol. III, pp. 24–41; 33.
99 Ruge, 'Selbstkritik des Liberalismus', p. 90.
100 Ruge, 'Das Verhältniß von Theorie und Praxis', p. 31.
101 August von Cieszkowski, *Prolegomena zur Historiosophie* (Berlin: Veit und Comp, 1838), pp. 18, 116–17.
102 Max Stirner, *Der Einzige und sein Eigenthum* (Leipzig: Wigand, 1845), pp. 242, 203.
103 ibid., p. 230.
104 ibid., p. 244.
105 ibid., p. 269.
106 Karl Marx, *Ökonomisch-philosophische Manuskripte*, in Marx, *Frühe Schriften*, edited by J.-J. Lieber and P. Furth (Stuttgart: Cotta, 1962), pp. 506–665; 593–94.
107 Karl Marx, *Thesen über Feuerbach*, in Karl Marx and Friedrich Engels, *Werke*, 43 vols (Berlin: Dietz, 1958–68), pp. 5–7; 6.
108 Marx, *Ökonomisch-philosophische Manuskripte*, p. 566.
109 ibid., p. 567.
110 ibid., p. 568.
111 ibid., p. 562.
112 ibid., p. 596.
113 Karl Marx, *Zur Kritik der politischen Ökonomie* (Berlin: Dietz, 1971), p. 15.
114 Friedrich Engels and Karl Marx, *Die Deutsche Ideologie*, in *Werke*, Vol. III, pp. 26–27, 69.
115 Karl Marx, *Das Kapital*, in *Werke*, Vol. XXIII, p. 85.
116 Karl Marx, *Zur Judenfrage*, in *Werke*, Vol. I, pp. 347–377; 366.
117 Marx, *Zur Kritik der politischen Ökonomie*, p. 15.
118 Karl Marx, *Zur Judenfrage*, p. 364.
119 Karl Marx, *Kritik des Hegelschen Staatsrechts*, in *Werke*, Vol. I, pp. 203–333; 263.
120 Friedrich Engels and Karl Marx, *Die heilige Familie*, in *Werke*, Vol. II, pp. 7–223; 118.
121 Marx, *Zur Judenfrage*, pp. 352-53.
122 ibid., p. 360.
123 Engels and Marx, *Die heilige Familie*, p. 233.
124 Marx, *Zur Judenfrage*, p. 360.
125 Engels and Marx, *Die heilige Familie*, p. 63.
126 Karl Marx, *Verhandlungen des 6. rheinischen Landtags. Debatten über das Holzdiebstahlgesetz*, in *Werke*, Vol. I, pp. 109–47; 121–2.
127 Engels and Marx, *Die heilige Familie*, p. 62.
128 Karl Marx, 'Das philosophische Manifest der historischen Rechtsschule', in *Werke*, Vol. I, pp. 78–85; 79.
129 Karl Marx, *Debatten über das Holzdiebstahlgesetz*, pp. 143–44.
130 ibid., p. 146.
131 ibid., pp. 119, 116.
132 ibid., p. 119.
133 Marx, *Zur Judenfrage*, p. 364–65.
134 Marx, *Ökonomisch-philosophische Manuskripte*, p. 597.
135 ibid., p. 593.
136 ibid., p. 370.
137 Eduard Gans, *System des Römischen Civilrechts im Grundrisse nebst einer Abhandlung über Studium und System des Römischen Rechts* (Berlin: Ferdinand Dümmler, 1827), pp. 198–99.
138 Eduard Gans, 'Naturrecht', in: *Philosophische Schriften*, edited and introduced by Horst Schroeder (Glashütten im Taunus: Detlev Auvermann, 1971), pp. 37–154; 75.

139 ibid., p. 355.
140 Marx, *Zur Judenfrage*, p. 355.

6 Positivism and organic theory

1 On Hugo's relation to legal positivism, see F. Eichengrün, *Die Rechtsphilosophie Gustav Hugos: Ein geistesgeschichtlicher Beitrag zum Problem von Naturrecht und Rechtspositivismus* (Haag: Nijhoff, 1935), pp. 113–14; see also, Heinrich Weber, *Gustav Hugo: Vom Naturrecht zur Historischen Schule. Ein Beitrag zur Geschichte der deutschen Rechtswissenschaft* (Göttingen: Vandenhoeck und Ruprecht, 1935), pp. 25–26.
2 Wilhelm von Humboldt, *Ideen zu einem Versuch, die Gränzen der Wirksamkeit des Staats zu bestimmen*, in *Werke*, Vol. I, pp. 56–233, pp. 90, 142–45, 147.
3 ibid., p. 109.
4 Paul Johann Anselm Feuerbach, *Anti-Hobbes, oder über die Grenzen der höchsten Gewalt und das Zwangsrecht der Bürger gegen den Oberherrn* (Erfurt: Henning'sche Buchhandlung, 1798), p. 26.
5 Paul Johann Anselm von Feuerbach, *Kritik des natürlichen Rechts als Propädeutik zu einer Wissenschaft der natürlichen Rechte* (Alktona: Verlagsgesellschaft, 1796), p. 115.
6 Feuerbach, *Anti-Hobbes*, pp. 86–87.
7 Feuerbach, *Kritik des natürlichen Rechts*, p. 238.
8 Feuerbach, *Anti-Hobbes*, pp. 269, 257.
9 Karl Salomo Zachariä, *Die Wissenschaft der Gesetzgebung. Als Einleiting zu einem allgemeinen Gesetzbuch* (Leipzig: Gerhard Fischer, 1806), p. viii.
10 ibid., pp. 221–23.
11 Karl von Rotteck and Karl Welcker, *Das Staats-Lexikon*, 15 vols (Leipzig: Brockhaus, 1834–43), Vol. VI, p. 733.
12 Karl von Rotteck and Karl Welcker, *Das Staats-Lexikon*, Vol. XV, pp. 66–67.
13 Friedrich Christoph Dahlmann, *Die Politik, auf den Grund und das Maß der gegebenen Zustände zurückgeführt*, introduced by O. Westphal (Berlin: Hobbing, 1924), pp. 124–32.
14 ibid., p. 132.
15 Robert von Mohl, *Das deutsche Reichsstaatsrecht* (Tubingen: H. Laupp, 1873), p. 50.
16 ibid., p. 40.
17 Lorenz von Stein, *Geschichte der sozialen Bewegung in Frankreich von 1789 bis aufunsere Tage* (Darmstadt: Wissenschaftliche Buchgesellschaft, 1959), Vol. I, p. 138.
18 Anton F. J. Thibaut, *Ueber die Nothwendigkeit eines allgemeinen bürgerlichen Rechts für Deutschland* (Heidelberg: Mohr und Zimmer, 1814), p. 25.
19 ibid., p. 12.
20 Anton F. J. Thibaut, *System des Pandekten-Rechts*, 2 vols (Jena: Johann Michael Manke, 1803), Vol. I, p. 35.
21 Anton F. J. Thibaut, *Versuche über einzelne Theile der Theorie des Rechts* (Jena: Johann Michael Manke, 1798), pp. 154–55.
22 ibid., p. 162.
23 ibid., pp. 202–5.
24 Thibaut, *System des Pandekten-Rechts*, p. 26.
25 Anton F. J. Thibaut, *Theorie der logischen Auslegung des Römischen Rechts* (Altona: Johann Friedrich Hammerich, 1799), pp. 194–95.
26 G. F. Puchta, *Cursus der Institutionen*, 3 vols (Leipzig: Breitkopf & Härtel, 1841), Vol. I, p. 4.

27 G. F. Puchta, *Lehrbuch der Pandekten* (Leipzig: J. A. Barth, 1838), p. 11.
28 ibid., p. 11. James Q. Whitman has convincingly emphasized that representatives of the Historical School were committed to defending the privileged position of the university jurists. See Whitman, *The Legacy of Roman Law in the German Romantic Era: Historical Vision and Legal Change* (Princeton, NJ.: Princeton University Press, 1990), p. 122.
29 ibid., p. 79.
30 ibid., p. 11.
31 ibid., p. 92.
32 Puchta, *Cursus der Institutionen*, Vol. I, p. 100.
33 ibid., p. 64.
34 ibid., p. 65.
35 Puchta, *Cursus der Institutionen*, Vol. II, p. 268.
36 For a still excellent critical explanation of the construction of the personality of the state in Roman law, see Rudolf Sohm, *Ein Lehrbuch der Geschichte und des Systems des Römischen Privatrechts* (Leipzig: Duncker und Humblot, 1899), p. 189.
37 Puchta, *Cursus der Institutionen*, Vol. I, p. 29.
38 ibid., p. 29.
39 Carl Friedrich von Gerber, *System des deutschen Privatrechts*, 6th edn (Jena: Fr. Mauke, 1858), p. 19.
40 On Gerber's position between Roman and Germanic law, see Peter von Oertzen, *Die soziale Funktion des staatsrechtlichen Positivismus* (Frankfurt am Main: Suhrkamp, 1974), p. 220.
41 Gerber, *System*, p. 3.
42 ibid., p. 62.
43 ibid., p. 166.
44 Carl Friedrich von Gerber, *Grundzüge eines Systems des deutschen Staatsrechts* (Leipzig: Bernhard Tauchnitz, 1865), p. 19–20.
45 ibid., pp. 71–73.
46 ibid., pp. 173–75.
47 ibid., pp. 19–20.
48 Oertzen, *Die soziale Funktion*, p. 182.
49 Gerber, *Grundzüge*, p. 137.
50 Rudolf Jhering, *Geist des römischen Rechts auf den verschiedenen Stufen seiner Entwicklung,* 3 vols, (Leipzig: Breitkopf und Härtel, 1852), Vol. I, p. 12.
51 ibid., p. 29.
52 Jhering, *Geist des römischen Rechts*, Vol. II/1, p. 316.
53 Jhering, *Geist des römischen Rechts*, Vol. I, pp. 104, 211.
54 ibid., pp. 216–17.
55 ibid., pp. 79–80.
56 ibid., pp. 217–18.
57 ibid., p. 203.
58 Rudolf Jhering, *Geist des römischen Rechts*, Vol. III, p. 317.
59 Rudolf von Jhering, *Der Zweck im Recht*, 2 vols (Leipzig: Breitkopf und Härtel, 1877–83), Vol. II, p. 133.
60 Rudolf von Jhering, *Der Besitzwille: Zugleich eine Kritik der herrschenden juristischen Methode* (Jena: Gustav Fischer, 1889), p. 538.
61 ibid., p. 481.
62 Rudolf von Jhering, *Der Zweck im Recht*, Vol. I, p. 47.
63 Rudolf von Jhering, *Der Kampf um's Recht*, 2nd edn (Wien: Manz, 1872), p. 51.
64 Jhering, *Der Zweck im Recht*, Vol. I, p. 222.
65 Jhering, *Geist des römischen Rechts*, Vol. II/1, p. 266.
66 ibid., p. 128.

67 Jhering, *Der Zweck im Recht*, I., p. 48.
68 ibid., pp. 301, 455.
69 ibid., p. 499.
70 ibid., p. 344.
71 ibid., p. 460.
72 See Bernhard Windscheid, 'Die Aufgaben der Rechtswissenschaft', in Windscheid, *Gesammelte Reden und Aufsätze* (Leipzig: Duncker und Humblot, 1904), pp. 100–116; 112.
73 Paul Laband, *Das Staatsrecht des deutschen Reiches*, 4th edn, 4 vols (Leipzig and Tubingen: J. C. B. Mohr, 1901), Vol. I, pp. 89–90.
74 ibid., p. 27.
75 ibid., p. 9.
76 ibid., pp. 195–96.
77 Paul Laband, *Das Staatsrecht des deutschen Reiches*, Vol. II, p. 5.
78 Georg Jellinek, *System der subjektiven öffentlichen Rechte* (Freiburg: J. C. B. Mohr, 1892), p. 9.
79 ibid., p. 10.
80 ibid., p. 77.
81 Georg Jellinek, *Allgemeine Staatslehre* (Berlin: Häring, 1900), p. 439.
82 Georg Jellinek, *Die rechtliche Natur der Staatenverträge: Ein Beitrag zur juristischen Construction des Völkerrechts* (Vienna: Alfred Hölder, 1880), p. 28.
83 Jellinek, *System der subjektiven öffentlichen Rechte*, p. 10.
84 Jellinek, *Allgemeine Staatslehre* p. 621. On Jellinek's liberalism and his critique of Laband, see Christoph Schönberger, 'Ein liberaler zwischen Staatswille und Volkswille: Georg Jellinek und die Krise des staatsrechtlichen Positivismus um die Jahrhundertwende', in Stanley L. Paulson and Martin Schulte (eds), *Georg Jellinek. Beiträge zu Leben und Werk* (Tubingen: J. C. B. Mohr, 2000), pp. 3–32; 21.
85 Jellinek, *Allgemeine Staatslehre*, pp. 122–23.
86 ibid., p. 74.
87 ibid., p. 145.
88 Jellinek, *System der subjektiven öffentlichen Rechte*, p. 22.
89 Jellinek, *Allgemeine Staatslehre*, p. 226.
90 ibid., p. 184.
91 ibid., p. 204.
92 ibid., p. 323.
93 ibid., p. 308.
94 Hermann Kantorowicz, *Zur Lehre vom richtigen Recht* (Berlin: Walter Rothschild, 1909), p. 37.
95 Eugen Ehrlich, 'Freie Rechtsfindung und freie Rechtswissenschaft', in Ehrlich, *Recht und Leben: Gesammelte Schriften zur Rechtstatsachenforschung und zur Freirechtslehre,* selected and edited by M. Rehbinder (Berlin: Duncker und Humblot, 1967), pp. 170–202; 188; Hermann Kantorowicz, *Aus der Vorgeschichte der Freirechtslehre* (Mannheim: J. Bensheimer, 1925), p. 33; Gustav Radbruch, 'Rechtswissenschaft als Rechtsschöpfung', p. 365.
96 Ehrlich, 'Freie Rechtsfindung und freie Rechtswissenschaft', Ein Beitrag zum juristischen Methodenstreit', in *Archiv für Sozialwissenschaft und Sozialpolitik*, 22 (1906), pp. 192, 184.
97 Gnaeus Flavius [Hermann Kantorowicz], *Der Kampf um die Rechtswissenschaft* (Heidelberg: Carl Winter, 1906), p. 26.
98 Radbruch claimed, notably, that the construction of the state as the unquestionable origin of law in positivism is comparable to the construction of God in early Protestantism. See Radbruch, 'Rechtswissenschaft als Rechtsschöpfung', pp. 366–7.

99 Flavius, *Der Kampf*, p. 28.
100 ibid., pp. 8–9.
101 C. J. A. Mittermaier, *Lehrbuch des deutschen Privatrechts* (Landshut: Philipp Krüll, 1821), p. 40.
102 Jacob Grimm, *Deutsche Rechts-Alterthümer* (Göttingen: Dieterich, 1828), pp. xvi–xviii.
103 Eduard Albrecht, 'Grundsätze des deutschen Staatsrechts, systematisch entwicklelt von Dr Romeo Maurenbrecher', in *Göttingische gelehrte Anzeigen*, 150–51 (1837), pp. 1489–1504; 1491–92.
104 Karl Friedrich Eichhorn, *Deutsche Staats- und Rechtsgeschichte*, 5th edn, 4 vols (Göttingen: Vandenhoeck und Ruprecht, 1843), Vol. III, pp. 328–46.
105 Karl Friedrich Eichhorn, *Deutsche Staats- und Rechtsgeschichte*, 3rd edn, 4 vols (Göttingen: Vandenhoeck und Ruprecht, 1821), Vol. II, p. 278.
106 Karl Friedrich Eichhorn, *Deutsche Staats- und Rechtsgeschichte*, Vol. III, p. 403.
107 Karl Friedrich Eichhorn, *Deutsche Staats- und Rechtsgeschichte*, Vol. II, pp. 342–43.
108 ibid., p. 559. See also Karl Friedrich Eichhorn, *Einleitung in das deutsche Privatrecht mit Einschluß des Lehenrechts,* 5th edn (Göttingen: Vandenhoeck und Ruprecht, 1845), pp. 405–6.
109 Georg Beseler, *Volksrecht und Juristenrecht* (Leipzig: Weidmannsche Buchhandlung, 1843), pp. 69–70, 84.
110 Georg Beseler, *System des gemeinen deutschen Privatrechts*, 3 vols (Leipzig: Weidmann'sche Buchhandlung, 1847), Vol. I, pp. 353–54.
111 Beseler, *Volksrecht und Juristenrecht*, p. 173.
112 ibid., p. 173.
113 ibid., p. 174; and Beseler, *System des gemeinen deutschen Privatrechts*, Vol. I, p. 135.
114 Johann Caspar Bluntschli, *Allgemeines Staatsrecht* (Munich: Verlag der literarisch-artistischen Anstalt, 1852), p. 244.
115 Johann Caspar Bluntschli, 'Der Rechtsbegriff', in Bluntschli, *Vorträge gehalten zu München im Winter 1858* (Braunschweig: Friedrich Vieweg und Sohn, 1858), pp. 143–83; 183.
116 Johann Caspar Bluntschli, *Die neueren Rechtsschulen der deutschen Juristen* (Zurich: Ch. Beyel, 1841), p. 38.
117 Johann Caspar Bluntschli, *Deutsches Privatrecht,* 3rd edn, expanded (Munich: Cotta, 1864), p. 24.
118 Albert Hänel, *Deutsches Staatsrecht*, Vol. I: *Die Grundlagen des deutschen Staates und die Reichsgewalt* (Leipzig: Duncker und Humblot, 1892), p. 117.
119 ibid., pp. 106–7.
120 ibid., p. 131.
121 Otto von Gierke, *Das deutsche Genossenschaftsrecht*, Vol. I: *Rechtsgeschichte der deutschen Genossenschaft* (Berlin: Weidmann, 1868), p. 801.
122 Otto von Gierke, *Das deutsche Genossenschaftsrecht*, Vol. II: *Geschichte des deutschen Körperschaftsbegriffs* (Berlin: Weidmann, 1873), pp. 27–29.
123 ibid., p. 24.
124 ibid., p. 30.
125 ibid., p. 37.
126 Otto von Gierke, *Das deutsche Genossenschaftsrecht*, Vol. I: *Rechtsgeschichte der deutschen Genossenschaft* (Berlin: Weidmann, 1868), p. 1.
127 ibid., p. 13.
128 Gierke, *Das deutsche Genossenschaftsrecht*, Vol. II, p. 134.
129 Otto von Gierke, *Deutsches Privatrecht*, Vol. I: *Allgemeiner Teil und Personenrecht* (Leipzig: Duncker und Humblot, 1895), p. 470.
130 Otto von Gierke, *Deutsches Privatrecht*, Vol. I, p. 29.

131 ibid., p. 126.
132 ibid., p. 702.
133 Otto von Gierke, 'Labands Staatsrecht und die deutsche Privatrechtswissenschaft', in *Jahrbuch für Gesetzgebung*, 7/4 (1883), pp. 1–99; 4.
134 ibid., p. 18.
135 ibid., p. 12.
136 ibid., pp. 3–5.
137 Gierke, *Das deutsche Genossenschaftsrecht*, Vol. II, p. 474.
138 ibid., p. 886.
139 ibid., pp. 563, 622.
140 Otto von Gierke, *Das deutsche Genossenschaftsrecht*, Vol. III, *Die Staats-und Korporationslehre des Althertums und des Mittelalters* (Berlin: Weidmann, 1881), p. 609.
141 Otto von Gierke, *Das deutsche Genossenschaftsrecht*, Vol. IV: *Die Staats-und Korporationslehre der Neuzeit* (Berlin: Weidmann, 1913), p. 403.
142 Otto von Gierke, *Naturrecht und deutsches Recht* (Frankfurt am Main: Rütten und Loening, 1883), p. 28.
143 ibid., p. 32.
144 Hugo Preuß, *Gemeinde, Staat, Reich als Gebietskörperschaften. Versuch einer deutschen Staatskonstruktion auf Grundlage der Genossenschaftstheorie* (Berlin: Julius Springer, 1889), pp. 110–11.
145 ibid., p. 156.
146 ibid., p. 161.
147 Hugo Preuß, 'Die Persönlichkeit des Staates, organisch und individualistisch betrachtet', in *Archiv für öffentliches Recht*, 4/1 (1889), pp. 62–100; p. 79.
148 Preuß, *Gemeinde, Staat, Reich*, pp. 206–7.
149 Preuß, 'Persönlichkeit des Staates', p. 87.
150 ibid., p. 73.
151 Preuß, *Gemeinde, Staat, Reich*, p. 235.
152 ibid., p. 222.
153 ibid., p. vii.
154 Hugo Preuß, *Das deutsche Volk und die Politik* (Jena: Eugen Diederich, 1915), pp. 55 56.
155 Hugo Preuß, 'Die Bedeutung der demokratischen Republik für den sozialen Gedanken', in Preuß, *Staat, Recht und Freiheit. Aus 40 Jahren deutscher Politik und Geschichte* (Tubingen: J. C. B. Mohr, 1926), pp. 481–97; 489.
156 ibid., p. 492.
157 ibid., p. 494.

7 The vitalist interlude

1 Friedrich Nietzsche, *Jenseits von Gut und Böse*, in Nietzsche, *Werke*, edited by Giorgio Colli and Mazzino Montinari, 8 vols (Berlin: de Gruyter), Vol. VI/2: 1–255; 10.
2 Friedrich Nietzsche, *Zur Genealogie der Moral*, in *Werke*, Vol. VI/2, pp. 257–430; 265.
3 Friedrich Nietzsche, *Der Anti-Christ*, in *Werke*, Vol. VI/3, pp. 163–251; p. 198.
4 ibid., p. 192.
5 ibid., p. 175.
6 Nietzsche, *Die fröhliche Wissenschaft*, in *Werke*, Vol. V/2, pp. 1–335; 150.
7 Friedrich Nietzsche, *Unzeitgemäße Betrachtungen*, in *Werke*, Vol. III/1, pp. 153–423; 267.
8 Nietzsche, *Jenseits von Gut und Böse*, p. 215.
9 ibid., p. 303.

10 Nietzsche, *Zur Genealogie der Moral*, p. 357.
11 ibid., p. 287.
12 ibid., pp. 307–8.
13 Nietzsche, *Der Antichrist*, p. 186.
14 Nietzsche, *Zur Genealogie der Moral*, p. 329.
15 ibid., pp. 328–29.
16 ibid., p. 309.
17 ibid., pp. 307–9.
18 ibid., pp. 310.
19 Friedrich Nietzsche, *Die Geburt der Tragödie*, in *Werke*, Vol. III/1, pp. 1–152; 40.
20 Nietzsche, *Zur Genealogie der Moral*, p. 314.
21 ibid., pp. 310, 314, 322.
22 ibid., p. 322.
23 Nietzsche, *Der Anti-Christ*, p. 175.
24 ibid., p. 175.
25 Wilhelm Dilthey, *Einleitung in die Geisteswissenschaften: Versuch einer Grundlegung für das Studium der Gesellschaft und der Geschichte*, in *Gesammelte Schriften*, 26 vols. (Leipzig/Berlin: B. G. Teubner, 1923), Vol. I, pp. 130–31.
26 ibid., pp. 131.
27 ibid., p. 377.
28 ibid., p. 358.
29 Wilhelm Dilthey, 'Ideen über eine beschreibende und zergliedernde Psychologie', *Die geistige Welt: Einleitung in die Philosophie des Lebens*, in Dilthey, *Gesammelte Schriften*, Vol. IV, pp. 139–237; 195.
30 Wilhelm Dilthey, *Der Aufbau der geschichtlichen Welt in den Geisteswissenschaften* (Frankfurt am Main: Suhrkamp, 1970), p. 142.
31 Dilthey, *Einleitung in die Geisteswissenschaften*, p. 224.
32 Georg Simmel, *Die Philosophie des Geldes* (Frankfurt am Main: Suhrkamp, 1989), p. 289.
33 ibid., p. 597.
34 ibid., p. 270.
35 ibid., p. 665.
36 ibid., p. 675.
37 ibid., p. 609.
38 ibid., pp. 610–11.
39 Georg Simmel, *Das individuelle Gesetz: Philosophische Diskurse* edited by M. Landmann (Frankfurt am Main: Suhrkamp, 1968), p. 203.
40 Ferdinand Tönnies, *Gemeinschaft und Gesellschaft: Grundbegriffe der reinen Soziologie*, new edn, on basis of 8th edn (Darmstadt: Wissenschaftliche Buchgesellschaft, 1979), pp. 149–50.
41 ibid., p. 181.
42 ibid., p. 154
43 ibid., pp. 198–99.
44 Max Weber, *Wirtschaft und Gesellschaft. Grundriß der verstehenden Soziologie*, 5th edn, edited by Johannes Winckelmann (Tubingen: J. C. B. Mohr, 1921), p. 13.
45 Max Weber, *Die protestantische Ethik und der Geist des Kapitalismus*, in Weber, *Gesammelte Aufsätze zur Religionssoziologie*, 3 vols (Tubingen: J. C. B.Mohr, 1920), Vol. I, pp. 17–206; 111, 203.
46 ibid., p. 184.
47 ibid., p. 199.
48 Weber, *Wirtschaft und Gesellschaft*, pp. 181, 198, 439.
49 ibid., p. 439.
50 ibid., p. 513.

51 See Max Weber, 'Der Nationalstaat und die Volkswirtschaftspolitik', in Weber, *Gesammelte politische Schriften* (Tubingen: J. C. B. Mohr, 1988), pp. 1–25.
52 Weber, *Wirtschaft und Gesellschaft*, p. 124.
53 ibid., p. 125.
54 ibid., p. 126.
55 Max Weber, 'Politik als Beruf', in Weber, *Gesammelte politische Schriften*, pp. 505–60; 554.
56 ibid., pp. 140–41.
57 ibid., p. 142.
58 ibid., p. 123.
59 Max Weber, 'Parlament und Regierung im neugeordneten Deutschland', in Weber, *Gesammelte politische Schriften*, pp. 306–443; 391.
60 Max Weber, 'Deutschlands künftige Staatsform', in Weber, *Gesammelte politische Schriften*, pp. 448–83; 469.
61 See Gneist's analysis of 'ministerial responsibility' as the cornerstone of a legal state: Rudolf von Gneist, *Der Rechtsstaat* (Berlin: Springer, 1872), pp. 162–63, 175.
62 Weber, 'Parlament und Regierung', p. 424.
63 Rudolf Sohm, *Kirchenrecht*, 2 vols, Vol. I, *Die geschichtlichen Grundlagen*, (Leipzig: Duncker und Humblot, 1892), p. 22.
64 ibid., p. 28.
65 ibid., p. 699.
66 Weber, 'Politik als Beruf', p. 558.
67 ibid., p. 559.

8 Neo-Kantianism

1 Adolf Trendelenburg, *Naturrecht auf dem Grunde der Ethik* (Leipzig: S. Hirzel, 1860), p. 282.
2 Karl David August Röder, *Grundzüge des Naturrechts oder der Rechtsphilosophie*, 2nd edn (Leipzig: Carl Winter, 1860), p. 79.
3 Hermann Cohen, *Kants Begründung der Ethik*, 2nd edn (Berlin: Bruno Cassirer, 1910), p. 306.
4 ibid., p. 79.
5 Paul Natorp, *Sozialpädagogik: Theorie der Willenserziehung auf der Grundlage der Gemeinschaft*, 4th edn (Stuttgart: Fr. Frommann, 1904), p. 46.
6 Heinrich Rickert, *Die Grenzen der naturwissenschaftlichen Begriffsbildung: Eine logische Einleitung in die historischen Wissenschaften* (Tubingen: J. C. B. Mohr, 1902), p. 702.
7 Rickert, *Der Gegenstand der Erkenntniß*, p. 434.
8 ibid., pp. 436–37.
9 Hermann Cohen, *System der Philosophie, Zweiter Theil:Ethik des reinen Willens* (Berlin: Bruno Cassirer, 1904), p. 1.
10 ibid., p. 269.
11 ibid., pp. 309, 177.
12 Hermann Cohen, *System der Philosophie: Logik der reinen Erkenntniß* (Berlin: Bruno Cassirer, 1902), pp. 174–75.
13 Cohen, *Ethik des reinen Willens*, p. 71.
14 ibid., p. 302.
15 Stammler was in Marburg in the early 1880s and was a friend of Natorp, although he later denied any direct connection with Cohen's neo-Kantian orthodoxy. See, on this, Claudius Müller, *Die Rechtsphilosophie des Marburger Neukantianismus. Naturrecht und Rechtspositivismus in der Auseinandersetzung zwischen Hermann Cohen, Rudolf Stammler und Paul Natorp* (Tubingen: J. C. B. Mohr, 1994), pp. 12–13.

16 Rudolf Stammler, *Theorie der Rechtswissenschaft* (Halle: Buchhandlung des Waisenhauses, 1911), pp. 18–19.
17 Rudolf Stammler, *Recht und Kirche. Betrachtungen zur Lehre von der Geminschaft und der Möglichkeit eines Kirchenrechtes* (Berlin: de Gruyter, 1919), pp. 24–5.
18 Stammler, *Theorie der Rechtswissenschaft*, p. 45.
19 ibid., p. 69.
20 Paul Natorp, 'Recht und Sittlichkeit', *Kant-Studien*, 18 (1913), pp. 1–79; 22.
21 Rudolf Stammler, *Die Lehre vom richtigen Recht* (Berlin: Guttentag, 1902), p. 53.
22 Rudolf Stammler, *Wirtschaft und Recht nach der materialistischen Geschicht-sauffassung: Eine sozialphilosophische Untersuchung*, 3rd edn (Lepzig: Veit & Comp., 1914), p. 550.
23 Natorp, 'Recht und Sittlichkeit', pp. 53, 60.
24 ibid., p. 70.
25 Rudolf Stammler, *Sozialismus und Christentum. Erörterungen zu den Grundbegriffen und den Grundsätzen der Sozialwissenschaft* (Leipzig: Felix Meiner, 1920), p. 96.
26 ibid., p. 181.
27 Stammler, *Die Lehre vom richtigen Recht*, p. 201.
28 Stammler, *Sozialismus und Christentum*, p. 198.
29 Natorp, *Sozialpädagogik*, p. 86.
30 Stammler, *Theorie der Rechtswissenschaft*, p. 397.
31 Cohen, *Ethik des reinen Willens*, p. 74.
32 ibid., p. 242.
33 ibid., p. 246.
34 ibid., p. 304.
35 Eduard Bernstein, *Die Voraussetzungen des Sozialismus und die Aufgaben der Sozialdemokratie* (Stuttgart: Dietz, 1899), pp. 123–4.
36 Cohen, *Ethik des reinen Willens*, p. 304.
37 Stammler, *Sozialismus und Christentum*, p. 69.
38 Stammler, *Wirtschaft und Recht nach der materialistischen Geschichtsauffassung*, pp. 184–5.
39 Natorp, *Sozialpädagogik*, p. 196.
40 Franz Staudinger, *Ethik und Politik* (Berlin: F. Dümmler, 1899), p. 81.
41 ibid., p. 146.
42 Karl Vorländer, *Kant und Marx: Ein Beitrag zur Philosophie des Sozialismus* (Tubingen: J. C. B. Mohr, 1911), p. 34.
43 See, especially, Max Adler, *Politik und Moral* (Leipzig: Verlag Naturwissenschaften, 1918), pp. 74–5.
44 Karl Kautsky, *Ethik und materialistische Geschichtsaufassung* (Berlin: Dietz, 1922), p. 129.
45 Stammler, *Theorie der Rechtswissenschaft*, pp. 21–2, 45.
46 Stammler, *Die Lehre vom richtigen Recht*, pp. 102–3.
47 Stammler, *Recht und Kirche*, p. 11.
48 ibid., p. 24.
49 Stammler, *Wirtschaft und Recht*, p. 591.
50 Paul Natorp, 'Kant und die Marburger Schule', in *Kant-Studien*, 17 (1912), pp. 193–221; 198.
51 Cohen, *Ethik des reinen Willens*, p. 18.
52 Cohen, *Kants Begründung der Ethik*, p. 272.
53 Heinrich Rickert, *Der Gegenstand der Erkenntniß: Einführung in die Transzendentalphilosophie*, 6th edn (Tubingen: J. C. B. Mohr, 1928) p. 259.
54 Emil Lask, *Rechtsphilosophie,* in Wilhelm Windelband (ed.), *Die Philosophie im Beginn des zwanzigsten Jahrhunderts: Festschrift für Kuno Fischer* (Heidelberg: Carl Winter, 1907) pp. 269-320; 272.

55 Stammler, *Recht und Kirche*, p. 24.
56 Cohen, *Ethik des reinen Willens*, p. 201.
57 ibid., p. 235.
58 ibid., pp. 217–18.
59 ibid., p. 228.
60 An important commentary on this is found in Eggert Winter, *Ethik und Rechtsgemeinschaft: Eine historisch-systematische Untersuchung zur Ethik-Konzeption des Marburger Neukantianismus im Werke Hermann Cohens* (Berlin: Duncker und Humblot, 1980), pp. 300, 304, 314, 308, 317.
61 Julius Binder, *Rechtsbegriff und Rechtsidee: Bemerkungen zur Rechtsphilosophie Rudolf Stammlers* (Leipzig: Deichert, 1915), p. 100.
62 ibid., p. 308.
63 Friedrich Meinecke, *Weltbürgertum und Nationalstaat: Studien zur Geschichte des deutschen Nationalstaats* (Munich: Oldenbourg, 1908), pp. 1, 7.
64 Friedrich Meinecke, 'Wilhelm von Humboldt und der deutsche Staat', in Meinecke, *Staat und Persönlichkeit* (Berlin: Mittler, 1933), pp. 81–97; 86.
65 Erich Kaufmann, *Kritik der neukantischen Rechtsphilosophie: Eine Betrachtung über die Beziehungen zwischen Philosophie und Rechtswissenschaft* (Tubingen: J. C. B. Mohr, 1921), p. vi.
66 ibid., p. 52.
67 ibid., p. 63.
68 ibid., p. 62.
69 ibid., p. 3.
70 ibid., p. 61.
71 Max Scheler, *Der Formalismus in der Ethik und die materiale Wertethik: Neuer Versuch der Grundlegung eines ethischen Personalismus*, 2nd edn (Halle: Niemeyer, 1921), pp. 104–7, 544.
72 See Alfred Schütz, 'Scheler's Theory of Intersubjectivity and the General Thesis of the Alter Ego', in *Philosophy and Phenomenological Research*, II (1941–42), pp. 323–47; 337.
73 Max Scheler, *Die Stellung des Menschen im Kosmos* (Darmstadt: Otto Reichel, 1928), p. 58.
74 Scheler, *Der Formalismus in der Ethik*, p. 160.
75 ibid., pp. 547–55.
76 Max Scheler, 'Ordo Amoris', in Scheler, *Gesammelte Werke*, 2nd edn, 16 vols (Bern: Francke Verlag, 1957), Vol. X, *Schriften aus dem Nachlaß*, Vol. I, *Zur Ethik und Erkenntnislehre*, pp. 345–76; 356.
77 Max Scheler, *Vom Ewigen im Menschen*, Vol. I, *Religiöse Erneuerung* (Leipzig: Verlag der neue Geist, 1921), p. 199.
78 Max Scheler, 'Absolutsphäre und Rechtsetzung der Gottesidee', in *Schriften aus dem Nachlaß*, Vol. I, pp. 179–253; 240.
79 Scheler, *Vom Ewigen im Menschen*, p. 722.
80 Heinz Heimsoeth, *Metaphysik der Neuzeit* (Munich: R. Oldenbourg, 1934), pp. 102–3.
81 ibid., p. 231.
82 Karl Jaspers, *Philosophie*, 3 vols (Munich: Piper, 1994), Vol. I, p. 28.
83 Karl Jaspers, *Psychologie der Weltanschauungen* (Munich: Piper, 1985), p. 308.
84 Karl Jaspers, *Die geistige Situation der Zeit*, 9th edn (Berlin: de Gruyter, 1999), pp. 51, 65.
85 Paul Natorp, *Der Deutsche und sein Staat* (Erlangen: Verlag der Philosophischen Akademie, 1924), p. 54.
86 ibid., p. 86.
87 ibid., p. 88.
88 ibid., p. 40.

89 Paul Natorp, *Sozialidealismus. Neue Richtlinien der sozialen Erziehung* (Berlin: Julius Springer, 192), p. 22.
90 ibid., p. v.
91 ibid., p. 80.
92 ibid., pp. 243–44.
93 Martin Heidegger, *Sein und Zeit*, 16th edn (Tubingen: Niemeyer, 1986), p. 53.
94 ibid., p. 118.
95 ibid., p. 119.
96 Heidegger, *Kant und das Problem der Metaphysik*, 6th edn (Frankfurt am Main: Vittorio Klostermann, 1998), p. 156.
97 ibid., p. 158.
98 ibid., p. 156.
99 ibid., p. 206.
100 Heidegger, *Sein und Zeit*, pp. 120–21.
101 Martin Heidegger, *Kant und das Problem der Metaphysik*, p. 242.
102 Martin Heidegger, *Einführung in die Metaphysik*, 6th edn (Tubingen: Niemeyer, 1998), pp. 33–34.
103 ibid., p. 16.
104 Martin Heidegger, *Über den Humanismus* (Frankfurt am Main: Klostermann, 1949), p. 13.
105 Martin Heidegger, *Über den Ursprung des Kunstwerkes* (Stuttgart: Reclam, 1960), p. 79.
106 Martin Heidegger, *Phänomenologie des religiösen Lebens*, in *Gesamtausgabe*, planned for 102 vols (Frankfurt am Main: Klostermann, 1975–), Vol. LX, pp. 127, 80.
107 Georg Lukács, *Geschichte und Klassenbewußtsein* (Neuwied: Luchterhand, 1968), p. 273.
108 ibid., p. 266.
109 ibid., p. 281.
110 ibid., p. 282.
111 ibid., p. 247.
112 ibid., p. 207.
113 ibid., p. 328.

9 The Weimar Republic

1 Hans Kelsen, *Das Problem der Souveränität und die Theorie des Völkerrechts: Beitrag zu einer reinen Rechtslehre* (Tubingen: J. C. B. Mohr, 1920), p. 12.
2 Hans Kelsen, *Der soziologische und der juristische Staatsbegriff: Kritische Untersuchung des Verhältnisses von Staat und Recht* (Tubingen: J. C. B. Mohr, 1922), pp. 93–94.
3 Hans Kelsen, *Wesen und Wert der Demokratie* (Tubingen: J. C. B. Mohr, 1929), p. 76.
4 Kelsen, *Das Problem der Souveränität*, p. 114.
5 ibid., p. 109.
6 Hans Kelsen, *Reine Rechtslehre* (Vienna: Deuticke, 1934), p. 64.
7 Hans Kelsen, *Über Grenzen zwischen juristischer und soziologischer Methode* (Tubingen: J. C. B. Mohr, 1911), p. 10.
8 See Hans Kelsen, 'Zur Theorie der juristischen Fiktionen', in *Annalen der Philosophie: Mit besonderer Rücksicht auf die Probleme der Als-Ob-Betrachtung*, Vol. I (1919), pp. 630–58; 634.
9 Kelsen, *Reine Rechtslehre*, p. 120.
10 ibid., p. 59.
11 ibid., pp. 120–21.

12 Kelsen, *Über Grenzen zwischen juristischer und soziologischer Methode*, p. 22–23.
13 Hans Kelsen, *Hauptprobleme der Staatsrechtslehre* (Tubingen: J. C. B. Mohr, 1911), pp. 378, 434, 570. For an important essay on Kelsen's hostility to the dualistic tendencies in ius-naturalism, see Kazimierz Opalek, 'Kelsens Kritik der Naturrechtslehre', in Werner Krawietz, Ernst Topitsch and Peter Koller (eds), *Ideologiekritik und Demokratietheorie bei Hans Kelsen* (Berlin: Duncker und Humblot, 1982), pp, 71–86; esp. 73–75.
14 Hans Kelsen, *Allgemeine Staatslehre* (Berlin: Julius Springer, 1925), p. 37.
15 Kelsen, *Reine Rechtslehre*, p. 128.
16 Kelsen, *Allgemeine Staatslehre*, p. 76.
17 ibid., p. 131.
18 Hans Kelsen, *Staatsform und Weltanschauung* (Tubingen: J. C. B. Mohr, 1933), p. 25.
19 Kelsen, *Das Problem der Souveränität*, p. 21.
20 Kelsen, *Der soziologische und der juristische Staatsbegriff*, p. 253.
21 ibid., p. 227.
22 Kelsen, *Staatsform und Weltanschauung*, p. 18.
23 For Kelsen's own commentary on this interpretation, see Kelsen, *Reine Rechtslehre*, p. vii.
24 See Adolf von Harnack, 'Protestantische Kultur', in Harnack, *Aus der Friedens- und Kriegsarbeit* (Giessen: Töpelmann, 1916), pp. 205–12; Ernst Troeltsch, 'Der metaphysische und religiöse Geist der deutschen Kultur', in Troeltsch, *Deutscher Geist und Westeuropa*, edited by H. Baron (Tubingen: J. C. B. Mohr, 1925), pp. 59–79; 67, 78.
25 Freidrich Naumann, *Geist und Glaube* (Berlin: Buchverlag der Hilfe, 1911), p. 64.
26 Friedrich Naumann, *Demokratie und Kaisertum* (Berlin: Buchverlag der Hilfe, 1900), p. 142.
27 See Naumann's speech in the *Reichstag* on basic rights: *Verhandlungen der verfassunggebenden Nationalversammlung,* Vol. 329 (Berlin: Druck und Verlag der Norddeutschen Burchdruckerei und Verlags-Anstalt, 1920), p. 2190.
28 Karl Renner, *Die Rechtsinstitute des Privatrechts und ihre soziale Funktion: Ein Beitrag zur Kritik des bürgerlichen Rechts* (Stuttgart: Fischer, 1965), p. 202.
29 Hugo Sinzheimer, *Ein Arbeitstarifgesetz: Die Idee der sozialen Selbstbestimmung im Recht* (Munich: Duncker & Humblot, 1916), p. 35.
30 See Hugo Sinzheimer, 'Das Rätesystem', in Sinzheimer, *Arbeitsrecht und Rechtssoziologie: Gesammelte Aufsätze und Reden*, edited by Otto Kahn-Freund and Thilo Ramm, 2 vols (Frankfurt am Main: Europäische Verlagsanstalt, 1976), Vol. I, pp. 325–50.
31 Gerhard Anschütz, *Drei Leitgedanken der Weimarer Reichsverfassung* (Tubingen: J. C. B. Mohr, 1923), pp. 6, 31.
32 See Theodor Litt, *Individuum und Gemeinschaft: Grundfragen der sozialen Theorie und Ethik* (Leipzig: Teubner, 1919), p. 22.
33 Hermann Heller, *Staatslehre*, edited by G. Niemeyer, 4th edn (Leiden: Sijthoff, 1970), p. 69.
34 Hermann Heller, 'Ziele und Grenzen der deutschen Verfassungsreform', in Heller, *Gesammelte Schriften*, edited by M. Drath, F. Borinski and G. Niemeyer, 3 vols (Leiden: Sijthoff, 1971), Vol. II, p. 414.
35 Hermann Heller, 'Die Krisis der Staatslehre', in Heller, *Gesammelte Schriften*, Vol. II, pp. 5–30; 7.
36 Hermann Heller, *Die Souveränität: Ein Beitrag zur Theorie des Staats- und Völkerrechts*, in Heller, *Gesammelte Schriften*, Vol. II, pp. 31–202; 49.
37 ibid., p. 202.
38 ibid., p. 62.

39 ibid., p. 71.
40 Hermann Heller, 'Der Begriff des Gesetzes in der Reichsverfassung', in Heller, *Gesammelte Schriften*, Vol. II, pp. 203–47; 227.
41 Heller, *Souveränität*, p. 65.
42 ibid., p. 113.
43 ibid., pp. 96–97.
44 Heller, *Staatslehre*, p. 183.
45 ibid., pp. 190–91.
46 ibid., p. 263–64.
47 ibid., p. 260.
48 ibid., p. 269.
49 ibid., p. 215.
50 ibid., p. 214.
51 ibid., p. 263.
52 Gustav Radbruch, *Grundzüge der Rechtsphilosophie* (Leipzig: Quelle & Meyer, 1914), pp. 153–54.
53 Gustav Radbruch, *Einführung in die Rechtswisssenschaft* (Leipzig: Quelle und Meyer, 1913), pp. 50–51.
54 Gustav Radbruch, *Der Mensch im Recht. Heidelberger Antrittsvorlesung* (Tubingen: J. C. B. Mohr, 1927), p. 12.
55 ibid., p. 17.
56 Radbruch, *Grundzüge*, p. 143.
57 Smend, 'Protestantismus und Demokratie', pp. 307–8.
58 ibid., p. 297.
59 Rudolf Smend, 'Verfassung und Verfassungsrecht', in Smend, *Staatsrechtliche Abhandlungen*, pp. 119–277; 226.
60 ibid., p. 263.
61 ibid., p. 182.
62 ibid., p. 219.
63 For critical analysis of Smend's politics, see Reinhold Aris, 'Krisis der Verfassung', in *Neue Blätter für den religiösen Sozialismus*, 3/1 (1932), pp. 19–29; 26; see also Hans Kelsen, *Der Staat als Integration: Eine prinzipielle Auseinandersetzung* (Vienna: Julius Springer, 1930), p. 87.
64 Smend, 'Protestantismus und Demokratie', p. 305.
65 Hans Gerber, *Freiheit und Bindung der Staatsgewalt* (Tubingen: J. C. B. Mohr, 1932), pp. 22–23.
66 Hans Gerber, *Die Idee des Staates in der neueren evangelisch-theologischen Ethik* (Berlin: Juncker und Dünnhaupt, 1930), p. 56.
67 Otto Koellreutter, *Staat, Kirche und Schule im heutigen Deutschland* (Tubingen: J. C. B. Mohr, 1926), p. 15.
68 Carl Schmitt, *Der Wert des Staates und die Bedeutung des Einzelnen* (Tubingen: J. C. B. Mohr, 1914), pp. 48, 95.
69 Jeff Seitzer has repeatedly made this point in our conversations on this matter, and I agree with him.
70 Carl Schmitt, *Politische Theologie* (Berlin: Duncker und Humblot, 1922), p. 46.
71 ibid., p. 43.
72 ibid., p. 43.
73 Carl Schmitt, *Die geistesgeschichtliche Lage des heutigen Parlamentarismus* (Berlin: Duncker und Humblot, 1923), p. 45.
74 ibid., p. 11.
75 ibid., pp. 19–20.
76 ibid., p. 22.
77 ibid., p. 41.
78 ibid., p. 22.

79 Carl Schmitt, *Der Leviathan in der Staatslehre des Thomas Hobbes: Sinn und Fehlschlag eines politischen Symbols* (Stuttgart: Cotta, 1995), p. 118.
80 Schmitt, *Die geistesgeschichtliche Lage*, p. 12.
81 Carl Schmitt, *Der Begriff des Politischen* (Berlin: Duncker und Humblot, 1932), p. 94.
82 Schmitt, *Die geistesgeschichtliche Lage*, p. 36.
83 Carl Schmitt, *Der Hüter der Verfassung* (Berlin: Duncker und Humblot, 1931), p. 90.
84 Carl Schmitt, *Die Diktatur, von den Anfängen des modernen Souveränitätsgedanken bis zum proletarischen Klassenkrieg* (Berlin: Duncker und Humblot, 1919), p. 136.
85 Carl Schmitt, *Volksentscheid und Volksbegehren: Ein Beitrag zur Auslegung der Weimarer Verfassung und zur Lehre von der unmittelbaren Demokratie* (Berlin and Leipzig: Duncker und Humblot, 1927), p. 34.
86 Carl Schmitt, *Verfassungslehre* (Berlin: Duncker und Humblot, 1928), p. 65.
87 ibid., p. 200.
88 Carl Schmitt, *Hüter der Verfassung*, p. 159.
89 At one point, for instance, Schmitt denounced the 'total parties' or the 'activist parties' seeking to 'dominate the state' in late-Weimar politics (Carl Schmitt, 'Weiterentwicklung des totalen Staats in Deutschland', in Schmitt, *Verfassungsrechtliche Aufsätze aus den Jahren 1924–1954: Materialien zu einer Verfassungslehre*, Berlin: Duncker und Humblot, 1958), pp. 359–71; 362–63. More famously, he also went to great pains to show that the supposed neutrality of law under the parliamentary systems made it easy for parties to 'get their hands on legal power' in order entirely to destroy the constitution. In this analysis, he implicitly suggested that the president should use decisive powers to prevent the assumption of power, by legal means, by the NSDAP (Carl Schmitt, *Legalität und Legitimität*, p. 37).
90 Ernst Jünger, *Der Arbeiter: Herrschaft und Gestalt*, in *Werke*, 18 vols (Klett: Cotta, 1964), Vol. VI, pp. 312–13. Oswald Spengler, *Der Mensch und die Technik* (Munich: Beck, 1932), p. 81.
91 Schmitt, *Die geistesgeschichtliche Lage*, p. 45.
92 Schmitt, *Hüter der Verfassung*, p. 131.
93 ibid., p. 13.
94 Schmitt, *Politische Theologie*, p. 16.
95 ibid., p. 46.
96 ibid., p. 38.
97 Schmitt, *Verfassungslehre*, p. 87.
98 Konrad Beyerle, *Die Bedeutung der neuen Reichsverfassung für Volk und Vaterland* (Berlin: Verlag der Reichszentrale für Heimatdienst, 1919), pp. 5–6; Joseph Mausbach, *Kulturfragen in der deutschen Verfassung: Eine Erklärung wichtiger Verfassungsartikel* (Monchengladbach: Volksvereins-Verlag, 1920), p. 12; Peter Tischleder, *Der Staat: Staatsidee, Staatsgewalt, Staatszweck, Völkergemeinschaft* (Monchengladbach: Volksvereins-Verlag, 1926), esp. p. 21; Franz Xaver Kiefl, *Die Staatsphilosophie der katholischen Kirche und die Frage der Legitimität in der Erbmonarchie* (Regensburg: Manz, 1928), p. 37.
99 Schmitt, *Verfassungslehre*, p. 209.
100 Carl Schmitt, *Römischer Katholizismus und politische Form* (Munich: Theatiner-Verlag, 1925), p. 34.
101 ibid., p. 218.
102 Carl Schmitt, 'Der Führer schützt das Recht', in Schmitt, *Positionen und Begriffe im Kampf mit Weimar-Genf-Versailles 1923–1939* (Hamburg: Hanseatische Verlagsanstalt, 1940), pp. 199–203.
103 Otto Koellreutter, *Deutsches Verfassungsrecht. Ein Grundriß* (Berlin: Junker und Dünnhupt, 1935), p. 12.

104 ibid., p. 191.
105 Otto Koellreutter, *Grundfragen des völkischen und staatlichen Lebens im deutschen Volksstaate* (Berlin: Pan-Verlagsgesellschaft, 1935), p. 10.
106 Julius Binder, *Grundlegung zur Rechtsphilosophie* (Tubingen: J. C. B. Mohr, 1935), p. 156.
107 Karl Larenz, *Rechtsperson und subjektives Recht: Zur Wandlung der Rechtsbegriffe* (Berlin: Juncker und Dünnhaupt, 1935), p. 19.
108 Karl Larenz, *Die Methode der Auslegung des Rechtsgeschäfts. Zugleich ein Beitrag zur Theorie der Willenserklärung* (Leipzig: Deichert, 1930), p. 91.
109 Larenz, *Rechtsperson und subjektives Recht*, p. 21.
110 Karl Larenz, *Deutsche Rechtserneuerung und Rechtsphilosophie*, in *Recht und Staat in Geschichte und Gegenwart* 109 (1934), pp. 5, 26.
111 Larenz, *Rechtsperson und subjektives Recht*, p. 24.
112 Roland Freisler, *Richter und Gesetz* (Berlin: Spaeth und Linde, 1936), pp. 8, 11.
113 Ernst Rudolf Huber, *Verträge zwischen Staat und Kirche im Deutschen Reich* (Breslau: Marcus, 1930), p. 127.
114 Ernst Rudolf Huber, *Neue Grundbegriffe des hoheitlichen Rechts* (Berlin: Duncker und Dünnhaupt, 1935), p. 19.
115 Ernst Rudolf Huber, *Verfassungsrecht des Großdeutschen Reiches* (Hamburg: Hanseatische Verlagsanstalt, 1939), p. 164.
116 Ernst Forsthoff, *Der totale Staat* (Hamburg: Hanseatische Verlagsanstalt, 1933), p. 41.
117 ibid., p. 13.
118 Ernst Forsthoff, *Recht und Sprache: Prolegomena zu einer richterlichen Hermeneutik* (Halle: Niemeyer, 1940), p. 19.
119 ibid., p. 3.

10 Critical theory and the law

1 See Rudolf Hilferding, *Das Finanzkapital. Eine Studie über die jüngste Entwicklung des Kapitalismus* (Vienna: Verlag der Wiener Volksbuchhandlung Ignaz Brand, 1910), esp. p. 295.
2 See Friedrich Pollock, 'Die gegenwärtige Lage des Kapitalismus und die Aussichten einer planwirtschaftlichen Neuordnung', in Pollock, *Stadien des Kapitalismus*, edited by Helmut Dubiel (Munich: Beck, 1975), pp. 20–39; 26.
3 For controversies about the use of this term, see Max Horkheimer, *Gesammelte Schriften*, edited by A. Schmidt and G. Schmid Noerr, 18 vols (Frankfurt am Main: Fischer, 1985), Vol. XII, pp. 398–417.
4 Frederick Pollock, 'State Capitalism: Its Possibilities and Limitations', in *Studies in Philosophy and Social Science*, 9 (1941), pp. 200–25; 222.
5 Herbert Marcuse, 'Der Kampf gegen den Liberalismus in der totalitären Staatsauffassung', in Marcuse, *Kultur und Gesellschaft*, 2 vols (Frankfurt am Main: Suhrkamp, 1965), Vol. I, pp. 17–56; 49.
6 Max Horkheimer, 'Autoritärer Staat', in *Gesammelte Schriften*, Vol. V, pp. 293–319; 294.
7 ibid., pp. 300–1.
8 ibid., p. 304.
9 Otto Kirchheimer, 'The Legal Order of National Socialism', in *Studies in Philosophy and Social Science*, 9 (1941), pp. 456–75; 462.
10 Otto Kirchheimer, 'Changes in the Structure of Political Compromise', in *Studies in Philosophy and Social Science*, 9 (1941), pp. 264–89; 280, 288.
11 Franz Neumann, *Behemoth: The Structure and Practice of National Socialism* (New York: Harper Torchbooks, 1966), p. 634.
12 ibid., p. 467.

13 Kirchheimer, 'The Legal Order of National Socialism', p. 475.
14 Franz Neumann, 'Types of Natural Law', in *Zeitschrift für Sozialforschung*, VIII (1939/40), pp. 338–61; 361.
15 Franz Neumann, 'Der Funktionswandel des Gesetzes im Recht der bürgerlichen Gesellschaft', in *Zeitschrift für Sozialforschung*, VI (1937), pp. 542–96; 547.
16 Friedrich Pollock, 'Bemerkungen zur Wirtschaftskrise', in *Stadien des Kapitalismus*, pp. 40–71; 68.
17 Marcuse, 'Der Kampf gegen den Liberalismus', pp. 23, 27.
18 Horkheimer, 'Autoritärer Staat', p. 308.
19 Max Horkheimer, 'Vorbemerkung [zu der *Theorie der Planwirtschaft*]', in *Gesammelte Schriften*, Vol. III, pp. 221–24; 223.
20 Kirchheimer, 'Changes in the Structure of Political Compromise', p. 272.
21 Otto Kirchheimer, 'Weimar – und was dann? Analyse einer Verfassung', in Kirchheimer, *Politik und Verfassung. 10 Analysen* (Frankfurt am Main: Suhrkamp, 1964), pp. 9–56; 56.
22 Otto Kirchheimer, 'Das Problem der Verfassung', in Kirchheimer, *Von der Weimarer Republik zum Faschismus: Die Auflösung der demokratischen Rechtsordnung*, edited by W. Luthardt (Frankfurt am Main: Suhrkamp, 1976), pp. 64–68; 67.
23 Otto Kirchheimer, 'Legalität und Legitimität', in *Die Gesellschaft*, 9/1 (1932), pp. 8–26; 14.
24 Neumann, 'Funktionswandel des Gesetzes', p. 552.
25 Neumann, *Behemoth*, p. 10.
26 Franz Neumann, 'Über die Voraussetzungen und den Rechtsbegriff einer Wirtschaftsverfassung', in Neumann, *Wirtschaft, Staat, Demokratie: Aufsätze 1930–1954*, edited by Alfons Söllner (Frankfurt am Main: Suhrkamp, 1978), pp. 76–102; 81–85.
27 Neumann, 'Über die Voraussetzungen und den Rechtsbegriff einer Wirtschaftsverfassung', pp. 80–81.
28 Neumann, 'Funktionswandel des Gesetzes', p. 553.
29 Neumann, 'Über die Voraussetzungen und den Rechtsbegriff einer Wirtschaftsverfassung', pp. 80–81.
30 Franz Neumann, 'The Concept of Political Freedom', *Columbia Law Review*, 53/7 (1953), pp. 901–35; 928.
31 Otto Kirchheimer, 'Bemerkungen zu Carl Schmitts Legalität und Legitimität', in *Von der Weimarer Republik zum Faschismus*, pp. 113–52; 116.
32 ibid., p. 116.
33 Marcuse, 'Der Kampf gegen den Liberalismus', pp. 30–31.
34 Theodor W. Adorno, *Kants Kritik der reinen Vernunft*, in Adorno, *Nachgelassene Schriften*, edited by R. Tiedemann, planned for 13 vols (Frankfurt am Main: Suhrkamp, 1995), Vol. IV/4, pp. 87–88.
35 Theodor W. Adorno, *Negative Dialektik* (Frankfurt am Main: Suhrkamp, 1966), p. 240.
36 Max Horkheimer and Theodor W. Adorno, *Dialektik der Aufklärung. Philisophische Fragmente* (Frankfurt am Main: Fischer, 1969), p. 15.
37 Max Horkheimer, *Traditionelle und Kritische Theorie*, in *Gesammalte Schriften*, Vol. III, pp. 162–216; 184.
38 Franz Neumann, 'Die soziale Bedeutung der Grundrechte in der Weimarer Verfassung', in Neumann, *Wirtschaft, Staat, Demokratie*, pp. 57–76; 63.
39 Marcuse, 'Der Kampf gegen den Liberalismus', pp. 30–31.
40 Horkheimer and Adorno, *Dialektik der Aufklärung*, pp. 32–33.
41 Adorno, *Kants Kritik der reinen Vernunft*, p. 87.
42 Max Horkheimer, 'Materialismus und Metaphysik', in *Gesammelte Schriften*, Vol. III, pp. 70–105; 99.
43 Adorno, *Kants Kritik der reinen Vernunft*, pp. 168–69.

44 Max Horkheimer, 'Theismus – Atheismus', in Horkheimer (ed.), *Zeugnisse: Theodor W. Adorno zum sechzigsten Geburtstag* (Frankfurt am Main: Europäische Verlagsanstalt, 1963), pp. 9–20; 18.
45 This is exemplified in Adorno, *Negative Dialektik*, p. 397.

11 The dialectics of refoundation

1 See, for example, Helmut Coing, *Die obersten Grundsätze des Rechts: Ein Versuch zur Neugründung des Naturrechts* (Heidelberg: Schriften zur süddeutschen Juristen-Zeitung, 1947), p. 7.
2 See Julius Ebbinghaus, 'Zu Deutschlands Schicksalswende', in Ebbinghaus, *Sittlichkeit und Recht: Praktische Philosophie 1929–1954* (Bonn: Bouvier, 1986), pp. 117–278.
3 Gerhart Husserl, *Recht und Zeit: Fünf rechtsphilosophische Essays* (Frankfurt am Main: Vittorio Klostermann, 1955), p. 57.
4 Werner Maihofer, *Recht und Sein: Prolegomena zu einer Rechtsontologie* (Typescript, 1953), p. 147.
5 Ernst Bloch, *Naturrecht und menschliche Würde* (Frankfurt am Main: Suhrkamp, 1961), p. 310.
6 Karl Jaspers, *Die Atombombe und die Zukunft des Menschen* (Munich: Deutscher Taschenbuchverlag, 1961), p. 279.
7 ibid., p. 279; Karl Jaspers, *Von der Wahrheit* (Munich: Piper, 1947), p. 809; Hannah Arendt, *The Human Condition* (Chicago, Ill.: University of Chicago Press, 1958), p. 257.
8 Karl Jaspers, *Vom Ursprung und Ziel der Geschichte* (Frankfurt am Main: Fischer, 1955), p. 192.
9 Karl Jaspers, *Freiheit und Wiedervereinigung* (Munich: Piper, 1990), p. 104.
10 Karl Jaspers, *Wohin treibt die Bundesrepublik?* (Munich: Piper, 1966), p. 190.
11 Karl Jaspers, *Vom Ursprund Ziel der Geschichte*, pp. 180–81.
12 ibid., p. 173.
13 ibid., pp. 180–81.
14 Martin Heidegger, 'Die Frage nach der Technik', in Heidegger, *Gesamtausgabe*, Vol. VII, pp. 5–36; 7.
15 ibid., p. 26.
16 Martin Heidegger, 'Überwindung der Metaphysik', in *Gesamtausgabe*, Vol. VII, pp. 67–98; 79, 85.
17 ibid., p. 70.
18 ibid., p. 123.
19 Hannah Arendt, *The Human Condition*, pp. 194, 198.
20 Karl Jaspers, *Von der Wahrheit*, p. 796.
21 Karl Jaspers, *Die Atombombe*, p. 188.
22 Karl Jaspers, *Vom Ursprung und Ziel der Geschichte*, p. 97.
23 Ulrich Scheuner, 'Das repräsentative Prinzip in der modernen Demokratie', in Max Imboden (eds), *Festschrift für Hans Huber zum 60. Geburtstag* (Bern: Stämpfli, 1961), pp. 222–46; 223. See also Hans Huber, 'Das Recht im technischen Zeitalter', in Huber, *Rechtstheorie, Verfassungsrecht, Völkerrecht: Ausgewählte Aufsätze 1950–1970*, edited by K. Eichenberger, Richard Baumlin *et al.* (Bern: Stämpfli, 1971), pp. 57–75; 73.
24 See Gerhard Leibholz, *Das Wesen der Repräsentation und der Gegenstand der Demokratie im 20. Jahrhundert* (Berlin: de Gruyter, 1960), p. 171. Leibholz changed his mind about this, and in his later works he made a constitutional distinction between associations situated in the private sphere and genuinely political organs, see Gerhard Leibholz, *Strukturprobleme der modernen Demokratie*, 3rd edn (Karlsruhe: C. F. Müller, 1967), p. 331.

25 See Hans Huber, 'Staat und Verbände', in *Rechtstheorie, Verfassungsrecht, Völkerrecht*, pp. 361–86; 379. Also, of a slightly later date, see Theodor Eschenburg, 'Die Verbände', in Eschenburg, *Zur politischen Praxis in der Bundesrepublik*, Vol. II, *Kritische Betrachtungen 1961–1965* (Munich: Piper, 1966), pp. 167–86; 184.
26 Scheuner, 'Das repräsentative Prinzip in der modernen Demokratie', p. 223.
27 See Otto Stammer, *Politische Soziologie und Demokratieforschung: Ausgewählte Reden und Aufsätze zur Soziologie und Politik* (Berlin: Duncker und Humblot, 1965), pp. 116–36; 117. Also, Ulrich Scheuner, 'Politische Repräsentation und Interessenvertretung', in *Staatstheorie und Staatsrecht: Gesammelte Schriften*, edited by J. Listl and W. Rüfner (Berlin: Duncker und Humblot, 1978), pp. 337–46; 344.
28 Heidegger, 'Die Frage nach der Technik', p. 29.
29 Heidegger, 'Über den Humanismus', pp. 76–77.
30 Heidegger, 'Die Frage nach der Technik', p. 13.
31 Hans Freyer, *Herrschaft und Planung: Zwei Grundbegriffe der politischen Ethik* (Hamburg: Hanseatische Verlagsanstalt, 1933), p. 22.
32 Hans Freyer, *Theorie des gegenwärtigen Zeitalters* (Stuttgart: Deutsche Verlags-Anstalt, 1955), p. 97.
33 ibid., p. 103.
34 ibid., p. 91.
35 Hans Freyer, 'Das soziale Ganze und die Freiheit des Einzelnen unter den Bedingungen des industriellen Zeitalters', in Ernst-Wolfgang Böckenförde (ed.), *Staat und Gesellschaft* (Darmstadt: Wissenschaftliche Buchgesellschaft, 1976), pp. 199–220; 216.
36 ibid., p. 216.
37 ibid., p. 220.
38 Arnold Gehlen, *Die Seele im technischen Zeitalter: Sozialpsychologische Probleme in der industriellen Gesellschaft* (Hamburg: Rowohlt, 1957), p. 109.
39 ibid., p. 9.
40 Arnold Gehlen, 'Industrielle Gesellschaft und Staat: Über einige Triebkräfte des politischen Lebens der Gegenwart', *Wort und Wahrheit*, XI (1956), pp. 665–74; 667.
41 In his early works, Freyer saw the 'will to dominate' (*Herrschaftswille*) as one of the 'fundamental psychological facts' of external organization in human society (Hans Freyer, *Soziologie als Wirklichkeitswissenschaft: Logische Grundlagen des Systems der Soziologie*, Berlin and Leipzig: B. G. Teubner, 1930, p. 44). This claim was slightly toned down in his works after 1945, but even here he still viewed administrative operations as processes of power application that control human behaviour through 'long-distance steering' (Freyer, *Theorie des gegenwärtigen Zeitalters*, p. 103).
42 Arnold Gehlen, 'Soziologische Voraussetzungen im gegenwärtigen Staat', in Ernst Forsthoff (ed.), *Rechtsstaatlichkeit und Sozialstaatlichkeit. Aufsätze und Essays* (Darmstadt: Wissenschaftliche Buchgesellschaft, 1968), pp. 320–39; 338.
43 Helmut Schelsky, 'Der Mensch in der wissenschaftlichen Zivilisation', in Schelsky, *Auf der Suche nach Wirklichkeit. Gesammelte Aufsätze* (Düsseldorf: Diederich, 1965), pp. 439–80; 456.
44 ibid., pp. 455–56.
45 ibid., p. 459.
46 ibid., p. 468.
47 Karl Jaspers, *Wohin treibt die Bundesrepublik?*, p. 190.
48 Dolf Sternberger, *Lebende Verfassung: Studien über Koalition und Opposition* (Meisenhem am Glan: Anton Hain, 1956), p. 23.
49 Wolfgang Abendroth, 'Zum Begriff des demokratischen und sozialen Rechtsstaates im Grundgesetz der Bundesrepublik Deutschland', in Abendroth,

Antagonistische Gesellschaft und politische Demokratie (Neuwied: Luchterhand, 1967), pp. 109–38; 110.

50 See, especially, Hermann Klenner, *Studien über die Grundrechte* (Berlin: Staatsverlag der deutschen demokratischen Republik, 1964), p. 26. Klenner's quasi-idealist accounts of the socialist constitution found their opponent in the works of Karl Polak, who set out a purely materialist-sociological analysis of constitutional reality, and derived valid law, 'the new socialist law', from the material evolution of the class and its interpretation by the party, the 'organizer of the transformation of all society' (see especially Karl Polak, *Die Dialektik in der Staatslehre*, 3rd edn, Berlin: Akademie Verlag, 1963, pp. 279, 284).

51 Klenner, *Studien über die Grundrechte*, p. 51.

52 Freyer, *Theorie des gegenwärtigen Zeitalters*, p. 68.

53 ibid., p. 157.

54 Helmut Schelsky, 'Über die Stabilität von Institutionen, besonders Verfassungen: Kulturanthropologische Gedanken zu einem rechtssoziologischen Thema', in *Auf der Suche nach Wirklichkeit*, pp. 33–58; 50.

55 ibid., p. 43.

56 ibid., p. 44.

57 ibid., p. 52.

58 Ernst Forsthoff, 'Verfassungsprobleme des Sozialstaats', in Forsthoff (ed.), *Rechtsstaatlichkeit und Sozialstaatlichkeit: Aufsätze und Essays* (Darmstadt: Wissenschaftliche Buchgesellschaft, 1968), pp. 145–64; 163.

59 ibid., p. 158.

60 Ernst Forsthoff, 'Begriff und Wesen des sozialen Rechtsstaates', in Forsthoff, *Rechtsstaat im Wandel: Verfassungsrechtliche Abhandlungen 1950–1964* (Stuttgart: Kohlhammer, 1964), pp. 27–56; 37–38.

61 Ernst Forsthoff, *Der Staat der Industriegesellschaft: Dargestellt am Beispiel der Bundesrepublik Deutschland* (Munich: Beck, 1971), pp. 67–68.

62 Forsthoff, 'Begriff und Wesen des sozialen Rechtsstaates', p. 54.

63 Forsthoff, *Der Staat der Industriegesellschaft*, p. 42.

64 Forsthoff, 'Begriff und Wesen des sozialen Rechtsstaates', p. 51.

65 Forsthoff, *Der Staat der Industriegesellschaft*, p. 168.

12 Habermas and Luhmann

1 Jürgen Habermas, *Strukturwandel der Öffentlichkeit. Untersuchungen zu einer Kategorie der bürgerlichen Gesellschaft*, new edn (Frankfurt am Main: Suhrkamp, 1990), p. 142.

2 ibid., p. 327.

3 ibid., p. 153.

4 ibid., p. 225.

5 ibid., p. 225.

6 ibid., p. 96.

7 ibid., p. 112.

8 ibid., p. 292.

9 ibid., p. 312.

10 ibid., p. 334.

11 Jürgen Habermas, *Technik und Wissenschaft als Ideologie* (Frankfurt am Main: Suhrkamp, 1968), p. 98.

12 Jürgen Habermas, *Legitimationsprobleme im Spätkapitalismus* (Frankfurt am Main: Suhrkamp, 1973), p. 14.

13 Habermas, *Strukturwandel*, p. 326.

14 ibid., p. 193.

15 ibid., p. 186.

16 Claus Offe, *Strukturprobleme des kapitalistischen Staates* (Frankfurt am Main: Suhrkamp, 1972), p. 25.
17 Habermas, *Legitimationsprobleme*, p. 97.
18 ibid., p. 54.
19 ibid., p. 106.
20 ibid., p. 104.
21 ibid., p. 153.
22 ibid., p. 138.
23 ibid., pp. 20–21.
24 Jürgen Habermas, *Theorie des Kommunikativen Handelns,* 2 vols (Frankfurt am Main: Suhrkamp, 1981), Vol. I, *Zur Kritik der funtionalitischen Vernunft*, p. 488.
25 Jürgen Habermas, *Zur Rekonstruktion des Historischen Materialismus* (Frankfurt am Main: Suhrkamp, 1976), p. 262.
26 ibid., pp. 267, 265, 266.
27 Jürgen Habermas, *Nachmetaphysisches Denken* (Frankfurt am Main: Suhrkamp, 1988), p. 32.
28 Jürgen Habermas, *Staatsbürgerschaft und nationale Identität. Überlegungen zur europäischen Zukunft* (St Gallen: Erker, 1991), p. 22.
29 ibid., p. 14.
30 ibid., esp. p. 22.
31 ibid., p. 23.
32 Jürgen Habermas, *Faktizität und Geltung: Beiträge zur Diskurstheorie des Rechts und des demokratischen Rechtsstaats* (Frankfurt am Main: Suhrkamp, 1992), p. 328.
33 ibid., p. 466.
34 Habermas, *Staatsbürgerschaft und nationale Identität*, p. 16.
35 ibid., p. 16.
36 Ulrich K. Preuß, 'Zum Begriff der Verfassung', in Preuß (ed.), *Zum Begriff der Verfassung: Die Ordnung des Politischen* (Frankfurt am Main: Fischer, 1994), pp. 7–36; 29.
37 Jürgen Habermas, *Die Postnationale Konstellation* (Frankfurt am Main: Suhrkamp, 1998), p. 135.
38 ibid., p. 155.
39 Habermas, *Staatsbürgerschaft und nationale Identität*, p. 25.
40 ibid., p. 502.
41 Habermas, *Faktizität und Geltung*, p. 429.
42 ibid., p. 492.
43 ibid., p. 465.
44 Niklas Luhmann, *Das Recht der Gesellschaft* (Frankfurt am Main: Suhrkamp, 1993), p. 416.
45 Niklas Luhmann, 'Soziologische Aufklärung', *Soziale Welt*, 18/2–3 (1967), pp. 97–123; 114.
46 Niklas Luhmnn, 'Politische Planung', in *Jahrbuch für Sozialwissenschaft*, 17 (1966), pp. 271–96; 283.
47 Niklas Luhmann, 'Soziologische Aufklärung', p. 109.
48 ibid., p. 97.
49 Niklas Luhmann, *Die Politik der Gesellschaft* (Frankfurt am Main: Suhrkamp, 2000), p. 12.
50 Niklas Luhmann, *Soziale Systeme* (Frankfurt am Main: Suhrkamp, 1984), p. 144.
51 Luhmann, 'Soziologische Aufklärung', p. 106.
52 Luhmann, 'Soziologie des politischen Systems', in Luhmann, *Soziologische Aufklärung. Aufsätze zur Theorie sozialer Systeme* (Cologne: Westdeutscher Verlag, 1970), pp. 154–77; 159.

53 Niklas Luhmann, 'Komplexität und Demokratie', *Politische Vierteljahresschrift*, 10 (1969), pp. 314–25; 315.
54 Niklas Luhmann, 'Selbstlegitimation des Staates', in *Archiv für Rechts-und Sozialphilosophie*, Beiheft: *Legitimation des modernen Staates* (1981), pp. 65–83; 69.
55 For a more detailed account of this, see Michael King and Chris Thornhill, *Niklas Luhmann's Theory of Politics and Law* (Basingstoke: Palgrave, 2003), esp. pp. 74–75.
56 For an account of this, see Niklas Luhmann, *Die Wirtschaft der Gesellschaft* (Frankfurt am Main: Suhrkamp, 1988), p. 325.
57 Niklas Luhmann, *Politische Theorie im Wohlfahrtsstaat* (Munich: Günter Olzog, 1981), p. 122.
58 Luhmann, *Die Politik der Gesellschaft*, p. 94.
59 Niklas Luhmann, *Macht*, 2nd edn (Stuttgart: Enke, 1988), p. 41.
60 Luhmann, *Die Politik der Gesellschaft*, p. 97.
61 Niklas Luhmann, 'Klassische Theorie der Macht: Kritik ihrer Prämissen', in *Zeitschrift für Politik*, 6/2 (1969), pp. 149–70; 168.
62 Luhmann, *Das Recht der Gesellschaft*, p. 424.
63 Luhmann, *Politik der Gesellschaft*, p. 390; Niklas Luhmann, *Das Recht der Gesellschaft*, p. 425.
64 Niklas Luhmann, 'Machtkreislauf und Recht in Demokratien', in *Zeitschrift für Rechtssoziologie*, 2/2 (1981), pp. 158–67; 166.
65 Niklas Luhmann, 'Widerstandsrecht und politische Gewalt', in *Zeitschrift für Rechtssoziologie*, 5/1 (1984), pp. 36–45; 40.
66 Niklas Luhmann, 'Soziologie des politischen Systems', p. 159.
67 Niklas Luhmann, *Legitimation durch Verfahren* (Frankfurt am Main: Suhrkamp, 1983), pp. 167, 209.
68 Niklas Luhmann, 'Politische Verfassungen im Kontext des Gesellschaftssystems, I', in *Der Staat*, 12/2 (1973), pp. 1–22; 11.
69 Niklas Luhmann, *Grundrechte als Institution: Ein Beitrag zur politischen Soziologie* (Berlin: Duncker und Humblot, 1965), p. 37. For an exemplary discussion of this, see Gert Verschraegen, 'Systems Theory and the Paradox of Human Rights', in Michael King and Chris Thornhill (eds), *Luhmann on Law and Politics: Critical Appraisals and Applications* (Oxford: Hart, 2006), pp. 101–25.
70 Luhmann, *Grundrechte als Institution*, p. 37.
71 Luhmann, *Die Politik der Gesellschaft*, p. 391.
72 Luhmann, 'Soziologie des politischen Systems', p. 167.
73 Niklas Luhmann, 'Die Paradoxie des Entscheidens', in *Verwaltungs-Archiv*, 84 (1993), p. 294.
74 Luhmann, *Die Politik der Gesellschaft*, p. 47.
75 Luhmann, *Das Recht der Gesellschaft*, p. 176.
76 Niklas Luhmann, *Protest. Systemtheorie und soziale Bewegungen* (Frankfurt am Main: Suhrkamp, 1996), p. 71.
77 See Jürgen Habermas, 'Theorie der Gesellschaft oder Sozialtechnologie? Eine Auseindersetzung mit Niklas Luhmann', in Habermas and Luhmann, *Theorie der Gesellschaft oder Sozialtechnologie – Was leistet die Systemforschung?* (Frankfurt am Main: Suhrkamp, 1975), pp. 142–290; for later reflections on this, see Jürgen Habermas, *Die neue Unübersichtlichkeit* (Frankfurt am Main: Suhrkamp, 1986), p. 181.
78 On Habermas's suggestion that Luhmann converts 'metaphysics into metabiology', see Jürgen Habermas, *Der philosophische Diskurs der Moderne* (Frankfurt am Main: Suhrkamp, 1985), p. 430.

Index